LIFE, HEALTH & ANNUITY REINSURANCE

Second Edition

John E. Tiller, Jr., FSA
Denise Fagerberg Tiller, FSA

ACTEX Publications, Inc.
Winsted, Connecticut

Copyright © 1990, 1995
by ACTEX Publications, Inc.

All rights reserved. No portion of this book
may be reproduced in any form or by any means
without the prior written permission of the
copyright owner.

Requests for permission should be addressed to
    ACTEX Publications
    P.O. Box 974
    Winsted, CT 06098

Manufactured in the United States of America

10 9 8 7 6 5 4 3 2

Cover Design by MUF

Library of Congress Cataloging-in-Publication Data

Tiller, John E.
    Life and health reinsurance/John E. Tiller, Denise E. Fagerberg.
    p. cm.
    Includes bibliographical references and index.
    ISBN 1-56698-183-2
    1. Reinsurance--United States. 2. Insurance, Life--United States.
    3. Insurance, Health--United States. I. Fagerberg, Denise E.
II. Title.

HG8083. T55 1990
368.3'0122--dc20   90-44071
                                                      CIP

ISBN: 1-56698-183-2

Introduction

The reinsurance mechanism is critical to the smooth and efficient functioning of the primary life and health insurance market. Yet, for many years, the available insurance literature that focused on this specialized field was very sparse. In 1990, the first edition of this text was published, filling that gap in the literature by providing a comprehensive survey of reinsurance concepts, products and practices.

The second edition, like the original text, is comprehensive. It defines basic reinsurance terms, describes traditional reinsurance products, introduces contemporary uses of reinsurance, discusses treaty wording and administrative practices, and summarizes current practices in the legal, regulatory, and accounting environment.

The book will be useful to students and experienced practitioners alike regarding historical and generally accepted practices within the life and health reinsurance industry.

A basic introduction to life, health, and annuity reinsurance had been overdue for some time. As an individual who has enjoyed both a personal and professional involvement with the world of reinsurance for most of my business career, it is a pleasure to commend the authors on their original text, and to thank them for this timely update of their valuable work.

William K. Tyler, FSA
Lincoln National Life Insurance Company

Preface

This book was written to provide the life and health insurance industry with both basic and advanced information regarding the various aspects of reinsurance in one source. It documents the basic principles which the authors believe apply to life, health, and annuity reinsurance, as well as the widely used applications and practices. Some examples and applications of these principles regarding specific products or features are included to enhance the reader's understanding. Some major historical developments are discussed to allow the reader to better understand how today's practices and applications evolved, as well as to demonstrate the flexibility of reinsurance in real life.

This book is intended to be a reference for both experts and novices involved in either ceding or assuming reinsurance. In analyzing a specific reinsurance need or agreement, the reader should be aware that a seemingly infinite number of legitimate variations of reinsurance are possible in practice. It is this diversity which creates the intellectual richness of the field.

It is not possible for one book to contain all the knowledge which would be necessary to describe, analyze, or document every possible reinsurance transaction. To attempt this would be folly, as every product variation by every company would have to be addressed. Since new applications for reinsurance are still being introduced, an exhaustive list of legitimate uses would be impossible. However, the principles of reinsurance remain relatively constant. The intent of this book instead is to focus on those principles and unique aspects of reinsurance. For example, GAAP accounting is not explained, but rather the unique application of GAAP to various situations.

The reader is assumed to have a basic knowledge of individual life, health, and annuity products and practices in the United States, as well as an understanding of basic statutory, GAAP, and tax accounting. The book takes the reader from the very basic definitions and uses of reinsurance to very advanced applications. While both authors are Fellows of the Society of Actuaries, an actuarial background is not necessary for understanding the concepts presented in the book except for the discussions of pricing and retention limit determination in Chapters Eight and Nine.

The book is intended primarily for United States and Canadian audiences, but the basic principles apply internationally. Considerations specific to international reinsurance transactions are discussed in Chapter Eighteen.

The book is arranged in four parts. Part One, consisting of Chapters One through Five, addresses the basic terminology of life, health, and annuity reinsurance and builds to working models of the more popular plans of reinsurance, including the coinsurance hybrids. It is recommended that all readers review these chapters, at least for vocabulary and general understanding.

Chapter One introduces many of the basic reinsurance terms and presents a discussion of the uses of reinsurance, the various classifications of reinsurance, the classifications of reinsurers, and the operational effects of reinsurance.

Chapter Two is devoted to a detailed discussion of automatic reinsurance. The normal requirements for automatic reinsurance, the methods of determining the amounts of automatic reinsurance, and the methods of allocating automatic reinsurance are covered.

Underwriting and facultative reinsurance considerations are presented in Chapter Three. The uses of facultative reinsurance are discussed as well as the considerations in developing a facultative program.

Chapter Four discusses traditional reinsurance and addresses the operation, uses, and characteristics of coinsurance, modified coinsurance, and yearly renewable term reinsurance. A simplistic model is developed to illustrate the effects of each plan on, and differences in results for, both the ceding and the assuming companies.

Preface vii

Financial reinsurance is discussed in Chapter Five. Models are used to illustrate the effects of coinsurance, modified coinsurance, funds withheld coinsurance, funds withheld modified coinsurance, and combinations of coinsurance and modified coinsurance. These models have evolved over a number of years and have been tested in seminars and lectures as well as in written formats.

By studying the models in Chapters Four and Five, the reader can gain an understanding of the various plans of reinsurance, including both similarities and differences. This understanding should be helpful in designing a reinsurance program to fit the needs of a particular situation.

Part Two is comprised of Chapters Six through Nine and deals with the administrative and functional considerations of reinsurance.

Chapter Six addresses the document known as the reinsurance treaty or reinsurance agreement. The normal terms and provisions contained in a typical treaty are reviewed.

Chapter Seven discusses reinsurance administration for both ceding and assuming companies. Typical procedures and functional responsibilities for both individual cession and self-administered reinsurance are described.

Chapter Eight deals with management of reinsurance by the ceding company. Four basic approaches for setting retention limits are described. Methods of evaluating the financial and nonfinancial aspects of reinsurance proposals are discussed, as well as certain considerations for managing facultative, financial, and inforce reinsurance. Many systems and methods exist for pricing individual life insurance products; it would be impractical, if not impossible, to document all of these. This chapter has been designed to assist the reader in identifying the considerations necessary to reflect reinsurance in the pricing of the ceding company's products.

Assuming company considerations are discussed in Chapter Nine. As in Chapter Eight, the reader is assumed to have an understanding of the principles of pricing individual life insurance products. The principles of reinsurance pricing are the same as for direct products, although the risks, guarantees, and benefits may be different. This chapter discusses many of the special considerations which arise in pricing reinsurance. The discussions of reinsurance pricing, experience refund formulas, bonuses, and chargebacks, in particular, will also be of interest to ceding company personnel involved in soliciting and evaluating reinsurance proposals or in administering and reporting ceded reinsurance.

Part Three, which includes Chapters Ten through Fourteen, covers regulatory, accounting, and tax considerations for companies operating in the United States. The reader is assumed to have an understanding of the basic principles of insurance regulation, statutory and GAAP accounting, and federal taxation of life insurance companies. These chapters are designed to build upon that knowledge through a discussion and application of those principles to the special requirements of reinsurance.

These chapters address the most fluid areas of the topic since changes occur almost continuously. While the reader is urged to do independent research regarding current guidelines when reviewing or designing a reinsurance agreement, the underlying premises and considerations should remain as discussed in these chapters. Material in these chapters was current as of August 1995.

Chapter Ten addresses the regulatory environment and the special concerns of regulators in various states in the United States. A major concern surrounds risk transfer analysis and requirements. It is almost impossible to separate any discussion of the regulatory issues from those of insolvency in Chapter Eleven and those of statutory accounting in Chapter Twelve.

Chapter Eleven is devoted to an examination of insolvency and its effect on the operation of a reinsurance treaty. This is especially important to those involved in long-term reinsurance commitments.

Statutory accounting in the United States is the subject of Chapter Twelve. Although modifications and refinements in reporting requirements and standards typically occur annually, the principles remain relatively unchanged.

GAAP accounting is discussed in Chapter Thirteen. While the details are also subject to modification by the accounting profession, this chapter documents the considerations unique to reinsurance transactions.

Chapter Fourteen addresses basic tax implications and principles, both state and federal, as they apply to reinsurance transactions. The bulk of this chapter is devoted to United States federal income taxation and its influence and effect on reinsurance agreements.

Part Four of the book is made up of Chapters Fifteen through Twenty-two and describes certain special topics and applications.

Chapter Fifteen covers aspects of nonproportional reinsurance: stop loss, catastrophe, and spread loss. While not as well known as the plans of reinsurance discussed earlier, these types of reinsurance are common in the field of health reinsurance and may even play a key role in the management of life insurance operations.

Preface

Chapter Sixteen discusses the unique aspects of assumption, including the effects on policyholders, the financial effects on both the ceding company and the assuming company, and strategic considerations.

Chapter Seventeen deals with the producer owned reinsurance company concept, including the business, financial, regulatory, and tax considerations. Agent-owned and captive reinsurance companies are discussed also.

Reinsurance transactions involving United States life insurance companies and companies domiciled in Canada, the United Kingdom, Australia, Continental Europe, Japan, and offshore locations are reviewed in Chapter Eighteen. The basic considerations of international reinsurance are also discussed.

Chapters Nineteen through Twenty-two address the reinsurance of specific insurance products or features. These chapters provide discussion of some of the special considerations which might be involved in reinsuring these products, applying the principles discussed in the previous chapters. Chapter Nineteen reviews considerations specific to the reinsurance of accident and health insurance. Chapter Twenty discusses the reinsurance of annuities, and Chapter Twenty-one addresses other lines of insurance, such as credit and group, and certain products, benefits, and provisions which require special consideration for reinsurance. Chapter Twenty-two covers the treatment of deficiency reserves, dividend options, conversions, and reissues and changes, and discusses reinsurance with affiliates and the role of insurance intermediaries.

Fairview, Texas	John E. Tiller, Jr.
August 1995	Denise Fagerberg Tiller

First Edition Acknowledgments

This book was made possible by the efforts of a number of people, whose contributions we gratefully acknowledge. These include many people with whom we have had discussions regarding reinsurance over the past sixteen years or so. It is impossible to remember all such conversations, but we thank all of these people just the same. Of course, the work experience provided by our employers, both past and present, and our clients was a major opportunity to increase our understanding of reinsurance.

In the same vein, we acknowledge the contributions of the many people whose books, papers, study notes, journal articles, and meeting discussions contributed to our knowledge of the reinsurance topic. In this regard, there is a wealth of information to be found in the Transactions and the Record of the Society of Actuaries, and we recommend this material to the interested reader.

Part of our early reinsurance education resulted from our preparation for the Society of Actuaries examination on that topic. We would like to acknowledge the authors of the various examination study notes, especially the late John C. Wooddy, FSA.

Many individuals were involved in the manuscript reviews leading to the publication of this book, and we wish to thank all of them. If we have left anyone out, please accept our sincere apologies.

Specific chapters of the first draft of the manuscript were reviewed by the following persons: John E. Bailey, FSA, Northwestern Mutual Life Insurance Company; Cecil D. Bykerk, FSA, Mutual of Omaha Insurance Company; Sue Ann Collins, FSA, Tillinghast / Towers Perrin; Deborah A. Gero, FSA, Tillinghast / Towers Perrin; Robert P. Johnson, FSA, Atrium Corporation; Donald C. Kiefer, FSA, Northwestern Mutual Life Insurance Company; Denis W. Loring, FSA, Equitable Life Assurance Society; Richard S. Miller, FSA, Tilling-hast / Towers Perrin; Thomas W. Reese, FSA, Tillinghast / Towers Perrin; Irwin T. Vanderhoof, FSA, I.T. Vanderhoof Consulting; Diane Wallace, FSA, D.B. Wallace Company; Michael R. Winn, FSA, Lewis & Ellis Inc.; A. Greig Woodring, FSA, General American Life Insurance Company; James W. Ylvisaker, FSA, Cologne Life Reinsurance Company; and Melville J. Young, FSA, Tillinghast / Towers Perrin.

In addition to these selected chapter reviewers, the first draft was reviewed in its entirety by the following persons: David M. Holland, FSA, Munich American Reassurance Company; Peter B. Patterson, FSA, Mercantile & General Reinsurance Company; Jack M. Turnquist, FSA, Totidem Verbis; William K. Tyler, FSA, Lincoln National Life Insurance Company; and William W. Zeilman, FSA, Life Reassurance Corporation of America.

Several draft versions following the initial review were used as study notes by the Society of Actuaries Education and Examination program for their Course I-550 exam. In connection with this, valuable editorial improvements were made by Bruce D. Moore, FSA, Prudential Insurance Company of America, and his contribution is gratefully acknowledged.

The final draft was again submitted for a complete review by Cecil Bykerk, and by review teams at Lincoln National (headed by Bill Tyler, and including Mike Higgins, Larsh Rothert, and Jim Schibley), Mercantile & General (headed by Pete Patterson, and including Steve Abba, Bill Caulfield-Browne, Bill Hazewood, Martin Kirr, Renate Nellich, Leo Penney, and Bob Tiessen), and Munich American (headed by Craig M. Baldwin, FSA, and including David Bruggeman, Maureen Fuller, Bob Orean, and Becky Underwood).

Other contributions to the final text for which we are extremely grateful include the following: Dave Holland for providing us with the updates of NAIC proceedings and with general encouragement; Robert Kaufman of Creative Strategies and Ardian Gill, FSA, and Kirk Roeser, FSA, of Gill and Roeser, Inc. for providing us with a basic glossary of reinsurance terms upon which the glossary included in this text is based;

First Edition Acknowledgments xiii

Darlene M. Cox, American United Life Insurance Company, for providing the reporting and auditing guidelines developed by the Reinsurance Section of the Society of Actuaries, reproduced as Appendix B and Appendix C; and Lincoln National Life Insurance Company for providing the sample reinsurance treaty reproduced as Appendix A.

Jim Schibley of Lincoln National deserves special thanks for his time in discussing legal and regulatory points of reinsurance with us.

Special thanks is also due to Bill Tyler of Lincoln National for writing the Introduction to the text, in addition to his valuable contributions to the manuscript review.

Certain individuals also provided us with specific information or made themselves available to discuss technical points. These include Diane Wallace, FSA, of D. B. Wallace Company; Richard S. Miller, FSA, and Melville Young, FSA, of Tillinghast / Towers Perrin; William E. Simms, Shigeko Kagawa, and Phillip Kruse of Transamerica Occidental Life Insurance Company; Richard N. O'Brien; Gordon Dowsley of Crown Life Insurance Company; LeRoy H. Christenson, FSA, of American United Life Insurance Company; Carolyn Cobb of the American Council of Life Insurance; and Sheldon D. Summers, FSA, and John O. Montgomery, FSA, of the California Department of Insurance.

We also wish to acknowledge the contributions of Tillinghast / Towers Perrin. Not only did the management and our colleagues show much encouragement throughout the project, but the firm also provided typists for much of the book.

We would like to express our appreciation to the people at ACTEX Publications, who took the project from manuscript form to a finished textbook. The principal persons involved in this phase of the project were Dick London, FSA, managing editor, Marilyn J. Baleshiski, format and layout editor, and Marlene F. Lundbeck, the graphic artist who designed the text's cover.

Finally, our very, very special thanks go to our friend, Jack M. Turnquist, FSA, of Totidem Verbis in Dallas for his technical review and assistance in topic selection, organization, and expression. Without Jack's contributions, this work would be of less value, although probably shorter. Nor should we forget Jack's wife Edith who opened her home to us while we worked with Jack.

J.T. & D.F.T.

Second Edition Acknowledgments

As with the first edition, this book would not exist in its current form without the contributions of many people. There were many individuals with whom we have had discussions over the years. They may be nameless, but the sum total of their comments and issues have been part of the research behind this book. Likewise, we recognize the valuable contribution of our several work experiences and the contributions of our employers, partners, employees, and clients.

We would once again like to acknowledge the contributions of the many people who took the time and exerted the effort to prepare books, papers, study notes, journal articles, newsletter articles, and meeting discussions. We would like to remind the reader of extensive wealth of material to be found in such publications; we are especially aware of the value of the various Society of Actuaries publications, including those of the Reinsurance Section.

We would like to reaffirm our gratitude to those who contributed to the first edition. That work provided the backbone for this second edition.

In particular, we need to express our deepest gratitude to the individuals who provided support and comment specifically for this second edition, and to their employers who granted them time to assist us. If we have omitted anyone, please accept our sincere apologies.

Second Edition Acknowledgments

First, it is appropriate to thank those who voluntarily noted errors or misstatements in the first edition. The honor of being first to submit a noticed error goes to Bill Harmon of Davis and Harmon. Several anonymous actuarial students preparing for course I-550 submitted notes of errors or questions, as did Donald P. Minassian of Butler University.

The material and presentations provided in the Society of Actuaries Seminar "Reinsurance Regulations: Critical Knowledge for Tough Times" was of special value in organizing and analyzing the various recent regulations pertaining to reinsurance transactions. The presenters in that seminar were Gerald Kopel (Chairperson, from Alexander Reinsurance Intermediaries), Eugene L. Copeland (Security Life of Denver Insurance Company), G. Michael Higgins (The Lincoln National Life Insurance Company), Denis W. Loring (Equitable Life Assurance Society), and Jeremy Starr (The Guardian Life Insurance Company).

Formal review of parts of the draft of the second edition was conducted by several individuals including: William K. Tyler of The Lincoln National Life Insurance Company, along with Kenneth J. Clark and G. Michael Higgins; Lee H. Christensen of American United Life Insurance Company, along with Chuck Lineback, Michael Barnett, and Sara Murphy; Paul A. Schuster of Reinsurance Group of America Inc., along with David B. Atkinson; P. James Householder of Cologne Life Reinsurance Company; Monica Hainer of London Reinsurance Group; Ian Pickering of KPMG Peat Marwick (United Kingdom); and Gregory L. Stephenson and Steven H. Mahan of KPMG Peat Marwick LLP (United States). In addition, assistance at various points was supplied by David L. White, Jr., Angie Tatum, and Elizabeth Rogalin of KPMG Peat Marwick LLP.

Additional thanks goes to Gill and Roeser for the continued use of the material which was the basis for the glossary in the first and second editions. Again, special thanks is given to Lincoln National for permission to use one of its treaties as the source for Appendix A.

We would like to express our appreciation to Bill Tyler for authoring the Introduction to the second edition, as he did for the first edition.

Appreciation is also given to the staff at ACTEX Publications for taking the manuscript from draft form to a finished product. Marilyn J. Baleshiski deserves most of the praise for dealing with our last minute deadlines, John's handwriting, and non-functioning PC disks. Thanks also to Dick London for both his assistance and insistence in developing the final product, and to Denise A. Rosengrant who proofread the entire manuscript.

It would be inappropriate to close these acknowledgments without recognizing those whose encouragement and inspiration motivated us. First, there were the many actuarial students and reinsurance practitioners who were kind enough to compliment us on the first edition. Producing a text of this size is not an easy process, and the kind observations were very much appreciated.

Second, we should thank both our parents and our children. Our parents, John and Jo Tiller and Egon and Marguerite Fagerberg, are not actuaries or even "insurance people." However, at early ages they filled us with a need to be productive and to "do your best." That drive helped us to gain the knowledge necessary and to endure the turmoil of writing this book. Our children forfeited nights, afternoons, and weekends of fun and attention so we could undertake and complete this project. But, we also wanted them to be proud of the finished product.

Third, there are those who provided professional inspiration over the years. There have been many, but three individuals stand out from the rest. While none of these three were directly involved in this second edition, each was in our minds as a role model at several points. These three are Jack M. Turnquist, Irwin T. Vanderhoff, and the late James C. H. Anderson. As actuaries and as individuals, these men were leaders.

Thanks to all of you who helped.

J. T. and D. F. T.

Contents

Introduction iii

Preface v

First Edition Acknowledgments xi

Second Edition Acknowledgments xiv

PART ONE
BASIC TERMINOLOGY OF
LIFE, HEALTH, AND ANNUITY REINSURANCE

1 Introduction 3
  Uses of Reinsurance 4
  Classifications of Reinsurance 11
  Classifications of Reinsurers 16
  Effects of Reinsurance on Company Operations 21

2 Automatic Reinsurance 25
Requirements for Automatic Reinsurance 26
Determining the Amount of Automatic Reinsurance 36
Using Multiple Automatic Treaties 38
Effecting Automatic Reinsurance 41
Automatic Reinsurance Considerations 42

3 Underwriting and Facultative Reinsurance 43
Ceding Company Uses of Facultative Reinsurance 44
Facultative Reinsurance Considerations:
          The Ceding Company 49
Reinsurer Uses of Facultative Reinsurance 52
Reinsurer Considerations 54
Facultative Reinsurance Variations 56

4 Traditional Reinsurance 59
Comparative Model 60
Plans of Traditional Reinsurance 62

5 Financial Reinsurance 107
Uses of Financial Reinsurance 107
Terminology 110
Comparative Model 112
Plans of Financial Reinsurance 118
Regulation and Taxation 167
Security Considerations 169

PART TWO
ADMINISTRATIVE AND FUNCTIONAL CONSIDERATIONS

6 The Reinsurance Treaty 177
Definition of Risks Reinsured 179
Terms and Specifications 181
Administration 183
Special Provisions 194
Preparing the Treaty 202

7 Reinsurance Administration — 205
Basic Administrative Procedures 206
Ceding Company Administration 208
Reinsurer Administration — Indemnity Reinsurance 218
Reinsurer Administration — Assumption 231
Reinsurer Administration — Fronting 232

8 Managing Ceded Reinsurance — 233
Retention Limits 233
New Business 246
Inforce Reinsurance 252
Facultative Reinsurance 253
Financial Reinsurance 254

9 Managing Assumed Reinsurance — 257
Pricing 258
Retention Limits 270
Retrocession Agreements 270
Inforce 271
Financial Reinsurance 279

PART THREE
REGULATORY, ACCOUNTING, AND TAX CONSIDERATIONS

10 Reinsurance Regulations — 285
Reserve Credit 286
Mirror Image Reserves 297
Unauthorized Reinsurers 299
Trusts, Escrow Accounts,
 Letters of Credit, Funds Withheld 303
Other Areas of Regulation 306
IRIS 313
Federal Regulation 313

11 Insolvency and Reinsurance 315
Model Act 316
The Insolvency Clause 318
Ceding Company Insolvency 323
Reinsurer Insolvency 324
Policyholder Rights 325
Managing the Insolvency Risk 326

12 Statutory Accounting for Reinsurance 331
Balance Sheet 332
Summary of Operations 336
Capital and Surplus Account 338
Cash Flow 339
Exhibits 340
Schedules 344
Other Annual Statement Items 348
Other Considerations 349

13 GAAP Accounting for Reinsurance 355
Background 356
GAAP and Reinsurance 356
GAAP for Ceded Reinsurance 365
GAAP for Assumed Reinsurance 372
Financial Reinsurance 381
Other Considerations 382

14 Tax Effects of Reinsurance 383
State Taxes 384
United States Federal Income Tax 386
Tax Planning 404
Other Tax Related Issues 406

PART FOUR
SPECIAL TOPICS AND APPLICATIONS

15 Nonproportional Reinsurance 413
Stop Loss 414
Catastrophe Coverage 417
Spread Loss 418
Reserve Considerations 418

Contents   xxi

16 Assumption   **421**
   The Assumption Process   422
   Financial Effects   426
   Strategic Considerations   429

17 Producer Owned Reinsurance Companies   **435**
   Captive Reinsurers   436
   Agent Owned Reinsurance Companies   441
   Reinsurers of Credit Insurance   446
   Captives and Other Special Purpose Reinsurers   449

18 International Reinsurance   **451**
   Motivations for International Reinsurance   452
   Considerations   454
   Selected International Reinsurance Markets   461

19 Health Reinsurance   **471**
   Disability Income   471
   Long Term Care   478
   Major Medical and Comprehensive   480
   Other Benefits   486

20 Annuity Reinsurance   **487**
   Annuity Products   488
   Special Considerations   495
   Structuring Reinsurance   500

21 Reinsurance of Other Lines and Products   **501**
   Credit Insurance   501
   Group Life and AD&D Insurance   506
   Select and Ultimate Term Insurance   509
   Nonguaranteed Elements in Life Insurance Contracts   510
   Deposit Term   513
   Increasing Benefits   514
   Accelerated or Living Benefit Riders   516
   Joint Life   517

22 Selected Additional Reinsurance Topics   **519**
   Deficiency Reserves   519
   Dividend Options   521
   Conversion, Reissue, and Change   521
   Replacement Programs   522
   Reinsurance with Affiliates   524
   Reinsurance Intermediaries   527

Appendix A   **529**
    Sample Reinsurance Agreement

Appendix B   **563**
    Guidelines for the Reporting of
       Self-Administered Reinsurance

Appendix C   **585**
    Guidelines for the Auditing of Administration and
       Reporting of Individual Life Reinsurance Assumed

Glossary   **609**

Bibliography   **629**

Index   **633**

About the Authors

To
ELIZABETH ELAINE, VICTORIA JO, and ALEXANDRA JEAN
our other collaborations,
and to KATHERINE MARIE and MARY ELIZABETH.

Perhaps some day the Tiller girls will be able to use this book to help
answer the age-old question facing all actuarial offspring:
"What do your parents do?"

Basic Terminology of Life, Health, and Annuity Reinsurance | Part One

1 Introduction

In the simplest terms, reinsurance refers to insurance purchased by an insurance company to cover all or part of certain risks on insurance policies issued by that company. Reinsurance is the process whereby one insurance company, referred to as the reinsurer, for a consideration, agrees to indemnify another insurance company, referred to as the ceding company or the reinsured, against all or part of a loss which the ceding company may incur under certain policies of insurance which it has issued. The fundamental principle of reinsurance is that a transfer of risk occurs. The risk transferred can be either a single risk, or any combination of the risks on the underlying policies.

This book is concerned only with reinsurance risks transferred on individual and group life, health, and annuity policies.[1] The risks transferred under a reinsurance arrangement on these policies may include mortality, morbidity, lapse, surrender, expense, and investment performance. Depending on the terms of the reinsurance arrangement, the reinsurer's participation in any one of these risks can vary from none to total.

---

[1] For information on reinsurance for property and casualty coverages, see Strain [25].

In this chapter, many of the basic terms used are introduced and defined. The uses of reinsurance, classifications of reinsurance, classifications of reinsurers, and the operational effects of reinsurance are discussed.

USES OF REINSURANCE

Reinsurance is one of the major risk management tools available to insurance companies, providing these companies with protection against adverse fluctuations in experience. Reinsurance is also a powerful financial planning tool. It can be used to increase or decrease the statutory earnings and surplus for either the ceding company or the reinsurer in any given year. The most common reasons why an insurance company would purchase or sell reinsurance are discussed below.

Mortality/Morbidity Risk Transfer

Perhaps the most common reason for an insurance company to purchase reinsurance is to enable that company to issue a policy on a single life for an amount in excess of the limit which it considers to be prudent for its relative financial size. This predetermined limit is called the retention limit. If there is no retention limit, or if the limit is set at too high a level, a company could face insolvency if it experienced a number of large claims over a short period of time. The retention limit is normally set at a level which will enable the company to use reinsurance as a tool to smooth out fluctuations in statutory earnings and surplus which could result from variations in the claim frequency and volume.

Lapse or Surrender Risk Transfer

Generally, an insurance company cedes business to cover excessive mortality or morbidity risks but, on occasion, a company may cede reinsurance to cover the risk of excessive lapses or surrenders. The lapse or surrender risk is the greatest on products with large first year surplus strain, particularly on products where the first year commission or the sum of first year commission and the first year cash value exceeds the first year premium.

Products with steeply increasing premiums and products with heavy policy loan activity also are prone to high lapses or surrenders. Excessive voluntary terminations may lead to deterioration in future mortality or morbidity experience. Also, a high level of surrenders can create disintermediation or other investment exposures.

Investment Risk Transfer

In some cases, the ceding company may reinsure a block of business in order to take advantage of the reinsurer's investment facilities or otherwise shift part of the investment risk to the reinsurer. Prior to 1980, such reinsurance was relatively rare. It may be used when the reinsurer has access to particular investments which are not available to the ceding company or when the ceding company wishes to avoid a high concentration of assets arising from a single product or from a large single annuity.

Since the early 1980's, several factors have combined to cause more investment risk to be transferred to the reinsurer. Increasing demand for and sales of interest sensitive products, such as single premium annuities and universal life, have created an increasing realization of the need for protection in the investment arena on the part of many ceding companies. High profile life insurance insolvencies and other regulatory problems have caused regulators to focus more attention on the asset side of the balance sheet and the interaction of reinsurance, asset performance, and solvency.

The result of these environmental changes is that most coinsurance and modified coinsurance treaties written by 1994 transferred meaningful investment risk participation to the reinsurer, unless the products reinsured had little investment risk, such as term insurance.

New Business Financing

A common use of reinsurance is to finance the acquisition of new business. In certain circumstances, the acquisition costs and reserve requirements associated with the writing of new business may be such that a successful sales effort would depress statutory earnings to the point of possible impairment of the company's statutory capital and surplus position. In this situation, the insurance company may seek a reinsurer to share the burden of the acquisition costs.

In most cases, the sharing of acquisition costs will be in proportion to the mortality or morbidity risk sharing. Where permitted by state regulations, the reinsurer may provide a proportionately larger amount of the first year surplus strain, increasing its expected profit margins in later years to recover its additional investment.

Underwriting Assistance

An insurer may seek reinsurance for underwriting needs. In the early days of reinsurance, all reinsurance was underwritten by the reinsurers. Today, the reinsurers are still the underwriting experts. Many insurance companies use an underwriting manual developed by a reinsurer, and the reinsurer may provide training for the insurer's underwriters.

The availability of an experienced reinsurance underwriter provides the insurer's underwriter the opportunity to have a difficult case reviewed, to seek a second opinion, or to obtain a more competitive rating. The reinsurer, which typically sees a greater number of large or complicated risks, often makes more aggressive underwriting decisions than a ceding company due to more advanced underwriting knowledge and techniques and because it has a wider spread of these less common risks. Competitive pressure among reinsurers may also lead to more aggressive underwriting decisions.

The reinsurer may be willing to reinsure all or a large portion of a difficult case, enabling the insurance company to place the case for its agent. An insurance company may maintain an underwriting relationship with several reinsurers in order to offer its agents the best possible underwriting service on difficult cases. In fact, several reinsurers may share the risk on a given policy.

Gaining Product Expertise

An insurance company entering a new line of business or embarking in otherwise unfamiliar territory, may form a partnership arrangement with a reinsurer because of the reinsurer's expertise in this particular area. The ceding company may receive assistance from the reinsurer in product development. In some cases, the ceding company may utilize the reinsurer's administration systems for a fee or in exchange for ceding reinsurance on the product. Typically, such an arrangement lasts for only a short period of time until the insurer has gained sufficient experience to administer the business itself.

Divesting a Product Line

An insurance company may cede reinsurance in order to exit from a certain product line or geographic area. It may choose to cede the business by the means of an assumption reinsurance agreement,[2] or through indemnity reinsurance.

Fronting

On occasion, a direct insurer will issue insurance policies to specified applicants at the request of another company, then reinsure all or substantially all of the risks on the insurance to the other company. This process, known as fronting, has been relatively widely used by property and casualty insurers. Until recently, fronting was relatively rare for life and health products as its use was traditionally resisted by regulators.

Fronting is becoming more prevalent for life and health products, with increasing acceptance from regulators. The ceding company receives a fee or portion of the profits on the business it has issued for the reinsurer. Fronting may be used in the circumstance of a company desiring to do business in a certain jurisdiction where it is not yet licensed. In order to secure business in that jurisdiction, the company finds an appropriately licensed company willing to write the insurance on its own policy forms and reinsure it. The reinsurer, in this circumstance, may perform policy administration and underwrite the policies as well.

Several states have very specific regulations regarding fronting. Quality of service and certainty of benefit payments to policyholders are of primary concern to regulators as they have no jurisdiction over unlicensed insurers.[3]

---

[2] See Chapter 16, Assumption.
[3] See Chapter 10, Reinsurance Regulations.

Increasing Ceding Company Sales and Profits

While there is a cost to reinsurance, there are advantages for a company to write business and cede the excess risk. Some of the most common advantages are discussed below.

(1) Because reinsurers normally have lower issue and administrative expenses,[4] reinsurance frequently can be purchased at a relatively low marginal cost to the ceding company. Within reason, the insurance company can cede a large portion of the risks on an insurance policy and still maintain an acceptable level of profit on the total policy. A small profit is generally considered superior to no profit at all.

(2) The company's agency force can write business with the company which might otherwise be placed with competitors having higher retention limits, providing a sales tool to smaller and medium-sized companies. This increases the insurance company's sales and enables the agents to earn more commissions with one company, encouraging loyalty.

(3) The insurance company's underwriters can gain valuable experience in underwriting larger amounts of insurance which will be useful when retention limits are increased. This would not be possible if all large policies were declined.

(4) If the reinsurance contract contains a recapture provision, the company may increase its retention limit at some future point and recapture amounts on previously issued policies up to the new retention limit, subject to the terms of the reinsurance contract.[5] This might allow the company to generate more future profits from currently reinsured policies.

Surplus Planning and Management

On occasion, an insurance company may have a need for increased statutory surplus. A temporary provision of increased surplus is

---

[4] For a discussion of reinsurance expenses, see Chapter 9, Managing Assumed Reinsurance.

[5] See Chapter 6, The Reinsurance Treaty.

Introduction

frequently referred to as surplus relief. Surplus relief can be provided in a number of ways, including the use of surplus relief reinsurance. In a surplus relief transaction,[6] the ceding company's statutory earnings and surplus are increased in the year in which the relief is provided. The amount of the relief is repaid to the reinsurer out of future statutory earnings.

There are several reasons why a company might wish to increase its surplus position. These include the following:

(1) The company has been overly successful in issuing new policies with resultant acquisition expenses reducing its surplus below prudent or required levels.
(2) The company must increase its surplus in order to obtain a license in a new jurisdiction.
(3) The company's surplus may have been temporarily reduced because of poor mortality, morbidity, or surrender experience.
(4) The company needs to increase its surplus to meet risk based capital (RBC) or other statutory requirements.
(5) The company desires to improve or maintain its rating with A. M. Best, Moody, Standard and Poor, or other insurance company rating agencies in order to increase agent, policyholder, or stockholder confidence in the company or to permit it to market in certain situations.
(6) The company wishes to meet certain objectives regarding policyholder dividends, shareholder dividends, or debt service.

Tax Planning

Historically, reinsurance has had powerful applications in tax planning[7] for both ceding companies and reinsurers. Some examples of these applications are discussed below.

(1) A company may wish to assume life insurance or cede health insurance in order to maintain or secure life insurance company

---

[6] For a discussion of surplus relief, see Chapter 5, Financial Reinsurance.

[7] See Chapter 14, Tax Effects of Reinsurance.

status for federal income tax purposes. Conversely, it may cede life insurance or accept health insurance in order to secure or retain a non-life insurance company status for federal income tax purposes.

(2) A company may wish to cede insurance and use the increased statutory earnings in order to utilize expiring tax loss carryforwards. The company can use reinsurance to change the timing of taxable income for federal income tax purposes.

The federal tax laws and regulations are complex and constantly changing, so use of reinsurance to assist in tax planning requires considerable expertise.

Increasing Reinsurer's Profit

As with directly issued insurance and annuity contracts, insurance companies accept reinsurance anticipating a profit. There are several ways in which a company can participate in the reinsurance marketplace; these are discussed later in this chapter.

Increasing Reinsurer's Inforce

Some companies may assume reinsurance in order to increase the size of the company. A company may do this to take advantage of underutilized administrative capacities, to develop a larger base of policies over which to spread administrative or overhead expenses, or to augment inforce amounts when direct sales do not meet business plans.

Limiting Catastrophic Claims

When a jet airliner crashes or a hotel burns, an insurance company may incur claims on two, three, or more individuals. While a single event involving multiple claims is not a common occurrence, such an event can have a dramatic effect on a company's earnings. Multiple deaths from a single event will affect both large companies and small companies. For partial protection, many companies purchase catastrophic insurance coverage, or cat cover.[8]

---

[8] See Chapter 15, Nonproportional Reinsurance.

Catastrophic coverage generally provides for the reinsurer to pay claims in excess of a certain limit, subject to a minimum number of claims and subject to a maximum amount of reinsurance per event. Coverage is usually limited to accidental deaths due to catastrophes such as plane crashes or earthquakes and does not include deaths due to epidemics, wars, insurrections, or natural causes. This coverage often excludes specific concentrations of lives such as sports teams, airline personnel, and other organizations or groups which would involve a large single conveyance transportation exposure. Coverage for these concentrated risk groups may sometimes be obtained from domestic or foreign syndicates and pools.[9]

Limiting Total Claims

While the major purpose of retention limits is to help smooth out fluctuations in earnings caused by large individual claims, some insurers, particularly smaller ones, are concerned with fluctuations caused by excessive claims in any one year. In order to provide protection against this risk, some companies purchase stop loss reinsurance coverage.[10]

A stop loss program provides for the reinsurer to reimburse the company for all or a specified percentage of retained claims in excess of a specified amount up to a defined maximum. This specified amount, referred to as the attachment point, is usually expressed as a percentage of the expected claims. The contract usually limits the amount of any claim to be included in the stop loss calculation to the company's retained portion of the claim. Claims from all causes generally are covered under a stop loss agreement.

CLASSIFICATIONS OF REINSURANCE

In this section the different ways in which reinsurance may be classified or distinguished are discussed, and several new terms are introduced.

---

[9] Lloyds of London is the best known provider of such coverages, although certainly not the only one.

[10] See Chapter 15, Nonproportional Reinsurance.

Ceded/Assumed/Retroceded

Ceded refers to the transfer of an insurance risk from the company which originally issued the policy, called the ceding company or the reinsured, to another insurance company, called the reinsurer. The portion of insurance passed to the reinsurer is known as the cession. In most traditional individual life, health, and annuity reinsurance arrangements, a cession is defined in terms of the individual policy. However, a cession may also refer to a group of policies such as in a stop-loss agreement.

Assumed refers to the acceptance of an insurance risk from the ceding company by the reinsurer. The reinsurer may also be referred to as the assuming company.

The reinsurer is not obligated to retain all risks which it has assumed. It may decide to retrocede to another company all or some portions of the risks it has assumed. The company that accepts the retroceded risks is known as the retrocessionaire. The reinsurance passed in this situation, known as the retrocession, is usually defined in terms of an individual policy.

Indemnity/Assumption

A reinsurance arrangement is defined by a written agreement commonly referred to as a reinsurance treaty. Such an agreement identifies the risks being transferred, defines the manner in which the risks are to be transferred, and describes the basic administrative and accounting procedures which both parties are to follow.

A reinsurance agreement may be written on either an indemnity or assumption basis. The differences between these two types of transactions lie in the relationship among the owners of the insurance policies, the ceding company, and the reinsurer.

Under indemnity reinsurance, the policyholders have no contractual relationship with the reinsurance company, and in fact, the policyholders rarely have any knowledge of the reinsurance agreement. The policyholders remit premium payments to the insurance company that issued the policy and look to that company for the payment of benefits. The ceding company remits the reinsurance premium to the reinsurer and looks to the reinsurer for reimbursement on claims for ceded policies.

Should the reinsurer fail to meet its obligations to the ceding company, the ceding company still has full liability to the policyholder. A recapture provision in the reinsurance contract, allowing the ceding company to regain all or a portion of its liabilities under the policies reinsured upon the occurrence of some specified conditions, is a common feature of indemnity reinsurance treaties, but is not mandatory.

Assumption is the permanent transfer of insurance liabilities from one company to another.[11] Under assumption, the assumption company assumes the position formerly occupied by the company which originally issued the insurance. The exact manner in which this is done will vary with state regulatory requirements. In most situations, the policyholders are given assumption certificates by the assumption company and the original insurance company ceases to have any contractual obligation to the policyholders. From the date of assumption forward, the policyholders remit premium payments to the assumption company and look to the assumption company for payment of benefits. Because assumption involves a permanent transfer of risk, the accounting treatment and income tax effect of the transaction may differ from the treatment given to indemnity reinsurance.

Assumption transactions are less common than indemnity reinsurance. Unless otherwise specified in this book, reinsurance will refer to indemnity reinsurance and special reference will be made to assumption and assumption companies where applicable.

Proportional/Nonproportional

Reinsurance may be conducted on either a proportional or a nonproportional basis. If business is ceded on a proportional basis, the portion of the benefit for which the reinsurer is responsible is defined at the time of the cession by a formula relating to the ceding company's retention limits. As an example, a company issues a $400,000 annually renewable term insurance policy and reinsures the amount in excess of its $100,000 retention. In this situation, the company retains 25% of the risk in all years.

---

[11] See Chapter 16, Assumption.

There are other methods of determining the proportion of reinsurance ceded, and the proportion may vary by policy duration. In each case, however, the proportion by duration is fixed at issue by some formula and is dependent upon the parameters for that policy only.[12]

Proportional reinsurance is conducted using traditional coinsurance, modified coinsurance, and yearly renewable term plans of reinsurance.[13]

When nonproportional reinsurance is used, the amount for which the reinsurer is liable is not fixed in advance.[14] Rather, the amount of reinsurance benefit is dependent on the amount of claims incurred during the contract period. The primary nonproportional plans of reinsurance are stop loss and catastrophe. When stop loss coverage is purchased, the company only collects on a claim if total claims exceed a defined attachment point. If a company purchases catastrophe coverage, it collects only if multiple deaths occur from a single covered event.[15]

Automatic/Facultative

A reinsurance treaty may allow business to be ceded on either an automatic or facultative basis.[16] An automatic reinsurance treaty provides that the ceding company is allowed to cede risks issued in excess of its retention limit, subject to certain specific criteria, to a specific reinsurer at a predetermined cost without submitting underwriting papers to the reinsurer for approval.[17]

A facultative reinsurance treaty provides that a reinsurer must approve each individual risk before it has any liability.[18] Variations

---

[12] See Chapter 4, Traditional Reinsurance.

[13] *Ibid.*

[14] Life and annuity reinsurance is largely proportional in nature. Property and casualty reinsurance is almost totally nonproportional. Health reinsurance is mixed, but nonproportional coverages predominate due to the nonfixed nature of many health coverages.

[15] For a further discussion of stop loss and catastrophic reinsurance, see Chapter 15, Nonproportional Reinsurance.

[16] In property and casualty reinsurance, automatic coverage is known as "treaty" business. This term is sometimes used for automatic life, health, or annuity reinsurance.

[17] See Chapter 2, Automatic Reinsurance.

[18] See Chapter 3, Facultative reinsurance and Underwriting.

include the conditional automatic treaty where the reinsurer provides an underwriting service to the ceding company and the facultative obligatory treaty where the reinsurer can decline a risk only when it has previously retained its full retention on the individual involved.

Excess/Quota Share

An excess treaty covers risks ceded in accordance with a scheduled system of retention limits. The retention limits usually vary by age and underwriting classification of the insured.

Alternatively, the reinsurance treaty may provide that a fixed percentage of each risk will be ceded. This is known as quota share reinsurance.

In most instances, quota share reinsurance applies to the first dollar of coverage. However, quota share can be used in combination with an excess risk arrangement.

Experience Rated/Non-Experience Rated

At one time, most reinsurance treaties were written on an experience rated or refund basis; the ceding company shared in a portion of any profits realized on the reinsurance in excess of a certain level.[19] Premiums on experience refund treaties frequently are higher than the premiums on comparable non-refund treaties.[20] This provides the reinsurer with an additional margin for fluctuation. In today's market, most reinsurers and ceding companies prefer the use of non-refund treaties.

Traditional/Financial

Two basic classifications of reinsurance are defined in this book: traditional and financial. Traditional reinsurance refers to reinsurance arrangements where the primary purpose is the transfer of risk.[21]

---

[19] In many parts of the world, a reinsurance experience refund is known as a profit commission.

[20] Alternatively, commission allowances may be lower than for a non-refund treaty.

[21] See Chapter 4, Traditional Reinsurance.

Financial reinsurance refers to reinsurance arrangements where the primary purpose is the achievement of a specific business objective such as increasing statutory surplus, reducing taxes, or acquiring blocks of business.[22] While financial reinsurance involves risk transfer, the risk transfer is secondary to the business purpose.

The distinction between traditional and financial reinsurance may not be immediately obvious in the treaty. These differences will be discussed throughout this book.

CLASSIFICATIONS OF REINSURERS

Insurance companies may assume reinsurance for a number of different reasons. Their degree of involvement ranges from an occasional reinsurance transaction to a full-time commitment of all resources. The various classifications of reinsurers are described in this section. A reinsurer may fall into more than one classification.

Authorized Reinsurer

An authorized reinsurer is a reinsurer which is licensed or accredited in the ceding company's state of domicile, or domiciled in a state with substantially similar laws as the ceding company's state of domicile. A company ceding reinsurance to an authorized reinsurer is usually allowed to take credit on its statutory financial statement for the reserves ceded.

Accredited Reinsurer

If a reinsurer is not licensed in the ceding company's state of domicile, it may become accredited[23] by showing the following:

(1) It meets the financial conditions of the ceding company's state of domicile.

---

[22] See Chapter 5, Financial Reinsurance.

[23] For a discussion of authorized and accredited reinsurers, see Chapter 10, Reinsurance Regulations.

Introduction

(2) It is licensed in at least one state.
(3) It has submitted to that state's jurisdiction and allows its books and records to be examined.
(4) Its directors and management personnel are of acceptable character and experience.

A ceding company will usually get full financial statement credit for reserves ceded to an accredited reinsurer.

Professional Reinsurer

All companies that assume reinsurance do so with the expectation of earning a profit. In this book, the term professional reinsurers refers to those companies that actively seek to assume reinsurance either as a major line of business or as their only line of business. A distinguishing feature of professional reinsurers is a sales staff dedicated to reinsurance activities.

Professional life reinsurers have specialized actuarial and accounting departments to meet the special needs of the reinsurance line. Most professional reinsurers offer the full range of reinsurance plans and services for both traditional and financial needs. However, a few reinsurers specialize in facultative or financial reinsurance while others provide such treaties only as an accommodation to clients with automatic treaties. Most domestic professional reinsurers are authorized or accredited in all fifty states.

Occasional Reinsurer

The term occasional reinsurer is used to refer to a company that does not actively seek reinsurance in the general market, but participates in certain reinsurance pools. Many companies participate in two large government sponsored pools: Federal Employees' Group Life Insurance (FEGLI) and Servicemen's Group Life Insurance (SGLI). These pools offer very low exposure to risk and require little administrative effort. Use of these pools is more to spread profits than to spread risks; their existence may satisfy political rather than economic needs.

Reinsurers sometimes offer selected clients reciprocity in their own retrocession pools in exchange for participation in the client's automatic reinsurance. The retrocession pool is made up from the reinsurer's assumed business. The amount of reciprocity reinsurance typically is proportional to the amount ceded the reinsurer, but the ratio of ceded to accepted volume is subject to negotiation.

Reciprocity arrangements historically were profitable to the retrocessionaires until the overall poor persistency experienced by the insurance industry in the late 1970's and early 1980's. Ceding companies found they could achieve lower reinsurance costs with less total risks by obtaining the best price rather than the best reciprocity. Many professional reinsurers can not afford to retrocede reinsurance assumed on competitive coinsurance rates unless competitive retrocession rates are used in the pools. Consequently, reciprocity is used less frequently today.

Special Purpose Reinsurer

Some insurance companies actively seek to acquire blocks of business. This is often done to utilize excess administrative capabilities or to increase the inforce insurance base for the purpose of spreading overhead and other expenses. Most special purpose reinsurers tend to specialize in one type of business. In many situations, assumption would be preferred over indemnity reinsurance.

Financial Reinsurer

A few insurance companies specialize in providing financial reinsurance. Most companies in this market have excess surplus available for investment. In order to participate in this market, a company must have a staff knowledgeable in the areas of tax and financial planning. Most financial reinsurance requires relatively little administrative effort when compared to traditional reinsurance since most of the administration is usually done by the ceding company.

Companies operating only in the financial reinsurance market may maintain a small sales staff to seek out clients. More often, they work

Introduction

with professional, full service reinsurers in the capacity of a retrocessionaire, with consultants or reinsurance intermediaries, or with a combination of these. Many professional reinsurers maintain active relationships with financial reinsurers and share large financial surplus strain treaties.

Retrocessionaire

Some companies act only as professional retrocessionaires serving professional reinsurers. As discussed earlier, some companies have participated in reciprocal pools with professional reinsurers. However, because of the highly competitive coinsurance marketplace, reinsurers frequently must retrocede assumed business on more competitive and, therefore, less profitable terms.

Professional retrocessionaires are those companies that are willing and able to assume risks from professional reinsurers at competitive rates. The underwriting function is very important to the professional retrocessionaire because it is involved in a large portion of jumbo policies.

Pool Participant

Prior to 1980, there were a few special reinsurance pools,[24] each involving a group of three to ten nonprofessional reinsurers that would cede a portion of their risks to the pool and, in return, assume a proportion of the risks contained in the pool. These pools were operated on an experience rated basis and were, in essence, a sort of spread loss coverage.[25] The primary purpose of these pools was to smooth out mortality fluctuations at no long term cost to any participant. Under the terms of the pool agreement, a company was usually required to remain in the pool until its experience account was positive.

These pools were established by companies whose overall mortality and underwriting characteristics were perceived to be homogeneous.

---

[24] This use of the term "pool" differs from that used later in the text. In Chapter 2, the term "pool" is used to describe a method of dividing reinsurance.

[25] See Chapter 15, Nonproportional Reinsurance.

When companies began to generate larger volumes of reinsurance and commercial reinsurance costs became very competitive, pools could no longer easily be kept in balance. While pools continued to exist for a few products, the members now purchase commercial reinsurance for the large volume plans, such as term insurance.

Joint Venture Reinsurer

Sometimes a life insurance company may have a particular expertise in a given product area which it can market to other insurance companies utilizing a joint venture approach. In such an arrangement, the insurance company with the expertise forms an informal partnership with an inexperienced insurance company and assists it in developing a particular insurance product. In return for the assistance, the inexperienced company agrees to cede to the other company some portion of the risk on the policies written on the new products. The reinsurer may allow the ceding company to use its administrative systems for a fee until the ceding company can develop its own.

Joint ventures tend to be more common in situations involving difficult or new products, such as long term care or variable life, or products viewed as having greater risk, such as term insurance or disability income.

Producer Owned Reinsurance Companies

A substantial volume of reinsurance is ceded to producer owned reinsurance companies.[26] These are companies formed and controlled by a separate entity in order to assume business from a specific source, usually from an affiliated or related party. In the credit insurance arena, many credit insurance companies have been formed to reinsure business produced by a particular credit insurance source such as an automobile dealership. Banks, savings and loans, and other financial institutions often form insurance companies in order to assume certain insurance coverages written on their customers.

---

[26] See Chapter 17, Producer Owned Reinsurance Companies.

Introduction

In the past decade, some life insurance companies have assisted their agents in forming captive insurance companies. The insurance company cedes a portion of the business written by the agents to the agent-owned company in order that the agents may share in the overall profitability of the business which they write. Companies expect that by giving the agents a stake in the future profitability of the business, the agents will be stimulated to produce higher quality business and to be more loyal to the insurer.

Affiliate Reinsurer

It is common for reinsurance transactions to occur among affiliated insurance companies. The affiliated companies may have a reinsurance pool in which all companies participate, or a subsidiary may cede part or all of its reinsurance to its parent or to a larger affiliate. Reinsurance pools of affiliated companies may have spread loss characteristics or they may use traditional risk transfer arrangements. Reinsurance among affiliates is frequently financially motivated.

Syndicate Member

There are certain syndicates of professional reinsurers in North America and Europe which provide specialty reinsurance such as accidental death and health coverage and also stop loss and catastrophe protection. Syndicates usually have staffs dedicated to marketing, underwriting, administration, and claims.

EFFECTS OF REINSURANCE ON COMPANY OPERATIONS

Reinsurance affects many areas of an insurance company's operations. The major areas are regulation and compliance, accounting, pricing and profitability, valuation actuary and the actuarial opinion, administration, and underwriting. Some of the key issues are summarized briefly below.

Regulation and Compliance

Reinsurance is less regulated than individual insurance because the perceived need for regulation is not as great. Policyholders are not parties to the reinsurance treaties. The insurance companies which are parties to the treaties are considered to be sophisticated buyers. In most states, reinsurance treaties do not need approval of the insurance department. However, it is important to determine that reinsurance treaties comply with all existing regulations,[27] particularly in the areas of reserve credits and insolvency.

State regulations are constantly changing in the United States; federal regulation is a distinct possibility. Regulation in other countries will affect reinsurance transactions which cross international borders. Reinsurance agreements should be constructed with the most recent regulatory changes in mind.

Accounting

Reinsurance transactions have an effect on the statutory balance sheet and summary of operations.[28] Accounting is primarily oriented towards statutory and cash information. For example, an insurance company must determine when it is appropriate to take reserve credit on reinsurance ceded.

Accounting and financial reporting needs should be addressed when the reinsurance treaty is drafted. Procedures must be communicated to the accounting department, in order that proper recognition be given to reinsurance premiums, allowances and claims, and proper information be provided for statutory purposes at a minimum.

Companies that prepare financial statements in accordance with Generally Accepted Accounting Principles (GAAP) must apply these principles to all reinsurance transactions. For traditional reinsurance, appropriate GAAP treatment is fairly well defined. However, in the area of financial reinsurance, the appropriate GAAP treatment is less well

---

[27] See Chapter 20, Reinsurance Regulations.

[28] See Chapter 12, Statutory Accounting for Reinsurance.

Introduction

defined and subject to greater latitude. Special treatments or different methods are frequently used to arrive at a common result.[29]

Tax accounting and reporting are also important and normally differ from statutory, cash, and GAAP needs. Tax needs must also be considered in developing accounting and reporting standards.

Pricing and Profitability

The cost of reinsurance will affect the overall profitability of a life insurance company and should be reflected in pricing. The actuarial department should be involved in the analysis of reinsurance proposals and in evaluating the overall reinsurance program. This periodic evaluation will normally include a retention limit study.[30]

The Valuation Actuary and the Actuarial Opinion

In the United States, the role of valuation actuary is becoming increasingly important. The valuation actuary's review of the insurance company's liabilities is very important and calls for a detailed study of all components of these values. All reinsurance reserves, reserve credits, and receivable and payable items must be carefully evaluated.[31]

Administration

The proper administration of reinsurance is necessary to ensure that all policies requiring reinsurance are ceded and that the reinsurance coverage on these policies is maintained throughout their life. Today, many companies have taken on more of the administrative responsibility for reinsurance using self-administered programs.[32] Valuation actuary considerations have also increased the ceding company awareness of the need to establish sound administrative procedures. The valuation actuary of the reinsurer may need to rely on the evaluation of the ceding company's valuation actuary with respect to self-administered business.

---

[29] See Chapter 13, GAAP Accounting for Reinsurance.
[30] See Chapter 8, Managing Ceded Reinsurance.
[31] See Chapter 12, Statutory Accounting for Reinsurance.
[32] See Chapter 7, Reinsurance Administration.

Underwriting

An insurance company's underwriting philosophy and facultative reinsurance program are closely related.[33] A company uses facultative reinsurance for many reasons and may have relationships with several reinsurers for different purposes. The insurance company underwriter may have daily contact with the reinsurer's underwriter and may develop a longstanding relationship.

---

[33] See Chapter 3, Underwriting and Facultative Reinsurance.

2 Automatic Reinsurance

The basic distinctions between automatic and facultative reinsurance were discussed in Chapter 1. This chapter is devoted to a more detailed discussion of automatic reinsurance. Chapter 3 provides a corresponding discussion of facultative reinsurance.

Originally all reinsurance was facultative, with individual underwriting evaluation and terms for each risk. As underwriting standards and insurance company practices became more defined, automatic reinsurance was developed. An automatic agreement allows reinsurance to be placed with a specific reinsurer with reliance upon the ceding company's selection criteria. This saves companies both time and expense and avoids unnecessary duplication of effort.

Automatic reinsurance is a contractual arrangement[1] whereby an insurance company is allowed to cede insurance issued in amounts over its retention limit, subject to certain criteria, to a specific reinsurer at a predetermined cost without obtaining the reinsurer's underwriting approval. The reinsurer is obligated to accept all policies which meet the

---

[1] See Chapter 6, The Reinsurance Treaty

criteria for automatic cession and the ceding company is obligated to cede all such policies. An exception is that the ceding company is permitted to cede a case facultatively to that reinsurer or another, if they are uncomfortable with the risk assessment.[2]

Automatic reinsurance is a form of proportional reinsurance, that is, the portion of each policy which is reinsured is determined in advance according to a formula stated in the treaty. Historically, the formula would result in a proportional sharing of the risk throughout the life of the individual policy, subject to recapture. Today, it is not uncommon for the proportion of reinsurance to diminish as the total net amount at risk decreases.

Automatic reinsurance may be ceded on an excess basis using a schedule of retention limits stated in terms of an amount of insurance, or it may be ceded on a quota share basis where the retention is stated in terms of a percentage of the risk. In the latter event, the ceding company is not required to keep its normal retention, but rather a percentage of each policy as specified in the treaty.

REQUIREMENTS FOR AUTOMATIC REINSURANCE

An automatic reinsurance treaty contains several requirements[3] which each policy must meet before it qualifies as an automatic cession. These requirements are usually designed to permit the majority of policies requiring reinsurance to be ceded automatically. These requirements concern the amount of risk that the ceding company must retain, and places limits on the maximum amount of automatic reinsurance that can be ceded on a life as well as a limit on the maximum amount of insurance inforce on the life. Other requirements cover underwriting and issue rules, residence of the insured, and plan of insurance to assure the reinsurer that the business reinsured meets the standards anticipated in its pricing.

---

[2] For further discussion of facultative reinsurance, see Chapter 3.

[3] Requirements typically included in an automatic life reinsurance treaty are discussed in this chapter. Requirements peculiar to accident and health reinsurance and annuity reinsurance are discussed in Chapters 19 and 20, respectively.

Full Retention

Probably the most critical requirement for automatic reinsurance is that the ceding company keep its full retention at issue on any policy ceded under the treaty.[4] This indicates that the ceding company has evaluated the risk and is willing to accept it under its own underwriting terms. This does not necessarily mean that the risk must be standard, as many companies include substandard risks in their automatic reinsurance. Without this condition, the ceding company would be free to select against the reinsurer as it pleased, holding a smaller or no retention on poorer risks.

The term full retention refers to the established retention schedule of the company. All companies have a schedule of retention limits, usually approved by its Board of Directors. Many companies have scheduled a lesser retention for lower and higher issue ages and for the higher substandard ratings where the risks are perceived to be greater or where the number of risks is small. Although grading retention limits is widely accepted in practice, it may not be justifiable in theory.[5]

Retention limits may vary by product, by source of business, or by line of business. Retention limits on accidental death coverage or waiver of premium may differ from the basic limits. These scheduled variations in retention limits do not violate the full retention rule. A violation occurs when the actual amount retained deviates from the established schedule for that product, issue age, and rating.

The retention limit for life insurance may be expressed as a flat amount of coverage, such as $250,000 per life. In a pool or quota share situation where the company cedes a percentage of all risks, the retention condition is met if the ceding company keeps its stated percentage of the

---

[4] Requirements for maintaining retention subsequent to issue are discussed in Chapter 6, The Reinsurance Treaty.

[5] See Chapter 8, Managing Ceded Reinsurance.

coverage issued, subject to a maximum amount per life. In a quota share situation, the normal retention limit may be thought of as being modified by the terms of the reinsurance treaty.

The full retention requirement applies to all policies issued on any one life by the ceding company. For example, if a company has filled its retention on a given life due to previously issued policies, a new policy may qualify for automatic reinsurance even if no portion of the risk on this policy is retained by the company, provided the other conditions are met. In most of these instances, the reinsurer requires that the rating class of the risk not have deteriorated since the last underwriting.

As an example, assume that ABC Life Insurance Company receives an application for $400,000 on the life of John Doe, age 35. Further assume that ABC Life has the right to cede automatically up to $400,000 of coverage per life to its reinsurer using the retention schedule shown in the table below.

ABC LIFE INSURANCE COMPANY INDIVIDUAL LIFE RETENTION SCHEDULE		
Issue Age	Standard Through 200% Extra Mortality	Over 200% Extra Mortality
0 - 18	$ 50,000	$ 25,000
19 - 65	100,000	50,000
Over 65	50,000	25,000

If there is no other insurance inforce with ABC Life on John Doe, and he is classified as a standard risk, ABC Life could automatically cede the $300,000 in excess of its retention. If John Doe already has $100,000 of life insurance inforce with ABC Life, ABC could cede the entire $400,000 of insurance.

The retention limit requirement applies at the time of policy issue. Under certain conditions, the ceding company may have the right to take out additional reinsurance at a later time. Additional reinsurance might be necessitated for financial reinsurance purposes or to permit the sale of a block of business. However, some treaties specifically prohibit the placement of any additional reinsurance on policies covered by that treaty.

Companies periodically revise their retention schedules. The retention in effect at the date of the current coverage is applicable regardless of any amounts of reinsurance which may have been placed on the same life.

In filling the new retention, all insurance currently inforce on the life must be considered.

Retention limits for various products are expressed in terms appropriate to each product. For example, some companies limit their retention or issue amounts on individual annuities to a maximum deposit amount per contract or individual. Disability income retention limits may be expressed as a maximum amount of benefit per month, a reduced benefit period, or a combination of these two. Medical expense insurance may call for retention limits which include both a maximum per occurrence and a maximum per year for each individual.

Minimum Cession

Many reinsurance treaties provide that, to qualify for automatic coverage, the cession must be for an amount in excess of a stated minimum. The purpose of this provision is to avoid the inordinate expense associated with administering very small cessions.

Binding Limit

The binding limit, or automatic capacity, is an important element of the automatic reinsurance formula. This is the amount of risk on a given life which the ceding company can cede automatically to the reinsurer and which the reinsurer must accept if all other conditions for automatic reinsurance are met. For purposes of determining the amount of risk when applying this limit, any amounts of insurance previously issued on the life by the ceding company that are currently reinsured with the reinsurer are added to the amounts to be ceded under the current cession.

The binding limit may be stated either as a multiple of the ceding company's retention or as an amount of insurance. It may be restricted at certain issue ages or substandard ratings. Even though the binding limit for the reinsurer is not exceeded, a specific risk may not qualify for automatic reinsurance because of insurance coverage with other carriers, as described in discussion of jumbo limits.

The binding limit is determined by the ceding company's underwriting ability, its retention limit, and its needs. A company with inexperienced underwriters may have a lower binding limit than a company with experienced underwriters, even if the first company has a higher retention limit. A company which writes large policies with great frequency may find it more convenient and desirable to have a higher binding limit than a company where large policies are rarely encountered.

In most situations, both the reinsurer and the ceding company would like the binding limit set at a level such that the majority of the policies requiring reinsurance can be ceded automatically. This lowers administrative expenses for both companies and allows the ceding company to issue policies more quickly. Higher binding limits also provide the reinsurer with more reinsurance by eliminating the need to compete with other carriers for facultative business on the larger policies.

The advantages of a higher binding limit must be balanced with the reinsurer's desire to review the larger cases which need specialized underwriting expertise. Automatic binding authority granted by a reinsurer must also be coordinated with the reinsurer's retention and retrocession arrangements. On a very large case, the reinsurer may need to check its own retention on the insured before accepting the risk or make special retrocession arrangements. Reinsurers also have limits and controls on their retrocession capacity and must follow the rules of their binding authority.

Prior to the late 1970's, binding limits of two, three, or four times the ceding company's retention were quite common. The automatic multiple tended to decrease as the retention limit increased. Years of high inflation and plummeting term insurance rates led to increasingly larger issue amounts. This caused insurance companies to seek higher binding limits to lower administrative costs and to shorten the time needed to issue a policy. Today, some companies have binding limits of several million dollars in excess of their retention limits. Such high limits are no longer as unusual as they once were since reinsurers have responded to competitive pressure and improved underwriting techniques. Today, binding limits are typically four to six times the retention, although much higher multiples are sometimes encountered.

If the sum of the amount applied for and the amount inforce in the ceding company exceeds the sum of the ceding company's retention limit and binding limit, automatic reinsurance is not allowed and the case must be submitted facultatively. Exceptions to this practice may be granted by the treaty.

In the previous example, assume ABC Life has a binding limit of $400,000 above its $100,000 retention, so it is able to reinsure automatically up to $400,000 on the life of John Doe. If John Doe previously had more than $100,000 of insurance inforce with ABC Life, resulting in more than $500,000 of insurance in total, ABC Life would not be able to cede this case automatically. It would be required to submit its underwriting papers for facultative review by this or other reinsurers.

Jumbo Limit

In order to qualify for automatic reinsurance, most companies require that the total amounts of insurance inforce and applied for in all companies on the individual life not exceed a specified amount, called the jumbo limit. Any amounts to be replaced are generally included. Some reinsurers do not include amounts of insurance applied for with other companies in this definition. Today's jumbo limits are frequently in the range of $5,000,000 to $15,000,000.

The purpose of the jumbo limit is to allow the reinsurer to check its retention and capacity on the life in question. When amounts of insurance approach these levels, the reinsurer may already have filled all or part of its retention on the life and would be required to retrocede all excess amounts to other carriers. Since this is difficult and costly, the reinsurer may decline to participate or may accept the risk only at a higher premium.

The jumbo limit is also used to ensure that the reinsurer can participate in the risk evaluation of large amounts. The reinsurer normally has more expertise in financial underwriting analysis and other problems associated with large policies. The reinsurer may also use the jumbo limit as a means to assure its retrocessionaires of consistent quality in the underwriting of risks.

Participation Limit

A reinsurer may decline to participate in the reinsurance on a given life if the total coverage currently inforce and applied for in all companies exceeds a specified maximum called its participation limit. If the participation limit is exceeded, the reinsurer will not accept any coverage, even on a facultative basis, irrespective of whether it currently has any reinsurance coverage on the life. Life insurance participation limits for a single individual may range from $25,000,000 to $75,000,000.

Participation limits may be used with individual life insurance risks but are most commonly applied to benefits such as accidental death and disability income. The limit may vary by line of business or type of benefit. Participation limits are sometimes a result of concern about excessive risk on exceedingly large insurance amounts. Other reinsurers believe that insurance above certain amounts is not a feasible solution to any real problem and represents speculation by the insured.

Facultative Exclusion

Another important requirement for automatically ceding reinsurance is that the ceding company must not have previously tried to reinsure the case facultatively. Automatic coverage is based on an agreement that the ceding company will cede to the reinsurer all business which fits a certain definition and the reinsurer will accept this business with no further conditions.

Most treaties will not allow the ceding company to submit a risk which qualifies for automatic cession to another reinsurer for review and also retain any automatic coverage rights. When the ceding company submits the case to another reinsurer, it is deemed to be voluntarily waiving its automatic privilege; the automatic reinsurer is no longer bound by the terms of the agreement relative to that case.

Further, unless specifically stated, once a policy on a specific life has been submitted for facultative review, all future applications on that life will not qualify for automatic reinsurance. Exceptions may be granted if the original case submitted facultatively was not taken out or if the original reason for facultative submission no longer applies. Examples include changes in the ceding company's retention or binding limits which would allow the case to qualify, or changes in underwriting standards.

This requirement protects the automatic reinsurer from anti-selection. Clearly, applications that the ceding company was unable to place elsewhere facultatively represent an unfavorable class of risks. The automatic reinsurer would be placed in an unfair position if such risks were ceded automatically even if the ceding company kept its normal retention. This requirement helps to maintain the partnership and good faith aspects of a reinsurance relationship.

This requirement also protects the reinsurer in the event of a claim arising prior to policy issue, facultative acceptance, or rejection of the application. Normally, the automatic reinsurer would be responsible for a defined portion of a claim under the coverage provided by the life insurance policy's conditional receipt. If a case is sent out facultatively, the automatic reinsurer is freed from this obligation unless there is specific coverage afforded by the treaty. Such special coverage is granted only in exceptional circumstances and subject to very clear, extensive rules on coverage and administration of applications, underwriting, and claims.

Normal Underwriting

Reinsurance treaties require that normal new business underwriting standards be applied to each cession. It is critical that the reinsurer be aware of the underwriting standards being applied to new issues and that these standards be consistently applied in all cases. Because the reinsurer has relied on the underwriting standards in setting the price for the automatic reinsurance, any deviation from these standards could adversely affect the reinsurer's profitability.

The definition of normal underwriting standards varies by treaty. In some instances it may include guaranteed or simplified issue for certain designated plans of insurance or markets. Where limited underwriting is included, the requirements, such as minimum group participation levels, may be specified in the treaty.

Failure to adhere to agreed upon underwriting standards may lead to denial of reinsurance coverage by the reinsurer. Reinsurers expect to be notified of any change in underwriting and some require that any approval of the change be in writing. Arbitration and legal action have resulted from violations of underwriting requirements.

A problem arises when an external replacement is involved or when underwriting standards are waived for business reasons such as with multiple life sales. Occasional deviations from normal underwriting standards may be handled on a facultative basis. If such risks are encountered frequently, separate automatic terms may be prepared.

Replacements and Continuations

Another requirement concerns insurance coverage resulting from the internal replacement or continuation of a policy. For reinsurance purposes, a continuation is defined as a new policy replacing an existing policy where the new policy lacks at least one of the following characteristics: new business underwriting, full first year commissions, new suicide period, or new contestable period. Reinstatements, reduced paid up, extended term, and decreases are generally not considered continuations. Re-entries, term conversions, and contractual increases in amounts generally qualify as continuations but are usually handled under separate provisions in the agreement. Often, the treaty will specify that the original policy must terminate within six months in either direction from the new policy date.

The widespread use of formal internal replacement programs has caused several reinsurers to address specifically the requirements related to replacements in the treaty.

The traditional requirement covering a continuation is that the new policy remain with the original reinsurer on terms appropriate for the original issue age and current duration of the original policy. For example, if an insurance policy issued four years ago to a man aged 35 and currently reinsured on a YRT basis is rewritten as a different plan of insurance without new full evidence of insurability and with a lesser first year commission, the original reinsurer would charge a YRT premium on the second policy appropriate for an issue age 35 in the fifth duration, not that appropriate for a new issue at age 39.

If the original reinsurer is reinsuring all new issues on the new plan, the reinsurance premium on the continuation would be the reinsurance premium on the new plan based on the original issue age and current duration. Alternatively, the reinsurer could charge a single premium and use the new issue age premiums.

Continuation rules are based on the fact that neither party can unilaterally terminate inforce reinsurance coverage. Moving coverage to another reinsurer on a continuation is considered a unilateral termination by the ceding company.

A reinsurer on the new plan can deny coverage if the underwriting rules are not followed and the ceding company attempts to place the continued policy with it; the requirements for automatic reinsurance would not have been met. In this event, the ceding company may have no reinsurance coverage at time of claim.

The ceding company must be aware of all the reinsurance implications of continuations. As stated, the cost of such reinsurance will typically be based upon the current duration of the original policy. This cost will normally be higher than the normal reinsurance cost for new issues. Therefore, in contemplating any replacement, conversion, or continuation program, the ceding company must take into account the appropriate cost of reinsurance in establishing the terms, conditions, and charges for these program. Multiple reinsurance treaties will complicate the situation.

If the ceding company wishes to involve a new reinsurer on a continuation, the ceding company should negotiate rules with both reinsurers. A reputable reinsurer would not replace another reinsurer on a given risk without obtaining the first reinsurer's written permission. This practice is desirable not merely because it is courteous, but it also clearly establishes the liability on the policy. Without this agreement, all three parties may be involved in a disputed settlement at time of claim.

Residence

In some instances, a treaty may require that the life reinsured be a resident of the United States, Canada, or some other specific region. Some companies impose a citizenship requirement. Frequently problems are encountered with the insuring of foreign risks, including the inability to obtain reliable medical data and claim information and the exposure to less predictable mortality.

Legal Authorization

Reinsurers often require that the reinsurance be generated from policies written in territories where the ceding company is legally authorized to do business. In addition, there may be a requirement that the policies are written in conformity with applicable regulations.

Plan of Insurance

Prior to the mid-1970's, it was common for one reinsurance agreement to apply to all plans of insurance. Today, it is more typical for a reinsurance agreement to apply to one or more specified plans of insurance. Ceding companies may have different reinsurers for different plans of insurance.

Other Restrictions

Other restrictions may be contained in the reinsurance treaty. Certain aviation risks are sometimes excluded from automatic reinsurance coverage. A reinsurance treaty might also exclude all business from a certain source, or be written so as to include only business from certain sources.

DETERMINING THE AMOUNT OF AUTOMATIC REINSURANCE

When an application meets the requirements for automatic reinsurance, the amount of coverage to be reinsured must be determined. The two approaches used to determine the amount ceded are the excess and the quota share bases.

Excess

When reinsurance is ceded on an excess basis, the ceding company reinsures amounts in excess of those specified in its retention schedule. The retention schedule may be the normal schedule for the company or a special schedule for a specific product.

Quota Share

A quota share arrangement is a form of reinsurance where the ceding company states its retention in terms of a level percentage of the risk on each policy issued up to its maximum retention. If the reinsurance is shared by more than one reinsurer, each receives a specified percentage.
 The quota share arrangement will result in more reinsurance being ceded on a given block of business than under the excess arrangement, as a portion of each policy issued is reinsured rather than only a portion of those policies which have amounts in excess of the retention limit.

Probably the most common use of a quota share arrangement is in those situations where the ceding company expects to write a substantial number of policies needing reinsurance. This may be because of large amounts per life, or because significant surplus strain is expected and the ceding company needs financial assistance. In this case, one or more reinsurers are employed and self-administration is typically utilized. This results in a predetermined equitable sharing of risks and strain among reinsurers and fairly simple administration.

Another use of a quota share arrangement is for a joint venture. These arrangements are usually created when the ceding company is entering a new product line or market where it lacks the experience to make its normal commitment. The ceding company will seek a more experienced company to assist it in entering the market and compensates the company by ceding to it a portion of the business.

Quota share arrangements are also used in situations where it would be inconvenient or impossible to individually identify amounts reinsured in excess of a certain limits. Examples of this include group life insurance or accidental death benefits. In its purest form, a quota share agreement is the most convenient method to provide surplus relief on a block of inforce policies as the ceding company can simply apply a level percentage to its premiums, claims, and reserves to determine the reinsurer's share. Appropriate adjustments can be made for previously reinsured amounts.

Quota share arrangements typically apply for only coinsurance or modified coinsurance since a basic purpose is to simplify administration by using percentage of premiums, reserves, and claims for reinsurance. The use with yearly renewable term would require the calculating of individual net amounts at risk and yearly renewable term premiums.

While quota share agreements are almost always automatic in nature, facultative arrangements are possible. For example, a company with a significant new marketing opportunity might seek a quota share reinsurer to provide both financial depth and underwriting capacity. In this instance, the arrangement would technically be facultative, but if the reinsurer turned the application down, the ceding company would be unlikely to look further.

In the previous example, ABC Life might have chosen to enter into a quota share arrangement because of the strain involved in this particular product. Under this arrangement, if ABC Life had chosen to retain 10% of each risk up to its normal retention and split the reinsurance evenly between XYZ Re and 123 Re, it would retain $40,000 of the insurance issued on John Doe and cede $180,000 to XYZ Re and $180,000 to 123 Re.

USING MULTIPLE AUTOMATIC TREATIES

A ceding company may reinsure a product on an automatic basis with more than one reinsurer in order to increase its facultative outlets, reduce its dependence on one reinsurer, or increase its automatic capacity. Or the ceding company may perceive that the practice will result in a more competitive situation, and therefore, in better price or service. However, a company will rarely use more than three or four reinsurers on any product as it is not cost-efficient for the ceding company or for the reinsurers. An insurance company may have different reinsurers for different products.

Splitting and allocating business among reinsurers must be done in a systematic manner so there is no confusion or uncertainty as to which reinsurer is responsible for which risks. Additionally, all reinsurers should believe they are receiving a fair cross-section of risks. Several methods which may be used to divide automatic insurance among reinsurers are described below.

Alphabet Split

The most common method of dividing individual cession automatic reinsurance among reinsurers is the alphabet split. Under this method, reinsurers are assigned a portion of the alphabet and automatically receive reinsurance based on the first letter of the insured's last name. In the previous example, if ABC Life reinsures all business for surnames beginning with letters A through K with XYZ Re and for all surnames beginning with L through Z with 123 Re, XYZ Re would automatically receive the $300,000 of reinsurance to be ceded on John Doe's life.

Joint life and joint and last survivor policies present a special problem if the insurers have different surnames. The treaties must be clear regarding how the reinsurers are to be assigned in such cases. It is usually desirable to place all coverages arising from a given policy with the same reinsurer. Any clear and fair rule, such as following the established alphabet split using the surname of the oldest insured, may be acceptable.

Based on typical distribution of United States surnames, the A to K, L to Z split should result in approximately equal shares. An A to G, H to O, and P to Z division should result in an appropriate three-way division. An A to D, E to K, L to R, and S to Z should result in each reinsurer receiving about one-fourth of the reinsurance. Actual splits can vary with the individual company's markets and experience.

Splits of reinsurance need not be equal to all reinsurers. One reinsurer may receive much more or less business on a given plan of insurance than other reinsurers of the same plan. Historic relationships, services provided, and available capacity may influence the distribution of reinsurance among reinsurers.

Pooling

Automatic reinsurance may be ceded through a pooling arrangement. Under this method each reinsurer receives a certain percentage of the reinsurance on each life reinsured. The portion of reinsurance going to each reinsurer need not be the same. From the prior example, ABC Life may form a reinsurance pool and cede 75% of each risk to XYZ Re and 25% to 123 Re. In this situation, XYZ Re would automatically receive $225,000 of the reinsurance on John Doe, with 123 Re receiving the remaining $75,000.

The ceding company may choose to use the pooling method in order to obtain a larger automatic binding capacity, since the mortality fluctuation risk is spread more evenly among the reinsurers in a pool. A larger binding limit may reduce the ceding company's administrative and reinsurance costs as well as reduce the turnaround time involved in submitting facultative papers. However, reinsurers typically will not agree to a new total binding limit significantly larger than the normal binding limit for the company.

Pools usually exist only when the ceding company is administering the pool itself in some automated manner. If traditional individual cession administration is used, the ceding company's paperwork is increased as a result of the number of cession cards required on each policy. In a pool, it is usually important that all reinsurers have identical terms, except for percentage shares. This facilitates the reinsurance administration and simplifies claim settlement. Some minor terms may differ, allowing for the idiosyncrasies of the various reinsurers.

In some situations, a pool may have a lead reinsurer. This company may take the lead in pricing, facultative underwriting, establishing and reviewing administrative procedures, claim settlement, or any additional matters agreed upon by the ceding company and the pool participants. Sometimes, the lead reinsurer may have somewhat more favorable terms or a larger share of the reinsurance. Lead reinsurers are not common in life insurance, but are frequently used in nonproportional, accident and health, and property and casualty reinsurance.

Layering

Under a layering arrangement, an insurance company will cede all amounts in excess of its retention up to a given limit to one reinsurer then cede the excess over this limit up to a second limit to a second reinsurer. The first reinsurer will normally receive the majority of the reinsurance as it receives the first reinsurance on all risks, but there are exceptions if the first layer is relatively narrow.

Layering was created to extend a company's total binding authority and to introduce a new reinsurer into the program. The first layer of coverage was normally defined by the ceding company's binding limit with the first reinsurer. A second reinsurer, wishing to build a relationship with the ceding company, might agree to automatically accept business in excess of this binding limit up to another limit.

Sometimes, the second excess arrangements involve an alphabet split and a flip-flop or switch. Under a flip-flop arrangement, the first reinsurer receives the first excess of reinsurance on one portion of the alphabet, while the second reinsurer receives the second excess. The relationships flip-flop, or switch, on the other portion of the alphabet, with the second reinsurer receiving the first layer.

A layered arrangement complicates the ceding company's administration as two cessions are required on the policies issued for amounts in excess of the first layer. Layering is probably the method least favored by reinsurers. As second, third and even fourth layers of coverage are secured, the reinsurers in all levels may find the overall quality of the business declining since the ceding company is underwriting large cases alone. Layering has become less popular as administrative procedures have been simplified and automatic limits raised.

Issue Age

On occasion, companies have split reinsurance by issue ages, having determined the cost difference by age between reinsurers to be significant. Reinsurers normally look carefully at such arrangements before agreeing to them. It is not uncommon for a reinsurer to provide a quote which will produce gains at some ages and losses at others. Obviously, the reinsurance of lives only at those ages where losses or small profits are expected is not wise.

Agent

Reinsurance may also be divided based on the writing agent. This method is used primarily for credit reinsurance, fronting, or reinsurance involving agent-owned companies, but it may be used in other situations.

Other Methods

Any reasonable method may be used to allocate reinsurance. A few companies have allocated reinsurance based on state of residence. One company has traditionally split its reinsurance based on the policyholder's residence at issue being east or west of the Missouri River. Even and odd years of birth may also be employed. In certain cases, reinsurance has been split by smoker status. As with splitting reinsurers by issue age, splitting reinsurers by smoker status may enable the ceding company to achieve a better cost, but a reinsurer may be reluctant to agree if the reinsurer's pricing contemplated one class subsidizing another.

EFFECTING AUTOMATIC REINSURANCE

If the application from the ceding company meets the automatic cession criteria, the reinsurance treaty will define the notification procedure. If more than one reinsurer is involved, the treaty will define how a reinsurer is chosen for a given policy.

The type of notification required depends on the type of policy being reinsured and the type of administration being used. If individual cession administration is used, the ceding company merely notifies the reinsurer when the application for insurance is processed by sending an automatic cession notification. This notification contains the information necessary to allow the reinsurer to set up its records. Historically, this notification was a physical cession card. Today, the cession card is sometimes sent in a computer readable form rather than on paper. Use of electronic data transfer is expected to become more common. If the ceding company is performing the basic administrative functions under a self-administered reinsurance arrangement,[6] the reinsurer will only receive a listing containing this information for all new cessions occurring during a defined period, usually monthly or quarterly.

The reinsurer normally does not receive a copy of the application or underwriting papers on an automatic cession although the reinsurer has the right to inspect the ceding company's records. Sometimes the reinsurer routinely requests to review papers, or to receive copies of all or some underwriting files to determine if underwriting standards are being maintained. Other reinsurers may do this as part of an audit process, or not at all. The procedure may depend upon the ceding company and its relationship with the reinsurer.

AUTOMATIC REINSURANCE CONSIDERATIONS

Automatic excess reinsurance is a very popular method because it is both time and cost efficient for both parties. Because the terms and conditions are outlined in advance in the reinsurance treaty, the ceding company does not need to go through the process of finding a reinsurer separately for each and every policy which exceeds its retention. This saves the ceding company much time and administrative expense, and allows it to issue the majority of its policies on a timely basis. If the reinsurance is to be shared among two or more reinsurers, the ceding company can usually negotiate uniform terms and conditions with minor exceptions. Uniformity in pricing terms is more difficult to achieve on a facultative basis.

The reinsurer anticipates its full retention. It does not have to compete on underwriting decisions with other reinsurers which saves each reinsurer time as well as the expense of underwriting.

Automatic reinsurance is the most effective way to handle quota share reinsurance due to the large volume of policies normally involved.

---

[6] See Chapter 7, Reinsurance Administration.

3 | Underwriting and Facultative Reinsurance

Under facultative reinsurance, the ceding company sends, or submits, its underwriting file on an application to the reinsurer for an underwriting decision. The reinsurance underwriter, after reviewing all the data he has requested, makes a decision as to the appropriate mortality or morbidity assessment on the individual. The range of possible decisions includes to rate preferred, standard or substandard, to defer decision to a later date, to accept at a stated rating subject to additional information or restrictions, and to decline or reject. The underwriter's decision is also known as the action or the offer. The ceding company typically is given a certain time period, such as 60, 90, or 120 days, to accept a reinsurer's offer in writing.

Facultative reinsurance is a process of offer and acceptance. It is generally held that the reinsurer's underwriting decision is an offer to reinsure the risk at the stated rating and terms. The ceding company is not obligated to cede reinsurance on the facultative offer, but has no automatic coverage once a submission for facultative underwriting is made. The ceding company has the option to accept or reject the reinsurer's offer. If the ceding company decides to reject the offer, it may retain the risk at its own rating, accept another reinsurer's offer, or decline the risk itself. Before reinsurance is in effect, the ceding company must accept the offer made by the reinsurer.

Acceptance is usually accomplished by sending an individual cession notice or a separate notice of facultative acceptance. If the offer is not specifically accepted or declined by the ceding company within that period, it is deemed to be withdrawn by the reinsurer. Some reinsurers automatically send notification of withdrawal of the offer to minimize administrative errors and legal exposure.

Facultative reinsurance is utilized when a cession does not meet the requirements for automatic reinsurance, or when the ceding company voluntarily requests the reinsurer underwrite an application. The ceding company may make such a request in order to reduce its exposure on a questionable risk or to allow the reinsurer to make a decision regarding a questionable impairment. Facultative reinsurance is a form of proportional reinsurance[1] as the amount of reinsurance on each policy is determined at the time it is ceded.

A key point regarding facultative reinsurance is that the terms of the cession — underwriting action, price, and retention, as well as the choice of reinsurer are negotiated separately for each policy. The administration and special provision articles of the given facultative treaty will generally apply, but specific terms can vary for each risk. Facultative risks can have a full retention by the ceding company, no retention, or any mutually agreed upon sharing of the risks.

CEDING COMPANY USES OF FACULTATIVE REINSURANCE

A ceding company may submit an application for facultative underwriting in order to obtain excess capacity, underwriting assistance, or a competitive underwriting rating. Facultative applications are frequently employed with experimental underwriting programs.

---

[1] This point refers to most life and annuity reinsurance. In reinsuring property and casualty or health coverages, facultative coverages are frequently non-proportional. Life reinsurance coverages which are non-proportional, such as stop-loss, are essentially facultative as underwriting and price-setting are done annually.

Excess Capacity

A ceding company must submit for facultative reinsurance any application that does not qualify for automatic reinsurance because the amount exceeds its binding limit or jumbo limit. Normally, the facultative submission can go to any reinsurer.

Under the terms of some automatic treaties, the ceding company is required to submit facultative applications to the automatic reinsurer first. More commonly, the ceding company is under no contractual obligation to submit a facultative application to the reinsurer that would have been on the risk automatically if the application been for an amount within the automatic binding limit.

Even without contractual obligations, the ceding company may choose to submit a standard case to only the appropriate automatic reinsurer because it is less costly to submit an application to only one reinsurer. However, if the company is involved in a substandard shopping program, there may be some obligation to submit clean or standard cases to all the reinsurers to "sweeten the pot" by allowing all reinsurers an equal chance at more preferred business.

Underwriting Assistance

The reasons for seeking underwriting assistance may be quite varied. The primary purpose is get a second opinion or underwriting assistance on difficult cases involving multiple or complicated medical impairments. Reinsurance underwriters see impaired and questionable risks with far more frequency than underwriters from traditional life insurance companies which write little brokerage business. Often, if there is previous reinsurance inforce on a particular life, the reinsurance underwriter may be familiar with the insured or have additional information on the case. This is especially likely for risks involving very large amounts of insurance or unusual underwriting considerations. Care must be taken to respect the confidentiality of records.

In the case of second opinion submissions, the amount applied for may fall within the ceding company's retention. Depending on the ceding company's and the reinsurer's decisions, the ceding company might cede some, none, or all of the risk.

If an insured has very complex financial dealings, perhaps involving large amounts of insurance already in force, the ceding company may send the application out for facultative review to reinsurers whose underwriters are more experienced in dealing with financial underwriting.

On occasion, an underwriter simply feels uncomfortable with an application and submits the case facultatively, stating that his company will keep no retention. On the other hand, the reinsurer may require the ceding company to retain a portion of the risk as a condition of a facultative offer.

A ceding company will sometimes submit a case to the reinsurer as a courtesy. While the ceding company's underwriter could be comfortable with his decision, he could recognize an area of concern and allow the reinsurer to make its own decision to agree with him. In this case, the ceding company would keep its retention and the reinsurer could decide to accept no reinsurance on that policy.

A reinsurer provides underwriting assistance for several reasons. In the case of automatic treaty clients, the reinsurer would prefer to review questionable cases itself rather than to have them ceded automatically and possibly erode assumed profit margins. Reinsurers also provide this service in an attempt to minimize the need for their automatic treaty clients to establish relationships with other reinsurers. In any event, the reinsurer expects to make a profit.

Shopping for Competitive Underwriting Ratings

Ceding companies frequently submit cases facultatively in order to get the most competitive ratings, a practice known as shopping. The ceding company searching for the best underwriting rating will send a particular application to a number of reinsurers, typically three or four. Often, these are formal programs where the participants and the criteria for selecting submissions to the program and accepting offers are agreed upon in advance.

The ceding company generally accepts the best offer received from the first reinsurer to make that offer. Sometimes the case will be split among equally competitive reinsurers. "Best" may refer to either the lowest underwriting rating, the lowest overall cost, or the most timely, depending on the sophistication and objectives of the ceding company.

The ceding company may retain little or none of the risk. Some companies base their participation decision on the level of competitiveness of the reinsurer's decision. One company established rules that if the best reinsurance decision matched its own, it would keep its full retention. If the reinsurance decision was one table[2] lower, it would reduce its retention by 25%; if two tables, 50%; and if three tables, 75%. If the reinsurance decision was four or more tables lower, the ceding company would retain nothing.

While the insurer usually will issue the policy at the reinsurer's rating, a few insurers will issue at one table rating higher than that quoted by the reinsurers. This may be done to cover the administrative costs of shopping, or for other economic reasons. Generally, the reinsurer would want the right to approve such actions.

Some direct writing companies view shopping programs as a valuable service to agents, enabling their agents to place difficult cases through them at a better rating than their normal underwriting would allow. This supposedly results in improved agent morale and loyalty as well as lower premiums and a psychological advantage to the policyholder. Shopping can also add to the ceding company's profit as long as it adjusts its retention in accordance with its perception of the adequacy of the reinsurer's rating.

As an example, suppose ABC Life's underwriters find that the proposed insured has an abnormal EKG which would result in a substandard table rating based on their underwriting manual. The agent, however, feels he cannot place the case with a substandard rating, so the underwriter sends the case to several reinsurers to determine if any of them will accept the case on a standard basis. XYZ Re, which specializes in abnormal EKG's and has a good relationship with ABC Life, offers to take the case on a standard basis. Because ABC Life's underwriting manual would have required a rating, it allows XYZ Re to reinsure the entire amount.

The primary disadvantage of shopping is the increased costs and the potential for decreased profit margins. When a case is submitted

---

[2] A table, as referred to in this text, means an underwriting rating equivalent to 25% extra mortality. Thus, a Table 2 case would have expected mortality equal to 150% of standard.

facultatively, underwriting papers must be sent to the reinsurer. Added costs include not only those for supplies, telephone and facsimile transmission, and express delivery, but also for significant clerical and underwriting time.

Shopping for a more competitive risk rating may subject the ceding company to reduced profit margins as the result of higher mortality costs in relation to the premium received on the retained portion of the risk. Companies frequently attempt to control this by reducing retention on shopped cases, sometimes retaining nothing.

Reinsurance premiums on shopped facultative business are often higher than those on other sorts of facultative business. This is because of the higher costs associated with extra mortality in a facultative shopping program and the higher underwriting costs per case placed.

Shopping programs may inhibit the development of the issuing company's underwriting staff. In some companies, the most difficult cases are sent to the reinsurers, leaving the underwriters little opportunity to gain real experience with these cases. Shopping may cause agents to lose confidence in the issuing company's underwriters, believing that the underwriters cannot handle the more difficult impairments.

Instead of alleviating pressure on the underwriter, a shopping program may actually add some pressure as agents lobby to have cases shopped even though such cases would normally not qualify for facultative treatment. Agents have even been known to ask for a specific reinsurer's underwriting action.

Shopping became very popular in the mid 1970's, as facultative underwriting moved from being an accommodation to
automatic clients to becoming a "loss leader" or "door opener." Facultative reinsurance has often been viewed as a stepping stone to an automatic arrangement; that is, the reinsurer could use a facultative arrangement to prove itself to the client in the hope of being included in the automatic reinsurance arrangements.

As more companies in the late 1970's and early 1980's entered the reinsurance market, the facultative market became highly competitive. These companies used competitive facultative underwriting to gain a market share.

Many competitive shopping programs of the early 1980's produced very poor mortality and persistency results. Procedures used in the

1990's have become more stringent. Some reinsurers have curtailed participation in larger shopping programs where single risks are submitted to more than four reinsurers. Some reinsurers will not participate if the placement ratio[3] of the ceding company drops below a certain level because of the high costs associated with these programs. In order to control anti-selection by the ceding company, reinsurers may require the ceding company to retain a minimum portion of the risk, for example, 10%. Some reinsurers offer facultative facilities as a service to their automatic treaty clients only.

Previous Facultative Submission

Generally, most reinsurance treaties require that once a case is submitted for facultative reinsurance, all future issues on that life must be submitted for facultative reinsurance. Exceptions may be allowed if the original case was not taken out or if certain circumstances have changed, such as a change in retention, change in underwriting standards, or expiration of a temporary extra premium period.

FACULTATIVE REINSURANCE CONSIDERATIONS: THE CEDING COMPANY

Both direct underwriting and facultative services are changing rapidly due to technological advances. On-line underwriting manuals are available to many underwriters, providing the latest information and guidelines on impairments. Artificial intelligence and other computer techniques are performing initial screening and classification of applications, in some instances applying the final underwriting decision. Electronic data imaging (EDI) allows almost instantaneous transfer of information. Time periods for gathering information and responding are continually being shortened.

In developing a facultative reinsurance program, the ceding company must weigh the costs versus the benefits. Even if the reinsur-

---

[3] A placement ratio is the ratio of the number of paid cessions from a given ceding company to the number of risks submitted to the reinsurer for evaluation.

ance terms are the same, facultative reinsurance costs may be higher than automatic reinsurance because of the costs of multiple submissions.

Time is also a consideration. Even with the use of facsimile machines and EDI there will be some delay before the company receives an acceptable offer. If more than one offer is received, the direct writing company must compare the offers. Reinsurance should be in place before a policy is issued or the ceding company may find itself on the entire risk without reinsurance.

The amount of reinsurance ceded on a facultative basis will vary among ceding companies based on each company's perception of the advantages and disadvantages of facultative reinsurance.

Advantages

Some of the advantages of facultative reinsurance to the ceding company include the following:

(1) It allows the ceding company to issue policies in excess of its binding limits, providing more profit potential and better service to its agents. This also permits the company to compete with larger insurance companies with higher retentions or binding limits.
(2) A ceding company may be able to issue a policy at a more competitive rating than is available based on its own underwriting manual. The reinsurer may allow the ceding company to retain something less than its normal retention in this instance.
(3) The ceding company can use the reinsurer's underwriting expertise on difficult cases rather than be committed to using internal resources.

Disadvantages

While there are clear advantages to the use of facultative reinsurance in a reinsurance program, there are several disadvantages to the ceding company. These include the following:

(1) Facultative submissions are a time-consuming process. The company could possibly lose the case in a competitive situation if

the other company involved does not need to submit the case facultatively or if the competing company has a quicker response from its reinsurers.

(2) Conditional receipt coverage is usually lost in the facultative process unless the ceding company is able to negotiate special coverage. Any claim incurred under the conditional receipt prior to securing a facultative offer could be quite costly.

(3) Submitting a case facultatively is more expensive as the underwriting files must be submitted to each facultative reinsurer. Facultative cases frequently involve large amounts of insurance or unusual impairments, with underwriting files which contain several hundred pages each. Because of the time element, these files are usually sent via a facsimile machine or express mail to each reinsurer. Obviously, the more reinsurers involved, the more costly this becomes. An individual reinsurer may require additional underwriting information or reports which would add to the expense and the time required.

(4) For self-administered pool business, facultative cessions require special handling and may be an administrative burden. Retention requirements and reinsurance rates may vary by reinsurer for facultative cessions. These factors add complexity to the reinsurance administrative system and, if not considered initially, may be quite difficult to address later.

(5) The field force may lose confidence in the company's underwriters, believing they cannot handle the more difficult impairments or are too conservative when they follow the company's underwriting standards. This may cause agents to push for more shopping, adding pressure on the underwriters to shop cases that do not meet normal shopping guidelines.

(6) If the ceding company maintains a retention on facultative policies and competitive underwriting by the reinsurer results in reducing the rating on the portion retained, overall mortality ratios may rise.

(7) Facultative reinsurance premiums may be higher than automatic reinsurance premiums, increasing costs.

(8) Once a life is placed on a facultative basis, all future policies issued on that life must be issued on a facultative basis unless special arrangements are made.

(9) If notification procedures are not followed or a ceding company fails to obtain the additional information requested by the reinsurer or to fulfill other conditions set by the reinsurer, the ceding company may find it does not have reinsurance coverage.
(10) Reinstatement of facultative polices usually requires reinsurer approval.
(11) The reinsurer may exert more control over facultative claims.

REINSURER USES OF FACULTATIVE REINSURANCE

All professional reinsurers provide facultative reinsurance coverage. Before the creation of automatic reinsurance, facultative reinsurance was the only coverage available. Today, reinsurers have different philosophies regarding facultative reinsurance. Each reinsurer may offer facultative facilities for one or more of the following purposes.

Quality Control

Facultative reinsurance is used as a quality control device by the reinsurer. The reinsurer sets a binding limit for each automatic treaty to allow it to review larger applications prior to accepting them.

Primary Business Source

For some reinsurers, facultative reinsurance remains the primary business source. These companies have built a longstanding reputation on underwriting knowledge. Ceding companies seek them out because of this expertise. These companies participate on a facultative only basis in many reinsurance programs. More recently, most of these reinsurers have sought automatic business.

Accommodation to Automatic Clients

Some reinsurers focus on automatic reinsurance and offer facultative coverage only as an accommodation to automatic clients. Normally, it wants to provide reinsurance capacity on the large applications in excess of the ceding company's binding or jumbo limit. In most instances, these applications fall into the standard rating class and represent profitable business.

A reinsurer which uses facultative reinsurance only as an accommodation to automatic clients will seldom participate as a facultative-only reinsurer of other companies.

Experimental Underwriting Programs

Experimental underwriting programs have been important in the development of the modern life insurance industry. Prior to World War II, very little mortality data existed on impaired insured lives since very few insurance companies had any significant experience and there was no central source to pool data. After the war, reinsurers were instrumental in initiating formal experimental underwriting programs covering important impairments such as diabetes and coronary heart disease. Today, most experimental underwriting programs involve special markets such as the elderly or foreign risks.

A reinsurer has an advantage in developing such programs because it can readily pool the experience of several companies in order to broaden the database and increase the statistical significance of the results. Experimental underwriting programs have allowed companies to study the mortality under these impairments and have assisted in the development of modern underwriting manuals.

In order to develop an experimental underwriting program today, a company must avail itself of all the most modern clinical information concerning the impairments to be studied. This information is used to develop an appropriate rating which is low enough to attract business but high enough to avoid loss. The mortality results are monitored carefully, with adjustments in underwriting being made quickly when they appear necessary.

The successful programs of the past have generally involved only a few impairments which were often highly rated or considered uninsurable. Today's experimental underwriting programs may involve a larger number of impairments and less highly rated risks.

Experimental underwriting programs are, to some degree, research programs and, as such, are quite involved. The underwriting rules must remain flexible and should be established to insure as many risks as possible in order to facilitate the gathering of significant data. However, the premium level must be set so as to minimize the potential for loss. Establishing a reserve to cover extra claims is a good budgeting and control technique.

Experimental programs established by reinsurers may be reinsured on a quota share basis in order to spread the risks. The ceding company would be notified that a certain action was an experimental decision so it could make an informed decision about its own retention. Ceding companies may be allowed to lower their normal retention or even retain nothing if they participate in an experimental program established by a reinsurer.

Automatic Reinsurance Marketing Tool

Many reinsurers use their underwriting expertise as a marketing tool for automatic coverage. The reinsurer may supply the ceding company with an underwriting manual which it developed, and may provide training services for ceding company underwriters.

Facultative reinsurance has often been viewed as a stepping stone to an automatic reinsurance agreement. The reinsurer would use a facultative arrangement to prove itself to the client in the hope of being added to the next automatic treaty.

Around 1980, competition for automatic reinsurance became very intense and spread into the facultative market. Some reinsurers made quotes on facultative shopping programs as a loss leader to attract new automatic clients and to increase market share. Poor results ended this practice.

REINSURER CONSIDERATIONS

Since any given risk is generally ceded to the reinsurer offering the lowest overall cost, facultative reinsurers are concerned about the relationship of underwriting action, underwriting expense, additional mortality, and price. These considerations are discussed below.

Underwriting Action

Reinsurers have different underwriting specialties and philosophies. Some specialize in specific impairments or in financial underwriting. Since underwriting is not an exact science, underwriting actions vary by company and, to an extent, by underwriter within a company.

Cost Control

The reinsurer's ultimate cost is related to the placement ratio for any facultative client. Placement ratios vary by client and are related to the number of reinsurers participating in the program. Low placement ratios result in a high cost per cession. A low placement ratio also indicates anti-selection because so few cases are placed. A placement ratio less than the ratio expected due to the proportion of reinsurers involved indicates that the reinsurer is not receiving its appropriate share of all business.

A reinsurer's underwriting expenses per application differ from those of the ceding company for a number of reasons. For a given degree of underwriting complexity, the reinsurance underwriter may review more cases in a day than his counterpart in a traditional insurance company.

Since the ceding company builds the underwriting file and pays for any tests or reports, it is the placement ratio that effects the ultimate per cession costs of reinsurance underwriting. The reinsurer must determine an acceptable placement ratio level in its pricing structure, and a reinsurer may decline to participate in a program where the placement ratio is below its objective.

Additional Mortality

Because of deviations in offers, facultative mortality is more difficult to predict than automatic mortality. In any mortality rating category, an insurer would normally expect a range of risks, with some lives being better and some being worse than the assumed average for the category. In a competitive facultative situation, the actual average may shift to the higher than expected mortality side, since the better risks in each rating classification or underwriting category are more likely to be placed with a lower rating by some other reinsurer.

Facultative Pricing

It is very difficult to relate underwriting action to pricing. Aggressive underwriting leads to higher mortality costs. If the pricing mortality assumption is less than the mortality that the underwriting action will produce, the reinsurer will lose by placing these cases. Coordinating pricing and underwriting requires good communication between underwriters and actuaries and careful monitoring of results.

Given the difficulties involved in pricing facultative reinsurance, there may be significant diversity in the price of facultative reinsurance to the ceding company. The ceding company may cede facultative reinsurance to its automatic reinsurer at the same premium or allowances as its automatic business as an accommodation. However, if placement ratios are low or the automatic price is extremely competitive, the automatic reinsurers may charge a higher price for facultative coverage. A reinsurer may also look at a ceding company's mix of automatic and facultative business in determining its facultative price. The greater the proportion of facultative, the greater the need for higher facultative prices.

A facultative only outlet may sometimes follow the automatic reinsurance terms for competitive reasons. However, if placement ratios are not adequate or if the reinsurer feels it is not getting an opportunity to review the better cases, the reinsurer may charge a higher price. Also, if the reinsurer uses much more aggressive underwriting than the ceding company, higher reinsurance rates may be justified.

FACULTATIVE REINSURANCE VARIATIONS

Two variations of facultative reinsurance are facultative obligatory and conditional automatic. These are special arrangements which have elements of both facultative and automatic reinsurance. Another variation, the facultative pool, is sometimes used as a time and cost savings device.

Facultative Obligatory

A company may have a facultative obligatory arrangement with the reinsurer. Under such an arrangement, the ceding company has no obligation to cede a particular risk to the reinsurer, but the reinsurer is obligated to accept any risks using the ceding company's underwriting evaluation, within certain limits. Generally, the reinsurer may refuse the risk only if its retention has already been filled on the risk from other policies. A time limit such as 48 hours may be set for refusing the risk.

This privilege is usually granted only to ceding companies in which the reinsurer has absolute trust as to both integrity and underwriting skill. This form of reinsurance is most frequently encountered in a professional retrocessionaire market.

Conditional Automatic

In a conditional automatic situation, an insurance company has a contractual relationship with a reinsurer such that the insurer must cede policies to the reinsurer which fulfill certain criteria. However, the reinsurer underwrites each case and retains the right to refuse to issue those risks which it finds uninsurable by its own standards. Generally, the reinsurer is given a time limit of 48 or 72 hours to evaluate and reject the risk; otherwise it is bound.

Conditional automatic reinsurance is generally used only in situations where the ceding company does not have underwriters of its own and relies on the reinsurer to underwrite all applications. It may also be used when the ceding company has underwriters, but the company is not a member of the Medical Information Bureau.[4] Such an agreement allows the ceding company access to valuable information in exchange for ceding a portion of the risk to the reinsurer.

---

[4] Members of the Medical Information Bureau (MIB) submit coded underwriting information on applicants to the MIB and receive coded information concerning impairments from the MIB regarding new applicants. The insurance company must independently verify this information, but it is regarded as a very useful underwriting tool.

Facultative Pools

In order to reduce the time and expense involved in facultative underwriting, a few companies have formed facultative reinsurance pools. In a facultative pool, a wheel may be used whereby the reinsurers take turns underwriting the cases or the ceding company may underwrite the cases using a previously agreed upon underwriting manual. The reinsurers share in all cases placed in the pool. The ceding company may also participate in the pool or it may hold no retention.

A facultative reinsurance pool would be formed as a time and cost savings device. For example, if three reinsurers participated on an equal basis, each reinsurer would only have to underwrite a third of the cases and would have a placement ratio equal to the insurer's direct placement ratio, thus reducing its costs.

Valuable time can be saved since the ceding company will not have to wait for responses from several reinsurers. Larger savings in time and expense result if the ceding company is responsible for underwriting. The reinsurer's expense savings may be reflected in lower reinsurance premiums.

In order to have a successful reinsurance pool, the reinsurers must have compatible or clearly understood underwriting philosophies. The rules for selecting policies for the pool must be clear and easy to follow. Normally, highly substandard lives or large amounts of insurance will not be placed in the pool. The pool might be limited to those lives which the ceding company would rate through Table 4, or perhaps Table 8, and issued for amounts less than $1,000,000.

If the ceding company performs all the risk evaluation, the rules for evaluating the risks must be carefully defined. In the event the ceding company performs the risk evaluation, the underwriting actions should be audited periodically.

The use of facultative reinsurance pools is limited. The ceding company must be able to generate enough business to produce a significant cost savings to interest reinsurers.

4 Traditional Reinsurance

Although reinsurance has many uses, they can be divided into two broad categories: traditional and financial. Each category has its own marketplace, buyers, and providers.

The traditional reinsurance market encompasses reinsurance which exists primarily for mortality, morbidity, investment, or persistency risk sharing, involving newly issued[1] life, health and annuity policies. This chapter is devoted to individual life insurance but the basic principles apply to other products. Traditional reinsurance can be issued on automatic or facultative bases, and can be proportional or nonproportional. This chapter describes the operation and characteristics of each of the traditional, proportional reinsurance plans, the procedures used to calculate reinsurance premiums and allowances, and the principal uses and considerations for each plan.

---

[1] While some or the same general considerations applicable to the reinsurance of newly issued policies may apply to the reinsurance of inforce blocks of business, the latter is generally restricted to financial reinsurance transactions or the sale or transfer of business using assumption. See Chapter 5, Financial Reinsurance, and Chapter 16, Assumption, for further discussion of these considerations.

COMPARATIVE MODEL

For the purpose of illustrating the effects and differences of the traditional reinsurance plans, a simplistic, one-policy model is presented. It is assumed that ABC Life Insurance Company issues a $400,000 nonsmoker whole life policy on the life of John Doe, a nonsmoking male age 35. ABC Life retains $100,000 of the risk according to its normal retention schedule and cedes the balance to XYZ Re. ABC Life and XYZ Re each have $500 of surplus on hand on January 1 of the calendar year. XYZ Re has issue expenses of $30 per cession and maintenance expenses of $15 per cession.[2]

Assumptions

For ease of presentation, the following simplifying assumptions and approaches are utilized:

(1) Investment income is assumed to be earned only on assets present at the beginning of the calendar year and not on cash flows.
(2) Policy and reinsurance premiums are assumed to be paid on an annual basis, eliminating the need for deferred premium calculations.
(3) Expenses are assumed to be incurred at issue and on policy anniversaries.
(4) No deaths or surrenders are assumed, since the illustration is based on a single life insurance policy.
(5) Federal income tax effects are ignored.
(6) All calculated amounts are rounded to the nearest dollar.
(7) The effects of Federal Income Tax are ignored.

The principal assumptions are summarized as follows.

---

[2] A reinsurer usually has lower issue expenses because it has no underwriting costs on automatic reinsurance and no agency development expenses. Its maintenance expenses are lower because it does not have to perform the same degree of policyholder and agent services as the ceding company, and accounting functions are simpler.

POLICY ASSUMPTIONS

Insured:	John Doe
Issue Age:	35, age nearer birthday
Underwriting Class:	Standard nonsmoker
Issue Date:	7/1/XX
Plan of Insurance:	Whole Life
Face Amount:	$400,000
Premium Rate per $1000:	$10
Annual Policy Fee:	$25
Reserve Basis (Statutory):	1980 CSO NS, ANB, 5.5% CRVM
Cash Value Basis:	1980 CSO NS, ANB, 7.0% MIN
Mean Reserves per $1000	
Year 1:	$0.80
Year 2:	$8.56
Commissions	
Year 1:	90%
Year 2:	10%
Premium Tax:	2.5%
Expenses	
Underwriting and Issue:	$350 per policy
Maintenance:	$25 per policy annually

COMPANY AND REINSURANCE ASSUMPTIONS

	ABC Life	XYZ Re
Initial Surplus:	$500	$500
Investment Rate of Return:	10%	10%
Retention Limit:	$100,000	$2,000,000
Reinsurance Expenses		
Issue:	(included in	$30
Maintenance:	policy expenses)	$15

Illustrations Before Reinsurance

In order to provide a base for comparative purposes, statutory financial statements for both companies are developed before any reinsurance occurs. Tables 4.1A and 4.1B show the Gains from Operations and Balance Sheets, respectively, for the first calendar year, and Tables 4.2A and 4.2B for the second calendar year.

PLANS OF TRADITIONAL REINSURANCE

The primary proportional reinsurance plans in the traditional market are (a) yearly renewable term, frequently referred to as YRT, (b) coinsurance, sometimes referred to as full coinsurance or original terms reinsurance, and (c) modified coinsurance, frequently referred to as mod-co. These three plans are discussed in detail and their relative effects on the financial statements of ABC Life and XYZ Re are illustrated.

Yearly Renewable Term Insurance

Yearly renewable term, or risk premium reinsurance (RPR), is a plan of reinsurance for which the premium rates are not directly related to the premium rates of the original plan of insurance. Under YRT reinsurance, the ceding company reinsures the mortality or morbidity risk only. The amount reinsured in any one year is not based on the face amount of the policy, but rather on the net amount at risk. The ceding company retains responsibility for establishing the policy reserves and the payment of all surrender values, dividends, commissions, and expenses involved in issuing and maintaining the policy.

Of the three traditional plans of reinsurance, YRT generally is considered the simplest plan to administer on an individual cession basis because the reinsurer does not need client/plan-specific records for premiums, allowances, cash values and reserves. It is usually less costly for the ceding company, given the same experience assumptions, because administration is simpler and the lapse and investment risks are smaller.

TABLE 4.1A

STATUTORY FINANCIAL STATEMENTS
BEFORE REINSURANCE — YEAR 1

GAIN FROM OPERATIONS

	ABC LIFE	XYZ RE
Revenue:		
Premiums:		
Gross	$ 4,025	$ 0
Ceded	0	0
Net	4,025	0
Investment Income:		
Surplus	50	50
Reserves	0	0
Total	50	50
Reinsurance Allowance	0	0
Mod-co Adjustment	0	0
TOTAL REVENUE	$ 4,075	$ 50
Benefits:		
Claims	$ 0	$ 0
Surrenders	0	0
Reserve Increase:		
Gross	320	0
Ceded	0	0
Net	320	0
Mod-co Adjustment	0	0
TOTAL BENEFITS	$ 320	$ 0
Expenses:		
Commissions	$ 3,622	$ 0
Acquisition	350	0
Maintenance	25	0
Premium Tax	101	0
TOTAL EXPENSES	$ 4,098	$ 0
GAIN FROM OPERATIONS	$ (343)	$ 50

TABLE 4.1B

STATUTORY FINANCIAL STATEMENTS
BEFORE REINSURANCE — YEAR 1

BALANCE SHEET

	ABC LIFE	XYZ RE
Assets:		
Invested Assets	$ 477	$ 550
TOTAL ASSETS	$ 477	$ 550
Liabilities and Capital:		
Policy Reserves:		
Gross	$ 320	$ 0
Ceded	0	0
Net	320	0
TOTAL LIABILITIES	$ 320	0
Surplus	$ 157	$ 550
TOTAL CAPITAL	$ 157	$ 550
TOTAL LIABILITIES AND CAPITAL	$ 477	$ 550

TABLE 4.2A

STATUTORY FINANCIAL STATEMENTS
BEFORE REINSURANCE — YEAR 2

GAIN FROM OPERATIONS

	ABC LIFE	XYZ RE
Revenue:		
Premiums:		
Gross	$ 4,025	$ 0
Ceded	0	0
Net	4,025	0
Investment Income:		
Surplus	16	55
Reserves	32	0
Total	48	55
Reinsurance Allowance	0	0
Mod-co Adjustment	0	0
TOTAL REVENUE	$ 4,073	$ 55
Benefits:		
Claims	$ 0	$ 0
Surrenders	0	0
Reserve Increase:		
Gross	3,104	0
Ceded	0	0
Net	3,104	0
Mod-co Adjustment	0	0
TOTAL BENEFITS	$ 3,104	$ 0
Expenses:		
Commissions	$ 402	$ 0
Acquisition	0	0
Maintenance	25	0
Premium Tax	101	0
TOTAL EXPENSES	$ 528	$ 0
GAIN FROM OPERATIONS	$ 441	$ 55

TABLE 4.2B

STATUTORY FINANCIAL STATEMENTS
BEFORE REINSURANCE — YEAR 2

BALANCE SHEET

	ABC LIFE	XYZ RE
Assets:		
Invested Assets	$ 4,022	$ 605
TOTAL ASSETS	$ 4,022	$ 605
Liabilities and Capital:		
Policy Reserves:		
Gross	$ 3,424	$ 0
Ceded	0	0
Net	3,424	0
TOTAL LIABILITIES	$ 3,424	0
Surplus	$ 598	$ 605
TOTAL CAPITAL	$ 598	$ 605
TOTAL LIABILITIES AND CAPITAL	$ 4,022	$ 605

Net Amount at Risk Calculation. The net amount at risk in any policy year is usually defined as the face amount of the policy less the terminal reserve and this amount is actually calculated for most YRT cessions. However, simplifying assumptions sometimes are made to facilitate the calculation of net amounts at risk. Some common specifications are discussed in the following sections.

In the use of any simplified method, the reinsurer and the ceding company should agree clearly on the method to be used. In addition, it should be clear that the reinsurance premiums and death benefits will be based on the assumed net amount at risk, not the actual net amount at risk at the time of death.

Level Term Policies. For level term plans of less than twenty years, reserves are generally minimal and, consequently, are usually ignored for reinsurance purposes. The net amount at risk in all years is taken to be the initial reinsured face amount.

For level term policies of twenty years or longer, the "tenth year cash value" method may be used. The first duration net amount at risk is the initial reinsured face amount. In durations two through ten, the net amount at risk usually is determined by using the tenth year cash value.[3] The cash value is used because it is available from the policy form. Reserves are generally available from a separate file. The tenth year cash value divided by nine is the assumed annual decrease in the net amount at risk in years two through ten.

In years eleven through twenty, the net amount at risk is determined by a straight line interpolation between the face amount less the tenth year cash value and the face amount less the twentieth year cash value. A similar approach is used for each successive ten year period.[4]

For example, assume that ABC Life issues a $100,000 term to 65 policy. The tenth year cash value for issue age 35 is $36.00 per

---

[3] In practice, longer period term plans may use a level net amount at risk assumption for simplicity, ignoring any reserves. The choice may be left to the ceding company and may depend on the detail information available within the reinsurance administration system.

[4] This "tenth year cash value" method of estimating net amount at risk is used frequently not just for term insurance products but also for any life plans with predetermined benefits and reserves.

thousand and the twentieth year cash value is $76.00 per thousand. The policy terminates at age 65 with no value.

In the first year, the net amount at risk is $100,000. One-ninth of the tenth year cash value is $400. In the second year, the net amount at risk reduces by $400 to $99,600. The net amount at risk reduces by $400 each year until the tenth year when the net amount at risk is $96,400.

The difference between the tenth and twentieth year cash values is $4,000; one-tenth of the difference is $400. The net amount at risk is, therefore, reduced by $400 each year from year ten to year twenty. The difference between the twentieth year cash value and the cash value at age 65 is $(7,600). In each of the last ten years, the net amount at risk is increased $760.

Decreasing Term Policies. The net amount at risk under decreasing term policies is usually agreed upon in advance based on a formula or table of values. This is particularly useful if decreases occur monthly or if the coverage was designed for use with adjustable interest rate mortgages. A common method is to use the initial reinsurance face amount as the net amount at risk in the first policy year. In years two through ten, the annual reduction in the net amount at risk is one-ninth of the difference between the tenth year death benefit and the first year value. In years eleven through twenty, the net amount at risk is decreased by one-tenth of the difference between the tenth and twentieth year death benefits.

For example, assume ABC Life reinsured a $100,000 thirty year decreasing term policy with a tenth year death benefit of $93,000 and a twentieth year death benefit of $68,800. The first year net amount at risk is $100,000. The second year net amount at risk is $99,222; in the third year $98,444; and so on, reducing $778 each year. In years eleven through twenty, the annual reduction is $2,420. In the final ten years, the annual reduction is $6,880.

Permanent Policies. The most common simplifying method for calculating the net amount at risk is to assume that the initial terminal reserve is zero so that the initial net amount at risk is equal to the face amount reinsured. For years two through ten, the net amount at risk is reduced annually by one-ninth of the tenth year cash values. For years eleven through twenty, the net amount at risk is reduced each year by one-tenth of the difference between the tenth and twentieth year cash values. This is repeated for each subsequent ten year period, and is analogous to the method used for level term policies.

Universal Life. The principal for net amount at risk calculations is the same as for permanent plans. However, the variable amounts of cash value and face amounts create administrative problems.

For some universal life policies, the direct policyholder death benefit is a level amount plus any accumulated account or cash values. Thus, for the direct policy the net amount at risk remains level. Calculation of net amount at risk for reinsurance purposes is simple; the reinsured death benefit is level at the initial amount at risk.

If, however, the original policy death benefit remains level, the net amount at risk fluctuates with the accumulation of account values, and according to certain IRS rules regarding policyholder taxation.[5] The reinsured amounts can be recalculated as frequently as the ceding company and reinsurer deem necessary. Because of this complexity, self-administration or some form of computerized administration is frequently used for universal life and other interest sensitive products. Often, these systems provide for a monthly calculation of the net amount at risk and reinsurance premium. However, in many instances, the monthly changes in the net amount at risk are relatively small and annual approximations may be adequate and less expensive.

Retention Determination.[6] Once the net amount at risk to be reinsured on a YRT basis is calculated, it is important to determine the amount of the risk to be retained. Four methods are commonly used, as described below:

Pro Rata. This is the original proportional method. Under this method the ceding company retains a constant percentage of the net amount at risk. This is calculated as the ratio of original face amount ceded to total original face amount of the policy.

---

[5] See Section 7702 of the Internal Revenue Code.

[6] Retention limits are most often determined on a per life basis. For a discussion of the complexities of using a per policy approach, see Chapter 6, The Reinsurance Treaty.

For example, if ABC Life issues a $1,000,000 whole life policy and cedes $900,000, on the pro rata method it would always reinsure 90% of the policy. If the tenth year terminal reserve is $55,000, the net amount at risk reinsured in the tenth year is 90% of $945,000, or $850,500.

Under the pro rata method, the amount retained will drop below the ceding company's retention limit if the net amount at risk decreases. The pro rata method is the preferred method for reinsuring decreasing term policies as it assures that the policies will be reinsured for the entire term period, although it can result in very small amounts of reinsurance in later policy durations. This method can be used for all plans of insurance.

While the pro rate method may resemble quota share reinsurance, it is not quota share reinsurance. Under a quota share arrangement, the same portion of each policy is reinsured. Under the pro rata method, the portions reinsured vary by the face amount and the initial retention.

Level or Constant Retention. Under the level or constant retention method, the company retains a fixed amount of the net amount at risk. The entire decrease in net amount at risk is allocated to the reinsured portion. If the net amount at risk is a decreasing amount, the amount reinsured under this method will decrease each year more rapidly than under the pro rata method and the reinsurer eventually may have no risk on the policy. While the amount of risk borne by the ceding company and the reinsurer are not in the same proportion each year, this is still referred to as proportional reinsurance because the net amount at risk can still be determined in advance.

If, in the previous example of the $1,000,000 whole life policy, ABC Life keeps a level $100,000 retention, the first year net amount at risk reinsured is $900,000, and the tenth year net amount at risk reinsured is $845,000, the total net amount at risk less $100,000. This tenth year reinsured amount is $5,500 less than that obtained using the pro rata method above. This difference is equal to the tenth year terminal reserve on the original retention.

Constant Risk Reinsured. This is a relatively rare method under which the reinsurance is a constant amount and the ceding company absorbs the reduction. Under this method the amount retained decreases as the reserves increase under the entire policy. In the example of the $1,000,000 whole life policy, ABC Life would always reinsure $900,000, or the entire net amount at risk under the original policy, if less. In the tenth year, the net amount is $945,000, and ABC Life would only retain $45,000.

Formula Retention. Under this method, the net amount at risk and retention are determined by an initially agreed upon formula. This method is often used in the case of decreasing term policies.

Premium Scales. YRT reinsurance rates are usually specific for a given age, duration, and sex. If the plan reinsured distinguishes premiums between smokers and nonsmokers or uses preferred risk discounts, these distinctions are usually reflected in the reinsurance YRT premium scale. Normally, a select period of five, ten, fifteen, or even twenty years is used, with fifteen years being the most common today. The select rate structure is used to reflect expected mortality experience for underwritten lives and provides the ceding company with lower reinsurance costs in the early years.[7]

In some cases, there is no first year premium. The so called "zero first year premium" scale is used to assist the company in reducing its surplus strain on new issues. In effect, the reinsurer assumes statutory surplus and earnings strain to the extent of first year claims.

Sometimes a production bonus or negative first year premium is used to further reduce the surplus strain for the ceding company. Persistency bonuses may be employed, although infrequently, to reward good experience. If used, such bonuses most often are paid on thirteen month experience. The reinsurer may charge an annual cession fee for YRT reinsurance to cover maintenance expenses.[8] This fee is similar

---

[7] Outside the United States and Canada, long select periods are rare. Most commonly there is no select period for YRT rates and attained age aggregate rates are used, although a 50% discount is sometimes applied to the first year rate. Much of this business is subject to experience rating, so any excess YRT premium is shared with the ceding company.

[8] Cession fees are relatively rare today, but are used in this book to illustrate principles of reinsurance and to demonstrate some of the variety of reinsurance terms available.

in purpose and amounts to the policy fee charged the policyholder for a direct policy.

Reinsurers may have several YRT scales available. The scales may vary by the anticipated production of the account, the anticipated average size, the anticipated experience, or the type of products reinsured. If a large volume of production is expected on a particular plan of insurance or if there are special product considerations, the reinsurer may develop a YRT scale specifically for the product. These scales are often designed and stated in coinsurance terms, that is the reinsurance premiums are stated in terms of percentages of the basic plan premium. This approach is commonly used for interest sensitive products where the reinsurance premiums can be stated in terms of a percentage of the cost of insurance rates for the policy. This may simplify the ceding company's administration.

Prior to the mid-1970's many YRT scales in the United States and Canada were experience rated. On an experience rated basis, the reinsurer would return a portion of the excess of premiums received over benefits paid. Experience refund scales were usually 10%-20% higher than non-refund YRT scales. Today, most YRT rate scales in the United States and Canada are not experience rated.

Traditionally, reinsurance YRT scales guaranteed in the reinsurance treaty are equal to the valuation net premiums. These rates are usually far in excess of the actual YRT rates being charged. The non-guaranteed or indeterminate premiums[9] approach has been used to allow the reinsurer to avoid establishing deficiency or additional reserves on assumed YRT reinsurance. While the reinsurer has the contractual right to raise rates to the guaranteed level, it is understood by the parties that there is no intention to do so. Some treaties go so far as to reference the reserve requirements. However, the fact that the reinsurer can raise rates should not be ignored; the reinsurer does have the right to do so. This approach is similar to that used by most insurance companies on direct issues of certain term and other indeterminate premium products.

---

[9] Indeterminate premium policies provide that the insurance company may change premiums, subject to a guaranteed maximum premium, under conditions outlined in the policy.

Most reinsurance YRT rate scales are calculated on a policy year basis, but calendar year YRT rate scales are also in use. Calendar year YRT rate scales are most frequently used with some sort of simplified administrative procedures. Since terminal reserves on the one year term coverage are zero, calendar year scales allow the reinsurer to avoid the necessity of setting up any reserve at the end of the year.

Many universal life products are reinsured on a monthly renewable term basis (MRT). The MRT rates may be stated in terms of the monthly cost of insurance rates, and generally increase on policy anniversaries.

Premium Calculation. The reinsurance premium for a specific policy year on a given YRT cession is equal to the reinsurance YRT rate per $1,000 appropriate for the policyholder's age, sex, policy year, and smoker status times the number of thousands of net amount at risk reinsured. Adjustments for substandard rating are made as necessary, and the cession fee, if any, is then added. Premiums are generally paid on an annual basis, although modal premiums are used on occasion. For variable benefit products such as universal life, monthly calculation of net amounts at risk and reinsurance premiums is most common.

In the case of a substandard table rating, the YRT reinsurance premium is increased to reflect the table rating. The substandard extra premium may take the form of a separate scale or, more commonly, a multiple of the basic YRT premium scale. There is no uniformity in the manner in which substandard table premiums are calculated when distinct smoker and nonsmoker YRT rates are being used. Some reinsurers use the traditional multiple of the nonsmoker or smoker YRT rate for table ratings. Other reinsurers have introduced special substandard rate scales which do not distinguish between smoking habits, thus avoiding potential double discounting which might occur when a multiple of a nonsmoker table is used as a substandard rate and the double surcharging when a multiple smoker table is used on a substandard life. Substandard charges may be waived after a period of years if the ceding company also removes the rating on the underlying policy.

Temporary or flat permanent extra ratings are typically coinsured. Frequently, unsophisticated allowances are granted; that is, the allowances are not individually priced. For ratings extending for more than five years, allowances of 75% to 85% for the first year and 10% to 15% renewal are typical. For ratings of five years or less, allowances of 10% to 15% in each year are typical.

Reinsurance premiums for ancillary benefits such as waiver of premium, guaranteed insurability options, payor death and disability, and monthly income are generally coinsured, again using standard allowances such as 75% to 85% for the first year and 10% to 15% renewal.

Accidental death benefits are usually reinsured on a YRT basis with a rate which rarely varies by age or duration. Term life insurance riders would generally be reinsured using the same YRT rates used for the base policy. Administration is often on a bulk basis.

Uses of Yearly Renewable Term. Yearly renewable term reinsurance is generally used for reinsuring traditional whole life products. It is also frequently used in reinsuring interest sensitive products. In this situation, a special YRT scale is usually developed, with no first duration premium and renewal YRT premiums expressed as percentages of the cost of insurance (COI) rates in the universal life policy. Such a scale resembles the coinsurance of the COI's and may be referred to as a "zero first year" schedule.

Special YRT rates scales may also be developed for use with specific products. In this case, the YRT rate scale is developed to match the slope of the term premium scale, with the YRT rates stated in terms of percentages of the base term rates. In essence, YRT is being used to emulate coinsurance in these situations. Yearly renewable term is also used in reinsuring certain disability income benefits. Annuities cannot be reinsured on a YRT basis.

Other Considerations. Yearly renewable term reinsurance is used to transfer only the mortality or morbidity risks involved in an insurance policy. Because YRT reinsurance involves only limited investment risk, little persistency risk, no cash surrender risk, and little or no surplus strain, the reinsurers will usually have a lower profit objective for YRT reinsurance. Therefore, YRT usually is obtainable at a lower effective cost than either coinsurance or mod-co.

For products with fixed benefits, the net amount at risk and retention schedules can be determined in advance and the administration of such contracts is fairly straightforward. For products with flexible benefits such as interest sensitive products where the cash value can grow quite rapidly, the administration is usually handled by the ceding company. One YRT premium scale is usually applicable to all amounts of insurance issued on a given product, where under coinsurance or mod-co, premiums and allowances may vary by size of the ceded policy. Also, under YRT the reinsurer need not be concerned with policy loans, cash surrenders, or the payment of policy dividends.

Assuming annual premiums are paid, the reserve credit is equal to the unearned portion of a one year term insurance benefit. The ceding company need only adjust the reinsurer's values to account for items in transit. Yearly renewable term reinsurance does not provide relief for deficiency reserves.

In fact, little surplus relief is available because one year term reserves are generally quite small. If the company needs help with the initial surplus strain and wants to use YRT reinsurance, it may negotiate a zero first year scale. If more relief is needed, it may negotiate production bonuses or a negative first year premium. These, of course, add to the cost of the reinsurance in renewal durations.

When a reinsured policy goes on a nonforfeiture status, the appropriate YRT premium must continue to be paid. In the case of extended term or reduced paid up insurance, the reinsurance amount must be adjusted to reflect both the new death benefit and the new net amount of risk pattern. The original YRT premium scale[10] usually is continued based upon the original terms at issue.[11]

YRT Reinsurance Illustrations. In the illustrative example, assume ABC Life has an automatic YRT reinsurance treaty with XYZ Re utilizing assumptions shown below.[12]

---

[10] In some treaties, a "loaded" YRT premium scale is specified for use with extended term insurance.

[11] This concept of maintaining the original issue age, duration, sex, underwriting status, and smoker status is known as using "point-in-scale" YRT premium rates.

[12] As with the other examples in this chapter, the accounting here is on a statutory basis. Results and values may, and likely will be, different for tax or GAAP purposes.

YRT ASSUMPTIONS

Amount Reinsured:	$300,000
YRT Premiums per $1000	
Year 1:	$0.65
Year 2:	$0.77
Annual Cession Fee:	$15.00
YRT Reserve Basis:	1980 CSO NS, ANB, 5.5%
YRT Mean Reserves per $1000	
Year 1:	$0.80
Year 2:	$0.84

Mean reserves per $1,000 of net amount at risk are $.5(1000c_x)$ because the YRT rates are not guaranteed.

First Year Results. The first year YRT rate premium for John Doe's issue age and nonsmoker status is $.65 per $1,000 of coverage with a $15 cession fee. ABC Life would remit a premium of $210 to XYZ Re. The premium tax on the $210 reinsurance premium is $5. The net payment to XYZ Re is $205, but the $210 premium is normally paid by the ceding company at issue. The $5 premium tax reimbursement from the reinsurer is not paid until early in the next calendar year, but would be accrued when the premium is paid. At the end of the first calendar year, the total policy reserve is $320. The YRT mean reserve on the ceded portion is $240. ABC Life is left with a net reserve of $80. Tables 4.3A and 4.3B show the statutory Gains from Operations and Balance Sheets, respectively, for the first year of the YRT transaction for ABC Life and XYZ Re.

ABC Life's net loss in the first year has been reduced to $308, a reduction in loss of $35 from that shown in Table 4.1A. This $35 is equal to the difference between the reinsurance premium and the sum of the reinsurance reserve credit and the premium tax reimbursement, shown as the reinsurance allowance. XYZ Re now has a net loss of $30 for the year, some $80 less earnings than in the pre-reinsurance scenario.

TABLE 4.3A

STATUTORY FINANCIAL STATEMENTS
YRT — YEAR 1

GAIN FROM OPERATIONS

	ABC LIFE	XYZ RE
Revenue:		
Premiums:		
Gross	$ 4,025	$ 210
Ceded	210	0
Net	3,815	210
Investment Income:		
Surplus	50	50
Reserves	0	0
Total	50	50
Reinsurance Allowance	5	0
Mod-co Adjustment	0	0
TOTAL REVENUE	$ 3,870	$ 260
Benefits:		
Claims	$ 0	$ 0
Surrenders	0	0
Reserve Increase:		
Gross	320	240
Ceded	240	0
Net	80	240
Mod-co Adjustment	0	0
TOTAL BENEFITS	$ 80	$ 240
Expenses:		
Commissions	$ 3,622	$ 0
Acquisition	350	30
Maintenance	25	15
Premium Tax	101	5
TOTAL EXPENSES	$ 4,098	$ 50
GAIN FROM OPERATIONS	$ (308)	$ (30)

TABLE 4.3B

STATUTORY FINANCIAL STATEMENTS
YRT — YEAR 1

BALANCE SHEET

	ABC LIFE	XYZ RE
Assets:		
Invested Assets	$ 272	$ 710
TOTAL ASSETS	$ 272	$ 710
Liabilities and Capital:		
Policy Reserves:		
Gross	$ 320	$ 240
Ceded	240	0
Net	80	240
TOTAL LIABILITIES	$ 80	$ 240
Surplus	$ 192	$ 470
TOTAL CAPITAL	$ 192	$ 470
TOTAL LIABILITIES AND CAPITAL	$ 272	$ 710

This is equal to the $30 difference between the reinsurance premium and the reinsurance reserve it has assumed, plus $45 of issue and maintenance expenses and $5 of premium tax reimbursement which it incurred on the ceded policy.

In comparing the Gains from Operations of Table 4.1A with those of Table 4.3A, the sum of the gains for the two companies is the same, except for the additional $45 expense ($30 acquisition and $15 maintenance) incurred by XYZ Re in handling the reinsurance. In particular, the total of the premiums and reserves for the two companies remains constant.[13] While correct in principle, this constant sum principle will not always be maintained in practice due to timing or administrative reasons to be discussed subsequently.

A comparison of the Balance Sheets of Table 4.1B to those of Table 4.3B shows that ABC Life's invested assets have been reduced by $205, representing the reinsurance premium less premium tax reimbursement, while XYZ Re's invested assets have increased by the $210 of YRT premiums less $50 of expenses.

Second Year Results. The net amount at risk per thousand in the second year is $991, calculated using the second year terminal reserve. Assuming a traditional proportional sharing in the net amount at risk, the death benefit reinsured in the second year is $297,000, calculated by multiplying the 300 units reinsured by the net amount at risk.

The YRT premium for the second year is $244. This is calculated as $.77 per $1,000 times 297.3 plus the $15 cession fee. The reinsurance allowance for premium tax is $6.

The statutory reserve credit is calculated based upon the amount at risk ceded. Assuming that $.5(1000c_{36})$ is $.84, the correct reserve credit is 297.3 times $.84, or $250.

Tables 4.4A and 4.4B show the effect of the YRT transaction in the second calendar year. The YRT premium increases to $244. The YRT reserve at the end of the calendar year is $250, an increase of $10 over

---

[13] In this text, it is assumed that the reserve assumptions and methods used by the ceding company and the reinsurer are identical and that the inforce records of the two parties agree. This frequently is not the situation in practice.

TABLE 4.4A

STATUTORY FINANCIAL STATEMENTS
YRT — YEAR 2

GAIN FROM OPERATIONS

	ABC LIFE	XYZ RE
Revenue:		
Premiums:		
Gross	$ 4,025	$ 0
Ceded	244	0
Net	3,781	244
Investment Income:		
Surplus	19	47
Reserves	8	24
Total	27	71
Reinsurance Allowance	6	0
Mod-co Adjustment	0	0
TOTAL REVENUE	$ 3,814	$ 315
Benefits:		
Claims	$ 0	$ 0
Surrenders	0	0
Reserve Increase:		
Gross	3,104	10
Ceded	10	0
Net	3,094	10
Mod-co Adjustment	0	0
TOTAL BENEFITS	$ 3,094	$ 10
Expenses:		
Commissions	$ 402	$ 0
Acquisition	0	0
Maintenance	25	15
Premium Tax	101	6
TOTAL EXPENSES	$ 528	$ 21
GAIN FROM OPERATIONS	$ 192	$ 284

TABLE 4.4B

STATUTORY FINANCIAL STATEMENTS
YRT — YEAR 2

BALANCE SHEET

	ABC LIFE	XYZ RE
Assets:		
Invested Assets	$ 3,558	$ 1,004
TOTAL ASSETS	$ 3,558	$ 1,004
Liabilities and Capital:		
Policy Reserves:		
Gross	$ 3,424	$ 250
Ceded	250	0
Net	3,174	250
TOTAL LIABILITIES	$ 3,174	$ 250
Surplus	$ 384	$ 754
TOTAL CAPITAL	$ 384	$ 754
TOTAL LIABILITIES AND CAPITAL	$ 3,558	$ 1,004

the previous year. XYZ Re now shows a net gain of $284 while ABC Life has a net gain of $192. The combined net gain for both companies of $476 is less than the corresponding combined net gain of $496 without reinsurance shown in Table 4.2B. The $20 difference in net gain is attributable to $15 of maintenance expense incurred by XYZ Re and the $5 of lost investment income on XYZ Re's surplus due to its increased expenses in the first year.

Of importance in this, and in each of the reinsurance examples, is the fact that total liabilities for both companies remain unchanged while the total of the assets of both companies decrease only to the extent that the reinsurer incurs issue and maintenance expenses. Because of these increased expenses, the total of the investment incomes is also decreased. The combined surplus of both companies is decreased by the cumulative amount of these additional expenses and lost investment income.

Coinsurance

Under a coinsurance arrangement, reinsurance coverage ceded to the reinsurer on an individual policy is in the same form as that of the direct policy issued to the policyholder. The reinsurer receives its proportionate share of the gross premium from the ceding company. The reinsurer provides a reimbursement to the ceding company in recognition of the commissions and other out-of-pocket expenses incurred on the ceded portion. This reimbursement is called the expense allowance.

The allowance may or may not cover all of the expenses and commissions incurred by the ceding company. Timing of the payments would match the timing of these expenditures only coincidentally. Occasionally, the allowance may exceed the commission and expenses of the ceding company, providing an additional element of profit. If the allowances do not cover all expenses, especially in renewal durations, the ceding company may need to establish a liability for the present value of any shortfall.[14]

In a coinsurance arrangement, the reinsurer establishes its proportionate share of the policy reserves. It shares proportionately in the risk

---

[14] See the discussion of the Model Regulation on Credit for Life and Health Reinsurance in Chapter 10, Reinsurance Regulation.

Traditional Reinsurance 83

of loss due to excessive mortality or morbidity, lapses, and cash surrenders, and in the investment risks inherent in the contract. The reinsurer also shares in the surplus strain of new issues, the proportion being a function of the relation of the first year expense allowance to the acquisition expense of the reinsurer. Although other methods for determining the retention may be used on occasion, the level retention method is almost always used for coinsurance.

Coinsurance Premiums and Allowances. In most cases, the reinsurance premium used for coinsurance is proportionate to the gross premium paid by the policyholder. Many modern insurance products feature "banded" premiums; that is, the gross premium rate per $1,000 will vary with the face amount of the policy to reflect decreasing per thousand administrative expenses and improved mortality as additional underwriting is used. There are three common methods used to determine reinsurance premiums and allowances for banded policies.

(1) Perhaps the most common method is to base the reinsurance premium on the gross premium rate charged the policyholder and to use a common set of allowances for all bands of banded policies. This method is probably the simplest to understand and to use.
(2) The second method is to base the reinsurance premium on the gross premium rate charged the policyholder and vary the coin-surance allowances by the policy band. This method complicates reinsurance administration, but is sometimes necessary for the reinsurer to have reasonably consistent profit margins for all policy bands. This usually leads to an equitable cost to the ceding company on all bands as well.
(3) The third method is to base the reinsurance premium on a specified band of premium rates regardless of the size of the policy. Typically, the reinsurance premium would be based on the premium rate for the highest amount policy band. Thus, the reinsurance premium for the reinsured portion will never exceed the lowest premium received by the insurance company. One set of allowances is then used for all sizes, resulting in a common net reinsurance premium rate (reinsurance premium rate less allowance) for all

policy sizes. This can simplify the administration. The use of a common net reinsurance rate based on the highest band's premium results in an additional margin on reinsurance for the ceding company on policies written on the lower bands.

Many insurance policies utilize policy fees to help cover the insurance company's maintenance expenses. Under most coinsurance agreements, the reinsurer allows the ceding company to retain the entire policy fee to offset direct expenses and no cession fee is charged. On some occasions, especially for quota share coinsurance agreements, the policy fee will also be coinsured.

Most modern insurance products also recognize a difference between smoker and nonsmoker mortality in the premium structures. Some companies' products may offer a preferred risk category also. The coinsurance premiums usually follow these underwriting classifications, with the reinsurance premium based on the gross premium rate, subject to the banding considerations discussed above. Coinsurance allowances generally vary by the smoker/nonsmoker/preferred risk classifications since the reinsurer's mortality, morbidity, and persistency assumptions and profit objectives will seldom exactly parallel the ceding company's assumptions.

Coinsurance allowances occasionally vary by age, especially if the ceding company's commission scale varies by age. The reinsurer also may vary the allowances by age in order to obtain reasonably consistent profits by age where the reinsurer's mortality, morbidity, and persistency assumptions of profit objectives do not parallel the ceding company's assumptions.

Coinsurance allowances may also vary be sex, but this situation is encountered infrequently.

Some traditional coinsurance agreements are experience rated, providing for the periodic determination of experience refunds. The refund is generally expressed as a proportion of any gain, where the gain is based on a formula reflecting premiums, benefits, allowances, interest, and changes in reserves for the period. Because the ceding company would share only in profits and not in losses, the reinsurance premiums net of allowances on an experience rated basis are higher than similar net reinsurance premiums for a non-refund agreement. Today, most traditional coinsurance is on a non-experience rated basis.

Traditional Reinsurance

In the early years of coinsurance, allowances would rarely equal or exceed 100% of premium in the first policy year. At various points in history, such as the late 1970's and early 1980's, many reinsurers routinely offered first year allowances in excess of 100% of the first year premium on certain products. This was done to alleviate surplus strain and in response to competitive pressures.

The granting of allowances, which, together with cash values, exceed 100% of premium in the first year subjects the reinsurer to an added risk of loss from lapse or surrender. To counteract this, reinsurers will sometimes include a charge back provision in the treaty. In general, a chargeback provision requires the return to the reinsurer of the excess of allowances and cash values paid over premiums received in the event of an early policy termination.

Occasionally, a reinsurer may reward a ceding company for high production or good persistency by means of a bonus. These bonuses may be stated as a percentage of premium or as an amount per $1,000. However, since persistency and production are difficult to monitor, such bonuses are employed rarely.

Many modern insurance products also feature indeterminate or non-guaranteed premiums. Coinsurance premiums and allowances generally are based on the current premium being charged on these products. The reinsurer would retain the right to recalculate coinsurance premiums and allowances should the premium charged for the product ever be changed.

Coinsurance Premium and Allowance Calculations. Under coinsurance, reinsurance allowances are uniquely developed for the product involved. Premiums generally are paid to the reinsurer on an annual basis regardless of the mode of payment received by the ceding company.

Substandard extras are somewhat complicated in their administration. Allowances will usually vary according to type of extra and the period of time to which they apply. Permanent table extra premiums are normally coinsured with the same allowances as the base policy. Flat extra premiums which apply for more than five years may use a more generalized allowance, such as 75% to 85% in the first year and 10% to 15% renewal. Temporary extra premiums which apply for five years or less may have allowances of 10% to 15% in all years. The reinsurance of a term rider attached to the base policy should theoretically have allowances unique for that rider, but sometimes, for the sake of simplicity, the base plan's allowances are used.

Ancillary benefits such as waiver of premium, guaranteed insurability options, payor death and disability, and monthly income are coinsured using generalized allowances such as 75% to 85% first year and 10% to 15% in renewal years. Generally, accidental death benefits are reinsured using a flat YRT rate per thousand.

In the illustrative example, assume that the whole life product has five bands: $10,000 to $99,999, $100,000 to $249,999, $250,000 to $499,999, $500,000 to $999,999, and $1 million and over. Assume that the appropriate standard basic rate for John Doe is $10 per $1,000 plus a policy fee of $25. XYZ Re has offered ABC Life the following allowances:

Policy Year	Expense Allowance
1	100.0%
2-10	15.0
Over 10	7.5

XYZ Re will allow ABC Life to retain the entire policy fee. XYZ Re will also reimburse ABC Life for ABC's premium tax paid of 2.5% on the ceded portion of the premium.

The ceded premium is $3,000. The initial expense allowance is 100% of the ceded premium, or a reimbursement of $3,000. The premium tax reimbursement is $75. For this illustration, this reimbursement will be added to the allowance for the ceding company, even though the timing of payments differ.

In the second policy year, the reinsurance premium will again be $3,000. The expense allowance is 15% of $3,000 or $450. The premium tax reimbursement remains $75, making the total of allowance and premium taxes $525.

Had XYZ Re agreed to base the reinsurance premiums and allowances on the $1 million band where the premium was only $8 per $1,000, the premium calculation would have been modified. The reinsurance premium would have become $8 times 300 or $2,400. The premium tax reimbursement would have been calculated on this lower amount for a total of $60. In the first policy year the allowance would

Traditional Reinsurance 87

have been 100% of $2,400. In the second policy year the allowance would have been 15% of $2,400 or $360. The total of allowances and premium taxes would then have been $2,460 in the first year and $420 in the second year.

Uses of Coinsurance. Coinsurance is applicable to any type of insurance: life, disability, medical, or annuity. For life insurance, coinsurance is used today most commonly for reinsuring term products which have little or no cash value buildup and, therefore, minimal investment risk. However, coinsurance is used with cash value products if there is a desire to pass strain or investment risk to the reinsurer. As discussed previously, care must be taken to meet statutory requirements regarding transfer of investment risks when coinsuring products other than term insurance.

Policyholder Dividends. While it was stated earlier that under a coinsurance arrangement, the reinsurer shares in the operating results of the basic plan, there are certain common exceptions. Until the early 1990's, reinsurers usually declined to share in policyholder dividends paid on participating policies. This was because the common dividend formulas cover not only the underlying mortality and morbidity experience of the plan but also include the ceding company's investment and expense results and profit criteria. Most importantly, dividend formulas include the experience on all business, not just the segment reinsured. The result on retained and reinsured business may differ dramatically, but dividend results tend to reflect the results on retained business.

If a large portion of a block of participating policies is ceded without reinsurer dividend participation, the ceding company may have a problem because it is not holding the assets underlying the reserves and therefore is not receiving the investment benefits. However, coinsurance allowances without dividend participation will be larger than coinsurance allowances which include dividend participation; this increased allowance is intended to offset, at least partially, the dividends.

Sometimes reinsurers agree to participate in a current dividend scale, but not in any future revisions to the scale, up or down. Alternatively, participation in subsequent revisions may be subject to future negotiations. When the reinsurer participates in the dividends, the dividend is actually an additional allowance.

At the time of this writing, New York State Regulation 102 required the reinsurer to participate proportionately in policyholder dividends, including any changes to the dividend scales, if reinsurance reserve credit was to be taken by the ceding company.[15] To date, no other state has adopted such regulation.

Other Considerations. Reinsurers rarely participate in policy loans under coinsurance. Policy loans would represent an additional risk to the reinsurer as well as an additional administrative problem. It is not inconceivable that the total of all policy loans on a block which is largely reinsured could exceed the retained assets.

Because the ceding company is assessed premium taxes on the entire premium collected and not just on the retained portion, common practice is for the reinsurer to reimburse the ceding company in some manner. In some cases, the reinsurer will make provisions for assumed premium taxes in determining the overall expense allowance structure. The ceding company would be responsible for any increases in premium taxes and no special accounting or payments are necessary.

In other cases, the reinsurer will provide for an exact premium tax reimbursement. Any increases or decreases in the premium tax rate would then be passed on to the reinsurer. Other agreements may call for premium tax reimbursement on a fixed percentage or some other mutually agreed upon basis. Treatment of guaranty fund assessments or premium tax offsets are discussed in many newer treaties.

Policies on nonforfeiture status can present a special reinsurance problem. If the insured elects the reduced paid up insurance option, the amount of reinsurance is adjusted proportionately to reflect the reduced amount, and no further premiums are received. If the extended term option is elected, the reinsurer will provide extended term insurance for the appropriate duration, again, with no further premiums. In some instances, especially if the benefit is small, the reinsurer may pay the

---

[15] See Chapter 10, Reinsurance Regulation.

Traditional Reinsurance 89

surrender value to the ceding company at the time the nonforfeiture option is elected and have no further liability.

Because the reinsurer does not normally participate in policy loans, if a policy goes on the automatic premium loan option, the reinsurer will continue to receive its normal premium and pay the normal allowances.

If the reinsurer is admitted or accredited in the ceding company's state of domicile, the ceding company is permitted to reduce its required reserve for the risks reinsured through a reinsurance ceded reserve credit. If the reinsurer is not admitted or accredited in the ceding company's state of domicile, it may be subject to special requirements[16] before the ceding company can take a credit. Coinsurance will pass the basic policy reserves as well as all policy deficiency reserves to the reinsurer on the ceded risk. The calculation and treatment of the reserve credit is under scrutiny by industry and regulatory groups at this time.[17] While the details of the credits may change, the basic principles remain as stated above.

The administration of coinsurance is relatively complex. It involves not only the calculations of premiums and payment of death benefits but also the calculation of expense allowances and reserves and the payments of cash surrenders.[18]

Coinsurance Illustrations. In the illustrative example of ABC Life, assume that ABC Life enters into a coinsurance treaty with XYZ Re using the following allowances:

Policy Year	Expense Allowance
1	100.0%
2-10	15.0
Over 10	7.5

XYZ Re has also agreed to reimburse for premium tax. In this case, the premium tax rate is 2.5%.

---

[16] See Chapter 10, Reinsurance Regulations.
[17] *Ibid.*
[18] See Chapter 7, Reinsurance Administration.

First Year Results. Tables 4.5A and 4.5B show the results of the coinsurance for the first year. ABC Life shows ceded premium of $3,000, leaving a net retained premium of $1,025. It has received a reinsurance expense allowance, including the premium tax reimbursement, of $3,075 from XYZ Re. ABC Life's reserve increase has been reduced to $80 due to the reinsurance reserve credit allowed on the ceded business. Its expenses remain unchanged from the other examples. ABC Life now has a statutory loss in the first year of $28 as compared to a loss of $343 without reinsurance and a loss of $308 with YRT.

The difference in the net losses between the results with no reinsurance and with coinsurance is $315. This is equal to the reinsurance premium less the expense allowance, premium tax reimbursement, and the reinsurance reserve credit. The difference of $280 in the gains between the YRT and coinsurance situation is attributable to lower net reinsurance premium (premiums less allowance) and the higher premium tax reimbursement. The reserve credits are the same.[19]

XYZ Re now has $3,000 of premium and a $240 reserve increase. Its total expenses have risen to $3,120 because of the coinsurance expense allowance and the higher premium tax reimbursement. XYZ Re has a net loss of $310 in the first year under the coinsurance arrangement as opposed to a $50 gain without reinsurance and a $30 loss with YRT. The difference between the net loss with coinsurance and net gain without reinsurance is equal to the sum of the reserve increase, the premium tax reimbursement, and the additional expenses incurred in the reinsurance transaction. The difference in the results for coinsurance and YRT lies in the expense allowance and the higher premium tax reimbursement, offset in part by the higher premium.

At the end of the first calendar year, ABC Life has $472 of surplus while XYZ Re has $190 of surplus. The combined surplus of both companies in the coinsurance illustration is $45 less than the combined surplus without reinsurance because of the additional expenses incurred at XYZ Re. It is equal to the combined surplus in the YRT illustration.

---

[19] In this illustration, the YRT and coinsurance mean reserves are the same in the first year because the base plan is a whole life plan with CRVM reserves. Obviously, not all plans will have a first year mean reserve equal to $.5(1000c_x)$, the YRT reserve.

TABLE 4.5A

STATUTORY FINANCIAL STATEMENTS
COINSURANCE — YEAR 1

GAIN FROM OPERATIONS

	ABC LIFE	XYZ RE
Revenue:		
Premiums:		
Gross	$ 4,025	$ 3,000
Ceded	3,000	0
Net	1,025	3,000
Investment Income:		
Surplus	50	50
Reserves	0	0
Total	50	50
Reinsurance Allowance	3,075	0
Mod-co Adjustment	0	0
TOTAL REVENUE	$ 4,150	$ 3,050
Benefits:		
Claims	$ 0	$ 0
Surrenders	0	0
Reserve Increase:		
Gross	320	240
Ceded	240	0
Net	80	240
Mod-co Adjustment	0	0
TOTAL BENEFITS	$ 80	$ 240
Expenses:		
Commissions	$ 3,622	$ 3,000
Acquisition	350	30
Maintenance	25	15
Premium Tax	101	75
TOTAL EXPENSES	$ 4,098	$ 3,120
GAIN FROM OPERATIONS	$ (28)	$ (310)

TABLE 4.5B

STATUTORY FINANCIAL STATEMENTS
COINSURANCE — YEAR 1

BALANCE SHEET

	ABC LIFE	XYZ RE
Assets:		
Invested Assets	$ 552	$ 430
TOTAL ASSETS	$ 552	$ 430
Liabilities and Capital:		
Policy Reserves:		
Gross	$ 320	$ 240
Ceded	240	0
Net	80	240
TOTAL LIABILITIES	$ 80	240
Surplus	$ 472	$ 190
TOTAL CAPITAL	$ 472	$ 190
TOTAL LIABILITIES AND CAPITAL	$ 552	$ 430

Traditional Reinsurance

The combined assets of the two companies are also $45 less than the combined assets of the two companies with no reinsurance and equal to the combined assets of the two companies in the YRT illustration. The total reserve liability of both companies is the same in all illustrations. It is important to note that liabilities did not disappear, and that assets and surplus were not created by the reinsurance transactions.

Second Year Results. In Tables 4.6A and 4.6B, the accounting results for the second calendar year of the coinsurance transaction are shown. The retained gross premium net of ceded premium remains $1,025 for ABC Life. Its reinsurance allowance, including premium tax reimbursement, is $525. The total reserve on the policy is now $3,424, resulting in a reserve increase of $3,104. The ceded reserve is $2,568, resulting in ceded reserve increase of $2,328, leaving ABC Life with a net reserve increase of $776. ABC Life's other expenses remain unchanged. ABC Life now has a net gain of $301 as opposed to a gain of $441 without reinsurance and $192 with YRT.

XYZ Re has received $3,000 of premium and has a $2,328 reserve increase, with a net gain of $175. This compares to the $55 net gain without reinsurance and a net gain of $284 with YRT.

ABC Life's net surplus has grown to $773 and XYZ Re's has increased to $365. The combined surplus for both companies is $65 less than the combined surplus for both companies with no reinsurance. The $65 is equal to the $45 expenses incurred in the first year of the reinsurance transaction by XYZ Re plus the $5 of lost investment income resulting from those additional expenses and the $15 maintenance expense incurred by XYZ Re in the second year.

Combined assets for both companies have also been reduced by this amount from that shown in the "Before Reinsurance" illustration. Combined surplus and assets in the coinsurance illustration are equal to the combined total of assets and surplus in the YRT illustration. Combined policy reserves are equal in all three illustrations.

Modified Coinsurance

Modified coinsurance differs from coinsurance in that the statutory reserve on the ceded portion of the policy is an obligation of, and held

TABLE 4.6A

STATUTORY FINANCIAL STATEMENTS
COINSURANCE — YEAR 2

GAIN FROM OPERATIONS

	ABC LIFE	XYZ RE
Revenue:		
Premiums:		
Gross	$ 4,025	$ 3,000
Ceded	3,000	0
Net	1,025	3,000
Investment Income:		
Surplus	47	19
Reserves	8	24
Total	55	43
Reinsurance Allowance	525	0
Mod-co Adjustment	0	0
TOTAL REVENUE	$ 1,605	$ 3,043
Benefits:		
Claims	$ 0	$ 0
Surrenders	0	0
Reserve Increase:		
Gross	3,104	2,328
Ceded	2,328	0
Net	776	2,328
Mod-co Adjustment	0	0
TOTAL BENEFITS	$ 776	$ 2,328
Expenses:		
Commissions	$ 402	$ 450
Acquisition	0	0
Maintenance	25	15
Premium Tax	101	75
TOTAL EXPENSES	$ 528	$ 540
GAIN FROM OPERATIONS	$ 301	$ 175

TABLE 4.6B

STATUTORY FINANCIAL STATEMENTS
COINSURANCE — YEAR 2

BALANCE SHEET

	ABC LIFE	XYZ RE
Assets:		
Invested Assets	$ 1,629	$ 2,933
TOTAL ASSETS	$ 1,629	$ 2,933
Liabilities and Capital:		
Policy Reserves:		
Gross	$ 3,424	$ 2,568
Ceded	2,568	0
Net	856	2,568
TOTAL LIABILITIES	$ 856	$ 2,568
Surplus	$ 773	$ 365
TOTAL CAPITAL	$ 773	$ 365
TOTAL LIABILITIES AND CAPITAL	$ 1,629	$ 2,933

by, the ceding company, rather than the reinsurer. The reinsurer is responsible for funding any increases in the reserve, less a credit for investment income. As in coinsurance, the reinsurer receives its portion of the gross premium on all policies ceded on a mod-co basis and reimburses the ceding company for its commissions and related expenses by means of an expense allowance. Mod-co, like coinsurance, transfers surplus strain on the reinsured portion of new issues to the reinsurer as well as a proportional share of the risk of loss from lapse, surrender, and death.

Assets equal to the reserve are provided to, and become the property of, the ceding company through the mod-co reserve adjustment, discussed subsequently in this section. These assets, and therefore the investment risk, are retained by the ceding company, unless special considerations are made in the formula for the interest element in the mod-co reserve adjustment. From an economic viewpoint, mod-co may be compared to coinsurance where the assets supporting the reserves represent a directed investment back to the ceding company. The reinsurer credits interest to the ceding company through the mod-co reserve adjustment.

Origins of Mod-Co. The first use of mod-co is unclear. One explanation is that mod-co was originally created to satisfy reinsurance problems experienced by New York companies which were not allowed to take credit for reserves on policies reinsured to companies not licensed to do business in New York. Another explanation is that mod-co was developed for ceding companies that believed they could realize a better investment return on the assets underlying the reserves than the reinsurer would assume in its pricing.

Mod-Co Premiums and Allowances. The premium and expense allowance considerations for mod-co are similar to those for coinsurance. The mod-co reinsurance premium is generally proportional to the gross annual premium of the policy ceded with the proper consideration for banding; smoker, nonsmoker and preferred risk classifications; indeterminate premiums; and the policy fee. Allowances follow the same pattern as in coinsurance; any differences in allowances between mod-co and coinsurance on a particular plan of insurance would arise from

Traditional Reinsurance 97

different tax implications or differences in the investment income assumption of the reinsurer on coinsurance and the interest rate used in the mod-co reserve adjustment.

Mod-Co Premium and Allowance Calculations. The premium and allowance calculations for mod-co are also similar to those for coinsurance. The treatment of substandard extra premiums is also the same. Term riders attached to the base policy may be reinsured using modified coinsurance or coinsurance at the discretion of the ceding company and the reinsurer. Ancillary benefits such as waiver of premium benefits may be reinsured using either modified coinsurance or coinsurance, but are usually coinsured. Generally, accidental death benefits are reinsured using a flat YRT rate.

Mod-Co Reserve Adjustment. Under a mod-co treaty, the reinsurer receives its proportionate share of the gross premium as in coinsurance, but the ceding company maintains the entire reserve on the reinsured policies. In order for the ceding company to do this, the reinsurer returns the increase in statutory reserves for the ceded portion to the ceding company. This is done through a mechanism know as the modified coinsurance reserve adjustment, or simply the mod-co adjustment. The mod-co reserve adjustment is determined as follows:

> The ending policy reserves, less
> the beginning policy reserves, less
> interest on the beginning policy reserves.

If the result is positive, the reinsurer pays that amount to the ceding company. If the result is negative, the ceding company pays the reinsurer. Historically, the calculation is normally done on a calendar year basis, but it is more likely to be done quarterly today. The reserves referred to in the above formula are, of course, the proportionate share of the statutory reserves which are held for annual statement purposes.

The interest rate used to determine the interest credited on the beginning reserves held by the ceding company is known as the mod-co interest rate. It is a very important element in determining the overall cost of modified coinsurance and degree of risk transfer. It is defined in the reinsurance treaty. The method for determining this rate has changed in recent years with the introduction of the Credit for Reinsurance Model Regulation. However, many inforce treaties have older provisions which will be discussed first.

Historically, the interest rate could be defined in terms of the ceding company's portfolio rate, its rate of return on assets underlying the block of business reinsured, its rate of return on new money, or an outside index. In the past, a fixed rate was sometimes used. If the mod-co interest rate is equal to the ceding company's rate of return on the assets underlying the reserves, the result to the ceding company would be the same as if coinsurance had been used. The same would be true relative to the reinsurer if the mod-co interest rate equaled the reinsurer's rate of return.

In the past, except in rare instances, the reinsurer does not participate in any capital gains and losses on the assets of the ceding company. Depending upon the actual performance, this can work to the advantage or disadvantage of either party. In general, the reinsurer is believed to have less investment risk under mod-co because it has no direct exposure to default or disintermediation risk. However, reinsurers usually prefer to manage their own assets and not to assume a credit risk by transferring the assets to another party.

In the past, if the ceding company believed it could secure significant capital gains, then it would prefer mod-co to coinsurance. Under coinsurance, the reinsurer retains all capital gains and losses on the assets underlying the reserves on the business ceded to it. Of course, under coinsurance, the reinsurer assumes the asset default risk while under mod-co the ceding company has this risk.

While regulation varies by state, the NAIC's Model Regulation[20] and typical actuarial practice now require that all significant risks be transferred if reserve credit or surplus enhancement is to result from a reinsurance agreement. For underlying policies involving certain investment risk if defined in the Model Regulation, the reinsurer must participate in the asset performance of the assets underlying the business ceded. This includes participation in capital gains and losses and all defaults and timing risks. For other policies, such as term insurance and

---

[20] See Chapter 10, Reinsurance Regulation.

certain health and whole life policies, the mod-co interest rate may be the result of the entire investment portfolio of the ceding company, including capital gains and losses, defaults, and timing risks. Most treaties being written today define the mod-co interest rate in a manner to be in compliance with the Model Regulation. The regulations do not apply to modified coinsurance alone. Interest payments under funds withheld coinsurance are to be treated in the same manner.

Uses of Mod-Co. Modified coinsurance is used primarily in reinsuring products which develop cash values. This allows the ceding company to retain the assets for investment purposes while still obtaining the surplus relief aspects of coinsurance. This has a particular advantage for participating products or for interest sensitive products where the interest element in the dividend or cash value formula plays a major role.

Mod-co was popular when the ceding company desired to maintain tax basis reserves calculated in accordance with Section 818(a)(2)[21] of the Life Insurance Company Income Tax Act of 1959 for all policies on the block reinsured. The 818(a)(2) reserves were an approximate revaluation of reserves maintained on a modified reserve basis to a net level basis.

In the early 1980's, many companies used modified coinsurance to reinsure vast amounts of individual life products in order to reduce federal income taxes. This tax reduction was accomplished by transforming investment income to underwriting income, moving investment income out of the ceding company through the mod-co reserve adjustment and returning it through the experience refund formula as underwriting gain.[22] This practice was halted after revisions were made to the tax code section (820) which enabled it.

Other Considerations. Mod-co eliminates some of the problems of coinsurance. Because the ceding company maintains the policy reserves, there is no question about reserve credits. The use of mod-co eliminates the problem of participation in policy loans by the reinsurer as the ceding company holds the assets. Mod-co also allows the ceding company more

---

[21] See Chapter 14, Tax Effects of Reinsurance.
[22] *Ibid.*

control over investments. This is important in developing policyholder dividend scales or interest credits and in matching assets and liabilities. In addition, mod-co allows the ceding company to maintain a higher level of assets and, therefore, attain a higher comparative asset ranking than would coinsurance. While the dividend participation concerns still remain, the magnitude of the participation requirement is greatly diminished.

The main drawback to the use of mod-co is that it is somewhat more complicated to administer than coinsurance because of the reserve adjustment calculation.

Mod-Co Illustrations. For the purpose of illustrating the effect of modified coinsurance on ABC Life and XYZ Re, it is assumed that XYZ Re has granted the same allowances as were used in the coinsurance example. It is further assumed that the mod-co interest rate is equal to the portfolio rate of 10% earned by both companies. Given these two conditions, the statutory net income and surplus for both companies are unchanged from those coinsurance example.

First Year Results. Tables 4.7A and 4.7B show the statutory Gains from Operations and Balance Sheets for the first year of the modified coinsurance transaction.

ABC Life shows the same ceded premium and reinsurance allowances as in the coinsurance illustration from Table 4.5A. Now, however, ABC Life has an additional revenue item called mod-co adjustment. The first year mod-co adjustment is calculated as follows:

ABC LIFE
MOD-CO RESERVE ADJUSTMENT — YEAR 1

Ending Policy Reserves:		$ 240
Less: Beginning Policy Reserves	$ 0	
Interest on Beginning Policy Reserves	0	0
Mod-co Adjustment:		$ 240

TABLE 4.7A

STATUTORY FINANCIAL STATEMENTS
MODIFIED COINSURANCE — YEAR 1

GAIN FROM OPERATIONS

	ABC LIFE	XYZ RE
Revenue:		
Premiums:		
Gross	$ 4,025	$ 3,000
Ceded	3,000	0
Net	1,025	3,000
Investment Income:		
Surplus	50	50
Reserves	0	0
Total	50	50
Reinsurance Allowance	3,075	0
Mod-co Adjustment	240	0
TOTAL REVENUE	$ 4,390	$ 3,050
Benefits:		
Claims	$ 0	$ 0
Surrenders	0	0
Reserve Increase:		
Gross	320	0
Ceded	0	0
Net	320	0
Mod-co Adjustment	0	240
TOTAL BENEFITS	$ 320	$ 240
Expenses:		
Commissions	$ 3,622	$ 3,000
Acquisition	350	30
Maintenance	25	15
Premium Tax	101	75
TOTAL EXPENSES	$ 4,098	$ 3,120
GAIN FROM OPERATIONS	$ (28)	$ (310)

TABLE 4.7B

STATUTORY FINANCIAL STATEMENTS
MODIFIED COINSURANCE — YEAR 1

BALANCE SHEET

	ABC LIFE	XYZ RE
Assets:		
Invested Assets	$ 792	$ 190
TOTAL ASSETS	$ 792	$ 190
Liabilities and Capital:		
Policy Reserves:		
Gross	$ 320	$ 0
Ceded	0	0
Net	320	0
TOTAL LIABILITIES	$ 320	$ 0
Surplus	$ 472	$ 190
TOTAL CAPITAL	$ 472	$ 190
TOTAL LIABILITIES AND CAPITAL	$ 792	$ 190

Traditional Reinsurance 103

ABC Life now has the entire reserve increase reflected in its gain from operations, and an additional income item representing the mod-co adjustment. Its expenses remain unchanged. ABC Life has a net loss of $28, identical to that in the coinsurance illustration.

XYZ Re receives its $3,000 of premium, the same as in the coinsurance example. However, in this case, it has no reserve increase as it is not holding any reserve on this policy. It has an additional cash benefit item for the mod-co adjustment of $240. XYZ Re's expenses remain unchanged, and it has a net loss in the first year of $310, again identical to its financial position under the coinsurance transaction.

The Statutory Balance Sheet shows that the surplus of ABC Life has been reduced to $472 and that of XYZ Re has been reduced to $190. These values are identical to those for the coinsurance illustration. ABC Life shows all $320 of the policy reserves on its statutory balance sheet and holds assets of $792. XYZ Re's assets equal its surplus because it has no liabilities; it has paid the mod-co reserve increase in cash. Combined assets for both companies are the same as in the coinsurance illustration. The assets have been redistributed to reflect the fact that ABC Life is maintaining the entire reserve.

Second Year Results. Tables 4.8A and 4.8B show the statutory Gains from Operations and Balance Sheets resulting from modified coinsurance in the second year. The second year mod-co adjustment is developed as follows:

ABC LIFE
MOD-CO RESERVE ADJUSTMENT — YEAR 2

Ending Policy Reserves:		$ 2,568
Less: Beginning Policy Reserves	$ 240	
Interest on Beginning Policy Reserves	24	(264)
Mod-co Adjustment:		$ 2,304

This mod-co adjustment appears as a revenue item for ABC Life and as a benefit item for XYZ Re.

TABLE 4.8A

STATUTORY FINANCIAL STATEMENTS
MODIFIED COINSURANCE — YEAR 2

GAIN FROM OPERATIONS

	ABC LIFE	XYZ RE
Revenue:		
Premiums:		
Gross	$ 4,025	$ 3,000
Ceded	3,000	0
Net	1,025	3,000
Investment Income:		
Surplus	47	19
Reserves	32	0
Total	79	19
Reinsurance Allowance	525	0
Mod-co Adjustment	2,304	0
TOTAL REVENUE	$ 3,933	$ 3,019
Benefits:		
Claims	$ 0	$ 0
Surrenders	0	0
Reserve Increase:		
Gross	3,104	0
Ceded	0	0
Net	3,104	0
Mod-co Adjustment	0	2,304
TOTAL BENEFITS	$ 3,104	$ 2,304
Expenses:		
Commissions	$ 402	$ 450
Acquisition	0	0
Maintenance	25	15
Premium Tax	101	75
TOTAL EXPENSES	$ 528	$ 540
GAIN FROM OPERATIONS	$ 301	$ 175

TABLE 4.8B

STATUTORY FINANCIAL STATEMENTS
MODIFIED COINSURANCE — YEAR 2

BALANCE SHEET

	ABC LIFE	XYZ RE
Assets:		
Invested Assets	$ 4,197	$ 365
TOTAL ASSETS	$ 4,197	$ 365
Liabilities and Capital:		
Policy Reserves:		
Gross	$ 3,424	$ 0
Ceded	0	0
Net	3,424	0
TOTAL LIABILITIES	$ 3,424	$ 0
Surplus	$ 773	$ 365
TOTAL CAPITAL	$ 773	$ 365
TOTAL LIABILITIES AND CAPITAL	$ 4,197	$ 365

Investment income has been redistributed between the two companies. Since the mod-co interest rate is equal to the investment income rate, ABC Life's investment income has increased by an amount equal to the mod-co interest while XYZ Re's investment income has decreased by the same amount.

As ABC Life is holding the entire reserve on this policy, it reflects the entire reserve increase of $3,104 in determining its gain from operations. The benefits and expenses remain unchanged, so ABC Life has a net income of $301 and XYZ Re has a net income of $175. The net incomes are again identical to the respective net incomes in the coinsurance illustration for both companies.

The Statutory Balance Sheet shows the statutory surplus has increased by the amount of the net income for both companies. The statutory reserves on the entire block are carried on ABC Life's balance sheet. The combined assets for both companies are equal to the combined assets for both companies in the coinsurance illustration. The assets of ABC Life are higher than in the case of coinsurance because it is holding the entire reserve.

Had the treaty called for a different mod-co interest rate, the results would have been different and would no longer equal those for the coinsurance illustration. For example, if that mod-co interest rate had been 7.5%, the mod-co adjustment would have been $2,310; ABC's gain would have been $307 and that of XYZ Re $169. The total of the earnings did not change, only the allocation.

5 | Financial Reinsurance

Reinsurance is a versatile tool for financial planning. In this chapter, the terminology, uses, and mechanics of financial reinsurance are discussed. To illustrate the financial effect of each plan of reinsurance on the ceding company and the reinsurer, a simple annuity model is developed for comparative purposes. The basic plans of financial reinsurance are defined and illustrated. A brief discussion of regulation, taxation, and security considerations is also included.[1]

USES OF FINANCIAL REINSURANCE

Financial reinsurance is useful for several purposes. The most common uses are surplus relief, tax planning, and strategic business planning. Financial reinsurance is based on differences in timing for statutory or tax earnings and on any statutory reserves redundancy. GAAP account-

---

[1] For more information regarding regulation and taxation, see Chapter 10, Reinsurance Regulations, and Chapter 14, Tax Effects of Reinsurance.

ing usually does not recognize financial reinsurance and is not considered in this chapter. Most financial reinsurance is structured in a manner that little, if any, cash exchanges hands except for fees or risk charges earned by the reinsurer.

Surplus Relief

The most common use of financial reinsurance is to provide the ceding company with assets or reserve credits in order to improve its current statutory earnings and surplus position. This process is commonly referred to as surplus relief.

For internal purposes, XYZ Re sets up an outstanding surplus account to track the funds advanced to ABC Life. The beginning balance in the account is $100.

Surplus relief creates an increase in statutory surplus for the ceding company in the year in which the relief is given and a corresponding reduction in the statutory surplus of the reinsurer. If the business reinsured produces adequate future gains, the reinsurer recovers all of its investment plus a profit. The ceding company's earnings in future years are decreased by the same amount that the reinsurer's earnings are increased.

In surplus relief, the reinsurer commits cash or other assets to, or assumes liabilities of, the ceding company. Surplus relief differs from a loan in that the repayment of the relief is tied to the future cash flow or statutory earnings on the block reinsured and is not guaranteed as to timing or ultimate recovery.

Because the reinsurer is repaid from the future earnings, it is important to the reinsurer that the value of future statutory earnings of the reinsured block exceed the amount of surplus relief granted by an adequate margin. The risk or profit charge assessed on a surplus relief agreement tends to be significantly less than the profit which would be expected if the reinsurer were to reinsure the same block of business in the traditional market. Since it expects less profit, the reinsurer usually looks for additional security in this type of transfer.

The value of future earnings is in part attributed to a redundancy in statutory reserves. The amount of redundancy is estimated by an analysis such as a gross premium valuation or an actuarial appraisal. In most surplus relief situations, the present value of the cash flows and the reserves released on the block reinsured significantly exceeds the amount

Financial Reinsurance 109

of surplus relief granted. The excess profits are returned to the ceding company by paying experience rating refunds or allowing termination of the treaty once the surplus relief and charges have been recovered.

Tax Planning

Reinsurance is used in tax planning,[2] although not to the extent it once was. In the most common tax planning application, a company cedes reinsurance, creating a taxable gain, which is used to offset current or carry forward tax losses. This is especially useful if a company has expiring tax loss carry forwards.

Any resulting statutory gain to the ceding company represents a corresponding loss to the reinsurer. Consequently, this type of reinsurance often resembles surplus relief, although the transfers are more commonly permanent. As in the case of surplus relief, the reinsurer recovers its initial statutory loss through the future statutory earnings on the reinsured block.

A company might also assume reinsurance to create a loss in order to offset other taxable gains. The ceding company usually has the right to terminate the reinsurance rather than pay the ongoing cost of the reinsurance once the initial gain has been repaid.

A company may cede health insurance or assume life insurance in order to qualify as a life insurance company for tax purposes. It may also cede life insurance or assume health insurance in order to qualify as a non-life insurance company if it considers this to be advantageous.

Strategic Business Planning

A company may wish to acquire reinsurance for a number of business related purposes. Reinsurance may be used to increase future profits, utilize excess administrative capacity, or assist the company in entering a new market. Conversely, a company may cede or sell reinsurance to exit a certain market. Reinsurance may also be used as part of the financing in a leveraged buy-out.

In most instances, reinsurance for business planning purposes is of a permanent nature and specific provision for recapture is not usually included in the treaty. Assumption is commonly used for this purpose.

---

[2] See Chapter 14, Tax Effects of Reinsurance.

TERMINOLOGY

The remainder of this chapter will focus on financial reinsurance which provides the ceding company with a gain in the first year of the transaction to fill a temporary or permanent financial need. Many of the commonly used reinsurance terms take on special meanings in financial reinsurance transactions. These terms are discussed below.

Initial Reinsurance Premium

The initial premium, or consideration, for reinsurance of a block of inforce is typically equal to the policy reserve, although it may be a higher or lower amount. In subsequent accounting periods the reinsurance premium on any form of coinsurance is usually the gross premium paid on the policies reinsured. Allowances are used to adjust the effective amount of renewal premium.

Allowances

Allowances refer to the amounts paid by or allowed by the reinsurer to the ceding company. In financial reinsurance, the initial allowance provides the gain in the first year of the transaction. It may be stated as a percentage of the initial premium, as an amount per unit of coverage, or as a flat amount per transaction. In renewal years, allowances may be paid to provide for the ceding company's commission and maintenance expenses and to adjust the expected results to a mutually agreed upon level.

For example, allowances may be set at a level above the ceding company's commission and expense level to allow the ceding company a continuing profit from the business. Alternatively, lower allowances may be used to give the reinsurer some additional profit margin.[3] In general, higher initial allowances should lead to lower renewal allowances and vice versa. Of course, the higher the allowances, the longer the period before the reinsurer recoups its initial strain.

---

[3] There may be regulatory consequences of establishing allowances at too low a level. See Chapter 10, Reinsurance Regulations.

Financial Reinsurance

Risk Charge

The term risk charge[4] refers to the portion of the reinsurance premium which the reinsurer retains for providing the reinsurance. The risk charge is normally stated in terms of the amount of the outstanding surplus or gain. The amount of the risk charge depends on the nature of the risks assumed, the size of the transaction, the reinsurer's profit objectives, the market conditions at the time, the ceding company's stability, tax considerations, company relationships, and the reinsurer's expenses for analysis, administration or intermediaries. Historic risk charges have varied between 1% and 5% of the outstanding surplus relief each year. The risk charge is negotiable on each treaty.

Experience Refund

Most financial reinsurance transactions provide for an experience refund. An experience refund is a mechanism used to identify and return some portion of the statutory earnings on the reinsured business to the ceding company. In the financial reinsurance area, experience refunds typically are not paid to the ceding company until the initial allowance has been recovered by the reinsurer from the statutory earnings on the reinsured business.

The payment of negative experience refunds, that is, payments by the ceding company to the reinsurer for poor experience, is uncommon. Treaty provisions creating such refunds will usually result in a disqualification of statutory reserve credits for the reinsurance transaction.[5] However, the use of loss deficit carryforwards or a requirement of repayment of accumulated losses prior to termination or recapture are not prohibited as long as the reinsurer is not allowed to terminate the agreement unilaterally forcing the ceding company into a loss position. Options in the agreement which permit the ceding company unilateral authority to terminate the treaty and pay the reinsurer for any accumulated losses are allowed.

---

[4] The risk charge is also known by other names, such as risk and profit charge or expense and risk charge.

[5] See Chapter 10, Reinsurance Regulations.

Outstanding Surplus Account

All or a defined portion of any statutory gains on the business reinsured, after provision for the risk charge, experience refund, and interest accumulated on the outstanding initial allowance, are used to repay the initial allowance. In order to track this repayment, the reinsurer will establish an outstanding surplus account or outstanding initial allowance account for each treaty. Most financial reinsurance treaties preclude termination or recapture while the reinsurer's accumulated results are in a deficit position. Conversely, most such arrangements may be terminated by the ceding company after the accumulated surplus relief has been repaid.

There is no guarantee that gains will develop in renewal years. To the extent gains are achieved, the risk charge is paid and the surplus account is reduced. To the extent losses result, such losses are added to the accumulated surplus account. Losses are generally accumulated with interest, especially if the reinsurer paid the initial allowance in cash.

The periodic risk charge may be paid as due or may be paid only to the extent that there are profits from the reinsurance, with any unpaid amounts carried forward. The first practice is utilized less frequently today because of regulatory concerns.

COMPARATIVE MODEL

In order to better understand how the various plans of financial reinsurance will affect the ceding company and the reinsurer, a simple illustration has been constructed using a single premium deferred annuity. The values used for premiums, reserves, investment income, and commissions have been arbitrarily chosen to simplify the illustrations and are not meant to be representative of an actual product. The risk charge and experience refund factors have also been arbitrarily chosen and should not be construed to represent those found in actual practice. A number of minor items which might affect the annual statement have been ignored for the sake of simplicity.

The single premium deferred annuity product was chosen to avoid renewal premium flows and to highlight the financial result from the reinsurance transaction. In practice, such annuities are often used for

Financial Reinsurance

financial reinsurance. Since the persistency on these products is usually very high and the reserves are large, single premium deferred annuities are capable of supporting large initial allowances. The administration is relatively simple since there are no renewal premiums, and the mortality risk is small. Any other type of insurance product could have been illustrated.

Assumptions

It is assumed that ABC Life sells $1,000 of single premium deferred annuities, issued December 31. It pays its agents $100 of commissions. Its reserves on December 31 are $1,000. ABC Life is assumed to have no other assets or surplus in order to emphasize the marginal effect of the transaction.

XYZ Re is assumed to have $100 of free surplus available for the reinsurance transaction. As ABC Life is administering the reinsurance, XYZ Re's expenses are minimal and will not be considered. Both ABC Life and XYZ Re earn 10% on invested assets held at the beginning of each year but not on the cash flows. Taxes and maintenance expenses are ignored in order to highlight the reinsurance transaction.

Benefits of $5 are assumed to be incurred in the second calendar year. The second year reserve increase on the remaining contracts is assumed to be $70.

Illustrations before Reinsurance

Tables 5.1A and 5.1B show the statutory Gains from Operations and Balance Sheets for ABC Life and XYZ Re for the year the annuities were issued before any reinsurance transaction. This shows ABC Life with $1,000 of premiums, $1,000 of reserves, and $100 of commissions and expenses for a gain of $(100). ABC Life, therefore, has $900 of invested assets and $1,000 of reserve liabilities, leaving it with a surplus for this particular transaction of $(100). XYZ Re's statutory balance sheet shows $100 of surplus.

Tables 5.2A and 5.2B show the results for the second calendar year had ABC Life had sufficient surplus from other sources to cover the $100 of strain and had not, therefore, entered into any sort of reinsurance arrangement. The negative $10 investment income on surplus demonstrates that ABC Life has to support the reserves on the plan.

TABLE 5.1A

STATUTORY FINANCIAL STATEMENTS
BEFORE REINSURANCE — YEAR 1

GAIN FROM OPERATIONS

	ABC LIFE	XYZ RE
Revenue:		
Premiums:		
Gross	$ 1,000	$ 0
Ceded	0	0
Net	1,000	0
Investment Income:		
Surplus	0	0
Reserves	0	0
Total	0	0
Reinsurance Allowance	0	0
Mod-co Adjustment	0	0
TOTAL REVENUE	$ 1,000	$ 0
Benefits:		
Claims and Surrenders:		
Gross	$ 0	$ 0
Ceded	0	0
Net	0	0
Reserve Increase:		
Gross	1,000	0
Ceded	0	0
Net	1,000	0
Experience Refund	0	0
Mod-co Adjustment	0	0
TOTAL BENEFITS	$ 1,000	$ 0
Expenses:		
Expenses and Commissions	$ 100	$ 0
TOTAL EXPENSES	$ 100	$ 0
GAIN FROM OPERATIONS	$ (100)	$ 0

TABLE 5.1B

STATUTORY FINANCIAL STATEMENTS
BEFORE REINSURANCE — YEAR 1

BALANCE SHEET

	ABC LIFE	XYZ RE
Assets:		
Invested Assets	$ 900	$ 100
Accounts Receivable	0	0
TOTAL ASSETS	$ 900	$ 100
Liabilities and Capital:		
Policy Reserves:		
Gross	$ 1,000	$ 0
Ceded	0	0
Net	1,000	0
Accounts Payable	0	0
TOTAL LIABILITIES	$ 1,000	$ 0
Surplus	$ (100)	$ 100
TOTAL CAPITAL	$ (100)	$ 100
TOTAL LIABILITIES AND CAPITAL	$ 900	$ 100

TABLE 5.2A

STATUTORY FINANCIAL STATEMENTS
BEFORE REINSURANCE — YEAR 2

GAIN FROM OPERATIONS

	ABC LIFE	XYZ RE
Revenue:		
Premiums:		
Gross	$ 0	$ 0
Ceded	0	0
Net	0	0
Investment Income:		
Surplus	(10)	10
Reserves	100	0
Total	90	10
Reinsurance Allowance	0	0
Mod-co Adjustment	0	0
TOTAL REVENUE	$ 90	$ 10
Benefits:		
Claims and Surrenders:		
Gross	$ 5	$ 0
Ceded	0	0
Net	5	0
Reserve Increase:		
Gross	70	0
Ceded	0	0
Net	70	0
Experience Refund	0	0
Mod-co Adjustment	0	0
TOTAL BENEFITS	$ 75	$ 0
Expenses:		
Expenses and Commissions	$ 0	$ 0
TOTAL EXPENSES	$ 0	$ 0
GAIN FROM OPERATIONS	$ 15	$ 10

TABLE 5.2B

STATUTORY FINANCIAL STATEMENTS
BEFORE REINSURANCE — YEAR 2

BALANCE SHEET

	ABC LIFE	XYZ RE
Assets:		
Invested Assets	$ 985	$ 110
Accounts Receivable	0	0
TOTAL ASSETS	$ 985	$ 110
Liabilities and Capital:		
Policy Reserves:		
Gross	$ 1,070	$ 0
Ceded	0	0
Net	1,070	0
Accounts Payable	0	0
TOTAL LIABILITIES	$ 1,070	$ 0
Surplus	$ (85)	$ 110
TOTAL CAPITAL	$ (85)	$ 110
TOTAL LIABILITIES AND CAPITAL	$ 985	$ 110

Table 5.2A shows that ABC Life now has net income in the second year of $15 while XYZ Re has net income of $10 from the investment income on its surplus. Table 5.2B shows ABC Life's invested assets have grown to $985, its reserves to $1,070, and its surplus is now $(85). XYZ Re's assets and surplus have grown to $110 as the result of investment income.

PLANS OF FINANCIAL REINSURANCE

In addition to the three basic reinsurance plans, financial reinsurance utilizes certain hybrid plans. This section defines and illustrates the financial reinsurance use of the three basic plans as well as the following three hybrid plans: funds withheld coinsurance, funds withheld mod-co, and partially modified coinsurance.

Yearly Renewable Term Insurance

Under the YRT plan of reinsurance the reinsurer holds reserves appropriate for a yearly renewable term product. In the case of a whole life product, the amount of the credit can be quite small in relationship to the basic product reserves, especially in renewal years. Because YRT reserves are relatively small, YRT does not provide any significant relief to the ceding company unless the product being reinsured is also of the YRT form. The gain is provided by a first year allowance or a negative first year premium.

The reinsurer assesses the ceding company a risk charge to cover the risks assumed, the use of its surplus, its expenses incurred, and a provision for profit. An experience refund may be used to return any excess profits to the ceding company. The reinsurer tracks the repayment of the initial allowance through a special account.

Uses of YRT. The most common use of the YRT plan for financial reinsurance would be with an interest sensitive life product where the reinsurer did not wish to become involved in the accumulation element of the basic contract. Yearly renewable term could also be used with any form of whole life insurance when the reinsurer did not wish to become involved in the investment risks.

If a term product is being reinsured, YRT reinsurance could be used. Under these circumstances, the reinsurer might create a special YRT rate scale expressing the rates as percentages of the underlying term policy premium rates. In this instance, there would be little difference between the use of coinsurance or YRT. Yearly Renewable Term reinsurance is also used for health policies but it is not suitable for annuities.

In surplus relief situations, YRT is most effective if it is based on a premium scale which features no first year premium, or if it provides a bonus per unit of production with higher renewal rates. The higher renewal rates are needed to recoup the initial strain. A chargeback may be applied for lapses within a certain period.

YRT reinsurance could be used in circumstances where the ceding company wanted to minimize asset transfer. If an inforce block of business is involved, the initial premium on a coinsurance basis would be the outstanding policy reserves. For many companies, this may be a sizable sum of money. The initial YRT premium would normally be considerably less than the reserves on a mature block of whole life policies.

Advantages. The use of YRT reinsurance will limit the reinsurer's investment and lapse risk since there is no reserve or cash value buildup. This could be particularly useful if the initial policy reserves are large and the reinsurer does not have the facilities to manage adequately the assets it would receive in a coinsurance transaction.

Yearly renewable term reinsurance may have a lower ongoing cost than any form of coinsurance if the risks are limited to mortality or morbidity.

Disadvantages. The low cost of YRT reinsurance limits the amount of possible future profits, thereby limiting the amount of the initial allowance or bonus which the reinsurer can provide. Because of the limitations in the initial allowance, the use of YRT reinsurance is limited in financial reinsurance applications. However, within regulatory limits, higher renewal YRT premiums will allow a higher initial allowance.

Another drawback of using YRT in financial reinsurance is that it is relatively difficult to administer. Financial reinsurance most commonly is administered on a simplified basis. Yearly renewable term does not lend itself to this type of administration. The reinsurance premium is calculated as a product of the YRT rate times the net amount of risk, and this calculation must be made for each policy. As will be discussed later, the administration of any form of coinsurance, if reinsured on a quota share basis, is relatively simple for a ceding company to perform.

Because of the drawbacks of YRT reinsurance, it rarely is used in financial reinsurance applications and will not be illustrated here. If used, YRT normally is teamed with a form of coinsurance.

Coinsurance

Under a typical coinsurance arrangement involving inforce insurance, the initial reinsurance premium is equal to the reserve and the reinsurer pays the ceding company an allowance which provides the initial gain. In subsequent years, the allowance generally covers the ceding company's maintenance and commission expenses.

An alternative treatment is to set the initial premium equal to the initial reserves less the desired gain of the ceding company. Renewal premiums could also be defined without reference to the policy gross premium and specific expense allowances. This particular treatment will not be used in this book, but the net economic effect is the same if the reduction in premium is equal to the allowance to be granted.

The reinsurance premiums net of allowances in subsequent years are used by the reinsurer to fund reserve increases, to pay claims, to cover its administration costs, and to provide a margin for adverse deviations. The reinsurer also includes a charge to reimburse it for the investment made in the first year of the contract.

In the traditional coinsurance market, pricing is done using the same techniques that the ceding company actuary used in developing the original product. Today's traditional coinsurance market is highly competitive. As a consequence, coinsurance allowances frequently have little provision for adverse deviation in experience results. The immediate benefits of larger allowances are considered preferable to the alternative of experience refunds by most ceding companies.

In the financial reinsurance market, pricing is not so precise. Generally, future profits are anticipated to be more than sufficient to repay the surplus relief together with the risk charges. Accordingly, most financial coinsurance treaties provide an experience rating feature whereby the reinsurer returns some or all of these excess profits to the ceding company. At some predetermined interval, an accounting is made of all reinsurance premiums received, claims and allowances paid, risk charges, interest earned, and the reserve increase for the period. The reinsurer may refund to the ceding company a portion of the profits in excess of any loss carry forwards or amounts used to repay the initial investment as experience unfolds, or it may use the entire earnings to repay its investment.

During the life of an arrangement, the reinsurer will generally keep a record of the repayment of the initial allowance in an outstanding surplus account. Once the balance of this account reaches zero, the reinsurance is generally terminated as there is little need for ongoing reinsurance coverage. The treaty may sometimes provide that reinsurance may be terminated before the relief is entirely repaid if the ceding company is able to transfer funds equal to the amount of outstanding relief to the reinsurer. Upon termination of the reinsurance, the assets equal to the reserves held by the reinsurer are returned to the ceding company.

Coinsurance can be used with any insurance product: life, health, or annuity. It works as well on term insurance as it does on interest sensitive life and annuity products.

Advantages. When an inforce block of business is being reinsured, pure coinsurance is probably the simplest to administer if a quota share method is used. Once previously reinsured amounts have been identified and removed, the quota share percentage can be applied to all premiums, claims, surrenders, and reserves. Under this method, the ceding company can easily provide the reinsurer with the information necessary for preparation of its statutory financial statements. From a regulatory viewpoint, pure coinsurance is probably the cleanest form of reinsurance because there are fewer questions regarding risk transfer in coinsurance.

Disadvantages. The chief disadvantage of coinsurance is the need to transfer assets. The ceding company must transfer control of the assets equal to the reserves to the reinsurer. In the case of the reinsurance of an inforce block, this may represent a significant portion of the assets of the ceding company. In the case of an interest sensitive or participating product, the ceding company may have to give the reinsurer control of or veto power over the dividend or interest rate determination. In addition to creating regulatory concerns, this could be a distinct disadvantage in competitive situations.

Another disadvantage is that it requires the reinsurer to manage the assets, subjecting it to additional investment risk which some reinsurers might find undesirable. Also, if the reinsurance is terminated, the reinsurer must transfer assets in an amount equal to the reserves to the ceding company. There is always a risk that capital gains or losses in an asset transfer may result in unfavorable cash, statutory, tax, or even GAAP consequences.

If the reinsurer is not licensed or admitted in the ceding company's state of domicile, the ceding company may be unable to take credit in its statutory annual statement for the reserves being held by the reinsurer unless the reinsurer provides some specific form of security acceptable to the state. This could be expensive and burdensome. Failure to secure the right to a reserve offset would defeat the surplus relief. In fact, if the desired reserve credit were greater than the intended surplus relief, the surplus position would be worsened.

Coinsurance also subjects the ceding company to an additional insolvency risk. Should the reinsurer become insolvent, the ceding company may be unable to obtain full reimbursement for benefits reinsured and, on termination, may not receive the full amount of policy reserves.

Coinsurance Illustrations. If ABC Life did not have at least $100 of available surplus in the first year, it would need reinsurance. Assume that ABC Life enters into a coinsurance treaty with XYZ Re on December 31, reinsuring 100% of this block of business, and XYZ Re grants ABC Life an allowance equal to 10% of the premium.

First Year Results. Tables 5.3A and 5.3B show the first year results of the coinsurance transaction.

ABC Life has ceded $1,000 of premium to XYZ Re, leaving it with a net premium of $0. The $100 of reinsurance allowances from XYZ Re gives ABC Life a total revenue of $100. This $100 is used to offset the $100 of commissions and expenses incurred in issuing the policies. This leaves ABC Life with a gain of $0. XYZ Re now has $1,000 of accepted premium and a $1,000 of reserve increase. Its commissions are $100, leaving it with a gain of $(100).

TABLE 5.3A

STATUTORY FINANCIAL STATEMENTS
COINSURANCE — YEAR 1

GAIN FROM OPERATIONS

	ABC LIFE	XYZ RE
Revenue:		
Premiums:		
Gross	$ 1,000	$ 1,000
Ceded	1,000	0
Net	0	1,000
Investment Income:		
Surplus	0	0
Reserves	0	0
Total	0	0
Reinsurance Allowance	100	0
Mod-co Adjustment	0	0
TOTAL REVENUE	$ 100	$ 1,000
Benefits:		
Claims and Surrenders:		
Gross	$ 0	$ 0
Ceded	0	0
Net	0	0
Reserve Increase:		
Gross	1,000	1,000
Ceded	1,000	0
Net	0	1,000
Experience Refund	0	0
Mod-co Adjustment	0	0
TOTAL BENEFITS	$ 0	$ 1,000
Expenses:		
Expenses and Commissions	$ 100	$ 100
TOTAL EXPENSES	$ 100	$ 100
GAIN FROM OPERATIONS	$ 0	$ (100)

TABLE 5.3B

STATUTORY FINANCIAL STATEMENTS
COINSURANCE — YEAR 1

BALANCE SHEET

	ABC LIFE	XYZ RE
Assets:		
Invested Assets	$ 0	$ 1,000
Accounts Receivable	0	0
TOTAL ASSETS	$ 0	$ 1,000
Liabilities and Capital:		
Policy Reserves:		
Gross	$ 1,000	$ 1,000
Ceded	1,000	0
Net	0	1,000
Accounts Payable	0	0
TOTAL LIABILITIES	$ 0	$ 1,000
Surplus	$ 0	$ 0
TOTAL CAPITAL	$ 0	$ 0
TOTAL LIABILITIES AND CAPITAL	$ 0	$ 1,000

Financial Reinsurance 125

The statutory Balance Sheet for ABC Life shows that it has neither assets nor net retained reserves after the transactions. XYZ Re has $1,000 of invested assets, $1,000 of reserves, and no surplus. When the coinsurance illustrations are compared to those for no reinsurance in Tables 5.1A and 5.1B, it can be seen that the net income, invested assets, policy reserves, and surplus have merely been redistributed between the two companies. The transaction does not create any new invested assets, surplus, or liabilities.

XYZ Re prepares a reinsurance report. The report summarizes the transaction and indicates the net amount of funds to be transferred. The reinsurance report below shows that ABC Life owes XYZ Re $900, which is the premium net of allowances. This amount is paid in cash.

ABC LIFE
REINSURANCE REPORT
COINSURANCE — YEAR 1

Ceded Premium:		$1,000
Less: Allowances	$100	
Benefits	0	
Mod-co Adjustment	0	
Experience Refund	0	(100)
Total Due XYZ Re:		$ 900

For internal purposes, XYZ Re sets up an outstanding surplus account to track the funds advanced to ABC Life. The beginning balance in the account is $100.

ABC LIFE
OUTSTANDING SURPLUS ACCOUNT
COINSURANCE — END OF YEAR 1

Beginning Balance:		$ 0
Plus: Statutory Gain		(100)
Less: Investment Income on Surplus	$ 0	
Risk Charge	0	0
Ending Balance:		$(100)

Second Year Results. In the second year of the reinsurance transaction, shown in Tables 5.4A and 5.4B, XYZ Re earns $100 of investment income on its $1,000 of assets. For the purpose of this illustration, XYZ Re agreed to allow ABC Life to share in a portion of the profits, so it pays ABC Life an experience refund of $1. The experience refund has been included in the illustration to demonstrate its effect. Normally, an experience refund would not be paid until the outstanding surplus account has been repaid.

XYZ Re also reimburses ABC Life for 100% of the $5 of benefits paid. XYZ Re is responsible for the entire reserve increase of $70. At the end of the second year, XYZ Re now has a gain of $24 while ABC Life has a gain of $1 from the experience refund.

The statutory Balance Sheet for ABC Life shows that it has assets of $1 and surplus of $1. XYZ Re has assets of $1,094, reserves of $1,070, and surplus of $24. When the statutory Gains from Operations and Balance Sheets for the second year of the coinsurance transactions are compared to the corresponding values in the no reinsurance example, it can be seen that, again, the total income, assets, liabilities, and surplus have merely been redistributed between the companies; nothing has been created.

The reinsurance report for the second year of the coinsurance transaction shown below indicates that XYZ Re has paid ABC Life a total of $6, $5 for benefit reimbursements and $1 of experience refund.

ABC LIFE
REINSURANCE REPORT
COINSURANCE — YEAR 2

Ceded Premium:			$ 0
Less: Allowances	$ 0		
Benefits	5		
Mod-co Adjustment	0		
Experience Refund	1		(6)
Total Due XYZ Re:			$ (6)

TABLE 5.4A

STATUTORY FINANCIAL STATEMENTS
COINSURANCE — YEAR 2

GAIN FROM OPERATIONS

	ABC LIFE	XYZ RE
Revenue:		
Premiums:		
Gross	$ 0	$ 0
Ceded	0	0
Net	0	0
Investment Income:		
Surplus	0	0
Reserves	0	100
Total	0	100
Reinsurance Allowance	0	0
Mod-co Adjustment	0	0
Misc (Experience Refund)	1	0
TOTAL REVENUE	$ 1	$ 100
Benefits:		
Claims and Surrenders:		
Gross	$ 5	$ 5
Ceded	5	0
Net	0	5
Reserve Increase:		
Gross	70	70
Ceded	70	0
Net	0	70
Experience Refund	0	1
Mod-co Adjustment	0	0
TOTAL BENEFITS	$ 0	$ 76
Expenses:		
Expenses and Commissions	$ 0	$ 0
TOTAL EXPENSES	$ 0	$ 0
GAIN FROM OPERATIONS	$ 1	$ 24

TABLE 5.4B

STATUTORY FINANCIAL STATEMENTS
COINSURANCE — YEAR 2

BALANCE SHEET

	ABC LIFE	XYZ RE
Assets:		
Invested Assets	$ 1	$ 1,094
Accounts Receivable	0	0
TOTAL ASSETS	$ 1	$ 1,094
Liabilities and Capital:		
Policy Reserves:		
Gross	$ 1,070	$ 1,070
Ceded	1,070	0
Net	0	1,070
Accounts Payable	0	0
TOTAL LIABILITIES	$ 0	$ 1,070
Surplus	$ 1	$ 24
TOTAL CAPITAL	$ 1	$ 24
TOTAL LIABILITIES AND CAPITAL	$ 1	$ 1,094

At the close of the year, XYZ Re updates its outstanding surplus account for ABC Life. XYZ Re's risk charge is assumed to be 3% of the outstanding surplus account at the beginning of the year. The beginning balance is reduced by the statutory gain from operations less the investment income it would have earned on the surplus had no transaction taken place and less a risk charge of $3. The ending balance is now $89.

ABC LIFE
OUTSTANDING SURPLUS ACCOUNT
COINSURANCE — END OF YEAR 2

Beginning Balance:		$ (100)
Plus: Statutory Gain		24
Less: Investment Income on Surplus	$ 10	
Risk Charge	3	(13)
Ending Balance:		$ (89)

XYZ Re's entire gains were not applied to reducing the outstanding surplus account. Of the $24 gain, $10 was allowed to XYZ Re for investment income it would have had without this transaction. Of the remaining $14 of income attributable to it entering into the reinsurance agreement, $3 is XYZ Re's return for providing the reinsurance, leaving $11 to reduce the outstanding surplus account.

Modified Coinsurance

Modified coinsurance has been a particularly popular method of providing financial reinsurance since the ceding company maintains the reserves and the assets in support of these reserves. As in a coinsurance arrangement, there is a proportionate sharing of premiums, benefits, and reserve increases.

Under the typical financial reinsurance arrangement involving modified coinsurance on an existing block of policies, the premium in the initial transaction will be equal to the reserves on the portion of the policies reinsured. The renewal premiums will typically be equal to the gross premiums on the portion of the policies reinsured. The reinsurer will pay the ceding company an allowance. If a first year gain is desired, it will be provided through the initial allowance. In renewal years, the allowance will help cover ceding company expenses.

The reinsurer uses the premium which it retains to pay claims and reinsurance expenses, to fund the reserve increase, and to repay any surplus committed to the agreement. Generally, it is anticipated that there will be a gain at the end of each accounting period. The reinsurer may allow the ceding company to participate in this gain through the use of an experience refund formula. As in the coinsurance example, the experience refund is generally calculated for each accounting period as the premiums received less allowances, claims, reserve increase, and a risk charge, less any repayment of the outstanding surplus relief. In most contracts, an experience refund is not paid unless the reinsurer's surplus account is positive.

As in the coinsurance case, the reinsurer also maintains a scorecard account for the outstanding surplus relief. This scorecard is tallied at the end of every accounting period. When the balance of the surplus account is zero, the ceding company may terminate the treaty.

The mod-co reserve adjustment is the same as that discussed in Chapter 4. If the initial transaction involves a block of inforce policies, the initial mod-co adjustment is equal to the policy reserves at the inception of the contract.

Advantages. Like coinsurance, mod-co is applicable to all plans of insurance. The major advantage of mod-co to the ceding company is that it avoids the necessity of liquidating or transferring ownership of assets to the reinsurer when an inforce block of business is involved. It is considered superior to coinsurance if a participating block or a block of interest sensitive products is being reinsured, as it allows the ceding company to retain control of the investment policy for the block of business.

The use of mod-co also eliminates the reserve credit problem found in coinsurance if the reinsurer is not licensed in the ceding company's state of domicile. Under mod-co, the reinsurer may deduct the entire reserve increase for federal income tax purposes, as it has paid the amount to the ceding company, even if the reserve does not otherwise qualify as a tax deductible item.[6]

---

[6] On the other hand, the ceding company will have taxable income and no tax deductible reserve increase to match with it.

Financial Reinsurance

The reinsurer may prefer the use of mod-co to avoid the necessity of managing assets. This might be particularly significant in the case of an occasional or specialty reinsurer that does not have a special staff dedicated to the administration of reinsurance investments.

Disadvantages. The main disadvantage of mod-co is that it is more complicated to administer than coinsurance because of the mod-co adjustment. Special transactions are required in the case of surrenders and death.

Transfer of assets back to the reinsurer in the event of treaty termination can create exposure to capital losses for the ceding company, just as transfer of the initial mod-co adjustment to the ceding company can create problems for the reinsurer.

If the reinsurer has doubts about the solvency of the ceding company during the projected life of a financial reinsurance arrangement, the reinsurer will generally prefer coinsurance. Coinsurance will allow it to maintain control of the assets. In the case of the ceding company insolvency, the reinsurer might look to offset claims by the amount of the policy reserves if it held the assets supporting the reserves.

Mod-Co Illustrations. For illustrative purposes, it is assumed that ABC Life enters into a mod-co reinsurance agreement with XYZ Re on essentially the same terms as the previously illustrated coinsurance agreement using a 10% mod-co interest rate.

First Year Results. Tables 5.5A and 5.5B show the statutory Gains from Operations and the Balance Sheets for the first year under this arrangement.

As in the coinsurance example shown in Table 5.3, ABC Life shows a ceded premium of $1,000 and $100 of reinsurance allowances. However, it now has received a mod-co adjustment as a revenue item in the amount of $1,000, and it carries the entire $1,000 reserve increase in its income statement as a benefit. XYZ Re shows $1,000 of accepted premium and $1,000 mod-co adjustment to reflect the initial reserve increase.

The statutory balance sheet shows that ABC Life now has $1,000 of assets and liabilities while XYZ Re has none. With respect to assets and liabilities, this is the exact opposite of the coinsurance example of Table 5.3. Earnings, however, are the same for the coinsurance example. Again, no invested assets, liabilities, or surplus have been created.

TABLE 5.5A

STATUTORY FINANCIAL STATEMENTS
MODIFIED COINSURANCE — YEAR 1

GAIN FROM OPERATIONS

	ABC LIFE	XYZ RE
Revenue:		
Premiums:		
Gross	$ 1,000	$ 1,000
Ceded	1,000	0
Net	0	1,000
Investment Income:		
Surplus	0	0
Reserves	0	0
Total	0	0
Reinsurance Allowance	100	0
Mod-co Adjustment	1,000	0
Misc (Experience Refund)	0	0
TOTAL REVENUE	$ 1,100	$ 1,000
Benefits:		
Claims and Surrenders:		
Gross	$ 0	$ 0
Ceded	0	0
Net	0	0
Reserve Increase:		
Gross	1,000	0
Ceded	0	0
Net	1,000	0
Experience Refund	0	0
Mod-co Adjustment	0	1,000
TOTAL BENEFITS	$ 1,000	$ 1,000
Expenses:		
Expenses and Commissions	$ 100	$ 100
TOTAL EXPENSES	$ 100	$ 100
GAIN FROM OPERATIONS	$ 0	$ (100)

TABLE 5.5B

STATUTORY FINANCIAL STATEMENTS
MODIFIED COINSURANCE — YEAR 1

BALANCE SHEET

	ABC LIFE	XYZ RE
Assets:		
Invested Assets	$ 1,000	$ 0
Accounts Receivable	0	0
TOTAL ASSETS	$ 1,000	$ 0
Liabilities and Capital:		
Policy Reserves:		
Gross	$ 1,000	$ 0
Ceded	0	0
Net	1,000	0
Accounts Payable	0	0
TOTAL LIABILITIES	$ 1,000	$ 0
Surplus	$ 0	$ 0
TOTAL CAPITAL	$ 0	$ 0
TOTAL LIABILITIES AND CAPITAL	$ 1,000	$ 0

The reinsurance report prepared for the initial transaction shows the $1,000 of ceded premium less the allowances of $100 and the mod-co adjustment of $1,000. In this case, XYZ Re pays ABC Life $100. This compares to the $900 payment made by ABC Life to XYZ Re at the inception of the coinsurance treaty.

ABC LIFE
REINSURANCE REPORT
MODIFIED COINSURANCE — YEAR 1

Ceded Premium:		$ 1,000
Less: Allowances	$ 100	
Benefits	0	
Mod-co Adjustment	1,000	
Experience Refund	0	(1,100)
Total Due XYZ Re:		$ (100)

As in the coinsurance example, XYZ Re creates a special outstanding surplus account for this treaty. At the inception of the treaty, the outstanding surplus account indicates that XYZ Re has advanced $100 to ABC Life.

ABC LIFE
OUTSTANDING SURPLUS ACCOUNT
MODIFIED COINSURANCE — END OF YEAR 1

Beginning Balance:		$ 0
Plus: Statutory Gain		(100)
Less: Investment Income on Surplus	$ 0	
Risk Charge	0	(0)
Ending Balance:		$(100)

Second Year Results. In the second year of the mod-co transaction, the mod-co reserve adjustment must first be calculated. This calculation was not shown for the first year as the transaction was made on December 31. Assuming a mod-co interest rate of 10%, the calculation is as follows:

ABC LIFE
MOD-CO RESERVE ADJUSTMENT — YEAR 2

Ending Policy Reserves:		$ 1,070
Less: Beginning Policy Reserves	$1,000	
Interest on Beginning Policy Reserves	100	(1,100)
Mod-co Adjustment:		$ (30)

The calculation indicates that ABC Life owes $30 to XYZ Re. This occurs because the interest element in the adjustment plus the reserves released by termination exceeded the reserve increase for the remaining policies. The mod-co adjustment is reflected in the statutory Gains from Operations shown in Table 5.6A.

As ABC Life held all of the assets involved in the transaction, it has earned $100 of investment income. As in the coinsurance example, it has earned a $1 experience refund. It shows the entire $70 reserve increase as a benefit. It also shows that XYZ Re has reimbursed it for the claims incurred. ABC Life's statutory Gain from Operations also shows that it has paid XYZ Re a $30 mod-co adjustment. As a result, ABC Life has a gain of $1 while XYZ Re has a gain of $24, just as in the coinsurance example. This occurs because the mod-co interest rate is equal to the investment income interest rate for both companies. The statutory Balance Sheet for ABC indicates that it has $1,071 of assets, $1,070 of liabilities, and $1 of surplus. XYZ Re has assets and surplus of $24 and no reserve liabilities.

The reinsurance report prepared for the second year of the transaction shows the $5 of benefits and $1 experience refund netted against the mod-co adjustment of $30. In this case, ABC Life pays XYZ Re $24.

TABLE 5.6A

STATUTORY FINANCIAL STATEMENTS
MODIFIED COINSURANCE — YEAR 2

GAIN FROM OPERATIONS

	ABC LIFE	XYZ RE
Revenue:		
Premiums:		
Gross	$ 0	$ 0
Ceded	0	0
Net	0	0
Investment Income:		
Surplus	0	0
Reserves	100	0
Total	100	0
Reinsurance Allowance	0	30
Mod-co Adjustment	0	0
Misc (Experience Refund)	1	0
TOTAL REVENUE	$ 101	$ 30
Benefits:		
Claims and Surrenders:		
Gross	$ 5	$ 5
Ceded	5	0
Net	0	5
Reserve Increase:		
Gross	70	0
Ceded	0	0
Net	70	0
Experience Refund	0	1
Mod-co Adjustment	30	0
TOTAL BENEFITS	$ 100	$ 6
Expenses:		
Expenses and Commissions	$ 0	$ 0
TOTAL EXPENSES	$ 0	$ 0
GAIN FROM OPERATIONS	$ 1	$ 24

TABLE 5.6B

STATUTORY FINANCIAL STATEMENTS
MODIFIED COINSURANCE — YEAR 2

BALANCE SHEET

	ABC LIFE	XYZ RE
Assets:		
Invested Assets	$ 1,071	$ 24
Accounts Receivable	0	0
TOTAL ASSETS	$ 1,071	$ 24
Liabilities and Capital:		
Policy Reserves:		
Gross	$ 1,070	$ 0
Ceded	0	0
Net	1,070	0
Accounts Payable	0	0
TOTAL LIABILITIES	$ 1,070	$ 0
Surplus	$ 1	$ 24
TOTAL CAPITAL	$ 1	$ 24
TOTAL LIABILITIES AND CAPITAL	$ 1,071	$ 24

ABC LIFE
REINSURANCE REPORT
MODIFIED COINSURANCE — YEAR 2

Ceded Premium:			$	0
Less:	Allowances	$	0	
	Benefits		5	
	Mod-co Adjustment		(30)	
	Experience Refund		1	24
Total Due XYZ Re:			$	24

After the financial statement is prepared, XYZ Re updates its outstanding surplus account for the ABC Life treaty. It reduces the beginning balance by its statutory gain attributed to this account less investment income attributed to the amount financed and less the risk charge on the amount advanced of $3. This again results in an ending balance of $89. These amounts are equal to those of the coinsurance transaction, as the same interest rates were used.

ABC LIFE
OUTSTANDING SURPLUS ACCOUNT
MODIFIED COINSURANCE — END OF YEAR 2

Beginning Balance:				$ (100)
Plus:	Statutory Gain			24
Less:	Investment Income on Surplus	$	10	
	Risk Charge		3	(13)
Ending Balance:				$ (89)

Funds Withheld Coinsurance

Funds withheld coinsurance looks like regular coinsurance in many ways. The reinsurer follows the ceding company's plan values and calculations of the premiums, allowances, experience refunds, and risk charges are all similar. When looking at the initial statutory gain from operations, it is impossible to tell the difference between coinsurance and funds withheld coinsurance. In order to see the difference between the two, the statutory balance sheet and reinsurance reports must be examined.

The only difference between coinsurance and funds withheld coinsurance is that in the initial funds withheld coinsurance transaction, the reinsurer retains the allowance and the ceding company retains the initial premium. If the allowance exceeds the initial premium, the reinsurer would set up an accounts payable item while the ceding company would have an accounts receivable asset. Should the initial premium exceed the allowance, the reverse would be true.

In subsequent accounting periods, the net balance of the funds withheld will increase or decrease as profit emerges, surplus is repaid, and the reserves increase or decrease. Until the net balance of the funds withheld reaches zero, no cash will change hands other than the reinsurer's risk charge. Since the ceding company is maintaining the assets underlying the reserves while the reinsurer holds the reserves on its financial statements, an interest adjustment much like the mod-co interest adjustment is made.

Advantages. The major advantage of funds withheld coinsurance is that no cash changes hands in the initial transaction and cash flow is minimized throughout the life of the treaty. This is particularly advantageous to the company with the net accounts payable item.

The use of funds withheld coinsurance also lessens the ceding company's insolvency risk should the reinsurer become insolvent. The ceding company, which has retained the assets underlying the reserves, is in a better position than it is under the regular coinsurance arrangement.

Use of funds withheld coinsurance may increase the risk to the reinsurer should the ceding company become insolvent as compared to a mod-co transaction. In the event of the ceding company's insolvency, the reinsurer will need to assert a claim on the assets supporting its reserve liability. On the other hand, the reinsurer should be able to use the amount it owes the ceding company for the allowance to offset any monies owed it by the ceding company.

Funds withheld coinsurance is also a legitimate alternative to mod-co if the funds stay with the ceding company. If the reinsurer is nonadmitted, the ceding company can still take reserve credit up to the amount of funds it is holding.

Disadvantages. The major drawback of funds withheld coinsurance is that it is more complicated than regular coinsurance. The receivables and payables must be tracked carefully. An interest adjustment must be made for the company with the net accounts receivable to reflect any foregone investment income.

Like coinsurance, funds withheld coinsurance may still result in a reserve credit problem for the ceding company if the reinsurer is not licensed or admitted in its state of domicile and the funds being withheld are with the reinsurer. However, the problem is alleviated somewhat because the ceding company is holding the assets behind the reserves.

Funds Withheld Coinsurance Illustrations. Assume ABC Life enters into a funds withheld coinsurance agreement using the same terms as previously.

First Year Results. Tables 5.7A and 5.7B illustrate the financial effect in the first year of a funds withheld coinsurance arrangement involving ABC Life and XYZ Re. In examining the Gains from Operations for both companies and comparing the results with those in Table 5.3A for the coinsurance transaction, there is no visible difference in earnings. The difference is in the statutory Balance Sheets.

The Balance Sheet shows that XYZ Re has an accounts receivable item of $900 while ABC Life has an accounts payable liability of $900. The combined gains, invested assets, policy reserves, and surplus for the two companies remain unchanged from any of the previous examples. In this case however, a "paper asset" and a "paper liability" in the amount of the initial funds withheld have been created.

The reinsurance report for funds withheld coinsurance shows a total due XYZ Re of $900, just as in the coinsurance example. In this case however, ABC Life does not remit the $900. This is the amount of its initial accounts payable and the amount of XYZ Re's initial accounts receivable.

TABLE 5.7A

STATUTORY FINANCIAL STATEMENTS
FUNDS WITHHELD COINSURANCE — YEAR 1

GAIN FROM OPERATIONS

	ABC LIFE	XYZ RE
Revenue:		
Premiums:		
Gross	$ 1,000	$ 1,000
Ceded	1,000	0
Net	0	1,000
Investment Income:		
Surplus	0	0
Reserves	0	0
Total	0	0
Reinsurance Allowance	100	0
Mod-co Adjustment	0	0
Misc (Experience Refund)	0	0
TOTAL REVENUE	$ 100	$ 1,000
Benefits:		
Claims and Surrenders:		
Gross	$ 0	$ 0
Ceded	0	0
Net	0	0
Reserve Increase:		
Gross	1,000	1,000
Ceded	1,000	0
Net	0	1,000
Experience Refund	0	0
Mod-co Adjustment	0	0
TOTAL BENEFITS	$ 0	$ 1,000
Expenses:		
Expenses and Commissions	$ 100	$ 100
TOTAL EXPENSES	$ 100	$ 100
GAIN FROM OPERATIONS	$ 0	$ (100)

TABLE 5.7B

STATUTORY FINANCIAL STATEMENTS
FUNDS WITHHELD COINSURANCE — YEAR 1

BALANCE SHEET

	ABC LIFE	XYZ RE
Assets:		
Invested Assets	$ 900	$ 100
Accounts Receivable	0	900
TOTAL ASSETS	$ 900	$ 1,000
Liabilities and Capital:		
Policy Reserves:		
Gross	$ 1,000	$ 1,000
Ceded	1,000	0
Net	0	1,000
Accounts Payable	900	0
TOTAL LIABILITIES	$ 900	$ 1,000
Surplus	$ 0	$ 0
TOTAL CAPITAL	$ 0	$ 0
TOTAL LIABILITIES AND CAPITAL	$ 900	$ 1,000

ABC LIFE
REINSURANCE REPORT
FUNDS WITHHELD COINSURANCE — YEAR 1

Funds Withheld Beginning Balance:				$ 0
Ceded Premium:		$ 1,000		
Less: Allowances	$100			
Benefits	0			
Mod-co Adjustment	0			
Experience Refund	0	(100)		
Total Due XYZ Re:		$ 900		
Less: Risk Charge Paid		(0)		900
Funds Withheld Ending Balance:				$ 900

XYZ Re, again, establishes an outstanding surplus account in its ABC Life file. In the initial transaction, the account shows that XYZ Re has advanced ABC Life $100 which will be repaid out of future gains.

ABC LIFE
OUTSTANDING SURPLUS ACCOUNT
FUNDS WITHHELD COINSURANCE — END OF YEAR 1

Beginning Balance:			$ 0
Plus: Statutory Gain			(100)
Less: Investment Income on Surplus	$	0	
Risk Charge		0	0
Ending Balance:			$ (100)

Second Year Results. Tables 5.8A and 5.8B show the statutory Gains from Operations and Balance Sheets in the second year for the funds withheld coinsurance transaction. The transaction no longer looks like pure coinsurance.

A strange thing has occurred in the second year of this transaction — ABC Life now shows ceded premium of $90 and XYZ Re has gross premiums of $90. This $90 represents the investment income on the $900 which ABC Life retained rather than paying to XYZ Re. Statutory accounting rules on the treatment of this particular item are not specific and some companies treat it as some form of miscellaneous revenue.

The investment income is now divided between the two companies in the same manner as was the case with no reinsurance since each maintained its original amount of invested assets. XYZ Re still pays ABC Life the $1 experience refund and reimburses it $5 for benefits. XYZ Re is holding all the reserves on its books. Again, this results in a $1 gain for ABC Life and a $24 net income for XYZ Re.

The statutory Balance Sheet shows that the accounts receivable item has grown to $981. ABC Life's invested assets have grown to $982 which is exactly $3 less than its invested assets in the no reinsurance example shown in Table 5.2B. The difference is attributable to the risk charge which it paid XYZ Re. Conversely, XYZ Re's invested assets are $3 higher than in the no reinsurance example because of the receipt of this $3 of risk charge. Again the combined gains, invested assets, policy reserves, and surplus remain unchanged for both companies as in the previous examples.

In order to see the growth of the funds withheld balance, the reinsurance report must be examined. It shows an initial funds withheld balance of $900. ABC Life now has ceded premium of $90, the amount of the foregone investment income on the withheld funds. It nets the benefits and experience refund against this amount for a total due XYZ Re of $84. However, ABC Life pays XYZ Re only $3, the amount of the risk charge. The remaining $81 increases the funds withheld balance.

ABC LIFE
REINSURANCE REPORT
FUNDS WITHHELD COINSURANCE — YEAR 2

Funds Withheld Beginning Balance:			$ 900
Ceded Premium:		$ 90	
Less: Allowances	$ 0		
Benefits	5		
Mod-co Adjustment	0		
Experience Refund	1	(6)	
Total Due XYZ Re:		$ 84	
Less: Risk Charge Paid		(3)	81
Funds Withheld Ending Balance:			$ 981

TABLE 5.8A

STATUTORY FINANCIAL STATEMENTS
FUNDS WITHHELD COINSURANCE — YEAR 2

GAIN FROM OPERATIONS

	ABC LIFE	XYZ RE
Revenue:		
Premiums:		
Gross	$ 0	$ 90
Ceded	90	0
Net	(90)	90
Investment Income:		
Surplus	0	0
Reserves	90	10
Total	90	10
Reinsurance Allowance	0	0
Mod-co Adjustment	0	0
Misc (Experience Refund)	1	0
TOTAL REVENUE	$ 1	$ 100
Benefits:		
Claims and Surrenders:		
Gross	$ 5	$ 5
Ceded	5	0
Net	0	5
Reserve Increase:		
Gross	70	70
Ceded	70	0
Net	0	70
Experience Refund	0	1
Mod-co Adjustment	0	0
TOTAL BENEFITS	$ 0	$ 76
Expenses:		
Expenses and Commissions	$ 0	$ 0
TOTAL EXPENSES	$ 0	$ 0
GAIN FROM OPERATIONS	$ 1	$ 24

TABLE 5.8B

STATUTORY FINANCIAL STATEMENTS
FUNDS WITHHELD COINSURANCE — YEAR 2

BALANCE SHEET

	ABC LIFE	XYZ RE
Assets:		
Invested Assets	$ 982	$ 113
Accounts Receivable	0	981
TOTAL ASSETS	$ 982	$ 1,094
Liabilities and Capital:		
Policy Reserves:		
Gross	$ 1,070	$ 1,070
Ceded	1,070	0
Net	0	1,070
Accounts Payable	981	0
TOTAL LIABILITIES	$ 981	$ 1,070
Surplus	$ 1	$ 24
TOTAL CAPITAL	$ 1	$ 24
TOTAL LIABILITIES AND CAPITAL	$ 982	$ 1,094

Financial Reinsurance

At the end of the accounting period, XYZ Re updates its outstanding surplus account for the ABC Life treaty. As in the previous examples, the ending balance is $89.

ABC LIFE
OUTSTANDING SURPLUS ACCOUNT
FUNDS WITHHELD COINSURANCE — END OF YEAR 2

Beginning Balance:			$ (100)
Plus: Statutory Gain			24
Less: Investment Income on Surplus	$	10	
Risk Charge		3	(13)
Ending Balance:			$ (89)

Alternatively, this may be looked at as follows, ignoring XYZ Re's investment income on its original assets:

ABC LIFE
OUTSTANDING SURPLUS ACCOUNT
(ALTERNATIVE CALCULATION)
FUNDS WITHHELD COINSURANCE — END OF YEAR 2

Beginning Balance:			$ (100)
Plus: Reinsurer Premium			90
Less: Benefits	$	5	
Reserve Increase		70	
Experience Refund		1	
Risk Charge		3	(79)
Ending Balance:			$ (89)

This result is the same as in the original calculation. The alternative calculation is more likely to be used in practice.

Funds Withheld Modified Coinsurance

Funds withheld modified coinsurance looks like regular mod-co in the initial transaction. The initial premium, allowance, and mod-co adjustments will be the same. The difference between the two is that under funds withheld mod-co, the reinsurer retains the initial allowance, setting up an accounts payable item for that amount. The ceding company then sets up a corresponding receivable item for the same amount.

Advantages. The principle advantage of funds withheld mod-co is that the reinsurer retains the initial allowance. It is freed from having to liquidate any assets to pay the allowance and minimizes future capital loss exposure. The reinsurer also has a lessened risk in the event of the ceding company's insolvency compared to regular mod-co as it is holding the assets underlying the initial allowance.

Disadvantages. A major problem of funds withheld mod-co is that it adds just one more layer of complexity to the administration of the treaty. The mod-co adjustment is complicated because the ceding company did not receive the allowance in cash. A special adjustment must be made to the interest element to reflect the fact that the ceding company has not earned interest on the allowance.

This form of reinsurance may be viewed as a violation of the NAIC Model Life and Health Reinsurance Agreement Regulation.

Funds Withheld Mod-Co Illustrations. Assume that ABC Life has entered into a funds withheld mod-co transaction with XYZ Re on the same basic terms as the mod-co transaction.

First Year Results. Tables 5.9A and 5.9B show financial effect in the first year of the funds withheld mod-co initial transaction. When looking at the statutory Gains from Operations for both companies, the transaction looks exactly like mod-co transaction shown in Tables 5.5A and 5.5B. The difference appears in the statutory Balance Sheets. In this example, ABC Life has an accounts receivable asset of $100 while XYZ Re has an accounts payable liability of $100. Combined gains, invested assets, policy reserves, and surplus for both companies remains unchanged from the other examples.

TABLE 5.9A

STATUTORY FINANCIAL STATEMENTS
FUNDS WITHHELD MODIFIED COINSURANCE — YEAR 1

GAIN FROM OPERATIONS

	ABC LIFE	XYZ RE
Revenue:		
Premiums:		
Gross	$ 1,000	$ 1,000
Ceded	1,000	0
Net	0	1,000
Investment Income:		
Surplus	0	0
Reserves	0	0
Total	0	0
Reinsurance Allowance	100	0
Mod-co Adjustment	1,000	0
Misc (Experience Refund)	0	0
TOTAL REVENUE	$ 1,100	$ 1,000
Benefits:		
Claims and Surrenders:		
Gross	$ 0	$ 0
Ceded	0	0
Net	0	0
Reserve Increase:		
Gross	1,000	0
Ceded	0	0
Net	1,000	0
Experience Refund	0	0
Mod-co Adjustment	0	1,000
TOTAL BENEFITS	$ 1,000	$ 1,000
Expenses:		
Expenses and Commissions	$ 100	$ 100
TOTAL EXPENSES	$ 100	$ 100
GAIN FROM OPERATIONS	$ 0	$ (100)

TABLE 5.9B

STATUTORY FINANCIAL STATEMENTS
FUNDS WITHHELD MODIFIED COINSURANCE — YEAR 1

BALANCE SHEET

	ABC LIFE	XYZ RE
Assets:		
Invested Assets	$ 900	$ 100
Accounts Receivable	100	0
TOTAL ASSETS	$ 1,000	$ 100
Liabilities and Capital:		
Policy Reserves:		
Gross	$ 1,000	$ 0
Ceded	0	0
Net	1,000	0
Accounts Payable	0	100
TOTAL LIABILITIES	$ 1,000	$ 100
Surplus	$ 0	$ 0
TOTAL CAPITAL	$ 0	$ 0
TOTAL LIABILITIES AND CAPITAL	$ 1,000	$ 100

The reinsurance report shows how the initial funds withheld amount is calculated. As in regular mod-co, the report shows that XYZ Re owes ABC Life a balance of $100 after the initial transaction. XYZ Re does not pay this amount, and instead sets up an accounts payable item.

ABC LIFE
REINSURANCE REPORT
FUNDS WITHHELD MODIFIED COINSURANCE — YEAR 1

Funds Withheld Beginning Balance:				$ 0
Ceded Premium:			$ 1,000	
Less: Allowances	$ 100			
Benefits	0			
Mod-co Adjustment	1,000			
Experience Refund	0		(1,100)	
Total Due XYZ Re:			$ (100)	
Less: Risk Charge Paid			0	(100)
Funds Withheld Ending Balance:				$ (100)

The outstanding surplus account for the ABC Life treaty again shows an initial balance of $100.

ABC LIFE
OUTSTANDING SURPLUS ACCOUNT
FUNDS WITHHELD MODIFIED COINSURANCE
END OF YEAR 1

Beginning Balance:			$ 0
Plus: Statutory Gain			(100)
Less: Investment Income on Surplus	$ 0		
Risk Charge	0		0
Ending Balance:			$ (100)

Second Year Results. In the second year of the funds withheld mod-co transaction, the companies must first calculate the mod-co adjustment:

ABC LIFE
MOD-CO RESERVE ADJUSTMENT — YEAR 2

Ending Policy Reserves:		$ 1,070
Less: Beginning Policy Reserves	$ 1,000	
Interest on Beginning Policy Reserves	90	(1,090)
Mod-co Adjustment:		$ (20)

In the regular mod-co example, the mod-co reserve adjustment resulted in a $30 payment to XYZ Re. In the funds withheld mod-co example, this amount is reduced to $20 because ABC Life did not have all the necessary assets to support the reserves. It offsets its reserve increase by the amount of investment income on the funds retained by XYZ Re. This is reflected in the statutory Gains from Operation shown in Table 5.10A.

The only difference in the statutory Gains from Operations in the funds withheld mod-co arrangement as compared to that for the regular mod-co arrangement is in the case of funds withheld. XYZ Re now has earned investment income on the amount of the retained allowance and has received a correspondingly smaller mod-co adjustment. ABC Life has earned less investment income and paid a smaller mod-co adjustment. The gain to ABC Life remains $1, while the gain to XYZ Re remains $24 as in the previous examples.

The statutory Balance Sheet in Table 5.10B shows that ABC Life's invested assets have grown to $982, the same as in the funds withheld coinsurance illustration, which is $3 less than the invested assets in the no reinsurance illustration. Again, this $3 is the risk charge which ABC Life paid XYZ Re. XYZ Re's invested assets are now $113, which is the same as in the funds withheld coinsurance situation and exactly $3 more than in the no reinsurance example.

The reinsurance report for the second year shows a decrease in the funds withheld balance of $11. The total amount due is $14, but only the $3 risk charge is paid.

Financial Reinsurance

TABLE 5.10A

STATUTORY FINANCIAL STATEMENTS
FUNDS WITHHELD MODIFIED COINSURANCE — YEAR 2

GAIN FROM OPERATIONS

	ABC LIFE	XYZ RE
Revenue:		
Premiums:		
Gross	$ 0	$ 0
Ceded	0	0
Net	0	0
Investment Income:		
Surplus	0	0
Reserves	90	10
Total	90	10
Reinsurance Allowance	0	0
Mod-co Adjustment	0	20
Misc (Experience Refund)	1	0
TOTAL REVENUE	$ 91	$ 30
Benefits:		
Claims and Surrenders:		
Gross	$ 5	$ 5
Ceded	5	0
Net	0	5
Reserve Increase:		
Gross	70	0
Ceded	0	0
Net	70	0
Experience Refund	0	1
Mod-co Adjustment	20	0
TOTAL BENEFITS	$ 90	$ 6
Expenses:		
Expenses and Commissions	$ 0	$ 0
TOTAL EXPENSES	$ 0	$ 0
GAIN FROM OPERATIONS	$ 1	$ 24

TABLE 5.10B

STATUTORY FINANCIAL STATEMENTS
FUNDS WITHHELD MODIFIED COINSURANCE — YEAR 2

BALANCE SHEET

	ABC LIFE	XYZ RE
Assets:		
Invested Assets	$ 982	$ 113
Accounts Receivable	89	0
TOTAL ASSETS	$ 1,071	$ 113
Liabilities and Capital:		
Policy Reserves:		
Gross	$ 1,070	$ 0
Ceded	0	0
Net	1,070	0
Accounts Payable	0	89
TOTAL LIABILITIES	$ 1,070	$ 89
Surplus	$ 1	$ 24
TOTAL CAPITAL	$ 1	$ 24
TOTAL LIABILITIES AND CAPITAL	$ 1,071	$ 113

ABC LIFE
REINSURANCE REPORT
FUNDS WITHHELD MODIFIED COINSURANCE — YEAR 2

Funds Withheld Beginning Balance:			$ (100)
Ceded Premium:		$ 0	
Less: Allowances	$ 0		
Benefits	5		
Mod-co Adjustment	(20)		
Experience Refund	1	14	
Total Due XYZ Re:		$ 14	
Less: Risk Charge Paid		(3)	11
Funds Withheld Ending Balance:			$ (89)

XYZ Re, at the close of the accounting period recalculates the outstanding surplus account for the ABC Life treaty. The result is, of course, the same as in the other examples. In this situation, it is equal to the funds withheld balance.

ABC LIFE
OUTSTANDING SURPLUS ACCOUNT
FUNDS WITHHELD MODIFIED COINSURANCE
END OF YEAR 2

Beginning Balance:			$ (100)
Plus: Statutory Gain			24
Less: Investment Income on Surplus	$	10	
Risk Charge		3	(13)
Ending Balance:			$ (89)

The alternative calculation of the outstanding surplus account is as follows:

**ABC LIFE
OUTSTANDING SURPLUS ACCOUNT
(ALTERNATIVE CALCULATION)
FUNDS WITHHELD MODIFIED COINSURANCE
END OF YEAR 2**

Beginning Balance:				$ (100)
Plus:	Reinsurance Premium	$	0	
	Mod-co Adjustment		20	20
Less:	Benefits	$	5	
	Experience Refund		1	
	Risk Charge		3	(9)
Ending Balance:				$ (89)

Partially Modified Coinsurance

Partially modified coinsurance,[7] or part-co, is a combination of coinsurance and modified coinsurance. In a part-co treaty, the initial coinsurance reserves are set equal to the initial reinsurance allowance. The remaining reserve liabilities are reinsured on a modified coinsurance basis. This results in no cash transfer at the inception of the treaty. In renewal years, the proportions of the coinsurance and modified coinsurance are adjusted.

The adjustment may be scheduled in the treaty or it may be allowed to float with the increase in coinsurance reserves and the surplus relief repayment. Some states disapprove of the coinsurance percentage increasing from its initial point because this typically indicates increased surplus relief without the reinsurer paying its share of cash losses. This is not necessarily improper, but it does call for explanation.

Advantages. The chief advantage of part-co is that there is no cash transaction initially. It also eliminates the need to create the paper assets and liabilities required under a funds withheld situation. In this sense, there is less regulatory question about the transaction.

---

[7] This combined form of reinsurance is also referred to as "co/mod-co" or "split co/mod-co."

Financial Reinsurance

Disadvantages. The chief disadvantage of part-co is that it is very complicated to comprehend and to administer. If the coinsurance reserves are going to follow the amount of the outstanding surplus, two statutory gains from operations calculations must be made. The preliminary statutory gain from operations calculations is necessary to determine the amount of the surplus repayment. The finalized statutory gain from operations will then be created to show the change in reserves from coinsurance to modified coinsurance, or vice versa.

Part-Co Illustrations. Assume that ABC Life has entered into a part-co transaction with XYZ Re. Since the initial allowance was $100, the initial amount of the coinsurance reserves is equal to $100. This is equal to 10% of the total reserves. The initial mod-co reserve is set at $900. Other assumptions are unchanged.

First Year Results. Tables 5.11A and 5.11B illustrate the financial effect in the first year of the initial part-co transaction. The statutory Gain from Operations shows that ABC Life receives a mod-co adjustment of $900 and is holding $900 in mod-co reserves. XYZ Re's statutory Gain from Operations shows that it is holding $100 of coinsurance reserves and has paid out a $900 mod-co adjustment.

The statutory Balance Sheet for ABC Life shows that it has retained its $900 of invested assets and has decreased its reserve liabilities to a matching $900. XYZ Re has kept its $100 of invested assets and has increased its reserve liabilities to $100.

The reinsurance report for the initial transaction shows ceded premium of $1,000 less allowances of $100 and a mod-co adjustment of $900 for a total amount due of $0. No cash has been transferred.

ABC LIFE
REINSURANCE REPORT
PARTIALLY MODIFIED COINSURANCE — YEAR 1

Ceded Premium:			$ 1,000
Less:	Allowances	$ 100	
	Benefits	0	
	Mod-co Adjustment	900	
	Experience Refund	0	(1,000)
Total Due XYZ Re:			$ 0

TABLE 5.11A

STATUTORY FINANCIAL STATEMENTS
PARTIALLY MODIFIED COINSURANCE — YEAR 1

GAIN FROM OPERATIONS

	ABC LIFE	XYZ RE
Revenue:		
Premiums:		
Gross	$ 1,000	$ 1,000
Ceded	1,000	0
Net	0	1,000
Investment Income:		
Surplus	0	0
Reserves	0	0
Total	0	0
Reinsurance Allowance	100	0
Mod-co Adjustment	900	0
Misc (Experience Refund)	0	0
TOTAL REVENUE	$ 1,000	$ 1,000
Benefits:		
Claims and Surrenders:		
Gross	$ 0	$ 0
Ceded	0	0
Net	0	0
Reserve Increase:		
Gross	1,000	100
Ceded	100	0
Net	900	100
Experience Refund	0	0
Mod-co Adjustment	0	900
TOTAL BENEFITS	$ 900	$ 1,000
Expenses:		
Expenses and Commissions	$ 100	$ 100
TOTAL EXPENSES	$ 100	$ 100
GAIN FROM OPERATIONS	$ 0	$ (100)

TABLE 5.11B

STATUTORY FINANCIAL STATEMENTS
PARTIALLY MODIFIED COINSURANCE — YEAR 1

BALANCE SHEET

	ABC LIFE	XYZ RE
Assets:		
Invested Assets	$ 900	$ 100
Accounts Receivable	0	0
TOTAL ASSETS	$ 900	$ 100
Liabilities and Capital:		
Policy Reserves:		
Gross	$ 1,000	$ 100
Ceded	100	0
Net	900	100
Accounts Payable	0	0
TOTAL LIABILITIES	$ 900	$ 100
Surplus	$ 0	$ 0
TOTAL CAPITAL	$ 0	$ 0
TOTAL LIABILITIES AND CAPITAL	$ 900	$ 100

The outstanding surplus account established for the ABC Life treaty again shows that XYZ Re has provided it with $100 of surplus.

ABC LIFE
OUTSTANDING SURPLUS ACCOUNT
PARTIALLY MODIFIED COINSURANCE — END OF YEAR 1

Beginning Balance:			$ 0
Plus:	Statutory Gain		(100)
Less:	Investment Income on Surplus	$ 0	
	Risk Charge	0	0
Ending Balance:			$ (100)

Second Year Results. At the end of the second year of the part-co treaty, both companies calculate the preliminary gain from operations. The first calculation is the preliminary mod-co adjustment. Ninety percent (90%) of the reserves were ceded on a mod-co basis, therefore, $63 of the reserve increase is on a mod-co basis. The mod-co reserve adjustment is as follows.

ABC LIFE
PRELIMINARY MOD-CO RESERVE ADJUSTMENT — YEAR 2

Ending Policy Reserves:			$ 963
Less:	Beginning Policy Reserves	$ 900	
	Interest on Beginning Policy Reserves	90	(990)
Preliminary Mod-co Adjustment:			$ (27)

This $(27) mod-co adjustment compares to the $(30) mod-co adjustment made in the pure mod-co illustration and to the $(20) mod-co adjustment in the funds withheld mod-co illustration. Coinsurance reserves have increased from $7 to $107.

Tables 5.12A and 5.12B present the preliminary statutory financial statements for the second year for ABC Life and XYZ Re. The preliminary statutory Gains from Operations reflect the division of 10% coinsurance and 90% modified coinsurance.

The preliminary statutory Balance Sheet shows that ABC Life has invested assets of $964 and XYZ Re has invested assets of $131. ABC Life has mod-co reserves of $963, while XYZ Re has coinsurance reserves of $107. As in the other examples, the gain and statutory surplus is $1 for ABC Life and $24 for XYZ Re.

Now that the preliminary gains from operations have been calculated, XYZ Re can calculate the outstanding surplus account.

ABC LIFE
OUTSTANDING SURPLUS ACCOUNT
PARTIALLY MODIFIED COINSURANCE — END OF YEAR 2

Beginning Balance:		$ (100)
Plus: Statutory Gain		24
Less: Investment Income on Surplus	$ 10	
Risk Charge	3	(13)
Ending Balance:		$ (89)

As in the other cases, the outstanding surplus account shows that $11 has been repaid out of XYZ Re's gain on the business. This surplus repayment is used to calculate the final mod-co adjustment, as shown below:

ABC LIFE
FINAL MOD-CO RESERVE ADJUSTMENT — YEAR 2

Preliminary Mod-co Adjustment:		$ (27)
Plus: Coinsurance Reserve Increase	$ 7	
Surplus Repayment	11	18
Final Mod-co Adjustment:		$ (9)

TABLE 5.12A

PRELIMINARY STATUTORY FINANCIAL STATEMENTS
PARTIALLY MODIFIED COINSURANCE — YEAR 2

GAIN FROM OPERATIONS

	ABC LIFE	XYZ RE
Revenue:		
Premiums:		
Gross	$ 0	$ 0
Ceded	0	0
Net	0	0
Investment Income:		
Surplus	0	0
Reserves	90	10
Total	90	10
Reinsurance Allowance	0	0
Mod-co Adjustment	0	27
Misc (Experience Refund)	1	0
TOTAL REVENUE	$ 91	$ 37
Benefits:		
Claims and Surrenders:		
Gross	$ 5	$ 5
Ceded	5	0
Net	0	5
Reserve Increase:		
Gross	70	7
Ceded	7	0
Net	63	7
Experience Refund	0	1
Mod-co Adjustment	27	0
TOTAL BENEFITS	$ 90	$ 13
Expenses:		
Expenses and Commissions	$ 0	$ 0
TOTAL EXPENSES	$ 0	$ 0
GAIN FROM OPERATIONS	$ 1	$ 24

TABLE 5.12B

PRELIMINARY STATUTORY FINANCIAL STATEMENTS
PARTIALLY MODIFIED COINSURANCE — YEAR 2

BALANCE SHEET

	ABC LIFE	XYZ RE
Assets:		
Invested Assets	$ 964	$ 131
Accounts Receivable	0	0
TOTAL ASSETS	$ 964	$ 131
Liabilities and Capital:		
Policy Reserves:		
Gross	$ 1,070	$ 107
Ceded	107	0
Net	963	107
Accounts Payable	0	0
TOTAL LIABILITIES	$ 963	$ 107
Surplus	$ 1	$ 24
TOTAL CAPITAL	$ 1	$ 24
TOTAL LIABILITIES AND CAPITAL	$ 964	$ 131

The original mod-co adjustment is changed to reflect the $7 increase in coinsurance reserves which are to be reinsured on a mod-co basis as well as the transfer of coinsurance reserves to mod-co reserves in the amount of the surplus repayment of $11. This $18 transfer of coinsurance reserves to mod-co keeps the coinsurance reserves equal to the amount of outstanding surplus. For the next year, coinsurance reserves will be $89 (107−18), or 8.32% of the total of $1,070. The mod-co reserve will be $981 (900+63+18).

When this transaction has been calculated, the Final Statutory Financial Statements are calculated for both companies. These are shown in Tables 5.13A and 5.13B.

The mod-co adjustment is now $9. The distribution of coinsurance and mod-co reserves has been adjusted to reflect the transfer of the increase in coinsurance reserves and the surplus repayment of $11. Notice that the $11 surplus repayment equals XYZ Re's release of reserve. Also, the $9 mod-co adjustment equals the sum of XYZ Re's share of benefits ($5), the experience refund ($1), and the risk charge ($3). All other things being equal, the $3 is the only cash transfer necessary. However, in the event of negative experience, XYZ would be required to pay ABC Life.

The gains for both companies remain the same. ABC Life's invested assets are now $982 on its statutory Balance Sheet. This is the same as in the funds withheld transactions. XYZ Re's invested assets are now $113, again, the same amount as in the funds withheld examples. ABC Life's mod-co reserves are now $981, while XYZ Re's coinsurance reserves are $89, the amount of the outstanding surplus.

ABC LIFE
REINSURANCE REPORT
PARTIALLY MODIFIED COINSURANCE — YEAR 2

Ceded Premium:			$ 0
Less: Allowances	$	0	
Benefits		5	
Mod-co Adjustment		(9)	
Experience Refund		1	3
Total Due XYZ Re:			$ 3

TABLE 5.13A

FINAL STATUTORY FINANCIAL STATEMENTS
PARTIALLY MODIFIED COINSURANCE — YEAR 2

GAIN FROM OPERATIONS

	ABC LIFE	XYZ RE
Revenue:		
Premiums:		
Gross	$ 0	$ 0
Ceded	0	0
Net	0	0
Investment Income:		
Surplus	0	0
Reserves	90	10
Total	90	10
Reinsurance Allowance	0	0
Mod-co Adjustment	0	9
Misc (Experience Refund)	1	0
TOTAL REVENUE	$ 91	$ 19
Benefits:		
Claims and Surrenders:		
Gross	$ 5	$ 5
Ceded	5	0
Net	0	5
Reserve Increase:		
Gross	70	(11)
Ceded	(11)	0
Net	81	(11)
Experience Refund	0	1
Mod-co Adjustment	9	0
TOTAL BENEFITS	$ 90	$ (5)
Expenses:		
Expenses and Commissions	$ 0	$ 0
TOTAL EXPENSES	$ 0	$ 0
GAIN FROM OPERATIONS	$ 1	$ 24

TABLE 5.13B

FINAL STATUTORY FINANCIAL STATEMENTS
PARTIALLY MODIFIED COINSURANCE — YEAR 2

BALANCE SHEET

	ABC LIFE	XYZ RE
Assets:		
Invested Assets	$ 982	$ 113
Accounts Receivable	0	0
TOTAL ASSETS	$ 982	$ 113
Liabilities and Capital:		
Policy Reserves:		
Gross	$ 1,070	$ 89
Ceded	89	0
Net	981	89
Accounts Payable	0	0
TOTAL LIABILITIES	$ 981	$ 89
Surplus	$ 1	$ 24
TOTAL CAPITAL	$ 1	$ 24
TOTAL LIABILITIES AND CAPITAL	$ 982	$ 113

The reinsurance report in Year 2 shows a total due from ABC Life to XYZ Re of $3.

ABC LIFE
OUTSTANDING SURPLUS ACCOUNT
(ALTERNATIVE CALCULATION)
PARTIALLY MODIFIED COINSURANCE — END OF YEAR 2

Beginning Balance:			$ (100)
Plus:	Final Mod-co Adjustment		9
Less:	Final Coinsurance Reserve Increase	$ (11)	
	Benefits	5	
	Experience Refund	1	
	Risk Charge	3	2
Ending Balance:			$ (89)

REGULATION AND TAXATION

Prior to about 1984, financial reinsurance was in an "anything goes" situation; that is, there was very little effective regulation. The early 1980's saw extensive activity in the financial reinsurance marketplace. A large number of these reinsurance transactions resulted in the reclassification of the components of taxable income and significant reduction in federal income tax revenues from the life insurance industry. Reinsurance also figured prominently in a number of insurance company insolvencies, primarily in the property and casualty area. The excessive use in reinsurance in these two situations, and a cavalier treatment of reserve credits and treaty provisions, brought about many changes in the way such reinsurance is viewed by regulators and tax authorities.

One of the major changes concerns the tax treatment given to reinsurance transactions. Section 845[8] of the Tax Reform Act of 1984

---

[8] See Chapter 14, Tax Effects of Reinsurance.

grants the IRS broad authority to change individual company tax returns if significant tax avoidance is found to be present. While substantial tax avoidance is not defined, a disproportionate sharing of risks and tax benefits is an indication of such avoidance. Since inforce blocks are typically very stable, it is possible that the use of such blocks to secure surplus relief, at least in the ways most prevalent in the market, might be judged to be disproportionate.

In many cases, reinsurance transactions have been used to mask the true financial condition of a life insurance company. Often very little, if any, risk was actually transferred to the reinsurer. There have been insolvencies where reinsurance transactions have only postponed the inevitable liquidation without providing any significant benefit, risk transfer, or economic security to the insolvent company. This has caused state insurance departments to review reinsurance agreements closely for risk transfer.[9]

The Internal Revenue Service (IRS) and state insurance departments are both concerned that a reinsurance treaty provide legitimate risk transfer. Several state insurance departments have recently begun to challenge certain reinsurance treaties, disallowing reserve credits and receivable assets, based on an apparent lack of risk transfer. It would appear that the departments have valid concerns. Specific reinsurance treaty terms which have caused concern include the following:

(1) Scheduled gains to the reinsurer, regardless of the underlying experience of the block of reinsurance.
(2) Reinsurer never having to pay out benefits, just building up a payment due liability.
(3) Reinsurer having the right to terminate the agreement or automatic termination of the agreement if either:
 (a) the reinsured becomes insolvent;
 (b) the reinsured has a change in management; or
 (c) the business reinsured proves to be unprofitable.

The appearance of these and similar terms cause negative reactions by the regulators. As a result, several states have come to challenge all "cashless" reinsurance. However, it appears that most, if not all, states

---

[9] See Chapter 10, Reinsurance Regulations.

will accept reinsurance agreements of a cashless nature if the transaction satisfies that state's risk transfer regulations.

Conditions which should be included in treaties in order to gain acceptance include the following:

(1) The reinsurer must have an actual obligation to pay benefits should experience reach a certain level.
(2) Gains to the reinsurer must be based on the actual experience of the reinsurance.
(3) No event, such as insolvency or management change, should automatically terminate the reinsurance in force. However, reinsurance may be terminated due to a certain level of earnings being attained, or if a warranty is violated.
(4) Inforce reinsurance cannot be terminated unilaterally by the reinsurer, except for nonpayment of premiums.
(5) Interest paid or credited via the reinsurance should be reasonable in relation to the investment markets or the assets involved.
(6) The relevant significant risks of the underlying policies should be transferred to the reinsurer, including capital loss, disintermediation, and asset default risks if they are deemed relevant.
(7) The ceding company should not be forced to pay back losses except for voluntary termination.

State regulators object to allowing reserve or receivable credits when the risk transferred is disproportionate to reserve credit. Adherence to the guidelines above should assist in qualifying agreements.

SECURITY CONSIDERATIONS

In recent years, the use of funds withheld and similar cashless reinsurance programs has come under criticism from both state regulators and the IRS. This criticism results from the apparent lack of risk transfer often associated with these types of agreements. In response to this criticism, and for other reasons relating to protection of assets, preserving reserve credits, minimizing currency fluctuations, and protection in the event of insolvency of either party, the use of trusts, escrow accounts, and letters of credit has increased in recent years.

Trusts and Escrow Accounts

With these concepts, a trust or escrow account is established to hold, identify, or further segment the relevant assets of one or both parties to a reinsurance transaction. A trust is used to secure amounts that are owed or might become owed from the company that establishes the trust to the company that is the beneficiary of the trust. Equitable title to the assets is in the trustee.

A common use of a trust is to transfer assets relating to reserves of an inforce block. The trust enables the investment performances to be tied to the assets owned and for the same assets or replacements to be transferred back upon recapture. In the examples above, consider the coinsurance model. In this model, the transactions would be the same except the assets held by the reinsurer would be placed in the trust. Trusts can be used in any reinsurance agreement, but they are most common as alternatives to funds withheld transactions.

Escrow accounts are frequently confused with trusts, but the differences are probably greater than their similarities. Escrow accounts are used to earmark assets, usually for potential transfer under specified conditions, rather than actually transferring the ownership of the assets as is the case with a trust. In a typical transaction, an escrow account might be used to support a funds withheld agreement.

In a funds withheld coinsurance case, the assets left with the ceding company would be placed in an escrow account. The escrow agreement would outline the various rights of companies. If certain conditions were to occur, the assets in escrow would be transferred to the reinsurer. Events which could trigger such a transfer might include the following:

(1) Surplus dropping below an agreed upon level.
(2) Change in management.
(3) Financial performance of the reinsurance below expected levels.

Trusts and escrow agreements are valuable tools to add protection to one or both parties in a reinsurance agreement while maintaining flexibility. The treatment of trusts and escrow agreements is not standardized in all states and is currently under review. Any agreement contemplating use of either of a trust or escrow account should be

Financial Reinsurance 171

reviewed in the light of the latest developments for the state insurance department involved.

Trusts can be used to segregate assets or provide reserve credits. If the purpose is to secure reserve credits, the trusts are subject to regulations such as the Model Law on Credit for Reinsurance.

Advantages. The use of the trusts and escrow accounts has the following potential advantages:

(1) Assets are separate and identifiable.
(2) Investment income can be limited to the performance of specific assets.
(3) If the reinsurer is not licensed or admitted in the ceding company's state of domicile, a properly structured trust or escrow will permit the ceding company to take appropriate reserve credit.
(4) In the event of recapture, the assets of the trust or escrow account can be used to effect payment, thereby reducing or eliminating dispute over market values.
(5) A trust is a true transfer of ownership and should be less suspect to both state regulators and the IRS.
(6) Upon default, the beneficiary has the right to withdraw assets as a secured creditor. Additionally, the trust or escrow account may be constructed to give certain privileges and rights to each party. In such instances, these are valuable tools providing assurance that the secured party receives its contractual benefits to the extent of the trust assets, not at a reduced value determined by a liquidator.

Disadvantages. Potential disadvantages in the use of a trust include the following:

(1) Use of a trust or escrow account creates additional expense which may or may not be of significance in a given agreement.
(2) A trust or escrow account can result in restrictions on investment management. The degree of control of either party or the investment policy may be negotiable, but unless some real element of management transfer is effected, it may be held that investment risk transfer did not occur.

(3) Transfer of assets into a trust is a transfer of ownership and may necessitate recognition of capital gains and losses for tax purposes, or the recognition of current market values for statutory statement purposes. The agreement should specify which party takes the capital gains or losses.
(4) If a trust is used to transfer ownership of assets, the company giving up the assets will suffer a reduction in the magnitude of assets it reports.
(5) Should the need to reverse the asset transfer occur, returning ownership to the original party, a depreciation in market values could create a surplus strain. This is occasioned because some assets may be carried for statutory purposes at book values in excess of market values. On transfer, new book values are established based on current market values. In some cases, it may be possible to avoid this by having assets returned at book value.

Letters of Credit

When a reinsurer is not licensed or admitted in the ceding company's state of domicile, state insurance departments are reluctant to give annual statement credit for the reserve liability ceded to the reinsurer as that state insurance department does not have the authority to enforce the terms of the contract or supervise the financial operations of the reinsurer. This problem can be avoided through the use of mod-co or a trust. However, as noted earlier, the use of mod-co places the assets outside of the control of the reinsurer. The use of a trust or escrow account may give the reinsurer more control over the assets but administration of a trust or escrow account is more expensive. A letter of credit is another solution.

Most states allow a ceding company to take annual statement credit for the reserve liability ceded to a non admitted reinsurer if the reinsurer provides the ceding company with a letter of credit for the amount of the reserves. A letter of credit is obtained from a financial institution and provides that the beneficiary, in this case the ceding company, may draw the funds on demand.

The chief advantage of a letter of credit is that it may be obtained for a nominal fee, often as low as .20% to .35% per year, although in certain situations the fee can exceed 1%.

Financial Reinsurance

Letters of credit also require very little administration. The major disadvantage of a letter of credit from a reinsurer's viewpoint is that the ceding company may actually draw down on the letter without warning. In this situation the reinsurer would be required to reimburse the financial institution.

From the ceding company's viewpoint, the major concern regarding letters of credit is its ability to withdraw the funds when actually needed. Most rules covering letters of credit address the specific concerns. These rules are discussed in Chapter 10, Reinsurance Regulations.

The Securities Valuation Office (SVO) of the National Association of Insurance Commissioners (NAIC) is authorized to develop a list of acceptable providers of letters of credit.

Administrative and Functional Considerations

Part Two

6 The Reinsurance Treaty

A reinsurance agreement, or treaty, is a legal contract between two insurance companies.[1] The treaty documents the arrangement between the reinsurer and the ceding company. In the past, the treaty frequently referred to a "gentlemen's agreement" between the two parties, meaning that the parties relied on mutual integrity and goodwill to resolve disputes or uncertainties in the event the treaty language was unclear or incomplete. In many instances, the documentation was poor and the parties often relied on side letters and notes.

In today's world, proper documentation is essential. Reinsurance transactions may be quite complex, involving large sums, and business relationships more distant. The parties to the agreement can no longer rely on good faith and memory.

As regulators and companies focus on the importance of reinsurance to financial solvency, the treaty has taken on increasing importance. Regulation and good business practice have combined to evolve the treaty

---

[1] See Schibley [22].

into the entire agreement, with thorough documentation and less emphasis on the "gentlemen's agreement" nature.

The reinsurance treaty is made up of a number of clauses or articles. These clauses deal with four major areas:

(1) Definition of Risks Reinsured.
(2) Financial Terms.
(3) Administration.
(4) Special Provisions.

In the case of indemnity reinsurance, the reinsurance treaty is solely between the ceding company and the reinsurer. The treaty does not create any legal relationship between the reinsurer and any of the ceding company's policyholders. In the event of the insolvency of the ceding company, the policyholders are not allowed to bypass the ceding company and deal directly with the reinsurer except in the case of a cut-through endorsement.[2] The reinsurer is also not a party to any disputes between the ceding company and the policyholders. Likewise, failure of a reinsurer to reimburse for a claim does not relieve the ceding company of any obligation to any policyholder.

An assumption treaty transfers the contractual policyholder obligations of the ceding company to the assumption insurer. The precise nature of the assumption or reinsurance arrangement will dictate the provisions of the treaty. In this chapter, the provisions described pertain primarily to indemnity reinsurance arrangements.[3]

The common terms of most reinsurance arrangements are discussed in this chapter.[4] For illustration purposes, a sample indemnity reinsurance treaty is provided as Appendix A. The actual language will vary to fit the needs of both parties.

---

[2] For further discussion of a cut-through endorsement, see Chapter 11, Insolvency and Reinsurance.

[3] Provisions and characteristics appropriate to assumption reinsurance are described in Chapter 16, Assumption.

[4] For further information, see "Discussion of Reinsurance Provisions in a Life Reinsurance Agreement," by the Treaty Committee of the Reinsurance Section, Society of Actuaries, August 1994.

DEFINITION OF RISKS REINSURED

One purpose of the reinsurance treaty is to define the conditions a risk must meet in order to qualify for reinsurance. These conditions vary between automatic and facultative reinsurance.

Automatic Reinsurance Treaty Provisions

An automatic reinsurance treaty sets forth very specific conditions which a policy must meet in order to qualify for reinsurance. Other provisions relate to the placing and timing of the reinsurance. The purposes of these are to facilitate the handling of policies requiring reinsurance and to assure that the reinsurer receives the type and quality of business it anticipated in pricing. These were discussed in some depth in Chapter 2 and are summarized here for reference:

Qualifications. The typical conditions which a policy must meet to qualify for automatic reinsurance include the following:

(1) The policy has been underwritten in accordance with agreed upon rules.
(2) The policy has been issued in accordance with normal guidelines.
(3) No facultative submission has been made to any reinsurer.
(4) The insured resides in a designated area and the ceding company is authorized to sell the reinsured product there.
(5) The ceding company maintains its full retention per the terms of the agreement.
(6) The table rating and issue age fall within predetermined limits.
(7) The amount to be ceded is not less than the specified minimum cession size.
(8) The amount ceded to the reinsurer on all policies inforce in the ceding company does not exceed the binding limit.
(9) The total amount applied for and inforce in all companies does not exceed the jumbo limit.
(10) The reinsurer may reserve the right to request and review underwriting papers after issue.

Allocation among Reinsurers. If the application for insurance meets the conditions and limits for automatic insurance and the policy is issued, the risk is ceded to the automatic reinsurer. If more than one reinsurer is participating in the automatic reinsurance, the treaty will define the method used to allocate the reinsurance. The common methods of allocation include the following:

(1) Assigning each reinsurer a portion of the alphabet and ceding by surname.
(2) Giving each reinsurer a stated percentage of each risk.
(3) Giving one reinsurer all cessions up to a certain amount, ceding any excess to a second reinsurer up to another amount, and so on.
(4) Assigning each reinsurer a group of issue ages or years of birth.
(5) Assigning the reinsurer by agent or source of business.

Commencement of Liabilities. The treaty defines when the reinsurer's liability begins on any policy reinsured. Under an automatic reinsurance treaty, the reinsurer's liabilities commence simultaneously with those of the ceding company as long as the automatic conditions have been met, even if the reinsurer has not been notified of the cession.

Conditional Receipt. If the application meets the conditions and limits for automatic reinsurance, and if the application included conditional receipt coverage, the automatic reinsurer may provide protection during the period covered by the conditional receipt, subject to any limitations the reinsurer may place on the coverage in the treaty. Before providing conditional receipt coverage, the reinsurer would want to review the wording of the receipt and the rules governing its use.

Facultative Reinsurance Treaty Provisions

Most automatic treaties provide for facultative submissions. Some treaties provide only facultative coverage. The purpose of the conditions set forth for facultative reinsurance is to facilitate the handling of those policies which do not qualify for automatic reinsurance or which require special consideration. They also assure that the reinsurer has adequate opportunity to evaluate such risks. These conditions are discussed below.

Qualifications. Any application may be submitted for facultative review. After its underwriting risk analysis, the reinsurer may decline the risk or it may make an offer to the ceding company stating its conditions for accepting the risk. These conditions will usually include the following:

(1) The underwriting classification.
(2) The amount of the risk the ceding company must retain, if any.
(3) The amount of the risk the reinsurer will accept.

Sometimes the reinsurer's offer will require the submission of additional information satisfactory to it, or impose other conditions, before coverage can be effected.

Commencement of Liabilities. The treaty defines when the reinsurer's liability begins on any reinsured policy. This reinsurance liability normally begins when the ceding company has met the necessary conditions and accepted the reinsurer's offer. Some treaties require that the ceding company must accept the offer in writing. The reinsurer may also place a time limit for the ceding company's acceptance, such as 60 to 120 days. Failure by the ceding company to make such a formal acceptance of the offer within the prescribed time period will relieve the reinsurer of any liability.

Conditional Receipt. Once an application has been submitted for facultative review, it no longer qualifies for automatic coverage. In this case, conditional receipt coverage is lost unless special provision has been made by either the automatic or facultative reinsurer.

TERMS AND SPECIFICATIONS

The financial terms and specifications are part of the treaty. These terms and specifications, which are common to automatic and facultative treaties, include the policy forms, forms of reinsurance, premiums, and expense allowances.

Policy Forms

The treaty defines the policy forms covered. Some treaties may cover all of the ceding company's policy forms, but it is not unusual for a treaty to cover only one policy form. On occasion, a treaty may be drafted to cover a single policy in a special circumstance.

Forms of Reinsurance

The reinsurance treaty specifies whether the policies covered under the treaty are reinsured on a coinsurance, mod-co, or YRT basis. If the reinsurance is to be on a YRT basis, the method for determining the net amount at risk will be defined in the treaty.

Any two, or even all three, plans of reinsurance may be integrated into a single treaty, and the treaty will define when and how each plan is to be applied. The reinsurance treaty may also require that facultative submissions be reinsured on a different basis than the one used for automatic reinsurance.

Coverage on supplemental benefits may be reinsured on a different basis from that used for the basic coverage. Disability and accidental death benefits may be excluded from the treaty and reinsured separately or retained by the ceding company. The ceding company may fill its life retention on the base policy and term riders first, then apply any accidental death benefits. Alternatively, accidental death benefits might have a separate retention schedule or be reinsured under a separate bulk ADB treaty. Disability benefits for monthly income, lump sums, and waiver of premium might be reinsured in a different proportion from the life benefit. The treatment of extraordinarily high issue ages or benefits should be discussed before formalizing the agreement.

This provision also outlines the reinsurer's liability for dividends, cash surrender values, premium tax reimbursements, and other benefits.

Premiums and Allowances

If coinsurance or mod-co is involved, the treaty defines the reinsurance premiums and allowances. If YRT reinsurance is involved, the YRT premium rate scale and discounts will be included in the treaty. The terms for reinsuring ancillary benefits, substandard ratings, and riders will be defined in the treaty.

Waiver of premium is usually reinsured using a percentage of the premium charged by the ceding company. Accidental death benefits are usually reinsured using a special premium scale. Substandard waiver or ADB premiums are generally multiples of the waiver or ADB premium.

The reinsurance of substandard flat extra premiums may be administered in a different form from the basic coverage, usually using generalized allowances.[5] Any agreed upon changes in premiums, such as the removal of substandard extra premiums after 20 years or at age 65, should be defined in the treaty.

Coinsurance Limit

In a coinsurance or mod-co treaty, the reinsurer may set a coinsurance limit. Any amounts reinsured on a single life in excess of this limit are reinsured on a YRT basis or priced individually. A coinsurance limit is employed because of the reinsurer's own retrocession costs.

ADMINISTRATION

Much of the reinsurance treaty deals with administrative procedures. The type of data needed, the type of administration, and the timing of reports should be specified in the treaty. The standard treaty clauses dealing with administrative matters are discussed below.

Notification

The reinsurer must be notified when a risk is ceded. The form and timing of the notification depends on the type of administration used: individual cession or self-administration.

---

[5] See Chapter 7, Reinsurance Administration.

Individual Cession. Under an individual cession arrangement, the contract specifies that the ceding company is to deliver a reinsurance cession record[6] to the reinsurer. This record contains the information required for the reinsurer to set up its accounting and valuation records and to search its own records to determine if any portion of its retention has been used previously. Such notification is generally required within 30 days after the delivery of the policy.

Self-Administration. When the ceding company performs basic reinsurance administration, the ceding company provides the reinsurer with a listing of all cessions on new issues at predetermined intervals. This listing contains the basic information of the reinsurance cession record, or at least enough data to provide an audit trail and to avoid uncertainty regarding liability.

The information may be sent as hard copy or in computer-readable form. The reinsurer reviews information and searches its records to determine if it has reinsured any of the lives previously. Notification is usually provided monthly.

Under the terms of some reinsurance agreements, the ceding company performs all the basic administrative functions and provides the reinsurer with summary data at pre-determined intervals. These arrangements are referred to as bulk reinsurance. Policy level detail is not provided.

Premium Accounting

The reinsurance treaty describes the billing procedures to be used. The procedures will vary between individual cession and self administration. In either case, the reinsurer retains the right to terminate reinsurance for cessions where the premiums are in default. The reinsurer normally gives the ceding company a 30-day grace period and a 30-day notice of termination. During this 30-day grace period the reinsurer will continue to be liable for claims. The reinsurer may allow the ceding company to reinstate terminated reinsurance within the 60-day period after the effective date of termination if all unpaid reinsurance premiums are paid

---

[6] *Ibid.*

in full. No evidence of insurability is required. However, the reinsurer is not liable for claims occurring after the termination of the reinsured policy and prior to reinstatement.

Individual Cession. Most reinsurance treaties specify that the reinsurance premiums are payable on an annual basis regardless of how the insurance premiums are payable to the ceding company. Under an individual cession treaty, the reinsurer sends the ceding company a monthly billing statement listing first year and renewal premiums which are due during that month, less refunds and allowances. If the statement shows that a net reinsurance premium is due the reinsurer, the ceding company must pay this balance within a specified period of time. If the statement shows a balance due the ceding company, the reinsurer must pay the ceding company within a certain period of time.

Self-Administration. Under a self-administered treaty, the ceding company periodically prepares a statement with the same type of information as is normally contained on the individual cession premium billing report. The reinsurance premiums on a self-administered treaty may be payable at specified intervals regardless of the basis of payment of the basic coverage or the premiums may be payable on the same mode as the basic coverage.

The ceding company will also provide a policy exhibit in addition to a listing of individual policies. Under a bulk agreement, policy level detail is not provided.

In a financial reinsurance arrangement, the reinsurance premiums are normally calculated on the same mode as the ceding company receives them; this greatly reduces the administrative effort required of the ceding company. Reinsurance premium payment is normally on a net basis and enacted on a quarterly or annual basis.

Reductions and Terminations

This section of the reinsurance treaty outlines administrative procedures in the reapportionment of liabilities should one of the policies reinsured under the agreement be changed from its original terms.

If reductions are dealt with on a by-life basis, a ceding company with multiple policies on the same insured must determine the effect of the change on the reinsured policy, whether or not the reduced policy was reinsured. A by-life reduction reduces reinsurance to maintain the ceding company's full retention. In a by-life reduction, reinsurance is reduced on the policy which was reduced or terminated. The balance of the reduction is then applied to other inforce policies, either on a first-in-first-out or last-in-first-out basis. If a number of reinsurers are involved, reductions will be proportionate. Administration will be further complicated if the ceding company varies retention limits by plan and the life involved is insured on multiple plans.

Alternatively, reductions may be made on a per-policy basis. In this case, reinsurance is affected only on the policy being reduced or terminated. If the affected policy carries little or no reinsurance, the company may find itself with more reinsurance than is necessary. This would cause problems at recapture.

When deciding to use a by-life provision, the ceding company should consider what it wishes to have happen in the event it issued three policies on one life, retaining one entirely and reinsuring the others with two different reinsurers, and the first policy terminates. In order to use the by-life basis, the ceding company must be able to connect all policies on the same life.

Treaties often require that the ceding company fill-up, or maintain, its full retention by recapturing a portion of the reinsurance in the event of the termination or reduction of any policy reducing the amount retained on the life of an insured.

Changes and Continuations

Historically, reinsurance treaties normally contained a single clause for "Reductions, Terminations, and Changes." In the early 1990's, practitioners realized that modern products afforded policyholders many options to change coverage terms. This necessitates that treaties define how reinsurance will be continued through changes in the risk characteristics. Since changes are so important, treaties now contain separate clauses for "Reductions and Terminations" and "Continuations."

The continuation provision defines the rights and obligations of the ceding company and the reinsurer when a continuation occurs. Continuations are generally defined as a new policy replacing a policy issued earlier where the new policy lacks at least one of the following new business characteristics:

(1) New business underwriting.
(2) Full first year commission.
(3) New suicide period.
(4) New contestable period.

Some treaties also require the concurrent termination of the original policy, generally within six months in either direction from the issue date of the new policy.

Internal replacements and policy exchanges are considered continuations. Re-entries, term conversions, and contractual increases, while theoretically continuations, are normally handled under separate provisions.

In most cases, the reinsurance premium will be based on the treaty's current YRT or coinsurance schedules for either the original plan or the new plan, using the point-in-scale premiums or allowances appropriate for the original issue age. Alternatively, the reinsurer may charge a single premium and treat the continuation as a new issue. If the duration is based on the original issue date, the recapture period will be measured from the original issue date. The treatment may vary depending on which party initiated the continuation, whether it was contractual or non-contractual, whether or not it is a new plan, and the extent of new business characteristics.

The treaty may specify that the provision is applicable even if the new plan is not covered by the treaty. In this case, the ceding company and reinsurer may negotiate a solution.

Because there are many possible continuation scenarios, the treaty may provide guidelines for making exceptions. It may call for repricing if a significant increase occurs and the original pricing assumptions appear inadequate. If a new risk classification is involved, such as preferred risk or joint life, new rates may be required.

Re-entries

A re-entry is a specialized form of a continuation involving an inforce select and ultimate policy reverting to an earlier duration (usually first year) based on the attained age. The re-entry provision is a part of the policy contract. Treatment of re-entries may vary depending on the extent of new underwriting evidence, size of commissions, duration, and age.

The treaty should state whether or not the recapture period is restarted. The handling of the suicide and contestable periods should be clearly stated.

Conversions

A term conversion is also a form of continuation, and the reinsurer would expect to cover the continued policy unless other arrangements were negotiated prior to writing the treaty. The continued policy is generally reinsured using point-in-scale premiums or allowances based on the original issue date and age. If the reinsurer does not reinsure the converted policy, special arrangements may be made to cover the converted policy.

The handling of term conversions should be specified in the treaty. In many cases, both parties expect the volume of conversions to be relatively insignificant. However, should the ceding company decide to promote conversions, the original terms of the agreement may not be appropriate.

Reduced Paid-up and Extended Term Insurance

When a policy goes on a non-forfeiture option, the amount of insurance may increase because of dividends, or decrease because of policy loans. This provision should describe how the amount of reinsurance is treated. Generally, increases and decreases are shared proportionately. Under the reduced paid-up option, the reinsurance may be canceled if the benefit falls below a specified dollar amount. The ceding company may retain the right to recapture reduced paid-up and extended term insurance.

Policy Dividends

Most reinsurance treaties do not have a separate dividend provision. Most reinsurers prefer not to participate in policy dividends because the ceding company must be free to make changes in the dividend scale and the performance of the reinsured portions is likely to differ from the performance of the retained business. Usually, the reinsurer will provide additional allowances in lieu of dividend participation.

Should the reinsurer elect to follow the dividend scale, the ceding company should promptly notify the reinsurer of any changes in the scale.

Under a YRT treaty, term additions from dividends are usually reinsured on a level net amount of risk basis to simplify administration. Some reinsurers will cover term additions only if elected at policy issue. Any subsequent election would require facultative approval.

New York Regulation 102, effective September 1, 1993, requires the reinsurer to fully reimburse dividends declared by the ceding company if the reinsurance is on a coinsurance or modified coinsurance basis.

Increase in Retention and Recapture

Neither party may unilaterally terminate existing reinsurance under a treaty, but a treaty may be terminated with respect to new business upon proper notification. A standard exception allows the reinsurer to terminate the treaty for inforce business for non-payment of premiums. Such termination may be treated as surrenders or lapses of the underlying policies, with payment of any surrender benefits reinsured after deduction of any reinsurance premiums due.

Many reinsurance treaties provide that if the ceding company increases its retention on risks reinsured under the treaty, the ceding company may, at its option, recapture amounts reinsured under the agreement subject to written notification of the reinsurer and subject to the terms of the recapture clause. Most reinsurance treaties require that a policy must be reinsured for a specified period of time[7] before recapture is allowed. This is designed to allow the reinsurer to recover its acquisition expenses.

---

[7] 12 See Chapter 8, Managing Ceded Reinsurance.

The general conditions for recapture permit the ceding company to recapture reinsurance on each life for which it retained the applicable maximum retention in effect at the time of the cession. If the policy is reinsured by more than one reinsurer, the reduction in reinsurance may be in proportion to the amount of reinsurance on the life carried by all reinsurers or applied to the top automatic layer first.

The ceding company must recapture reinsurance on all like risks under the same treaty; that is, it cannot pick and choose which specific cessions it wishes to recapture and which it does not. If recapture of a block of life insurance is effected, any basic life reinsurance on disabled lives must be recaptured along with the non-disabled lives; reinsurance of the waiver of premium claim usually stays in effect.

Risks may be recaptured on the anniversary following the increase in retention, provided that the recapture duration has been attained. Reinsurance cannot be recaptured and then ceded to another company. The treaty may allow recapture under certain circumstances such as the reinsurer raising rates.

Provisions requiring recapture under certain circumstances such as a change in ownership, financial conditions, or upon insolvency were included in some financial reinsurance agreements prior to 1984. Today, regulators are concerned about the potential for abuse of these provisions. While regulation does not necessarily forbid such treaties for economic purposes, reinsurance reserve credits or surplus benefits are not allowed for such treaties and their use is very rare.[8]

Reinstatement

If the policy reinsured under the treaty has lapsed for nonpayment of premiums to the ceding company and has subsequently been reinstated according to the reinstatement rules of the ceding company, the treaty generally provides that reinsurance can be reinstated on the policy by payment of all premiums in arrears by the ceding company. Interest may be paid to the reinsurer to the extent the ceding company collects it.

---

[8] See Chapter 10, Reinsurance Regulation.

This provision reduces administrative work for both parties. However, under certain circumstances involving facultative cessions, the reinsurer may require some evidence of insurability. The reinsurer may also require evidence if it holds a substantial share of the risk or the length of time between lapsation and reinstatement exceeds 90 days.

Expenses

The reinsurance treaty generally provides that the ceding company is responsible for all expenses in connection with issuing and maintaining the policy. This includes the cost of medical reports and tests which the reinsurer may require on facultative submissions.

Claims

The claim section of the reinsurance treaty outlines the terms and conditions under which the reinsurer is liable for claims incurred under the reinsurance agreement. None of the treaty terms prevent the ceding company from settling a claim with a beneficiary. The treaty defines the notification process and approval requirements the ceding company must follow before the reinsurer is obligated to reimburse the claim. If the ceding company does not follow these steps, or if bad claims management practices are used, the reinsurer may deny liability.

When a claim involving a reinsured risk is incurred, the ceding company is required to inform the reinsurer within a defined period of time. Normally, if the contestable period of the reinsured policy has expired, and if the ceding company has retained more than 50% of the risk, the reinsurer will abide by the claim as it is settled by the ceding company. When the ceding company requests reimbursements for the claim, it must deliver copies of all papers concerning the claim to the reinsurer.

If the ceding company retained less than 50% of the insurance, or if the claim exceeds a predetermined limit, some treaties require the ceding company to submit all claim papers to the reinsurer first and await the reinsurer's response on the claim before settling the claim. The treaty may also require that facultative claims be submitted for the reinsurer's approval.

If a claim is incurred during the contestable period of the policy, regardless of the size or amount retained, some reinsurers require the ceding company to submit claim papers prior to settling the claim. In such event, the ceding company usually will wait for the reinsurer's response before settling the claim.

The types of restrictions placed on the ceding company's authority may vary. Reinsurers may have a greater expertise in claim review, especially for unique or large claims. Restrictions involve obtaining one or more of the following from the reinsurer:

(1) Opinion.
(2) Concurrence.
(3) Advice and consultation.
(4) Recommendation.
(5) Approval.
(6) Direction.

To avoid unnecessary delay in payment to the claimant, the treaty may provide that the reinsurer must respond within a limited period of time. If no response is given, the ceding company may assume that the reinsurer has no objection to the proposed settlement. A longer time limit is usually placed on contestable claims as the questions concerning these claims may be more involved.

Even if the ceding company has full claim settlement authority, it is expected to act in good faith. The parties should consider what constitutes good faith while negotiating the treaty.

If the ceding company contests a reinsured claim, and if such contest results in a reduction of its liability, the reinsurer would also share in this reduction in proportion to the amount of reinsurance ceded on the life. If more than one reinsurer is involved, all would share proportionately in relation to the amount of coverage reinsured with each company.

However, if a reinsurer declined to participate in the contest of the claim, it could "bail out" and discharge all of its liability by paying the full amount of the reinsurance to the ceding company. Under this circumstance, the reinsurer would not share in any subsequent reduction or increase in the liability. Such an action by a reinsurer is infrequent and could possibly hamper the ceding company's defense if the beneficiary became aware of the reinsurer's action.

The claim provision will explain the handling of changes in benefits due to the misstatement of age or sex. Generally, changes are shared proportionally. In the case of misrepresentation or suicide, if the ceding company returns policy premiums rather than paying the policy benefits, the reinsurer will refund the reinsurance premiums. If the ceding company pays reduced benefits in the case of suicide, the reinsurer will pay its share of the reduced benefits. The provision might limit the total amount the ceding company recovers from all reinsurers on a claim to the amount paid to the beneficiary.

The ceding company is expected to pay all routine expenses in connection with settling claims, including the cost of routine investigation reports, although some reinsurers may pay part of this expense. The reinsurer may share expenses in connection with the settlement of the claim which are not routine. These non-routine expenses would normally be incurred in connection with the contest of a claim, or by a decision on an individual claim. The expenses would be shared in proportion to the reinsurance ceded under the contract. However, in the rare event where the reinsurer has declined to participate in the contest of the claim and has paid the full amount of the reinsurance to the ceding company, the reinsurer would not share in any expenses of the contest.

The treaty typically requires that the ceding company provide timely notice of a claim. This is particularly important in the case of a litigated claim when extra-contractual or punitive damages may be involved. If the notice is late, the reinsurer may deny coverage. Case law has supported this position.

The reinsurer will normally share state-required interest payments. If the reinsurer does not pay benefits within a specified time period, the treaty may impose an interest charge.

The claims provision may also define what, if any, extra-contractual damages are covered, when they are covered, and how they will be shared. Alternatively, this may be addressed in a separate provision.

The payment of reinsurance proceeds under a life policy is generally made in a lump sum. The reinsurer normally does not participate in settlement options. However, the reinsurance proceeds for an in-benefit annuity contract or the benefits under a health policy are generally paid as incurred.

Provisions for handling payments of accelerated death benefits should be included. Joint life and second-to-die policies also require special consideration. Multiple reinsurers may also complicate claim settlement.

In a financial reinsurance agreement, the ceding company generally has much more latitude in settling claims. Under most such treaties, claims can be settled without reinsurer review.

SPECIAL PROVISIONS

The remainder of the treaty focuses on problem prevention and solving. These special provisions have evolved over the years in response to the change in the basic nature of reinsurance relationship from that of a long-standing partnership to more of a business relationship.

Oversights, Errors, and Omissions

The oversights, errors, and omissions clause covers unintentional clerical errors and oversights. Under common law, any deviation from the agreement could result in the non-deviating party being freed from its obligation. This clause, unique to reinsurance treaties, is intended to avoid this result and to minimize disputes and the need for arbitration or litigation. The treaty may state that only clerical errors are covered. These oversights and errors most frequently involve the failure of the ceding company to notify the reinsurer of a cession or incorrect entries made in the completion of the cession record.

A non-clerical error is a decision a company took which had negative consequences, such as deciding not to check for previous inforce insurance on a life or failing to correct an administrative error on a timely basis. In these circumstances, the reinsurer would be relieved of responsibility. Unfortunately, the distinction between clerical and non-clerical errors is sometimes unclear.

The clause provides that both companies will be restored to the position they would have occupied if the oversight had not occurred. Some reinsurers require that the oversight be corrected within a reasonable period of time after its discovery. This clause should provide that favorable and unfavorable errors are to be identified and corrected in a timely manner.

The Reinsurance Treaty

In the event of the failure of a company to provide the reinsurer with information concerning a cession, the ceding company would be required to pay all reinsurance premiums from the date of the cession, often with interest. If a claim is incurred, the reinsurer would be expected to reimburse the ceding company for its share of the claim upon the receipt of the back premiums. However, should the oversight involve the reinsurance of a facultative submission which the reinsurer had previously notified the ceding company it would not accept, or the failure of the ceding company to fulfill underwriting requirements on a particular facultative case, the reinsurer would deny liability in the event of any claim.

In many cases, errors are found long after they are committed making it difficult to restore both parties to the original position. Documentation is often unavailable. Large errors, particularly those involving claims, are more likely to be discovered than are small errors, which are more likely to involve premiums. Audits generally find only systematic errors and not individual errors.

Extra-Contractual Damages

The original concept of the gentlemen's agreement did not anticipate the large awards for extra-contractual or punitive damages which have been incurred in recent years. In some instances, the ceding company perceived that the reinsurer had "deeper pockets" and contended that the reinsurer should cover all costs of extra-contractual damages in excess of the ceding company's retention. Reinsurers have responded by adding provisions to the treaty regarding extra-contractual damages.

There are three basic types of extra-contractual damages:

(1) *Ex gratia* payments, or amounts the ceding company is not obligated to pay.
(2) Compensatory damages, or damages directly related to claim denial.
(3) Punitive or exemplary damages due to intentional or negligent conduct.

Most reinsurers will not participate in *ex gratia* payments. Some will participate in compensatory damages. Most do not wish to participate in punitive damages. The extra-contractual damage clause holds that the reinsurer has no liability for any extra-contractual damages awarded against the ceding company as a result of the acts, omissions, or a course of conduct committed by the ceding company in connection with any insurance ceded under the treaty. Some reinsurance treaties provide that if the reinsurer was in some way a party to the act, omission, or course of conduct which resulted in the award of such damages, it will share a portion of the damages with the ceding company.

The amount of control over claims retained by the reinsurer may affect its liability in the case of punitive damages. It is important that the reinsurer not make the ceding company be perceived as its agent in settlement claims; otherwise it may become directly liable to the policyholders.

The amount of payment for extra-contractual damages is usually in proportion to the amount of the risk reinsured. However, the amount may not be fixed in advance as the circumstances are difficult to predict and define. As such, the concept of the gentlemen's agreement still comes into play in this situation.

Extra-contractual damages are generally the result of specific actions by one of the parties. Therefore, it may be reasonable for the reinsurer to share in the cost to the extent it participated in the action or the decisions leading to the action. On the other hand, if the reinsurer had no participation in the decisions or action, particularly in situations arising from underwriting or policy administration issues, it may be equally reasonable for the reinsurer not to share in the extra expense.

It may be difficult to determine the degree to which the reinsurer may have been a party to the act which resulted in the damages. Different reinsurers have different opinions as to the requirements of equity on the decision whether to participate in extra-contractual or punitive damages.

Inspection of Records

The reinsurer reserves the right to inspect any of the records of the ceding company which pertain to the reinsurance ceded under the terms of the agreement. As a matter of good business practice, the reinsurer should audit both individual cession and self-administered accounts on a regular basis. Depending on the size of the account and its history, the audit may be conducted annually or less frequently. This audit ensures that cessions meet the conditions of the treaty and have been properly underwritten, recorded, and accounted for. This audit is particularly vital for self-administered accounts as the reinsurer maintains very few records on the policies reinsured.

In the case of a reinsurance pool, prior agreement should be reached concerning making information gathered by one pool member available to other members.

Arbitration

The arbitration clause exemplifies the gentlemen's agreement concept. In the event that any disagreement or claim arises out of the contract, both parties to the contract agree that such disagreement is to be settled amicably and with good faith. If the parties cannot agree among themselves, these disputes are settled through arbitration rather than litigation in the courts.

Arbitration is considered faster, more flexible, easier, and less costly than court proceedings. Most believe that it is more appropriate to use insurance experts who are familiar with insurance issues rather than the courts. Arbitration does not require public disclosure and the parties are not bound by the formalities of court proceedings.

The clause generally explains the arbitration procedures, often citing the Uniform Arbitration Act. Typically, the treaty will specify many details of the arbitration procedure. Alternatively, some treaties may specify that arbitration will be conducted in accordance with the Commercial Arbitration Rules of the American Arbitration Association which are in effect at the date of the disagreement.

The typical arbitration clause calls for three arbitrators who are current or past officers of life insurance companies other than the two parties to the contract. Each party to the contract appoints one arbitrator and the two arbitrators select a third. If one company fails to appoint an arbitrator or if the two arbitrators are unable to agree to a third arbitrator, the treaty will specify a method for selecting the third arbitrator.[9] The arbitrators determines how the expenses are apportioned.

The arbitration clause will specify how either party can initiate arbitration proceedings. It may place time constraints on submitting facts and scheduling hearings. Formal written notification of the decision is required.

The terms of arbitration clauses vary relative to the guidelines provided for the arbitrators in considering the dispute. Some treaties require that the intent of the parties, equity, and normal business practices be considered rather than a strict application of the law. Newer treaties direct that the arbitrators first look to the terms of the treaty and, only if they are unclear, should equity be considered. These newer treaties frequently make reference to the rules of the American Arbitration Association as guidance to the arbitrators.

The decision of the arbitrators is final and is usually not appealed. The appropriate court may be approached to enforce a decision. Some states will not enforce arbitration agreements because of laws granting all citizens the right to a trial. If the laws of both parties' states of domicile do not enforce arbitrations and they desire it, the provision should either provide that the laws of another state be used or that the case be submitted to federal court which would then mandate arbitration.

Assignment and Transfer

The assignment clause holds that reinsurance ceded under the agreement cannot be sold, assigned, or transferred by either party without prior written approval of the other party. If written approval is not obtained, the other party reserves the right to terminate the reinsurance.

Parties to the Agreement

The reinsurance treaty creates a contractual relationship between the reinsurer and the ceding company. An indemnity reinsurance treaty

---

[9] In the past, many treaties have specified that in the event the first two arbitrators cannot agree on a third, the President of the American Council of Life Insurance (ACLI) will choose the third one. The ACLI, however, has requested that it not be so named. In this event, the President of the American Arbitrations Association might be used to choose the third arbitrator.

specifies that it does not create any relationship between the reinsurer and the ceding company's policyholders or beneficiaries. This prevents these policyholders and beneficiaries from taking action against the reinsurer, even in the event of an insolvency of the ceding company. The reinsurer normally finds that desirable.

In some states, it has been possible to provide for a direct liability to this policyholder through a "cut-through" clause which provides for direct claim payment in the event of the insolvency of the ceding company. The Insurers Rehabilitation and Liquidation Model Act provides that, in the event of the insolvency of the ceding company, payments must be made to the ceding company or its receiver unless another payee is specified in the contract.

Insolvency

In order for the ceding company to take statutory financial statement credit for reserves on reinsurance ceded in most states, the reinsurance treaty must contain an insolvency clause which guarantees that reinsurance is payable to the liquidator without decrease or diminution in the event of the insolvency of the ceding company.[10] It normally does not prohibit the reinsurer's right to offset payments by monies owed it.

The insolvency clause is necessary because the basic reinsurance agreement provides that the reinsurer is required to pay only those claims which represent actual losses incurred by the ceding company. When an insolvency occurs, the liquidator may be able to pay only a portion of each claim, but the reinsurer should not benefit from a windfall. If the reinsurer has received full payment of premiums, it should pay full benefits.

The reinsurer should retain the right to be notified of and investigate pending claims and pursue any defense available. The expense of such defense is, subject to court approval, chargeable to the ceding company in proportion to the ceding company's benefit.

Most states require that an insolvency clause be included in a treaty before reinsurance reserve credit is allowed. The clause is reflected in the NAIC Insolvency Model.

---

[10] See Chapter 11, Insolvency and Reinsurance, and Chapter 10, Reinsurance Regulations.

Definition of the rights of a ceding company in the event of insolvency of a reinsurer is a less common part of a treaty. The ceding company may want a provision granting it the option to unilaterally terminate and recapture reinsurance in the event of reinsurer insolvency. In the event of such a termination, the reinsurer, its liquidator, receiver, or statutory successor would remain liable for any outstanding benefits incurred prior to termination. This provision enables the ceding company to avoid paying premiums to an insolvent entity with the likelihood of receiving reduced benefits in return. The ceding company may even find that its claim comes after that of individual policyholders of the reinsurer. Some states will not permit such a provision.

Offset

The offset clause in most reinsurance treaties provides that mutual debits and credits may be offset against each other, even in the event of the insolvency of one of the parties to the treaty. That is, any reinsurance premiums or other amounts due the reinsurer may be deducted from any amounts owed the ceding company or its successor by the reinsurer.

Mutuality is the key for determining the validity of offset in an insolvency. Mutuality of capacity must exist between the parties; that is, they must be viewed as debtors and creditors of each other. Most states will allow offsets arising from multiple agreements between the same parties. However, the NAIC Model Rehabilitation and Liquidation Act prohibits offsets where the parties both cede and assume business. Offsets are not allowed between one party and the affiliate of another.

Mutuality of time refers to the date of liquidation or rehabilitation, establishing pre and post-liquidation debts. Only debts from the same period may be offset.

Some state regulations or laws prohibit or restrict the use of offset provisions. For example, California requires that any reference to offset be in a separate provision and not part of the insolvency clause. Offset may be allowed without an explicit provision. However, offset may be disallowed as it creates a preference or priority for the reinsurer in an insolvency.

The offset clause is more fully discussed in Chapter 11 dealing with insolvency.

Letters of Credit

The Letter of Credit provision would specify what recoverables or reserves are covered by the Letter of Credit, and under what circumstances the ceding company can draw upon the Letter of Credit.

Several states' regulations or laws and the NAIC Models address requirements for Letters of Credit.[11] It is important that specific state regulations be followed and that the parties to the agreement understand the circumstances under which the Letter of Credit may be drawn upon.

Entire Agreement

The NAIC Model Regulation for Life and Health Reinsurance Agreements adopted in 1992 requires all coinsurance and mod-co treaties contain a provision stating that the agreement is the entire agreement between the parties. Side letters and other understandings between the parties are not allowed. Further, any change or modification to the agreement must be made by amendment to the agreement and signed by both parties.

Duration of the Agreement

The duration of agreement clause affirms that the treaty cannot be terminated with respect to the inforce business except by mutual consent. It provides that the reinsurance take effect as of the effective date of the treaty. The agreement can be amended by written agreement of both parties. New reinsurance may be terminated by either party by giving written notice. Typically, 90 days is required for such notice. Terminating new reinsurance will not affect existing reinsurance. The reinsurer may not be liable for any claims or refunds not reported within a certain period of time following termination, such as 180 days.

Following this clause, the treaty is executed by the signatures of officers of both companies. Often there is a separate clause for the execution of the treaty.

---

[11] See Chapter 10, Reinsurance Regulations.

Schedules, Exhibits, and Amendments

Schedules and Exhibits are attached to clarify and explain items that may vary or cannot be placed in the basic agreement. Amendments typically add or delete items that have changed since the effective date. As noted above, the new NAIC Model Regulation requires that all changes must be made by formal amendment and signed.

Examples of items to be attached to the treaty include the following:

(1) Retention schedules.
(2) Binding limits, jumbo limits, issue age limits, coinsurance limits, minimum cession amounts.
(3) Plans, riders, and benefits reinsured.
(4) Reinsurance rates and calculation methods.
(5) Underwriting rules and guidelines.
(6) How the reinsurer's share is determined.
(7) Recapture period.
(8) Sample forms or report formats.

PREPARING THE TREATY

The reinsurance treaty is the basic tool available to both parties to the reinsurance agreement for accounting and administrative purposes. As such, the wording should be clear and unambiguous. Those persons drafting the treaty should be familiar with the purpose of the treaty. If a professional reinsurer is involved in the arrangement, the reinsurer generally provides the treaty. In some instances, when a nonprofessional reinsurer is involved, the ceding company may prepare the treaty.

Review

Both parties should carefully review any reinsurance treaty before placing it in effect. The reviewers would normally come from the accounting, actuarial, administrative, and legal areas of the company. The goal of any review is to assure that the treaty accomplishes its purpose, clearly defines the intent of the parties, and does not violate any regulations.

Pre-Approval and Filing

In most states, reinsurance treaties do not need to be approved by the state insurance department. Some states require that treaties, or only treaties between affiliates, be filed and approved prior to execution. Other states require only that a copy of the executed treaty be filed with the department. The insurance department reviews all treaties at the time of the triennial examination.

In some circumstances, a ceding company may seek pre-approval of the treaty before signing it. This is generally done for financial reinsurance agreements or when the company has questions about the treaty's acceptability. The pre-approval process is frequently used for treaties that are attempting to do something new for which there are few precedents.

Standardization of Provisions

Professional reinsurers have constructed treaties with standardized provisions for the ease of their administration. However, provisions of treaties will vary among reinsurers. It is to the ceding company's advantage to standardize provisions among the reinsurers that might be sharing the reinsurance on any given product. For example, it would be useful to have the same claim procedures for all reinsurers. It would also be useful to have the same binding limits, coinsurance limits, jumbo limits, and minimum cessions for all treaties which include new issues.

Use of Side Letters

In the past, side letters were frequently used in conjunction with reinsurance treaties. These side letters spelled out the intent of the treaty. Sometimes, the side letters were the precursor of the treaty. The side letter states the intent to put the treaty into effect as of a certain date. This is done in situations where the companies are not able to draft the treaty before the effective date. Side letters sometimes were used to clarify the intent of a reinsurance treaty when the intent was not obvious in the treaty itself. In other cases, side letters were used to circumvent the terms of the main treaty, or to provide additional security to the reinsurer.

The use of side letters is discouraged today. Regulators are interested in clear and unambiguous treaties without hidden purposes, conditions, or terms. Many states preclude the use of side letters in coinsurance treaties. Modern treaties often contain a clause which states that the treaty constitutes the entire agreement between the parties. If side letters do exist, the regulators typically require that they be fully disclosed and included in the overall analysis of the treaty.

Industry Practices

While the reinsurance treaty is very important, the common practices of ceding companies and reinsurers are also relevant in administering and interpreting a reinsurance agreement. The typical treaty is more abbreviated than most legal contracts and good faith is assumed of both parties. Common industry practices are assumed or implied; terms and phrases of art are widely used without definition. Any reinsurance agreement should be reviewed with such practices and understandings in mind and any significant deviation from them should be specifically referenced.

Pitfalls

There are many pitfalls in the drafting of a reinsurance treaty. Even the work of professional reinsurers should be reviewed since they may make mistakes. Particular care should be taken when reviewing a treaty prepared by a nonprofessional reinsurer.

The most common mistake made in drafting a treaty is to copy another company's reinsurance treaty. This presupposes that the other company drafted its treaty correctly. This is not always the case. Also, if the purposes of the two treaties are not exactly the same, the new treaty may not accomplish the desired results. Any company copying another's reinsurance treaty should be sure it understands the purpose of both treaties and carefully review the treaty before finalizing it.

The person drafting the reinsurance treaty should understand the rules and regulations governing the conduct of reinsurance. If the contract violates these regulations, the ceding company may not receive reserve credit on its statutory statement for the reinsurance ceded, or may even increase its total liability.

7 Reinsurance Administration

To some degree, reinsurance transactions affect almost every area of the typical insurance company. Reinsurance influences such diverse functional areas as accounting, actuarial, agency, claims, data processing, investment, legal, policyholder service, underwriting, and executive. Reinsurance administration activities include: drafting treaties, enforcing treaties, ceding individual policies, making premium payments (net of reinsurance allowances), paying claims and surrender benefits, handling facultative submissions, making policy changes, valuing and opining on policy reserves, and recapturing as the result of an increase in retention.

This chapter explores the basic principles of reinsurance administration, especially as they pertain to proportional reinsurance. Just as treaties vary according to the particular provisions and companies involved, so does the administration. However, the basic functions of treaty negotiation, premium calculation and payment, and claims determination and collection remain for all treaties, even those for nonproportional coverages.

This chapter focuses on the functions involved in reinsurance administration rather than the medium used for administration. Much of the discussion centers on the established manual processes used by all companies at one time or another. Computer technology and applications are rapidly changing how information is collected and transmitted, but has not yet greatly affected what information is involved.

There is a significant blurring of definitions between individual cession and self-administration. Ceding companies provide electronic files containing information on the reinsured risks along with accounting summaries and the reinsurer feeds that information into its individual risk accounting system. To the ceding company, this is self-administration, but the reinsurer has all the data and controls that it has under a manual individual cession process. Bulk account clients may provide no detailed information to the reinsurer, but the accounting summaries provided are backed by detailed computer systems containing all the individual data. Those bulk systems are subject to audit by the reinsurer, giving it assurance that the individual data is accurate.

Electronic data imaging rather than typing, key punching, or photocopying is used to store data, but the data is largely the same. Electronic funds transfer may be preferred over physical checks. In these and other examples, technology speeds up the process and improves accuracy, but the end result is the same. Information is exchanged, liability is established, and payments are made.

BASIC ADMINISTRATIVE PROCEDURES

The goal of effective reinsurance administration is to see that all policies requiring reinsurance are ceded in accordance with treaty provisions, and that payments and information regarding the policy status and policy values flow on a timely basis between the ceding company and reinsurer.[1] In order to have effective reinsurance administration, one must first understand the basic transactions and the methods available for administering reinsurance.

---

[1] In the chapter, examples pertain to proportional reinsurance, including financial reinsurance. For a discussion of administration of nonproportional reinsurance, see Chapter 15.

Reinsurance Transactions

The administrative processing of a typical insurance policy begins with the reception of the application, followed by the underwriting and issue of an individual policy. Throughout the lifetime of most policies, premium and commission accounting and reserve valuations occur on a regular basis. While an insurance policy is inforce, there may be scheduled changes in premiums and benefits or nonscheduled changes in these amounts at the policyholder's request. Depending on the nature of the contract, the policyholder may take out a loan, receive annuity, dividend, or disability benefits, surrender all or a portion of the policy, apply for accelerated benefits, or elect a nonforfeiture status. Eventually, all policies terminate through either death, conversion, maturity, expiration, lapse, or surrender.

Reinsurance transactions tend to mirror the basic transactions affecting the original policy. For example, in a traditional reinsurance arrangement, the reinsurance is ceded at the time of policy issue. Nonscheduled changes in the reinsured policy, such as a change in benefits, change of plan, or the removal of a substandard or smoker classification, normally affects the reinsurance and must be reported to the reinsurer promptly. In some instances, the ceding company can make such noncontractual changes unilaterally without the reinsurer's concurrence. In other situations, the reinsurer must give its approval or else it is not bound by the insurer's action.

The reinsurer cannot prohibit a noncontractual policy change, as it is not a party to the contract between the ceding company and the policyholder. However, the reinsurer can insist that it be kept in the same position as though no change had occurred. This is accomplished by treating the reinsurance as though no change had occurred and the original policy were in force.

Changes in premium rates affect coinsurance and mod-co. Policy loans or changes in the dividend scale may or may not affect the reinsurance depending on the terms of the reinsurance treaty.[2] Changes

---

[2] New York law requires that the reinsurer follow the ceding company's dividend scales on products reinsured on a coinsurance or mod-co basis.

in the state premium tax rate may also affect the reinsurance reimbursement. Benefit payments will normally result in some sort of reinsurance transaction, unless the benefit involved is a disability or annuity benefit reinsured on the basis of a cumulative amount of claims payments. Termination of a policy results in termination of reinsurance ceded on that policy and may affect reinsurance ceded on other policies in force on the same life. A change to nonforfeiture status also may affect the reinsurance.

Administrative Methods

Two major methods are used to administer reinsurance. The traditional method is known as individual cession administration. Under this form of administration, the ceding company and reinsurer both maintain individual records for each policy ceded and the reinsurer provides the ceding company with premium, allowance, and reserve reports. This form was developed when reinsurance records were kept on individual cards, first as paper records and then as individual computerized data cards. Today, the reinsurer's records are kept on a computer; the ceding company's records may be on a computer data base or on an index card system.

The second type of administration is called self-administration. This may also be called bulk or bordereaux. Under this type of administrative arrangement, the ceding company maintains individual records of each policy, but the reinsurer does not. The reinsurer relies on the ceding company to provide all of the information necessary for processing the reinsurance.

CEDING COMPANY ADMINISTRATION

Efficient ceding company administration requires that employees in all areas understand their responsibilities in the reinsurance administrative process and the requirements of each reinsurer. These requirements vary between individual cession administration and self-administration.

Functional Responsibilities

In general, the insurance company functional units responsible for underwriting, new business, and claims are also responsible for reporting the companion reinsurance transaction to the reinsurer.[3] The exception to this is the company that has such a large volume of insurance ceded that it can justify having a special reinsurance department to handle the administration. Some of the reinsurance duties of the various functional areas are discussed below.

The underwriting department has primary responsibility for seeking facultative reinsurance. When an application for insurance is received, the underwriter will determine if a facultative decision is necessary, either because the application does not meet the requirements for automatic reinsurance or because of impairments or financial conditions.

If facultative underwriting is needed, the underwriter submits all the underwriting papers to selected reinsurers. After receiving and evaluating the reinsurers' offers, the underwriter chooses and notifies the reinsurer with which the cession is to be placed. Should the reinsurer place conditions on its offer or ask for further evidence, the underwriter is responsible for fulfilling the requirements.

The underwriting department will often have primary control in choosing facultative-only outlets and in the design and implementation of a facultative shopping program. It may have input in choosing automatic reinsurers as the choice may affect its facultative arrangements.

The policy issue department may be involved in the actual cession of reinsurance on individual policies. Employees in this area must be familiar with the terms and conditions of each treaty and with the reinsurance arrangement for each policy form. Under a traditional individual cession treaty, the issue department fills out the cession record and forwards it to the reinsurer. The ceding company also is responsible for checking the monthly reports provided by the reinsurer to ascertain that the cessions were properly recorded.

---

[3] Actually, in many companies, the administration of reinsurance falls in the actuarial department. In some, especially those companies too small to have an actuarial department, reinsurance is administered by the underwriting department.

In a self-administered situation, the ceding company does not fill out the individual cession record but, depending on the system design, may be involved in some manner in the processing of the cession. With either type of administration, it is important for the ceding company to forward cession information on a timely basis so that the reinsurer can process retrocessions, where necessary.

The accounting department typically handles direct premium and commission payments as well as the accounting for reinsurance premiums and allowances and for any reinsured benefit payments. In the case of individual cession administration, this department will work from documents provided by the reinsurer. In the case of self-administration, the reports will be prepared internally. The accounting department also prepares financial statements integrating the reinsurance transactions.

The actuarial department normally solicits automatic reinsurance proposals for new products, evaluates the proposals, and chooses the reinsurers, with input from other functional areas. Actuaries generally have the primary responsibility in designing, soliciting, and evaluating financial reinsurance programs. This department may perform expense studies periodically to allocate reinsurance expenses. It may also solicit facultative reinsurance proposals and work with the underwriting department in evaluating facultative costs. It will interface with the data processing department in developing experience reports.

The actuarial department is also responsible for reserve valuation for both individual cession and self-administered contracts. In the individual cession situation, the actuarial department will calculate the ceded reserves credits, check those with the reserve calculation provided by the reinsurer, and coordinate the financial statement reporting of such values. This is particularly important in jurisdictions where mirror image reserves are required. In self-administered cases, the actuarial department may provide the reinsurer with additional information concerning the reserves, frequently including an actuarial opinion concerning the adequacy of the reserves.

The claim department is responsible for investigating claims and notifying the reinsurer of any reinsured claims. Because the agreements may vary greatly, the department should review the claims provisions of the reinsurance agreements associated with the claim. Depending on the terms of the particular agreement, the claim department may be able to settle claims without the reinsurer's recommendation, or it may be required to submit claim papers to the reinsurer for review prior to payment of the claim. In either situation, the reinsurer usually wants the ceding company's claim department to forward claim documentation. The claim department may be responsible for verifying claim information on the monthly reinsurance report and for the annual or quarterly claims pending reports.

The data processing department is often involved in the creation of the reinsurance database either for internal use for individual cession reinsurance or for the administration of a self-administered contract. Data processing works with the other areas to produce the reports necessary to track the experience of the reinsured business and is involved when a new product, having special reinsurance processing needs, is developed.

The agency department may become involved in choosing the reinsurer, particularly if it believes that the company should have a reinsurance relationship with a particular company for facultative services, agent morale, or additional sales. In this situation, the agency department generally is concerned with the reinsurer's product or underwriting reputation. It should be remembered that the policyholder's contract is with the ceding company, not the reinsurer. Use of the reinsurer's name in advertising or agency recruitment is usually prohibited by the reinsurer.

The executive area may become involved in making the decision to seek a special financial reinsurance arrangement. Senior management will be concerned with the financial implications and risks involved in the transaction. The executive area would also approve changes in retention limits. On occasion, the executive area will be involved in selecting automatic reinsurers. Generally, its concern would focus on the reinsurer's reputation and any longstanding relationships.

The primary reinsurance function of the investment department involves identifying and transferring assets, if necessary, or coordinating investment policy with the reinsurer in certain investment-oriented or financial reinsurance transactions. In a traditional reinsurance arrangement, the investment department may be involved with products such as annuities which feature a large investment element. These products require a higher-than-average rate of return for competitive purposes and the investment policy must be coordinated with the reinsurer. Reinsurance payments may have a significant effect on cash flow.

The legal department should review all treaties prior to execution. It should be involved from the beginning in the case of financial reinsurance or reinsurance involving new or controversial methods. The legal department is responsible for compliance with state law. It may draft the treaty or work with a treaty drafted by the reinsurer. In either event, it should ascertain that the treaty language is clear and unambiguous and that the treaty accomplishes its aim. Should disagreements arise, the legal department may negotiate the solution. The legal department often is involved in claims settlement, especially if either the ceding company or the reinsurer is considering payment for less than the full amount.

The policyholder service department notifies the reinsurer of any policy changes which affect reinsurance. Under individual cession reinsurance administration, the policyholder service area fills out a form similar to the cession record notifying the reinsurer of the change in reinsured policy. Its responsibility in the self-administration situation will vary with the type of administrative system.

The policyholder service department may be responsible for reviewing the monthly reports sent by the reinsurers documenting all the policy changes reported during the month, or it may share this responsibility with another unit. At least annually, the ceding company should review the inforce listings provided by the reinsurer and check the policy data against its own records.

Individual Cession Administration

Individual cession administration has been in use since the beginning of reinsurance. Procedures for ceding, reporting, and record keeping are well-defined with only slight variations among reinsurers.

Individual Cession Record. When reinsurance is ceded on an individual cession basis, the ceding company notifies the reinsurer by filling out an individual cession record. This record contains the policyholder's name, date of birth, sex, plan of insurance, amount of insurance, amount reinsured, policy or cession number, underwriting class, premium, smoker status, riders, and other information necessary for the reinsurer to set up its computer records. Historically, this record was a paper document called a cession card. This record is increasingly being provided on some form of electronic data.

Records and Reports. The ceding company's reinsurance records may consist of only a copy of the cession card or it may have its reinsurance records on a computer system. Under an individual cession arrangement, the reinsurer sends the ceding company a monthly billing report listing all policies with anniversaries falling within the month. This report provides sufficient information to enable the ceding company to trace the policy on its records. The report also lists all changes, such as lapses, deaths, surrenders, and increases or decreases in amount of premium, reported since the last monthly report. The report shows the reinsurance premium due less any allowances.

The ceding company should check the reinsurer's report against its records to determine if the records are in agreement. The underreporting of lapses and deaths can result in significant loss of income. Once the monthly premium report has been checked and corrections made, it is approved for payment.

At least annually, the reinsurer provides the ceding company with the listing of all inforce policies detailing the reserve information necessary for the company to complete its statutory financial statements. The ceding company verifies these listings to determine that all cessions have been properly recorded. The actuarial department reviews the reserves for reasonableness. For interim financial statements, the ceding company generally uses other methods of producing statutory reserves.

Because there may be items in transit or because the reinsurer may use a different valuation basis for its reporting purposes, it may be appropriate for the ceding company to make its own reinsurance reserve calculations for statutory purposes.[4] This calculation is difficult if the necessary reinsurance information is not contained in the basic policy records on a computer file. Companies which prepare GAAP financial statements must make provision to adjust the GAAP values to reflect

---

[4] For a more thorough discussion of valuation considerations, see Chapter 12, Statutory Accounting for Reinsurance.

reinsurance ceded.[5] This function is usually divided between the actuarial and accounting departments.

For a ceding company with a modest amount of reinsurance business, individual cession administration may be the most economical as it is usually less expensive to verify reports than it is to develop and maintain an administrative system that is capable of producing the reports to the reinsurer's specifications. Now that it is possible to transfer reinsurance data electronically via disk, tape, or direct computer interface, individual cession reinsurance may become even more economical.

Self-Administration

Individual cession administration was created long before modern data processing equipment and was designed to remove the burden of detailed reinsurance administration from the ceding company. As modern data processing systems were developed for insurance administration, reinsurance needs were frequently neglected. Self-administration places the responsibility for reinsurance record-keeping with the ceding company and may require complex data processing applications.

Considerations. Depending on the volume and complexity of the plans reinsured, the ceding company will use either individual cession or self-administration for traditional reinsurance. Financial reinsurance is nearly always on a self-administered basis. A ceding company may chose to self-administer the business for any of a number of reasons, including the following:

(1) The volume involved may be so great as to make self-administration more economical for the ceding company to administer the business using a computer system than preparing individual cession forms.
(2) The ceding company and the reinsurer may be involved in a quota share arrangement which is most easily administered by the ceding company. Frequently, in this situation, the amounts of risk per life are small, so the reinsurer will not need to retrocede any risks, thus eliminating one reason for individual risk information.

---

[5] For a discussion of GAAP treatment for reinsurance ceded, see Chapter 13, GAAP Accounting for Reinsurance.

(3) The product reinsured may be complex or necessitate special calculations that the reinsurer normally is not prepared to make. An example would include interest sensitive products where the net amount at risk is calculated monthly.
(4) The ceding company may believe that it can administer the reinsurance more economically than the reinsurer and that the reinsurer will pass the cost savings on to the ceding company in the form of lower reinsurance costs.

Reporting. In a self-administered system, the ceding company is responsible for providing the reinsurer with all relevant information regarding the ceded policies. This reinsurance information usually is communicated on paper, but it can be communicated with the use of disks, tapes, or direct interfacing between computers. The ceding company must provide the reinsurer with premium reports, policy change reports, and claim information, as well as the information necessary to complete its annual statement.

Standardized formats for transferring this information between the ceding company and the reinsurer are evolving. Although the reinsurer may have its own requirements, the details of this information transfer are usually subject to negotiation. Some of the considerations include the frequency and timing of the reports, the physical form of the report, and the format of the reports. Of course, computer-to-computer methods require careful coordination.[6]

Many reinsurers require that reports be received monthly, although in some instances, quarterly reporting is permitted. While the reinsurer prefers that the reports be received in time for its normal financial reporting cycles, this is not usually feasible if the reinsurer has an early financial reporting deadline. In most cases, the reinsurer makes estimates for its financial reporting purposes. The reinsurer then accepts the reports in arrears and "trues-up" its estimates with actual experience.

---

[6] Such methods are relatively new and standards are emerging. Basically, these techniques involve the ceding company producing an electronic individual cession card for both new business and changes which the reinsurer can use with manual intervention. See Appendix B, Guidelines for the Reporting of Self-Administered Business for an example.

The amount of detail required in the reports is subject to negotiation. The detail should be sufficient to allow the reinsurer to determine the applicable treaty and independently calculate the reinsurance premium. Typically, detailed information on an individual policy level is required for new business, changes, and claims. The reinsurer may require that detailed reserve reports be provided at least on an annual basis. In any event, the ceding company must maintain sufficient policy detail information in its office for audit purposes. When detail is required, the reports normally contain the policy number or cession number, insured's name, sex, date of birth, issue age, policy duration, policy date, plan name or plan code, underwriting class, amount issued, amount reinsured, and reinsurance premium and allowances.

The type of transaction must be identified. The most common transactions include the payment of first year and renewal premiums, including reinsurance premiums and allowances due, reported separately for life, ADB, waiver of premium, other supplemental benefits, and riders. Transactions which must be documented include not taken, lapse, surrender, reinstatement, conversion, increase or decrease in face amount, recapture, death, expiration, and other policy changes. The effective date of the transaction must be included. If facultative reinsurance is being ceded on a self-administered basis, a facultative indicator is necessary.

System Design. Entering into a self-administered reinsurance arrangement is not a step to be taken lightly by the ceding company. The ceding company must have a complete reinsurance system, requiring either a significant amount of systems development or the purchase of a reinsurance administrative system. If the ceding company cannot devote the time and the money to building or buying such a system, it should not enter into such an arrangement.

In designing the system, it should be made as flexible as possible in order to adapt to future products. The systems design should allow for coinsurance, mod-co, and YRT rates; variations in smoker and sex classifications; and different retention limits by plan or policy. Special consideration should be given to the differing treatment needed for supplemental benefits, riders, automatic and facultative cessions, replacements and continuations, recaptured risks, multiple policies on the same life, and multiple reinsurers on the same policy. It must also interface with the company's other administrative systems.

When reinsurance is ceded under a quota share arrangement, for either traditional or financial reinsurance, the reporting is not normally as complex.[7] Quota share arrangements are used to keep things simple. Percentages are applied to the pertinent amounts such as premiums, claims, reserves, and other benefits. Multiple policies on one life are usually ignored. In the case of financial reinsurance, a special adjustment for reinsurance already in force may be required. The ceding company is still required to provide all of the necessary information for the reinsurer to complete its financial statements and usually produces a special report of all ceded policies annually.

Facultative Cessions. Facultative cessions often create special problems in a self-administered reinsurance arrangement. The ceding company may keep a reduced or no retention on facultative submissions. This may require special handling in the administrative system. If facultative reinsurance is to be handled through the self-administered system, the company may have to require that facultative business be placed only with those reinsurers that are in the automatic arrangement to minimize administrative problems. This may limit the ceding company's ability to place certain substandard policies at a competitive rate.

The reinsurer requires special notification of facultative cessions. This handling normally occurs outside the automated system. If the automatic reinsurance is ceded on a pool basis with each reinsurer receiving a percentage of each policy ceded, facultative policies must be handled separately since these are not normally shared. The reinsurer also may charge different premiums or grant different allowances for policies reinsured on a facultative basis, again complicating systems development. For these reasons, it is not uncommon for facultative policies to be handled on an individual cession basis.

---

[7] For certain situations, even the reporting for quota sharing arrangements can become somewhat complex. For example, if the ceding company's share exceeds its retention, individual excess reinsurance will be needed. Facultative coverage always requires special notices.

Appendix B contains the "Guidelines for Reporting Self-Administered Reinsurance" developed by the Reinsurance Administration Committee of the Reinsurance Section of the Society of Actuaries. These guidelines provide more detail on the considerations in self-administered reporting and illustrate sample report formats.

Choice of Method

Before deciding to enter into a self-administration arrangement with a reinsurer, the ceding company must look at the system, the costs, the anticipated volume, and its reasons for pursuing self-administration. It must make an honest estimate of the costs and of the anticipated reinsured volume to see if the volume will justify the costs of the administrative system.

If, for example, the ceding company's only purpose for entering the self-administered reinsurance arrangement on a universal life product is to calculate the reinsurance premiums on a monthly basis to match the monthly changes in the net amount of risk, it may find that a mutually agreed upon approximation procedure will produce satisfactory results on an individual cession method for far less cost.

The ceding company must also make a realistic estimate of the time required to complete the system. More than one insurance company has committed to producing monthly reports on a self-administered basis and found itself manually processing these reports each month for a year or more after the first cession was made.

REINSURER ADMINISTRATION — INDEMNITY REINSURANCE

The reinsurer has many of the same basic functions as the ceding company. The major difference between the two is in the market: the ceding company markets to individuals and corporations while the reinsurer markets to insurance companies.

Reinsurance Administration

Functional Responsibilities

Almost every unit in a professional reinsurance company has a dual function. The first function is its primary purpose, such as accounting, pricing, or underwriting. The second function is marketing assistance.

Basic Functions. A professional reinsurer's functional organization is much like that of a direct writing insurance company. Its various functional personnel perform much the same duties as their ceding company counterparts.

One major difference in the work performed by a reinsurer occurs because of the volume and complexity of the transactions involved. For example, the reinsurance underwriter will review many more complex cases than his ceding company counterpart and tends to become more expert.

The reinsurance pricing actuary prices hundreds of products in a given year, far more than his direct counterpart. He is able to do so because he works within the confines of the final product design and does not have the complex implementation or policy form problems faced by a ceding company actuary.

The reinsurance valuation actuary will normally have far more plans to value than the typical ceding company valuation actuary. This results in an enormous valuation file. Much time is spent creating and maintaining valuation records. The reinsurance valuation actuary faces particularly complex problems in preparing GAAP reserves for reinsurance assumed. The major problem for both statutory and GAAP reporting occurs with the self-administered business where the valuation actuary has very little data on which to base his calculations.[8]

The reinsurance claims department is not responsible for the administrative aspects of a claim such as checking wills and beneficiaries or building the claim file. However, reinsured claims tend to be large and are often very complex. Reinsured claims often require extensive review and discussion with the ceding company claims personnel. Sometimes, legal counsel is required. Even if the direct company is able

---

[8] Some of these problems are discussed in Chapter 13, GAAP Accounting for Reinsurance.

to settle its claims without reference to the reinsurer, the reinsurer is often consulted on large and complicated claims as it may have more experience in these unusual circumstances.

Since a reinsurer does not deal directly with policyholders as a ceding insurance company does, the reinsurer does not have a policyholder service department as such. It does, however, have an administrative department dedicated to creating new cessions, billing premiums, making policy changes, and processing terminations. This department interfaces with the ceding company's policyholder service department. Service to the reinsurer's policyholders, the ceding companies, is not centralized in any one department but is shared among all the departments.

The reinsurer may have a service department which responds to special requests from its clients or prospects. Such a department may coordinate visits to the reinsurer by reinsurance client or prospective client staff, prepare information for distribution, or provide training.

A reinsurance company is responsible not only for preparing its own financial reports, but it must also provide premium and allowance reports for its client companies and check client reports. It prepares special financial reports for treaties which include experience refund provisions. Premium tax reimbursement calculations and claim accounting also need to be performed. Retrocession accounting and administration is also necessary.

Marketing. The second major difference between the functions of a reinsurer's personnel and those of the ceding company occurs because of the differences in the clients and the products. The ceding company has two clients: the agent and the policyholder. The reinsurer has only one client: the ceding company. The ceding company must service both the agent and the policyholder.

Servicing the agent includes paying commissions, issuing policies promptly, and developing new products for the agents to sell. Servicing the policyholder involves issuing the policies, collecting premiums, providing information on policy values, making policy changes, and paying policy benefits.

The reinsurer performs the same functions, but services only the ceding company. This involves developing reinsurance products, billing and collecting premiums, paying allowances, and paying reinsurance benefits. It also includes answering accounting questions, providing assistance in systems development, providing underwriting services, and providing assistance in product development.

A ceding insurance company may have an extensive portfolio of products to sell with several whole life, interest sensitive whole life, term, annuity, disability, and medical policies. The reinsurer has six generalized products: coinsurance, mod-co, mortality risk reinsurance, health reinsurance, financial reinsurance, and underwriting expertise. It uses these products to cover the range of the ceding company's portfolio and its needs.

A consequence of this difference is that the reinsurer has a different marketing organization than a direct writing company. A reinsurer does not employ commissioned agents.[9] Instead, most professional reinsurers use sales representatives who are compensated through a salary and incentive bonus package. Because the reinsurance marketplace is relatively small in comparison to the direct insurance marketplace, the reinsurer employs only a few sales representatives. The number of sales representatives for a single professional reinsurer in the United States and Canada ranges from about four to twelve.

The reinsurance client is very sophisticated and the reinsurance sales representative must deal with the key decision makers, usually from the actuarial and underwriting departments. At times, the accounting, legal, and agency departments as well as the chief executive officer become involved. Because of this, the reinsurance sales representative should have a strong knowledge of insurance products as well as general knowledge of insurance regulation, taxation, administration, and underwriting. Frequently, the sales representative will take a more technically qualified individual, such as an underwriter or an actuary, on a client visit to discuss specific matters.

---

[9] Most life reinsurance, and much of health reinsurance, is conducted through sales representatives who work for one reinsurer. Most property and casualty reinsurance, as well as many non-proportional life and health reinsurance agreements, are negotiated through reinsurance intermediaries who do not represent a single company, but who purport to search the market for the best quotes. Compensation for intermediaries is on a commission basis. See Chapter 22, Selected Additional Reinsurance Topics.

Sales representatives are usually assigned to a specific geographic area and call on clients and prospects in that area. During the course of the reinsurance representative's call on a client, he may have to discuss a variety of subjects. When the insurance company wants a reinsurance proposal, the sales representative obtains the information necessary for the reinsurance pricing actuary to prepare the proposal. The representative also gathers other pertinent information, such as proposed administrative procedures or changes in marketing.

While a reinsurer may have only a handful of representatives calling on clients on a regular basis, the reinsurer's total sales and service team is much larger. This team may include accountants, actuaries, administrators, underwriters, and data processing personnel who may be called upon in specific sales situations. In a direct sales situation, only the underwriter might have contact with the agents or applicants on any regular basis. It would be rare for an accountant, actuary, or data processing staff member to speak to an individual applicant or policyholder. However, because of the nature of the reinsurance client and product, it is common for these specialists to be involved with the ceding company on a regular basis.

The reinsurance accountant is most likely to become involved in the sale of financial reinsurance or a self-administered program. The accountant would work with the reinsurance actuary to explain the reporting mechanisms involved in the contract to the ceding company's accountant and actuary. The accountant might also be involved with the reinsurance administrator to explain the reinsurer's reporting requirements for self-administration to the ceding company. At any time during the life of a self-administered arrangement, the accountant may be in contact with his ceding company counterpart to answer questions or obtain information.

The reinsurance actuary is involved in preparing proposals for any of the traditional reinsurance products and for financial reinsurance. In pricing a traditional reinsurance product, the actuary needs to understand the direct product and the assumptions used to develop it. In some instances the material given to the sales representative may be incomplete or unclear. In this situation the actuary may have to contact his ceding company counterpart. In some circumstances, the actuary may be involved by the sales representative early in the product development process to advise the ceding company actuary on product trends, experience, pricing assumptions, and the regulatory and tax aspects of the product involved.

In a financial reinsurance sales situation, the reinsurance actuary usually develops earnings projections. In order to prepare these projections, the reinsurance actuary needs the product features of the plans involved and the experience of the block. The actuary may be called upon to present the projections to the ceding company in order to explain how the proposed reinsurance arrangement will operate.

Data processing personnel are sometimes involved in self-administered arrangements. If the ceding company is embarking on its first attempt at designing a reinsurance administration system, the reinsurer's data processing personnel may play an important advisory role during the design and implementation of the administrative system. In a traditional reinsurance sales situation, the data processing people may be called upon occasionally to discuss systems modifications necessary for unique product design features.

The reinsurance underwriter plays the major role in marketing the underwriting services of the reinsurer. The reinsurance underwriter may have almost daily contact with some of the clients, and a relationship built between the underwriters may be vital to the success of a reinsurance relationship. The success or failure of the underwriting service affects the success of the reinsurance program.

The successful reinsurer has to offer competitive products and service to its clients. Service crosses all areas of the company. To be effective, the reinsurer should have knowledgeable people in all positions that deal with the clients. Because there is relatively little product differentiation, the successful reinsurer must have a competitive price, provide good service, and be flexible and innovative in its approach.

Individual Cession Administration

Under an individual cession reinsurance arrangement, the reinsurer is notified of an automatic cession when it receives the individual cession record from the ceding company. If it is paper copy, this cession record is sent to the reinsurer's administrative department. This department is responsible for keying the data contained in the record into the reinsurance administration system. This system is similar to the administration systems of most direct writing companies. The system records will contain all of the pertinent information necessary to administer and value the policy such as plan of insurance, plan of reinsurance, and premium and allowance schedules.

If electronic transfer of data is used, the reinsurer has staff who are responsible for translating the data into a format which can be interpreted by the reinsurer's system. The ceding company's data is then transferred from the ceding company's storage medium into individual records on the reinsurer's administrative system. The resulting records look substantially the same as those produced from paper and drive the same reinsurer reports, such as premiums, inforce tracking, and valuation.

When an individual cession record is processed, the reinsurer's computer system searches or indexes its inforce file for other reinsurance on the same life. If any reinsurance inforce combined with the new cession causes the total amount to go over the reinsurer's retention, the reinsurer retrocedes the excess.

Retrocessions are usually handled under an automatic retrocession arrangement, but large amounts may require individual underwriting and acceptance by the retrocessionaire.

The reinsurance administration department receives notification of all nonscheduled changes in reinsured policies. It updates the individual policy records to reflect the current status of the reinsured policy.

Each month, the reinsurer sends each ceding company a billing report listing all policies with anniversaries falling within that month. The report shows the reinsurance premium due as well as the allowance. This report also shows all the changes reported to the reinsurer. Sometimes, the changes result in a premium refund to the ceding company. The ceding company then remits the reinsurance premium due net of refund and allowances.

At least annually, the reinsurer provides the ceding company with a reserve report listing all inforce policies. This report provides the ceding company with all the pertinent information necessary for it to identify the policies on its records. This report also includes the statutory policy reserves for the ceding company's annual statement.

Annually, usually shortly after the close of the calendar year, the reinsurer prepares a premium tax reimbursement report for each treaty which provides for this allowance. A check is then sent to the ceding company along with the report.

Also, about this same time of year, the reinsurer prepares experience refund reports for all treaties which include that provision for distribution to clients. Checks are included for those clients qualifying for experience refunds.

Self-Administration

When self-administration became popular in the 1980's, reinsurers and ceding companies entered into these arrangements somewhat blindly with the hope that the arrangement would be beneficial to both parties. This did not always prove to be the case. Many of the problems encountered could have been avoided by a more thorough appraisal of the factors involved.

Considerations. Before entering into a self-administered arrangement with any company, the reinsurer must consider the following:

(1) The ceding company's willingness and ability to produce the necessary reports on a timely and accurate basis.
(2) The ceding company's likelihood of producing a volume of business sufficient to justify the expenses involved in its administration.
(3) Its ability to verify and certify the policy reserves.
(4) Its GAAP reporting requirements.
(5) Its ability to produce the necessary experience studies.
(6) Its ability to audit these accounts on a timely basis.

The reinsurer must accurately judge the ceding company's ability to produce the necessary reports. If the ceding company must go for several months on a manual basis before the system is complete, both companies will suffer. If the information is not accurate or is not received on a timely basis, self-administration may be more expensive for the reinsurer than individual cession administration would have been.

When an insurance company prepares its statutory annual statement, the actuary must provide an actuarial opinion stating that, among other things, the reserves are computed in accordance with commonly accepted actuarial standards and make a good and sufficient provision for all unmatured obligations of the policies. It is, of course, impossible to opine on reserves that are supplied on a "blind" basis, that is, with no individual policy identification. Even if reserves are provided on a policy level basis, it will be difficult to form an opinion on reserves if sufficient policy detail is not provided.

One option available to the reinsurer is for the ceding company's actuary to provide an actuarial opinion similar to that provided for the statutory annual statement, limited to the reserves on the policies ceded to the reinsurer and for the reinsurer's actuary to place reliance upon this opinion when rendering his. While there are no guidelines as yet regarding actuarial opinions for reserve items prepared by the ceding company, as self-administered arrangements become more common and as regulators take more interest in reinsurance practices, such opinions should become more common.

For the reinsurers that prepare GAAP financial reports, self-administered reinsurance creates a whole new set of problems. It is almost impossible to transform a single statutory reserve amount total to the corresponding GAAP benefit reserve total, let alone develop the corresponding expense reserve or deferred acquisition cost asset. In order to calculate GAAP benefit and expense reserves, a breakdown of inforce by age and duration is needed. The reinsurer may ask the ceding company to provide this breakdown or it may prepare this from a computer file provided by the ceding company. Alternatively, the reinsurance actuary may create and rely on a relatively simple model for GAAP benefit reserves and DAC, modifying the model occasionally as new data is available. In any case, a good deal of work may be involved, diminishing the cost benefits of self-administration.

From the reinsurer's point of view, a further drawback of self-administered treaties is that it loses valuable data for statistical studies. Experience studies enable the reinsurer to monitor its business and establish pricing assumptions. In the case of self-administered reinsurance, the reinsurer must either look to the ceding company to prepare the experience studies or obtain the data from the ceding company in a form compatible with its computer system. At a minimum, it must receive the data in a form which is understandable and useful for analysis. As an alternative, the reinsurer may opt to view experience on a treaty level basis only, foregoing lower level detail entirely.

The growing need for audits and their associated costs, together with the increasing demand for valuation and experience data, has offset much of the anticipated cost advantages from self-administration. Many reinsurers now have full audit teams, and auditing has become an important part of the reinsurance process.

Reporting. It is not always easy for the ceding company to produce timely and accurate reinsurance reports providing the necessary information. In the negotiation process, the reinsurer, generally being the most knowledgeable about such matters and having an overriding interest in receiving this information, must take the initiative in the negotiations and very clearly state its needs. This should include the nature and the format of the reports as well as the timing. Samples of reports and written specifications should be presented early in the process. The reinsurer would, as much as possible, like to standardize reports from clients to alleviate problems for its personnel. This is not always possible, particularly if the reinsurer is involved in a pool with other reinsurers.

In a self-administered reinsurance situation, the reinsurer does not receive individual cession records. In the place of these records, the reinsurer receives a listing of all policies issued within a given time period, commonly 30 or 90 days. This listing will provide most, if not all, of the information contained on the reinsurance cession card. The reinsurer usually checks all new issues against its current inforce file to ascertain that it has no other insurance inforce. If it has already used all or part of its retention on a given insured, the reinsurer may need to retrocede any portions of the policy in excess of its retention.

Since the purpose of self-administered reinsurance is to lower the reinsurer's administrative costs, the reinsurer will not, as a rule, create an individual policy record for each policy on the listing. Instead, these listings are maintained on file for future reference. In fact, if the amounts involved are low, the reinsurer may not even index the amounts received for retention purposes, thus accepting that it will occasionally be over its retention on some lives.

The reinsurer also receives at the same interval a listing of all terminations and changes since the prior report. The reinsurer should be able to verify changes by tracing the policies back through the prior listings. This verification may be done on a random basis for control and audit purposes and is particularly important in case of any benefit payments. The report also contains a recap of all transactions, called a policy exhibit or reconciliation, showing the beginning balance, any increases and decreases, and the ending insurance balance. The beginning balance must match the ending balance from the previous month. Any discrepancies are reported to the ceding company.

The ceding company also produces a billing report on the same frequency, incorporating the issues, terminations, and changes. Financial reinsurance agreements almost always are administered by the ceding company. Because these arrangements usually involve a quota-share method of ceding reinsurance, administration is greatly simplified since the ceding company need only to apply a common percentage to all policy values.

Self-administration became popular in the traditional reinsurance markets with the advent of interest sensitive life products. Many ceding companies were concerned that the net amount of risk could change dramatically from period to period and desired a monthly calculation of reinsurance premiums in order to reflect any changes in the net amount of risk. It was not feasible for reinsurers to perform a monthly calculation of the fund of the universal life product, so that task fell on the ceding company.

One premise behind the idea of self-administration is that the reinsurer's administrative costs will be decreased because it will not have to make entries into its administrative system and produce monthly reports or valuations. The reinsurer often priced these products with a lower expense assumption to reflect this cost savings, thereby returning the savings in the form of increased allowances or decreased reinsurance premiums. This made the reinsurer more competitive in the marketplace. In order to achieve the pricing results, it is important that the reinsurer realizes these cost savings.

Lower reinsurer expenses are not always achieved. The time and related expense of making estimates and then truing up accounting every period can be expensive. The cost of monitoring self-administration, auditing, and individual indexing and retrocession offset much of the savings from self-administration. The loss of data and tracking ability causes concerns which has led to even more auditing and monitoring.

Self-administration often is acceptable for financial reinsurance due to the quota share nature of that business and the relatively small amounts at risk involved. Elsewhere, electronic transfer of individual cession is viewed as being superior to traditional self-administration, with stronger audit trails and better experience data.

System Design. Because building a system to administer reinsurance is a large undertaking for any company, the reinsurer may be called upon to provide advice in the systems design. The reinsurer may help the ceding company evaluate its current capabilities, and it may help the ceding company with its cost estimates for systems development. The reinsurer should help the ceding company evaluate its needs and, if the anticipated volume of reinsurance does not justify the cost of a system, the reinsurer should suggest alternatives to self-administered reinsurance.

For example, on an interest-sensitive life product, the companies may agree to the use of projected net amounts at risk for a period of three to five years under an individual cession arrangement unless actual values vary by more than 10% from those anticipated in a given year. If such a variation occurs, a new set of values will be developed for use for a new period. Both reinsured benefits and premiums would be calculated and paid based on the agreed-upon estimates.

Criteria for Self-Administration. It is beneficial to both the reinsurer and the ceding company if the reinsurer develops the accounting criteria for self-administration. As part of any self-administration proposal, the reinsurer should clearly describe its reporting requirements. These reporting requirements cover premium and allowance accounting, the information necessary for the reinsurer to prepare reserves for statutory statement purposes, to calculate satisfactory GAAP reserves, and to perform experience studies.

Auditing

Auditing is an important tool for reinsurers. This is a very time-consuming process and is needed to ensure that all business is being properly ceded and administered. It is desirable for a reinsurer to audit the ceding company's records on site every two to three years.

A primary purpose of any reinsurance audit is to satisfy the reinsurer that it is receiving all the business it is entitled to receive under the terms of the treaty, and that it is receiving only that business. Obviously, when pricing a reinsurance treaty the reinsurer anticipated a certain degree of profit, so it is important to the reinsurer that all eligible risks are being ceded to it. Risks which are being incorrectly ceded to it may represent lost profits to the proper reinsurer. If such incorrect cessions result from errors in issue or underwriting procedures, they may not meet the requirements of any reinsurer and are likely to have very poor experience. This part of the audit generally is conducted by randomly selecting and reviewing individual risk files.

The reinsurer is also interested in confirming that all premiums, allowances, and reserves are being calculated correctly. This is verified by randomly selecting policies and checking the values produced by the ceding company's administrative system. The reinsurer also reviews benefit payments to make sure that proper procedures have been followed.

During the course of an audit, the reinsurer verifies that the ceding company has sufficient controls in its administrative processing to ensure that its procedures are being followed correctly. The reinsurer assures itself of agreement with the ceding company regarding the terms and conditions of the treaty. To this end, the reinsurer checks that the ceding company's treaty is up-to-date and consistent with the reinsurer's version.

The reinsurer is interested in reviewing underwriting practices. It verifies that the proper new business underwriting rules are followed at all times and reviews rules concerning underwriting classification and conditional receipts. It also reviews rules used for continuations, changes, reentries, reinstatements, and conversions.

The reinsurer's audit team may consist of some combination of an accountant, an actuary, an administrator, an underwriter, and a claims examiner. The exact composition of the team will vary from client to client because of different needs and problems. An audit requires a great deal of preparation. Before going to the client's office, the audit team should be thoroughly familiar with the relevant treaties and the existing reinsurance reports. It may wish to review the systems documentation before the actual audit begins. Based on this information, the audit team develops a plan for proceeding with the audit. When the audit is completed, a report is written for the reinsurer's management. Depending on the nature of the findings, all or portions of the report may be discussed with the ceding company's management.

REINSURER ADMINISTRATION — ASSUMPTION

When a company considers purchasing a block of inforce policies, the process involves several functional areas.

Functional Responsibilities

The decision to purchase a block of inforce insurance will have a long-term effect on the purchasing company. The decision is usually based on a desire to expand into a new area, to employ an underutilized administrative capability, or to increase the inforce base to increase the size of the company or decrease per unit expenses.

Before a company assumes a block of inforce insurance, careful analysis is required. The actuarial department will review experience studies and perform earnings projections or review projections prepared by the ceding company. The data processing department, in conjunction with the other service areas, will study the systems needs. The investment department will review the assets underlying the reserves. The legal department will draft the treaty or review the treaty prepared by the ceding company. The agency department may provide input concerning the effect the acquisition will have on its marketing efforts. The executive department will review results to ascertain that the goals are met.

After the assumption agreement is finalized, the administration of the policies is moved to the assuming company. The data processing department and the other service areas will be involved in the conversion process. Once the conversion is completed, the daily administration — policyholder service, billing, commission accounting, and claims — should follow the normal functions. However, the actuarial and accounting departments will have to make separate provisions for the block for GAAP and tax purposes. The actuarial department may also wish to track the experience of the assumed block separately.

REINSURER ADMINISTRATION — FRONTING

There are several possible administrative scenarios in the event of fronting. These are discussed briefly in Chapter 10, Reinsurance Regulation. The reinsurer usually performs both direct and reinsurance administrative chores, providing direct and ceded information to the fronting insurer. Administrative functions frequently are undertaken as a third party administrator, or TPA, rather than as an insurer. The ceding company is responsible for all its normal reporting requirements and policyholder obligations, even if the reinsurer is actually performing the administration.

8 Managing Ceded Reinsurance

Ceded reinsurance can have a significant effect on the operations and financial results of a life insurance company. Most companies will have several reinsurance agreements in force at any time, using a number of different reinsurers to cover a wide variety of products. Since the early 1980's, each major new product usually had its own special reinsurance arrangements.

An insurance company must manage this array of ceded reinsurance just as it manages its direct insurance operations, with attention to both proper administration and monitoring of results. This chapter discusses the evaluation of new and existing reinsurance programs for automatic, facultative, and financial reinsurance.

RETENTION LIMITS

One of the key factors in any automatic reinsurance program is the retention limits. Each product line has its own retention limits: ordinary life, group life, group health, annuity, disability, and medical. Sometimes, a company has different retention limits for different products and supplemental or ancillary benefits within a product line. Frequently, a company will vary retention limits by issue age or underwriting classification.

Some companies allow each line to maintain independent retentions, but most establish a combined or company retention. The combined retention is less than the sum of the limits of all the lines. For example, a company may have a $500,000 limit each for individual life insurance and group life insurance, but have a company limit of $750,000. If the company already had $350,000 of retention on an insured under a group policy, it would retain only $400,000 on an individual policy issued on the same life, not $500,000.

The key purpose of the retention limit is to allow the insurance company to manage fluctuations in earnings caused by fluctuations in claims. Retention limits normally increase as the size of a company increases, because the probability of fluctuation in the expected amount of claims reduces as the amount of inforce increases.

The retention limit usually grows as the company's surplus grows, since the company is better able to withstand larger fluctuations in experience.

Most insurance companies wish to maintain retention limits which balance lower reinsurance costs against the need for protection from adverse claim fluctuations. Periodically, a growing insurance company will review its retention limits in terms of reinsurance costs and claim fluctuation protection. There are four basic analytical approaches which may be used to evaluate a company's retention limit:

(1) Ratio method.
(2) Model office projection.
(3) Rosenthal's approximation.
(4) Pentikäinen's approach.

Ratio Method

The ratio method[1] is perhaps the most common and certainly the easiest and most practical method to use in evaluating a retention limit increase. The company begins by examining the changes in the ratios of the

---

[1] This is also known as the "quick and dirty" method.

retention limit to surplus, the retention limit to the amount of insurance inforce, the retention limit to premiums, the retention limit to assets, and the retention limit to expected claims since the last retention increase.

There are no published or accepted standards or guidelines concerning these ratios. A company would rarely make a radical change in the established ratio unless it had reason to believe that the ratio was unrealistic. The company would consider any changes in risk patterns or reinsurance costs in establishing new ratios.

The second step of the ratio method is to review these ratios for peer companies with similar amounts of surplus and inforce and with similar growth patterns. A company would generally not want to be out of line with other companies in the peer group.

The ratio approach is used by companies that do not have the resources to do more technical work. It also is used by other companies in conjunction with another method. There are certain advantages to the ratio method. It does not take much time, it is easy to perform, and the results are easily communicated to nontechnical executives.

Even if another formal method is used for analysis, senior management and board members usually want to know how the company's proposed retention limits will compare to its peer group of companies in any event. To the extent that the historic ratios of the retention limit to the other values are reasonable and the company was able to find a good match with the other companies used in the ratio comparison, this method is probably adequate.

There are disadvantages of the ratio method. There are no set standards for the ratios, and the use of a small sample of peer companies may result in such a broad range of data that the results are difficult to interpret. There may be competitive pressures to set the retention at the higher end of the range which might not be appropriate. Because the costs of reinsurance are not directly reflected in this method, separate consideration of such costs is necessary since they should constitute a major consideration in setting retention limits.

Model Office Projection

A more sophisticated approach to a retention limit increase is to develop a model of all inforce reinsurance where the company has kept its stated retention, and to explore the financial effect of any changes in the retention limits. Separate models by broad substandard and preferred underwriting classifications may be informative. Automatic and facultative cessions should be separated, with the focus placed on automatic business. This approach may be used in conjunction with any of the analytical approaches.

The actual construction of the model may be very difficult. A company may have coinsurance, mod-co, and YRT cessions in its reinsurance portfolio. Several reinsurers may provide coverage, each on a different cost basis. In fact, some policy forms may be ceded to several reinsurers, with each reinsurer on a different cost basis.

Many direct administrative systems provide no information regarding reinsurance other than the fact of its existence. Often, information regarding the company or companies to which the excess coverage is ceded, how much is ceded, the plan of reinsurance, the reinsurance premium, or the recapture provisions is not contained in the computer system. For many companies, this information is available only in a separate reinsurance cession file, which may simply be an index card system, or in the reinsurance treaty. Transferring this information to a computer readable form could be a formidable task.

Simplifying assumptions may be necessary. For example, it could be assumed that only amounts in excess of a company's retention on any one policy have been ceded. This assumption ignores the existence of multiple policies on one life, which would result in the amount of risk assumed to be retained on some lives being greater than the normal retention limit of the company. An estimated adjustment can be developed to account for this.

If several YRT reinsurance premium scales are in use, the model may use the two or three most prevalent scales. Similar coinsurance or mod-co treaties may be modeled as one. Treaties producing a trivial amount of reinsurance may be modeled into similar treaties with more substantial amounts reinsured.

The anticipated mix of new direct product sales and reinsurance needs should also be considered. If the mix is different from that of the inforce being modeled or if different reinsurance needs are expected, the model should recognize these facts and be modified accordingly. The primary purpose of the study is to establish retentions for future issues.

Once the model has been validated against current experience, a single test can be run with the proposed retention limit or a Monte Carlo approach may be used. In this latter approach, several scenarios can be constructed using different claim frequencies to test the retention limits. The retention limit chosen will be the one which best balances reinsurance costs, including both reinsurance premiums and the administrative costs of ceding reinsurance, against the retained mortality costs.

The effect of recapturing the reinsurance inforce eligible for recapture should be included in the model as a separate feature. This will allow the company both to include the savings due to recapture, if any, in the reinsurance costs and to determine if it wishes to recapture any business.

The advantage of the model office approach is that it places a value on the financial benefits or cost of the change in the retention limit. This value can be used by management in the decision making process.

A disadvantage of a model office is that the result is only as good as the model; actual results may not equal those expected. Models are also very time consuming to build and typically require extensive computer resources.

Rosenthal's Approach

For the purposes of this discussion, it is assumed that the reader is familiar with the concepts of individual and collective risk theory.[2]

The basic concept behind individual risk theory is that, in a group of insured lives, a claim probability can be associated with each life, and the amount of the claim is known in advance. The claim probabilities may change over time, but the probability of a claim for one member of the group is independent of the claim probability for another member.

The gain or loss on any given policy in any given period is the basic random variable. The total gain on the portfolio is equal to the sum of the gains of the individual policies. This distribution of gains is assumed to follow the normal curve.

Assume there are n_x^z policyholders in a group of N insured lives with amount of insurance Z and probability of dying during the year of q_x. It follows that $p_x = 1 - q_x$. Ignoring interest and lapses, the net premium for any policyholder is the expected value of a claim, Zq_x. If the policyholder survives, the gain is Zq_x; if he dies, the loss is $Z - Zq_x = Zp_x$.

---

[2] If not, the reader is encouraged to read Chapters 2, 11, 12, and 13 of Bowers, *et al.* [2].

The expected value of the gain for one policyholder is

$$E(gain) = Zq_x p_x - Zp_x q_x = 0.$$

The variance of the gain for one policyholder is

$$V(gain) = [Zq_x - E(gain)]^2 p_x + [-Zp_x - E(gain)]^2 q_x$$

$$= (Zq_x)^2 p_x + (-Zp_x)^2 q_x$$

$$= Z^2 p_x q_x (q_x + p_x)$$

$$= Z^2 p_x q_x.$$

The expected value of the gain for all n_x^z members of the cell with amount of insurance Z and probability of dying q_x is equal to the summation of all the expected gains for each individual, or zero. The variance of the cell gain is equal to the sum of the variances

$$V(cell\ gain) = \sum_{n_x^z} V(gain)$$

$$= Z^2\ n_x^z\ p_x\ q_x.$$

The variance of the class gain, where Z is fixed and x varies, is equal to the sum of the variances

$$V(class\ gain) = \sum_x V(cell\ gain)$$

$$= \sum_x Z^2\ n_x^z\ p_x\ q_x.$$

The variance for the total portfolio of N lives is equal to the sum of the variations over all amount classes Z

$$V(total\ gain) = \sum_Z V(class\ gain)$$

$$= \sum_Z \sum_x Z^2\ n_x^z\ p_x\ q_x.$$

This involves a great many calculations, one for each policyholder. Rosenthal [21] developed an approximation for the variance. Let σ_R^2 represent Rosenthal's approximation, given by

$$\sigma_R^2 = Npq \sum_Z \frac{Z^2 N_z q_x}{Nq},$$

where

$$N = \sum_Z \sum_x n_x^z,$$

$$N_z = \sum_x n_x^z,$$

q = *average value of q_x over the entire portfolio*,

and

q_z = *average value of q_x over amount class Z*.

The Rosenthal approach involves estimating the variance in the amount of claims in a portfolio which would be in excess of the retention limit. The variance calculated can be used to determine the size of the risk reserve or claim fund necessary to absorb claims with a certain probability.

The Rosenthal approximation states that the approximation is conservative if, as is believed to be the case, there is a positive correlation between the series of Z's and the associated q's, that is, the approximation of the variance tends to be larger than the actual variance. As such, the probability that claims do not exceed a certain value based on the approximation tends to be less than the actual probability. However, there is no guarantee that this relationship will be true in every case and obviously the results may not be appropriate if a normal approximation is not appropriate. Furthermore, events may not be independent, which also affects the actual results as compared to those modeled.

For a given retention limit, the Rosenthal approximation can be used to calculate the probability that actual claims do not exceed those expected by a predetermined amount. This predetermined amount is the maximum claim loss[3] the company is willing to absorb in any year.

The advantage of the Rosenthal approximation is that it assigns a value to the probability that losses in a year will exceed the fund provided for this loss. Management can use this information in its decision making process. The disadvantages are that it is a nontrivial calculation. The results may be difficult to interpret and the implications difficult to communicate to non-technical management. One question that needs to be addressed is "What is a suitable level of safety?" Similarly, "Is an 85% level sufficient?" "Is 99% sufficient or too conservative?"

Pentikäinen's Approach

Pentikäinen [18] investigated the retention limits of Finnish insurance companies to study the probability of ruin within one year. This approach uses ruin theory[4] to evaluate a retention change. Ruin theory is used to estimate the probability that claims will exceed the claim fluctuation fund or risk reserve. The risk reserve at time t, denoted $U(t)$, is defined as

$$U(t) = u + K(t) + \lambda m - X(t),$$

where

u = initial risk reserve at $t=0$,
$K(t)$ = net risk premium = expected claim amount,
λm = security loading where m is the expected number of claims and λ is the security loading factor (addition to net premiums), and
$X(t)$ = aggregate amount of claims, a random variable.

---

[3] In this analysis, "loss" can be considered to be any unfavorable claim deviation, or the excess, if any, of actual claims over expected claims.

[4] For a discussion of ruin theory, see Bowers, et al. [2].

Managing Ceded Reinsurance

Further, if p_1 is the first moment of the claim function, or the average claim amount, then mp_1 is the expected amount of aggregate claims, or $K(t)$.

For the purpose of this illustration, the following definitions will be used:

M = retention limit
u' = initial risk reserve on January 1
$K'(1)$ = net risk premiums or expected claims
$U(u', 1)$ = probability of ruin within one year

For various portfolios of insurance, Pentikäinen plotted the logarithm of the ratio of the retention limit to mean claim amount, M/p_1, against the logarithm of j, where

$$j = \frac{u' + \lambda m}{[p_1 \cdot K'(1)]^{1/2}}.$$

Pentikäinen discovered that for a given value of the probability of ruin, the curves for the various portfolios were fairly close together for values of M/p_1, up to 50. Assuming a 1% chance of ruin within one year, he found that the straight line

$$\log j = \frac{1}{2}[\log(M/p_1) + \log 1.9] = \log 1.9(M/p_1)^{1/2}$$

would give a conservative, or lower, value of M than the actual curves.

It then follows that

$$\log \frac{u' + \lambda m}{[p_1 \cdot K'(1)]^{1/2}} = \log 1.9(M/p_1)^{1/2},$$

so that

$$\frac{u' + \lambda m}{K'(1)^{1/2}} = 1.9 M^{1/2},$$

and

$$M = \frac{(u' + \lambda m)^2}{3.61 K'(1)}$$

or

$$M \doteq \frac{(u' + \lambda m)^2}{4 K'(1)}.$$

If M is at least fifty times the average claim amount, and there are at least 500 expected claims, Pentikäinen estimated the error in his formula to be 10-30% and seldom more than 50%.

For any given risk reserve or claim fluctuation fund U, values of M can be developed from the aggregate amount of expected claims and the security loading expressed in terms of the number of expected claims. These values of M can be used in management's discussions regarding a retention limit increase. The difficulties include quantifying the security loading, quantifying the expected claims, and interpreting the results, as well as communicating results to senior management.

Practical Considerations

Despite the obviously technical questions involved, setting a retention limit is still generally the result of a team effort involving input from the actuary, underwriter, financial officer, and marketing officer, as any retention changes will affect these areas. A final check is the general attitude of the company toward risk and risk avoidance. It has been said that the retention limit should be the largest amount of a claim that the CEO would be willing to see on his desk on any given morning.

Regardless of the method used, once the data is assembled, the actuarial department will make a recommendation regarding a new retention limit and justify the recommendation to others. If accepted, the board or its designee will formally adopt the new retention limit and set an effective date. Reinsurance administrative staff then communicate the new limits to the reinsurers and notify them of any intention to recapture. Formal notification and amendments to existing treaties are the best form of documentation.

Management objectives and risk tolerance of the organization are also important. The board often will wish to evaluate risk and reward tradeoffs. If the added profit of retaining business is small, the board may prefer to eliminate the risk of higher retention. It is important that in making this decision, the facts given the board include all costs, such as lost risk profits, additional investments needed to support new business, required surplus, and the expense of administration of reinsurance.

Many companies use reinsurance, in the form of coinsurance, to finance growth. A retention increase will reduce the volume of reinsurance, requiring the ceding company to finance this additional business itself.

While small retention increases may not be cost effective, it may be possible to reduce the number of cessions significantly with only a modest increase in retention, generating significant savings in administrative costs. For example, a company with a $75,000 retention may eliminate almost half of its cessions by increasing its retention to $100,000. This will result in greatly reduced administrative costs to both ceding company and reinsurer.

Reinsurance costs per unit may be affected in either direction by a larger retention. A retention increase may increase the average size cession by decreasing the number of small cessions. This may allow the reinsurer to offer more favorable terms and an additional savings. Most companies can tolerate a modest increase in retention with no significant change in their exposure to fluctuation.

On the other hand, a company that generates a large volume of reinsurance as the result of a relatively low retention may receive more competitive reinsurance terms and better service than a company that produces very little reinsurance due to a higher retention.

Frequency of Reviews. Few companies review retention limits as often as annually; relatively small changes in the retention limit may be more of a nuisance than a real cost saving item. In general, a meaningful review should be made about every five years.

Corridors. As small cessions are relatively very expensive to administer, the minimum cession size must be considered. This may be accomplished via a minimum cession definition, say $25,000, where the ceding company agrees to keep its normal retention, say $75,000, plus an amount up to, but not including, the minimum. If the issued amount were $100,000 or more, the $75,000 retention would apply; if an amount less then $100,000 were issued, the entire amount would be retained.

Alternatively, a corridor approach may be utilized. Under this method, the retention is the issued amount for all issues up to $99,999, and $75,000 for larger issues. The economic and mechanical effects are the same as for the minimum cession approach, but the treaty definition and wording are different.

The use of corridors or minimum cession limits may appear to violate the technical retention limit, $75,000 in this discussion. However, if approved by the company's board or management and communicated to the reinsurers, these methods are perfectly acceptable. It is advisable to include such practices in the company's published retention schedule and to document them in the reinsurance treaties.

Variations. Many companies have reduced retentions for very high and low issue ages, say for 65 and above and 18 and below, and for certain substandard issues, say above Table 4. The theory behind this practice is that any given ceding company will not have enough exposure at the extreme ages to smooth out fluctuations.

From a practical viewpoint, if all issue ages and substandard classes are adequately priced and underwritten, there is little need to have significant variations in retention limits by issue age or substandard classification. However, this may be reasonable for some mutual companies where dividend classes are based on very fine distinctions. A consistent retention limit will simplify administration and may create expense savings.

Supplemental or Ancillary Benefits. Companies may have separate retention schedules for the various supplemental or ancillary benefits. Waiver of premium would normally follow the retention schedule of the base policy. Accidental death benefits usually have a separate retention schedule. Sometimes, accidental death benefits are 100% reinsured.

Recapture of Reinsurance Inforce. Once a decision has been made to increase the retention limits, the next decision facing the insurance company is whether to apply this retention increase to inforce business. The decision will involve considering the costs of reinsurance to the expected mortality costs. While the company is under no obligation to increase the retention on all inforce reinsurance, it is supposed to notify its reinsurers of any intention to recapture at the time of the retention increase.

Failure to notify the reinsurer of plans to recapture is generally accepted as a forfeiture of the right to recapture. Definitive correspondence is recommended in either event, and recapture is best documented in a formal amendment.

Retention increases via recapture can be applied on a treaty by treaty basis. If the ceding company decides to increase its retention under a certain treaty, it must recapture all business reinsured under that treaty. It can, however, choose not to recapture business written under a specific treaty. Once a company passes on a recapture option, it may not recapture that business following a subsequent retention increase. The company must exercise its recapture rights at the earliest opportunity or lose any future rights. This is to partially protect the reinsurer from anti-selection.

Retention increases on inforce business as the result of recapture should not affect the remaining reinsured risks. For example, assume a company increases its retention from $75,000 to $100,000, and it had ceded $175,000 of a $250,000 risk. After the expiration of the specified recapture period, the company can recapture $25,000 of the $175,000. The remaining $150,000 remains reinsured on the original terms as though the first $25,000 had never been reinsured. Following another retention increase, the company could recapture up to its new retention.

Recapture is affected on all risks which are eligible for recapture at the time of the retention increase. The typical rules for recapture include the following:

(1) The policy must have reached the recapture duration.
(2) The company must have retained its normal retention.
(3) Quotashare and reduced retention cessions are usually not eligible for recapture.
(4) Facultative cessions are eligible for recapture only if the ceding company kept its full retention at issue.

After the initial recapture, recapture is effected on the policy anniversary on which the risks first become eligible. Thus, a recapture program may take years to be completed.

Other Factors. A good deal of judgment is used is setting the retention limits. The company may choose to set a limit lower than the theoretical limit for several reasons.

(1) It simply may not feel comfortable with the maximum claim amount produced by the theoretical retention limit.
(2) It may wish to set a lower limit for a certain policy form which it feels has a higher degree of risk than the rest of its portfolio.
(3) The surplus strain on a given policy form may be so great that it must lower the retention in order to issue the policies.
(4) It may be able to get a better reinsurance cost if it maintains a lower retention on certain policy forms.

NEW BUSINESS

Reinsurance is frequently a vital concern in the development of a new product, especially for an innovative product design or marketing structure or a price competitive plan. It is desirable to have a reinsurance agreement in place, at least verbally, before a new policy form is introduced.

Assessing Needs

Before soliciting reinsurance proposals on a new product, the ceding company should review its needs and make some preliminary decisions about its wants and desires. The major points it must consider include the following:

(1) The plan of reinsurance.
(2) The form of administration,
(3) The recapture period, retention limits, facultative needs and any special terms needed.

The ceding company should decide if it wants coinsurance, mod-co, or YRT on any new product. Either coinsurance or mod-co would be the primary choice if surplus strain were anticipated to be a problem. Mod-co or YRT would be chosen if the ceding company wanted to maintain the assets in support of the reserves.

The ceding company may choose YRT because of its low annual cost. If the company wishes to use YRT, it may decide to use its existing YRT agreements or it may decide to solicit a special YRT scale designed to fit the new product. If the underwriting to be used is different from that normally used, a different YRT scale will be needed. In any event, the company should verify that the treaty will cover the new products.

The ceding company should choose between self administration and individual cession administration early in the product development process. Should it decide on self administration, the company should consider the demands of self administration during the product development and implementation process.

Before soliciting any reinsurance proposal, the ceding company should determine any special needs it may have for the product. It may desire a special retention, or a special recapture provision. The company should consider how many automatic reinsurers it would like to have participate, the automatic capacity needed, the division of reinsurance among the reinsurers, and any facultative needs.

Soliciting Proposals

When coinsurance or modified coinsurance is to be used, reinsurance proposals are requested late in the product development process after premiums, cash values, and reserves have been generated since this information is vital to the reinsurance pricing actuary. This information is also necessary if a customized YRT scale is desired.

Occasionally, the insurance company works closely with one particular reinsurer throughout the product development process in order to benefit from the reinsurer's expertise in a new product area. At other times, reinsurance cost, terms, and capacity may be vital components of the viability and profitability of a new product, so one or more reinsurers will be involved early. At such times, the reinsurers may provide tentative reinsurance proposals early in the product development process.

Usually, it is not difficult to find reinsurers interested in submitting a proposal on a new product. Most professional reinsurers have sales representatives who call on clients or prospects on a regular basis. The representative is expected to gather the information pertinent for developing a proposal. This information will include the premiums and other policy values, commissions, underwriting standards, and the general marketing plan. The representative may also ask questions regarding company mortality and persistency experience on similar products.

If the company is venturing into a new product line, market, or underwriting program, the sales representative may ask for information regarding the pricing assumptions and their source. All of this information is necessary for the reinsurance pricing actuary to develop a proposal with the appropriate assumptions. The ceding company actuary should also make known any special needs or preferences his company may have regarding the plan of reinsurance, administration, slope of the reinsurance premium scale, and recapture periods.

Evaluating Costs

When all the reinsurance proposals have been gathered, the task of financially evaluating the proposal generally falls on the ceding company's pricing actuary. Because reinsurance costs may vary by duration, issue age, and policy size, the most straightforward method of evaluating the proposals is to reprice the product at the various issue amounts with the normal company retention and original pricing assumptions with the inclusion of reinsurance costs. This permits the calculation of the return on investment. If the pricing system does not provide for the inclusion of reinsurance costs, special adjustments can be made with relatively little effort.

A typical alternative is to determine the expected profit from the various reinsurers' points of view, using a common set of assumptions. The proposal generating the lowest profit should be the lowest cost to the ceding company. Sensitivity testing is advisable.

YRT. The YRT comparison is perhaps the most simple to perform. A simple spread sheet program can be written to calculate and compare the present value of YRT premiums using the anticipated net amounts at risk, discounted with interest and survivorship. The net amount at risk assumptions may make a critical difference in this comparison and should be chosen carefully when an interest sensitive product is involved.

Alternatively, the death benefit cost for the policy as a whole, including both the retained and ceded portions, can be determined by weighting the mortality rates and the proposed YRT premiums in proportion to the retained and ceded coverage. The resulting weighted values are used as the mortality assumption.

Coinsurance. If the profit test system does not allow direct input of reinsurance allowances, the profit tests can be run on the ceded portion only, treating allowances as commissions. Expenses, other than those directly related to ceding reinsurance, would be excluded as these must be supported by the retained portion alone.

The resulting "profit" reflects the ceding company's reinsurance cost on the amount ceded. The total profit on the combined ceded and retained portions can be found by deducting the reinsurance cost from the profit for the entire amount issued assuming no reinsurance. The drawback of this approach is that it does not permit the calculation of the return on investment.

Care must be taken not to oversimplify the assumptions, especially regarding average size, premium bands, and expenses. Reinsurance will typically occur with much greater frequency for policies issued at higher amount bands which have lower per unit premiums, higher expenses for medical underwriting, and, perhaps, better mortality. Persistency may also be different on reinsured policies.[5] All factors must be taken into consideration when setting the assumptions for determining present values of reinsurance costs.

Another, simplistic approach is to compare the present value of reinsurance premiums net of allowances using anticipated mortality, persistency, and interest. This is similar to the YRT comparison. However, the values produced would be useful only to compare relative net reinsurance premiums among reinsurers, and not to evaluate the true

---

[5] Larger policies are often associated with more informed buyers, which can affect experience, with both positive and negative implications.

reinsurance costs as they do not consider the effect of cash values, reserves, and interest.

Mod-Co. The evaluation of mod-co proposals is more difficult because of the effect of the mod-co interest rate. For the sake of simplicity, mod-co could be treated as coinsurance, with the earned interest rate being the mod-co interest rate. This method fails to recognize any gains or losses resulting in the difference, if any, in the interest actually earned and that credited via the mod-co interest adjustment. Given current regulation in the United States, such differences may be expected to be small. This is not the case in all parts of the world.

As an alternative, the original profit test can be modified to test both the ceded and retained portions together by adjusting the premiums and commissions to reflect the ceded premiums and allowances, adjusting the mortality to reflect the lower amount at risk, and adjusting the investment income to reflect the mod-co interest rate. Special adjustments can also be made to recognize the differences in earned interest and the mod-co interest rate.

Administrative Expense. When evaluating the reinsurance costs of any new product, the ceding company should have an understanding of the administrative expense involved in ceding reinsurance. However, evaluating these costs is not always easy. The major problem is identifying the actual expenses. A functional cost study is probably necessary, looking at both the fixed and marginal expenses associated with reinsurance.

Evaluating Nonfinancial Aspects

Price is not the only criterion in evaluating reinsurance proposals. The ceding company must be able to work with the reinsurer. There are many other factors which contribute to a satisfactory reinsurance arrangement. These will vary by company.

Service. The ceding company must be assured that it receives prompt and accurate service from its reinsurers. Cessions and claims must be processed promptly and all reports produced on a timely basis. When dealing with a new reinsurer, it may be difficult to evaluate the service issue. Often, service does not become an issue unless actual service does not meet expectations

Administrative Requirements. The ceding company should review administrative requirements. It will want little variation in requirements among reinsurers as this would complicate its own procedures. A ceding company would wish to avoid any burdensome or unusual requirements.

Underwriting Expertise. For many companies, underwriting service is very important. It may not be necessary that all automatic reinsurers provide the desired underwriting service. However, the company may maintain automatic reinsurance relationships with its desired facultative reinsurers. The degree of underwriting support to be provided by the reinsurer, and the level of competitiveness, should be discussed and agreed upon in advance. Sometimes a reinsurer will not offer facultative services on a selected automatic treaty, or it may do so only with higher costs or with a minimum placement ratio.[6]

Product Knowledge. Some companies depend on their reinsurer to provide them with the latest product information. They may seek information about product features, experience trends, regulation, and taxes.

Stability. For some companies, the stability of the reinsurer is important. Some companies view new entrants to the reinsurance market as less stable or less tested and prefer to deal with established reinsurers. Most companies want to work with a reinsurer that they expect to be in the reinsurance business for years to come. Individual perceptions of stability vary, but few companies wish to deal with a reinsurer that is in a precarious financial position or that is perceived as being less than fully committed to the business of reinsurance.

---

[6] See Chapter 3 for a discussion of facultative reinsurance and placement ratios.

Capacity. The ceding company should be satisfied that the reinsurer will be able to accept all of its business. For most companies this is not a problem, because reinsurers are able to retrocede. Capacity may be a problem in facultative situations involving large amounts, if the reinsurer does not have adequate facultative retrocession facilities.

Capacity problems may be a function of the reinsurer's surplus rather than mortality risk protection. This problem can occur in either excess new business or financial reinsurance situations when the reinsurer does not have sufficient surplus to cover the surplus strain and does not have a ready source of surplus or retrocession capacity.

Other. Choosing a reinsurer can also be an emotional decision. Some companies have built longstanding relationships with one or two reinsurers. There is a certain sense of security and trust involved in knowing a group of people over a long period of time. The administrative procedures are all in place, and everyone knows how things work. In addition, the individuals at one company know who to contact at the other company with special requests or problems.

In any event, the reinsurer and terms should be settled before a product is introduced. If a formal treaty is not feasible, at least a letter of intent is desirable. Failure to choose a reisurer and agree on terms can leave a ceding company without any reinsurance coverage if early claims occur.

INFORCE REINSURANCE

Periodically, every insurance company should review its ceded reinsurance portfolio. This review may be conducted in conjunction with the retention limit review. The purpose of this review is to examine individual reinsurance arrangements.

Reviewing Procedures

The major purpose of a reinsurance review is to assure that procedures are being followed correctly. It should ascertain that policies requiring reinsurance are ceded properly, that policy changes and lapses are reported promptly, and that claim procedures are followed correctly.

Improving Operations

The company should look for ways to streamline procedures without sacrificing accuracy in order to lower its administrative expense.
 The company may wish to standardize certain treaty provisions relating to the administration of its contracts. This could greatly simplify new business and claim procedures. It should be kept in mind that changes in treaties typically affect only new cessions. Existing reinsurance will not be affected unless both parties explicitly agree to such a change.

Recapturing Business

As discussed earlier, a company may choose to recapture eligible business after a retention increase. The decision to recapture will be based on comparing the present value of reinsurance premiums and expenses to the present value of reinsurance benefits less the cost of recapturing. An actuarial model is useful in this analysis. Recapturing inforce business may provide additional stability for the retention increase, creating an inforce block of larger retained risks at once.
 Rules regarding minimum cessions must be maintained. Contracts involving only a handful of policies or involving the cession of amounts less than a selected amount, for example, $10,000, should be reviewed. It may be economical to both the ceding company and the reinsurer for these small cessions to be recaptured.

FACULTATIVE REINSURANCE

Periodically, the ceding company should review its facultative program to determine if its needs are being met and if its costs are reasonable. This review may be done annually.

Facultative Criteria

One part of the facultative review is to examine how policies are selected for the facultative program. In some companies, this may be a very informal procedure, the decision being left to the underwriter's discretion. However, an increasing number of companies have formal guidelines. For example, a company could decide to submit all applications rated above Table 4 for facultative review. In such a situation, the ceding company would want to determine if its needs have changed and it requires a different criterion. If the company finds it is making a large number of exceptions to the rules, it may wish to modify the rules to cover the exceptions.

Service

The ceding company should also examine its placement ratios with its various facultative reinsurers. Dealing with a large number of facultative reinsurers can be very expensive. If the company finds that a particular reinsurer is not providing the underwriting service needed, it may be beneficial to both parties to redefine or even terminate the relationship.

Costs

The costs of facultative reinsurance should be an ongoing concern for all ceding companies. As mentioned in Chapter 3, reinsurance costs can vary a great deal by reinsurer. If an application is sent to more than one reinsurer for facultative offers, it is wise to look at both the table rating and the reinsurance premiums before placing the case. The reinsurance cost for a given rating from one reinsurer may be greater than that for a higher rating from another reinsurer.

The ceding company should periodically evaluate the internal costs and perceived benefits of its facultative reinsurance program. Facultative submissions can be expensive. The ceding company must consider if the costs of the facultative submission on the borderline applications is justified by its expenses in relation to the reinsurance premiums and claim recoveries on such business and any enhancement to agent relations.

FINANCIAL REINSURANCE

An insurance company enters into a financial reinsurance agreement for some specific purpose. These are usually one time agreements that do not involve new cessions, although this need not be the case. Termination may be accomplished at any point that the reinsurer's experience reaches a specified level. Because of the nature of these arrangements, the needs assessment and ongoing monitoring for the business are different from those of traditional reinsurance.

Assessing Needs

The needs assessment process in financial reinsurance will vary according to the motivation for the transaction. In a financial reinsurance transaction for surplus relief, the company generally realizes that it has a need for surplus but must ask itself "how much" and "for how long." The company should also consider the various alternatives to reinsurance.

The company must also consider which block it wishes to reinsure. Typically, an older block of business with stable experience and large reserves is chosen.

Monitoring Results

Although the underlying treaty is for the life of the business,[7] most financial reinsurance transactions are of a short term nature. While the recapture period on traditional reinsurance is seldom less than ten years, most financial transactions can be terminated at any time subject to the provisions of the treaty. One common provision is that the reinsurer is not to be left in a loss position. The treaty may provide that the ceding company must pay to the reinsurer any accumulated losses as a price for termination. Such termination should be voluntary, at the ceding company's option.

While the terms often are used interchangeably, termination of a treaty or coverage under a financial treaty is different from recapture. Recapture refers to reducing inforce reinsurance following a retention increase. Termination refers to voiding a treaty or coverage, usually without the requirement of a retention increase. In fact, the concept of retention increase and recapture is alien to most financial reinsurance where the amounts reinsured are part of the ceding company's normal retained amounts.

---

[7] See Chapter 10, Reinsurance Regulations, and Chapter 5, Financial Reinsurance.

The reinsurance treaty defines the ceding company's rights to recapture or terminate coverage. Additional transactions can be negotiated subsequent to the signing of the treaty, but only with the agreement of both the ceding company and the reinsurer.

While the reinsurer will be monitoring all of its experience rated accounts, the ceding company will find it useful to track the results periodically.

Changing Conditions and Needs

The ceding company must continually monitor internal and external conditions that may affect its financial reinsurance transactions. The two major external factors most frequently affecting financial reinsurance are regulation and taxation. Changes in these areas may occur at any time, and if any changes occur that would diminish the desired financial effect, termination should be considered.

Internal changes in the ceding company can also affect reinsurance. While most reinsurance treaties do not require termination upon a change of management or ownership of the ceding company,[8] the ceding company may wish to terminate the reinsurance if one of these events occurs. New management or ownership may have a different philosophy concerning financial reinsurance or financial conditions may change as a result of this change in ownership. In some instances, new ownership will negotiate a financial reinsurance agreement in order to help finance the acquisition of the ceding company.

---

[8] See Chapter 5, Financial Reinsurance.

9 | Managing Assumed Reinsurance

Any reinsurer, whether it is a professional reinsurer or another type, must manage its assumed reinsurance portfolio, both assumed and retroceded. This chapter primarily addresses professional reinsurers' activities, but the considerations are equally important to other types of reinsurers. In addition, ceding companies that understand the concerns and operations of the reinsurer can avoid misunderstandings and improve relationships.

This chapter covers issues concerning the pricing of reinsurance[1], the setting of retention limits for assumed reinsurance, the managing of retrocession agreements, the monitoring of inforce assumed reinsurance, the designing and pricing of special features, and the special considerations of financial reinsurance.

---

[1] The material in this chapter applies primarily to traditional reinsurance. While the same principles apply to financial reinsurance, different techniques, such as model office projections, are more commonly used.

PRICING

Reinsurance pricing follows the same principles as traditional insurance pricing. The reinsurance pricing actuary reviewing an insurance plan of a particular ceding company must put itself in the shoes of his counterpart at that company and evaluate the plan in terms of the anticipated experience for the ceding company. The chief difference between direct pricing and reinsurance pricing is that the reinsurance actuary wears "several pairs of shoes" in one day and frequently produces a pricing quote in a week or less, a much shorter time frame than is given the direct pricing actuary. This is possible because the reinsurance actuary usually begins with the direct insurer's finished product.

Original Policy Values

The reinsurance pricing actuary must evaluate each plan of insurance from each company separately in order to develop appropriate pricing assumptions for the pricing of specific reinsurance plans. The pricing process begins with the original policy values supplied by the ceding company.

While the usefulness of the various values will vary depending upon the plan of reinsurance desired, the values are always of some significance. For example, in YRT the cash surrender values, or reserves, affect the net amounts at risk and benefits, and, therefore, affect the reinsurance premiums to be received. The design of the product and its compensation influence overall persistency.

Premiums. The policy premiums are important when pricing coinsurance or mod-co because the allowances, and, therefore, the net reinsurance premiums, are based on the policy gross premiums. In the case of an interest sensitive product, the reinsurance may be on a YRT basis, with the YRT premiums being calculated as the cost of insurance rates less an allowance. While this may look like coinsurance of the cost of insurance rates, the reinsurance is really YRT.

While the gross premiums are used to develop the reinsurance allowances, the policy premium scales can also give an indication of the anticipated persistency. The persistency of the underlying policy is of importance not only for coinsurance or mod-co, but also for YRT. These considerations are discussed later in this chapter.

In today's market, most policy forms will have two or more premium bands. The reinsurance pricing actuary may perform profit tests on all premium bands if time permits. If time does not permit, the reinsurance actuary may only review bands for amounts over the ceding company's retention.

In some instances, the reinsurance pricing actuary may price only the premiums applicable for amounts of insurance falling in the highest band. These premiums are the smallest and the persistency on this band is probably the least favorable. Allowances based on the highest band may be applied to all bands. This will generally produce larger profits to the reinsurer because the lower band premiums are larger, resulting in a larger net reinsurance premium. Also, persistency is usually better for the lower bands. However, nonmedical underwriting may negate the additional profits.

Alternatively, the high band premiums and allowances may apply to all issues, regardless of the ceding company's actual gross premiums. In this case, the ceding company receives the benefit of the larger premium on the lower bands.

If a significant amount of reinsurance is anticipated at the lower bands where nonmedical underwriting is used, the reinsurance pricing actuary may want to price these bands separately. In any event, the actuary should review all bands to see if, in his judgment, testing of other bands is needed.

Most traditional reinsurance premiums are collected on an annual basis regardless of the premium mode although the unearned reinsurance premium is refunded in the event of an off-anniversary termination. The underlying distribution by premium mode of the product being reinsured is of interest to the pricing actuary to the extent that it affects persistency. For example, monthly premium business often has higher lapse rates than annual premium business, and certainly less premium is collected in any policy year due to off-anniversary terminations.

The primary exception to this annual premium mode rule is reinsurance involving interest sensitive products: excess interest whole life, universal life, variable life, and variable universal life where the reinsurance premium is calculated in the normal fund calculation cycle.

Normally, this is a monthly calculation, and reinsurance premiums follow this pattern. However, reinsurance premiums may be remitted on a quarterly basis in arrears. Any lost interest and the monthly lapse patterns should be reflected in the pricing.

Policy Fee. In most coinsurance and mod-co situations, the ceding company is allowed to retain the policy fee to cover its ongoing expenses, and the policy fee would be ignored in pricing. If the reinsurer is to participate in the policy fee, the fee should be considered in the pricing. The reinsurer should consider the effect on minimum reserves of including or excluding the policy fee.

Cash Values. The original policy cash values are important in profit testing in order to determine surrender costs. Cash values are readily available on conventional products, but must be estimated in the case of interest sensitive products. For these products, the reinsurance pricing actuary should test several likely scenarios based on his judgment or the judgment of the ceding company's actuary.

Reserves. Policy reserves are also an important part of the expected profit analysis. In the case of conventional products, the reserves are generally provided by the ceding company, or may be calculated given the statutory reserve basis. In the case of interest sensitive products, the reinsurance pricing actuary must again use his best judgment. Both statutory and tax reserves are necessary for proper evaluation. For simplicity, cash values are sometimes used in lieu of the statutory and tax reserves, but this practice can distort expected profits.

Benefits. The reinsurance pricing actuary must carefully study the policy benefits and reflect these in profit testing. The pricing actuary must be aware of any automatic increases or decreases in the benefits and the point at which these changes may occur. If the policyholder has different options at any given point, the pricing actuary must examine each option.
   Policy benefits affect mortality, morbidity, and persistency, and are discussed subsequently.

Net Amount at Risk. The net amount at risk is important in pricing because it determines the benefit costs. In a YRT case, it also deter-

Managing Assumed Reinsurance 261

mines the flow of premium income. If the net amount at risk is overstated in a YRT profit test, the expected profits may be overstated.

Because it is usually more readily available, the cash value may be used to determine the net amount at risk when pricing YRT reinsurance. For decreasing term coverage, the net amount at risk for reinsurance purposes depends on the death benefit schedule of the product and the retention method being used.

If the ceding company retains a level retention on decreasing term risks, the amount reinsured may reduce quickly, causing the reinsurance to terminate prior to the contractual end of the term of the policy. In this case, it may be necessary to reduce first year allowances. A pro-rata retention will allow the reinsurer to continue to receive premiums and provide coverage throughout the term period, possibly permitting higher first year allowances. When providing reinsurance on mortgage protection products which do not follow a fixed amortization schedule but which vary with variable rate mortgages, the reinsurance actuary may wish to look at several scenarios to determine the average expected profitability of the product.

When pricing a YRT scale for an interest sensitive product, the choice of the net amount at risk may be quite difficult. Points to consider include the following:

(1) If large amounts of pour-in money are received, initial cash values may be quite large.
(2) In the case of flexible premium products, it may be difficult to predict premium levels. Premiums may not necessarily follow "target" premiums.
(3) Products sold on "vanishing" or a limited premium basis may result in reduced cash values in later years, compared to policies where premiums are expected every year. As a rule, "minimum" premium plans will produce minimal cash values.

The retention method used is also important. The same considerations apply as in the decreasing term situation.

Commissions. The reinsurance pricing actuary should examine the commissions paid by the ceding company on the policy. The ceding company usually desires that the reinsurance allowances cover its commission costs, and the reinsurance pricing actuary attempts to do this wherever possible.

Commission patterns affect persistency results, as will be discussed later in this chapter.

Assumptions

In setting pricing assumptions, the reinsurance pricing actuary looks at the original policy values, the type of agent used in making the sale, the market for the policy, the ceding company's underwriting philosophy, the ceding company's recent experience, and the ceding company's pricing assumptions.

Mortality. One of the most critical assumptions in pricing any sort of life insurance product is the mortality assumption.[2] The pricing actuary at a direct writing company is concerned with the expected nonmedical, paramedical, medical, simplified issue, or guaranteed issue mortality appropriate for his company. The reinsurance actuary must consider these assumptions for each company reinsured.

Intercompany mortality studies[3] have shown significant variation in mortality results by contributing company. A primary reason for this variation is the difference in underwriting standards among companies. While one company's underwriters may classify a specific life as a standard risk, a company using a more conservative underwriting approach may consider the life to be substandard by perhaps four tables or more.

Other factors which have a significant effect on mortality results include the type of agents, the market, and geographic concentration. For example, companies which specialize in the rural market often have

---

[2] Discussion here focuses on life insurance and mortality. For health reinsurance, the morbidity considerations would be similar, with emphasis on the risk characteristics of the benefits reinsured and any premium adjustment features.

[3] This information is collected by the Committees on Mortality and Morbidity Experience Studies among Lives Individually Insured and published annually in the *Transactions, Society of Actuaries, Reports.*

very good mortality results at ages over 30, but may have very poor mortality results at younger ages due to a higher than average rate of accidental deaths. Companies which have a loyal career agency force tend to have better mortality than companies which have a substantial volume of brokerage business. The business insurance market tends to have worse mortality than the family market. Of course, no rule is ironclad, and individual analysis of each pricing request is advised.

Mortality will also vary by product type. Historically, term insurance mortality experience has been worse than that on permanent products due to antiselection at both issue and renewal.

Insurance plans with poor persistency experience tend to have poor mortality experience. Individuals who lapse are normally the healthy lives who could qualify for new insurance coverage, leaving the persisting group with poorer than average mortality.

Select and ultimate term has been a particular problem to the insurance industry. Pricing such a product is truly a challenge for both the direct writer and the reinsurer. In fact, the reinsurance experience on such products in the early 1980's was so poor that several reinsurers withdrew from this particular market, refusing to reinsure these plans.

In order to price a select and ultimate product, it is necessary to determine exactly how reentries are to be handled.

It is important to know how frequently reentry will be allowed, the degree of underwriting which will be used on reentries, as well as the amount of commission which will be paid upon reentry. The mortality assumption for the reentry group and the no-reentry group are both affected by the level of reentry underwriting and commission. In general, the more lives which would qualify for reentry, the worse the mortality is on the remaining group which cannot requalify for new select rates. One problem facing the reinsurance pricing actuary is that the reentry rules often are not clearly defined or strictly followed. At this writing, there is little experience on which to base assumptions.

Select and ultimate products and other products with increasing premiums tend to have poorer persistency than level premium products. Products with reentry provisions present a special problem concerning the reentry assumptions. The interaction between mortality and persistency is very clear in these products.

If large volumes of reinsurance are expected to be placed on a facultative basis, the reinsurance pricing actuary must consider the expected facultative mortality. Factors which influence automatic reinsurance mortality will also influence facultative coverage. Facultative mortality is further influenced by the number of reinsurers participating in the underwriting program, the cause for the facultative submissions, and the placement ratios.

Persistency. Another critical pricing assumption is persistency. There can be significant first year policy strain in a coinsurance or mod-co arrangement, exposing the reinsurer to the risk that poor persistency will prevent it from recovering its initial investment.

Persistency varies by type of agent involved in the sale. Business written by brokers tends to be replaced more frequently as the brokers look for new first year commissions. Business placed by true career agents, and sometimes business placed by salaried agents, may have very good persistency.

The market also affects persistency. For example, the employer sponsored plan market will tend to have persistency related to employee turnover rates. Companies which have upscale policyholders who are frequently exposed to other insurance agents may have poor persistency.

Policy size is an important factor in persistency. Larger policies tend to move to new insurers more frequently than smaller policies because the commission dollars generated by a move are greater. Because reinsurers see large policies with great frequency, reinsurance persistency does not tend to be as good as the overall or retained persistency of the ceding company.

The commission scale may affect persistency. High first year commissions attract business. Policies which feature high first year commissions generally have low renewal commissions. Agents have been known to move policies periodically in order to obtain new first year commissions.

Persistency bonuses may improve short-term persistency on a product. Policies which have level commissions will tend to have better persistency than policies with heaped first year commissions.

The premiums and benefit patterns will also affect persistency. Policies with increasing premiums tend to have poorer persistency than level premium policies because the cost per thousand increases with increasing age. If a policy has select and ultimate premiums, any healthy person would be prudent to reenter or replace his policy periodically to secure the lowest rate. Decreasing term policies with level premiums often have poor persistency because the premium per unit of outstanding coverage increases each year. In later policy years, the amount of coverage may become trivial when compared to the premium, and the policyholder will lapse the policy.

Recapture. The reinsurance pricing actuary must reflect possible recapture of ceded business. Typically, this is done by increasing assumed lapses once the recapture duration is attained. Several factors influence the assumption, including the length of time since the last retention increase, the current retention limit, and the growth pattern of the company. Because it is so difficult to predict recapture by company, a generalized approach may be used.

Expenses. Because of the very competitive nature of the reinsurance market, expenses are a critical item in pricing reinsurance. The successful reinsurer may be able to provide for expenses of only 5% to 8% of premium in order to remain competitive. This level is much lower than the expense level of most direct writing companies.

Issue expenses for an automatic reinsurer would be substantially less than issue costs connected with the direct product as the reinsurer will have no underwriting costs or agency expenses. It will usually have relatively fixed sales and administration expenses. Facultative underwriting costs should be less than the underwriting costs of the direct writing company as the direct writer will pay for the various medical reports. Facultative underwriting costs are related to the placement ratios experienced by the reinsurer. To keep the underwriting costs down, the reinsurer must maintain a reasonable placement ratio on its facultative submissions.

The quest for ever lower reinsurance costs and the shift to universal life and other indeterminate products has necessitated moving some of the administrative burden of reinsurance from the reinsurer to the ceding company. Reinsurers attempted to pass along any administrative cost savings on to the ceding company. However, self-administered reporting has resulted in only marginal cost savings to the reinsurer. Reinsurers must spend a good deal of time reviewing the reports, auditing the accounts, and preparing financial statements. Overhead must also be considered. Given the relatively low level of most reinsurance expenses, little real cost savings may be realized.

Expenses may be allocated on several bases: per policy or unit issued, per policy or per unit inforce, or percent of premium. If charged on a per policy basis, pricing results will be more favorable for larger policies. This is an advantage to the reinsurer if pricing the higher premium bands. If expenses are charged on a per unit basis, smaller policies will be favored. When expenses are charged on a percent of premium basis, low premium reinsurance, such as term coinsurance and YRT, will show more favorable pricing results.

Normally, maintenance and routine issue expenses will be charged on a per policy basis which is related to the manner in which the expenses are incurred. Underwriting expenses may be charged on a per unit and/or a percent of premium basis, whichever is related to the manner in which these expenses are incurred. Overhead expenses may be charged in any reasonable manner.

If maintenance and issue expenses other than underwriting are allocated on a per policy basis, the average size assumption is quite important. The average size is dependent on the company's retention and the type of product involved. For example, term products generate larger size policies than whole life products. The average size of a company's reinsurance cessions tends to increase as the retention limit of the ceding company increases.

Premium Tax. Some reinsurers routinely reimburse ceding companies for premium taxes on reinsurance premiums. In this case, an explicit premium tax assumption is necessary. This assumption may be client-specific or the reinsurance pricing actuary may employ a generalized assumption based on the overall premium tax rate. In most situations, there is little difference between the client's rate and the reinsurer's rate, particularly for clients doing business in a number of states. Small regional companies may have rates which vary significantly and special consideration may be given to these accounts.

Federal Income Taxes. Reinsurers are subject to federal income taxes in some manner or another. In pricing products, the reinsurer must consider the expected amount and timing of any taxes payable to the Internal Revenue Service or its counterparts in other countries. This consideration includes the effect of the so-called DAC tax and excise taxes as well as normal taxes on income.[4]

Allowances. In some instances, specific reinsurance allowances are input in profit testing. The ceding company may provide the reinsurance pricing actuary with desired allowances which are used in the initial round of profit testing. In most cases, however, the pricing of coinsurance or mod-co is a matter of solving for allowances which provide the desired profit for the reinsurer.

Interest. The reinsurance pricing actuary must establish a reasonable interest assumption for investment income just as his direct counterpart does. This assumption is normally based on investment department and company objectives just as is the case for a direct company.

Reinsurance pricing involving term coinsurance or YRT scales gives little consideration to investment income. In pricing mod-co, the mod-co interest rate should be used, at least for interest on reserves. If pricing includes consideration of investment income on cash flows, the reinsurer's own earned rate should be used.

Special Facultative Considerations

Facultative reinsurance presents a particular set of problems for the reinsurance pricing actuary.

The major problem facing the reinsurance pricing actuary is relating underwriting action to pricing assumptions. It is very difficult to predict the effect of reinsurer underwriting actions on mortality experience. Aggressive underwriting is going to produce worse mortality experience

---

[4] See Chapter 14, Tax Effects of Reinsurance.

than that produced by conservative underwriting. However, aggressive reinsurance underwriting will result in more business and, hence, more premium. There is no precise method to determine how mortality will change when underwriting standards change, but past facultative mortality experience should be helpful.

Even though facultative underwriting is a function of the reinsurer's underwriting standards, some variation in facultative mortality exists by ceding company. Different ceding companies produce different facultative mortality experience because of the type of business being facultatively ceded. Some ceding companies using conservative underwriting standards may reinsure a large number of marginally substandard policies in order to keep the standard risk classification clean for dividend purposes. The reinsurer might consider these cases standard by its underwriting criteria. Other companies may send out only highly rated cases.

Facultative mortality varies by the level of the placement ratio. As placement ratios increase, mortality will tend to decrease because the reinsurer is receiving a better spread of risks.

Techniques

The reinsurance pricing actuary employs many of the same techniques that the ceding company pricing actuary uses. However, because of differences in the nature of the business, there are some problems which are unique to reinsurance pricing.

Age/Sex/Underwriting Distributions. In the ideal situation, one set of coinsurance allowances or one YRT rate scale will produce uniform profits for all age/sex/smoker cells. This ideal situation rarely, if ever, occurs because of differences in the mortality and persistency assumptions used by the reinsurer and ceding company. However, a common set of allowances is desirable to ease administration. In order to produce a common set of allowances, the profit levels must vary by cell and must be weighted by cell in developing the overall profit level, a process sometimes employed by direct insurers. Distributions may vary by company and product. Monitoring actual-to-expected results is vital to achieve the desired profit goals.

Profit Objectives. The reinsurance pricing actuary employs the same sort of profit goals as his ceding company counterpart. The most common goals are expressed as a percent of premium, per unit issued, percent of mortality, and return on investment. A combination of goals may be used. The most common goal is the percent of premium goal where the present value of future profits is divided by the present value of future premiums. This goal may vary by product type, with higher premium products often using a lower goal. This goal is appropriate for both permanent and term products.

The profit per unit issued or profits expressed as a percentage of the death benefit is appropriate in pricing term coinsurance and YRT because it directly reflects the major risk involved.

The return on investment goal is usually confined to cash value products. When used with term insurance, exceedingly large values may be produced even if actual dollar profits are small or negative. Risk/reward ratios are not necessarily properly recognized, in that a very small shift in experience, especially mortality, may entirely eliminate these high expected profits. If losses occur in later years, multiple return on investment values may result. Reinsurers review profit margins in all years and try to avoid negative margins after the first policy year.

Profit Test Years. Most reinsurers base their profit objectives on the profits arising over a period of ten or twenty years. The danger is that losses could develop after the period reviewed.

Sensitivity Testing. Because of the short time frame allowed to the reinsurance pricing actuary, sensitivity testing is performed infrequently. The pricing actuary normally tests one scenario for three to six ages for each smoker status. If time permits, different sets of assumptions may be used for certain cells. Females are priced separately only if they are expected to constitute a significant portion of the reinsurance assumed. The value of sensitivity testing should not be overlooked because a seemingly small variation in assumptions can have a large impact on results in a competitive field like reinsurance where profit margins are slim.

GAAP Considerations. Pricing most often is done on a statutory model. Success or failure of a reinsurance or insurance company frequently is judged on a GAAP or alternative management reporting basis. Accordingly, it may be advisable for the reinsurer's pricing actuary to prepare a GAAP or other management reporting projection to evaluate how a proposal will look in future financial reports. If the results do not meet management's objectives, it may be wise to develop an alternative proposal or decline the opportunity altogether.

RETENTION LIMITS

The reinsurer must examine its retention limits on assumed business periodically just as a ceding company must. The reinsurer may use any one or a combination of the techniques discussed in the previous chapter for ceding companies. A reinsurer with both assumed and direct business should consider the retention limits independently because the expected mortality will be different or organizational considerations may require separation of the profits for the two blocks of business. The reinsurer may find that it should keep a different retention on its assumed portfolio than it does on its direct portfolio.

RETROCESSION AGREEMENTS

Professional reinsurers have retrocession agreements in order to retrocede amounts over their retention limits. In the past, reinsurers often had retrocession arrangements with some of their client ceding companies. This was called reciprocity,[5] an uncommon practice today. Today's reinsurers will retrocede to other professional reinsurers or to professional retrocessionaires.

---

[5] See Chapter 1, Introduction.

Managing Assumed Reinsurance 271

A reinsurer may have more than one retrocession agreement for new business. Many have special retrocession agreements for selected business which allow the reinsurer to retrocede assumed policies on the original terms. This can result in cost savings and freedom in pricing for the reinsurer. Special facultative retrocession agreements may have YRT premium scales which vary by retrocessionaire.

A professional reinsurer might also have retrocession agreements for financial reinsurance contracts. This situation occurs when the reinsurer does not have sufficient surplus of its own and is acting on behalf of another insurance company. This other company has the surplus but does not have the expertise to design the arrangement and draft the treaty or does not have the proper resources or contacts to find companies needing surplus relief. Typically, each of these retrocession treaties is for a unique reinsurance treaty.

INFORCE

Periodically, the reinsurer must review its inforce assumed reinsurance portfolio. Unlike the ceding company which tends to look at its entire inforce block of ceded reinsurance, the reinsurer's review will often be at the treaty level. Some treaties call for an annual review of experience for experience refund, bonus, and chargeback calculations. The reinsurer will also want to review self-administered accounts and facultative programs periodically.

Experience Refunds

An experience refund is a mechanism to return some portion of the profits experienced on a block of ceded reinsurance to the ceding company. Experience refunds can be used for YRT, coinsurance, and mod-co.

Generalized Formula. In reviewing experience refund treaties, it is typical to find the refund formula defined in algebraic symbols. A typical generalized formula would be as follows:

$$ER = f\{P + I - A - C - S - RC - PT - LCF(1+i) - FIT - F\}$$

The symbols in this formula are defined as follows:

ER = Experience refund
f = Percent of gains to be returned to ceding company
P = Premiums incurred
A = Allowances incurred
C = Claims incurred (mortality or morbidity)
S = Surrender benefits incurred
PT = Premium taxes reimbursed
RC = Reserve charge (positive for increase, negative for decrease)
LCF = Loss or deficit carry forward
i = Interest rate to be used on LCF
I = Investment income from reserves and cash flow
FIT = Federal income tax adjustments, if any
F = Fee or risk and expense charge

Of course, some of these terms may not be necessary in a specific agreement, or other terms may be required to clarify or more easily accommodate a specific feature, such as a chargeback of allowances upon early lapse.

As can be seen, this is really a modified gain and loss statement. In theory, any item in the gain and loss can be included in the formula. Since reinsurance normally deals only with annual premiums, items such as due and deferred premiums are not needed. However, refund of premiums for off-anniversary terminations need to be recognized in calculating incurred premiums and allowances. If premiums other than annual ones are used for reinsurance, the experience refund formula can be adjusted to recognize that fact, if desired.

The experience refund formula can be made to accommodate any structure. For example, it is not uncommon to include only cash items. This is done largely to reduce administrative effort. In practice, certain modifications are common to certain types of treaties. Some typical simplification are noted below.

The loss carry forward is a unique feature, representing the reinsurer's accumulated past losses under the treaty. Its inclusion in the experience refund calculation simply provides that the ceding company will participate in excess gains on the block only after any losses incurred previously under that treaty by the reinsurer have been recovered. Such prior losses include any strain at issue and any prior increases in reserves. Otherwise, the ceding company would receive the benefit of future reserve releases without "paying" for the establishment of those reserves.

The interest rate applied to the loss carry forward may vary with several factors. For example, it is not uncommon for two different rates to be used, especially in financial reinsurance treaties. One, relatively low rate may apply to non-cash lapses, but another, higher rate may apply to any actual cash outlaid by the reinsurer. This higher rate compensates the reinsurer for loss of investment income on the "missing" cash. In some states, regulations[6] limit the interest rate which may be applied to any loss carry forwards.

The fee, or risk and expense charge, is another valuable feature. It represents the profit and expense load which the reinsurer extracts before any profits are shared with the ceding company. This fee may be stated as a percentage return on strain or losses, as a percentage of reinsured premiums, or as a flat amount per unit of inforce per year. In fact, any fee structure may be used, as long as both parties agree in advance. The fee may vary, depending upon the type of risk and the treaty structure.

Historically, the percentage of the profits which go to the ceding company was fairly uniformly set at 50%, but the percentage can be any mutually acceptable portion up to 100%.[7] Percentages less than 50% are rare in the United States and Canada, but relatively common elsewhere.

---

[6] See Chapter 10, Reinsurance Regulation.

[7] The reinsurer which gives 100% of the profit back presumably has satisfied its profit objectives through the risk and expense fee.

YRT. Since little or no reserves are involved in YRT reinsurance and surrender benefits are not considered, the experience refund formula in a YRT treaty may be simplified. A typical experience refund formula in a YRT reinsurance treaty may look like the following:

$$ER = f\{P - C - F - LCF(1+i)\}$$

Reserves are ignored as being insignificant and merely a timing matter. Allowances are not considered as the typical YRT treaty has no allowances.[8] In this example, premium taxes are also ignored, and presumably are covered by the expense and risk charge; they could be separately recognized.

Under a YRT treaty, the loss carry forward may be limited to a period of time. For example, a claim may be included in the loss carry forward calculation for only a limited period of time, say five or seven years. If the reinsurer cannot recover its fee by that time, it will "forgive" the loss (loss forgiveness) and exclude it from future loss carry forwards. Obviously, in this case, the order of losses is important and any gains should be applied to the oldest eligible loss first.

Coinsurance. The generalized formula is applicable for the coinsurance situation. No special treatment is necessary, although investment income must be clearly defined. Frequently, an annual statement rate is used to determine the interest rate applied to reserves, or a fixed rate or outside index may be used. Usually, investment income on cash flow is ignored, but some treaties make provision for it.

Mod-co. In theory, mod-co is no different than coinsurance in developing an experience refund. A key item is determining the interest rate to be used, which generally will be the mod-co adjustment interest rate. In some cases, the mod-co adjustment may be used directly in the formula.

---

[8] Actually, certain benefits and substandard extras are coinsured even under a YRT treaty and have allowances. If these benefits are included in the experience refund calculation, both the premiums and the allowances should be considered.

In this case, the formula would be

$$ER = f\{P-A-C-S-PT-LCF(1+i)-F-MCA\},$$

where *MCA* is the mod-co adjustment.

The interest rate used in the calculation of the mod-co adjustment may be limited or influenced by state reinsurance regulations, as discussed in Chapter 10, Reinsurance Regulations.

Bonuses

Some treaties call for the payment of production or persistency bonuses. Production bonuses vary by the level of production, which is generally measured in terms of new reinsurance ceded volume. The bonus would usually be stated in terms of cents per thousand of production. The reinsurer would generally review its new business reports for those accounts having production bonuses. The bonuses may be limited to a stated maximum volume per life.

Persistency bonuses may be paid for the achievement of a certain level of persistency. These bonuses are generally based on thirteen month persistency which is calculated by comparing first year volume of the previous year to the second year volume inforce at the end of the current year. Such bonuses are expressed as cents per thousand of inforce or percentages of premiums and may vary by level of persistency.

Production and persistency bonuses are used infrequently in the United States today, but are more common elsewhere.

Chargebacks

When first year allowances exceed first year premiums, a chargeback feature often is included in the treaty. A chargeback provides for the reinsurer to receive its unrecovered investment back on policies which lapse before premiums received exceed the allowances paid. In pricing, chargebacks may be handled as negative cash values.

Some sample chargeback calculations at various durations are illustrated below. For purposes of illustration, assume the following facts about a coinsurance treaty.

Premiums:	$1,200 annually

Allowances
    First Year:
    Renewal:
	
	140%
	20%

Premium Tax Reimbursement:	2%
Chargeback Provision:	Return of excess of allowance paid over premium received, if any, on a policy-by-policy basis.

Example 1 - Lapse at 12 months

Allowances		
First Year	$1,680	
Renewal	0	$1,680
Premiums		
First Year	$1,200	
Renewal	0	1,200
Chargeback		$ 480

Note that premium tax is not included in this chargeback calculation. That, of course, depends upon the terms of the chargeback provision.

Example 2 - Lapse at 15 months

Allowances		
First Year	$1,680	
Renewal	60	$1,740
Premiums		
First Year	$1,200	
Renewal	300	1,500
Chargeback		$ 240

Example 3 - Lapse at 24 months

Allowances		
First Year	$1,680	
Renewal	240	$1,920
Premiums		
First Year	$1,200	
Renewal	1,200	2,400
Chargeback		$ (480)

In Example 3, premiums exceed allowances, so no chargeback is incurred.

    Chargebacks may be defined according to any mutually acceptable terms. For example, chargebacks may be unlimited in time, as above, or limited to terminations within a specific period, such as 12, 13 or 24 months from issue. Also, chargebacks may apply to the excess of something other than 100% of premiums, such as 90% or 110% of premiums.

Chargebacks do not afford complete protection against excess lapses for a reinsurer. Chargebacks are collectible only to the extent that future allowances payable to the ceding company can be reduced. The ceding company usually does not guarantee the chargebacks; to do so could create a statutory liability for the ceding company. If lapses are high enough, the future allowances may not cover the chargeback and the reinsurer could lose some of its lapse protection.

Self-Administered Accounts

Periodically, the reinsurer should review self-administered accounts. The reinsurer should look at the experience of the account to determine if it is getting the volume and profits expected in pricing. It would also look at the timing and the quality of the reports received. If it is not receiving reports on a timely basis, or if reports are incomplete, the reinsurer must address the problem. The reinsurer may want to audit the account.

Facultative Reinsurance

The reinsurer should review large facultative accounts periodically to make sure that anticipated placement ratios are being met and that it is receiving proper notification of cessions. Poor administration can lead to poorly defined liabilities, uncertainty, and potential losses.

The reinsurer should periodically review the experience of all facultative accounts. This review can help in establishing pricing assumptions for mortality, persistency, and expenses.

Monitoring of Results

It is important that the reinsurer monitor its results to make sure that business goals are being met. Monitoring should include mortality and persistency experience studies for both automatic and facultative reinsurance and profits by account vis-à-vis pricing expectations.

Effect of Marketing

The experience of inforce business, as well as the relationships built up during the time that the inforce business is on the books, can have a significant effect on a reinsurer's marketing efforts. Ceding companies and reinsurers tend to build up relationships with individuals and companies. From this point of view, reinsurers sometimes will price more competitively for a long-term existing account then they will for a new account. This tendency was very strong up until the mid-1980's when pricing competition became so great that old relationships seemed to take a back seat to sound pricing considerations.

One of the major influences of inforce upon marketing is the current experience that the reinsurer is having on a given client's business. If experience is very good and the reinsurer has continuing faith in the ceding company, it will tend to protect the account with more competitive pricing on new products and a higher level of service overall. If, on the other hand, the block is performing poorly, the reinsurer can logically be expected to take that into consideration when pricing new plans.

On occasion, reinsurers have even been known to give a discount on profitable inforce reinsurance in order to maintain their position with respect to new business.

FINANCIAL REINSURANCE

Financial reinsurance creates certain unique problems for a reinsurer; most of these have been discussed previously. However, certain aspects of managing an assumed portfolio of financial reinsurance deserve additional comment.

Ceding Company Stability

In evaluating a prospect for financial reinsurance, the long-term stability of that client company and the expectations of future stability have a major influence on the reinsurer's evaluation and willingness to establish a financial reinsurance relationship.

In most circumstances, a traditional reinsurance treaty carries a fairly well-defined risk and the economic loss is largely related to the mortality, persistency, and expense experience on that block of business. The reinsurer accepts a risk and establishes a profit objective which it considers appropriate for that risk.

In dealing with financial reinsurance, the reinsurer typically takes a lower level of profit and expects a lesser exposure to normal insurance risk. However, the reinsurer may take a significant risk with respect to surplus loss.

A financial reinsurance treaty may involve the ceding company holding and managing a large block of assets backing reserves for the reinsurer. If the ceding company mismanages the business it has reinsured or the corresponding assets, the reinsurer can have a significant loss. Therefore, the stability of the ceding company, while important in traditional reinsurance, becomes much more important in the financial reinsurance field.

External Changes

In financial reinsurance, the reinsurer needs to be very concerned about the occurrence of certain external changes. These can be environmental changes such as a drastic change in the economy. However, more frequently they center about the ownership and management of the company.

In the past, some financial reinsurance treaties called for an immediate termination or recapture of the treaty, with any experience loss being repaid to the reinsurer, upon any significant change in management or ownership of the ceding company. In general, such clauses have been questioned because they leave the regulator with uncertainty as to the validity of reinsurance under all future circumstances. Since the reinsurer may not be able to rely on such clauses, the reinsurer needs to evaluate the management and ownership carefully.

Another type of external change involves evolution in the regulatory environment. New regulation may change the interpretation or application of certain treaty provisions. The reinsurer must be aware of any such changes in either the ceding company's state of domicile or the reinsurer's. New regulation may cause the reinsurer to want to renegotiate certain treaty terms.

Monitoring Results

Just as with traditional reinsurance, it is important for the financial reinsurer to monitor the experience. A typical way to do this would be to make a model office projection on a block of financial reinsurance at the time the treaty is written. Then, the reinsurer periodically compares the results of that projection with the actual results.

It is more common for subsequent changes to be made in a financial reinsurance treaty than in a traditional treaty. For example, if surplus relief is the initial objective of the treaty, the ceding company may desire to add additional business to the treaty in order to effect additional surplus relief. On the other hand, it may just wish to prolong the repayment of the surplus relief. Before any reinsurer would agree to this, it would want to review the existing reinsurance for trends and performance.

Any changes must be determined on a voluntary, negotiated basis. Any agreement outside the reinsurance treaty which is in place during the existence of the treaty should be considered a part of the treaty. An agreement, such as the ceding company agreeing to indemnify the reinsurer for any loss, likely would invalidate the reinsurance agreement for reserve credit or other surplus relief purposes as far as the regulators are concerned. Therefore, it is important for the reinsurer to monitor the results of financial reinsurance treaties and try to negotiate improved terms, if necessary.

Regulatory, Accounting, and Tax Considerations | Part Three

10 Reinsurance Regulations

Reinsurance, like other forms of insurance, is regulated by the laws and regulations of the various state insurance departments. Far fewer regulations exist for reinsurance than for other forms of insurance because reinsurance is a transaction between two insurance companies rather than a transaction between an insurance company and an unsophisticated policyholder.

State insurance department regulation is concerned with many facets of insurance. The primary concern of regulation is the ability of the policyholder to rely upon the insurer's promise of payment of benefits. Statutory reserves and statutory accounting are designed to strengthen this promise of payment.

Reinsurance, through the use of reserve credits or assets called receivables,[1] allows the ceding company to transfer some of the econ-

---

[1] Receivables include funds withheld as well as benefits and allowances in the payment or under claim review. In general, a receivable is a cash amount due or expected, while a reserve credit is like a promise to pay a future benefit. In any event, both a receivable and a reserve credit have the same effect of increasing a ceding company's surplus.

omic responsibility and hold lower reserves, thereby strengthening its balance sheet. Regulators establish rules defining the acceptability of reinsurance treaties and reserve credits for statutory accounting purposes.

These rules define the validity of a treaty only in statutory accounting terms, and not with respect to legal, economic, or tax purposes. A treaty may be proper in its economic and legal terms and of benefit to the ceding company, but not meet the standards for statutory accounting purposes.[2]

The occurrence of some prominent life and property and casualty insurance company insolvencies in the 1980's and 1990's created increasing concern that reinsurance transactions were being used or abused to mask a company's true economic position. In response, much of the recent regulatory activity has focused on reserve credits, mirror image reserving, nonadmitted reinsurers, and the use of trusts and letters of credit. This chapter deals with some of the important issues in reinsurance regulations.[3]

RESERVE CREDIT

Insurance regulations in most states do not prohibit reinsurance transactions. The insurance commissioner normally cannot disallow a reinsurance treaty, but can, instead, disallow any reserve credit or related asset.[4] If the reserve credit is disallowed, the ceding company would have to increase its reserves to the pre-reinsurance level. Much of today's regulation concerns reserve credit issues, but review of additional liabilities, such as extraordinary premium payments or interest guarantees, are under consideration.

---

[2] For example, a coinsurance treaty with a nonadmitted reinsurer may produce perfect indemnity coverage, but the treaty still would not qualify for reserve credit.

[3] Of necessity, this book discusses regulations as they are at the time of this writing, August 1995. Changes may have occurred since that time and the reader is advised to check current regulations before entering into any transactions.

[4] Actually, under statutory accounting, the appropriate treatment would be to take credit for the reinsurance as a reduction to the reserves, even though the reinsurer may not be admitted, and to establish a separate liability, as appropriate, for reinsurance in unauthorized companies. See Chapter 12, Statutory Accounting for Reinsurance.

Regulatory Concerns

One major purpose of these regulations is distinguishing true reinsurance transactions with an appropriate transfer of risk from transactions that are in essence loans where the reinsurer seldom, if ever, is exposed to meaningful insurance risk. The latter may be a legitimate business credit risk, but it is not a reinsurance risk and should not be accounted for as reinsurance on the ceding company's balance sheet.

Identifying what constitutes appropriate or sufficient risk transfer is a problem for regulators and company staff. This definition often is left to the discretion of the state regulator, resulting in possible disagreement and potential inconsistency. Some states have implemented specific regulations or legislation to address the issue, but it is difficult to define all situations in advance.

Regulatory Guidelines

Regulators want to ensure that the reinsurer will be able to pay its obligations to the ceding company when due and that the reinsurer will pay according to the terms of the agreement. Most states require that the reinsurer must be licensed or accredited in the ceding company's state of domicile or that the reinsurer must provide some security either through funds withheld, a trust account, an escrow account, or a letter of credit.

Two documents developed by the NAIC — the Model Law on Credit for Reinsurance and the Credit for Reinsurance Model Regulation — address the basic regulations used by most states for both life and health and property and casualty insurers. Many states have adopted one or both of these, frequently with modifications peculiar to a single state. A few states have gone well beyond the models in one or more areas. Since regulation of reinsurance is a constantly evolving process with changing rules, it is advisable to obtain a qualified advisor before entering into any significant reinsurance agreement.

Model Law on Credit for Reinsurance. The NAIC Model Law on Credit for Reinsurance establishes conditions that a reinsurer must meet in order for a domestic ceding company to take credit for reinsurance, either as an asset or as a reduction in liability for reinsurance ceded. Credit is allowed where reinsurance is ceded to a reinsurer under any of the following situations:

(1) The reinsurer is licensed to transact insurance or reinsurance in the state.
(2) The reinsurer is accredited as a reinsurer in the state. An accredited reinsurer is one which:
   (a) files with the Commissioner evidence of its submission to the state's jurisdiction;
   (b) submits to the state's authority to examine its books and records;
   (c) is licensed to transact insurance or reinsurance in at least one state, or in the case of a United States branch of an alien insurer, is entered through and licensed to transact insurance or reinsurance in at least one state;
   (d) files annually with the Commissioner a copy of its annual statement filed with the insurance department of its state of domicile and a copy of its most recent audited financial statement, and either
      (i) maintains a policyholder surplus of at least $20,000,000 and has not been denied accreditation by the Commissioner within 90 days of its submission, or
      (ii) maintains a policyholder surplus of less than $20,000,000 and whose accreditation is approved by the Commissioner.
(3) The reinsurer is domiciled and licensed in, or in the case of a United States branch of an alien reinsurer, is entered through a state which employs standards regarding credit for reinsurance substantially similar to those applicable under the Model Law, and the reinsurer:
   (a) maintains policyholder surplus of not less than $20,000,000, and
   (b) submits to the authority of the state to examine its books and records.
(4) The reinsurer maintains a trust in a qualified United States financial institution for payment of the valid claims of its United States policyholders and ceding insurers. Annually, the reinsurer must report to the Commissioner substantially the same information as that required on the NAIC Annual Statement to enable the

Commissioner to determine the sufficiency of the trust fund. In the case of a single reinsurer, the trust shall consist of an amount representing the reinsurer's liabilities attributable to business written in the United States and the reinsurer maintains a trusteed surplus of not less than $20,000,000. In the case of a group of individual unincorporated underwriters, such as Lloyd's, the trust shall consist of a trusteed account representing the group's liabilities attributable to business written in the United States and a trusteed surplus of $100,000,000 held for the benefit of the United States ceding insurers of any member of the group, and make available to the Commissioner an annual certification of the solvency of each underwriter by the group's domiciliary regulator and its independent public accountants.

The model act also provides the following:

(1) Credit is allowed for a reinsurer not meeting the above requirements only with respect to the insurance risks located in jurisdictions where such reinsurance is required by law or regulation of the jurisdiction.

(2) If the reinsurer is not licensed or accredited to transact insurance or reinsurance in the state, the reinsurer must also agree to perform its obligations under the terms of the agreement. In the event that the reinsurer fails to perform, it agrees to submit to any court of competent jurisdiction in any state of the United States and will abide by the final decision of that court, or of any appellate court in the event of an appeal. The reinsurer must further agree to designate the Commissioner or his chosen attorney as its true and lawful attorney for any action.

(3) A reduction from liability for reinsurance ceded to a reinsurer not meeting the above requirements is allowed in an amount not exceeding the liabilities carried by the ceding insurer in the amount of the funds held by or on behalf of the ceding insurer, including funds held in trust for the ceding insurer as security for payment of obligations under the reinsurance contract. The security may be in the form of:

(a) cash;
(b) securities listed by the Securities Valuation Office (SVO) of the NAIC and qualifying as admitted assets; or
(c) a clean, irrevocable, unconditional letter of credit by a qualified United States institution.[5]

Credit for Reinsurance Model Regulation. The model regulation provides guidance for implementing the model law. Unfortunately, the various state requirements are not only different, they are frequently in conflict with each other. For example, consider the specific rules in New York and California.

New York Regulations 114 and 133 and California Bulletin 87-10 further expand on the rules governing the banks permitted to be utilized for trusts and letters of credit.[6] The New York Regulations have specific rules concerning the actual form of the letter. The California regulation requires that all three parties must be unrelated and the agreement explicitly allows a conservator or liquidator to withdraw the funds from the trust or draw down the letters of credit.

Risk Transfer

Over the years, regulations have been introduced to define acceptable levels of risk transfer in order to obtain reserve credit. Various states have addressed this independently, and the NAIC has developed models.

Life and Health Reinsurance Agreements Model Regulation. The NAIC adopted the latest version of the Life and Health Reinsurance Agreements Model Regulation in September 1992. This model is required to be adopted by a state seeking accreditation with the NAIC and addresses many questions regarding risk transfer. While prompted by the need to define significant, meaningful, or adequate risk transfer

---

[5] The Securities Valuation Office maintains a list of qualified institutions.

[6] At this time, the future of these regulations is uncertain. The industry is attempting to modify some terms, but the effect of the regulation is likely to follow that of the cited provisions.

Reinsurance Regulations

for financial reinsurance transactions, the rules apply to all reinsurance except YRT, assumption, and certain forms of nonproportional reinsurance. The regulation applies to all life and accident and health companies except for companies regulated by substantially similar rules in their states of domicile.

The objective of the regulation is to deny reinsurance reserve credit for certain kinds of financial reinsurance transactions. The model regulation also attempts to provide guidelines to determine if "all of the significant risk inherent in the business being reinsured" has been transferred.

The regulation prohibits the ceding company from establishing any asset or reducing any liability in its statutory financial statements if, in substance or effect, any one of eleven conditions exist:

(1) Renewal expense allowances in any accounting period are not sufficient to cover anticipated allocable renewal expenses of the portion of the business reinsured. Renewal expenses include, but are not limited to, commissions, premium taxes, administration, claims, valuation, and maintenance costs. Denial of reserve credit may be overcome if a liability for the present value of the shortfall is established by the ceding company.

(2) The ceding company can be deprived of surplus or assets at the reinsurer's option or automatically upon the occurrence of some specified event. Termination of the agreement for non-payment of amounts owed under the contract such as premiums, tax reimbursements, or modified coinsurance adjustments is not considered a violation of this clause and thus may be included in an agreement.

(3) The ceding company must repay the reinsurer for losses under the agreement. Offsetting current or future experience refunds against past losses or payment of the reinsurer's losses in the event of voluntary termination by the ceding company is not in violation of this clause.

(4) The ceding company must, at specified points in time, recapture or terminate all or part of the reinsurance under the agreement.

(5) The agreement involves the possible payment by the ceding company of amounts not realized from the reinsured policies. For example, the model regulation specifically mentions payment of premiums or fees in excess of the direct premiums collected as being a violation.

(6) The agreement fails to "transfer all of the significant risk inherent" in the reinsured business. A table is provided, as discussed later in this section.
(7) The assets risks of credit quality, reinvestment, or disintermediation are significant for the business reinsured and the risk is not adequately transferred to the reinsurer. This is discussed at more length later in this section.
(8) Settlements are made less frequently than quarterly or amounts due from the reinsurer are not paid in cash within 90 days.
(9) The ceding company is required to make warranties or representations which are "not reasonably related" to the reinsured business.
(10) The ceding company is required to make warranties or representations regarding the future performance of the reinsured business.
(11) The agreement is principally for the purpose of surplus relief without transferring all significant risks and the expected potential liability to the ceding company is basically unchanged.

The model regulation further requires that reinsurance agreements be in writing. The current model regulation has been adopted in only a few states, but is expected to be adopted by all in the current or similar form.

A controversial part of the model regulation concerns an attempt to identify the elements of risk necessary to be transferred if reserve credit is to be granted (see item 6 above). The model regulation identifies six "risk categories:" mortality, morbidity, lapse, credit quality of assets, reinvestment, and disintermediation. It further identifies 17 product types, such as "health insurance-long term care and long term disability," "immediate annuities," or "traditional non-par permanent."

For each of the 17 product types, the model regulation states whether each of the six risk categories is significant. If a risk type is significant, that risk should be transferred to the reinsurer if reserve credit is to be allowed. If a risk type is not listed as significant, that risk can be left with the ceding company and reserve credit is still allowable. If a product does not fall within one of the 17 listed types, determination is to be made on a consistent basis.

Another controversial part of the model regulation is the determination of asset risk transfer (see item 7 above). The model states that if the credit quality, reinvestment, or disintermediation risk is significant, there are three methods acceptable to demonstrate risk transfer. These are physical transfer of the assets underlying the business, legal segregation of the assets in a trust or escrow account, or another mechanism acceptable to the commissioner which, by contract or contract provision, legally segregates the underlying assets.

However, the model allows the assets to be maintained on an unsegregated basis by the ceding company for all types of products except annuities, guaranteed investment contracts, other annuity deposit business, single premium whole life, flexible premium universal life, and fixed premium universal life contracts which permit dump-in premiums. For products where the ceding company may maintain the assets, asset and interest participation, including capital gains and losses, may be achieved through the following specified formula for an interest rate:

$$\text{Rate} = \frac{2(I+CG)}{X+Y-I-CG},$$

where

I = net investment income
(Exhibit 2, Line 16, Column 7),[7]

CG = capital gains less capital losses
(Exhibit 4, Line 10, Column 6),

X = current year cash and invested assets plus investment income due and accrued less borrowed money
(Page 2, Line 10A, Column 1, plus Page 2, Line 16, Column 1, less Page 3, Line 22, Column 1),

and

Y = X for the prior year.

This is a standard formula formerly contained in the annual statement to determine average investment earnings rate and is known as the

---

[7] References included in this formula are to the annual statement for 1992. Changes in the annual statement format may change these references from year to year.

Exhibit 2 rate. This rate was used for many years as the modified coinsurance interest rate for many modified coinsurance agreements. While it does not necessarily transfer the results of specific assets underlying certain business, it is a reasonable proxy which is administratively simple.

As of this writing, several states have adopted the model regulation verbatim or with minor modifications. California, for example, largely followed the model's terms, with somewhat different language and format, but few substantive differences. The major difference is the insistence that all universal life, not just that with dump-in premium provisions, provide for segregated assets.

New York has provided the major exception to the model regulation, adding two more reasons to disqualify an agreement. The first of these requires the interest rate applied to experience loss carryover for experience refunds cannot exceed the Exhibit 2 formula discussed above, or the actual earned rate on segregated assets.

The second additional New York requirement relates to participating and interest sensitive policies and contracts. Any reserve credits will be disallowed unless the reinsurer fully reimburses the ceding company for its proportion of dividends or other amounts credited. An exception may be granted if another provision for dividends and credits is approved by the superintendent of the New York department.

Insolvency

In order to take a statutory financial statement credit for reinsurance ceded, all reinsurance agreements are required to contain an insolvency clause. The insolvency clause states that the reinsurance is payable to the liquidator without diminution because of insolvency. The insolvency clause is required because the basic understanding in a reinsurance contract is that the reinsurer is required to pay only those claims which represent actual losses incurred by the ceding company. United States courts have ruled that the liquidator may first collect reinsurance proceeds without paying any part of the loss. In fact, the liquidator may apply only a portion of reinsurance proceeds to pay the claim. The remainder of the reinsurance proceeds may be used to pay portions of other claims.

The importance of this clause and its interpretation is that the basic terms of the treaty are not changed by the event of insolvency. If the ceding company continues to make premium payments, it is entitled to full claim payments. If, on the other hand, it fails to pay reinsurance premiums, the reinsurer is entitled to terminate the reinsurance in most states. Consequently, the offset provision, allowing either party to offset amounts payable to it by amounts due to it, may provide an alternative to termination.[8]

The most important case in this area of insolvency is the Fidelity & Deposit Company vs. Pink.[9] In this case, the Southern Surety Company of New York was declared insolvent and the New York Superintendent of Insurance, Lewis H. Pink, took possession of the assets to begin liquidation proceedings. Pink approved a claim for payment but did not actually pay it. However, he demanded reimbursement from the reinsurer. The reinsurer refused to pay stating the language of the treaty was quite clear that it was only responsible for actual losses. It argued that, as no claim was paid, there was no actual loss. The United States Supreme Court agreed with the reinsurer. Superintendent Pink responded by introducing Section 77 of the New York Insurance Law which requires the inclusion of the insolvency clause in reinsurance contracts. Most other states have adopted similar requirements.

Insurers Rehabilitation and Liquidation Model Act. Given the insolvencies and near-insolvencies of some prominent insurers, regulators have given increased attention to certain aspects of insolvency proceedings. To this end, this model act was proposed.[10]

The stated purpose of this act is to protect the interests of insureds, claimants, creditors, and the public in general. With respect to reinsurance transactions, some critics have expressed concern that one party, the insurance commissioner or his designee, is both a regulator and, as receiver, a participant in the actions.

---

[8] See Chapter 11, Insolvency.

[9] Fidelity & Deposit Company v. Pink, 302 U.S. 224, 82 L.Ed. 213, 58 S. Ct. 162 (1937), *reh'g. denied*, 302 U.S. 780, 82 L.Ed. 603, 58 S. Ct. 407 (1938).

[10] These comments are based on the January 1995 draft.

The Act recognizes a difference in rehabilitation and liquidation. Rehabilitation is the process of moving a company back to sound financial status with the future ability to continue operations independently. Liquidation occurs if rehabilitation is viewed as unfeasible and involves closing down the company as an independent entity. This often involves selling all assets and finding new carriers for much of the inforce.

With respect to reinsurance transactions under the model act, a rehabilitator would have the authority to affirm or reject existing agreements unilaterally. Even if he initially affirms an agreement, he can later reject it. A liquidator would have the power to affirm or disavow an agreement. These powers apply to a broad range of agreements, such as vendor contracts, and include reinsurance.

Historically, reinsurers have been able to claim priority for any amounts due for premiums, modified coinsurance funds or interest, and funds on deposit, but may have had to accept treatment as a general creditor for amounts overdue or otherwise owed it. The proposed act would drop any reinsurers in priority for distribution of funds for any purpose from the historical position of being an administrative expense, which comes before policyholder benefits, to being another general creditor, with little chance for payment.

Offset Provisions

The right of offset[11] is used by reinsurers and ceding companies to allow the reduction in amounts owed by Party A to Party B by any amounts owed by Party B to Party A. In normal conditions, this may be viewed as an administrative convenience, permitting only one transfer of cash for a lesser amount. However, in the event of insolvency of either party, especially the ceding company, offset provides significant assurance that premiums and amounts on deposit, or held for modified coinsurance reserves, are used for the benefit of the other party and not applied to general or policyholder obligations of the insolvent company.

Several states have determined that the right of offset, or set-off, and the treaty provisions which allow this right are a primary problem

---

[11] See Chapter 11, Insolvency and Reinsurance, for a more detailed discussion of offset, or set-off, rights.

in reinsurance. However, denial of set-off could create problems. Denial of the right of offset would, for example, allow reinsurance to remain inforce following non-payment of reinsurance premiums. Full denial of offset could lead to the interpretation that an insolvent ceding company need not pay renewal reinsurance premiums, but would have the right to collect reinsured benefits in full. Under this theory, the reinsurer would become a general creditor, coming after policyholders and employees in the priority for funds, a result which would create additional risk for the reinsurer.

At least two states — Missouri and Oklahoma — have adopted specific regulation or law aimed at limiting the right of offset and thus passing more risk to the reinsurer, at least in the event of insolvency. Missouri has legislation intended to disallow any reinsurance agreement which contains an offset provision.

Oklahoma law is somewhat different. It does not prohibit the use of offset in all instances. Instead, the law denies the right of offset if the ceding company is insolvent and the reinsurance agreement fails to transfer significant risk. If significant risk transfer is found to have occurred, offset is allowed.

MIRROR IMAGE RESERVES

The basic concept of mirror image reserves is that the ceding company is not allowed to take a reserve credit on its statutory annual statement for any reserves in excess of the amount of reserve the reinsurer is holding on the business. This is a complicated topic, subject to much debate. Only a few states currently have regulations in this area, and these differ significantly in their provisions.[12] The introduction of risk transfer regulation appears to have reduced the focus on mirror reserving concepts. Some of the arguments for and against mirror image reserving are presented.

---

[12] The fifth amendment to New York Regulation 20 required "worldwide" mirror reserves. This would obligate the ceding company to verify that its reinsurer and any of the reinsurer's retrocessionaires on a given block of reinsurance would be holding mirror reserves.

Regulatory Concerns

Regulators are concerned about liabilities that disappear or vanish in reinsurance transactions. They fear that adequate provision for all liabilities will not be made if the statutory reserves vanish in the transaction and are not being held by the reinsurer. This leads to concern over solvency and the ability of the ceding company to pay all policyholder obligations.

Differences in Reserves

There are a number of reasons for the ceding company and the reinsurer to hold different reserves.[13] These occur because of mechanical or logistical problems in communicating reinsurance information.

One of the most common reasons for reserves to differ between the ceding company and the reinsurer is because of the items in transit. There is always a lag between the reporting of new cessions, reinstatements, lapses, and other changes between the ceding company and the reinsurer. The reinsurer must close its books by a certain date in order to prepare its own financial statements and simply cannot wait an extra thirty to ninety days to make certain that it has the majority of all transactions reported. The reserves on items in transit are usually insignificant in comparison to the total reserve, and some ceding companies may not make any adjustment because of time pressure in preparing their own financial statements.

Reserves may differ because the reinsurer may be using a slightly different reserve valuation basis to simplify its procedures. The reinsurer is faced with valuing many different types of policies and may have only a handful of policies on any one policy form. Where possible, the reinsurer may try to group policy forms which are similar but not quite identical into a common valuation reserve basis. For example, the ceding company may be reserving a policy form using the Illinois Method, and the reinsurer may value it on a CRVM basis rather than setting up a unique reserve file for that product. The differences are usually trivial, but they do exist.

---

[13] This discussion covers statutory reporting. For tax purposes, special rules are in place to ensure a mirror reserving type of result. However, tax reporting is much slower, with most tax returns being filed in September following a year end.

Reserves also may differ when the reinsurance accounting is on a self-administered basis where the ceding company is supplying the reinsurer with the reserve information. If the ceding company is unable to produce the reserve reports before the reinsurer must close its books for the year, the reinsurer is forced to use the last reserve value it had from the ceding company or an estimate based on this old information. The reporting is typically from one to three months in arrears. Obviously, the longer the lag in reporting, the greater the difference in reserves will be.

Vanishing Reserves

Sometimes reserves vanish in a reinsurance transaction because the reserves are not required in the reinsurer's jurisdiction or the reserve requirements are less stringent and a lesser value is held. A prime example of this is deficiency reserves. Some states have a very stringent deficiency reserve requirements while some other states have no requirements at all. A reinsurer in a state which did not require deficiency reserves could accept business with deficiency reserves and not set up any of these reserves on its statutory statement, while the ceding company might take full credit for the deficiency reserves on its statutory statement.

The problem is not limited to deficiency reserves. The situation is quite common in offshore sites which use a more flexible valuation system, such as the United Kingdom or Bermuda.[14]

UNAUTHORIZED REINSURERS

Reinsurers which are neither licensed nor accredited to accept reinsurance on lives in the ceding company's state of domicile, or domiciled in a state with substantially similar laws as the ceding company's state of domicile, are called unauthorized reinsurers. While it is very rare for a professional reinsurer not to be admitted in all states, not all reinsurance

---

[14] See Chapter 16, International Reinsurance.

transactions take place with the professional reinsurers. Many reinsurance transactions take place between specialty reinsurers, producer owned insurers, or affiliates which are unauthorized in the ceding company's state of domicile.

Regulatory Concerns

Regulators have no jurisdiction over unauthorized reinsurers. This makes it very difficult to enforce contractual reinsurance benefits due to the ceding company. Regulators also have no control over the financial condition of unauthorized reinsurers. Should an unauthorized reinsurer become insolvent, the domestic ceding company's financial position could be severely impaired.

Fronting

A special subset of the unauthorized reinsurer problem concerns fronting. In this situation, the ceding company has issued policies on behalf of the reinsurer and may cede 100% of the risk to the reinsurer maintaining only a small fee for administration or use of its license. Regulators are concerned that the reinsurer is circumventing the regulations of its jurisdiction by using the status of the ceding company. The reinsurer may not meet the standards set by that state and may even have been denied admission. Should the reinsurer become insolvent, the ceding company might be financially impaired as it would be responsible for the risks without having any premiums or reserves.

Model Law. Until the early 1990's, fronting was viewed negatively by most regulators. Some states, most notably New York, has stringent laws prohibiting or tightly controlling the use of fronting. A more recent view is that fronting may not be bad, but that it must be carefully regulated. The regulatory bodies have reacted, most prominently with the Model Fronting Disclosure and Regulation Act. This act applies to property and casualty insurance and to most accident and health coverages, but life insurance, annuities, and credit life and health coverages are excluded. This leaves old rules and regulations for fronting in place for these excluded coverages.

The Fronting Disclosure and Regulation Act is directed primarily at disclosure, although prior approval may be required, depending on the relationship of premiums and surplus. Disclosure is required regarding the following:

(1) Total gross premiums written and ceded.
(2) The lines and classes of business ceded.
(3) The reinsurer's NAIC number, domicile, address, and chief operating officer.
(4) Total incurred losses on the ceded business.
(5) The collateral for unearned premiums and claim reserves, including IBNR.
(6) The name of the third party administrator, if any, performing underwriting or claims functions.

In additions, certain responsibilities are placed with the fronting, or ceding, company, such as the following:

(1) Perform due diligence on the reinsurer.
(2) Obtain and provide an independent actuary's opinion regarding rate adequacy.
(3) Provide a written agreement detailing the following:
  (a) The duties of each party.
  (b) Security arrangements for assets.
  (c) Appointment of the insurance commissioner of the state of domicile as an representative of the reinsurer with authority to accept or disburse funds.
  (d) The right of the ceding company to terminate the agreement with thirty day notice.
(4) An annual audit of the reinsurer for compliance.
(5) Suspension of the program upon disagreement.
(6) Maintenance of records regarding the agreement, accounting, collateral, and audits.

New York and Fronting. Before the proposal of model act, New York attempted to deal with fronting through a proposed regulation prohibiting certain transactions. While this regulation was never enacted, the prohibited transactions are included as an example of what future regulations may consider.

(1) New York licensed life insurance companies are prohibited from ceding directly or retrocede indirectly to an unlicensed insurer any policy covering residents of the state of New York if the reinsurance is a condition of the original placement of the policy with the licensed company and if the unlicensed insurer has the power to place such policies.
(2) No New York licensed insurer can cede 50% or more of its liability under any policy covering a resident of New York, either directly or indirectly, to an unlicensed insurer which controls or is controlled by or affiliated with the policyholder, producer, or any other entity which has the power to place these policies.
(3) No New York licensed insurance company is allowed to reinsure any part of its liability on a policy covering residents of the state to an unlicensed insurer if the reinsurer or any affiliate of the reinsurer performs any one or more of the following functions in connection with the policies reinsured: marketing, underwriting, policy owner service or claims.

The proposed regulation would have exempted group policies issued to multistate employers if less than 10% of the covered employees resided in New York and if the unlicensed reinsurer did not control or was not controlled by or affiliated with the policyholder or producer. Reinsurance transactions involving affiliates of the ceding company were not prohibited if these transactions were performed under a non-disapproved service agreement. Further, facultative underwriting was not considered underwriting for the purpose of fronting.

Effect of Regulations

As previously stated, unauthorized reinsurers are required to provide security through funds withheld, trust or escrow accounts, or letters of credit. Ceding companies will not receive reserve credit for reinsurance ceded to an unauthorized reinsurer if the reinsurer does not meet these guidelines. In that event, there are special reporting requirements in the statutory annual statement which highlight these transactions.

TRUSTS, ESCROW ACCOUNTS, LETTERS OF CREDIT, FUNDS WITHHELD

Trusts, escrow accounts, and letters of credit are the principal instruments used as security for reinsurance transactions. Security may also be provided by structuring the reinsurance with funds withheld. Recent regulation has focused on defining specifications regarding these instruments to assure that they are indeed security for the transaction, not meaningless pieces of paper. Likewise, limitations have been placed on the admissibility of assets under a funds withheld reinsurance treaty.

Regulatory Concerns

Regulators are concerned that funds set aside in a trust, escrow account, or letter of credit truly exist, are sufficient to cover the liabilities, and are actually available to the ceding company or its successor when necessary. Some recent insurance company insolvencies have demonstrated the difficulties experienced by the ceding company or the liquidator in actually obtaining funds seemingly committed by the reinsurance agreement. Regulators want to be certain funds are available.

While regulators have not dictated terms of a legal agreement, such as a reinsurance treaty, they have established rules for statutory accounting of liabilities and acceptable assets. Regulations, therefore, set forth the conditions which must be met if favorable accounting treatment is to be allowed. Among other things, these regulations may define the type of assets acceptable in a trust and the types of financial institutions which are acceptable as participants, using these instruments.

Trusts and Escrow Accounts

Section 10 of the Credit for Reinsurance Model Regulation sets forth the requirements for provisions to be included in a trust agreement. The requirements include that the beneficiary of the trust, normally the ceding insurance company, has a right to withdraw assets from the trust account at any time without notifying the grantor, normally the reinsurance company. The trust agreement must provide that the trustee will receive and hold all assets and that these assets must be in such a form that the trustee may negotiate any of the assets in the trust without the consent or signature of the grantor. Assets deposited in the trust account must be valued according to their current fair market value. The assets must consist only of the following:

(1) Cash,
(2) Certificates of Deposit, and
(3) Investments as specified by the Insurance Code.

The assets may not be investments issued by a company which is in any way affiliated with the grantor or the beneficiary. The reinsurer must transfer to the trustee legal title of all the assets in the trust.

The reinsurance agreement may provide that the ceding company or its successors will be able to withdraw assets from the trust only for the following purposes:

(1) To reimburse the ceding company for the reinsurer's share of premiums returned to the owners of policies reinsured under the reinsurance agreement on account of cancellations of such policies.
(2) To reimburse the ceding company for the reinsurer's share of surrender benefits or losses paid by the ceding company pursuant to the provisions of the policies reinsured under the reinsurance agreement.
(3) To fund an account with the ceding company in an amount at least equal to the deduction for reinsurance ceded from the ceding company's liabilities for policies ceded under the agreement. Such accounts shall include, but not be limited to, amounts for policy reserves, claims and losses incurred and unearned premium reserves.
(4) To pay any other amounts the ceding company claims are due under the reinsurance agreement.

Letters of Credit

A letter of credit is a document issued by a bank on the orders of one party, in this case the reinsurer, which provides that the beneficiary, in this case the ceding company, will be able to withdraw funds up to a specified limit. It is a guarantee of payment which can be enforced, yet the use of a letter of credit requires no physical disbursement of assets by the reinsurer unless the ceding company actually requests disbursement of the funds. The letter of credit must be in writing. The actual contract between the bank and its customer does not affect the beneficiary.

Rules covering the use of letters of credit in reinsurance situations vary from state to state, therefore, it is important to review the position of the insurance department in the specific states affected by a given treaty. Section 11 of the Credit for Reinsurance Model Regulation sets forth the requirements for letters of credit. It requires that the letter of credit must be "clean," "unconditional," "irrevocable," and "evergreen."

A "clean" letter of credit requires that the beneficiary present only a demand for payment to the issuing bank and that no further documentation is necessary. "Unconditional" means there can be no further qualifications outside the letter of credit. "Irrevocable" means that the letter of credit can be modified only with the consent of the parties specified in the contract. The rules also require that the letter of credit be "evergreen," that is, that the letter of credit will be renewed automatically unless the issuing bank gives advance written notice of non-renewal to both parties. This allows the parties to make other arrangements.

California requires the issuer be a member of the Federal Reserve System and be satisfactory to the Commissioner. The New York regulation requires that the reinsurance contract specifically call for the letter of credit. The NAIC Model Law on Credit for Reinsurance provides for the SVO to maintain a list of institutions qualified to provide acceptable letters of credit.

The financial institution issuing the letter of credit receives a fee commensurate with the degree of risk it is assuming by issuing the letter of credit. This fee is usually expressed as a percentage of the amount of the letter of credit and may be in the range of .20% to .30% per year, or up to 1%.

Funds Withheld

Another form of security is funds withheld by, or assets left on deposit with, the ceding company in support of the reinsurance. Either the ceding company withholds funds due the reinsurer or the reinsurer deposits funds with the ceding company in an amount at least equal to the reserve credit to be taken. The ceding company establishes a separate liability for the funds due the reinsurer and uses this as an offset in determining the liability for reinsurance in unauthorized companies.

This approach is generally viewed favorably by the regulators since the ceding company has in its possession assets sufficient to cover the reserve credit. The regulators do have a concern that the reinsurance agreement provide sufficient transfer of risk. In addition, they require that any interest paid or credited to the reinsurer on such funds be reasonable in relation to the ceding company's investment returns. If the regulators are not satisfied that these conditions have been met, they may disallow the offset in the determination of the liability for reinsurance in unauthorized companies.

OTHER AREAS OF REGULATION

In recent years, regulation of reinsurance has been under continuous review and scrutiny. New laws or regulations are proposed with regularity, partly because reinsurance is a major part of the capital structure of many companies, and, partly because, in some insolvent or troubled insurers, existing reinsurance was found to be of little or no economic benefit when financial problems occurred. Several common additional areas of formal regulation or practice are discussed in the balance of this chapter.

Reinsurance Treaty Approval

Unlike an insurance policy form, a reinsurance treaty usually does not require approval of the state insurance department in order to be put into effect, although some states require that a copy of the treaty be filed with the Commissioner. As mentioned earlier, state insurance departments usually do not disapprove or disallow insurance treaties but rather disallow reserve credits or disapprove specific statutory accounting treatment.

Having a reserve credit disallowed is highly undesirable. There are times when the parties to a financial reinsurance treaty may wish to consult with the state insurance department before effecting the treaty. This step is taken most often when the issues are known to be sensitive, when a new technique is used, or when the financial implications are significant.

Intercompany Reinsurance

Generally, the same rules apply to reinsurance between related companies as apply to independent entities. Some states do have special regulations regarding related party reinsurance, such as a requirement of prior approval of treaties. On the other hand, an unusual treaty between related parties may be viewed more favorably than one between unrelated parties, especially if both companies are domiciled in the same state and the stronger company is the reinsurer. Again, the primary concerns of the regulators are conformity with the applicable regulations and protection of policyholder interests.

Holding Company Regulation. The Model Insurance Holding Company System Regulatory Act concerns insurers under a parent company and covers many items not related to reinsurance. Two provisions relate to reinsurance between affiliated companies with common ownership or control.[15] These provisions apply to not only new reinsurance agreements, but also to modifications or amendments to existing agreements.

---

[15] "Control" is defined to mean the "power to direct or cause the direction of the management and policies" of a company. Control is commonly assumed to be present if one person or entity possesses the votes or proxies of ten percent or more of the voting securities. This definition is subject to debate and negotiation.

Under the first related party reinsurance provision, any reinsurance transaction with an affiliated party must be disclosed, regardless of size or materiality. Under the second provision, the state regulator has the right of prior approval of any material reinsurance transaction with an affiliated party. "Materiality" is defined as an event where the reinsurance premium or change in liabilities is five percent or more of the insurer's surplus.

Language is also present which appears to make this regulation applicable to any transaction where business is ceded to an unrelated third party and then retroceded to an affiliated party.

This particular regulation applies to the ceding company, which must make the necessary disclosure or obtain the appropriate approval from the insurance department in its state of domicile.

Assumption[16]

Recent insolvencies involving assumed contracts or policies and the resultant interest of the United States Congress has motivated the NAIC to focus attention on the assumption process.

Assumption Reinsurance Model Act. The purpose of the Assumption Reinsurance Model Act, adopted by the NAIC in January 1994, is to "protect and define the rights and obligations of policyholders, regulators and the parties to assumption reinsurance agreements." The scope of the act is for all authorized insurers, with certain exceptions:

(1) Transactions where the ceding party retains direct liability, otherwise known as indemnity reinsurance.
(2) Substitution of a new policy with a new insurer upon expiration of the old policy.
(3) Transactions resulting from a regulated merger.
(4) Transactions of an insurer in rehabilitation or liquidation.
(5) Transactions involving a guarantee association.
(6) A group policy transfer following a policyholder request.

---

[16] This section discusses recent regulation regarding assumption transactions. See Chapter 16, Assumption, for a more detailed look at assumption.

The act takes the position that assumption reinsurance is a novation of a previously valid agreement and requires the approval of both the policyholder and the insurer. Hence, assumption would not be valid if only the insurer approves, as has been the situation historically. This is a recognition of standard common law precedent.

The act requires notification of the policyholders, agents, and brokers. The notice would include the following:

(1) The date of transfer and novation.
(2) The name, address, and phone number of the assuming and transferring insurer.
(3) The policyholder's right to consent to, or reject, the transfer and novation.
(4) Procedures and time limit for consenting or rejecting.
(5) A summary of the effect consenting or rejecting will have on the policyholder's rights.
(6) A statement that the assuming insurer is licensed to write such business or otherwise authorized to assume the business.
(7) The name and address of the person at the transferring insurer to whom the policyholder should send written statement of acceptance or rejection.
(8) The address and phone number of the insurance department where the policyholder resides so the policyholder can obtain further information.
(9) Financial data for both companies including the following:
    (a) Rates for the last five years from two nationally recognized rating services and an explanation of the ratings.
    (b) Balance sheets from the previous three years.
    (c) A copy of Management's Discussion and Analysis that was filed as a supplement to the previous year's financial statement.
    (d) A explanation of the reason for the transfer.

For domiciled companies, preapprovals by the state insurance departments of domicile of both the direct insurer and the assumption company are required. If the assumption company is not licensed in all states where there are policyholders, those states may disapprove the transaction for those policyholders. Additional rules apply to foreign and alien companies.

The Model Act requires prior approval by the Commissioner when a domiciled insurer assumes or transfers risks under an assumption agreement. A licensed foreign insurer must file a copy of the notice of transfer and an affidavit that the transaction is subject to substantially similar requirements in the domicile of either the transferring or assuming insurer. If such requirements do not exist, the foreign insurer must obtain prior approval.

Many factors are included in the consideration for approval. The financial conditions of the two parties after both before and after the transaction and the effect of the transaction are of primary importance. The competence, experience, and integrity of the assumption carrier are considered, as well as the future administration of the business. The apparent fairness and reasonableness of future treatment of the policyholders of both companies is considered, especially the future dividends or distribution of surplus for participating policyholders.

The policyholders have the right to reject the transfer, although in practice if relatively few object, insurance departments may override such objection and authorize the assumption of all policies for administrative simplicity. If the policyholder has not objected in writing after two notices and a specified period of time, currently 24 months in the model act, the policyholder is deemed to have accepted the transaction. Also, payment of premium without reserving the right to reject is deemed to be acceptance.

Certain constitutional arguments enter into consideration of deemed acceptance. Some arguments hold that a unilateral novation by the insurer is not legal. Courts have decided in favor of the policyholder even after payment of premium. One purpose of the proposed act is to minimize uncertainty.

The model act recognizes at least one circumstance where novation can be unilateral. If the domiciliary state finds a company to be in hazardous financial condition, the commissioner may transfer inforce business and assets to another carrier without policyholder consent and provide an explanation to the policyholder.

In some states, even following all regulations and obtaining policyholder approval may not relieve the original insurer of future liability. Under the theory of "joint liability," both insurers are liable for benefits and the policyholder can approach either with a claim. This can be handled administratively by the new carrier acting in the name of the original company, but problems may arise if the assumption carrier fails to perform or does not perform to the policyholder's expectations.

Under the theory of "contingent liability," the original insurer is responsible if the assumption carrier fails to perform, such as in an insolvency. In any event, an original insurer can expect to be requested to perform by some policyholders if the new carrier becomes insolvent, so it is wise to pick an assumption insurer which is expected to be solvent until the last policy is terminated.

Miscellaneous Laws and Regulation

There are many laws and regulations which can, under certain circumstances, have an effect on reinsurance transactions. Some of these are discussed herein.

Required Provisions. Various states have addressed the need for specific provisions to be included in reinsurance agreements. These required provisions may vary according to the reinsurer, or may be required in all agreements. For example, the insolvency clause discussed in Chapter 6 normally is required if reserve credit is to be taken, regardless of the reinsurer involved. Certain provisions about letters of credit or assets held in trust are required only if an unauthorized or unaccredited reinsurer is involved.

Any person considering entering into a new reinsurance agreement or modifying an existing agreement is advised to review the current laws and regulations of the ceding company's state of domicile and other relevant states before finalizing the agreement.

Material Transactions. The Disclosure of Material Transactions Model Act applies to a broad range of possible transactions, with Section 3 specifically addressing "nonrenewals, cancellation or revision of ceded reinsurance programs." The responsibility under this act is for the ceding company to notify its domestic state regulators of any change in reinsurance programs which is material.

Materiality differs for life and casualty companies. For life, annuity, and accident and health insurance, any change of more than 50% in reserve credit from the prior annual statement is viewed as material, unless the amount then ceded was less than ten percent of the gross amount of reserve before any reinsurance credits. Accident and health insurance written in a property and casualty insurer is subject to the rules for property and casualty insurers; materiality is defined as a change of 50% or more in ceded reinsurance premiums.

If a transaction is determined to be material, specific reporting requirements are detailed.

Alien Reinsurers. A non-United States domiciled insurer is known as an alien insurer. Some alien insurers offer reinsurance in the United States through a branch of the alien carrier rather than a United States domiciled subsidiary.[17] The State of Entry Model Law applies to these carriers and provides rules regarding capital, assets deposited in the state, surplus requirements, reserve requirements, and reporting. Reinsurance to a branch is treated the same as reinsurance to a United States domiciled reinsurer, with the state of entry serving as its state of domicile. In particular, reserve credit regulation is the same as with a United States company.

To date, only twelve states have such legislation. Historically, Michigan has been the state of choice for entry of many life insurers and New York for many property and casualty insurers.

Some alien reinsurers choose to act without either a subsidiary or a branch. Reserve credit is taken as with unauthorized reinsurers. Specific regulation is proposed in the Non United States Insurers Model Act. This act is still under discussion and would be largely a gatekeeper, with minimum standards on deposits and reporting. It would apply to both direct insurance as well as reinsurance.

Intermediaries. Transactions and activities of reinsurance intermediaries, or brokers, are regulated by the Reinsurance Intermediary Model Act, discussed in Chapter 22, Selected Additional Reinsurance Topics.

---

[17] Reinsurance transaction with a United States domiciled subsidiary of an alien insurer is regulated as with any other United States domiciled carrier.

IRIS

The NAIC Insurance Regulatory Information System (IRIS) was developed to assist state insurance departments in overseeing the financial conditions of insurance companies. All companies are required to file annual statements in all states in which they are licensed. Because no state insurance department is able to review all licensed companies' financial statements quickly and thoroughly, IRIS was developed to help the insurance department select those companies which may require more immediate attention.

IRIS consists of a series of ratios which may be developed from the statutory annual statement. There are currently twelve IRIS ratios. Because reinsurance may affect the amount of assets, liabilities, surplus, investment income, premiums, benefits, or expenses reported in a company's annual statement, its use can affect, either favorably or unfavorably, a number of the ratios developed. A company should consider the effect on these ratios before entering into a significant reinsurance transaction. Alternative structuring of the treaty might produce significantly different effects on the ratios.

Certain of the ratios are intended to measure the effect of reinsurance. For example, Ratio #8 measures the amount of surplus relief. It is calculated by dividing commissions and expense allowances on reinsurance ceded by the capital and surplus of the company. A ratio of greater than 20% may trigger a further investigation into the nature of the reinsurance transactions. The greatest attention will be paid to those reinsurance agreements providing surplus relief.

FEDERAL REGULATION

During recent years, there has been interest in the United States Congress for applying some level of federal regulation or oversight to the insurance industry. The primary areas of concern which involve reinsurance are with protecting policyholders in the event of an insurer's insolvency or an assumption transaction. The prospect of federal intervention has been a catalyst for increased state and NAIC activity, including the introduction of many of the model laws and regulations discussed in this chapter. Thus far, no federal legislation regarding reinsurance has been passed, but that can change with the whims of Congress.

11 Insolvency and Reinsurance

Reinsurance treaties are unique legal contracts in that they affect not only the two parties to the transaction, but also the individuals insured by both parties, even those not covered by the reinsurance agreement. The ultimate worth of the treaty, and the ability to collect under its terms, must be clear, even in the event of an insolvency by one of the two parties. Therefore, special provisions are included in most reinsurance treaties clarifying the working of the treaty in such an event.

Few life insurance companies face insolvency. While some companies may approach the edge of solvency, most are able to avoid actual disaster by obtaining necessary funds from financial institutions, by slowing growth, by selling all or a portion of the business to another insurer, or by adding surplus through reinsurance transactions. If an insurer is declared insolvent, it is frequently due to some combination of fraud, excessive asset risk, mismanagement, underreserving, inexperience, or an uncontrollable external event such as a war or plague.

MODEL ACT

Insurance companies are specifically excluded from the Federal Bankruptcy Act. The NAIC developed the Insurer's Supervision, Rehabilitation and Liquidation Model Act to guide the State Insurance Departments in insolvency proceedings. The Model Act defines insolvency as either the inability to pay obligations when due or having admitted assets that do not exceed the sum of all liabilities plus the greater of the legally required capital and surplus or the total par or stated value of authorized and issued capital stock.

Conditions

The Model Act allows the Commissioner to take charge of the troubled company in any of the following situations:

(1) The continued operation of the company might prove financially hazardous to its policyholders, competitors, or the public.
(2) There is fraud, embezzlement, or other dishonesty.
(3) The periodic financial reports are not filed and no adequate explanation is provided.
(4) The insurer attempts to sell or reinsure all or almost all of its business without the prior consent of the Commissioner.

The Commissioner may, at his option, attempt to rehabilitate the company. If the rehabilitation is successful, the management of the company is turned over to an approved management team. If the rehabilitation is not successful or not attempted, the Commissioner can liquidate the company.

In the case of a liquidation, the Commissioner gathers the assets of the company. If a Guarantee Fund exists in the state, the fund will either assume the life, accident and health, and annuity business or assumption reinsure it with a solvent company. The insolvent insurer's creditors are then paid on a class by class basis from the remaining assets. All creditors of a given class must be paid in total before any creditors in the next class may receive any payment.

Priority of Distribution

The model act defines eight classes of unsecured creditors for distribution purposes after the claims of secured creditors have been satisfied. These classes and their definitions are as follows:

Class 1. The costs and expenses of administration approved by the receiver.

Class 2. The administrative expenses of the guaranty associations where such expenses would have otherwise been incurred by the receiver in evaluating coverages, settling claims, and in arranging ongoing coverage through transfer to other insurers and maintaining policies.

Class 3. All claims including federal, state, or local government claims for losses incurred, including third party claims, claims for unearned premiums, and claims of a guaranty association. All claims under life, health, and annuity policies are loss claims.

Class 4. Federal government claims other than those in Class 3.

Class 5. Debts due employees for services and benefits.

Class 6. Claims of any person except for those classified elsewhere.

Class 7. Claims of any state of local government for penalty or forfeiture.

Class 8. Surplus or contribution notes or similar obligations, premium refunds on assessable policies, and interest on claims of Classes 1 through 7.

Class 9. The claims of shareholders or other owners.

Historically, in most insolvencies, Class 1 and Class 2 creditors are paid in full. The policyholders may receive only a portion of the benefits from their policies. The federal government is usually paid before the policyholders. Class 6 general creditors seldom receive full value.

The Ceding Company's Position

In the event of a reinsurer's insolvency, a ceding company most frequently finds itself classified as a Class 6 creditor. On occasion, a ceding company has tried to assert that it is a policyholder and therefore in Class 3, but such attempts have been unsuccessful.

The Reinsurer's Position

In the case of a ceding company insolvency, the reinsurer is considered to be in Class 6, a general creditor, at least with regard to amounts owed at the time of insolvency. General creditors rarely receive full payment for amounts owed them, so a reinsurer must either accept the fact that it will lose some or all amounts owed it in the event of a client's insolvency or make other provisions which will improve its position. The use of a trust may allow a reinsurer to become a secured creditor, moving ahead of all unsecured creditors.

The administrator, receiver, or liquidator of a company in receivership may choose to maintain active reinsurance agreements, paying premiums in full when due and collecting full benefits when claims are incurred. If so, as discussed later, the reinsurer is obligated to maintain the terms of the agreement as though no insolvency or financial impairment had occurred. In such instances, the administrators have determined that the risk management or potential claim recovery value of the agreement exceeds the cost of future premiums.

THE INSOLVENCY CLAUSE

Most reinsurance agreements contain an insolvency clause stating that the reinsurance is payable to the liquidator without diminution because of insolvency.[1] The insurance company is denied reserve credit for

---

[1] See Chapter 6, The Reinsurance Treaty.

reinsurance ceded on its statutory financial statements unless this clause is included. The insolvency clause has been required by many states because the basic understanding in a reinsurance contract is that the reinsurer is required to pay only those claims representing actual losses incurred by the ceding company.

United States courts have ruled that the liquidator may collect reinsurance proceeds without paying any part of a loss. In fact, the reinsurance proceeds become part of the general assets of the ceding company, and are not identified with any specific policyholder. The liquidator may apply only a portion of the reinsurance proceeds to pay the specific claim reinsured. The remainder of the reinsurance proceeds may be used to pay portions of other claims or other expenses.

Purpose

The effect of the insolvency clause is to override the normal treaty mechanics whereby the reinsurer pays only its proportionate share of any claims paid. It really provides that, in the event of an insolvency, the ceding company may not be able to pay all claims incurred. Instead it may pay a lesser amount. However, the reinsurer may not use this lowered payment as a reason to reduce its payment. In this event, the reinsurer must pay its share of the amount which would have been due the policyholder absent the insolvency.

The insolvency clause is required for a treaty to generate reserve credit, but is not a requirement for a valid reinsurance agreement. For example, a coinsurance treaty which omitted this clause would have equal effect on cash flows, barring an insolvency, but would not provide reserve credits.

Nonproportional treaties may omit this clause altogether as reserve credits are not an issue. However, many treaties still include this clause as it provides clarification on a potential problem point. In any event, the clause should be useful in establishing the collectibility of claims due at year-end or at the point of insolvency.

Cut-Through

Until recently a "cut-through" or purchase of a claim has had unclear status in a liquidation. Reinsurers, from time to time, have attempted to pay a claim directly to the claimant, bypassing the liquidator without a specific authorization in the reinsurance contract. However, a liquidator is empowered to settle claims for less than their full value in a liquidation, and apply the remainder of the reinsurance proceeds to pay other claims.

In Ainsworth vs. General Reinsurance Corp.,[2] the U.S. Court of Appeals for the Eighth Circuit upheld a decision that General Reinsurance was liable to the receiver of Medallion Insurance Company for policy proceeds that had previously been paid directly by General Reinsurance to the policyholder. In this case, the reinsurer paid a reduced amount directly to the policyholder in exchange for a release discharging the primary insurance company and its receiver from all liability in connection with the claim. The receiver, however, filed an action to recover the 100% of proceeds due from General Reinsurance. The court found that Missouri's Statutory Code for insolvencies mandated that the receiver collect all reinsurance proceeds and that the reinsurer was not free to pay the policyholder without the receiver's consent. General Reinsurance had to pay the receiver as well as the policyholder.

Section 36C of the NAIC Rehabilitation and Liquidation Model Act allows cut-through provisions. Specific state regulations should be carefully researched.

Set-Off

In a reinsurance arrangement, large sums of money may pass back and forth between the reinsurer and the ceding company. These sums include premiums, expense allowances, and claim reimbursement. To simplify these transactions, frequently only the net balance is remitted. This is referred to as an offset or a set-off.[3] A set-off allows for the netting of amounts due arising out of different transactions.

In the event of the insolvency of one party to the contract, the right to set off becomes important. Courts have held that the inclusion of the

---

[2] Ainsworth v. General Reinsurance Corporation. 751 F.2d 962 (8th Cir. 1985).

[3] The term "set-off" or "offset" comes from the fact that amounts due are netted, or set-off against each other.

right to set off in a statute or a reinsurance agreement does not create this right, but merely affirms the already existing right of set-off. In most states the right of set off is a part of the law. This right cannot be overridden by the courts, but it can be eliminated or abridged by statute. In states where this right is normally granted, the two parties can eliminate it through negotiation and mutual agreement. If the right of set-off is prohibited by statute, the prohibition cannot be overridden by contract provisions.

In order to set off debts in a liquidation, the reinsurer must show that some equitable ground exists and that there is "mutuality." Mutuality of capacity is defined as debts that are "due to and from the same persons in the same capacity." In other words, there must be a relationship between the two parties, each acting as a principal and not as an agent or trustee. Mutuality of time provides that obligations incurred before liquidation be offset only against other obligations incurred prior to liquidation. Likewise, obligations incurred after liquidation may be set off only against other obligations incurred after liquidation. Under this concept, a party incurring obligations from one agreement can look to the obligations owed it from another agreement with the same party to offset payment of the debt.

The majority of states have enacted statutes concerning the right to set off in insurance company liquidations. However, only California, New York, Minnesota, New Jersey, Wisconsin, Missouri, Illinois, and Oklahoma have case law specifically interpreting the statutes. Other jurisdictions may look to these cases as precedent in interpreting their set-off statutes.

Historically, the right to offset was well accepted within a single reinsurance treaty. There was even fairly widespread belief that obligations incurred could be set off against amounts due under a separate treaty between the same two parties. However, a case now in the California courts has challenged this position.

In this situation, a group of property and casualty insurers, known collectively as Mission Insurance, became insolvent and had many reinsurance agreements with many reinsurers, including several between some of its companies and some Prudential companies. Prudential argued, in essence, that all treaties between any Mission Insurance company and any Prudential company should be combined for purposes of determining the offset. The California Insurance Commissioner disagreed, and essentially asked the court to invalidate the offset provisions.

The trial court agreed with the Commissioner and denied the right of set-off. Prudential appealed and the California Court of Appeals rejected the Commissioner's arguments, siding with Prudential and reversing the trial court.[4] The case is now on appeal to the California Supreme Court. The Court of Appeals' decision establishes the right to offset mutual debts and credits between ceding companies and reinsurers under California law. In any event, the final result of the litigation will provide an important precedent for states with similar laws.

Oklahoma has a unique statute regarding offset within reinsurance agreements. This statute denies the reinsurer the right of offset in the combined event of the ceding company becoming insolvent and the reinsurance treaty failing to transfer reasonable risks. The application of this statute has been tested in one court case.[5]

In the referenced case, American Standard Life accepted via indemnity reinsurance a relatively large block of premium-paying and paid-up traditional life insurance policies from Life Assurance Company of Pennsylvania (LACOP). A major portion of this business was retroceded from American Standard to another reinsurer that had previously reinsured the same block from LACOP. The reserve credit resulting from the retrocession was about three times the size of American Standard's capital and surplus

The interest adjustment on the modified coinsurance portion of the reserves was fixed in the reinsurance treaty at approximately 10.25%. In addition, the reinsurer's fee for providing the reinsurance was established as an additional premium above the premiums received by American Standard or the experience gains of the treaty. Both LACOP and American Standard became insolvent.

---

[4] Prudential Reinsurance Co. v. Superior Court. 265 California Reporter, 1986.

[5] State of Oklahoma *ex rel* Cathy J. Weatherford, Insurance Commissioner, Petitioner, v. Oklahoma Life and Health Guaranty Association, intervening petitioner, v. The Guardian Life Insurance Company of America, respondent; case number CJ-88-12013; tried by the District Court of Oklahoma County, Oklahoma, in July 1994.

Many issues were debated early in the litigation process, including the fact that the treaty was in force before the effective date of the statute. Following earlier judicial findings, the only issues at trial were the questions of risk transfer and the right of offset. Demonstrations were presented that American Standard had earned only approximately 3.0% on its assets while paying the reinsurer approximately 10.25% plus the additional fee. The reinsurer was unable to convince the court that there was a "real world" scenario where risk transfer was present.

Finding that reasonable risk transfer was not present, the Oklahoma District Court decided for the plaintiff. The reinsurer was ordered to pay all claims without offset for either assets nominally held by American Standard to back the modified coinsurance reserves or any future premiums. The reinsurer is entitled to recovery for the remaining assets of American Standard after all policyholders have been paid, standing as a Class 6 general creditor.[6] The case is now on appeal to the Oklahoma Supreme Court.

An argument against offset is that it gives "reinsurers an unlawful preference against creditors in higher statutory priority groups." In addition, it has been argued that reinsurers should not be "entitled to share as claimants" in the insolvent company's assets. The recent litigation has pointed out the need to review this situation. Section 34 of the NAIC Rehabilitation and Liquidation Model Act provides specific authority for offset.

CEDING COMPANY INSOLVENCY

When discussing insolvency, the focus is usually on a ceding company insolvency. There are many considerations, most of which should be addressed before entering into a reinsurance treaty.

In the event of the insolvency of an insurance company, the receiver or liquidator takes control of the company, begins to collect the assets, and pays claims. The insolvency clause clearly states that the receiver

---

[6] Actually, since the reinsurer filed its claim late, it currently stands behind all other general creditors in the order of payments. However, that is a matter of insolvency administration, not the reinsurance litigation.

or liquidator will receive the reinsurance proceeds on claims without reduction. The liquidator is under no obligation to pay the claim with the reinsurance proceeds, the proceeds could be used for the payment of any claim or expense. If the reinsurance is secured by a letter of credit, assets in trust, or an escrow account, the receiver or liquidator may actually draw out the funds.

The reinsurer is entitled to receive any monies owed it as a Class 6 general creditor. However, the reinsurer traditionally has had the right to offset any funds which it owes the liquidator of the ceding company by the amounts which the ceding company owes it. This is particularly important if there is a large amount of unpaid premiums, if the ceding company is maintaining the reserves under a mod-co arrangement, or if funds withheld coinsurance has been used and the ceding company is holding an accounts payable liability. In the absence of the right to set off, the reinsurer could be left in a critical situation. In the absence of the statutory right to do so, the reinsurer is not allowed to cut through or pay claims directly to the policyholder, bypassing the liquidator.

REINSURER INSOLVENCY

The reinsurer can also become insolvent. This could have a dramatic effect on the ceding company's financial position. The recent insolvency of several property and casualty reinsurers has increased regulatory concern about reinsurance transactions.

The presence of an indemnity reinsurance agreement does not relieve the ceding company of its obligations to the policyholder. In the event of a reinsurer insolvency, the ceding company would be required to make full benefit payment to its policyholders even if the policies were 100% reinsured. This could be a problem in the case of any situation which is largely coinsured or in a funds withheld mod-co arrangement. This could conceivably impair the ceding company's financial situation. In these situations, some protection would be afforded the ceding company if there is a letter of credit or trust securing the reserve credits.

The ceding company would receive benefit payments from the reinsurer as a Class 6 general creditor, not as a Class 3 policyholder. It is quite likely that, as a Class 6 creditor, the ceding company would not receive full reimbursement for the reinsured benefits. This situation is particularly critical where the ceding company reinsures 100% of the risk for a small administrative fee. This is one reason that fronting agreements should be considered only with caution.

The liquidator or reinsurer would expect to receive all monies which the ceding company owes to the reinsurer. The ceding company may be able to set off these monies by any amounts which the reinsurer owes it.

For those ceding companies utilizing reinsurance pools, the situation of the insolvency of a member of a reinsurance pool should also be considered. Unless otherwise specified in the treaty, each reinsurer is responsible only for its share of claims and liabilities. In the event of the insolvency of one member, the ceding company is in the same situation as it would be without the pooling arrangement; the pooling is merely an administrative tool. However, a pool could provide that the surviving members are responsible for the obligations of an insolvent member, but this would then be specified in the treaty. This latter approach is uncommon.

POLICYHOLDER RIGHTS

Policyholders are placed in Class 3 for benefit distribution in the case of ceding company insolvency. This places the policyholder ahead of the reinsurer and the other general creditors of the ceding company. While benefit payments may be delayed, state insurance departments work very diligently in the case of an insolvency to see that policyholders receive full benefit payment.

In the cases of the Equity Funding and Baldwin United insolvencies, the policyholders eventually received full benefit payment. In the event of the reinsurer insolvency, the policyholders would expect full benefit payment within a reasonable period of time from the ceding company. Should the reinsurer's insolvency push the ceding company into insolvency, the policyholders would be treated as Class 3 creditors.

MANAGING THE INSOLVENCY RISK

The two major tools that the reinsurer has in managing the insolvency risk are to carefully draft the reinsurance treaty and to carefully underwrite proposed clients. Conversely, the major tools available to a ceding company to avoid being in business with an insolvent reinsurer are similar: to carefully draft the treaty and to carefully select its reinsurers, giving weight not just to reinsurance costs and services, but also to financial condition and management.[7]

Contractual

From the contractual side, the most important provision for inclusion in the treaty is the set off clause. However, as pointed out earlier, this protection is not as invulnerable as it was once believed to be. The reinsurer might gain some additional protection by requiring that the ceding company maintain a trust to cover any unpaid premiums or fees. Inclusion of any requirements which would cause the reinsurance to be terminated in the case of a change of ownership or a change in management, or upon the insolvency of the insurer, would no doubt cause insurance regulators and the IRS to view this as other than a reinsurance contract.

The ceding company likely may gain added protection by requiring that a trust or letter of credit always be used to secure reserve credits. Such protection generally is regarded as unnecessary if the reinsurer is accredited, but there are no guarantees. Of course, there may be additional costs associated with such security.

The reinsurer may add a provision requiring quarterly or even monthly financial reports and conditions regarding asset and liability matching, investment restrictions, and the types of assets which the ceding company may purchase. These restrictions are not common in reinsurance treaties but often are required by institutional investors.

If the reinsurer is making a major financial commitment to the ceding company, the reinsurer may consider imposing some sort of

---

[7] See Chapter 8, Managing Ceded Reinsurance.

restriction on stockholder dividends paid.[8] The reinsurer may place restrictions on the type, amount, or source of new business which the company can issue if it believes that such business would be detrimental to the long term health of the insurer. The reinsurer may also use an "indeterminate premium" form of reinsurance, allowing itself the right to charge a higher premium or lower allowance later should it view future expectations differently.

As noted earlier, the forced termination of reinsurance upon certain conditions, such as a change in management or insolvency of the insurer will cause the contract to be viewed as a nonreinsurance transaction. The ceding company likely would have to reserve for that eventuality. Also, requiring that the ceding company pay the reinsurer any amount of a negative experience refund will result in similar treatment. There are two exceptions to this rule. First, the reinsurer need not pay any current or future experience refund if there is a cumulative negative experience refund balance. Second, the reinsurer can require that unpaid losses be paid upon voluntary termination of the reinsurance by the ceding company.

Some treaties include a chargeback allowance which permits the reinsurer to recover allowances paid in excess of premiums received in the event of lapse or surrender of the underlying policies. Any amounts charged back are actually additional premiums or reduced allowances, and as such are subject to the same exposure as other funds owed.

In any event, any company advancing funds or establishing significant liabilities under a reinsurance treaty would be well advised to discuss that treaty with the insurance department of the states of domicile of each party and to understand those states' interpretations of the treaty's provisions.

Underwriting

Perhaps the best safeguard against insolvency is informed underwriting. While a few companies seek surplus relief for purely cosmetic purposes,

---

[8] Designers of reinsurance treaties should be aware of the restrictions or cautions placed on representations and warranties in the Model Regulation on Reinsurance Credit for Life and Health Agreements. See Chapter 10, Reinsurance Regulations.

most companies seeking financial reinsurance have true financial problems, such as limited capital available. The reinsurer must do its underwriting homework. As a minimum, the reinsurer should obtain and review the proposed client's statutory annual statements for the last three to five years and, if possible, the last two triennial reports from the state insurance department. If the company produces GAAP financial statements, the reinsurer should review these also.

Other sources of information include the various publications of the A.M. Best Company and the National Underwriter. The Best's publications include a monthly magazine which contains news of new product trends and other happenings within the life insurance industry, a weekly newsletter, and an annual report which is available for personal computers. The National Underwriter is a weekly industry newsletter which features some of the current events in the life insurance industry. Reports from other rating agencies, such as Standard & Poor, Duff and Phelps, and Moody, may also be useful.

Before providing any surplus relief, the reinsurer should examine the client's existing statutory and GAAP surplus. It should particularly review existing surplus relief contracts. The reinsurer should be careful with any company that has a large amount of surplus relief inforce with other reinsurers as this indicates that surplus has been a problem over the years. There may not be sufficient profitable, unreinsured business available for the transaction. A review of the non-financially oriented reinsurance is also important.

The reinsurer should look at the company structure. In some circumstances, it may be necessary to investigate some of the affiliates of the ceding company, especially subsidiaries, as their success or failure may affect the company's position. The reinsurer should also appraise the client's managerial talent, and feel comfortable with the management team. The reinsurer must believe this management team can move the company in the necessary direction so that continued surplus relief will not be a permanent need.

In reviewing the company, it is important to look at the various products which the company has sold and is selling. Accident and health coverages can be very volatile. A company active in the term insurance market may also experience earnings fluctuations; companies with large amounts of annuity business may experience fluctuations with swings in experience due to changes in interest rates and economic conditions. The reinsurer may also choose to investigate any potential legal liabilities that could affect the company's financial position.

The reinsurer should examine the asset side of the company. Items to consider include the proportions and amounts of assets invested in real estate, the amount of assets invested in bonds and the quality of those bonds, and any commercial paper carried by the insurance company. The reinsurer should pay particular attention to assets invested in affiliates as the market value of these assets could be quite small in reality, or may be overstated in the statutory books. Current reinsurance receivables should also be reviewed.

If the review of the prospect company generates concern, the reinsurer may wish to discuss the company with the company's domestic state insurance department, or its own insurance department. Most reinsurance transactions are negotiated in confidence, so a reinsurer normally would contact an insurance department only with the ceding company's prior knowledge and permission.

As well as underwriting the company, the reinsurer must also underwrite the business to be reinsured. It is important to review the product design and past experience to make an estimate of the future experience of the block. The pricing margins should be reviewed to determine if the margins are adequate to repay the existing relief and provide a healthy flow of profits in the future. The existing reinsurance contracts on the policies to be reinsured should also be reviewed.

The focus of the above comments has been on financial reinsurance, as those examples are clearest and the insolvency risks involved are often the largest. The same cautions and considerations should, however, apply to all reinsurance treaties.

Selection of Reinsurers

An increasing number of ceding companies are choosing reinsurers not merely on the basis of price and services, but with great emphasis on the financial condition of the reinsurer. Some conditions used to screen reinsurers include the following:

(1) Minimum defined rating by one or more specified ratings agencies.
(2) Exceeding a minimum level of surplus.

(3) Being licensed or accredited in the ceding company's state of domicile.
(4) History of doing business over a specified period of time.

12 | Statutory Accounting for Reinsurance

Until the middle of the 1970's statutory accounting requirements for reinsurance were fairly simple. For the most part, data was accumulated on worksheets and either entered directly in the annual statement[1] or embedded in the overall numbers. As reinsurance became increasingly important to the financial structure and solvency of many insurers, more data has been required to be detailed in the annual statement.

This concern became apparent after the problems surrounding the Equity Funding scandal and increased with the concerns following the Baldwin United insolvency.[2] The insolvency of several primary property and liability insurers due to the failure of their reinsurers caused even more alarm among the regulators.

---

[1] In this chapter, the statutory report required to be filed annually with the various state insurance departments is referred to as the annual statement; the form developed by the NAIC Committee on Blanks used for the preparation and presentation of this annual statement is referred to as the convention blank.

[2] While reinsurance did not cause the insolvencies in either situation, it did play a prominent role as a vehicle for perpetrating one of the many frauds uncovered in the Equity Funding operations and in obscuring the true financial condition of the various insurance companies within the Baldwin United complex.

Throughout the 1980's and early 1990's, insurance regulators, actuaries, and accountants attempted to create uniformity in statutory accounting and to highlight reinsurance transactions in the convention blank. One desired result was to provide enough scrutiny of reinsurance transactions so that true reinsurance transactions be treated as such, while any transactions that are in effect only loans of surplus be treated as loans.[3] A further objective was that a modest audit trail be established to allow examiners and other interested parties to cross-check between the annual statements of the ceding company and of the reinsurer.

This chapter will discuss the reinsurance related entries in the annual statement. The reader may find it helpful to have a copy of a recent annual statement or convention blank at hand when reading this chapter. References to specific pages, exhibits, schedules, or lines are based upon the convention blank used to report for the year ended December 31, 1994. Convention blank format and specifications change annually and the reader is urged to check the latest NAIC and specific state instructions and requirements.

Unless otherwise noted, the discussion in this chapter will focus on statutory accounting for ceded reinsurance. Accounting for retroceded business is identical to that of ceded business. Most accounting for reinsurance assumed is the same as that for direct issues.

BALANCE SHEET

Pages 2 and 3 of the convention blank summarize the assets, liabilities, and surplus and other funds for life insurance companies. Special provision is made for reporting certain reinsurance items.

Assets

Invested assets normally are not affected by the presence or absence of reinsurance. Assets held on behalf of a reinsurer are usually reported as part of other assets of that generic type.

---

[3] The current regulatory standard for allowing reserve or surplus credit from reinsurance ceded is the transfer of all significant risks. See Chapter 10, Reinsurance Regulations.

Line 5 — Policy Loans. Coinsurance treaties usually provide that the reinsurer will not participate in policy loans. However, should the reinsurer share in policy loans, it would include the appropriate amount on this line. An interesting question arises concerning the treatment of such policy loans on the ceding company's statement. There is no specific provision for reduction of this asset even though coinsurance reserves are specifically deducted from the gross reserves in Exhibit 8. The commonly accepted treatment for a ceding company in this situation is to show the net policy loan asset on line 5; this would be the gross policy loans less those funded by the coinsurer.

Line 11 — Reinsurance Ceded. The subdivisions of line 11 summarize amounts due from reinsurers.

Line 11.1 — Amounts recoverable from reinsurers. This item reflects the reinsured portion of benefits which have been paid by the ceding company but not yet reimbursed by the reinsurer. Detail by reinsurer for this item is given in Schedule S, Part 1. This item is repeated in Exhibit 13 — Assets.

Line 11.2 — Commissions and expense allowances due. Normally, amounts shown here are the result of a lag in processing, but they may also represent amounts withheld by the reinsurer under a financial reinsurance treaty. This item is also shown in Exhibit 13 — Assets.

Line 11.3 — Experience rating and other refunds due. This receivable is normally due to the fact that most experience refunds are finalized and paid shortly after the end of the year. This item is also shown in Exhibit 13 — Assets.

Line 21 — Aggregate write-ins for other than invested assets. Accounts receivable representing amounts for funds withheld by the reinsurer may be shown on line 21 for aggregate write ins for other than invested assets.[4] If the amount represents allowances withheld, they would more likely appear on line 11.2; if they represent reserve adjustments or other amounts, line 21 may be more appropriate. The breakdown of the items

---

[4] Trust accounts or letter of credit provided for purposes of securing reserve deductibility are not reflected in the balance sheet.

aggregated on this line, as is the case with all aggregated write-in lines, is detailed at the bottom of the page.

Assumed Reinsurance Issues. Treatment of assumed reinsurance is usually straightforward. Any invested assets are reported with other such assets. Any amounts due the reinsurer are reported on the appropriate line. If premiums are due the reinsurer, they are included on line 14 for life insurance premiums and annuity considerations deferred and uncollected or on line 15 for accident and health premiums due and unpaid. Other amounts due for assumed reinsurance are more appropriately included on line 21.

Liabilities

In general, liability items are developed on a net basis with reference to reinsurance ceded. Liabilities arising from reinsurance assumed are treated just as though they arose from direct insurance policies, unless otherwise specified.

Line 1 — Aggregate reserve for life policies and contracts; Line 2 — Aggregate reserve for accident and health policies. The aggregate reserve for life policies and contracts, net of reinsurance ceded, is shown on line 1 of page 3. A similar reserve for accident and health policies, net of reinsurance ceded, is shown on line 2. The derivation of these amounts is discussed in more detail subsequently in the discussions of Exhibits 8 and 9.

Line 4 — Policy and contract claims; Line 4.1 — Life; Line 4.2 — Accident and health. The amounts shown for policy and contract claims on lines 4.1 and 4.2 are net of amounts recoverable from reinsurers and are developed in Exhibit 11, discussed subsequently.

Line 3 — Supplementary contracts without life contingencies; Line 5 — Policyholders' dividends and coupon accumulations; Line 6 — Policyholder dividends due and unpaid; Line 7 — Provision for policyholder dividends and coupons payable in the following calendar year. As is the case with policy loans, reinsurers seldom participate in supplementary contracts or policyholder dividends. If they do, the amounts shown on lines 3, 5, 6, and 7 are reduced accordingly.

Line 11.3 — Other amounts payable on reinsurance assumed. This item includes refunds payable and modified coinsurance reserve increases payable on reinsurance assumed. Commissions and expense allowances payable are excluded from line 11.3 and shown on line 12A. Claims payable are reflected in line 4 rather than line 11.3.

Line 12A — Commissions and expense allowances payable on reinsurance assumed. Commissions and expense allowances due on reinsurance assumed are shown in this separate line item.

Line 24.2 — Reinsurance in unauthorized companies. This item is the net amount of reserve credit taken for reinsurance in unauthorized companies over the amount of funds withheld, trusteed assets, letters of credit, and other funds held for the benefit of the ceding company. Detail is shown in Schedule S, Part 3b, column 4 less column 7.

The effect of the liability in line 24.2 is to remove any credit for reinsurance ceded given in lines 1, 2, 4, and elsewhere if the reinsurer is unauthorized and no security is provided. The appropriate reserve liability reflects the reinsurance if the treaty offers valid risk transfer, but an additional liability is required due to unauthorized status. In some ways, this liability can be considered to be earmarked surplus.

Line 24.3 — Funds held under reinsurance treaties with unauthorized reinsurers. This is the total amount from Schedule S, Part 3B, columns 5c and 5d, excluding letters of credit and trust agreements, to the extent that these funds were included as part of total assets on page 2 or not offset by a directly related credit offset on page 2.

This liability deals with deposits made by reinsurers to provide reserve credit. As discussed regarding line 24.2, reserve credit is taken in the appropriate liability item, but in this instance, assets are also given to the ceding company to secure the credit. Thus, the ceding company has both decreased liabilities and increased assets. The effect of the liability on line 24.3 is to avoid double-counting the effect of the transaction in surplus. Mod-co avoids this need as reserve liabilities are not reduced when the assets are paid to the ceding company.

Only deposited assets are included in this account. Letters of credit and trusts are not shown as assets on page 2 of the ceding company's annual statement.

Line 25 — Aggregate write-ins for liabilities. Any other amounts due reinsurers, such as those under a funds withheld arrangement with an admitted reinsurer, are usually shown as a write-in item on line 25, and detailed below.

Surplus and Other Funds

With regard to the balance sheet, reinsurance does not change surplus directly. Instead, the effect of reinsurance on each of the various liabilities and assets will affect the level of surplus. In the absence of other events, if a reinsurance transaction causes an asset to increase or a liability to decrease, surplus will increase. Likewise, a transaction which causes an asset to decrease or a liability to increase will cause surplus to decrease.

SUMMARY OF OPERATIONS

The Summary of Operations is shown on page 4 of the convention blank and the Analysis of Operations by Line of Business is shown on page 6. The comments which apply to page 4 also apply to page 6.

Income Items

Line 1 — Premium and annuity considerations. The premiums and annuity considerations shown on line 1 include premiums on reinsurance assumed and are net of premiums on reinsurance ceded. Line 1 must agree with Exhibit 1, Part 1, line 20d, column 1 less column 11.

Line 1A — Deposit-type funds. Should deposit-type funds be ceded to a reinsurer, the ceded amount would be deducted from the gross amount to determine this line item. For reinsurers, assumed amounts would be included in this amount.

Line 5 — Commissions and expense allowances on reinsurance ceded. The total from Exhibit 1, Part 2, line 25a, column 1, is entered on this line. For a ceding company, any amounts reimbursed for premium taxes are included in allowances on line 5.

Line 5A — Reserve adjustments on reinsurance ceded. This line normally reflects the modified coinsurance adjustment due from the reinsurer. It should be remembered that this item includes the increase in reserve less the appropriate investment income. This may be viewed as balancing other income items; the investment income portion of the modified coinsurance adjustment is included in the ceding company's net investment income on line 4 and the reserve increase is included in the amount shown on line 17.

Line 6 — Aggregate write-ins for miscellaneous income. This line is used for a variety of reinsurance related items. Some companies use this line to include allowances on annuity deposits reported on line 1A or for initial allowances when blocks of inforce business are ceded. Experience refunds earned are generally included here. Details are shown below in the *DETAILS OF WRITE-INS AGGREGATED AT ITEM 6 FOR MISCELLANEOUS INCOME* at the bottom of page 4.

Benefit and Expense Items

Lines 8 through 18 — Benefit payments and reserve items. All incurred benefit payments and increases in aggregate reserves on lines 8 through 18 are reported net of reinsurance ceded, including that ceded in unauthorized companies, and inclusive of reinsurance assumed.

Line 20 — Commissions on premiums and annuity considerations. This line excludes commissions on reinsurance ceded and assumed.

Line 21 — Commissions and expense allowances on reinsurance assumed. Amounts for reinsurance assumed from Exhibit 1, Part 2, line 26b, column 1 less column 11, is shown in this line. Some reinsurers include experience refunds incurred on this line.

Line 22 — General insurance expenses. The normal administrative expenses of reinsurance ceded and assumed are included in general expenses on line 22.

Line 23 — Insurance taxes, licenses, and fees. The premium tax on reinsurance assumed normally is included in line 23. In some instances, the reinsurer makes no specific allowance for premium tax reimbursement, but grants an overall allowance for all expenses. In such a situation, the total allowance should be included in line 21 and line 23 would reflect a zero amount for that reinsurance transaction.

Line 25 — Aggregate write-ins for deductions. This line may be used for a variety of reinsurance related items. Experience refunds incurred by reinsurers may be included here, as might amounts incurred under modified coinsurance adjustments. Ceding companies may use this line to reflect the amount of reserves transferred to reinsurers under an agreement covering an inforce block of insurance for surplus relief, rather than recording this amount on line 1 as premiums and considerations.

CAPITAL AND SURPLUS ACCOUNT

The Capital and Surplus Account is shown on page 4 following the Summary of Operations. A reconciliation of the change in capital and surplus funds for the year is provided. The effects of reinsurance, as reflected in the Summary of Operations, are included in the net income entered on line 35.

Line 38 — Change in liability for reinsurance in unauthorized companies. The change in the liability for reinsurance ceded in unauthorized companies is reflected on line 38 of the Capital and Surplus Account. Any change in liability for reinsurance ceded to unauthorized reinsurers is thus reflected directly in surplus and not in the Summary of Operations.

Line 46 — Aggregate write-in for gains and losses in surplus. The Life and Health Reinsurance Agreements Model Regulation makes specific provision for entries into this line when inforce business is ceded from a company. The net gain after tax from the initial transaction is entered into line 46. This amount may be calculated as the product of (1 minus the tax rate) and the pre-tax gain.

The expected tax amount, calculated as the product of the tax rate and the pre-tax gain, is entered in line 5, Commissions and expense allowances on reinsurance ceded, of the Summary of Operations. The tax liability will flow through on line 30, Federal income taxes incurred, of the Summary of Operations. Thus, the entire after-tax surplus gain on the effective date of the agreement goes directly to surplus without passing through the Summary of Operation.

The treatment for renewal periods is to recognize the gains through the Summary of Operations as they would have been without the reinsurance, less any expense and profit charges for the reinsurer and different tax effects. This amount may be calculated as the product of the after-tax rate and an amount equal to the pre-reinsurance gains on the business less any expense and profit charge to the reinsurer less any experience refunds credited to the ceding company. This amount is entered in line 5 as an allowance on reinsurance ceded. The experience refund is reported on line 6, Aggregate write-in for miscellaneous income.

The amount entered in line 5 is entered in line 46 of the Capital and Surplus Account, but as a negative of the line 5 amount. In effect, the portion of the surplus relief earned in that year is transferred from surplus and recognized in earnings.

There is no similar effect in the reinsurer's Capital and Surplus Account. All items are reflected in the appropriate line of the Summary of Operations and the net effect enters into the Capital and Surplus as part of the company's overall gains and losses.

Other Items. Reinsurance seldom has a direct influence on the other items of the capital and surplus account, but under special circumstances, it may. For example, some insurers reflect any change in contingency or deficiency reserves directly through surplus as a write-in on line 46 rather than through a change in reserves in the Summary of Operations. If this technique is followed, the change so reflected should be net of any credits for ceded contingency or deficiency reserves. Similarly, changes in reserves due to changes in valuation basis are reflected directly in surplus on line 39 and should be net of reinsurance.

CASH FLOW

The Cash Flow analysis appears on page 5. All reinsurance items should be reflected on the appropriate lines as cash actually received or disbursed, for both ceded and assumed reinsurance transactions. Since incurred and non-cash items are not shown in this analysis, there may be significant differences in the amounts shown relative to the corresponding items in the Summary of Operations. For example, amounts withheld do not affect the cash flow reporting.

One reinsurance item that is highlighted is on line 4, Allowances and reserve adjustments received on reinsurance ceded. This item consists of the sum of the cash portions of the amounts shown on page 4, line 5A, Reserve adjustment on reinsurance ceded, plus Exhibit 1, Part 2, column 1, line 26A, Reinsurance ceded commissions and expense allowance incurred, plus the change in line 11.2, Reinsurance commissions and expense allowances due, from page 2.

EXHIBITS

There are fourteen exhibits in the convention blank which support the Balance Sheet and the Summary of Operations. Reinsurance transactions may have a direct effect on the first twelve exhibits.

Exhibit 1, Part 1: Premium and Annuity Considerations

Exhibit 1 shows first year, single, and renewal premiums by line of business for the insurance company. Separate classification is provided for both reinsurance assumed and reinsurance ceded for deferred and uncollected premiums and for collected premiums. Total premiums are developed for first year, single, and renewal categories, and within these are shown for direct business, reinsurance ceded, and reinsurance assumed.

In most traditional reinsurance applications, reinsurance premiums are paid on an annual basis or on a monthly risk premium basis, resulting in no deferred premiums. Therefore any items shown in the breakdown of deferred and uncollected premiums for lines 3 and 13 for reinsurance ceded or assumed are normally unpaid premium items under traditional reinsurance arrangements. If reinsurance premiums are paid on a modal basis other than annual, as in some traditional treaties or in many financial reinsurance arrangements, both deferred and uncollected premiums are reflected in the reinsurance lines.

Exhibit 1, Part 2: Dividends and Coupons Applied, Reinsurance Commissions and Expense Allowances and Commissions Incurred

Reinsurance commissions and expense allowances incurred are summarized in Exhibit 1, Part 2. Separate lines are provided for ceded and assumed for first year, single, and renewal commissions and expense allowances. Experience refunds on reinsurance may be treated as allowances in the annual statement. If so, the appropriate amounts would be included in this part of the exhibit. This treatment is consistent with United States federal income tax practice regarding experience refunds.

The total ceded commissions and expense allowances are recorded on line 5 of the Summary of Operations while the total commissions and expense allowances on reinsurance assumed are recorded on line 21 of the Summary of Operations.

Exhibits 2, 3, and 4: Investment Income and Capital Gains and Losses

There are no special entries in these exhibits for reinsurance ceded or assumed. The nature of the reinsurance agreement will have an effect on assets. Transactions which increase invested assets will normally increase investment income and transactions which decrease assets will tend to decrease investment income.

Investment income pertaining to modified coinsurance is a part of the overall net investment income for the ceding company, and is not separately identified in its annual statement. The reinsurer does not include any amounts in investment income for mod-co.

Exhibit 5: General Expenses

The general administrative expenses associated with reinsurance ceded and assumed are incorporated with direct expenses shown in this exhibit. Any unusual expenses incurred as a result of reinsurance operations could be included in the aggregate write-in on line 9.3.

Exhibit 6: Taxes, Licenses and Fees

Specific reimbursement of premium taxes for reinsurance assumed are included in the amount reported on line 3 for premium taxes on direct premiums. Any premium tax reimbursed on reinsurance ceded would be reported in Exhibit 1 as reinsurance allowances.

Exhibit 7: Dividends and Coupons to Policyholders

This exhibit would include any amounts for dividends or coupons incurred for reinsurance assumed less corresponding incurrals of reimbursements for reinsurance ceded.

Exhibit 8: Aggregate Reserve for Life Policies and Contracts

Exhibit 8 shows the aggregate reserve for life policies and contracts by valuation basis for each benefit type and line of business. The reserves on reinsurance assumed are combined with those for direct business under the appropriate valuation basis, benefit type, and line of business. The reserve credit for reinsurance ceded is shown in total by benefit type and line of business. The reserve credit for reinsurance ceded includes that for reinsurance ceded in unauthorized reinsurers, as noted previously.

Only coinsurance and YRT reserves are reflected in Exhibit 8. The total net reserve in Exhibit 8 goes to line 1 on page 3. The total credits for reserves on reinsurance ceded should balance to the amounts detailed in Schedule S.

Exhibit 9: Aggregate Reserve for Accident and Health Policies

Exhibit 9 shows the aggregate reserve for accident and health policies by type of reserve and by line of business or type of policy. As was true in Exhibit 8, reserves for reinsurance assumed are included in the totals for direct business and should balance to those detailed in Schedule S. The reserve credit for reinsurance ceded is shown in total and for each line of business or policy type, but is not segregated by type of reserve. The net reserve is carried to page 3, line 2.

Exhibit 10: Deposit Funds and Other Liabilities Without Life or Disability Contingencies

Exhibit 10 shows the deposit funds and other liabilities without life or disability contingencies by line of business. Part A shows details of liabilities net of reinsurance ceded and includes any liabilities for reinsurance assumed. Part B shows the total deductions taken for reinsurance ceded for the current and previous year.

Exhibit 11: Policy and Contract Claims, Part 1

This exhibit details claims by line of business. Part 1 shows the net claims liability at the end of the current year together with the components for direct business, reinsurance assumed, and reinsurance ceded. The net liability, separated as to life and accident and health coverages, is carried to lines 4.1 and 4.2 on page 3. The credits for reinsurance ceded are listed by company in Schedule S.

Exhibit 11: Policy and Contract Claims, Part 2

Part 2 of Exhibit 11 develops the net claims incurred during the year together with the components for direct business, reinsurance assumed, and reinsurance ceded. The net incurred claims, separated as to benefit type, are carried to the appropriate lines of the Summary of Operations.

Exhibit 12: Reconciliation of Ledger Assets

Exhibit 12 shows the development of increases and decreases in ledger assets, reconciling the current year ledger assets with the previous year. Premium and benefit items are shown net of reinsurance.

Line 9 — Commissions and expense allowances on reinsurance ceded. This entry is developed in Exhibit 1, Part 2, column 1 total for reinsurance ceded.

Line 9A — Reserve adjustments on reinsurance ceded. This item represents the reserve increase received from reinsurers on modified coinsurance ceded. This item was reported on page 4, line 5A.

Line 12 — Aggregate write-ins for increases in ledger assets. Changes in ledger assets due to reinsurance transactions, such as surplus relief are reflected in this line.

Line 22A — Commissions and expense allowances on reinsurance assumed. This entry is developed in Exhibit 1, Part 2, column 1 as the total for reinsurance assumed.

Exhibit 13: Assets

Exhibit 13 recaps the assets shown on the Balance Sheet, dividing them into ledger assets, non-ledger assets, assets not admitted, and the net admitted assets. The lines in this exhibit correspond to the lines on page 2 and the admitted assets from this exhibit should agree with the counterparts on page 2, by line and in total.

SCHEDULES

Reinsurance ceded and assumed amounts are directly recognized in Schedules H, S, and T of the convention blank.

Schedule H: Accident and Health Exhibit

Schedule H summarizes the experience and reserves for accident and health insurance by line of business and type of policy and is divided into four parts.

Part 1 — Analysis of underwriting operations. This portion develops the underwriting gain. All values shown include reinsurance assumed and are net of reinsurance ceded.

Part 2 — Reserves and liabilities. This portion shows the reserves and liabilities for accident and health insurance. Premium reserves, policy reserves, and claim reserves and liabilities are shown, inclusive of reinsurance assumed and net of reinsurance ceded.

Part 3 — Test of the previous year's claim reserves and liabilities. Again, all figures shown are net of ceded reinsurance and include reinsurance assumed.

Part 4 — Reinsurance. Premiums written, premiums earned, incurred claims, and commissions are shown separately by line of business and type of policy for reinsurance assumed and for reinsurance ceded. No net numbers are developed.

Statutory Accounting for Reinsurance 345

Schedule S: Reinsurance

Schedule S itemizes information relative to all reinsurance, both ceded and assumed, by specific treaty. It is divided into several parts. Each part of Schedule S is divided so as to show the information separately for affiliate reinsurers and non-affiliate reinsurers. Each treaty with each company is identified in the appropriate parts of the schedule by the company's federal ID number, the effective date of the treaty, the company's name, and the location (city and state or country) of the company. This information is used by the insurance department staff to compare corresponding items in the ceding company's and reinsurer's annual statements and to verify the authorized status of reinsurers.

Part 1 — Amounts Recoverable on Paid and Unpaid Loss for All Reinsurance Ceded. Part 1 is a schedule for reinsurance ceded showing the amounts recoverable for paid and unpaid losses by treaty as of the end of the year. Paid and unpaid amounts are shown in separate columns. Separate lists and totals are shown for life and for accident and health. While amounts are shown by specific treaty, a treaty is not listed in this part unless there is a claim amount due or pending at the end of the year.

The total of amounts recoverable on paid losses for reinsurance ceded is shown on line 11.1 of page 2. This represents amounts paid by the ceding company which have not yet been reimbursed by the reinsurer and are normally a result of lags in payment.

The amounts recoverable on unpaid losses should agree with the total shown in Exhibit 11, Part 1 for reinsurance ceded. These amounts represent the reinsured portion of claims still pending or in the course of settlement and therefore not yet paid.

Part 2 — All Accident and Health Ceded. Part 2 is another ceded schedule listing certain values for each ceded accident and health reinsurance treaty as of December 31. The code for the line of business and type of reinsurance, premiums, unearned premiums, and the reserve credit for other than unearned premiums is shown.

Again, these listings and totals are separated for affiliates and non-affiliates. Grand totals are developed and should agree with the appropriate parts of Exhibit 1, Part 1 and Exhibit 9.

Part 3A — Reinsurance Ceded for All Life Insurance and Related Benefits. Part 3A lists certain information for reinsurance ceded on all life insurance and related benefits. This shows, by contract, the line of business and type of reinsurance code, the amount of reinsurance inforce, current and previous years' reserve credit, and ceded premiums. The total of the amount inforce at the end of the year corresponds to the reinsurance ceded at the end of the year shown on line 21 of the Exhibit of Life Insurance. The reserve credit taken should correspond to the reinsurance ceded totals of Exhibits 8, 9, and 10. The premiums should correspond to the appropriate lines in Exhibit 1, Part 1.

Part 3B — Data on Life and Accident and Health Reinsurance in Unauthorized Companies. Part 3B shows certain balance sheet and other items for life and accident and health reinsurance in unauthorized companies. Information is shown separately for life and accident and health coverages, identifying the reinsurer and the treaty.

Items shown are the reserve credit taken, any amounts recoverable on paid and unpaid losses, other debits, deposits by and funds withheld from reinsurers, and other miscellaneous credit balances. Any security for reinsurance ceded reserves are identified further as to whether the security is in the form of a letter of credit, a trust agreement, funds deposited by or withheld from the reinsurer, or another arrangement.

The excess, if any, of the sum of the reserve credit taken, the amounts recoverable on paid and unpaid losses, and the other debits over the sum of the deposits by and funds withheld from the reinsurer and the other miscellaneous credit balances is developed separately for each treaty. The sum of the positive excesses only is entered on line 24.2 of page 3 and represents that portion of the total reserve credits taken which is not admissible.

Any reserve or other credits for reinsurance in an unauthorized company is still taken in the same manner as credits for reinsurance in authorized companies. It is in Part 3B that the separate liability is developed for page 3, line 24.2. This additional liability is required because the reinsurer is not authorized and the insurance department cannot be as certain of collection as it would be with an authorized insurer. The net result is that surplus credit is allowed only to the extent of funds arising from the treaty which are readily available to the ceding company.

An unauthorized company is one which is not admitted either as a direct writer or as a reinsurer in the state of domicile of the ceding company. If the reinsurer is admitted in every one of the United States except the ceding company's domicile, it is still unauthorized. The domicile of the reinsurer has no direct influence on authorized status; it may be domiciled in another of the United States or in another country.

Part 3C, Section 1 — Data on Reinsurance Assumed for Life Insurance and Related Benefits. Part 3C, Section 1 shows information for reinsurance assumed on life insurance and other related benefits for each treaty. It shows the line of business and type of reinsurance code, amount of enforce at the end of the year, the reserve, premiums, and reinsurance payable on paid and unpaid losses. This is basically the comparable data to that which is developed in Part 3A for ceded life insurance and related benefits.

The total premiums should agree with Exhibit 1, Part 1, line 20b, columns 2 through 7. The total reinsurance payable on paid and unpaid losses should agree with Exhibit 11, Part 1.

Part 3C, Section 2 — Data on Reinsurance Assumed for Accident and Health. Section 2 of Part 3C shows data for reinsurance assumed on accident and health insurance for each treaty. It shows the line of business and type of reinsurance code, premiums, unearned premiums, reserve liabilities other than unearned premiums, and reinsurance payable on paid and unpaid losses, paralleling the data developed in Part 2 for ceded business.

The total premiums should agree with Exhibit 1, Part 1, line 20b, columns 8 through 10. The total reinsurance payable on paid and unpaid losses should agree with Exhibit 11, Part 1.

Part 3D — Five Year Exhibit of Reinsurance Ceded Business. Part 3D is divided into three sections and provides a five year history of reinsurance ceded. The purpose is to quickly show reinsurance trends. Section A covers operating items such as premiums, commissions and expense allowances, claims and other benefit payments, and the increase in reserves for reinsurance ceded.

Section B contains balance sheet items such a deferred and uncollected premiums, aggregate reserves, unpaid claims, amounts recoverable, and unpaid commissions and expense allowances for ceded reinsurance.

Section C covers reinsurance in unauthorized companies, separating amounts into funds withheld, letters of credit, trust agreements, and other.

Part 3E — Restatement of Balance Sheet to Identify Credit for Reinsurance Ceded. In this section, page 2 and page 3 items are shown as reported. The adjustments made for reinsurance ceded are highlighted, and the amounts are restated gross of reinsurance. The net credit items for reinsurance ceded are shown at the bottom of the section. This section permits the reader to quickly determine the effect of ceded reinsurance on the financial stability of the company.

Schedule T: Premium and Annuity Considerations

Schedule T allocates direct premiums and annuity considerations by state and territory; separate columns are used for life insurance premiums, annuity considerations, and accident and health insurance premiums.

Premiums for reinsurance assumed and reinsurance ceded are not allocated by state or territory but are added to and subtracted from the grand total at the end of the schedule. The total for direct premiums should agree with that in Exhibit 1, Part 1; reinsurance ceded and assumed totals in Schedule T may not agree with those in Exhibit 1 since Schedule T may not reflect large reinsurance transactions on inforce blocks.

OTHER ANNUAL STATEMENT ITEMS

Reinsurance affects three other analyses in the convention blank.

Analysis of Increase in Reserves and Deposit Funds During the Year

The analysis of the increase in reserves is shown on page 7. All items in this analysis are shown net of reinsurance. For example, reserves are shown net of ceded coinsurance amounts, but including the mod-co reserves held by the ceding company. The analysis includes any amounts for coinsurance and YRT assumed.

Exhibit 8A: Changes in Basis of Valuation During the Year

Any changes in the valuation basis of reinsurance assumed are shown in this exhibit. The changes shown are also net of any reinsurance ceded reserve credits.

Exhibit of Life Insurance

The Exhibit of Life Insurance on page 21 shows the increases and decreases in the life insurance inforce, number of policies, and current death benefits during the year separately for industrial, ordinary, credit, and group insurance. Reinsurance assumed during the year is shown on line 3. Deductions during the year for death, maturity, disability, expire, surrender, lapse, conversion, and all other decreases include those for reinsurance assumed. Any assumed reinsurance which is recaptured during the year is shown on line 17. The amount of reinsurance ceded at the end of the year is shown on line 21, but the number of policies affected is not given.

OTHER CONSIDERATIONS

Self-Administration

Because of the limited amount of data which is received on self-administered treaties, the reinsurance valuation actuary may be faced with many special problems. The information provided may consist only of summaries with very little detail. The reinsurer likely will rely on the accuracy of the information provided by the ceding company.

In most instances the reinsurer will review the information provided for reasonableness and ask questions of the ceding company as needed. The information will then be included in the various exhibits and schedules. The audit trails provided are different than those normally used by insurance companies. New procedures and audit practices will be required to handle self-administered accounts. This should not cause a problem, but individuals who participate in assembling financial statements should be aware that information will be gathered and documented in a different manner.

The ceding company should be aware that it is responsible not only for the reinsurance data in its own statement, but for corresponding information in its reinsurer's statement. This is different than the situation with individual cession reinsurance where the reinsurer has enough data to prepare its own statements independently.

Financial Reinsurance

Financial reinsurance should be treated the same as any other type of reinsurance for statutory accounting purposes. All entries in the annual statement should be made with equal care and attention to detail. Most financial reinsurance is self-administered so the considerations discussed earlier for self-administration apply.

In many instances, financial reinsurance is expected to be short term in nature, so attempts are sometimes made to avoid distortions in the annual statement. For example, the ceding company might use an aggregate write-in line rather than the premium line to show the transfer of a large amount of initial reserves. A reinsurer might choose to net an initial premium under a mod-co treaty with the initial mod-co adjustment in order to minimize the distortions to the elements of its statutory earnings and cash flow.

Statement of Actuarial Opinion

Reinsurance is an important element to consider in forming the actuary's statement of opinion as to the adequacy of a company's reserves. The considerations of the actuaries of the ceding company and the reinsurer are different, but somewhat parallel. The mechanics of the process are described elsewhere in this book, but a brief discussion of some of the issues involved is appropriate.

Reliance. The ceding company's actuary can generally obtain all of the data necessary to form an opinion regarding reserve credits. The assuming company's actuary is not always in the same position. Frequently, especially when dealing with self-administered reinsurance, the reinsurer relies on the ceding company for all data, including the calculation of the statutory reserves and other actuarial items. In such cases it is common for the reinsurer's actuary to rely upon the ceding company's actuary as to the accuracy, appropriateness, and adequacy of the reserves and other items for the block of business reinsured.

Statutory Accounting for Reinsurance

The preferred practice is for the ceding company's actuary to provide the reinsurer with a statement that, in his opinion, the reserves and other actuarial items are calculated in accordance with generally accepted actuarial standards, meet the standards of the relevant jurisdictions, and make a good and sufficient provision for the policy obligations. The reinsurer's actuary then includes a statement of reliance on this statement of opinion in the appropriate section of his own opinion.

This practice does not allow the reinsurer's actuary to rely blindly on such an opinion. For example, if the reserves clearly do not meet minimum standards or are inadequate, the actuary should not opine that they do. The terms and benefits of a reinsurance treaty may be different than those of the direct policies underlying the reinsurance. The actuarial opinion of the reinsurer must address its own liabilities, not those of the ceding company.

Qualified or Limited Opinions. The actuary of either company may find himself in a position where he must give a qualified or limited opinion. For example, a ceding company's actuary may be uncertain about the recoverability of benefits from a reinsurer, or may believe that a given treaty does not transfer adequate risk. In this case, he may qualify his opinion appropriately, stating his reasons or concerns.

Likewise, a reinsurer's actuary may qualify his opinion if he is uncertain about the derivation, accuracy, or adequacy of reserve amounts given him by a ceding company. In some instances, the ceding company will not produce information in time for the reinsurer to use it in its statement. In such a situation, it would be appropriate for the reinsurer's actuary to qualify his opinion stating that the reserves for certain blocks of assumed reinsurance had not been reviewed due to lack of available information. Another approach would be to limit his opinion by stating that it excluded such blocks of business. In either event, the amount and classification of the reserves in question should be identified.

Valuation Actuary. For the most part, the valuation actuary for the reinsurer has the same considerations and concerns as any other valuation actuary. In the end, he must give his opinion as to whether or not the reserves established make good and sufficient provision for all obligations of the company. On the other hand, the ceding company's actuary must consider whether his company can rely upon its reinsurers to perform and whether or not any meaningful risk transfer results from each reinsurance agreement.

In July 1989, the Actuarial Standards Board adopted Actuarial Standard of Practice No. 11 (ASP 11), entitled The Treatment of Reinsurance Transactions in Life and Health Insurance Company Financial Statements. This standard applies to any financial statements prepared for periods beginning after December 15, 1989. It applies not only to statutory, but also to GAAP and other financial statements.

The standard defines net statement liabilities to be the reserves, net of reinsurance reserve credits, plus any other liabilities, such as amounts due reinsurers, less any other assets arising from reinsurance transactions, such as amounts receivable from reinsurers. In GAAP accounting, the deferred acquisition cost asset is part of the net liability reviewed by the actuary. ASP 11 holds that it is the responsibility of the ceding company and the reinsurer to establish net statement liabilities for their respective obligations.

These net statement liabilities must satisfy all legal, accounting, and valuation requirements for the accounting system under consideration. These liabilities must also make appropriate provision for all unmatured obligations according to the actuary's best estimate of future experience. The net statement liability of the ceding company plus the net statement liability of the reinsurer may be more or less than that which the ceding company would hold if no reinsurance had taken place.

In determining the net statement liabilities, the actuary should review all financial features and ascertain that all risks transferred are recognized in determining reinsurance credits and net liabilities. The actuary must review all potential cash flows, understand and consider all contingent payments, and understand agreements when conditions of reinsurance do not parallel original insurance. If, during the review, additional assets and liabilities beyond reserves and other actuarial items arise, these must be considered in arriving at conclusions about net statement liabilities. In developing the net statement liabilities, any conditions where the indemnification responsibility of the reinsurer expires prior to termination of the benefits of the underlying policies must be considered, especially if the reinsurance can be terminated at the option of either party.

Statutory Accounting for Reinsurance

If the future obligations of the ceding company to the reinsurer exceed the ceding company's expected revenues, an additional liability may be indicated. The actuary must also consider the likelihood of collection and may wish to review the appropriate regulations concerning security for reinsurance. In particular, the ceding company's valuation actuary must look to the asset and interest guarantees made if the treaty involves mod-co or funds deposited with or held by the ceding company. Any guarantees must be included in the calculation of obligations and future cash flows.

The actuary may use cash flow testing to confirm the sufficiency of net statement liabilities, taking into account all aspects of policy and reinsurance cash flows. The actuary must demonstrate that all work conforms to the standard and provide adequate documentation. Any deviations from the standard must be disclosed with a statement concerning the nature, rationale, and the effect of the deviation.

Cash flow testing cannot be used to justify establishing reserves lower than the minimums required by law. Likewise, it is inappropriate to use reinsurance and projected high asset performance or low assumed persistency to circumvent minimum standards for reserves.

Any valuation actuary who has responsibility for reinsurance, either ceded or assumed, should read and be familiar with this standard.

Regulation. The valuation actuary must consider the regulatory standards and requirements of his company's state of domicile and other states which exert jurisdiction. In addition to satisfying minimum standards, certain other standards may apply.

For example, the Life and Health Reinsurance Agreements Model Regulation requires that the ceding insurer's valuation actuary "consider this regulation and any applicable actuarial standards when determining the proper credit" for reinsurance. This model regulation further requires that the actuary maintain adequate documentation, be prepared to describe the actuarial work performed, and demonstrate conformity with the regulation.

Future Trends

As stated at the beginning of the chapter, the Convention blank format and specifications change annually. While the Model Regulation on

Reinsurance contains accounting guidance, not all states have adopted it, or have adopted only portions of the Model. Consequently, there are variations by state. The NAIC is working toward a codification of statutory accounting into a comprehensive basis.

On September 19, 1994, the Technical Resource Sub-Group (TRG) to the Life Codification of Statutory Accounting Principles Working Group of the NAIC published a report on guidelines for modified coinsurance and coinsurance with funds withheld. In the report, the TRG recommends different accounting treatment for the two transactions.

For a mod-co transaction, the TRG recommends that the ceding company reduce premium income by premiums paid or payable to the reinsurer, net of experience refunds. Policy benefits paid by the reinsurer will reduce the ceding company's policy benefits. The expense allowances would be reported separately in the Summary of Operations, and the mod-co reserves would be included with the policy reserves. The mod-co reserve adjustment would be reported as a separate item in the Summary of Operations.

In a funds withheld coinsurance transaction, the treatment of premiums, benefits, and expense allowances would follow the mod-co treatment. The policy reserves would be reduced by the portion assumed by the reinsurer. The ceding company would establish a separate liability for the amounts withheld, with any interest due or payable recorded as interest on indebtedness.

For the reinsurer in a mod-co transaction, the statutory policy reserves would exclude the mod-co reserve, and the mod-co adjustment would be reported separately in the Summary of Operations. In a funds withheld transaction, the reinsurer would include the policy reserves and record the funds withheld as an accounts receivable. Any interest earned or receivable would be recorded as miscellaneous income.

The TRG further recommended that Schedule S be modified to separately report the amounts of the mod-co reserve and the funds withheld under coinsurance.

The TRG also recommended that the Risk Based Capital (RBC) Working Group should review and modify the C-2 and C-4 risk formulas to recognize the differences in the contracts with respect to the amount at risk. The TRG also recommended that the IRIS Ratio #12, Change in Reserve, should be reviewed and modified to reflect the differences in the contracts.

13 GAAP Accounting for Reinsurance

Generally Accepted Accounting Principles (GAAP) are the basis of an accounting system which is separate and different from statutory accounting.[1] Where statutory accounting is concerned primarily with solvency and security of policyholders, GAAP is used to estimate economic results and value of a company, primarily from the shareholders' position.

GAAP accounting is required for any company whose shares are publicly traded in the United States, regardless of country of incorporation.[2] Any other company, including mutual life insurers and privately

---

[1] A number of publications which address GAAP for insurance companies and reinsurance are available. These include Ernst and Ernst [5] and Robertson [20], as well as various statements and standards of the Financial Accounting Standards Board and pronouncements of the Securities and Exchange Commission.

[2] United States GAAP is discussed in this chapter. GAAP in other countries, including Canada, the United Kingdom, and Germany, have different rules and standards. If a foreign company's shares are traded in the United States, it must produce financial reports on both its domestic GAAP basis and the United States GAAP basis.

held stock companies, must follow the same standards and principles if it wishes to state that its financial reports have been prepared in accordance with GAAP.

Largely because of the long term nature of life insurance and annuity products, special guidelines apply to GAAP accounting for life insurers. In many ways, reinsurance is simply another line of life insurance business, but certain idiosyncrasies of reinsurance lead to different procedures. This chapter is intended to provide insight into the major principles of GAAP as applied to reinsurance.

GAAP accounting varies between countries. Unless otherwise noted, GAAP, as used in this book, refers to GAAP accounting standards as applied in the United States.

BACKGROUND

GAAP accounting differs from statutory accounting in its purpose and its application. Where statutory accounting is centered on issues of solvency and security for policyholders, GAAP is intended to provide a "best estimate" of the economic value of a company and its operations. Statutory accounting has specific rules, especially for minimum reserves, and utilizes seriatim valuation of assets and liabilities; GAAP accounting has guidelines and tolerates more modeling of liabilities.

GAAP requires the establishment of benefit reserves, maintenance expense reserves, and deferred acquisition cost assets (DAC), all calculated with GAAP assumptions. Benefit reserves provide for the present value of future policyholder or contract benefits, less the present value of "benefit premiums." Expense reserves provide for the present value of future maintenance expenses in excess of the present value of "expense premiums." DAC is a provision for unrecovered acquisition expenses which were deferred at time of issue or reinsurance.

In most instances, the two reserve items are liabilities and DAC is an asset. The sum of benefit reserves and expense reserves, less the DAC balance, is the net liability.

GAAP AND REINSURANCE

GAAP for insurance companies is governed by the general guidelines of GAAP and the Statements of Financial Accounting Standards promulgat-

GAAP Accounting for Reinsurance

ed by the Financial Accounting Standards Board (FASB). FASB Statement Numbers 60, 97, 91, 109, 113, 115, and 120, in particular, are applicable to insurance companies, for both direct operations and reinsurance transactions.[3] Accounting treatment may vary depending on which FASB Statement is applicable to a policy form, as discussed later.

Robertson's papers[4] offer the most detailed discussion of GAAP as applied to reinsurance of traditional products. Actuarial Standard of Practice 11 (ASB 11) is also relevant for actuarial aspects of GAAP accounting, in particular, benefit reserves and deferred acquisition cost (DAC) assets.

General Considerations

One of the central points of Robertson's papers is that the approach to GAAP accounting for reinsurance should vary by the type of the reinsurance involved (YRT, coinsurance, or mod-co) and by the position of the company (ceding company or reinsurer). The basic tenet of GAAP for reinsurance has been to recognize income in proportion to revenues. Reinsurance is subject to more variability than any other product line. Some products, such as a traditional YRT plan, may produce no statutory surplus strain and perhaps even a profit at issue, while some produce significant strain. The degree of adjustment required for restatement from statutory to GAAP will vary accordingly. Therefore, generalization is difficult.

There is also the question of materiality. The vast majority of reinsurance accepted is in companies that make reinsurance a major line of business. In those cases, it would seem obvious that GAAP should be uniquely defined for the reinsurance line. However, many companies find that the ceded portion of their business is relatively small and immaterial in the overall financial reporting, and therefore not deserving of extensive effort.

Some state insurance regulators have endorsed the concept of mirror image reserves for statutory purposes, suggesting a system

---

[3] It is assumed that the reader is familiar with GAAP principles and pronouncements. Other pronouncements are relevant to life and health insurance companies; the ones listed mentioned herein are those which have the greatest effect and interest.

[4] See Robertson [20].

whereby reserve factors are identical for the ceding and accepting companies. This clearly is not a valid approach for GAAP.

The assumptions a ceding company uses across an entire block of business may be inappropriate for the reinsurer on the reinsured portion of that same business. This is obvious for items such as expense factors, commission and allowance patterns, and other acquisition costs are considered. Different mortality or persistency assumptions may be appropriate on the reinsured and retained portions of the business. If reinsurance ceded is a small portion of its business, there is no need for the ceding company to develop unique assumptions for its ceded business.

The reinsurer most likely will have different assumptions, applicable to either that specific business or to its overall reinsurance assumed. Because of this, it is unlikely that the GAAP reserves, for either benefits or expenses, would be the same for the ceding company and the reinsurer on any block of business.

The seven FASB statements mentioned above directly relate to life insurance and, therefore, to reinsurance. The principles outlined in these pronouncements are applicable to direct issued business, ceded or retroceded business, and assumed reinsurance business. Sometimes, the nature of the reinsurance will cause the reinsured business to have a different character than the underlying direct issues.

FASB Statement No. 60

FASB Statement No. 60 is the basic pronouncement regarding GAAP accounting for life and health insurance. As later modified by FASB Statement No. 97, Statement 60 defines GAAP accounting for traditional life and health products, such as term insurance, whole life, individual disability income, fixed benefit payout annuities, and certain participating life sold by stock insurers.

Statement 60 calls for recognition of variable sales costs, such as commissions, allowances, and underwriting expenses, over the premium paying period of the policy. In general, these costs are recognized as level percentages of premiums based on GAAP assumptions applicable at the issuance of the policy. All acquisition costs must be amortized over the premium paying life of limited pay policies. The assumptions are "locked in" at issue and are changed only for loss recognition, that

GAAP Accounting for Reinsurance

is, if the net GAAP liability is insufficient to fund future benefits under the original assumptions.

However, even though acquisition expenses must be amortized over the premium paying period, profits must be recognized proportionately over the life of the policy. This involves deferring some of the profit from the premium paying period to the paid-up period.[5] In practice, the amounts to be deferred sometimes are so small that they can be ignored as immaterial.

Statement 60 defines short-duration and long-duration contracts, with differing GAAP accounting guidelines for each. Accounting for reinsurance transactions of short- or long-duration contracts usually, but not always, follows the treatment of the direct product. Examples of short-duration contracts include group term life and most credit life and disability products. Examples of long-duration contracts include both traditional individual life and universal life products, as well as individual long term disability insurance.

Statement 60 accounting is similar to statutory accounting; premiums are included in revenue. Benefit reserves are based on the same principles as statutory, that is, the present value of future benefits less future premiums. For this purpose, a GAAP net benefit premium is developed from GAAP assumptions regarding mortality or morbidity, interest, and persistency. The net benefit premium is a constant percentage of the gross premium, with no reduction as with CRVM reserves. DAC assets allow for any acquisition costs.

Except in rare instances, business which is treated under Statement 60 for direct issue purposes will be treated as Statement 60 for reinsurance ceded and assumed also. For ceding companies and reinsurers, YRT from Statement 60 products is treated under Statement 60 guidelines.

FASB Statement No. 97

FASB Statement No. 97 applies to two major types of business: limited premium paying period policies and investment contracts. Statement 97

---

[5] Special guidelines for limited payment and paid-up business were stated in Statement No. 97, amending the original treatment in Statement 60.

states the rule mentioned above that all acquisition costs must be amortized over the premium paying life of the policy. This applies not only to direct issues, but also to coinsurance and mod-co ceded and accepted. However, YRT with reinsurance premiums payable for life after the end of the direct premium paying period should be handled as Statement 60 cessions for both ceding and reinsuring company, even though the direct issue would be handled differently.

Policies and contracts with interest sensitive features, such as universal life and single premium deferred annuities, are treated differently than traditional policies. The portion of the premiums or deposits used for investment are treated as deposits, not premiums, and are not available to amortize acquisition costs. Instead, cost of insurance rates, surrender charges, other loads, and investment income, including capital gains and losses are considered to be revenue. Acquisition costs and other expenses are charges against that revenue stream.

Unlike Statement 60 accounting, Statement 97 accounting allows for unlocking of assumptions, essentially recognizing different outlooks for both the future and past experience. This unlocking feature does not apply to the limited pay provisions of Statement 97.

For interest sensitive contracts, benefit reserves are equal to the account value of the policy or contract. For universal life policies, a benefit reserve, such as the amount needed for one month's death benefit, is added to the account value for GAAP benefit reserves.

The presence of indeterminate premium elements or flexible payments will not cause a product to be classified as a Statement 97 product. For example, term insurance policies and YRT reinsurance which have current premiums less than a maximum schedule of rates normally are treated under Statement 60.

The treatment of YRT reinsurance from underlying Statement 97 products typically differs between ceding company and reinsurer. The ceding company includes the cost of YRT reinsurance ceded in its estimated gross margins used to amortize DAC, thus including the cost in its Statement 97 procedures. The reinsurer treats the YRT accepted under Statement 60 guidelines, regardless of the underlying source of the business.

FASB Statement No. 91

FASB Statement No. 91 accounting applies to contracts which contain no mortality or morbidity risks.[6] For example, a ten year certain only annuity could qualify for Statement 91 treatment. Such contracts are treated as bank deposits with some differences from FASB 97 products. Primarily, acquisition costs may be amortized somewhat differently and loss recognition is viewed differently, with losses being posted periodically as they occur, not as a present value in advance.

For reinsurance applications, if the plan is coinsurance or mod-co and all risks are transferred, the ceding company should account for the cession consistent with the direct issue. If only investment risks are transferred, it may be acceptable for the reinsurer to use Statement 91 treatment even if the underlying contract is of a Statement 97 type.

FASB Statement No. 109

GAAP requires a liability or an asset be established with respect to deferred taxes. To a large degree, this is a recognition of future tax that will be paid on income which has been recognized for GAAP accounting but not for actual tax accounting. Both ceding companies and reinsurers need to be alert to this issue in defining and accounting for reinsurance transactions.

For example, consider a block of inforce business that, when ceded to a reinsurer created a current tax loss, but that is expected to generate future profits. The reinsurer would be required to establish a deferred tax liability for the taxes on those future profits, partially offsetting the current tax saving. The current tax benefit would be in cash and the deferred tax amount would be a liability. This in effect defers some of the current income to pay the future tax bill.

Assuming the ceding company is in an opposite situation, it would show current taxable income, but establish an asset for future recovery, or, perhaps, reduce its deferred tax liability for that block.

---

[6] In practice, Statement 91 treatment is sometimes accorded to contracts which have a small, but very insignificant element of mortality or morbidity risk. Acceptability of this treatment must be discussed carefully with the insurer's audit firm.

Financial reinsurance often has a major tax deferral or savings component. The tax benefit of these transactions must be subjected to the deferred tax liability analysis and reporting.

The primary principle associated with deferred taxes, as with most GAAP items, is to match expenses with revenue.

FASB Statement No. 113

FASB Statement No. 113 is addressed solely at reinsurance transactions. It deals with three major concepts: risk transfer, the "geographic treatment" of ceded reserve credits, and the timing of earnings from reinsurance contracts.[7]

Risk Transfer. Risk transfer in a GAAP sense differs from risk transfer in a statutory sense. Risk transfer from the statutory view centers on whether the reinsurer will be responsible for payment of future benefit. Risk transfer from a GAAP sense deals more with the shifting of economic results and whether any transfer is permanent or temporary.

Accordingly, a "surplus relief" treaty may transfer significant risks to the reinsurer and qualify for reserve credits under statutory accounting. However, if there is a high likelihood that recapture will occur in a short period of time and that the only economic effect is the payment of a fee from the ceding company to the reinsurer, GAAP accounting would indicate that there be no shifting of assets and liabilities and that only the fee be part of premium income. In essence, the reinsurance would be recognized as being temporary in nature and the accounting would reflect this temporary nature.

Funding arrangements or reinsurance which provides only for financing of acquisition costs are treated largely as loans under GAAP accounting and not as reinsurance transactions. Likewise, reinsurance agreements whose only real purpose is to transfer additional reserves or surplus requirements, without meaningful insurance risks, are not treated as reinsurance under Statement 113 guidelines.

---

[7] FASB 113 actually deals with many more issues relating to reinsurance, but these three have the most relevance to life, health, and annuity reinsurance. However, FASB 113 should be reviewed carefully before a company enters into a significant or unusual reinsurance agreement.

GAAP Accounting for Reinsurance

For such agreements, the proper GAAP accounting is to either ignore any premiums and other amounts which are netted against each other, recognizing only the "fee" for the service as income. Some amounts may be treated as deposits rather than premiums or reserves. For GAAP purposes, such transactions are treated as though they do not exist except for permanent transfers, such as fees.

For most life and annuity products and many health products, it is required that there be "the reasonable possibility that the reinsurer may realize a significant loss from assuming" the reinsurance. There is little guidance as to what terms meet this condition. However, it is generally accepted that it all of the risks present in the original policies or contracts are transferred, then the conditions have been met.

Statement 113 is relatively recent in origin, having been applied for the first time at year end 1993. Standards of evaluation regarding risk transfer are still emerging.

Geographic Considerations. The second, or geographic, part of Statement 113 is clearer in its application.[8] With respect to indemnity reinsurance, GAAP recognizes rightly that the ceding company has not reduced its liabilities by entering into the reinsurance agreement. The company still has its full obligations to pay its policyholders, even if the reinsurer fails to pay its portion of any benefits. The reinsurance is a promise to reimburse and, as such, is an asset.

Under GAAP accounting, the balance sheet logically reflects this view of reinsurance. Instead of reducing liabilities with reserve credits, GAAP increases assets for the value of any such receivable. Liabilities remain the same as if no reinsurance were ceded. In practice, the new asset should be equal to the old reserve credit and GAAP equity is not affected.

Reinsurers account for reinsurance accepted in the same manner, establishing a liability for risks accepted and an asset for retrocessions.

---

[8] The term "geographic" is a term of usage and is not found in FASB Statement No. 113. It refers to the location of the balance sheet adjustment for reinsurance ceded, to either the asset or the liability side.

Timing of Earnings. Statement 113 describes the timing of earnings for reinsurance agreements. Earnings on reinsurance accepted are matched to revenues received. Earnings and costs on reinsurance ceded are matched to the revenues of the direct, underlying products. Earnings are not front-ended, or recognized at the time of the cession, unless assumption occurs.

In the event of indemnity reinsurance of an inforce block of business, any gain from the initial ceding commission or transaction is deferred and released over time. There is no GAAP gain or loss on the event of the initial transaction.

FASB Statement No. 115

FASB Statement No. 115 deals with asset values under GAAP. Prior to the introduction of this guideline, GAAP asset values were similar to statutory values, for example, bond values were carried at amortized cost. Under Statement 115, the company must state whether an asset is being held to maturity, available for sale, or part of a trading portfolio. Changes in current market values are reflected in the GAAP balance sheet and surplus, although the method of reflection varies according to the trading category of the asset. Under some circumstances changes in market value can lead to similar changes in reserves and the deferred acquisition asset balance.

Statement 115 does not have a direct effect on reinsurance. However, assets in trusts and funds withheld accounts are subject to the same rules. For example, lack of agreement on investment philosophy or intent could lead to unexpected results if one party trades securities which the other party expected to be held to maturity.

FASB Statement No. 120

FASB Statement No. 120 defines certain aspects of GAAP accounting for mutual life and health insurers. In particular, it addresses accounting for participating traditional life products. Stock life insurers offering participating policies can opt to follow Statement 120 or the accounting rules for stock companies. The primary issues addressed in Statement 120 are the recognition of dividends and reserving for future dividends.

The major point relevant to reinsurance concerns the change in character when business is reinsured. Participating business ceded to a reinsurer on a YRT basis falls under normal Statement 60 and Statement 97 guidelines. Coinsurance or modified coinsurance ceded on a fixed dividend scale would follow normal guidelines. If the reinsurer is following the ceding company's dividend scale, that reinsurer probably should follow the normal guidelines also. If the block is large and a valid argument can be made that the block constitutes a separate dividend class for the reinsurer, it may be feasible to treat the block according to Statement 120.

GAAP FOR CEDED REINSURANCE

Under statutory accounting principles, premiums paid for reinsurance ceded are deducted from premiums received and the net amount is reported as premium income. Claim reimbursements from the reinsurer are offset against total claim payments and, similarly, any cash value or other surrender benefits received from the reinsurer are offset against the appropriate transaction account. If an experience refund is payable, the refund is generally recorded as miscellaneous income, although refunds can be considered negative reinsurance ceded premiums.

For purposes of GAAP, all of these elements must be matched against the appropriate revenue or benefit base in a manner consistent with that required of the GAAP treatment for directly issued business. Although different techniques may be used, Robertson calls for the calculation of an annual "expected cost" of reinsurance according to GAAP valuation assumptions.

For reinsurance ceded purposes, the assumptions used in developing the valuation premium should be consistent with the original assumptions used in developing the direct GAAP reserves. However, ceded experience could be different from the overall block. For example, reinsured policies may be only larger ones with more extensive underwriting, lead to different mortality and persistency assumptions and experience. If experience is expected to be significantly different on the reinsurance ceded portion, different assumptions may be used.

As with statutory accounting, GAAP accounting usually involves calculating direct and ceded factors[9] for benefit reserves and deferred acquisition costs and using these to develop gross numbers. Unlike statutory accounting, GAAP does not reduce the benefit reserves for reinsurance ceded. GAAP reserves are not changed by reinsurance. Instead, an asset is established for the benefit reserve ceded.[10] Reinsurance is treated as a recoverable item, hence an asset, rather than a reduction in liability.

This treatment of reinsurance as an asset, rather than a contra-liability, is logical in light of the historical and legal position of reinsurance. Reinsurance treaties affirm that the ceding company maintains its obligations to all policyholders and specifically deny that any other party, such as the policyholder, has an interest in the transaction. GAAP recognizes this fact and the economic realities of reinsurance by leaving the benefit reserves intact and establishing an asset for expected recoveries.

The final net benefit reserve and net deferred acquisition cost asset are the important items. While the direct and ceded pieces may be calculated separately, it is the net value that matters.

Affiliated companies filing consolidated statements should use the same assumptions for reinsurance ceded and assumed from one entity to the other. Even if different assumptions are used at the individual company levels, any differences are eliminated in consolidation at a corporate level. Otherwise, ceding and accepting companies need not use the same assumptions.

The type and extent of GAAP reporting necessary for a ceding company will vary with the type of reinsurance and according to how material reinsurance is to the total balance sheet and earnings. For some companies, ceded reinsurance never has been considered to be material

---

[9] Traditional GAAP accounting under FASB 60 was accomplished largely through the use of reserve factors for benefits and DAC, similar to those used for statutory. Flexible premium and interest sensitive products have lead to more use of models and other accounting devices. The term "factors" is used in this book to include any combination of assumptions, methods, and inforce records which are used to generate benefit reserves, expense reserves, or DAC assets.

[10] Until 1993, GAAP followed statutory in reducing liabilities. The current treatment was required by FASB 113.

and no GAAP adjustments have ever been made. Even some large companies with significant volumes of reinsurance business use the statutory reserve adjustments for GAAP reporting for reinsurance ceded. This practice has become less common in recent years as the use of reinsurance has increased and as more of it is of a coinsurance type. The question of materiality should be kept in mind in reviewing GAAP procedures for reinsurance ceded.

Yearly Renewable Term

Yearly renewable term reinsurance requires the simplest accounting (GAAP, statutory, or tax) of any form of reinsurance. The easiest way to handle ceded YRT is merely to recognize the premiums, the claims and any experience refunds as incurred. Implicit in this treatment is an assumption that the YRT cash premium is relatively proportional to the mortality rates assumed throughout the life of the business; this may or may not be so.

For example, YRT may be purchased on a zero first year premium basis. In this case, the theoretically correct way to handle it would be to develop benefit reserves based upon the mortality assumption of the ceded business. An implicit first year premium equal to expected mortality plus profit and expenses, and an equivalent level allowance or loading, may be used to develop a deferred acquisition cost asset.

This procedure spreads the expected actual first year cost over the life of the business. Otherwise, the ceding company takes into earnings first year claim recoveries which are repaid in future years through higher reinsurance premiums than would be the case if a first year premium were paid. A simpler method is to develop a negative deferred acquisition asset to account for the zero premium.

As an alternative, some companies adjust the benefit reserves to accommodate the zero first year premium, arriving at the same net liability.

Coinsurance

Coinsurance is more complicated than YRT. Benefit reserve factors might reasonably be assumed to be the same for reinsurance ceded as for the original policy. The investment rate assumed should be that of the ceding company and not the reinsurer. Alternatively, it is possible to develop a net benefit reserve for the ceding company based strictly upon the retained portion of the policy, but most administrative systems do not allow this approach.

The amount and incidence of reinsurance expense allowances seldom match those of the actual acquisition expenses and commissions of the ceding company. If these are reasonably similar, it may be possible to use the same deferred acquisition cost factors to net ceded coinsurance out of the deferred acquisition cost asset developed for the corresponding directly written business. However, if the allowances and commissions are not similar and the ceded business is material, then separate deferred acquisition cost factors should be developed for the ceded portion of the business.

For a quota share coinsurance treaty, it may be possible to develop GAAP reserves and DAC based upon the net retained portion taking into account the percentage of the business retained versus the percentage ceded and the differing patterns of expense and allowances. In effect, a net balance may be developed for the entire block, based on net retained revenues and benefits.

Modified Coinsurance

In calculating GAAP factors for mod-co, the ceding company can take the same approach on deferred acquisition cost asset factors as it would for coinsurance. However, calculation of benefit reserve factors should be adjusted for the fact that the statutory reserve is held by the ceding company. This can be a complicated adjustment depending on the basis for selecting the interest rate used to calculate the mod-co adjustment.

In most cases, the ceding company's net earned rate is used in the mod-co interest adjustment. In this case, the same interest rate should be used for the reinsurance as is used for the originally written business. In statutory accounting, the ceding company holds the reserve under mod-co. However, under GAAP accounting, the ceding company will establish a receivable for the ceded benefit reserve, just as it would for coinsurance. Since it also holds the assets backing the statutory reserves, it must establish a liability for amounts on deposit in order to avoid taking double credit in its surplus.

GAAP Accounting for Reinsurance

While not technically correct, for GAAP purposes, mod-co may be viewed as involving a loan from the reinsurer to the ceding company, creating an asset in the amount of the statutory reserve and an interest obligation, as defined in the mod-co adjustment provisions of the treaty. This results in a total benefit reserve for the ceding company equal to the "benefit reserve calculated without considering reinsurance, reduced by the portion reinsured, plus the statutory reserve held by the reinsured company."[11]

The actual interest rates expected should be used in calculating the benefit reserves. One way to do this is to assume that the portion of the GAAP reserve which corresponds to the statutory reserve is earning interest at the rate established for the mod-co interest adjustment. Any remainder of the reserve should be assumed to earn interest at a rate consistent with the original interest assumptions.

A satisfactory approximation in most cases would be to use the same approach as for coinsurance, substituting for the interest rate assumed in the original policy pricing the one used in determining the mod-co adjustment. This introduces an error which is related to the product of (1) the difference between the mod-co interest rate and the direct interest rate and (2) the difference between the GAAP benefit reserve and the statutory reserve. For most companies this would be relatively small and immaterial.

Special Provisions

Certain reinsurance transactions require special consideration for GAAP.

Chargebacks. Some reinsurance treaties call for allowances at acquisition which exceed 100% of the first year premium. These treaties frequently call for a chargeback of excess allowances if a certain persistency level is not maintained. One such feature calls for a refund of all allowances in excess of 100% of premium for any policy which does not pay the 13th month premium. Such provisions require additional attention for GAAP if the reinsured inforce is significant.

---

[11] See Robertson [20].

For statutory purposes, there is no general requirement to make provision for this chargeback in most situations. For GAAP purposes this provision, like any other affecting cash flow, should be recognized. Those policies which lapse with a chargeback create negative statutory revenues; for GAAP purposes, the chargeback is charged against the revenue over the life of the policies.

This chargeback is an offset of overstated first year revenue. Just as the deferred acquisition cost asset spreads the excess first year acquisition expense and commission over the life of the policy, so should it spread chargeback expenses.

In effect, while first year allowances in excess of 100% create statutory and, generally, tax gains for the ceding company, they do not necessarily create immediate GAAP gains. GAAP accounting calls for both excess first year allowances and chargebacks to be spread over the life of the policies in proportion to expected premium revenues. This prevents inappropriate front-ending of GAAP earnings and reduces the ceding company's cost of surrender or termination.

Recapture. Most reinsurance agreements include some form of recapture provision. This leads to the possibility of termination of reinsurance even though the base policy has not terminated. Recapture generally is allowed only after a specific period of time has elapsed following the original policy cession, and then only if a retention increase has taken place. While it is appropriate for a reinsurer to take into account recapture, it is not necessarily required that a ceding company consider recapture in calculating reserves. If it does not, it will likely have GAAP gains or losses upon recapture.

If recapture is to be taken into account, it may be treated as an additional provision for termination in both the benefit reserve and the deferred acquisition cost calculations. Obviously, the earliest point of this additional termination provision is at the earliest point of recapture allowed in the contract. Companies which take recapture into account may introduce a significant increase to the termination rate at that point and a smaller increase thereafter. As a practical matter, most ceding companies ignore recapture in GAAP calculations.

Experience Refunds. Experience refunds, being subject to wide fluctuations, are difficult to handle in GAAP accounting. Good experience in one contract year can create a refund, while poor experience in another year can generate a smaller refund or no refund, perhaps even eliminating future refunds. Most companies choose to ignore experience refunds in calculating GAAP factors, allowing any refunds to flow through earnings as they are incurred on the statutory basis.

Theoretically, a test using GAAP valuation assumptions should be made to determine if an experience refund is expected. This test should be made in aggregate over the life of the block of business. If a refund is expected, then that refund should be taken into consideration along with other revenues. This will generally result in reducing the expected annual cost of reinsurance.

Self-Administration

Self-administration has created problems for reinsurers in the accounting arena, but it has not created particular problems for ceding companies. The problems for reinsurers are largely the result of a lack of information, but ceding companies have access to all the information. Since the principles of GAAP accounting do not vary with the manner in which reinsurance is administered, ceding companies should be able to handle GAAP in a straightforward manner, regardless of the type of administration.

Retrocessions

In determining GAAP benefit reserves and deferred acquisition cost assets for retroceded business, the principles of ceded reinsurance generally apply. To the extent the retroceded premiums or allowances are equal to the accepted premiums and allowances, then the assumed GAAP factors can be used for the retroceded factors. To the extent that different premiums or terms are included in the retrocession agreement, then different factors should be developed.

Again, the degree of materiality should be considered. If retroceded business is a very small portion of a company's reinsurance assumed operations, it may choose to greatly simplify its retroceded GAAP factors.

Facultative Cessions

Facultative cessions generally exhibit different mortality and persistency experience. Also, reinsurance expenses may be different from those for automatic business. Depending upon the volume and the differences involved, the insurer may develop different GAAP factors for facultative cessions.

GAAP FOR ASSUMED REINSURANCE

Reinsurers have unique problems in determining GAAP factors. Few treaties have enough experience to be independently credible; few are large enough to necessitate separate treatment for calculating GAAP factors. Trying to generalize factors for use with several treaties from different companies is difficult as premiums and allowances are generally distinct for each agreement. The reinsurer seldom has the option to avoid making GAAP adjustments.

Another problem faced by reinsurers is dealing with the type, or lack, of detail available. For individual cession business, the reinsurer has extensive detail on each life. However, many individual cession reinsurance treaties may have less than 100 cessions inforce; the expense and effort needed to develop special factors for all plans may be prohibitive. Self-administration or bulk accounts may have no meaningful detail available.

For large accounts, it is possible and practical to develop separate GAAP factors. The reinsurer should develop GAAP factors based upon its expected experience and the plan of reinsurance, but it may group several ceded treaties together for administrative simplicity. The reinsurer must decide whether a given contract is different enough from other contracts to be combined with similar contracts or whether separate assumptions are justified.

Yearly Renewable Term

In developing GAAP factors for a YRT scale, the reinsurer should consider the expense, persistency, and mortality assumptions used in

GAAP Accounting for Reinsurance

developing that scale. This is a straightforward procedure; the factors so developed can be applied to all business produced using the rate scale until a new GAAP era is started.

In practice, many reinsurers assume that the net benefit premium for GAAP is a constant percentage of the gross premium. This is true if the slope of the YRT scale is the same as the slope of the underlying mortality assumption at all issue ages and durations. In fact, this relationship is seldom exact, but the difference may be immaterial. If this assumption is made, then the only benefit reserve needed is the unearned portion of the net benefit premium. Many companies use some such approximation. To the extent that the two slopes are different, errors in GAAP reserves and earnings will result.

Just as with the ceding company, a zero first year premium YRT contract requires additional consideration, following regular GAAP guidelines. The recovery of the first year reinsurance claims and expenses is expected to come from future premiums. Economically, while this is no different than coinsurance on an annually renewable term plan with a 100% first year allowance, it creates problems as there are no first year "revenues."

The preferred method involves the development of an implied first year premium with an allowance of equal amount. A benefit reserve should be calculated based upon actual premiums to be received, adjusted for this implied first year premium. The implied first year premium and 100% allowance generates a deferred acquisition cost asset.

An alternative procedure which should produce algebraically the same net liability and earnings is to establish no deferred acquisition asset and to base benefit reserves on the zero premium received. This leads to a negative first year benefit reserve which is amortized over the life of the policy. Both procedures have been used. If persistency experience diverges from assumptions, more consistency between factors may be maintained with the latter approach.

Coinsurance

Coinsurance is more administratively complex to handle than YRT, as many more combinations of rates, allowances, and benefits are involved.

In theory, every plan from every insurer could have a separate set of factors based upon the expected premiums, interest, mortality, persistency, and allowances. Perhaps some reinsurers have tried to adhere to this approach, but most have found it administratively convenient to combine several plans.

This may produce some variations among plans, but these typically will offset each other. In fact, reinsurers can develop a model plan or a series of model plans for each of type of policy reinsured and, at the time of pricing, assign the product to a specific model plan. For large accounts or plans, separate factors should be developed.

In developing the factors, the reinsurer, like a direct insurer, should match revenues and expenses over the life of the policy, using realistic assumptions for mortality, persistency, and expense with reasonable provision for adverse deviation. Development of deferred acquisition cost factors is the same for coinsurance as for a direct issue, with allowances being used for commissions. The calculation of factors for coinsurance is not difficult, but the application and administration can be very tedious and complicated.

Modified Coinsurance

Mod-co may be treated exactly the same as coinsurance, except that the interest rate assumed for the benefit reserve should be consistent with that used for the mod-co adjustment. This can introduce a slight error since the statutory reserve will likely be different than the GAAP benefit reserve and the mod-co adjustment interest rate may be different from the rate which is assumed to be earned by the reinsurer. However, the reinsurer's assumed earned rate may be used as a matter of simplification unless there is a significant difference in anticipated rates.

If the difference between the reinsurer's assumed rate and the mod-co adjustment rate is significant, then the reinsurer's assumed rate should be used. Many reinsurers use their coinsurance assumed interest rate in the mod-co reserve factors for simplicity.

If the allowances, premiums, benefits, and mortality and persistency assumptions are the same, deferred acquisition costs and benefit reserves should be identical for mod-co and coinsurance.

GAAP Accounting for Reinsurance

Special Provisions

As was the case with ceded reinsurance, the following transactions require special consideration for GAAP.

Chargebacks. As noted in the section on ceded reinsurance, chargebacks need to be considered in developing GAAP factors. The benefit reserve factors do not change with the presence of a chargeback. However, the presence of a chargeback will have an effect on deferred acquisition cost factors. The additional first year allowance should be treated as an additional first year expense. A chargeback should be treated as income in the year in which it is expected to be received, based upon the lapse assumptions. An alternative method is to treat the additional first year allowance as an expense in the year it occurs and chargebacks as negative surrender values.

In any event, chargebacks should be recognized in determining the reinsured deferred acquisition cost and the revenue to which it should be related is the base premium, not an inflated premium including the chargeback. The total expense, including both the additional allowance and the chargeback, is spread in proportion to revenues over the life of the policy.

Recapture. Recapture is an interesting problem for reinsurers. While it is generally reasonable and appropriate for a ceding company to ignore recapture, it is probably not prudent for a reinsurer to do so since some ceding companies likely will exercise this option.

For example, the GAAP assumption might be that 50% of the business will be recaptured at the earliest opportunity, with an additional 5%-10% recaptured annually thereafter. Such an approach is reasonable. It likely will lead to faster amortization of acquisition costs, but the effect on benefit reserves is unpredictable.

It is reasonable to assume that if a block of business is producing negative results for the reinsurer and is expected to continue to produce negative results, then recapture will not occur. On the other hand, if the ceding company can prudently reduce reinsurance costs by recapture, it is reasonable to assume the company will exercise its recapture options subsequent to any retention increase. In short, recapture is more likely on profitable business than on unprofitable business.

It would be appropriate for a reinsurer not only to assume additional lapses for potential recaptures, but also to assume a deterioration in mortality on the remaining business following recapture, reflecting the fact that the accounts which do not recapture may choose not to do so because of negative expectations. Depending upon the premium and benefit patterns of the reinsurance, this could lead to either higher or lower benefit reserve factors in earlier durations.

Experience Refunds. In the past, a substantial part of the coinsurance and mod-co written on a traditional basis contained experience refund provisions. While less frequent today, refund business still occurs and significant blocks of inforce business are subject to experience refund rating. In addition, many YRT treaties were written with experience refund provisions. The presence of experience loss carryforwards introduces a computational complication in integrating experience refunds into the GAAP factors; timing differences as well as expected values must be considered.

In theory, when a contract is written with an experience refund provision, the expected refunds should be included in the determination of benefit. In practice, unless the refund amounts are expected to be significant, refunds for GAAP purposes often are recognized as incurred on a statutory basis.

An experience refund reserve is needed if the timing of GAAP earnings differs from the timing of the earning of the experience refund. For example, consider a coinsurance agreement covering normal life insurance issues with high first year commissions and an experience refund based on cumulative statutory earnings. Statutory earnings in the first several years will be negative due to the acquisition expenses and reserve requirements; there will be no experience refunds paid.

However, that business may show GAAP earnings in each year. The portion of those gross GAAP earnings which will be paid in future experience refunds should be "held" in the experience refund reserve until paid. Otherwise, current GAAP earnings will be overstated and future GAAP earnings will be reduced to provide for the experience refund.

If a loss occurs, the experience refund account is placed in a loss carryforward position. It is appropriate to review that individual account to determine if some or all of the loss is expected to be recovered in the future. To the extent that the loss is expected to be recovered in the future, that amount, discounted for interest, may be a valid GAAP asset.

Self-Administration

GAAP accounting for self-administered business is a significant challenge for a reinsurer. In principle, the application of GAAP to self-administered reinsurance[12] is the same as for individual cession business. The choices of an appropriate model and appropriate assumptions are identical in concept. The major difference is that the reinsurer seldom has sufficient detail to apply the factors accurately for self-administered business.

Even when the reinsurer receives detail by plan, issue age, and year of issue, the information often is not readily or economical usable. A dynamic worksheet approach to deferred acquisition costs and a concurrent review of statutory results may achieve the stated goals of GAAP, but the theoretical basis for the resulting financial entries may be weak.

The purpose of self-administration is to simplify administration for both the reinsurer and the reinsured while minimizing the volume of data transferred from one party to another. The systems used to produce reports are often those used for other purposes and the reinsurance data is only a by-product. There may be significant realistic limitations to the amount of detail available.

Models. To add additional administration for GAAP is self-defeating to the purpose of self-administration, so a model approach is both desirable and necessary. The construction of a model and the development of GAAP factors are essentially the same as for individual cession business, with differences due to the detail available. The same basic steps need to be undertaken for both individual cession and self-administered contracts. These are as follows:

(1) *Selection of Various Model Segments.* Some self-administered agreements include only one plan and others include many. In addition, it may not be practical to develop GAAP factors for every

---

[12] For a more detailed discussion of the intricacies of self-administered reinsurance and GAAP accounting, see Tiller [26].

contract. Some grouping is necessary. The grouping should be based upon plans of similar characteristics and expected profit levels. Smoker/nonsmoker and other significant underwriting categories and premium classifications should be recognized whenever possible. In most instances, GAAP accounting will require more segments than will statutory accounting since GAAP issue era groupings are used.

(2) *Assumption Selection.* Most companies have found that a few, perhaps three, issue age groups per plan are adequate. This should be consistent with the standard of the company on other products and lines. Other assumptions should be selected consistent with this standard.

(3) *Projection of New Issues.* A key part of modeling bulk accounts is a projection for new issues. This earnings projection should be made on both GAAP and statutory bases and should produce by-products such as inforce volume, inforce premium, and inforce statutory reserves. This projection will be used not only in determining deferrable expenses and initial reserves, but in the development of GAAP factors for the inforce.

(4) *Factor Application.* Once the factors have been developed for the model in the prior step, they can be applied to summaries of the inforce business which are provided by the ceding companies. In this case, factor application is identical in principle to that for individual cession business.

(5) *Model Validation.* Checking assumptions, especially persistency assumptions, is extremely difficult for self-administered contracts. For example, if a distribution of the inforce business by issue age within issue year is available, then a model can very easily be tested for credibility. Self-administered contracts generally do not provide that data and other tests have to be devised. In any event, comparisons should always be made of the aggregate statutory reserves, the volume inforce, and the premium produced by the model to that actually reported by the reinsured. These are general checks and can help identify problem areas.

With any model, actual results will differ from those projected over time. The purpose of the model validation is to determine the accuracy of results and to assist in determining when corrections or modifications to the model are necessary. Even if only one assumption, such as persistency, is out of line, the model can produce extremely inaccurate results. Since profit results vary by issue age, if the assumed issue age distribution is not representative, the model can produce distorted earnings.

While validation can never be perfect, it can provide a level of comfort for relying on the results. This modeling technique accomplishes, in effect, the substitution of a "per account" factor in the place of a "per thousand dollar unit" factor.

The most important consideration in developing GAAP factors for self-administered treaties is dealing with the data available or, more importantly, not available. The reinsurer must adapt itself to the data available on the submitted reports. The reinsurer should consider GAAP as well as statutory, tax, and cash reporting requirements when designing self-administration reporting forms.

Identification of substandard issues on self-administered business is sometimes difficult. The validation process should obviously take substandard business into account and assumptions should reflect the percentage of substandard policies. While not conceptually difficult, this is an extra layer of administration complexity.

Once a model has been validated, it needs to be checked at least annually. As long as the validation continues to show the model to be reasonable, it can continue to be used. If a check shows that actual results are deviating significantly from the model, then a new model may be appropriate, based upon more current assumptions. This need may conflict with GAAP rules regarding assumption lock-in for certain products, except in cases of loss recognition. It should, however, not be considered in the same light as a loss recognition or a recoverability issue, but rather as the correction of an accounting error.

Unless it is necessary due to loss recognition or recoverability problems, the underlying GAAP factors and assumptions should not be changed. But the model should be adjusted to reflect the appropriate age or smoker/nonsmoker distribution, for example. There is generally little reason to change the mortality or persistency in a model unless loss recognition or recoverability is involved. Even if persistency experience is significantly different, it is not appropriate to change the future expected persistency in the model. The inforce should be adjusted, effectively writing off the deferred acquisition asset in proportion to excess terminations.

Adjusting for Time Lag. The time lags in reporting are also a difficulty in self-administered agreements. While individual cession business is generally reported on a fairly current basis and has relatively few items in transit, a self-administered contract may have a whole quarter or, in some countries, an entire year of activity unreported.

Some reinsurers accept this and allow the books to be one reporting period behind for such clients. Others attempt to project both statutory and GAAP results through the end of the current accounting period, then adjust the estimates to actual results when results are received. The latter approach is technically correct, but extreme care must be taken that earnings are not distorted. Techniques which produce conservative statutory results may lead to excessive GAAP gains, creating a misleading impression of the performance of the reinsurer and management problems, since any excess earnings must be "made up" later.

Recoverability and Loss Recognition

Recoverability and loss recognition criteria are the same for self-administered reinsurance, individual cession reinsurance, and are directly written business. These types of tests should be performed on reinsurance accepted just as they are for direct written business. The mechanical procedures may differ for each of these three categories according to the data and systems available.

Loss recognition testing applies to the entire inforce business. Its purpose is to determine if the net liability being held, combined with future premiums and investment income, is sufficient to mature the current liabilities.

Reinsurers should perform loss recognition tests on their accepted business periodically. Assumptions should be the current best estimate of future experience. Inclusion of negative events should not occur until the events are demonstrated. For example, future deterioration in mortality due to AIDS should not be included until there was evidence that such negative experience was occurring.

This differs from the statutory position that would move to a negative assumption faster in order to protect the solvency of the company. In no event should loss recognition occur in order to protect future profits. Once loss recognition has occurred, future profits should be zero except for experience deviations from assumptions.

In performing loss recognition or recoverability tests for a direct writer, reinsurance ceded should obviously be taken into account. If a problem appears to be developing with either recoverability or loss recognition, additional refinement of models and investigation of experiences should be completed before a loss or reduction in deferral is accepted.

Recoverability testing refers to the DAC established for the current year's new issues or cessions. Using GAAP assumptions, it should be demonstrated that the net liability established is sufficient and that the DAC asset will be recovered from future earnings. If this cannot be demonstrated, the DAC asset should be reduced or the benefit reserve increased. Reinsurance costs and gains are part of this calculation.

Facultative Business

Facultative business provides a challenge for reinsurers, since experience will differ from that of automatic business. For individual cession business, facultative factors can be developed using different mortality assumptions. For some reinsurers facultative business is not material and it is not necessary to develop separate GAAP factors.

GAAP factors can take into account the weighted average of mortality and of persistency for facultative and automatic business and develop one set of factors to apply overall. If a company wishes to do the detailed administration, it can develop separate factors for facultative business. Facultative reinsurance can be a problem for self-administered treaties. It may be difficult to identify the proportion of facultative cessions reinsured.

FINANCIAL REINSURANCE

In theory, financial reinsurance treaties are treated the same as other reinsurance agreements. The economic effect on both the ceding and reinsuring companies is usually quite different from that of the gross numbers which flow through the reinsurance treaties. FASB 113 is especially important in determining the proper GAAP accounting for financial reinsurance.

First, it must be determined whether or not risk transfer has occurred. If not, then accounting for the transaction as deposits, if necessary, and recognizing only the fee in earnings is indicated. If risk transfer is sufficient to satisfy FASB 113 requirements, then accounting for financial reinsurance is the same as for any other reinsurance agreement.

OTHER CONSIDERATIONS

The principles discussed in the examples regarding life insurance should be of instructional value in applying GAAP accounting for accident and health reinsurance.

Special treaties, such as stop-loss and catastrophe covers, have a variety of options under GAAP accounting. Under traditional accounting for these policies, the gross premiums are taken into income along with the current year's claims, and the net result is the statutory earnings. Many companies follow the same approach for GAAP. Surplus is required to provide a cushion for claim fluctuations. However, some companies build up a catastrophe or contingency reserve under GAAP.

Under this approach, the net premiums are accumulated in a reserve fund, usually with interest. Incurred claims are deducted from the reserve fund. Net premiums are the product of the expected loss ratios and the respective gross premiums. Unless payments of future premiums are guaranteed or highly likely, the reserve fund should not go below zero. There must be a mechanism to release excess reserves should actual claims be lower than expected levels. This reserving approach has gained acceptance for both statutory and GAAP reporting for highly volatile benefits such as these.

14 | Tax Effects of Reinsurance

The tax effects of reinsurance involve many degrees of complexity, ranging from the seemingly mundane routine of premium taxes to exotic international tax issues. Since taxes can be a major expense of an insurance company, competent management may explore reasonable, legal options to reduce taxes along with other expenses.

Any reinsurance agreement can have significant tax consequences, either intended or unintended. Many reinsurance agreements have had a number of their terms dictated or influenced by tax considerations. In the past, some reinsurance transactions were motivated primarily by anticipated tax benefits for one or both parties.

The many and varied aspects of the taxation of insurance companies and the effects of reinsurance agreements are beyond the scope of this text. This chapter is designed to introduce the subject of taxation as it interacts with reinsurance and to describe some of the tax considerations that are typically part of the analysis of a reinsurance arrangement. The focus of this chapter is on taxation within the United States, but the analytical basis is similar everywhere. Some considerations of the taxation of reinsurance treaties which cross international borders are also included.[1]

Taxation is an extremely important subject which should be approached with caution. This book is not intended to be a handbook on taxation; specific court cases and precedents are not always cited. The facts and circumstances surrounding an agreement can change the tax treatment. It should be noted that tax laws, regulations, procedures, and practices are constantly changing. Qualified tax advisors or counsel always should be involved in the analysis whenever a reinsurance treaty has significant tax implications.

STATE TAXES

State taxation of life and health insurers is typically in the form of premium taxes, levied as a percent of premium collected. The actual percentage may vary according to the class of business involved, the state of domicile of the insuring company, or the state of residence of the insured. There may be a reduction in or offsets to premium taxes for other taxes paid to a state or for other reasons.

Another form of state taxation is receiving increased attention: payments to guaranty funds as the result of payments to or on behalf of the policyholders of failed insurance companies.

State Premium Taxes

In most jurisdictions of the United States, reinsurance is excused from a premium tax based upon the fact that the premium taxes for any business reinsured have already been paid by the direct company. Many reinsurance agreements call for the reinsurer to reimburse the ceding company for premium taxes on the reinsurance premiums to the extent that the reinsurer is not otherwise taxed on those premiums. Other agreements call for no explicit reimbursement for premium tax, but

---

[1] Additional international tax considerations are discussed in Chapter 18, International Reinsurance.

implicitly the reinsurer may have increased allowances or otherwise reflected the fact that it is not paying premium tax on this business.

The payment may be either an exact reimbursement based on the actual premium taxes paid or a specified percentage of reinsurance premiums. Economically, the latter is just an additional allowance. The specified percentage may be stated in the treaty or agreed upon for administrative convenience.

If the treaty calls for premium tax reimbursement, the reinsurer participates in any change in the premium tax rate. If the treaty specifies a percentage allowance, only the ceding company is affected by any change in premium tax rates.

Guaranty Fund Assessments

In most insurance company failures, state guaranty funds assess companies for cash contributions or stand-by guarantees of benefits to policyholders. Such assessments are typically made against companies writing similar types of business in the states of residence of the covered insureds. In most, if not all, states, assessments are made based on direct written premiums and exclude the effects of reinsurance. Furthermore, recovery of such assessments against future premium taxes incurred is common.

Under most reinsurance agreements, the reinsurer would not participate in any assessments. However, a reinsurer technically could be relieved of some premium tax reimbursement as the result of future reductions in premium tax for any assessments paid.

In most instances, such as a YRT treaty, the effects of a reinsurer participating in the assessments would be minimal and not worth any administrative effort. However, if the reinsurer is participating in coinsurance or modified coinsurance of a large block of business, the economic effects of participation or non-participation in a proportionate share of guaranty fund assessments may have significant economic consequences.

Lack of documentation of original intent may lead to confusion and disagreement. It is advisable for reinsurance agreements to address the subject of the reinsurer's participation in these and similar assessments, along with the terms of such participation. If the reinsurer is relieved of such participation, the treaty should state that agreement.

In the latter event, it may be equitable for the reinsurer to reimburse for premium taxes on a gross basis, before any offset for guaranty fund assessments. Of course, it is equally equitable for the reinsurer to participate in any future recoveries which relate to payments it makes, even if the recoveries do not derive from business it has reinsured.

Other State and Local Taxes

Other state and local taxes, licenses, and fees sometimes are charged on insurance or insurance company activities. Typically, these are not covered or reimbursed directly under any form of reinsurance, a practice which is administratively simple. It is expected that these costs are minimal and are included in normal operating costs when the ceding company analyzes its expenses. However, no law or regulation prevents the reinsurer from direct participation in such costs, if properly negotiated and documented in the treaty.

The reinsurer is responsible for any such taxes, licenses, or fees it incurs as a business entity.

UNITED STATES FEDERAL INCOME TAX

Tax law and the basis on which life insurance companies in the United States are taxed is fluid.[2] However, since 1958, taxes have been based upon total income or the principal components of earnings of the company, with some limitations on the deductibility of policyholder dividends or other expense items. Historically, companies have used reinsurance to change the timing of taxable income, most frequently to defer it, but sometimes to accelerate it.

---

[2] There are several references on taxation of insurance companies in general and life insurance companies in particular, including *Federal Taxation of Insurance Companies*, Partners of KPMG Peat Marwick, Research Institute of America, 90 Fifth Avenue, New York, NY 10010. The Internal Revenue Code (IRC) itself, the discussions in the various "Blue Books," and *The Congressional Record* are the ultimate sources.

Background

Taxation of life insurance companies has always been a complicated matter, due to the long-term nature of their liabilities. Over the last 80 years, the United States has used many bases for taxing life insurance companies. From 1958 through 1981, the Life Insurance Company Tax Act of 1959, commonly referred to as the 1959 Act,[3] applied.

Many of the current reinsurance practices with regard to financial reinsurance treaties and the effect of taxation upon reinsurance agreements evolved under the 1959 Act. Therefore, some basic understanding of the provisions of the 1959 Act is important in understanding the history of reinsurance taxation, the current law, and certain reinsurance practices.

Tax Phases. Under the 1959 Act there were three situations, or phases, of taxation. In the first of these, commonly known as "Phase I," taxes were based on investment income. Companies in this situation most frequently were large mutual insurers. Dividends could not be used to reduce taxable income.

"Phase II Negative" companies were taxed on the operating income of the company, including investment income. These companies were often smaller stock companies or companies showing significant growth and strain.

"Phase II Positive" companies, those where operating income exceeded investment income, were taxed on the sum of investment income and 50% of the excess of operating income over investment income. The untaxed operating income was placed in a notional deferred tax account, known as the Policyholders' Surplus Account, or PSA.

The accumulation of the PSA included certain other untaxed items and deductions, governed by "Phase III" tax rules. Even though the multiphase tax system has been replaced, amounts remaining in the PSA are still subject to taxation. The Phase III tax is assessed in the event of certain distributions, the loss of life company or insurance company status, the accumulation of amounts in excess of specified limits, or the liquidation of the company.

---

[3] Public Law 86-89; June 25, 1959; Sections 801-820 of the Internal Revenue Code.

Section 820 and Its Effect. In the late 1970's, it became obvious that the 1959 Act was not functioning properly, particularly for companies in a Phase I situation. At a time of high interest rates, the tax on marginal investment income often exceeded 100%. In addition, the investment income on tax qualified pension contracts of some life insurance companies was being heavily taxed despite the obvious intent of the law that such income would not be taxed. Companies in this situation were forced to either subsidize tax qualified business or be noncompetitive.

As a result, in the late 1970's companies in a Phase I position began to make increasing use of hitherto little used provision of the 1959 Act, Section 820. Under Section 820, modified coinsurance could be treated as though it were coinsurance for tax purposes. The effect was to make it possible to move investment income from the ceding company to the reinsurer, using the mod-co interest adjustment combined with a Section 820 election, and return it to the ceding company as operating income via an experience refund or a return of reinsurance premium.

The use of Section 820 resulted in the recharacterization of investment income as operating income for tax purposes, with a significant tax reduction. This allowed more dividends to be deducted from taxable income by the ceding company, lowering its taxes. Typically, the reinsurer was taxed only on the profit it retained from this business, and often the transfer of tax exempt investment income benefits sheltered this and other income from taxation.

Significant amounts of investment income "escaped" taxation through this treatment, and the total tax bill of the life insurance industry was drastically reduced. As the federal government became aware of this and other problems involved in taxing life insurance companies, it moved to change the law. The Section 820 election is no longer a part of the Tax Code.

Section 818(c) and Its Effect. Another provision unique to the 1959 Act was the more broadly used Section 818(c). This provision allowed for statutory modified reserves to be treated as net level premium reserves for tax purposes using either an exact recalculation or a formula approximation adjustment. Over time, this approximation was believed to over-estimate the actual difference, thus providing an additional tax benefit.

The 818(c) feature was important because it allowed for a tax deduction in excess of the actual statutory reserve at issue. This resulted in a significant tax loss at issue, with reduced tax deductions in renewal years for persisting policies and additional taxable gains at termination. After considering the time value of money, the effects on taxable income generally resulted in an overall gain to the company.

Policies issued on a modified reserve basis and reinsured on either a coinsurance basis or on a mod-co basis with the Section 820 election passed the 818(c) benefits to the reinsurer. Occasionally, the ceding company could not utilize all of these special deductions while the reinsurer could, resulting in lower total federal income taxes being paid by the two companies.

These tax savings were passed to policyholders in the form of lower premiums rates. Some observers believe that this tax benefit was one of the primary driving forces in the so-called term wars of the late 1970's and early 1980's, during which the industry saw repeated and significant drops in term insurance premium rates. The tax benefit also fueled a much increased use of reinsurance, including the concept of ceding companies reducing their normal retentions to obtain the benefit of favorable reinsurance costs.

Phase III Concerns. The 1959 Act placed limitations on the maximum amount which could be accumulated in the Policyholders' Surplus Account. These limits were expressed as functions of premiums or reserves. If the premiums and reserves both became too low, a Phase III tax would be incurred on the amount in excess of the limit.

A number of companies facing a potential Phase III tax turned to reinsurance as a solution. Assumed reinsurance was used to increase the level of premiums or reserves, thereby avoiding the imposition of a Phase III tax. At first, the IRS challenged the use of reinsurance in this manner, but the courts upheld this activity and the practice became relatively common. The later enactment of Section 845, as discussed subsequently, could cause new concerns for companies using this approach. While Phase III is no longer of major concern, the old balances of "untaxed" income are maintained for many stock insurance companies and represent a potential liability.

Another aspect of the Phase III situation was that only those companies that were taxed as life insurance companies were entitled to this deferral of taxation. Reinsurance was sometimes considered as a means to maintain life company tax status, using assumed business to increase the proportion of reserves treated as life insurance reserves.

Effects on the Industry and Congress. The use of reinsurance significantly reduced life insurance industry taxes for a period of time, and therefore played a major role in the development of life insurance taxation as it exists today. The application of reinsurance to obtain tax benefits made a number of people aware of the potential of financial reinsurance and educated a whole generation in the use of reinsurance for financial planning. The movement of surplus and tax benefits through reinsurance encouraged and subsidized the growth of cheaper term and term-like products.

The rapid growth of many life insurance companies was fueled by reinsurance financing in terms of both allowances and risk bearing, and much of this financing was motivated, or at least assisted, by tax benefits to the reinsurer. Many companies were writing large term and term-like policies with average sizes well in excess of their retention limits, requiring significant reinsurance.

Many reinsurers took advantage of the Section 818(c) election to generate tax losses. In some instances, plans with no pretax profit for either the direct writer or the reinsurer produced significant after-tax profits for both. This led to very high coinsurance allowances on some plans and helped to justify the rapid reduction in term insurance rates in the early 1980's, probably to the detriment of the life insurance industry.

Probably the most significant result of the tax-related reinsurance activity of the 1970's and 1980's was the change in the tax code. Congress changed the tax laws for life insurance effective for tax years 1982 and 1983, and again for tax years beginning in 1983 or later. Several of the changes were aimed directly at reinsurance. Congress and the IRS were very aware of the past use of reinsurance for tax reductions and viewed any use of reinsurance with considerable skepticism.

Reinsurance and Federal Income Taxes Today

The tax laws passed in 1982 and 1984 eliminated the provisions of Sections 818(c) and 820 from the Internal Revenue Code.[4] There are no similar provisions in today's tax law. However, many companies became aware of the advantages of shifting the timing of losses and gains from one company to another via reinsurance; that process continues today, both in the financial or surplus relief reinsurance transactions and in the more traditional lines. Just as reinsurance can be used to accomplish many financial purposes for a company, reinsurance can also be used to provide other, more sophisticated tax-related benefits.

A responsible practitioner should be aware that tax law for life insurers is under constant scrutiny, subject to seemingly continual change. There are numerous cases in litigation, as well as constant legislation and IRS activity regarding reinsurance. The law as of this writing is basically that as passed by Congress in 1984, with some modifications, in particular those made in 1990.

DEFRA. The 1984 law was part of a major overhaul of the federal income tax system of the United States, the Deficit Reduction Act of 1984, commonly referred to as DEFRA. The portions unique to insurance companies include Sections 801 through 847. Sections 801 through 818 specifically address life insurance companies and Section 845 addresses reinsurance. The primary changes to life insurance company taxation since DEFRA were made in 1990 and are discussed later in this chapter.

The principal changes in life insurance company taxation due to DEFRA were the elimination of the three phases and the establishment of specified "tax reserves" to be used in the calculation of taxable income. Companies are taxed mostly on total income, including both underwriting gains and investment income. There is no limitation of

---

[4] Some treaties which had included the Section 820 election remain inforce, but without the Section 820 tax treatment. Several legal actions resulted from disagreement with the IRS over the use of Section 818(c), but most of these have been settled at this date.

deductions such as those which caused the unreasonable anomalies of Phase I under the 1959 Act, but there is now a deferral of a portion of acquisition expenses. Stock and mutual companies are taxed in the same manner, except for the so-called "differential" tax.

Section 820 no longer exists. Accordingly, in determining life reserve ratios or another test involving reserves, the reserves for coinsured amounts is, for tax purposes, part of the assuming company's statement and the reserves for modified-coinsured amounts is part of the ceding company's accounts.

OBRA 90 and Section 848. The Omnibus Budget Reconciliation Act of 1990 (OBRA 90) was passed by Congress and signed into law by the President in late 1990. The most significant provision relating to life insurers was the new IRC Section 848. This required the capitalization and amortization of estimated policy acquisition costs. Rather than calculate and debate actual acquisition costs, the estimated acquisition costs are assumed to be the same for all companies, varying only by class of business (such as, individual life and individual annuities). Also somewhat contrary to typical thoughts of acquisition expenses, the Section 848 calculation applies to all premiums collected, not just to first year premiums or expenses.

The amortization period is always 120 months, except for certain "small" companies which have a 60 month amortization period. Amortization is typically believed to begin at mid-year, so a capitalized "expense" of 100 would be recognized for tax purposes as 5 (5%) in the year of capitalization, 10 (10%) in each of the next nine tax years, and 5 (5%) in the eleventh year.

The effect of this so-called "DAC-tax"[5] is to increase taxable earnings in any year in which a premium is collected and reduce taxes for the next ten years. By its eleventh duration, a given policy can be affecting this "DAC" calculation eleven times, with amortization for all eleven premiums collected thus far and capitalization of the amount associated with the eleventh year premium.

---

[5] The "DAC-tax" takes its nickname from its attempt to look somewhat like the deferred acquisition cost (DAC) asset established under GAAP accounting. It is also known as the "proxy DAC."

Tax Effects of Reinsurance

Reinsurance premiums are affected in the same manner as direct premiums, except that reinsurance assumed amounts are always amortized over 120 months, never 60 months. In short, the amount of premiums subject to this "DAC" calculation is direct premium plus reinsurance premium assumed less reinsurance ceded premium paid. The actual definition and calculation of "reinsurance premium" is complicated and is discussed later in this chapter.

Section 848 applies to all premiums, direct and reinsurance, except any initial consideration resulting in an assumption reinsurance transaction or an indemnity coinsurance or modified coinsurance transaction involving inforce blocks of business. Renewal premiums under such agreements are treated as any other premiums for purposes of the "DAC" calculation, but the initial consideration amounts have specific rules which are discussed separately.

Taxation of Gains and Losses. If a reinsurer provides statutory surplus for a company's growth, the reinsurer typically would have a statutory loss and could expect some degree of tax loss also. That loss creates a tax deferral on a current cash basis, allowing the reinsurer to shelter some of its income from taxes or at least defer the taxation. To the extent tax rates vary from one year to another or from one company to another, additional opportunities utilizing reinsurance may be created.

Historically, income from reinsurance has been taxable in the year it occurs, whether the company is a ceding company or a reinsurer. This continues to be the case. Losses due to reinsurance have been subject to various treatments, depending upon the facts of a particular situation.

Losses incurred by a ceding company are generally deductible in the year they occur. Typically, this would arise because reinsurance premiums exceed the sum of allowances, benefits, and reserve credits. However, in some circumstances it may be appropriate to spread a reinsurance cost over more than one tax year. This might occur in the event of a single premium intended to prepay mortality reinsurance on a YRT basis, where no reserve credit is taken. Such circumstances have been very rare.

Usually, a reinsurer will show a statutory loss, or surplus strain, when it puts new reinsurance on its books, especially in the case of a surplus relief agreement. This will typically translate into a tax loss, but the timing of that loss depends upon the terms and form of the reinsurance. In any event, normal tax reserves must be used and the other peculiarities of tax accounting must be observed.

Initial Amounts under Assumption Transactions. For many years there was uncertainty and controversy about the amount and timing of any deductions for ceding commissions under an assumption treaty or an indemnity agreement covering inforce business. Historically, any strain (excess of tax reserves and commission over initial premiums or considerations) was fully deducted in the year of incurral. Through a series of court cases and revenue rulings, the IRS eroded this position.

Under the IRS' position on assumption, any tax deductible strain incurred by the assumption insurer could not be deducted immediately, but must be amortized in the future, roughly in proportion to expected income over the "useful life" of the business.

Until late 1993, the rules for determining the useful life of the business assumed were not precise; generally, useful life was determined as either the expected life of the reinsurance agreement, if it could be determined, or the average life of the business assumed. Under this treatment, the assumption reinsurer would incur statutory strain without an accompanying tax deduction. However, the determination of useful life is such that the deductions typically could be "front-ended."

As part of OBRA 93, IRC Section 197 was added. This provides a 15-year amortization period for intangibles (tax strain) acquired after August 10, 1993. The amount to be capitalized and amortized in an assumption transaction is the excess of any amount paid by the acquiring company over the amount required to be capitalized under Section 848. Thus any ceding commission in excess of the amounts calculated as percentages of premium for DAC-tax purposes is capitalized in addition to the amounts capitalized for DAC-tax purposes.

Initial Amounts under Indemnity Reinsurance of Inforce Blocks. Until recently, the deductibility of initial ceding commissions was even less clear under an indemnity agreement than under an assumption agreement, especially if the reinsurance was of an inforce block of business. Historically, the strain calculated on a tax basis was considered deductible by the reinsurer in the year the strain was incurred.

In 1982, the IRS issued Revenue Ruling 82-69[6] which extended the capitalization and amortization treatment for assumption reinsurance to indemnity reinsurance of blocks of inforce business. The IRS position was challenged in the courts with mixed results; in some cases the court involved upheld the taxpayer's position while other courts agreed with the IRS. This created uncertainty as to the appropriate position to be taken by the reinsuring company.

In June 1989, the Colonial American case reached the United States Supreme Court. This case concerned the deductibility of the strain, or "ceding commission," in an indemnity reinsurance agreement. Under the agreement, a block of inforce business was ceded to Colonial American Life Insurance Company. Colonial American deducted the strain in the year it occurred. The IRS contended that this was really the acquisition of an asset and should be treated as would the acquisition of any asset under general tax accounting; specifically, the ceding commission should be capitalized initially and amortized over the useful life of the business.

The Supreme Court agreed with the IRS, clarifying the conflict which had existed between the different lower court opinions. As a consequence, the ceding commission or strain arising from indemnity reinsurance on inforce business should be amortized and not deducted immediately, a treatment identical to that accorded assumption reinsurance.

The situation was clarified further with the June 1990 release of Revenue Procedure 90-36.[7] This document describes an administrative procedure under which reinsurers can apply the Colonial American decision. A brief discussion of the pertinent points follows.

The Colonial American decision and Revenue Procedure 90-36 address the reinsurance of inforce blocks of business. Reinsurance allowances that parallel the expenses incurred by the ceding company for acquisition, administration, and service of new issues should be deductible by the reinsurer as incurred, in accordance with Letter Ruling 8752003 of the IRS.

Revenue Ruling 82-96 was largely restated as applying to indemnity reinsurance of blocks of inforce business. Ceding commissions spent for

---

[6] IRS Rev. Rul. 82-69. 1982-1 C. B. 102.
[7] Internal Revenue Bulletin 1990-27, July 2, 1990.

purposes of acquiring the block are to be treated as capital expenditures to acquire an asset and amortized over the anticipated life of the asset.

An "annual ceding commission" which is paid by the reinsurer to reimburse the ceding company for the reinsured portion of current expenses of servicing and administration may be deducted in the year in which they are incurred.

The amortization applies only to the portion of the business retained by the reinsurer. Any portion of the ceding commission which is attributable to business which is retroceded may be deducted in the year of the retrocession. This is consistent with the fact that any ceding commission received by the reinsurer from a retrocessionaire will be included in that year's taxable income.

The "up-front ceding commission" to be amortized is defined as "the excess of the increase in the reinsurer's tax reserve liabilities resulting from the transaction... over the value of the net assets received."

The ceding commission is to be amortized over the life of the reinsurance agreement. If possible, the expected life of the reinsurance agreement is to be used. This may be determined from the terms of the agreement, such as any rights of termination or recapture after a specified period of time. If the life of the reinsurance agreement is indeterminate, the "reasonably estimated life of the underlying policies" may be used. The amortization may be on a straight-line basis or done in a manner consistent with the anticipated income, including both premiums and investment income.

The revenue proclamation also proscribed rules for changing the accounting methods with respect to inforce agreements in order to comply with the proclamation and further provided that it applied only to life insurance companies, not to property and liability insurers.

The passage of Section 848 and release of final regulations regarding it in December, 1992, superseded the older regulations and the Colonial American decision for "specified contracts," as defined in the law. For specified contracts, the amounts to be capitalized and amortized regarding reinsurance transactions follows the rules for Section 848, based on the percentages applied to specific product types. However, this superseding does not apply to the reinsurance of products which are not specified contracts, such as IRA's.

The above discussion applies to both ceding and assuming companies with regard to reinsurance of new issues. However, there is not a mirror treatment in the event of assumption transaction. For a ceding company in an assumption, any gain or loss is recorded immediately, with no capitalization or amortization effect. In essence, the total current taxable income of the insurance industry is likely to be increased, as the ceding company reports any gains immediately, but the assuming company must amortize its corresponding investment. Similarly, the ceding company in a typical inforce block transaction reports any gains immediately, except that ongoing renewal premiums are subject to DAC-tax effects.

Life Company Status. An insurance company is taxed as either a "life company" or a "non-life company." While there are many nuances to consider, essentially a company is considered to be a life company for tax purposes if it meets three criteria:

(1) It is primarily engaged in the business of insurance.
(2) It is engaged in the issuance or reinsurance of life insurance policies or annuity contracts.
(3) Over 50% of its reserves are held for "life insurance" plans,[8] including annuities.

Life insurance companies are taxed differently than other companies. There may be advantages to a specific company to be taxed either as a life company or a non-life company. Reinsurance is one means of achieving the preferred status. One way to increase life reserves and thereby establish or maintain life company status is by assuming reinsurance. Ceding non-life reserves may accomplish the same objective. Ceding life reserves or assuming non-life reserves are ways to establish or maintain non-life status. Reinsurance has been used in both situations and its treatment has been upheld by the courts. However, the IRS may still challenge an agreement if significant tax avoidance results or if there is inadequate transfer of risk under the agreement.

---

[8] For tax purposes, noncancellable accident and health insurance policies are considered to be life insurance. A life insurance policy must meet the rules of Section 7702 or it is not considered to be life insurance for tax purposes.

Phase III Status. A potential Phase III tax liability arising from the 1959 Act still exists for many stock companies. Any amounts in the account were "frozen" with the enactment of DEFRA. The balance cannot be increased, but it can be lowered, and this would typically create a tax liability. If a company with a positive Policyholders' Surplus Account balance loses its life company status or if its premium income or life reserves drop below a certain level, a Phase III tax is incurred. Reinsurance has been used to maintain appropriate levels of reserves or premiums.

Small Company Status. Under DEFRA, a "small company" is allowed a special deduction which effectively reduces its taxable income by as much as 60 percent. This deduction is available only to a life company that has less than $15 million of taxable income and also less than $500 million of assets in its corporate group. The deduction grades from 60 percent for taxable income of $3 million or less to zero for taxable income of $15 million or more.

It is conceivable that reinsurance could be used to reduce either assets or income below the applicable limits.

Section 845. Congress, the Treasury Department, and the IRS apparently realized that they could never anticipate and legislate all situations in which reinsurance could be used. However, they were apprehensive about the possible usage of reinsurance to reduce insurance industry taxes significantly. To that end, DEFRA included the creation of Section 845. Although significant reduction of taxes through reinsurance was primarily a phenomenon of life insurance companies, this provision applies to all insurance companies, including property and casualty companies.

There are two parts to Section 845. Under the first part, Section 845(a), the IRS is given very broad latitude to reallocate tax items between two companies which are related. To many practitioners, this is merely a reaffirmation specific to reinsurance of a broader rule concerning related party transactions stated elsewhere in the Internal Revenue Code. Under IRS rules, related parties need not be fully controlled.

The Section 845(a) rules may apply when the transaction involves an agent or conduit between two related parties. Unlike Section 845(b) which applies to unrelated parties, Section 845(a) does not require the presence of "significant" tax avoidance before it can be invoked.[9]

Even prior to the enactment of Section 845, companies usually established "arm's length" standards for reinsurance when related parties were involved. It is uncertain what reinsurance terms will be considered unacceptable, given the IRS' broad powers to reallocate items in the tax returns.

Section 845(b) deals with reinsurance transactions between unrelated parties. Again, the IRS has broad latitude to reallocate income and deduction items between the two parties, but not as broad as provided under Section 845(a). Individual circumstances are important, so it may not be possible to generalize from a situation which was judged acceptable to another similar situation due to the differences in the circumstances.

The IRS has the option to reallocate various income and deduction items within a single company's return if there is a "significant tax avoidance effect." Significant tax avoidance is not defined, but is left to the discretion of the Treasury Secretary, or in effect, to the IRS. Evidence of fraud or intent to avoid taxation is not required, merely the presence of tax avoidance. For a given reinsurance transaction, the determination of significant tax avoidance involves an examination of the relationship of the resulting tax benefits and the risks transferred.

Congressional committee reports[10] give some guidance about certain reinsurance situations which might raise questions of tax avoidance, such as the following:

(1) The equity of a company is artificially reduced.
(2) The source or character of any item is changed or the taxation of income items is deferred.

---

[9] The effective dates of the two parts of Section 845 were different. Section 845(a) applied to any related-party transaction effective on or after September 27, 1983. Section 845(b) applied to any risks reinsured after December 31, 1984.

[10] Staff of the Joint Committee on Taxation, General Explanation of the Deficit Reduction Act of 1984. H.R. 4170. 98th Cong., and General Explanation of the Revenue Provisions of the Deficit Reduction Act of 1984, prepared by the Staff of the Joint Committee on Taxation. December 31, 1984.

(3) A loss which could only be used against earnings of one company can now be used by others in a consolidation (removal of the "separate return limitation year (SRLY) taint").
(4) Tax benefits are artificially transferred between taxpayers in different tax brackets.
(5) A loss carryover period is extended.

The presence of any of the above facts may trigger a review by the IRS. In their absence, some factors which may need examination were included in the committee report. These are to be explored in total, as no single factor may be determinative by itself. The committee's factors include the following:

(1) *Age of the Business Reinsured.* Older business is often held to have less lapse risk and therefore may be an indicator of a lowered level of economic risk transfer relative to the tax benefits.
(2) *Character of the Business Reinsured.* If the tax benefits of the business transferred are disproportionate to the risks transferred, there may be a question of tax avoidance.
(3) *Structure for Determining Potential Profits.* A reasonable sharing of future profits may indicate an absence of risk avoidance.
(4) *Duration of the Agreement.* A history of a long-term relationship may be an indicator of the absence of risk avoidance.
(5) *Provisions for Termination of the Agreement.* Provisions to protect the reinsurer's investment in the event of termination may be an indicator of the need for further investigation.
(6) *The Tax Positions of the Parties.* If both companies are in the same tax position (large/small, profit/loss, life/non-life), the chances for tax avoidance are much smaller.
(7) *The Financial Positions of the Parties.* Surplus relief for an otherwise insolvent company tends to indicate a lack of tax avoidance.

The law does not require that an adjustment be made to the tax returns of both parties to the reinsurance agreement; the IRS can reallocate items in one party's tax return and not change the other's. For example, the IRS could reclassify a reinsurer's commissions and allowances, eliminating its deduction, but leave the income the allowances generated for the ceding company with the ceding company. In effect, the application of Section 845 could result in double taxation. The IRS has the authority to reallocate items where only one party is a domestic taxpayer, subject to United States federal income taxes.

The background documentation of the development of Section 845 shows that Congress and the IRS intended for this provision to be used to prevent reinsurance abuses which distort taxable income. Certain exclusions and safe harbors were contemplated. As an example, taking over the business of a company near insolvency would normally not be subject to reallocation.

Proportionality is a safe harbor. Proportionality exists when allowances are constructed such that the strain is divided between the ceding company and the reinsurer roughly in proportion to the division of the business between the parties. The documented safe harbors include the following:

(1) YRT reinsurance to the extent that the agreement calls for the payment of premiums for an annual risk only and does not provide for direct sharing of expenses.
(2) Coinsurance of annual renewable term products.
(3) Coinsurance of new issues of a ceding company where expenses and income items are allocated between the two parties in proportion to the risk transferred.
(4) Coinsurance which covers inforce blocks of business where the initial ceding commission reasonably reflects the proper allocable share of any premium for the ceding company representing future profits on the business and any past expenses of the ceding company.

The IRS has not issued regulations for Section 845 and, in the opinion of many experts, is unlikely to ever do so. Because this is a relatively new provision and no regulations are forthcoming, there are no precedents upon which reliance can be placed. Care should be taken in interpreting the exclusions and safe harbors.

In 1993, the IRS made its first comprehensive ruling regarding the application of Section 845(b) regarding reinsurance between unrelated parties, with a conclusion which is unfavorable to the taxpayer. This situation involved two agreements between the same two unrelated parties. The point in question involved the resulting life company status of one of the parties. With both agreements in place, company A would be treated as a life company and qualify for the small company deduction, reducing A's taxes by about 60%. The IRS noted that A would save over $1 million in federal income taxes over three years, but would assume only minimal risk under the agreement in question.

In a Technical Advice Memorandum, the IRS did not explain the company's argument or discuss its own position at length, but merely states its position that, under Section 845(b) the reinsurance agreement can be disregarded in determining A's life company status.

The IRS is concerned about legitimate risk transfer as opposed to agreements where only paper liabilities are involved and no cash loss can ever be incurred by the reinsurer. Therefore, a major consideration in constructing an agreement which needs favorable tax treatment is that some meaningful element of risk be transferred from the ceding company to the reinsurer, *i.e.*, that it not be a sham transaction. The more risks that are transferred, and the greater the degree of those risks, the more likely it is that the desired tax treatment will result. This is an important reason to utilize experienced reinsurance and tax advisors when considering such a treaty.

Special Mutual Company Taxes. Under DEFRA, mutual life insurance companies have a special tax[11] assessed on their surplus. The rules for this are very complex, but the important fact is that for most mutual life insurers, additional surplus creates additional tax. For this reason, some mutual companies have found that they can use surplus to finance reinsurance. This has a twofold benefit: earnings are increased by the profits on the reinsurance and the special tax on surplus is reduced to the extent that the additional business generated from reinsurance requires surplus.

---

[11] This tax is technically a reduction in the deductibility of policyholder dividends for mutual companies and is known as the tax on differential earnings. The provision for these tax is contained in Section 809.

Alternative Minimum Tax. DEFRA introduced the concept of the alternative minimum tax, or AMT. AMT is a tax on certain tax-preferred income items and applies to all businesses, not just to certain insurance companies.

AMT is based on an adjustment to taxable income known as "adjusted current earnings," or ACE. The underlying tax policy is to include "economic income" in the AMT base. The current method of computation was introduced in 1990 and applies for any taxable year beginning after 1989.

A company's pre-adjustment alternative minimum taxable income (AMTI) is adjusted by 75% of the difference between the amount calculated as ACE and its pre-adjusted AMTI. This adjustment can be either positive or negative, although any negative amount is limited to the net adjustment from all prior years.

Earnings from reinsurance transactions is part of pre-adjusted AMTI, the same as earnings from direct insurance. Accordingly, reinsurance transactions normally would not affect the ACE adjustment.

Offshore and Foreign Treaties. Many foreign countries have tax bases which are significantly different from that of the United States. In the past, it was not uncommon for a United States insurer to reinsure business with a foreign based company to improve the total tax position of both companies by capitalizing on the differences of the two systems of taxation. That practice is much less common today. The presence of Section 845 allows for the reallocation of income and deduction items and therefore makes the use of an international reinsurance treaty less certain.

There is special provision regarding the DAC-tax and foreign treaties. If the reinsurer is not a United States taxpayer, the ceding company does not recognize the net effect of the reinsurance ceded transaction in its DAC-tax computation. However, business accepted by a United States taxpayer from a non-United States taxpayer is included in the DAC-tax calculations of the reinsurer.

However, saving taxes is not the only, nor even the primary, motivation for reinsurance treaties, either domestic or international. As a result, many international reinsurance treaties exist today. Certain provisions of the tax code and regulations apply to these treaties.

Reinsurance ceded outside of the country to a non-United States taxpayer calls for an excise tax. This tax is in lieu of an income tax on the reinsurer and is the responsibility of the ceding company. The current excise tax for life and health insurance products, both direct and reinsurance ceded, is 1% of premiums. The rate on property and casualty products currently is 4% of direct premiums and 1% of reinsurance ceded premiums.

The excise tax is waived for reinsurance to companies domiciled in certain countries. Any such waiver is granted as part of a tax treaty between the United States and the other country. Historically, the most important countries with such treaties have been the United Kingdom and France. The cost of the excise tax should be considered like any other expense.

The list of countries which have such treaties changes frequently; anyone involved with international reinsurance should check the current status of such treaties. The status could change after the initiation of a treaty, thus affecting the expenses involved in maintaining the agreement.

International reinsurance may be subject to other taxes, such as those pertaining to controlled foreign corporations, to passive income, or to foreign tax credits. While these topics are well beyond the scope of this book, it is important to identify all possible tax implications and include them in any analysis relating to reinsurance.

TAX PLANNING

Reinsurance usually is consummated for reasons other than tax savings. Overall financial stability and pretax income are typically the primary motivations. But tax considerations can be very important. Taxes are an expense, and it is a legitimate goal of management to reduce expenses.

It is not only reasonable but necessary to consider the tax implications in designing and analyzing reinsurance agreements; one design might lead to increased taxes while another might be tax neutral or might reduce taxes. In addition, reinsurance is a source of capital and should be analyzed as such, including the tax effects. Therefore, tax planning and reinsurance planning often go hand-in-hand.

Certain considerations are applicable in the vast majority, if not all, reinsurance transactions where significant tax benefits or questions are present. These and the specific use of tax loss carryovers are discussed below.

General Considerations

Tax planning involving reinsurance has become much more difficult since 1984. Prior to 1984, there were straightforward methodologies and specific provisions within the law favoring tax planning using reinsurance; the situation is almost completely reversed today. There are no specific provisions, such as the since repealed Sections 818(a)(2) and 820, allowing for any tax-favored reinsurance transaction.

To the contrary, Section 845 now grants the IRS broad reallocation authority; its potential application must be factored into any reinsurance planning program.

Nonetheless, many companies continue to enter into reinsurance transactions which result in significant tax benefits. This should be done with care and with the use of tax and reinsurance experts. One thing which is certain is that uncertainty will continue for some time in this arena. Tax planning using reinsurance is not impossible, but it is complicated.

If possible, a company would prefer to incur tax losses at high tax rates and gains at low rates. This is not always under the company's control, but to some extent reinsurance may assist in planning to maximize such opportunities. It should be kept in mind that effective tax rates can change, either because of legislative action or because a company's circumstances change. An example of this would include a company moving from a small company position to a normal tax position or moving into or out of the AMT situation.

Some tax planning opportunities, such as preservation of Phase III tax deferrals, maintenance of small life company status, or maintenance of life company status have been discussed earlier in this chapter. Perhaps the largest opportunity for using tax situations to optimize tax benefits is the matching of tax losses in one company with the provision of surplus and earnings by another company. This is a major consideration in structuring financial reinsurance. A similar opportunity exists when a company has a tax loss carryover.

Loss Carryovers

The tax code provides that if a corporation's taxable income is negative for a given year, the loss can be applied to income in other years. This is accomplished by the use of loss carryovers.

If a company has gains in prior years, it may use the current loss as a loss carry back to offset those gains and recover taxes previously paid. Any tax recovery is limited to prior taxes actually paid. The period of time for which losses can be carried back is subject to change by Congress, but is currently three years. Losses must be carried back to the earliest possible year and applied to that year first; any remaining losses are then applied to the next qualifying year.

If a company does not use the loss as a carry back, it may use it as a loss carry forward. In this case, the loss is carried into future tax years and used to reduce future taxable income. A loss carry forward may be less valuable than a carry back because a carry back will result in current cash income, where a carry forward has no current cash benefit. The actual benefits will vary according to the facts in the case. Currently, the limitation on tax loss carry forwards is fifteen years.[12]

Reinsurance can be used to take advantage of loss carryover situations. If a company has a loss carry forward, it might choose to use reinsurance to accelerate future income which would be sheltered from current taxes. In this manner, it could realize a current cash benefit from a loss carry forward. On the other hand, a reinsurer may create a current tax loss and use it as a carry back to recover taxes already paid.

OTHER TAX RELATED ISSUES

Taxation of life insurance companies is complex and the administration complicated. Reinsurance adds layers of additional complexity to this administration and the striving for compliance in an ever-changing environment. Some of these administrative or smaller issues are discussed in this section.

---

[12] The carry forward and carryback periods discussed here are for operating losses. Capital losses are determined separately and, currently, may be carried back for three years also, but forward for only five years.

Tax Effects of Reinsurance

Accounting for Reinsurance

Several aspects of reinsurance agreements call for special attention with respect to taxes. The most complicated of these is the calculation of reinsurance premiums, but other aspects may be troublesome. As an overall guide, it is better to be precise about accounting issues than to rely on simplistic estimates.

Calculation of Reinsurance Premiums. Reinsurance premiums, for both ceding and accepting companies, is precisely defined, in theory, under the regulations concerning Section 848. "Net premiums" are to be included in the tax return of an insurance company. IRC Section 848(d) defines "net premiums" as the excess, if any, of premiums and other considerations received over return premiums and other considerations incurred for such contracts. Premiums received includes both amounts received from policyholders and contractholders and amounts received from ceding companies for reinsurance accepted. This net premium is the amount subject to capitalization and amortization.

To prevent potential abuse, reinsurance ceded premiums can be used to reduce net premiums only when ceded to another company which is subject to United States taxation.

Under the final regulations for Section 848 issued in December 1992, a netting concept was adopted to ensure constancy of treatment by the ceding and assuming company. All reinsurance items incurred are to be netted, with the net negative of one company equaling the net positive of the other. Both parties are required to make this net calculation the first year, so timing is also consistent, resulting in mirror image treatment.

The items to be netted include all cash transactions, such as ceding commissions, annual allowances, reimbursements for benefits and claims, reinsurer participation in policy loans, experience refunds, termination payments, and modified coinsurance reserve adjustments, including the interest component. In the event of funds withheld agreements as well as modified coinsurance, the net cash settlement is followed. Thus, for tax purposes, reinsurance premiums are basically the net cash flows.

Regulations are in place to prevent "dumping" the DAC-tax liability on small companies which would pay no taxes. There are also special rules for dealing with insolvent ceding companies.

It should be noted that the definition of "premiums" for Section 848 purposes is unique to Section 848 applications and somewhat artificial. The resulting "premiums" may, and likely will be, different from "premiums" as used elsewhere in the tax return, such as in calculating taxable income or Phase III limitations. Premiums for those purposes correspond closely to the statutory use of the classification.

Tax Reserves. Reserves established for federal income tax accounting purposes differ from those established for GAAP or statutory purposes. Since 1984, insurance companies have been required to calculate reserves for tax return purposes based on specified mortality tables, interest rates, and methods. These specified bases are the same for reinsurance assumed and ceded as for direct issues.

Occasionally, questions arise regarding the proper basis for blocks of business that were reinsured other than when issued, at a much later date, such as would occur in an assumption or block indemnity transaction. The proper reserve is to be based on the original year of issue of the underlying business, not the first year of the reinsurance.

Unauthorized Reinsurance. Statutory accounting disallows reserve credit and receivables arising from reinsurance transactions with unauthorized reinsurers. GAAP accounting treats unauthorized reinsurance the same as authorized, allowing reinsurance treatment if the risk transferred is appropriate and there is no reason to doubt the collectability of claims. Tax accounting more closely parallels GAAP in this instance, with accounting treatment based on the economic nature of the transaction. Any amounts on deposit for security from unauthorized reinsurers is treated as a cash deposit in the determination of net reinsurance premiums.

Uncollectable Reinsurance. On occasion, a claim against a reinsurer will turn out to be uncollectable or a reinsurer will not be able to collect premiums from a ceding company, most often due to the failure of the other party. Treatment of the uncollected amounts on a tax return is uncertain. It is generally thought that a better case for taking a tax loss can be made if the loss has also been recognized for statutory purposes. For example, a ceding company which cannot collect from a reinsurer should reduce any reserve credits to zero and fully recognize any claims without benefit of reinsurance.

Documentation

The IRS has the ability to investigate all aspects of the financial results of an insurance company, including reinsurance. If proper treatment of a reinsurance transaction is important to the results of a company, then it is advisable that the reinsurance transaction be well documented. At a minimum, the contract and the accounting records should be clear and should be consistent both with each other and with the intent. It is also advisable that all memos or letters regarding the transaction be clear and consistent with the final result.

It is also advisable to be consistent, whenever possible, between statutory, GAAP, and tax accounting with respect to reinsurance. Tax examiners may ask to see the statutory or GAAP accounting for specific reinsurance transactions. Inconsistent treatment may lead to other questions. Failure to pass risk transfer tests in GAAP or statutory accounting may lead to questions under Section 845. If a transaction fails to pass risk on a statutory basis, it will be difficult to demonstrate risk transfer for tax purposes.

Policyholder Taxation

Policyholder taxation issues are not affected by indemnity reinsurance. The contract is between the policyholder and the issuing company, and, under normal circumstances, the issuing, or ceding, company has the responsibility for maintaining policyholder tax records and meeting compliance standards. Even in a joint venture, the company with its name on the policy has these responsibilities. If they are given to the reinsurer in an administrative capacity, there should be a separate contract for administrative matters, or at least a separate section in the reinsurance agreement outlining the responsibilities of each party.

Special Topics and Applications

Part Four

15 Nonproportional Reinsurance

In a life insurance company, proportional reinsurance is used to prevent any one claim from having a significant negative effect on earnings and surplus; nonporportional reinsurance is used primarily to reduce fluctuations in total claims. Proportional reinsurance always applies on an individual, risk by risk basis, regardless of overall claims results. Nonproportional reinsurance may be applied on an individual risk basis, used to limit claims on a block of business, or used to reduce the ceding company's exposure to a particular hazard. The reinsurer's participation in the risk depends upon the amount of the claim or claims, the number of claims, or some combination thereof.

It is not the intent of this book to discuss all of the applications and ramifications of nonproportional reinsurance. This chapter provides a brief introduction to the more common forms of nonproportional reinsurance used in life insurance: stop loss, catastrophe, and spread loss coverages. Under each of these forms, the reinsurance risk and coverage applies to a block of risks, not to individual risks.

Nonproportional forms of coverage are frequently used for accident and health as well as property and liability coverages for both blocks of business and individual risks. For a discussion of the use of nonproportional reinsurance for individual risks, see Chapter 19, Health Reinsurance.

STOP LOSS

Stop loss coverage provides protection against an excessive number or amount of claims in any given contract period. While stop loss coverage may be used alone, it is used more commonly in conjunction with proportional reinsurance.

Stop loss coverage sometimes is used to assist the ceding company in increasing its retention limit. Stop loss can provide a cushion from unfavorable overall claims experience following a retention increase. The use of recapture in conjunction with stop loss and increased retention must be considered carefully. Many reinsurers take the position that recapture and subsequent coverage under a stop loss agreement is an act of recapturing to cede the block to another reinsurer. This practice is not allowed under most recapture provisions.

For life insurance, stop loss applies to a block of policies, not just to one life.[1] In a stop loss arrangement, the reinsurer pays only covered claims in excess of an attachment point. This point usually is expressed in terms of a percentage of expected claims, subject to some minimum level of claims. The attachment point typically is set as an amount equal to at least one maximum claim above the expected amount of claims. A typical attachment point might be 110% of expected claims after deduction for reimbursements from any proportional reinsurance.

Certain types of claims may be excluded from the coverage, such as group coverages or certain blocks of small amounts at risk. When total covered claims have exceeded the attachment point, the stop loss reinsurer will pay a specified percentage of all additional net claims up to a predetermined maximum.

Terms of a typical stop loss agreement for life insurance might be as follows:

---

[1] For accident and health and other open-ended benefit coverages, stop loss may apply either in "aggregate" to collective risks or in "specific" form to a single risk. See Chapter 19, Health Reinsurance.

Nonproportional Reinsurance

Maximum Retention: $100,000 per life.

Expected Claims: $5,250,000 (defined by formula as, say, 105% of a specified experience table, where "true" expected claims would be $5,000,000).

Attachment Point: 110% of expected claims, subject to a minimum of $5,775,000.[2]

Limits: 90% of all covered claims in excess of the attachment point amount, up to a total maximum of $1,000,000, with a maximum on any single life of $100,000.

In this example, if actual claims were under $5,775,000, the stop loss coverage would pay nothing. If actual claims were, for example, $6,500,000, the reinsurer would pay 90% of the excess claims, which is 90% of $6,500,000 less $5,775,000, or $652,500. If actual covered claims equaled or exceeded $6,886,111, the reinsurer would pay $1,000,000. This assumes that the limit of $100,000 on each life has been applied in calculating covered claims, and that all excluded risks have been taken into account properly.

The premium charged for stop loss coverage is often expressed as a percentage of expected claims plus a fixed fee. In theory, stop loss net premiums are easy to calculate using risk theory methods. However, parameters such as epidemics, catastrophes, and other nonindependent events, as well as the high probability of fluctuation, must be considered and create significant complications. The actual calculation of claims and premiums may be difficult because of the problem of assembling the appropriate data.

The method used to determine expected claims is obviously critical and must be carefully defined in the reinsurance treaty. Coverage is restricted to net retained claims in order to avoid duplication of

---

[2] The $5,775,000 is calculated as 1.05 x 1.10 x $5,000,000. In this case the 10% margin exceeded the $100,000 minimum of one retention, so no additional amount was added.

reinsurance. Both expected and actual claims are determined on the net amount at risk, not the gross death benefit. The net premiums are then loaded to cover expenses and the risk of deviation. Sometimes, this loading is several times the net premium.

Stop loss coverage is relatively inexpensive and useful for protecting surplus. Proper use of stop loss could lead to lower long term reinsurance costs by allowing companies to establish higher individual risk retentions. The coverage is also closely aligned with most management needs, protecting overall surplus and earnings from all claim fluctuations, even those in the normally retained portion of the business.

However, few insurance companies purchase stop loss. Maximum coverage amounts, both overall and per life, are relatively small, so stop loss will not protect against all claim exposures to earnings. Stop loss cannot replace individual risk coverages, but can supplement those traditional coverages.

Stop loss coverages are not guaranteed to be renewable at a given rate, or even to be renewed at all. This uncertainty may cause ceding company managements to be reluctant to place much reliance on a stop loss agreement as a long range tool for surplus protection.

Furthermore, such coverages are not widely available. Relatively few North American reinsurers offer stop loss coverage on life insurance because it is a very low premium coverage with a risk of significant deviation. While the probability of a claim is low, the cost, when one occurs, is high. It is difficult to write enough stop loss coverage in any year to provide an adequate spread of risk and balance premiums and claims.

Those reinsurers that write stop loss coverage sometimes do so only as an accommodation to existing clients and with some reliance on the trend of improving mortality experience. The reinsurer has a very low probability of recouping any losses incurred on a case because the ceding company can terminate a contract rather than pay the increased premium which would likely result from a year of bad claims.

Administration of stop loss and accumulation of the necessary data, for both premium and claim computations, was very difficult. With proper use of modern computer technology, such problems are reduced, but not eliminated. Systems resources are still necessary, as well as very accurate coding of records.

CATASTROPHE COVERAGE

Catastrophe coverage, or cat cover, is more commonly used than stop loss for life insurance. Catastrophe coverage protects the ceding company against multiple single claims from a single event such as a plane crash, a fire, an earthquake, or some other accident or natural disaster. The covered events must be carefully defined and may exclude epidemics, wars, riots, nuclear hazards, or certain specified events. Certain types of risks may also be excluded such as sports teams, airline personnel, credit card and travel accident coverage, long term disability, and assumed reinsurance.

In effect, a cat cover protects the ceding company from unplanned, presumably random concentrations of risks or claims. Know concentrations usually are excluded from the catastrophe coverage, or a higher premium is charge.

Each agreement is individually negotiated and unique. The premium for the coverage is usually expressed in terms of a rate per million of mean inforce business. The contract will specify a minimum required number of individual claims and overall deductible per event as well as the maximum amount of claims covered. A per life limit is used to limit claims. Only the net amounts at risk will be used in determining premiums and claims.

Catastrophe is very useful and quite common as both large and small companies are exposed to multiple deaths from a single event. In fact, larger companies may have a higher probability of loss from any one accident because of a larger exposure. Usually, the coverage pays only after the occurrence of three, four, five, or more deaths from a single event. Large deductibles are common. Some companies desiring a large amount of catastrophe coverage purchase two or more contracts in layers. Each layer would have a deductible which would include all layers below it.

Catastrophe coverage is readily available and relatively inexpensive. However, because the probability of a catastrophic event is so small, the coverage is unlikely to replace a company's traditional proportional reinsurance portfolio or allow the company to increase its retention limit.

SPREAD LOSS

A spread loss agreement provides coverage if a company's losses in a given year exceeded a specified attachment point. The attachment point and reinsurer's participation can be defined in a manner similar to that used for stop loss. If a claim occurs, the reinsurer would pay the ceding company. The ceding company would then repay the amount of the claim with interest over a period of years, thus spreading the loss. The repayment is frequently accomplished by an increase in the premium following incurral of a claim.

In its traditional form, spread loss reinsurance is not really a form of reinsurance, but is more a means of changing the timing of cash flows. Premiums are somewhat arbitrary and are subject to negotiation.

This type of coverage may be useful for protecting the cash flow of a company but it does not ultimately protect surplus. Spread loss most likely would not qualify for statutory reserve credit or be treated as reinsurance for GAAP purposes. Any cash benefit received by the company would almost certainly require that a liability be established for future repayment.

The risks to the reinsurer are not among the normal ones of mortality, morbidity, persistency, interest, or default, but rather those of cash flow timing, credit, or insolvency. In essence, spread loss reinsurance is a type of loan. If the ceding company becomes insolvent during the period of time it owes the reinsurer a spread loss payment, the receiver would likely terminate the reinsurance agreement and the reinsurer would not be repaid. Any claim that the reinsurer paid would be repaid only subject to the continued solvency of the ceding company.

RESERVE CONSIDERATIONS

There are no firmly established standards for reserves for nonproportional reinsurance. Judgment, familiarity with Actuarial Standard of Practice No. 11, and, for GAAP, familiarity with Financial Accounting Standard 113 are important.

Ceding Company

One point common to most nonproportional reinsurance is that it seldom qualifies for any reserve credit in the convention blank. Since nonproportional reinsurance generally covers only risks beyond those covered by normal reserves, no reserve credit is taken.

However, it is possible to construct a stop loss agreement in such a manner that it transfers a risk which is covered by the basic reserves. For example, it is possible to construct a stop loss coverage with the attachment point set at 80% of the valuation mortality table rates. In this case, some reserve credit may be justified, but the situation is unclear.

Historically, reserve credits for nonproportional coverages have not generally been acceptable to regulators. Exceptions include claim recoveries not yet collected and, in some instances, unearned premium amounts. Given the recent introduction of Actuarial Standard of Practice No. 11 on reinsurance by the Actuarial Standards Board, acceptable forms of nonproportional reinsurance which permit reserve credit may be possible. The issue is not really the form of the reinsurance as much as it is the transfer of risk and the timing of cash settlements. Many regulators have historically insisted on proportionality[3] before they would permit any reserve credits.

If, in the course of producing the statutory annual statement, it is determined that monies are owed to a ceding company as the result of a nonproportional reinsurance agreement, that company may include those amounts as a credit just as it would for a proportional reinsurance ceded due and unpaid claim. The amount of credit would be subject to the normal rules regarding authorized and unauthorized reinsurers.

In reviewing reserve credits for nonproportional reinsurance, the terms of the specific agreement must be considered. In a normal stop loss or catastrophe coverage situation, any claims recoverable would be treated as any other reinsurance claims recoverable. However, in a spread loss situation, any claim due most likely would be offset by future premiums which would be an offsetting liability for the ceding company.

---

[3] In this context, proportionality is intended to convey the thought of the reinsurer paying a fixed percentage of each claim as it is incurred by the ceding company, not paying amounts following the depletion of some fund held by the ceding company or paying only after overall experience has exceeded some level.

On a GAAP basis, a benefit reserve credit might be appropriate for stop loss or catastrophe if a model based on GAAP assumptions demonstrates that a recovery is expected. Premiums typically would flow through as incurred. Unearned premiums may be included in both GAAP and statutory balance sheets, according to the terms of the treaty. This would be true for both the United States and Canada.

Under United States GAAP accounting, a typical spread loss agreement would not qualify for reinsurance accounting treatment, but would be treated as financing, or a loan, with deposit accounting treatment. In effect, a liability would be established for future repayment. In Canada, both statutory and GAAP accounting require the recognition of all future net cash payments, leading to the conclusion that spread loss would be of no benefit in financial reporting.

Reinsurer

For statutory purposes, some reinsurers take the gross premiums into earnings as earned during the year covered. Others reserve all or part of the net premium. If a reserve is established, a claim payment usually reduces the reserve before it affects surplus. Regardless of the practice regarding reserves, the reinsurer should maintain adequate surplus in relation to its risk for nonproportional reinsurance.

Under GAAP accounting,[4] all premiums normally would be earned during the period of coverage and all claims taken into earnings when they occur. In some instances, it may be permissible to report only the loading as earnings, establishing a benefit reserve from net premiums. If the reinsurer wishes to establish a benefit reserve, it should be able to demonstrate that a future claim is a reasonable likely event. It should also provide a computational mechanism for releasing the reserve over some period of time if a claim does not occur.

Under either statutory or GAAP, if a claim is incurred, the reinsurer should establish a reserve for the value of the amount it expects to pay, discounted consistently with other claim amounts.

---

[4] As with all GAAP accounting questions, treatment of accounting for nonproportional treaties should be discussed with the reinsurer's accounting firm.

16 Assumption

The majority of this book has dealt with indemnity reinsurance, which is by far a more common occurrence than is assumption. Assumption differs from indemnity reinsurance in one very major regard: under assumption the obligations and the relationship to the policyholder shifts from the original direct writing company to the assumption insurer.[1] The assumption insurer issues the policyholder a certificate of assumption which is to be placed with the policy. All contacts with the policyholder and the agent, including premium collection, commission payment, and benefit notification, are handled by the assumption insurer.

This treatment obviously differs from that of indemnity reinsurance where the policyholder is generally not aware of its existence. Basically, indemnity reinsurance allows the direct writer increased capacity and

---

[1] In the past, including the first edition of this text, the term "assumption reinsurance" was commonly used. Most people now recognize that indemnity reinsurance and assumption are very different processes and products. Accordingly, the term "assumption" is used without the added "reinsurance." The company accepting the responsibility to policyholders may be referred to as the assumption reinsurer, the assumption insurer, the assumption carrier, or, simply, the buyer.

ability to underwrite more risks than it otherwise could. Assumption, on the other hand, is the sale of the original insurer's interest in the block of business, a permanent transfer of all interest and obligations similar to the sale of any asset from one business to another.

Chapter 10, Reinsurance Regulation, discusses the specific laws and regulations pertaining to assumption, including the Assumption Reinsurance Model Act. This chapter discusses the business and practical aspects of assumptions.

THE ASSUMPTION PROCESS

The two companies, the ceding company and the assumption insurer, must negotiate an assumption agreement covering the sale or transfer of the block of business. Generally, there is no provision for recapture as the transfer is intended to be permanent in nature and the original direct insurer will have no further interest or obligations regarding the policies. Subsequent to the assumption, it is as though the policies had always been issued by the assumption insurer.

Typically, the ceding company would be responsible for any claims incurred up to the point of the assumption and the assumption insurer responsible for any thereafter. If both parties' objectives are to be met and disputes avoided, it is important that they agree upon the liabilities and any specific assets that are to be transferred.

In many states, the insurance department has either specified regulatory or assumed defacto power to approve or prevent an assumption transaction. In other states, the regulators believe that they have no control over this process. Most states require that an assumption insurer be directly licensed in the ceding company's state of domicile. Some regulators believe that as long as the assuming company is reasonably sound financially and is admitted as a reinsurer in that state, there should be no objection. The regulators are concerned about the benefits promised to the policyholders and generally review any assumption agreement to see if the policyholders would be adversely affected by the proposed transaction.

Effect on the Policyholder

Under the indemnity reinsurance process, the direct writing insurer has made promises to the policyholder based upon the terms of the policy. The policyholder can look to that company to perform, but he cannot look to the reinsurer. In fact, most indemnity reinsurance treaties carry a clear statement that no third party, including any policyholder, has any rights established under the reinsurance treaty. The indemnity reinsurance treaty is strictly a bilateral agreement between the ceding company and the reinsurer.

Under assumption, the opposite occurs. The assumption insurer assumes the direct obligation to the policyholder and the original writing company expects to be removed from any further policyholder obligations. In normal operation, the policyholder has all of his future dealings with the new carrier and no further contact with the original carrier.

The policyholder is not absolutely helpless. In legal theory, the policy is a two-party contract between the insurer and the policyholder and cannot be unilaterally transferred by either one of the parties without the consent of the other. In an assumption, if that consent is given, a novation, or new contract, is created between the policyholder and the assumption insurer. This consent can be either specific or implied. Some state regulators require the specific consent of the policyholder while others deem that the policyholder has consented if he pays premiums or submits claims to the assumption insurer.

Courts have been divided on this issue. Most recently, however, a California appeals court held that an original insurer was liable to the policyholder for benefits following the insolvency and default of the assumption insurer.[2] In this case, the court held that the submission of claims to the new insurer did not imply consent by the policyholder as he had no other course of action short of losing all benefits.

Both legal and regulatory decisions have been divided regarding the need for consent of the policyholder and what constitutes consent. Any parties considering entering into an assumption transaction are well advised to obtain competent legal counsel.

---

[2] Baer v. Associated Life Insurance Company, 248 California Reporter 1989.

Sometimes policyholders are concerned about an assumption, believing that the rules have been changed and promises modified, and that they have no say in the matter. This concern is greater if the new carrier is less well known or is viewed as being less sound than the original insurer.

For this reason, increased lapse rates frequently occur immediately after the assumption transaction; policyholders surrender the existing policies and replace them with those of companies of their own choosing, usually subject to new underwriting by the new carrier. This in turn may cause the mortality or morbidity of the remaining block to deteriorate, since less healthy risks cannot pass new underwriting. Consequently, the value of a block of business may change as the result of the assumption. This is known as the "shock lapse" effect.

Many assumption transactions result from a company selling business in order to generate immediate value. If a stronger company or one which specializes in that particular type of business assumes the policies, the policyholder may end up with a more secure position.

Certificates of Assumption

Once the assumption agreement is finalized, the assumption insurer has a limited period of time, such as 60 days, during which to notify the policyholders of the change in insurers. This is usually done through a certification of assumption which the assumption insurer issues to each policyholder, identifying the new carrier and describing how to contact that carrier. From that point forward, the assumption insurer typically takes over the responsibilities for policy administration.

The content of the required notice is detailed in Section 4A(2) of the Assumption Reinsurance Model Act. However, the insurance departments of the states of domicile of both the ceding company and the assumption insurer must approve the certificate of assumption. Either department may desire modification of the standard notice if it finds the notice to be unfair, inadequate, or misleading. The departments may differ in their requirements. As of this writing, not all states had adopted the Model Act.

The certificate of assumption becomes a part of the policy and the policyholder is advised to keep it with his policy just as he would any other endorsement or rider.

Original Insurer Responsibilities

Under assumption, the original carrier expects to have no further responsibilities to the policyholder. The two companies agree as to the consideration to be paid for the business. They also negotiate the type and amount of assets which should be transferred to meet the obligations and satisfy the reserve requirements of the reinsured policies. They should document specific agreement regarding responsibility for claims incurred prior to the assumption date and for claims in course of settlement and claims incurred but not reported as of the assumption date.

There are both ethical and business responsibilities on the part of the ceding company to ensure that the assumption insurer has the ability to pay future benefits. While there may not be a specific regulation or law requiring this, it would be prudent for the ceding company to exercise some reasonable judgment. For example, if the assumption insurer were to become unable to pay reasonable future benefits, and it was obvious that the reinsurer was financially unsound at the time of the transfer, some contingent liability might revert to the ceding company.

It is probable that if bad faith or fraud could be demonstrated, the original insurer would have liability for the failure of the reinsurer to perform. It is also logical that this liability would lessen over time. For example, if the assuming company was rated highly and apparently sound at the time of the transaction, but became insolvent 25 years later, it is unlikely that such action would prevail.

The legal profession has been reluctant to issue any clean opinion that a ceding company would be absolutely free of future liability following an assumption agreement. Until recently, there were few trial cases where the original company was found liable for the assumption insurer's failure to perform. The Baer case[3] caused many insurers to reassess their position regarding selling a block of business through assumption since they could become liable if the new carrier fails to perform. Adoption of the Assumption Reinsurance Model Act is expected to provide clarity and additional comfort to companies entering into assumption agreements.

---

[3] *Ibid.*

The intricacies of an assumption agreement will vary depending upon the parties involved, the type of business involved, the states involved in the transaction, and the economic conditions surrounding it. It is always important that both parties receive proper legal, tax, accounting, and actuarial advice as the agreement is being negotiated.

Once the assumption has taken place and the certificates issued, the original insurer has no further responsibilities beyond those outlined in the agreement, barring some legal action.

The block of business which is being sold or transferred using assumption may be subject to coverage under one or more indemnity reinsurance treaties. In the absence of any specific treaty provisions addressing termination or recapture in the event of subsequent assumption, the indemnity reinsurance coverages would normally remain in effect.

One view is that the indemnity reinsurer has economic interests which need to be taken into account as part of an assumption transaction. While the indemnity reinsurance need not continue, one common method of addressing those interests is to keep the indemnity reinsurance in force after the assumption.

The existing indemnity reinsurer, the ceding company, and/or the assumption insurer may wish to negotiate a termination or recapture of this coverage. In any event, the assumption insurer should take into account the terms and financial effects of all existing indemnity reinsurance agreements.

In order to protect itself from the effects of the business being sold to a less preferable ceding company, a reinsurer may require a clause in the original indemnity reinsurance agreement prohibiting the sell or further reinsurance of the underlying policies without the reinsurer's prior written consent.

FINANCIAL EFFECTS

Assumption has permanent effects on the statutory and GAAP financial statements of both the ceding company and the assumption insurer, as well as their tax returns. Some of these effects are discussed in this section.

Assumption 427

Ceding Company

The financial effects of assumption on a ceding company are fairly straightforward. For most purposes, it treats the transaction as a surrender. On a statutory basis, it would release its reserves, other than reserves for any retained claims in course of settlement and incurred but unreported claims, in compliance with the terms of the treaty. It would cease to receive premiums and pay commissions.

On the asset side, the ceding company typically would transfer any policy loans to the assumption insurer, eliminating its own account. It would also transfer assets to the assumption insurer as provided in the agreement. In some cases, the assumption insurer might promise future contingent payments to the ceding company based upon overall persistency, or a single target, such as persistency at a single future point. Such payments would be booked by each party when incurred. Any allowance would be reported as earned.

On a GAAP basis, the ceding company would normally write off its deferred acquisition cost asset and eliminate its benefit reserves, adjusting invested assets and cash according to the assets transferred. Again, reserves for any unsettled claims would be handled in accordance with the terms of the agreement. Treatment of any trailing commission or future commission would be dependent upon the terms of the agreement. In most cases, the amounts would probably fall directly through to earnings as they are incurred.

Tax treatment for the ceding company is relatively straight forward. In a typical assumption treaty, assets would be adjusted according to any net transfer involved and tax reserves would be set to zero. Any income flowing out of that transaction, including any ceding consideration, would flow through taxable income accordingly.

Assumption Insurer

Financial reporting of assumption for the assumption insurer is more complicated than it is for the ceding company. The treatment is similar to that used when a new policy is issued, but certain elements of accounting relating to the purchase of an asset apply to assumption.

Statutory Reporting. The assumption insurer will report assumption in the same manner as for indemnity reinsurance for statutory purposes. It will immediately establish the appropriate reserves for the risks assumed. For example, if an assumed policy is in its tenth policy year, the reinsurer should establish liabilities based on tenth year mortality, not that of a newly issued policy.

The assumption insurer will generally treat as an immediate expense the full amount of any initial consideration or allowance. Any initial allowance may be shown in the Summary of Operations of its annual statement on either line 20, as commissions on premiums and annuities for direct business; line 21, as commissions and expense allowances on reinsurance assumed; or on line 25, as a write-in item.

After the assumption, the treatment of premiums and commissions is just as though the assumption insurer had insured the business from issue. Any premiums received are shown on the direct premiums and considerations lines, not on the reinsurance premiums line; any commissions paid would be treated as direct commissions, not as reinsurance allowances. Assumption business is not reported in Schedule S.

GAAP Reporting. Typically, the assumption insurer under assumption will treat the block of business under a method similar to GAAP accounting for a purchase transaction. This would require that it match future earnings to future revenues on the block in a manner designed to produce no immediate GAAP gain or loss as a result of the original assumption transaction. The initial consideration and allowance are usually capitalized and amortized over future revenues.

Unless the assumption insurer is a professional reinsurer, this may involve a more detailed approach than it would apply to other blocks of reinsurance. It would definitely be more detailed than the GAAP reporting normally accorded financial reinsurance treaties.

GAAP deferred taxes for both parties would have to be computed according to their situations.

Tax Reporting. Tax reporting for the assumption insurer is clearly defined and has been for some time. Basically, the block of business is treated as the purchase of an asset and any ceding commission or strain resulting from the transaction must be amortized over the useful life of

Assumption

the block of business. The useful life may be determined to be the average life of the business, or it may have another definition. Competent tax counsel should be consulted in making this determination.

A major point to remember is that assumption does not create a major tax deferral. Although it may be possible to somewhat front-end the tax deduction, the operating mechanism still involves amortizing any net ceding commission. Prior to the Colonial American case,[4] it was believed that the deduction for assumption would be amortized, but indemnity reinsurance would create an immediate deduction. As discussed in Chapter 14, that is no longer the case. For the reinsurer, the tax treatment of indemnity reinsurance and assumption is the same for inforce blocks of business.

Reserves, as computed for tax purposes, are based on the rules applicable for the original issue dates of the policies, not the assumption date.

STRATEGIC CONSIDERATIONS

Assumption is most frequently the result of strategic decisions and considerations about allocation of resources. An understanding of some of these considerations and their implications is important to the understanding of the applications of assumption.

Ceding Company

Ceding companies may use assumption as a vehicle to implement a strategy to exit a given product line or to sell a block of business. Thereby, the seller will recognize immediately a gain representing a measure of the value of future gains on this business. Typically, the ceding company will receive a higher value from assumption than it would from indemnity reinsurance. Indemnity reinsurance may be subject to future recapture, which may reduce its value to the reinsurer.

---

[4] Colonial American Life Insurance Company v. Commissioner of Internal Revenue, No. 88-396.

Assumption may give the reinsurer more control over the future of the business and its administration. This, in turn, may offer more opportunities for profits.

Assumption involves a transfer of invested assets. The assumption insurer may believe that it can make more money from the assumed business than it can by investing its capital elsewhere. The ceding company may choose to recognize future gains now and free up both cash and its surplus for reinvestment elsewhere to its advantage. As previously mentioned, this strategy may allow some companies to focus on more preferred opportunities.

Both parties, but especially the ceding company, should realize that assumption is intended to be an irrevocable step. The ceding company may be able to repurchase the block of business, but normal assumption treaties do not include provisions for either recapture or repurchase. Any such provisions would have to be separately and carefully negotiated.

Just as assumption is less common than indemnity reinsurance, it is also more permanent. If a company wishes to stay in a line of business and to maintain its field force, it likely would use indemnity reinsurance, not assumption, to raise cash or surplus or to limit its risks.

A ceding company may use assumption if it decides it no longer wants to be at risk or deal with the policyholders and agents on a particular block or line of business. Assumption has been used by companies to exit from group life and health business or from other lines of business, such as credit or industrial insurance. Assumption allows the sale of a line or division of business without selling the entire company and without any transfer of ownership or control.

While this transfer is similar to the sale of stock, it does not require the involvement of investment bankers or SEC approval. Assumption is less likely to require stockholder approval or discussion, although approval of the board of directors is usually required to assure the other party of the legitimacy of the transaction.

As discussed earlier, the ceding company should be careful in its selection of an assumption insurer. If the assumption insurer becomes insolvent or otherwise fails to honor the original commitments to the policyholders, the original company may have a contingent liability. Therefore, it is logical that the ceding company perform reasonable due diligence on any perspective assumption insurer, including both its ability and its intentions to meet fully the guarantees and obligations towards the policyholders.

The risk of insolvency is difficult to analyze for the indefinite future. Therefore, some companies have required a trust for the assets committed to the obligations of its former policyholders. Such a trust can be referenced in the assumption agreement, allowing the original company to take over both the assets and the policies should the assumption insurer become insolvent. A more prudent standard might address minimum capital and surplus requirements.

This approach may not be fully acceptable to an insurance department trying to liquidate an insolvent company, but at least it will provide some protection for the ceding company and the policyholders. The insurance department may believe that this will lead to favored treatment for one group of policyholders at the expense of others. This can be partially mitigated by having future earnings from such a block be paid to the assumption insurer or its successor, except for reasonable administration fees.

Assumption Insurer

Assumption insurers typically enter into assumption agreements for strategic reasons which are perhaps the reverse of those of the ceding companies. While the ceding company may find that a block of business is too small for it to administer effectively, an assumption insurer may want to assume several blocks of similar business in order to benefit from its administrative capacity.

Recently, some insurers with excess administrative capacity have searched for blocks of a specific type of business, such as industrial insurance, traditional ordinary insurance, or universal life policies. They expect to administer the additional policies at a very low marginal cost. This, in turn, will drive down their effective expenses per unit. The cost per unit for one company may be increasing due to a shrinking line of business, but adding that same business to another company's inforce might reduce the latter's per unit costs. This differential in expense factors can make an assumption transaction attractive to both parties. In short, the business may be worth more to the assumption insurer than to the ceding company.

The assumption insurer must be careful, however, to ensure that it can effectively administer the business on a low cost basis. The cost of adding the new policies to the existing inforce system may be prohibitive, especially when including the cost of conversion to the new system.

An assumption insurer should consider the shock lapse factor; lapse rates almost always increase temporarily following notification to the policyholders of an assumption. This can affect the value both by reducing the future premiums and by leaving worse than average risks on the books.

There is not one specific reason why shock lapses occur. One theory is that any unusual activity causes insureds to reexamine their needs and their coverages. Frequently, assumption occurs after the original company has had publicized financial difficulties or changes in ownership. Such events may either disturb some policyholders or offer opportunities for agents, either the original ones or others, to leverage policyholder uncertainty or concern into replacement sales. Terminations continue after assumption largely because of the momentum developed prior to the assumption.

Frequently, shock lapses are the result of the former agents contacting the policyholders to offer new options, especially if the agents are allied with another insurer, not the assumption insurer. Accordingly, it is important for the buyer to consider the agency relationships before determining the price it can offer for a block of business.

On the other hand, persistency may improve following an assumption agreement. This can result if the new insurer is perceived by the agents and the policyholders as being more stable and desirable than the original company. This is most likely if the assumption occurs before the policyholders or agents have had time to develop significant concerns.

Companies sometimes use assumption to buy a field force and to build a larger line of business. This occurred in the group insurance business in the late 1980's. Several carriers decided to exit or limit their group business while others decided to increase their group business, in essence buying the customer lists and distribution capabilities of the ceding companies.

Companies may have excess surplus which they believe can be invested in an additional block of business for an acceptable return.

Sometimes, the blocks of business transferred are closed blocks and involve no field force or ongoing sales capabilities. These transactions should be viewed merely as investments. Of course, the considerations of persistency, mortality or morbidity, expense, and investment income should be reviewed carefully.

Insurance departments may utilize the assumption process as a method to provide for the security of policyholders of insolvent or financially impaired companies under their jurisdiction. This may be accomplished by soliciting bids. Since the insurance departments' primary concern is the security of the policyholders, this process can result in favorable terms to the successful bidder.

On occasion, the ceding company will continue to perform some or all of the administrative functions for the assumption insurer, at least for a period of time. This service usually is compensated for with a service or administration fee.

In some situations, a reinsurer may choose to defer any decision relative to assumption. An indemnity reinsurance agreement may be established which gives the reinsurer the right to assume the business directly at some point in time or upon the occurrence some of event. For example, the reinsurer may not be licensed in the appropriate states, so indemnity reinsurance might be used until it is licensed. Even if the reinsurer is licensed, indemnity reinsurance may be used until the appropriate regulatory approval for the assumption transaction is secured.

In other instances the buyer may prefer indemnity reinsurance, but want the right to convert to assumption if the ceding company's capital and surplus become too low. This may offer the reinsurer some protection and clarity in the event the ceding company were to become insolvent or otherwise impaired. However, such contingency actions are difficult to guarantee when insurance departments' approvals are required.

Other reasons may lead the two parties to prefer the "right of assumption" feature over immediate assumption. In any event, the tax implications need to be carefully considered; the existence of the right of assumption followed by actual assumption within a few years may lead the IRS to contend that the treaty was assumption all along and was never indemnity reinsurance.

The buyer must also consider its state licenses. For indemnity reinsurance, it is generally sufficient for the reinsurer to be licensed in the ceding company's state of domicile. Even if it is not licensed in that state, most regulatory concerns can be satisfied by placing assets backing the reserves in trust or escrow. This is not the situation for assumption. The assumption insurer has a direct relationship with the policyholders and the regulators may want more authority or protection.

Some experts contend that the assumption insurer must be licensed as a direct insurer, or at least be an authorized reinsurer, in all states where the affected policyholders reside. Others contend that it is sufficient to be licensed only in the ceding company's state of domicile, especially if the insurance departments of both that state and the buyer's state of domicile approve the transaction. Certainly assumption transactions have occurred where the buyer was not licensed in all the involved states.

17 | Producer Owned Reinsurance Companies

For the most part, the transactions described in this text have been between a life insurance company and one of the reinsurers actively accepting reinsurance business in North America. These reinsurers are in the business of reinsuring for economic gain and are open to a broad range of ceding companies. They are independent of the producer of the business and are relatively indifferent as to the source of business, as long as that source is acceptable to the reinsurer.

Reinsurance is not limited to transactions involving such reinsurers. Numerous transactions take place between insurance companies and reinsurers with a corporate affiliation with the producer of the business. These reinsurers are often referred to as producer owned reinsurance companies. In addition, some reinsurers are formed for special purposes, such as joint ventures, or to reinsure an employee benefit program of its parent corporation. Such a company may be known as a captive reinsurer, or just a captive.

The primary purpose of producer owned reinsurance is to increase the sales of the direct insurer by sharing some of the underwriting and investment gains with the producer of the business. This sharing is accomplished through reinsurance.

CAPTIVE REINSURERS

A captive reinsurance company is an insurance company formed with the purpose of reinsuring insurance policies from a particular, captive source. The term "captive" reinsurer has a specific meaning to the IRS, which tends to view captives with skepticism. The term producer owned reinsurer is used to distinguish these reinsurers from true captives.

Purposes

The producer of the business that is reinsured is normally the owner of the reinsurance company. The owner may be called the sponsor. This chapter is primarily concerned with reinsurers formed to reinsure policies sold by certain key agents of insurance companies or to reinsure risks related to credit insurance.

Typically, the sponsor wants additional compensation for selling its business through a particular insurer. The insurer may not wish to pay such additional amounts directly and immediately, either because of statutory limitations or because the risk of loss would then be too great. The sponsor may also believe that it will receive tax advantages by participating in the underwriting and investments through reinsurance rather than collecting direct commissions. However, careful analysis is advised as underwriting and investment gains are subject to the actual experience of the block of business reinsured.

Location Considerations

Because of the limited purpose of these reinsurers, such companies are generally licensed in only one jurisdiction. In order to realize a reasonable return on investment, startup costs and ongoing administrative expenses need to be kept as low as possible. Most participants choose jurisdictions that have very low capitalization requirements, regulatory fees, and taxes. The amount of time required to establish a new company, the filing requirements, and the approval process are also considerations.

For these reasons, Arizona, Louisiana, or Texas are most frequently selected as the states of domicile of many producer owned reinsurers.[1] Because of the large number of companies domiciled in these states, some sponsors prefer to license the insurance company in another state. Delaware is currently a popular choice, as it is perceived to have a more prestigious license.

Offshore sites such as Bermuda, the Bahamas, Barbados, the Cayman Islands, Turks and Cacios, Nevis, and the Virgin Islands are also popular jurisdictions for the formation of captives. These islands often offer very attractive tax treatment as well as less stringent or more flexible reserving and capitalization requirements, lower fees, and quicker implementation.

Drawbacks to an offshore site include the perception that such sites are less prestigious or reputable than one in the United States, that premiums ceded outside of the United States may be subject to Federal Excise Tax, and that the reinsurer may be required to provide a trust or a letter of credit in order for the ceding company to take statutory reserve credit for reinsurance ceded.

State Insurance Regulation

Any insurance company chartered in one of the United States will have to comply with the insurance laws and regulations of that state. The insurance company must maintain the standards for capital, surplus, and reserves. Most producer owned reinsurers are licensed in only one state. Unless the ceding company is domiciled in the same state or the reinsurer provides appropriate security, the ceding company will not be allowed to take reserve credit on business ceded.

Sponsors often choose the domicile of the reinsurer based on the requirements for capital of that domicile. However, that question must be carefully studied. In at least one instance, a reinsurer has been forced

---

[1] This is not intended to imply that any state or jurisdiction is lax in its regulation of insurers. However, the capitalization requirements and the receptiveness to new companies do vary among jurisdictions. For example, Arizona has established a special category for reinsurance companies, with reduced capital and surplus requirements.

to meet the higher capital standards of another state because the vast majority of its risks were on lives residing in the second state.

SEC Regulations

Normal rules and regulations of the Securities and Exchange Commission (SEC) apply to the formation of a producer owned reinsurer if the formation of the reinsurer or the distribution of its shares takes place in the United States. Broad interpretation of these guidelines is usually applied. Even if there is a single owner, such as a corporation, the formation will probably at least have to be disclosed.

The SEC requires that companies with more than a minimum number of shareholders (currently 24) must be registered with the SEC. To avoid this registration, most reinsurers have a limited number of participants. Even so, the SEC requires a private placement memorandum which contains some of the same information that would be required in a prospectus, together with additional information as to the limited marketability of the shares and the risk of loss from the operation.

Ceding Company Motivation

Ceding companies work with producer owned reinsurers in order to increase their own profits. The increased profits are expected to result from an enhanced ability to attract, motivate, and retain producers resulting in an increased production of quality business.

Attracting New Producers. The willingness to cede business to a producer owned reinsurer can be a useful marketing tool for a ceding company to attract top quality producers. Many large producers expect to share in the profitability of their business. In fact, use of a reinsurer is often a prerequisite for any insurer wishing to write business with that production source; otherwise, the producer will go elsewhere.

Retention of Key Producers. Just as many companies have employee stock ownership plans as an incentive to retain key employees, insurance companies may cede insurance to a producer owned reinsurer in order to retain the key producers. Retaining high quality producers may boost the ceding company's retained profits.

More Production. If the producers realize a profit on the assumed reinsurance, it is anticipated that they will write more business in order to receive more profits. The ceding company benefits from the increase in volume of business, both in terms of the direct profits realized on the additional business and the ability to spread its costs.

Better Experience. Because the producers share in the profits of the business ceded, it is anticipated that they will write higher quality business in order to increase their share of the profits. Part of the expectation may be that the producers will place their more questionable risks with other insurers. High quality business also increases the ceding company's profits.

Reinsurer Motivation

In a producer owned reinsurance situation, the reinsurer is the producer of the business. The primary reinsurer motivations include more income, tax benefits, and increased influence and status.

More Income. Producers enter the reinsurance arrangements in order to receive income from the profits of the business. These profits are in addition to the normal commission income. If the producer is confident that he is writing high quality business, he can anticipate a steady flow of income from the reinsurance.

The individuals owning the stock of the reinsurer anticipate that it will increase in value over the years, presumably by retaining earnings and in recognition of future earnings from the business reinsured. Some insurers that promote these reinsurance programs encourage the producer-owner to view the reinsurance company as part of his retirement program.

Tax Benefits. The producer frequently expects to defer taxation and possibly reduce taxes by creating and using a captive. In the past, the producer hoped to replace current ordinary income taxes with capital gains treatment when he sold the shares of stock for an increased value at a later date. This strategy is desirable when capital gains are taxed at a lower rate than ordinary income. However, as recent experience has shown, the existence of a preferential rate for capital gains may or may not be available when the shares are sold.

A more common objective is to shelter income from current taxation, deferring the recognition of income and the payment of the tax into the future. A major reason for doing this is to permit reinvestment of income without first paying tax on it in anticipation of a lower tax rate in the future or upon retirement.

Increased Importance and Status. Normally, only the top producers of an insurance company are invited to participate in the reinsurance of their business. As partners in the future profitability of the business, they often exert a great influence on the sponsoring insurance company. These producers may receive special products, commissions, and service from the sponsoring companies.

Owning an insurance company may give some producers a feeling of increased status.

Tax Considerations

The tax considerations for reinsurance discussed earlier apply to producer owned reinsurance as well. In addition, a number of other factors require consideration in the producer owned situation because the benefits are frequently tied to stock ownership which, in turn, raises a number of income issues. Before entering into any sort of reinsurance arrangement, both parties should retain competent tax counsel to assist in the design and structure of the arrangement in order to increase the likelihood of obtaining the desired tax treatment.

If the reinsurer is domiciled in the United States, it will be taxed as either a life insurance company, a non-life insurance company, or a general corporation according to normal Federal Income Tax regulations.[2]

One benefit of a reinsurer is that it may qualify as a small life company, resulting in a lower effective tax rate. In order to qualify for

---

[2] See Chapter 14, Tax Effect of Reinsurance, for a discussion of tax status.

the special small life company deduction, the reinsurer usually must not be deemed to be a part of the sponsoring company.[3] Accordingly, the sponsoring company should own less than 80% of the voting stock or the total value of the reinsurer. If the sponsoring company has entered into an agreement to repurchase the stock in the future, the IRS may deem this to be constructive ownership of the shares.

If the reinsurer is domiciled outside of the United States, it may escape current United States taxation entirely, but it is still subject to the taxes of its domicile. Whenever the income is repatriated, it will be subject to United States taxation. The applicable regulations are very complex. For this reason, many offshore reinsurers take the Section 953(d) election, making them subject to current United States taxation. This election also eliminates the Federal Excise Tax on premiums ceded offshore.

AGENT OWNED REINSURANCE COMPANIES

An agent owned reinsurance company (AORC) is formed for the purpose of allowing key agents to participate in the profitability of their own business or as a means to defer compensation, either for tax or financial planning reasons. Typically, a select group of agents, chosen according to standards of quality and production, is invited to participate in the ownership of the reinsurer. The agents purchase shares in the reinsurer and the ceding company places a portion of all business written by these agents into the AORC.

The agents most likely to become involved in an agent owned company are those who are engaged in sophisticated upscale markets and those who use group marketing techniques such as salary savings. Competition to attract these agents is quite strong and is expected to grow. Companies which have established AORC's may be in a good position to retain these agents in the future.

---

[3] The small company deduction is available only to life companies of which the "controlled group" has less than $500,000,000 of assets.

Form of Reinsurance

The reinsurance arrangement generally involves coinsurance or mod-co. These arrangements are usually designed to minimize first-year surplus strain and to produce a positive cash flow in the first year of operation. Rarely will the sponsoring company cede more than 50% of the business placed by the participating agents in the reinsurer.

To control fluctuations in experience, the AORC will often limit its mortality exposure with relatively low retention limits, retroceding the balance of the risk on a YRT basis. In some cases, the retrocession may be to the ceding company. The level of actual risk sharing desired in the reinsurer will dictate the financial terms of the arrangements.

Some AORC agreements involve only YRT reinsurance. Under these agreements, the agent can participate in mortality experience, but has little or no exposure to investment, persistency, or expense risks and the profits that can arise from them. Some of these agreements are designed largely to increase commissions indirectly.

Ownership and Participation

In forming the reinsurer, it must be determined whether each agent will share in the overall profits and losses of the business, or if each agent will be assigned an account or a special series of stock which would reflect only the profits and losses from that agent's business.

The advantage of separating each individual agent's business is that the agent's financial incentives are then tied directly to the actual profitability of the business he sells. If profits are distributed in proportion to stock ownership rather than in relation to the business submitted and profits produced, some agents will gain a windfall from the efforts of others and the others will not receive the rewards anticipated. Agents with good experience may become dissatisfied if their profits are diminished due to the poor experience of business submitted by other agents.

Agent Considerations

There are several reasons for a life insurance agent to join an AORC. The principal ones include increasing his earnings through the profits of

Producer Owned Reinsurance Companies 443

the reinsurance company and deferring or reclassifying earnings for tax purposes.

Increased Earnings. An agent would not enter into a reinsurance agreement unless he anticipated that he would share in future profits as the result of the business which he produced in addition to his normal commission income.

There are drawbacks from the agent's view. The primary motivation of many agents is the level of first year compensation received on business written. In order to reduce surplus strain and the investment required in the AORC, the level of first year, and perhaps even renewal, commissions is sometimes reduced.

Participation in reinsurer is not a risk free endeavor; both the initial investment in the purchase of shares and any foregone commissions are exposed to loss as the result of the future experience and operations of the AORC. It is possible for losses on the business reinsured to reduce, not enhance, the agent's total compensation.

Further, most agents have very little knowledge of or control over the pricing of insurance products. These factors tend to limit an agent's willingness to defer immediate compensation in order to participate in an uncertain endeavor.

Taxation. One of the major considerations in forming an AORC will be the effect on the individual producer's personal federal income tax. Some of the factors which may influence income tax treatment are discussed below.

Buyback Agreement. If the arrangements with the agents include some predetermined buy-back formula for repurchasing their stock, the IRS may consider any change in value as current income. Despite this fear, many companies use such agreements with their AORC's because some agents prefer the added security.

Risk Participation. Most tax practitioners believe that the greater the degree of risk participation by the agent stockholders, the lower the likelihood that gains in the reinsurer will be treated as current income to the shareholders. The argument is that when there is a true risk sharing, any income deferred is exposed to the risk of loss and is therefore not current ordinary income.

Constructive Receipt. If the agent can, at his option, receive lower commissions on the policies which are placed in the reinsurance company in order to increase future profits, the IRS may argue that this optional reduction in commissions amounted to constructive receipt of the profits, at least to the extent of the commission reduction. This argument might be countered by allowing only one set of commission scales for use in any AORC.

Market Value. The IRS may argue that the price paid by the agent for stock in the company, usually the book value, is less than the true market value of the stock. This could result in the excess of the imputed true market value over the price paid for the stock paid being treated as ordinary income.

Risks. If several agents share in the experience of a common book of business, then the ownership of shares is more likely to be viewed as an investment. If a given agent's participation is tied directly to his business alone, there is more exposure to IRS challenge. Therefore, the risks and experience are important considerations.

Percentage Ownership. In order to receive the desired tax treatment, no producer should own ten percent or more of an AORC. Ownership of ten percent or more will cause the proportionate share of the reinsurer's income to be included in the agent's taxable income for the year. Therefore, AORCs usually have at least eleven agent shareholders.

Ceding Company Considerations

The ceding company, or direct insurer, typically sponsors an AORC in order to protect or build its distribution system and to increase its total earnings or premium income.

Distribution Systems. Good agents are valuable and there is always competition for their services. Many insurance companies consider the establishment of an AORC as an excellent recruiting and retention tool. In addition, some companies believe that good agents attract other good agents; having an AORC with some good agents shows the company's concern for its agents, and that will attract others.

If the reinsurer achieves adequate profits, the agents will be satisfied; otherwise they may become very unhappy. It is anticipated that the formation of an AORC that allows the agents to share in the profits of the business will create a team or partnership arrangement where the agents and the insurance company are working towards the same goal. However, formation of an AORC may also create an agent power structure which could make future negotiations difficult.

Earnings. Insurance companies forming AORCs believe that total profits will grow as a result. Their philosophy is that keeping, say, 50% of the profits on an agent's sales, while passing some of the strain and experience risk back to the agent, is better than receiving none of that agent's business.

The ceding company anticipates improving its profits by writing higher quality business and by writing more business. However, sponsoring an AORC will create an additional level of expense. The ceding company may have to supply the capital and surplus for the newly formed company.

The sponsoring company may have to commit home office staff to the formation and ongoing operations of the reinsurer. The sponsor may have to divert human and computer resources from other projects for some period of time. There is no guarantee that this additional effort will result in more or better quality production. In one way or another, the sponsoring company may pass on to the AORC the cost of capital to start the AORC and its marginal expenses, but it can rarely recover any overhead involved.

Control. The ceding company will want to maintain some degree of control over the AORC to ensure that funds are available to pay benefits and that any seed capital is protected. It is in the sponsoring company's interest to prohibit the reinsuring of business written by the agents with other carriers in its AORC.

Typically, the ceding company will provide the day-to-day management of the AORC. It will also retain management or voting control, frequently through the use of preferred stock. Under this approach, the ceding company's preferred stock has voting control and the agents' common stock provides for profit participation and ownership. The common stock reflects the value of the reinsured business. The preferred stock allows the ceding company to maintain control and to receive dividends for the use of capital. At some point, the management rights of the preferred stock might be transferred to the common stock.

The main disadvantages of separating each individual agent's business are that the agent's share of AORC income is more likely to be considered as current taxable income and the administration is more complicated. Also, the company may need to purchase stop-loss insurance for each agent's account so that a few early claims do not bankrupt an account.

In most successful AORC programs, the insurer has set high standards for continued agent participation in the AORC. If the standards are not met, the agent is disqualified and either bought out or not allowed to have any further business ceded to the reinsurer.

There is always the possibility that an agent could launch a minority shareholders lawsuit against the agent-owned company. Such a lawsuit might be filed because the agent wishes to remove his accumulated share of the profits before the scheduled time or because another agent has placed unprofitable business with the company, lowering the profits for the entire group. The risk of such lawsuits can be minimized if flexible rules for withdrawals are established at the beginning and if consistent underwriting standards and qualification standards are established and maintained. The sponsoring insurance company's exposure relative to such lawsuits might be reduced by not being a majority shareholder in the AORC or through the use of segregated classes of stock.

REINSURERS OF CREDIT INSURANCE

The credit insurance industry, unlike most branches of the insurance industry, is a producer dominated business. Credit insurance is normally sold in conjunction with retail or consumer credit, including credit cards.

Producer Owned Reinsurance Companies

The direct writer's primary customer is the producer, such as the financial institution or retailer involved in the loans being covered by the credit insurance.

In order to attract these producers, direct insurers frequently compete by paying commissions as high as possible. Insurance departments have sought to control this situation by regulating the level of premiums and commissions used in conjunction with credit life and credit disability coverages. In order to allow the sponsoring institution to share in the profits of the credit insurance business and thus retain its high volume outlets, insurance companies will reinsure a portion of the business written through that sponsor into a reinsurance company formed and owned by the sponsor.

Lenders, and therefore producers of credit insurance, include banks, thrifts, finance companies, automobile dealers, furniture dealers, and other retailers. Any of these may offer credit insurance as a service to their customers and as a source of profit to itself. These institutions may become sponsors of producer owned reinsurers.

In the case of banks, thrifts, or finance companies, most producer owned reinsurers are wholly owned subsidiaries. Sometimes, a group of producers, like automobile dealers, will join together and form an exotic reinsurance company. An exotic will have a different class of stock for each producer. Separate accounting is performed for each producer. Exotics help spread overhead and administrative costs.

Form of Reinsurance

Producer owned reinsurance of credit insurance is normally ceded on a coinsurance basis. The reinsurer often accepts 100% of the risk. Credit insurance on open end loans, such as monthly outstanding balance coverage sold in conjunction with revolving charge or credit card accounts, is usually coinsured using monthly premiums. The reinsurer does not have to set up reserves and does not experience a surplus drain.

In the case of single premium credit insurance coverages, cessions on a "written" basis[4] typically result in a significant surplus drain to the

---

[4] See Chapter 21, Reinsurance of Other Lines and Products.

reinsurer, especially in the case of credit disability coverage where the initial reserve is equal to the gross single premium. To alleviate this strain, the disability coverage, and sometimes the life coverage, may be ceded on an "earned" basis.[5]

Sponsor Considerations

Banks and other lending institutions have complicated regulations regarding the ownership of an insurer, or even an agency. Rules vary between federally chartered and state chartered institutions. Automobile dealerships and other retailers typically do not face such restrictions on their activities.

Profits and Leverage. One reason for forming a reinsurance company is the anticipation of making additional profits. The sponsor may also believe that it will gain more influence over the ceding company, resulting in better service and more control over the products.

Ceding Company Considerations

The ceding company's reasons for working with a credit reinsurer are similar to those for establishing an AORC. In particular, it expects higher sales and increased earnings from its credit insurance operation.

Sales Results. The ceding company anticipates increased sales by attracting and retaining large producers as the result of allowing the producers to share in the profits of the business. The insurer also may attract new producers by setting them up in the reinsurance business.

Profit. As in any endeavor, the ceding company hopes to make a profit on the business which it retains. The profits are anticipated to come from the volume and the quality of the business produced by the large producers.

---

[5] *Ibid.*

Any increase in profits may be partially offset by increased expenses. Depending on the terms of the reinsurance agreement, the ceding company may prepare all the necessary financial reports and perform many of the routine administrative functions for the reinsurer. The ceding company normally makes a charge for this service.

This charge is often stated in terms of a percentage of premiums and referred to as the reinsurers "retention." This charge is designed to cover the ceding company's expenses and to provide a margin for profit and contingencies. Sometimes, the distributor will perform all the administrative functions itself, including managing the assets and valuing the reserve liabilities.

CAPTIVES AND OTHER SPECIAL PURPOSE REINSURERS

The uses and structures of reinsurers appear to be limited only by the creativity of insurers and producers, subject to tax and regulatory considerations.

Many insurance companies are interested in using a joint venture with another entity to combine administrative capacity, distribution potential, and financial strength. Reinsurance is one means of allowing both parties to share in the risks and profits. This may be accomplished either by reinsuring business from one company to another or by using a jointly owned subsidiary to assume the risks underwritten by the venture.

Historically, most well-known captives have been formed to reinsure property and casualty risks, primarily workers' compensation and liability coverages. These captives were formed to provide the sponsor with more control over the price of the coverage, especially the fluctuations in price, and with tax advantages in some instances. Captives also have other special applications, such as improving corporate risk management with a self-insurance program.

The IRS has a long history of litigation against captives. The most common issue is whether the insurance premiums paid to a captive are a deductible expense of the parent corporation or sponsor. In most cases, the IRS has prevailed. Accordingly, competent tax counsel should be engaged prior to entering into any such arrangements.

Some noninsurance companies use captive reinsurers to participate in the risks and gain from the insurance benefits resulting from certain of their employee benefit plans. The terms of such participation are limited by the provisions of the Employee Retirement Income Security Act of 1974, commonly referred to as ERISA, and other statutes.

18 International Reinsurance

As used in this book, international reinsurance refers to the ceding or assuming of reinsurance involving a company domiciled outside of the United States and another company inside the United States. This chapter addresses only reinsurance involving Canada, the United Kingdom, Australia, Continental Europe, and offshore sites such as Bermuda and the Virgin Islands. The intention of this chapter is to introduce the basic concepts and considerations of international reinsurance. This should not be considered to be a full discussion of the topics of international reinsurance or of reinsurance in countries outside the United States.

The general principles of reinsurance discussed throughout this book are applicable to international reinsurance transactions. The three basic plans of reinsurance, coinsurance, mod-co, and YRT, are used throughout the world and the basic contract terms are universal. This should not be surprising since reinsurance was not invented in the United States. However, the use of certain plans varies by country. For example, in the German domestic reinsurance market, coinsurance is almost unknown, but mod-co is widely used. In Canada, coinsurance is common, but mod-co is very rare. YRT is the most universally used plan.

Edward Lloyd is credited with starting the first reinsurance underwriting system in his London coffee house in the late 17th century. However, widespread abuses ultimately led to strict government regulations which curtailed most English reinsurance activity. The German companies brought reinsurance to the United States, and German and Russian companies dominated the United States market until World War I. Since reinsurance was transacted on a coinsurance basis at that time, United States insurers were faced with major problems relating to the transfer of funds and recovery of benefits during the war. This encouraged the development of the domestic reinsurance industry.

While property and liability reinsurance is distributed worldwide, over fifty percent of the life reinsurance in the world originates in the United States. Most of this is written with domestic United States reinsurers. A number of these are foreign owned, but they operate as United States carriers and hold most of the assets relating to United States risks in the United States. Given the size of the market, foreign reinsurers choose to participate despite lower profits than may be achieved elsewhere in the world.

MOTIVATIONS FOR INTERNATIONAL REINSURANCE

Despite the excess capacity for reinsurance which currently exists in the United States market, a large number of international reinsurance transactions take place annually. Several factors might motivate a company to enter into an international reinsurance agreement.

Availability of Specialty Coverages

An insurance company may seek reinsurance outside of the United States either because it is unable to obtain the coverage domestically or because it can obtain the coverage at a better cost. The types of reinsurance most commonly purchased abroad are catastrophe and stop loss protection and certain forms of health reinsurance. Traditional life insurance risks are less likely to be reinsured internationally for a lower cost because of the current oversupply of such reinsurance capacity in the United States.

United States subsidiaries of foreign owned or controlled companies may retrocede portions of their accepted reinsurance to foreign subsidiaries and affiliates. Similarly, U.S. owned reinsurers may retrocede risks to foreign domiciled subsidiaries and affiliates.

Business Purposes

In some instances, a United States company doing business in a foreign country will be required to cede a portion of the business to a company in that country. In other instances, a United States carrier may cede domestic risks to a foreign insurer as part of an international business sharing. Group coverages on employees of international firms are sometimes shared among companies domiciled in several of the countries served by that firm.

Some United States insurers are part of a international family of insurers. Reinsurance between these companies may occur for many reasons. It may be an efficient way of sharing capital and surplus among the various companies, allowing the stronger to help finance the weaker. Many foreign reinsurance markets are much less competitive and therefore more costly than those of the United States and Canada. Therefore, it may prove to be more profitable to cede business to an affiliate than to buy coverage in the local reinsurance marketplace; any profits on this reinsurance would stay within the group.

Surplus Relief or Financing Growth

United States life insurance companies have fairly inflexible, perhaps stringent, statutory reserve requirements when compared to some parts of the world. In many instances, a United States company is required to set up a significantly greater reserve than would a foreign company for the same policy. This is particularly true for situations requiring the recognition of premium deficiencies and interest guarantees.

Since the use of surplus creates a cost, the reinsurer that incurs the least surplus investment can usually offer a better price. Much reinsurance has been placed outside of the United States, particularly in offshore sites such as the Bermuda, because of the different reserve requirements. Letters of credit and similar instruments are frequently used instead of "hard assets."

Insurers that need to finance growth may look to international insurers, especially if the need is long term in nature. Foreign insurers and reinsurers are more likely to take a longer term view of profits than a United States company.

Differences in Taxation

A domestic insurance company may place reinsurance outside the United States to take advantage of differences in tax laws. If an insurance company can reinsure business to a company in another country that has a lower effective tax rate or a more favorable tax standard, the benefits of lower taxes might be shared with the ceding company in the form of lower reinsurance costs.

Historically, tax related reinsurance has been common in offshore sites, but changes in the Internal Revenue Code have made it increasingly difficult to create any advantages from international reinsurance. However, it is probably safe to assume that few, if any, international reinsurance agreements result in more combined taxes being paid than if both parties were in the same country.

CONSIDERATIONS

Before entering into a reinsurance arrangement with a foreign company, the ceding company should complete an in-depth analysis of the regulatory, tax, and political situations involved. As with any reinsurance agreement, both parties should consider other aspects such as the quality of the management, the financial standing, and the security provided by the other party. The focus of this chapter is on the additional issues which occur in an international transaction. Certain key issues of general interest are discussed below.

Regulation

Regulation of insurance companies is significantly different in other countries. In some countries regulation is more liberal, granting the insurers a great degree of freedom. Elsewhere, the government may control nearly all aspects of the business. Quite frequently, reinsurers have more freedom of action than do direct writers.

Reserving. When a United States domestic insurance company cedes business to a nonadmitted reinsurer, whether it is domiciled in a neighboring state or halfway around the world, the ceding company is usually unable to take credit in its annual statement for the reserves on the business ceded. Many international reinsurance contracts are structured so that no asset transfer occurs to avoid this reserve credit problem. This may involve the use of mod-co or funds withheld coinsurance. Other treaties may be structured as stop loss in order to avoid the reserve credit issue.

Alternative solutions usually involve the use of a letter of credit, a surety bond, a trust, or escrow account.

Solvency Requirements. Most countries have specific solvency or surplus requirements. In the European Union (EU), the prescribed minimum solvency margin is the minimum amount of capital and free reserves which must be maintained to support the business. The solvency margin requirements form part of the first EU Life Directive which was published in 1979. All EU insurers are subject to the minimum EU solvency margin requirements; individual countries are free to apply more stringent requirements.

Solvency margin requirements represent additional capital which must be committed to support the business. There is general consistency between EU countries regarding the types of assets which are admissible for backing the solvency requirements, subject to the third EU Life Directive. The assets supporting the solvency margin requirements usually are invested in secure instruments such as government bonds so there is little or no risk of loss to the solvency capital. However, most companies' shareholders expect a higher return on the capital invested in the business, including amounts for solvency margin requirements. This added investment therefore affects the cost of products, both direct sales and reinsurance. The concept of solvency margins is similar to that of risk-based capital in the United States.

The classes of long-term business defined for solvency margin purposes are as follows:

Class	Business
I	Life and Annuity
II	Marriage and Birth
III	Linked Long Term
IV	Permanent Health
V	Tontines
VI	Capital Redemption
VII	Pension Fund Management

The solvency margin for a given company is based on a percentage of its amount at risk and a percentage of its reserves. For example, the formula for Class I, life insurance and annuity business, may be expressed as (a)(b)+(c)(d), where:

(a) is 4% of the policy reserves;
(b) is the greater of (1) and (2), where:

   (1) is the factor 50% for pure reinsurers (85% for all other companies), and
   (2) is the ratio of the policy reserves after reinsurance ceded to the policy reserves before reinsurance ceded;

(c) is a percentage of the sum at risk (defined below) for a given type of business; and
(d) is the greater of (3) and (4), where:

   (3) is the factor 50%, and
   (4) is the ratio of the sums at risk after reinsurance ceded to the sums at risk before reinsurance ceded.

The percentage which applies in item (c) to the sum at risk for all life business is 0.3% unless the policy provides death benefits only. The percentage is applied only to non-negative sums at risk. If death benefits only are provided, the following percentages apply:

(1) 0.10% for contracts with original durations of three years or less.
(2) 0.15% for contracts with original durations of over three years, but not more than five years.
(3) 0.30% for contracts with original durations of five years or more.
(4) 0.10% for a pure reinsurer.

The percentages vary by class and may be changed in the future. The life percentages were established in 1981 and have not been modified since then.

The guarantee fund is calculated as the greater of one-third of the margin of solvency of the minimum guarantee fund. The minimum guarantee fund is set at 800,000 European Currency units, or about 470,000 British pounds at December 31, 1994.

The solvency margin requirements may be met with certain items other than invested assets. In particular, the following three implicit items can be brought into account in meeting the minimum requirement:

(1) Future profits may be taken into account up to 50% of the average annual profits made in long term business during the last five years.
(2) When lower reserves are allowed according to the Zillmerized[1] method, but the allowance is not fully utilized, the difference in the reserve held and the fully Zillmerized amount may be taken into account.
(3) Hidden reserves may be taken into account at their full value.

The application of the solvency requirements varies somewhat by country. In the United Kingdom, the same requirements apply to both direct insurers and to reinsurers, subject to a lower sum at risk factor for pure reinsurers. In some other EU countries, pure reinsurers are considered to be general trading businesses and are not covered by insurance legislation.

---

[1] Zillmerized, or Zillmer, reserves are similar to full preliminary term reserves, including both an allowance for expenses in the first year and increased net premiums in renewal years. Zillmerized reserves are used in much of the world.

Taxation

Tax treatment of insurance companies and products varies significantly from country to country. The parties to any international reinsurance agreement should understand the ramifications to their company before entering into such an agreement. If the treaty benefits are to be optimized, both parties need to understand the tax implications to the other party.

The subject of taxation in every country is too broad and too fluid to be addressed in this book. Tax codes and bases are political in nature and are subject to sudden and major changes. This section is intended to provide insight into areas which should be considered in developing an international reinsurance treaty.

Income Taxes. As discussed previously,[2] Section 845 of the United States Internal Revenue Code gives the IRS broad powers to reallocate items in an insurance company's tax return if it believes that a reinsurance arrangement entered into by the company results in significant tax avoidance or is without a reasonable risk transfer. Specifically, this allows IRS the authority to reclassify elements of the tax return of the domestic insurer without requiring an offsetting treatment to the other insurer, whether domestic or foreign.

The tax bases of foreign domiciled reinsurers may vary significantly from those of domestic companies or from each other. The United States tax basis is essentially one of all gains from all sources. In the United Kingdom, the tax base for direct insurers is largely total investment income less insurance related expenses, with underwriting gains largely untaxed. Life reinsurance and pension business is taxed largely on profits, however. Other countries have different bases; some allow greater flexibility in establishing reserves or in determining taxable income.

Excise Tax. The United States imposes a federal excise tax on premiums involving domestic risks reinsured outside the country. This tax is set currently at 1% of all premiums reinsured for life insurance,

---

[2] See Chapter 14, Tax Effects of Reinsurance.

annuities, and health insurance. This tax is in lieu of United States federal income tax on the foreign reinsurer, but its payment is the responsibility of the United States ceding company, not the reinsurer. The excise tax is not incurred for business ceded to entities which are taxed in the United States as domestic taxpayers.

Reinsurance ceded to companies domiciled in the United Kingdom, France, and a few other countries is exempt from excise tax. This exemption is due to tax treaties which exist between the United States and these countries. As of this writing, reinsurance ceded to companies in Canada is not exempted, but discussions to alter this situation have been held.[3]

Obviously, this tax can add to the cost of reinsurance, so the benefits of the treaty must be carefully studied before it is consummated. The existence of the tax or any exemption should be verified before entering into an agreement. As with any tax, the situation is subject to change. Even if no excise tax is applicable at the time the treaty is signed, it is good practice to document which party will be responsible for the cost of the tax should one be imposed later.

Stamp Duties. Some countries have, from time to time, imposed a stamp duty; all insurance policies issued or reinsured must be stamped and a fee paid to the government. The duty is based on the amount of death benefit and is payable one time only. The amount of the duty may vary with the initial duration of the contract. If the reinsurance arrangement involves a significant amount of insurance being ceded to a company in a country with a stamp duty, the stamp duty can be quite costly.

The United Kingdom had a stamp duty, but it was removed in 1990.

Withholding Tax. At one time, the United States imposed a withholding tax on all investments by foreign companies in the United States. This withholding tax, in the amount of 30% of investment income, was removed by the Tax Reform Act of 1984. When it was in effect,

---

[3] The excise tax is not paid on business ceded to United States branches or subsidiaries of Canadian companies. Such organizations are taxed as domestic taxpayers.

companies domiciled in the United Kingdom and certain other countries were exempt from this tax. The topic is mentioned here because such a tax could be reenacted in the future; any revival of the withholding tax would affect new treaties, and possibly inforce agreements as well.

Foreign Tax Planning. Before entering into any agreement involving a foreign country, it is important to become familiar with the taxation system of that country. Many European countries and Japan have very conservative definitions of statutory earnings, with taxable income based on statutory earnings. Insurers operating there pay relatively little in income taxes until the later durations of a given policy.

Furthermore, the governments may function differently in these countries with respect to taxation. Typically, the government determines to raise a certain amount of tax from the insurance industry and can change the tax base and rules rather quickly to accomplish this objective. Companies in these countries have had little motivation to enter into tax related reinsurance agreements as the government would just adjust the rules to achieve the tax revenue objective.

Economic and Political Factors

In considering an international reinsurance arrangement, certain factors not usually relevant to domestic reinsurance, may be of overriding importance.

Currency Exchange Risk. In the event that the assets backing the policy reserves are transferred outside of the United States, the company is subject to the risk of fluctuations in the currency exchange rate. These fluctuations could cause wide swings in earnings or in asset values, potentially affecting the reserve credits. This risk can be eliminated for the ceding company if all amounts are based on its currency; the risk is then transferred to the reinsurer.

Inflation. Even a low rate of inflation can be a problem to a life insurer because of the long term nature of most risks coupled with guaranteed or fixed premiums. Severe inflation can quickly eat into profit margins. Before entering into any agreement in a foreign country, the insurance company should consider the economic situation in that country and the potential effect of inflation on the agreement.

Political Instability. Because of the risks involved in asset transfer, any insurance company contemplating reinsurance with a company in a foreign country should be aware of the political situation in that country. Not all countries have orderly changes in government, nor do all countries consistently respect private property rights, especially those of foreign individuals or companies.

While it may be quite difficult to predict political turmoil or coups, when these do occur, social and economic upheaval follows. Assets could easily be devalued or confiscated, investment income could be disrupted, or reinsurance premiums or benefits withheld.

SELECTED INTERNATIONAL REINSURANCE MARKETS

Most developed countries in the world, with the possible exception of China and certain of the former Soviet block countries, currently afford some degree of life and health reinsurance market potential. The following is a brief description of the principal international reinsurance markets dealt with by United States life insurance companies.

Canada

Perhaps the most important insurance "trading partner" for the United States is Canada. Many companies domiciled in either country do business in both with a variety of subsidiaries, affiliates, and branches. Life, annuity, and disability products are similar, as are most reinsurance programs.

United States life insurance companies regularly cede traditional reinsurance to a Canadian company. It is less common for a Canadian insurer to cede any business to a United States carrier. There are basic differences between the direct insurance markets of these countries. Differences in valuation and nonforfeiture laws have resulted in different products and practices.

The Canadian Market. Canadian insurance companies may be federally or provincially incorporated or registered. Most are federally registered and are under the jurisdiction of the federal Superintendent of Insurance. There are over 150 federally registered insurance companies, about sixty of which are incorporated in Canada. The remainder are branches of foreign companies.

The larger Canadian insurers are sophisticated and knowledgeable in the United States insurance market. Some are active in the United States reinsurance market. Most professional reinsurers in Canada have domestic United States branches which are licensed to do business in most, if not all, of the states.

By ceding reinsurance to a United States branch, all monies involved remain expressed in terms of U.S. currency, eliminating the currency exchange risk to the ceding company and the federal excise tax. The reinsurer is, however, exposed to currency exchange fluctuations in its combined balance sheet. The branch of the Canadian company can combine its financial results with its parent without triggering the excise tax. Because of this use of branches, a United States ceding company is typically indifferent to the choice between a domestic reinsurer or a United States branch of a Canadian reinsurer.

Reserves and Financial Reinsurance. Canadian valuation and nonforfeiture laws are less rigid than those of the United States. A Canadian valuation actuary has more freedom in setting reserves, but must file a lengthy report detailing and justifying his choice of assumptions.

The policy reserves are calculated using the actuary's best estimate of future experience, adjusted for specific provisions for adverse deviation (PADs) for each assumption. The effect is to release the present value of earnings at issue, except for the present value of the PADs. If the calculated reserve is less than the cash surrender value, the difference must be held in a strengthened reserve or as allocated surplus. Each assumption can change each year although, in practice, that is seldom the case. The same reserves are used for statutory and GAAP purposes, but tax reserves follow government dictated rules.

Premium deficiency or minimum reserves are not required, as such. The United States branch of a Canadian company is subject to the reserve requirements of its state of entry, but any deficiency reserves or other differences would normally be "lost" in the consolidated overall statement of the Canadian company.

Because of the valuation and nonforfeiture laws, surplus strain is minimal in Canada. Since reserves do not follow an outside set of assumptions, but rather the best estimate of future experience, surplus relief, as it is known in the United States, is not feasible. Reserves represent the present value of payments to and from the insurer; a reinsurance treaty is viewed not as transferring reserves, but rather as a stream of payments. If the reinsurer is expected to show a profit, the ceding company's reserves might actually increase as the cost of reinsurance is an expense item. Under a typical United States financial reinsurance treaty, the present value of payments is not altered except for the fees paid to the reinsurer.

Normally, no benefit such as reduced reserves or increased earnings can be derived from a "surplus relief" treaty. However, Canada does have specific surplus requirements based on specific formulae and driven by items such as assets by class, premiums by type, and reserve totals. It is possible to obtain some relief from these surplus requirements by using financial reinsurance.

These same rules allow Canadian reinsurers to accept financial reinsurance from United States' companies with little effect on their Canadian worldwide balance sheets. If profitable, the reserves would equal the present value of benefits less premiums, which would be positive. The United States required reserves would have to be posted in the branch or subsidiary which accepted the business. In the ultimate parent's balance sheet the reserves would be on a Canadian basis.

The issue of reserve credits for business ceded to non-admitted reinsurers is seldom a problem in Canada. Both common practice and regulation essentially prevent the use of non-admitted carriers.

Canadian life insurance companies are taxed like other Canadian corporations; there is little opportunity for tax-driven reinsurance.

Administration and Practice. In 1956, Canadian life insurance companies formed the Canadian Reinsurance Conference. This group meets annually and its purpose is to establish guidelines for the conduct of reinsurance. This is not a regulatory body and does not have any authority to police the business. However, its 1984 Reinsurance

Guidelines established standardized reinsurance procedures and is valuable in the administration of reinsurance. This document is used as a reference for generally accepted industry practices. No such guidelines exist in the United States but, because of the similarities between the countries, the Canadian guidelines are recommended reading.

United Kingdom

There are two distinct reinsurance markets in the United Kingdom, the conventional market and the specialty market of Lloyds.

Conventional Market. Insurance companies in the United Kingdom are regulated by the Department of Trade and Industry (DTI). The insurance market has historically been more savings oriented than that of the United States, with a large portion of sales coming from variable life type products. Valuation actuaries in the United Kingdom have far more discretionary powers in setting reserve liabilities than their United States counterparts,[4] but they are also more accountable for reserve adequacy. As a consequence, reserves may not necessarily be lower than those required in the United States.

In the past, some reinsurance between companies in the United States and the United Kingdom occurred because of the different tax structures of the two countries. United Kingdom life insurers are taxed on the excess of I, investment income, over E, expenses, including commissions and allowances on reinsurance accepted. This difference, $I - E$, determines taxable income. As noted, pension business is taxed on profits, not on $I - E$. As of January 1, 1996, life insurance is also taxed on profits, in effect.

The following example illustrates how this difference in tax systems motivated international reinsurance to the benefit of both parties. Companies ceded United States business involving relatively large amounts of commission and relatively little investment income to a United Kingdom company. The United Kingdom insurer reported higher

---

[4] The United Kingdom Insurance Companies Regulations 1994 established the minimum basis of policyholder liabilities. While an actuary may choose a more conservative basis, the regulations require consistency from year to year.

E, with little or no increase in I, thus reducing the amount of $I - E$ and, therefore, the insurer's tax bill. The tax saving was shared with the ceding company in the form of higher allowances. In effect, the reinsurer could lose money on the underwriting and make it up, and then some, from tax savings.

As in the United States, the use of reinsurance to exploit differences in tax systems and situations attracted the attention of tax authorities in the United Kingdom. Effective January 1, 1995, changes were introduced into the taxation of life insurers and reinsurers, partly to prevent the use of reinsurance as a tool for tax arbitrage between countries. Direct insurers now have investment income imputed on business ceded, effectively creating taxable income as though the business were retained. Life reinsurance is taxed, in effect, on profits, as it is in most countries.

Lloyds Market. Lloyds of London is composed of a group of syndicates. Historically, each syndicate was made up of a group of individuals known as Names. Membership has now been opened to corporations; this category is expected to show significant growth. Each Name has an unlimited liability and must show sufficient financial strength to qualify. Neither Lloyds nor the syndicates are insurance companies in the traditional sense. Lloyds acts only in the capacity of a clearing house and establishes requirements.

Lloyds syndicates may write life business, but only for death benefit coverage and only for terms of ten years or less. A handful of specialist life syndicates offers such coverage. Because of these restrictions, Lloyds is not a significant factor in life reinsurance.

Lloyds primarily handles property and liability risks, but it also offers a wide range of health and medical coverages, including accidental death benefits. It can and does offer stop loss and catastrophe coverages for life and health insurance.

In the past decade, there have been some major problems at Lloyds, involving the inability of some syndicates to pay in full and poor underwriting practices. The rules, regulations, and practices which govern Lloyds are changing. These changes will allow limitations on the risks assumed by each syndicate. They will also more clearly define capital requirements, risks assumed, and the administration of the business.

Australia

Life insurance in Australia is regulated under the Life Insurance Act of 1945 by the Life Insurance Commissioner. There are about fifty registered life companies, six of which are professional reinsurers.

The Australian life market is very competitive and more savings oriented than the United States market. Australia is far more advanced in the integration of financial services. The larger life companies have very large surpluses and many are having difficulties sustaining growth in the Australian market. Little need for surplus relief or financial reinsurance exists. In fact, some of these companies may find overseas investment or reinsurance attractive.

The tax situation in Australia is similar to that which existed in the United States under the 1959 Act. It might be possible to use mod-co to reclassify investment income as underwriting income to result in a more favorable tax for the Australian company, but a true transfer of risk would be necessary. To date, this has not been done to any significant extent.

Continental Europe

In general, the practices of Continental Europe are similar to those of the United Kingdom. Solvency margins are similar, as previously described. Taxes vary by country, as do reserve requirements. With the integration of the EU, even more similarity of practice is expected to emerge. However, doubt has been expressed that practices and regulations will ever be identical in all countries.

For decades, direct insurance in many continental European countries was priced on a tariff basis. Under a tariff system, life insurance premiums are defined by law on a basis of loaded statutory net premiums. A percentage of the profits, sometimes set by law, is returned to the policyholders as dividends. Competition is based on dividends and the strength of distribution systems.

The third EU Life Directive essentially eliminated the tariff system, introducing freedom of pricing in many EU countries. Life companies are also free to offer cross-border services in life insurance throughout the EU. This, in turn, has created increased competition in the life reinsurance marketplace. Companies and countries are responding to the changed environment at different rates.

Reinsurance tends to be organized in many pools, with risks shared in small pieces among many carriers. Reinsurance from companies in Europe tends to go to the larger reinsurers. It is very uncommon to find a reinsurer that is also a direct insurer. Europeans view this largely as a conflict of interest. Of course, many reinsurers and direct insurers have common or cross ownership.

Most life reinsurers are part of organizations or companies which offer both life and property and liability reinsurance. In general, the European reinsurers are more conservative in analyzing risk than are the United States and Canadian reinsurers. Both direct insurance and reinsurance markets tend to be less competitive than in the United States, Canada, and the United Kingdom, although that is changing.

Most reinsurance is administered on a bulk basis with a bordereau listing of inforce and details being provided to the reinsurer by the ceding company. Accounting is commonly on an annual basis, often six months or more after the close of a calendar year. As a result, reinsurers may have extra time to produce statutory reports. For example, in Germany, reinsurers do not have to produce statutory reports until November of the following year, some ten months after the date of the report.

Several large reinsurers based in Europe are active in the United States. They generally function through United States subsidiaries, although branch offices are occasionally used. Dutch, English, German, Swedish, and Swiss reinsurers have significant subsidiaries in the United States.

The principal Continental European reinsurance markets are described briefly.[5]

The Netherlands. The Dutch insurance market is well developed and one of the most sophisticated in all of Continental Europe. Dominated by three large companies, the Dutch market is not regarded as being competitive. All three companies enjoy comfortable market shares and profit margins.

---

[5] The reader should note that the following discussion pertains to the domestic reinsurance markets in each of these countries. When reinsurers headquartered in these countries participate in the United States or Canadian markets, their subsidiaries or affiliates follow the local practices, regulations, and customs. Profit objectives and ultimate, parental surplus levels may be affected, but not the coverages provided.

The domestic market is limited, and these three companies have looked for investment opportunities outside the Netherlands. These companies are familiar with United States reinsurance practices through their subsidiaries. In fact, two of these companies have United States subsidiaries which engage in life and health reinsurance.

Capital gains and all other taxable income are taxed at a rate of 45%. However, capital gains may be sheltered somewhat by rolling them into replacement assets.

Switzerland. Switzerland's life insurance market historically operated on a tariff system like that of many other countries in Continental Europe. The Swiss regulatory system is geared to producing conservative earnings.

Some of the largest reinsurance groups in the world are of Swiss origin and management. Several Swiss reinsurers are active in the United States reinsurance market.

France. The French life insurance market is relatively unsophisticated but growing. The market operated on a tariff premium basis, but is not as rigid as in some countries.

Germany. The German life insurance market operates on the tariff system. It is important to remember that the German life insurance market has been wiped out twice in this century because of wars and hyperinflation. Regulation of the German market is geared toward solvency. Because of the strength of the Deutschemark, German insurers have not been particularly interested in assuming currency exchange risks.

As an illustration of the different practices for life reinsurance around the world, it may be instructive to review briefly the German domestic market. Some of the largest reinsurance groups in the world are in Germany, although most had to be totally rebuilt after World War II. Mod-co and YRT are very common, but coinsurance is rare. In effect, coinsurance of the savings element of policies is prohibited as the assets backing reserves must be deposited with the ceding company. YRT rates, like direct rates, are relatively conservative. Most reinsurance is ceded on an experience rated basis, but the reinsurer keeps the majority of the profits.

Mod-co in Germany is dissimilar to mod-co in the United States. Premiums are those used for statutory reserve purposes, loaded for certain expenses. Allowances most often are those permitted in Zillmer reserve calculations with possibly some additional allowance to finance acquisition costs. The reinsurer seldom incurs a cash loss on issue.

The mod-co adjustment interest rate is the statutory reserve interest rate, regardless of the assets backing the reserves or the performance of those assets, a practice clearly disallowed in the United States. The ceding company shares in the profits through experience refunds.

Since there is little difference in rates, competition is based on relationships and service, capital strength, additional financing terms, and, sometimes, the level of profit participation. Reinsurance is much more of a partnership than in the United States and Canada.

Japan

The Japanese life insurance market is approximately two-thirds the size of the United States market and growing rapidly. There are only some twenty domestic life insurance companies operating in Japan, each of which is incredibly large in relation to the average United States insurer. In the past, the Japanese have tended to be very conservative and rather unsophisticated in insurance and reinsurance. However, most life insurers have very large surpluses and some have expressed interest in United States insurance company investments.

Offshore Sites

Offshore sites, such as Bermuda, Barbados, the Bahamas, the Cayman Islands, and the Virgin Islands, are popular jurisdictions for the formation of reinsurance companies. It is much easier to start a reinsurance company in the islands than in the United States, Canada, or the United Kingdom because of the lower capitalization requirements and lower fees. Also, a company can usually be formed more quickly in the Islands than in the United States.

The Islands offer very attractive tax treatment and less stringent reserve requirements, both of which add to their popularity. More investment flexibility is allowed, with higher yielding investments available. Unless exempted by tax treaty, any premiums ceded to the islands are subject to the United States federal excise tax. Recent tax rulings have curtailed certain other benefits.

These islands are the home to many producer owned reinsurance companies for the reinsurance of credit insurance, workers' compensation, and agent owned companies. While there is a certain exotic appeal to doing business in the islands, there is also a certain stigma because of the image of lower surplus and reserve requirements. This need not be the case; many island based reinsurers are financially solid and very well run.

19 Health Reinsurance

Most of the concepts of reinsurance, such as risk sharing, reserve credits, and accounting, are the same for both life and health risks. Reinsurance of accident and health risks is nearly always the result of traditional risk transfer needs. Financial reinsurance of accident and health plans, especially medical insurance is rare.

Accident and health reinsurance, however, involves some unique features and practices. In this chapter, some of these features and considerations of accident and health reinsurance are discussed, with reference to disability income and medical indemnity coverages as the primary plans of insurance.

Health insurance is written on both individual and group bases. The benefit structures and the reinsurance considerations are similar for both types of insurance. The discussion in this chapter applies to the reinsurance of both group and individual health insurance.

DISABILITY INCOME

A large volume of accident and health reinsurance is on disability income or loss of time coverages. These products cover permanent disability, and, in some instances, partial disability. Waiting periods and benefit periods can vary by cause, and policies may include features for cost of living increases, return of premiums, or return of cash value. Most policies cover disability from both accidental and medical causes, although some cover accidental disabilities only.[1]

Disability income products are reinsured for largely the same reasons as life products. The primary reason is for spreading of risk, especially large amounts of benefits. There can be a significant surplus strain associated with disability income claims. Even if the monthly cash benefit is relatively small, the necessary claim reserve can be significant for a small or moderate sized insurance company.

A second major reason for disability income reinsurance is product expertise. A company whose primary business is individual life may wish to offer disability coverages as an accommodation to its agents. The company may find the reinsurer's expertise to be valuable in areas such as product design, pricing, rate structure, policy forms and rate filings, underwriting, valuation, policy administration, and claims administration. The reinsurer's involvement can vary from providing excess risk coverage to providing virtually all administrative services related to a disability income line of business in addition to the risk coverage.

Retention Limits

There are three common approaches to setting retention limits for disability income coverages, one of which is unique to disability or periodic income coverages. To some extent, the retention limits and the type of reinsurance are interrelated. In determining its retention, a company usually would consider the present value of benefits as a guideline in determining the maximum monthly benefit to be retained. For example, if the disability income line were roughly the same size as the life insurance line, it might set limits for disability income which would produce present values of benefits which were roughly the same as the maximum retention for life insurance. If the disability income line

---

[1] For purposes of this text, hospital indemnity and other forms of periodic cash benefit coverages are considered to be disability income plans.

were smaller than the life insurance line, it might establish a lesser retention limit.

This method is logical if the claim reserve is viewed as a lump sum benefit at the time of claim incurral; the intent is to keep the maximum incurred benefit at a reasonable level. Of course, the potential effect of fluctuation and the carrier's attitudes on risk avoidance by product line are major considerations.

Fixed or Excess Share. A fixed, or excess share, reinsurance of disability income is a proportional reinsurance coverage which closely resembles the typical retention situation for life insurance, except the retention and the reinsurance coverage amounts are stated in terms of dollars per month of benefit, instead of a gross dollar amount. Under an excess share arrangement, the ceding company retains a fixed, level amount of disability income coverage for the entire benefit period. For example, a company may elect to retain $200 per month per life for a certain coverage type. If the carrier issued $500 of monthly benefit, it would cede $300.

Retention limits may vary by policy form or benefit period. The company may decide to retain less for longer benefit periods or shorter elimination periods. It may decide to retain 100% of any hospital indemnity coverages if the benefit amounts involved are relatively small. This type of variation in retention makes sense when the maximum possible present values of the various benefits are taken into consideration.

Quota Share. Quota share reinsurance is another form of proportional coverage where the ceding company retains a fixed percentage of each risk. This corresponds to the quota share method used in life reinsurance. The only difference between excess share and quota share reinsurance is in the determination of each party's share of the risk. The quota share method simplifies reinsurance administration and is often used when disability income is not a major product line of the ceding company, but rather an accommodation to its agents. Quota share coverages usually result in more reinsurance, with less earnings retained by the ceding company.

Extended Wait. Extended wait, or extended elimination period, reinsurance is a nonproportional coverage. Under this method, reinsurance benefits begin only after the claim has reached a specified duration. This period of delay in reinsurance participation is known as the extended wait or the extended elimination period. Since the ceding company's share of the benefit payments is larger before the expiration of the extended wait period than afterwards, this larger share can be viewed as a large deductible which must be met before reinsurance coverage begins.

For example, the ceding company may retain all amounts for the first two years of benefits and then reinsure 75% of amounts payable after that point. Alternatively, a flat amount, such as $200 per month, may be retained after the extended wait period. While the carrier could seek to cede 100% of the benefits after the extended wait period, reinsurers generally prefer to keep the direct insurer involved in the ongoing claim review and its economic implications.

Extended wait coverage is also used in combination with excess share or quota share reinsurance. This is especially true of lifetime accident and sickness benefits, where extended wait coverage eliminates the reinsurance administration of a number of short duration claims. The ceding company retains a portion of each claim for a given period and a lesser amount thereafter. This makes the reinsurance package as a whole into a nonproportional plan. The extended wait coverage and the basic coverages (excess share or quota share) may be with the same reinsurer or with different reinsurers, even for the same insured life.

Plans of Reinsurance

As with life insurance, there are three major plans of reinsurance for disability income: YRT, coinsurance, and mod-co. Unlike life insurance, these are seldom used in combination.

Yearly Renewable Term. The simplest and perhaps most common method of reinsuring disability income coverages is the use of YRT reinsurance. This is quite similar to the use of YRT reinsurance in the life insurance situation. Under this plan, a schedule of YRT premiums for $100 of monthly benefit is developed for each issue age, benefit period, and waiting period.

Health Reinsurance

YRT works particularly well in the case of the excess retention method and also can be used with the quota share method. For individual cessions, YRT is relatively easy to administer, especially for the reinsurer. In addition to less complicated administration and increased clarity, YRT offers relative ease in the event of recapture.

There are two major differences between YRT reinsurance for life insurance and disability income coverages. For life insurance, the amount of coverage reinsured is the net amount at risk, or the face amount of the policy less the policy reserve. For disability income coverage, the policy reserve does not enter into the determination of the amount reinsured.

The second difference concerns the amount of surplus relief available as the result of reserve credits. For life insurance, YRT does not develop significant reserves, and, therefore, does not provide meaningful reserve credits. However, in the case of disability income coverage, the per unit active life reserve under YRT may be close to that of the original policy.

Yearly renewable term reinsurance is often designed and priced to cover only total disability benefits. Such a product may be inappropriate for partial benefits.

Coinsurance. The use of coinsurance for disability income reinsurance closely parallels the use of coinsurance for life insurance. The reinsurer accepts the ceding company's premium on the business reinsured and pays an allowance to cover the ceding company's commissions and expenses. Normally, this allowance is larger in the first year to cover acquisition costs. The reinsurer then holds its share of all policy reserves and pays its share of policy benefits.

Coinsurance is used most frequently in the quota share retention method because it greatly simplifies administration. The ceding company need only apply the quota share percentage to its premiums, reserves, and benefits to determine the reinsurer's share. Allowances are easily determined from the reinsurance premiums. The pricing of allowances is unique to each ceding company's premium and benefit structure.

With coinsurance of life insurance, the policy cash values or reserves usually are paid to the ceding company at recapture. Most basic disability income coverages do not have cash values, although many have return of premium or cash value riders. Therefore, if coinsurance is used, a basis for recapture should be negotiated either at the time recapture is requested or at the time the treaty is written.

If the treaty provides for recapture, it must be clear regarding what amount, if any, is to be paid by the reinsurer to the ceding company on recapture, if disputes are to be avoided. This is more difficult than it is for life insurance because disability income reserves are less rigidly specified or defined than are life insurance reserves where cash values may represent a reasonable substitute.

Modified Coinsurance. Given the fact that disability income products can generate significant reserves, both for active lives and claims, mod-co could be a good choice for reinsurance. However, mod-co is rarely used. Funds withheld coinsurance is more likely to be chosen if the reinsurer is not authorized in the necessary jurisdictions.

Pricing

The reinsurance pricing actuary has to consider many factors in developing rates for disability income. While the process is generally the same as that for life reinsurance, some special characteristics merit further review.

Benefits. The reinsurance pricing actuary should study the policy form and rate charts carefully. Different definitions of disability will influence experience of the product, as will variations in occupational classifications, benefit periods, and elimination periods.

Market. The market environment of a product also affects its ultimate experience. The actuary should consider whether the product is sold as a major marketing effort or only as an accommodation to agents. The actuary must also consider if the product is going to be marketed only to certain income levels or occupational groups, or in certain geographic regions. Any of these factors can affect experience and rates. Also, it is important to determine whether the plan will be sold only as a stand alone policy, a rider, or both.

Health Reinsurance

Underwriting. Insurance claim management begins with good underwriting. This is particularly true for any accident or health product. The reinsurance pricing actuary or underwriter needs to evaluate the ceding company's underwriting rules, as well as its underwriters and their experience.

Claim Procedures. A company's claim procedures can have a significant effect on the profitability of any health product. Claims should be handled promptly and professionally in order to avoid adverse legal action, and not be allowed to continue beyond the point defined by the terms of the policy.

Retention. The ceding company's retention is also important to reinsurance experience. If an excess share retention is being used instead of quota share, the reinsurer will have a relatively narrow base of risks over which to spread its claim costs. Larger coverage amounts exhibit different experience than do smaller ones. The ceding company should have sufficient exposure to risk on the reinsured policies to ensure proper claims review and management. Otherwise, the company could pay claims with relative impunity to avoid hassles with policyholders and agents.

Experience. The ceding company's previous experience in the market may be an indicator of future experience. If the company has had little or no experience, the pricing actuary should be more cautious than with a company which has substantial positive experience.

Special Considerations

Administration of a disability income reinsurance agreement is similar to that of life reinsurance. Two points, recapture and valuation, warrant special discussion.

Recapture. As mentioned previously, recapture of disability income reinsurance may be complicated because of a lack of defined reserves and an absence of cash values. Any expectations or rules regarding recapture should be defined in the treaty. Otherwise, recapture should be considered to be prohibited, unless, of course, the parties can agree on terms later. Policies with open disability claims are not normally recaptured until the cessation of the claim.

Valuation. The reinsurer needs a flexible valuation system to develop the reserves for disability income products, as each ceding company's benefit and premium structure is likely to be different. All reinsured benefits should be considered in determining the reinsurer's reserves and the ceding company's reserve credits. Claim reserves must also be computed. Extended wait coverages will generate claim reserves when the claim is first incurred, not when the wait period is finally breached.

LONG TERM CARE

Long term care (LTC) products are, in essence, a form of disability income insurance. Many of the considerations are similar to those for disability income. However, there are some considerations which are unique to LTC, primarily its recent introduction and the social environment in which it exists.

Recent Introduction

Long term care products are relatively new to the market and are still evolving rapidly. The major claims from LTC occur after age 85, but the industry has little experience with insured lives at such high ages for any health insurance product.

Benefits. Benefits are evolving. There are standard benefits which are required by many regulators, but enhanced or optional benefits are introduced by many insurers on a continual basis. It is anticipated that the largest claim costs will occur on individuals after age 85, but even those insurers which were first in the market are just beginning to develop high age experience. A small improvement in persistency can actually generate significantly higher claim costs as more individuals remain insured to higher ages.

There is no uniformity in the basis for coverage. The original LTC and nursing home products provided benefits on an indemnity basis. The insured was reimbursed for covered expenses if such expenses were incurred. Some of the more recent products are based on a disability model. Under this program, the insured is entitled to payments if the defined medical events occur, even if no expenses are incurred.

Original plans covered only certain expenses in a nursing home. In fact, most plans were similar to hospital indemnity products, paying a flat amount per day if the individual was confined to a nursing home. More frills are available now, and benefits for home health care are common.

Reinsurers must know what benefits are being offered before they can make intelligent offers for reinsurance. Both parties need to ensure that communication about benefits and claims practice are clear in order to avoid future confusion and conflict.

Underwriting. Underwriting selection is not based on decades of experience, but on evolving analysis. Group products are sold to working individuals, most of whom are under age 60 at time of underwriting and are actively at work. Individual products are sold mostly to individuals who are over age 60 and not actively at work. "Normal" health at higher ages includes medical conditions which would be cause for substandard ratings or decline in younger individuals. Direct insurers may change underwriting criteria quickly as new evidence emerges. Reinsurers must ensure that underwriting standards are clear and that changes are not made without their knowledge or approval.

Pricing. Because the product is new and the environment is changing rapidly, pricing is a special challenge. Benefits offered and underwriting standards vary from insurer to insurer. There is no meaningful experience data for large amounts. Accordingly, the reinsurer's pricing actuary must review each request for proposal with care and attention to every detail.

Reinsurance Products. Most reinsurance thus far has been on a coinsurance basis. Many insurers which specialize in long term care and related products have chosen to retain all the risks. Many other insurers have looked to the reinsurers for assistance in entering the market. The result is essentially a joint venture, with the insurer providing marketing and the reinsurer product development, underwriting, and pricing advice. In many such instances, the insurer cedes the majority of the business to the reinsurer.

Social Environment

Perhaps more than any other product, the future of LTC is intertwined with social environmental issues. A major political issue of the past few years has been the future of health care in the United States, including LTC. In addition, social acceptance of nursing home care is in flux. Not many years ago, common practice was for individuals to care for their aged relatives in their homes.

It is increasingly common to place these people in nursing homes without social stigma. This may lead to greater per capita use of LTC benefits in the future than in the past. Alternatively, home health care benefits may make it easier to keep such people in private residences.

Capital investment in nursing homes is another major factor. Much of the construction of homes is funded by state agencies; the current move to lower taxes and less government, has led to slower construction. There is evidence of a correlation between the number of beds per capita available and the number of claims per capita.

In short, both reinsurers and direct insurers must keep the evolving social environment in mind when developing and managing long term care products.

MAJOR MEDICAL AND COMPREHENSIVE

Low limit hospital and medical expense insurance generate little need for reinsurance. However, major medical and comprehensive health insurance may expose a company to very large claims, necessitating reinsurance.

Insurance companies and employers with self-funded plans reinsure medical coverages for protection against adverse fluctuations in experience. Medical coverages usually provide benefits on an indemnity basis. The amount of a claim depends upon many factors, and is not a defined lump sum as for life insurance. Because of this, the majority of reinsurance on medical plans is nonproportional.

Health Reinsurance

Sometimes, an insurance company will enter into a joint venture with a reinsurer to provide medical coverage. The direct company may feel that it must provide the coverage to control the sales situation and market other products, such as group life. Alternatively, the reinsurer may have the expertise and the desire to enter a particular market but may not be licensed in a particular state. A joint venture could take advantage of the perceived better reputation of the direct company. In other instances, the insurer may be truly interested in entering the market.

Retention

The two methods used to determine retention for medical coverages correspond roughly to the quota share and extended wait methods used for disability income reinsurance.

Quota Share. The quota share method of reinsuring medical benefits is identical in practice to the quota share method used in life and disability income reinsurance. A fixed percentage of all policies is reinsured. Under this method, the reinsurer has an equal percentage stake in every claim. Coinsurance of major medical and comprehensive plans must be quota share, although that share may vary with the level of the deductible of the underlying policy.

Extended Deductible. The extended deductible is a nonproportional method of reinsurance developed for major medical which is applicable to individual policies. It corresponds to the extended waiting period used for disability income reinsurance. The reinsurer does not pay a claim until a certain level of payments to one individual or to all persons insured under a policy has been reached by the ceding company. For example, the reinsurer may agree to pay 75% of claims for any individual in excess of $25,000. If the amount of insurance benefit is $65,000, the reinsurer would pay $30,000.

The reinsurer's participation in claims may increase as the total amount of the claims increases to higher levels. This is accomplished by establishing different layers of reinsurance coverage.

Plans of Reinsurance

The two plans of reinsurance for major medical and comprehensive insurance are coinsurance and stop loss or excess reinsurance. Since active life reserves are only unearned premiums, and those tend to be monthly, asset management is of little concern. Even claim reserves tend to be of a short-term nature. Mod-co can be used, but funds withheld coinsurance is more likely if the reinsurer is not authorized in the appropriate jurisdictions. The concept of YRT does not apply to these coverages.

Coinsurance. Coinsurance of medical coverages is rare, but if used, it is typically on a quota share basis. The reinsurer shares in premiums, claims, and reserves in proportion to its share of the business. Expense allowances are negotiated and priced in a manner similar to those for other coverages. Coinsurance usually is intended to last for the life of the policy.

Medical coverages vary by renewability guarantees, such as guaranteed renewable, noncancelable, collectively renewable, and nonrenewable. The terms of the coinsurance agreement should reflect the original policy's terms. It may also define the reinsurer's participation in the renewal premium setting process, if any.

Stop Loss or Excess Reinsurance. Today, most reinsurance of medical coverages is done on a stop loss or excess reinsurance basis. Two kinds of stop loss are used and both can be applied to the same group of policies. Specific stop loss or excess reinsurance provides excess loss coverage on each individual insured. Aggregate stop loss or aggregate excess reinsurance provides protection on an entire group of employees or block of policies.

Specific stop loss or excess reinsurance provides payment if a claim exceeds a specified dollar amount. This amount is referred to as the trigger point, attachment point, or high deductible. The trigger point is usually defined as the dollar amount of medical expenses incurred during a calendar year from all causes. The trigger point may be defined in terms of all charges arising from a single cause without a time limit, but this is difficult to administer. A lifetime trigger point may be used, but this is rare.

Aggregate coverage is used if total retained claims exceed a specified amount. Aggregate coverage may have maximum limits and coinsurance participation also. Aggregate coverage is rare for group major medical insurance, but is often used in conjunction with specific stop loss in self-funded plans.

Specific and aggregate coverages are usually provided by the same reinsurer, but they need not be. Each stop loss coverage has a deductible and a maximum limit. Some insurers purchase additional protection by adding one or more excess layers of stop loss over the lower coverages, with the deductible of each higher layer equal to the sum of the deductible and maximum coverage of the next lower limit. This procedure, called layering, is not common.

Stop loss reinsurance is usually guaranteed for a period of one year. Rates may change with each period, or the reinsurer may decide to not renew the coverage. The ceding company can move the coverage to another reinsurer if more favorable terms are available. However, there is no guarantee that the desired coverage will be available in the future.

Pricing

Pricing medical reinsurance is a difficult process. Several factors affect the price and are discussed below.

Benefits. The reinsurer and the ceding company must agree on the benefits covered in advance if confusion and conflict are to be avoided. If the reinsurer does not cover certain experimental treatments or diseases, the ceding company may want to exclude these treatments or diseases from the direct coverage, rather than risk exposure to a potentially expensive claim without reinsurance.

Market. There are several distinct medical reinsurance markets, each with different characteristics. Each market requires specific expertise. The small writer usually lacks the strong underwriting, actuarial, and claims management resources necessary for success. The reinsurer in this market must provide such expertise.

Larger writers are more sophisticated. Reinsurance decisions are based primarily on cost. The reinsurer must be technically strong to avoid being selected against.

Reinsurers in the self-funded employer market need a strong underwriting background. Since most self-funded employers use third party administrators (TPAs), the reinsurer must be familiar with the TPA's claim practices.

Reinsuring health maintenance organizations (HMOs) requires special expertise. The relationship between the HMO and hospital provider is important to understand. The management of the HMO will also affect results as will the enrollment.

Medical costs will also vary by region and by type of group. The key rating parameters for a fast growing company will change rapidly. A company with poor sales results will often have poor experience. The reinsurer must be aware of the underlying characteristics of the ceding company's business to achieve success.

Claims. The ceding company's claim practices will have a significant effect on the results. The reinsurer must be satisfied with the company's ability and willingness to monitor claims or be able to assume the responsibility.

Retention. Several factors affect the retention limit. The ceding company's attitude is very important. Some companies have been known to lower retention limits if they feel the reinsurance premiums are inadequate. Since the ceding company's attitude affects underwriting and claims management, the reinsurer must be assured that the ceding company retains an appropriate amount of risk.

Experience. Because there are many unique markets, experience will vary significantly by company. Medical experience may change rapidly. The successful reinsurer studies the ceding company's past experience and monitors current experience.

Experience Refunds. Because medical reinsurance is a low frequency, high amount risk, most reinsurance is written on a nonrefunding or fully pooled basis. However, many companies ceding large amounts of group medical insurance want credit for good experience. Various methods for refunding are employed. Calculation of the experience refund is complicated by the long tail of the claims.

Special Considerations

There are more differences between medical coverages reinsurance and life reinsurance than there are between disability income reinsurance and life reinsurance. This is to be expected since the original benefits and forms are so different. Some of these differences necessitate different practices and procedures.

Covered Benefits. In developing the treaty for any medical reinsurance arrangement, the reinsurer and the ceding company must agree as to which benefits are covered and which are excluded. Among other things, this includes definitions of when coverage for individuals will begin, when coverage will end, and what claims are covered.

The ceding company and the reinsurer should discuss experimental procedures and whether such procedures are to be covered by the reinsurance agreement. Given the constant introduction of new medical techniques, medicines, and technology, there is little prospect of including an exhaustive list in the treaty. Therefore, it would be prudent to define a procedure for deciding on the role of the reinsurer regarding new procedures.

Recapture. Recapture of reinsurance on medical coverages is rare. Coinsurance is not really designed for recapture, and special terms would be needed. Stop loss is renewable for only short periods, so recapture is not a factor.

Administration. Administration of premiums and allowances, if any, is a fairly simple accounting procedure. Claims administration may be more difficult. If coinsurance is used, the reinsurer is responsible for a fixed percentage of claims and therefore reserves, so claims sharing is fairly simple. For stop loss however, running tallies of losses per individual policy or group are needed for coverage.

Incurred versus Paid Claims. Most medical reinsurance contracts are written on an incurred claims basis. Because of the long tail on most claims, exceptions are often made for self-funded employers. The use of paid claims expedites the calculation of experience refunds and lessens the complications of termination. However, the experience can be manipulated if paid claims are used.

Carryforward provisions. The carryforward provision of a stop loss or excess reinsurance agreement affects costs. Without a carryforward provision, a company with a large claim covering two calendar years could find itself liable for the entire claim if the amounts paid in each year are less than the deductible or trigger point. For example, if a company with a $50,000 deductible incurs a claim and pays $30,000 at the end of the year and $40,000 during the next year, it would not be reimbursed by the reinsurer in the absence of a carryforward provision.

The typical carryforward provision allows the ceding company to apply amounts paid on claims incurred in the last three months of the calendar year to the amounts paid in the next calendar year. Sometimes, if the amount paid during the last three months of the calendar year exceeds the deductible, no carryforward is allowed. In other agreements, the amount carried forward is the deductible reduced by the amount reimbursed. In the above example, if the company paid $60,000 in claims at the end of the calendar year, it would be permitted to carryforward $40,000.

OTHER BENEFITS

Many varieties of medical, accident, and health coverages exist, and more are being created. Reinsurance for each may be designed in a unique manner, but the principles described in this book would be expected to apply. These coverages include hospital surgical, dread disease, and travel accident benefits, among others. Stop loss, coinsurance, extended wait or extended deductible, and combinations of these may be applied as appropriate.

20 | Annuity Reinsurance

Until the mid-1980's, the reinsurance of annuities was relatively rare, largely because annuities were not a major product line with most insurers. However, as the "unbundling" of the protection and savings elements of insurance products spread, consumer interest in annuities grew and sales increased rapidly. This growth was spurred by high interest rates, demographic changes, and certain tax deferral opportunities offered by annuities.

Along with this growth in sales of annuities came a demand for reinsurance of annuities. This demand flowed from the sometimes high surplus strain created by the sale of annuities or a desire to access the reinsurer's investment management services, not from a need for mortality, morbidity, or even interest risk protection. This need has led to the creation of different reinsurance techniques designed to share investment and asset risks and to provide surplus relief, while meeting regulatory requirements.

The principles of both traditional and financial reinsurance discussed elsewhere in this book also apply to annuities. This chapter addresses certain of the various products sold as annuities and some of the specific points to be analyzed or documented in developing a reinsurance agreement covering annuities.

ANNUITY PRODUCTS

For purposes of this chapter, annuity products are classified in two major groups based upon the guarantees provided. The first group includes annuities with benefits that are sensitive to interest rates declared periodically by the insurer, based on its investment results. While some guarantees are present, the ultimate benefits are highly dependent upon the future interest credited to the contract. Included in this group are market value adjusted annuities and variable annuities. The other group includes those with guaranteed benefits, which are therefore independent of the insurer's investment results.

Interest Sensitive Benefits

Interest sensitive annuities function largely as tax-deferred savings accounts, with interest being credited to the contractholders' funds on deposit. Generally there are long term guarantees at or below the maximum permitted statutory valuation interest rate and shorter term (one to five years) guarantees based upon a current interest rate declared by the insurer. Annuity purchase rates are guaranteed, creating some long term risks regarding interest rates and mortality. In a number of contracts, these guarantees are relatively modest and provision is made for allowing more favorable rates based on the insurance company's current practice at the time of annuitization.

Interest sensitive annuities are used largely as asset accumulation vehicles and can be classified according to the premium payment expectations. Generally, they are known as deferred annuities because the annuitization is to occur in the future, not immediately at issue. The two principal types of interest sensitive products are single premium deferred annuities and flexible premium deferred annuities.

Single Premium Deferred Annuities. Single premium deferred annuities (SPDA's), as the name implies, are annuities purchased with a single premium and containing some long term guarantee as to annuity purchase rates. Generally, the contractholder can withdraw his money in a lump sum rather than accept a periodic payout, but there may be a penalty imposed for this option.

The primary risks of SPDA's are those relating to the reinvestment of assets and asset default and to disintermediation at time of withdrawal.

Favorable annuity purchase rate guarantees can create substantial risks if mortality improves rapidly or interest rates decline significantly. Surplus strain is created by acquisition expenses and by initial interest guarantees which exceed the applicable statutory valuation interest rates.

Frequently, the strain of acquisition expenses is partially offset during the first seven to ten contract years through the use of surrender charges which reduce both surrender values and reserves. As the surrender charges reduce, reserves increase accordingly. As a result, insurers may wait for many years before realizing statutory profits on their SPDA sales.

Reinsurance opportunities arise from the strain created at issue. While the strain per unit may be low when compared to that for life insurance, the large volumes of SPDA premium can create enormous strains for some carriers. In addition, rating agencies and regulators want annuity issuers to maintain additional surplus, often referred to as risk based capital or required surplus. Many insurance company managements insist on maintaining capital and surplus well above minimum regulatory levels, either to satisfy internally-imposed capital standards or obtain a high rating. Reinsurance can be arranged which both offsets the initial statutory strain and transfers or reduces the target capital requirement.

Initially, companies ceding annuity reinsurance tended to use financial reinsurance to create surplus relief. However, as regulators increased the requirements for reserve credits or balance sheet improvement, companies turned increasingly to more permanent forms of risk transfer reinsurance. Some ceding companies now use reinsurance to realize immediately a significant portion of future earnings on the SPDA's, creating statutory earnings and surplus which can be used to support other new issues or pay dividends.

Perhaps the largest problem in reinsuring SPDA's is negotiating and documenting mutually acceptable investment and interest crediting strategies. This will be discussed in more depth later in this chapter.

Flexible Premium Deferred Annuities. Flexible premium deferred annuities (FPDA's) are similar to SPDA's in that they are primarily accumulation products with permanent annuity purchase rate guarantees. Like SPDA's, strain is caused by acquisition expenses and interest rate guarantees. Unlike SPDA's, FPDA's are designed to permit the payment of renewal premiums, usually on a flexible basis, although scheduled payments may be planned at issue.

Commissions on first year premiums for FPDA's are higher than those on SPDA's, but renewal commissions tend to be somewhat lower. Interest guarantees are similar to those of SPDA's, so the higher commissions can lead to greater strain as a percent of premium. Surrender charges employed are similar to those on SPDA's.

The basic reinsurance considerations are the same for FPDA's as those for SPDA's, with two exceptions. SPDA's have only one premium, so there is no commitment regarding new money. FPDA's are designed to permit the payment of renewal premiums, so interest commitments on new money are important. This point must be considered in drafting the reinsurance agreement.

A more significant difference may be that a certain level of renewal premiums may be necessary to recover the initial strain created by the commission on the first year premiums. This situation is similar to that which occurs with most life insurance products with high first year commissions. The first year commission on an FPDA, however, is almost certain to be lower than that of a corresponding life insurance product.

Reinsurance pricing must take into account both the initial strain as well as the need for renewal premiums and the commitments regarding interest on those renewal premiums.

Guaranteed Benefits

Annuities which are designed to guarantee payments to a beneficiary provide a greater challenge to both the insurer and the reinsurer than do accumulation annuity products. At one time, all deferred annuities were of the guaranteed type. Today, this type of annuity is rare and virtually all guaranteed benefit annuities are variations of single premium immediate annuities (SPIA's). These products usually do not have any renewal premiums.

Rather than focus on crediting current interest on an accumulation account, these annuities guarantee the payment of predetermined amounts on specified future dates. Sales competition is based largely on purchase price, along with the rating, the stability, and the reputation of the issuing company. Since payments may be guaranteed for many years in the future, the reinvestment risk is more significant on these products than on interest sensitive annuities.

Just as the credited rate is important to the profitability of interest sensitive annuities, the interest rate assumed in pricing the guaranteed benefits, referred to as the pricing rate, is key to profitability of guaranteed benefit annuities.

Structured Settlement Annuities. Structured settlement annuities are SPIA's sold in response to a need to structure a series of payments, instead of a lump sum, typically as an award, payment of lottery winnings, or the settlement of a claim or lawsuit. For example, settlement of a workers' compensation claim for a job related disability may consist of a lifetime income, with lump sums at specified intervals for college expenses of dependents. Payments may increase annually as a provision for inflation. Some of the benefits may not become due for fifty or more years. This presents a significant risk regarding reinvestments as few investments are available for such long periods.

Commissions are fairly uniform and the structured settlement market is controlled by a relatively small group of brokers. Competition is based almost entirely on price, once the stability and integrity of the insurer are established. When market interest rates are high in comparison to statutory valuation interest rates, gross premiums, net of commissions, are much lower than initial reserves. This, of course, can create a significant surplus strain.

Reinsurance of structured settlement annuities has been rare, probably because most major writers of this business are large, well capitalized insurers. However, the high strain has led some insurers to seek reinsurance for surplus relief purposes. Like SPDA reinsurance, structured settlement reinsurance started as financial reinsurance to provide short term surplus relief, but traditional coinsurance and modified coinsurance are growing in usage.

The use of coinsurance implies that the reinsurer assumes most or all of the risks of asset default, lower interest rates, and reinvestment. The reinsurer will know the stream of benefit payments promised and may invest the funds it receives as it wishes.

The use of mod-co is more complicated as the assets and their management are left with the ceding company. Depending on the terms of a specific agreement, the reinsurer will assume the interest rate and reinvestment risks. The asset default risk, together with the opportunity for capital gains and losses and the recognition of unrealized capital gains and losses, may be left with the ceding company or passed to the reinsurer. In most jurisdictions today, regulations require participation in all aspects of investment and assets risks, including capital gains and losses.[1] In any event, the reinsurer will wish to be comfortable with the ceding company's investment philosophy and practices, both initially and for the long term.

Structured settlements may involve substandard lives where injury or medical impairment is anticipated to reduce normal life expectancy. If these settlements involve any payments contingent on survival, competition for the business will be affected by the insurer's underwriting practices as a higher substandard rating will result in a more competitive premium. Both insurers and their reinsurers are advised to examine the underwriting carefully to ensure acceptance of desirable risks while minimizing exposure to unprofitable segments of the market.

It is generally believed that any type of insurance or annuity can be reinsured on an assumption basis if agreement can be reached between the ceding company and a reinsurer. Structured settlement annuities may be an exception to this generalization. Many structured settlement annuities are issued at the direction of a court, specifying a particular insurer or rating for the insurer. Questions have been raised as to whether or not the original company can transfer structured settlement obligations through assumption reinsurance. This point should be addressed before any assumption reinsurance of structured settlement annuities is finalized.

Guaranteed Investment Contracts. Guaranteed investment contracts (GIC's), guarantee a lump sum payment at some specified point in the future. The periods of time involved are usually relatively short, such as three to seven years. Mortality risk and annuity purchase rate guarantees are usually limited, if they exist at all. The risks are basically those of asset default and interest guarantees.

Reinsurance on GIC's can arise from an insurer's desire to reduce its exposure to these investment risks. It is more likely, however, that reinsurance will result from the need for surplus relief. If interest guarantees exceed the statutory valuation interest rates, significant surplus strain can result; financial reinsurance is a common response.[2] In any event, the reinsurer must assume some of the guarantees in order for reserve credit to be granted.

---

[1] See Chapter 10, Reinsurance Regulation.

[2] See Chapter 5, Financial Reinsurance.

Traditional mod-co may be used to reinsure GIC's if the reinsurer is comfortable with the ceding company's investment practices. The treaty must be clear as to the reinsurer's participation in realized or unrealized capital gains and losses or in asset defaults, in accordance to relevant regulation.

Terminal Funding Annuities. Terminal funding annuities are a combination of deferred and immediate annuities sold in a specific application to fund pension obligations. The phrase "terminal funding" arose from the purchasing of annuities to fulfill obligations under pension plans which were being terminated. The most publicized usage has been in leveraged buy-outs or corporate takeovers where the pension plans were overfunded. Purchase of annuities to meet all earned commitments freed the excess funds for other uses, such as payment of corporate debt.

Terminal funding annuities, like structured settlements, are price-competitive. When market interest rates are higher than valuation interest rates, strain can result. Reinsurance considerations are similar to those of structured settlement annuities.

Variable Annuities

Historically, reinsurance of variable annuities has been infrequent. The investment risks are borne by the contract holder, so the need for risk transfer is small. However, strain can result from acquisition expenses and there are mortality guarantees. Reinsurers can participate in these elements, as well as extend "free look" provisions, death benefits, and annuitization guarantees or purchase rates.

Once annuitized, variable annuities may have either fixed or variable benefits. Fixed benefits are determined in the same manner as for SPDA's and FPDA's, based on annuity purchase rates. These rates have mortality and interest guarantees which can be reinsured in the same manner as any SPIA or deferred annuity. Even those benefits which are variable may have mortality and minimum interest guarantees which can be reinsured in a similar manner.

In recent years, the advent of joint ventures between producers and insurers has led to a wider use of reinsurance to share costs and profits of writing variable annuities and variable life insurance. Modified coinsurance is the preferred plan of reinsurance, but there are difficulties in putting it in place.

Some legal advisors believe that it is not possible to coinsure or mod-co separate account products. This is because of legal requirements that the premiums go directly into the separate account and not be diverted to any other purpose or paid to any other party. Coinsurance and mod-co necessitate the payment of the insurance or annuity funds to the reinsurer, which would be a diversion of funds. As a result, some insurers and reinsurers have developed reinsurance agreements which emulate mod-co without actually transferring funds. Other legal advisors appear to have a more lenient interpretation of the laws and regulations.

Writers of variable annuities frequently provide minimum death benefit guarantees to their contractholders. These may be either a guaranteed return of the initial amount deposited, regardless of the asset value of the account at the time of death, or increases in that amount at a set rate per annum. Reinsurers participate in these guarantees, providing coverage for what is basically a net amount at risk, or the excess of the minimum guaranteed amount over the account value.

This coverge is of a YRT nature in that no cash surrender or maturity values are provided by the reinsurer, only death benefits. The premiums for this coverage often are expressed as percentages of the account value, however, and not as a function of an issue age and duration cost of mortality. While the reinsurer does not participate directly in the asset performance as it would with coinsurance or mod-co, it is clearly affected by the performance of the underlying assets. If asset growth is high enough, the reinsurer has no risk. If asset performance is poor, the reinsurer's risk can be substantial.

Market Value Adjusted Annuities

Some insurers offer general account products called market value adjusted annuities which have some of the aspects of separate account variable annuities. The most common feature of market value adjusted annuities is to mark the account values to then current market values upon surrender or withdrawal. Interest may be credited as with a normal general account annuity, but if market values are different from book values at the time of surrender or withdrawal, the contractholder participates in the capital gain or loss implied.

Reinsurers can participate in these products in the same manner as they can with other annuities, either general account or separate account. Modified coinsurance is the most commonly preferred plan as it is important to have all assets invested together; otherwise, the reinsurer's result at time of surrender or withdrawal could be very different from that of the insurer due to different asset values.

SPECIAL CONSIDERATIONS

The basic principles of reinsurance discussed previously in this book apply to the reinsurance of annuities as well. This section addresses some of the unique aspects of such reinsurance.

Plans of Reinsurance

Although some attempts have been made to create a form of YRT reinsurance for annuities, most, if not all, annuity reinsurance is on a coinsurance or mod-co basis. Funds withheld versions and combinations of coinsurance and mod-co are frequently used to minimize cash flows, especially if surplus relief is the objective and recapture is expected.

Reserve Requirements

If coinsurance is used, the reinsurer is responsible for the reserves on the reinsured portion of the business.

Control of Assets

In any annuity reinsurance agreement it is necessary to determine which party will develop the investment strategy, manage the assets, own the assets, and establish the crediting or pricing interest rate. These functions do not necessarily always lie with the same party. A defined process for setting credited rates or pricing rates is necessary if the reinsurer is to make a profit on the business and the ceding company is to maintain good faith with its contractholders.

In a coinsurance agreement, the reinsurer has the responsibility for the assets backing the reserves, but the ceding company has the responsibility for setting the credited rates for any interest sensitive product. However, the ceding company usually does not have the right to unilaterally bind the reinsurer to any credited rate it desires. The reinsurer obviously needs the credited rate to be one that it can reasonably support with its investment income. Mutual trust and cooperation are vital to the success of an interest sensitive annutiy reinsurance program.

In a mod-co agreement, the ceding company both manages the assets and sets the credited rate. The reinsurer is not directly concerned with the earned rate on the assets, but rather with the mod-co adjustment interest rate. The reinsurer will want the modco adjustment interest rate to show a spread above the credited or pricing rate which is sufficient to meet its profit objectives. The ceding company will want the mod-co adjustment interest rate to bear a reasonable relationship to the earned rate so the ceding company is not otherwise subsidizing the reinsurer. Of course, regulations regarding risk transfer must be satisfied if statutory reserve credit or surplus improvement is to result from the reinsurance.

The ceding company retains the responsibility for and obligation of dealing with the contractholder, including establishing credited interest rates. The reinsurer either benefits from a large spread or suffers from one which is too small. Therefore, it is suggested that the two parties negotiate and document a planned investment strategy prior to signing a treaty. This should include a discussion of both the methodology for establishing credited or pricing rates and the management of assets. These may not be absolutely binding, but they will serve as a guide and document the original intention of the parties.

Some companies have turned to the use of trusts to ease the questions of asset control, ownership, and management. For example, the reinsurer in a coinsurance agreement can place the assets invested in support of the reinsured business into a trust for the benefit of the ceding company. These assets can be restricted to certain classes of investments based on maturity, quality, duration, and other significant features. The two parties to the reinsurance agreement should then agree on an investment strategy and a crediting strategy. Sometimes an independent third party investment manager is hired to manage the assets. While each party maintains its individual rights and obligations, this process can make it easier to agree on investment issues.

In addition, if the reinsurer fails to perform or develops solvency or solidity problems, the ceding company may be able to take control of the trusteed assets directly to protect both itself and its contractholders.

Transfer of Risk

If reserve credits or surplus relief are expected to result from an annuity reinsurance agreement, sufficient risk transfer is required. While mortality risks are inherent in some annuities, significant risk transfer involving other elements of annuities is possible. The reinsurer need not be involved in all risks on a contract for sufficient risk transfer to be present, but the reinsurer must participate in all significant risks. Significant risks are indentified by product type in the Life and Health Reinsurance Agreements Model Regulation.[3] Reserve credit or surplus relief will likely be allowed to the extent that any risk or risks have actually been transferred.

In particular, reserve credits should be allowed only for risk elements which are considered in the original insurer's reserves. For example, if the reinsurance agreement provides for payment by the reinsurer only in the event of annuitants living beyond the end of the mortality table, there should be no reserve credit granted. This may be a valid reinsurance need, but it is unlikely that any insurer would use that assumption in establishing its reserves.

There are several types of risk which can be transferred in a reinsurance agreement. The primary risk exposures are discussed in the following paragraphs.

Interest. The immediate element of risk in most annuities is the interest guarantee. Every annuity carries either an interest guarantee or a pricing interest assumption on the funds involved. The risk involved is whether or not the insurer will earn the interest assumed. If the reinsurer accepts that risk, then some risk transfer has occurred. For example, if an SPDA guarantees to credit a ten percent rate for the next twelve months and the reinsurance contract passes that guarantee to the reinsurer along with the assets, then the reinsurer has accepted the interest rate risk.

On the other hand, if a mod-co treaty contains a formula for the mod-co adjustment interest rate to be the contract credited rate plus a guaranteed spread, then the transfer of the interest rate risk is doubtful. This is especially obvious in that the minimum mod-co interest rate would be, by definition, the contractual guaranteed crediting rate plus the guaranteed spread, even if the ceding company earned far less than the guaranteed crediting rate.

In any event, the transfer of the interest risk is dependent upon the terms of the entire reinsurance agreement. Careful examination is advised to determine if any portion of the treaty might negate the risk transfer.

---

[3] See Chapter 10, Reinsurance Regulations.

Asset Default. Another major risk element in annuities is asset default. Except for some market value adjusted and variable annuities, any asset loss is absorbed by the insurer, not by the contractholder. This is especially true for immediate annuities. If the reinsurer participates in asset default risks, then transfer of risk has been achieved with respect to the asset default risk. This is most obviously the case with coinsurance in its simplest form, without funds withheld, additional guarantees, or other modifications. The reinsurer assumes the guarantees and manages the assets; if any of the assets fail, the reinsurer must meet all its obligations.

Participation in the asset default risk does not necessarily mean that reserve credits will result. Asset default is not a specific element of normal reserves. A reinsurance agreement which only protects the ceding company from capital losses may not reduce the ceding company's reserve liability even though the reinsurer is definitely at risk.

Voluntary Termination. A reinsurer can be exposed to the persistency risk for annuities just as it can for life insurance. This risk arises in at least three ways: contract surrender, partial withdrawal, or premium reduction or cessation.

For either SPDA's or FPDA's, there can be a risk that the contract will surrender before the acquisition expenses are fully recovered. Partial withdrawals which are higher than expected have much the same effect as increased surrenders. Higher than expected outward cash flows can also lead to disintermediation, where assets might have to be sold below their book value in order to fund the cash payments, compounding the risks associated with voluntary terminations. With flexible premium contracts, there is the added hazard that renewal premiums will not be as large as assumed, leading to lower profits or nonrecovery of all of the acquisition expenses.

Single premium immediate annuity contracts of the type discussed in this chapter generally do not have provisions for voluntary termination.

Mortality. There are several elements of mortality risk in the annuity business. Perhaps the highest degree of risk arises from the mortality associated with life contingent benefits of structured settlement annuities. Typically, reinsuring these contracts using either coinsurance or mod-co will transfer the mortality exposure. Similarly, terminal funding annuities include both of the mortality risks associated with pension funding: more individuals will live to collect benefits than assumed and beneficiaries will live longer than expected.

Most accumulation products also have exposure to mortality risks. In many annuities, surrender charges do not apply in the event of death. Higher than assumed mortality leads to fewer assets under management and higher cash payouts. On the other hand, improving mortality can make annuity purchase rate guarantees inadequate for the insurer and reinsurer.

Annuitization. The long term guarantees of annuity purchase rates and benefits are risks to insurers. As mentioned previously, if mortality improves significantly or interest rates drop significantly, these guarantees can cause losses to the insurer or its reinsurer.

Reinsurance agreements usually provide for the reinsurer to participate in the business after annuitization. Many agreements, however, allow the reinsurer to settle its participation in annuitizations by payment of a lump sum. These agreements may call for the payment of an amount related to the reserve or the accumulated value in lieu of a string of annuity payments. The ceding company is then solely responsible for the annuity benefits.

This is similar in concept to the life reinsurance situation where the beneficiary elects to receive a settlement option payout other than cash, but the reinsurance is settled as a lump sum payment by the reinsurer to the ceding company. This treatment is also equivalent to recapture upon annuitization.

Depending on the annuity purchase rates and the profit expected during the pay out period, the payment by the reinsurer may be equal to the full fund or some percentage thereof, either smaller or larger. Some treaties allow the reinsurer the option to select a lump sum settlement upon annuitization if the annuity purchase rate actually used is more favorable than that guaranteed in the annuity contract. If the reinsurer participates in the benefit pay out, it will change its reserves to reflect the new liabilities. Statutory reserves often increase when a contract annuitizes at more favorable purchase rates than those guaranteed in the contract. The reserves must now reflect the present value of the future benefits after amortization; during the accumulation phase, reserves reflected only the accumulation and cash values.

Administration

Reinsurance of annuities is nearly always done on a quota share basis with self-administration or simplified accounting if the volume of contracts reinsured is significant. Listings or other forms of notification are sometimes provided to the reinsurer showing contractholder names and pertinent data if the reinsurer is concerned about limits on amounts issued to single individuals.

If coinsurance is used, the reinsurer would be wise to request information regarding the liabilities which will enable it to select investments of appropriate maturity and yield. As mentioned previously, asset management is perhaps the single most important element of profitability for annuity writers or reinsurers.

STRUCTURING REINSURANCE

Clarity of asset management and of crediting strategies are the most important elements to consider in structuring an annuity reinsurance treaty. Care must be taken to define each party's responsibilities and rights. If coinsurance is chosen, the treaty should be constructed to ensure that the ceding company will be able to take reserve credits. This might mean that the reinsurer yields all rights to set crediting rates to the ceding company, regardless of the investment performance of the reinsurer. The treaty also should be clear regarding the reinsurer's participation in future premiums, expenses, and annuitizations.

Since relatively large sums of money are involved with annuities, it is perhaps even more important to be comfortable with the competency and integrity of the reinsurance partner than it is for the reinsurance of other types of business. Trust and cooperation are important because all elements of crediting strategy and investments cannot be defined in advance for all future years. New regulations, changing economic conditions, or new investment vehicles may arise which will have to be addressed by both parties. In spirit, reinsurance of annuities, especially those in the accumulation phase, is more of a partnership than an indemnity arrangement.

21 | Reinsurance of Other Lines and Products

The earlier chapters of this book have dealt with general issues regarding individual life, health, and annuity reinsurance. This chapter addresses special considerations which are unique to selected life insurance products or provisions.

Some of the products and problems discussed in this chapter are no longer current. Other products are new in concept and reinsurance procedures are still evolving. This discussion is not intended to be complete, as reinsurance is a dynamic tool, but to serve as a guide in responding to new reinsurance needs and opportunities.

CREDIT INSURANCE

Credit life and credit disability insurance are generally reinsured as a package. That is, a reinsurer will usually receive both the credit life and credit disability reinsurance from a particular company. While reinsurers may share the reinsurance ceded from a company, it would be uncommon for one reinsurer to receive only credit life, with another reinsurer receiving only the credit disability. However, it is not unusual for the reinsurer's share of the life insurance to be different than its share of the disability insurance.

Historically, most credit insurance has been issued on a single premium basis. However, monthly premium credit insurance currently is issued in conjunction with revolving credit loans or sometimes for loans of large amounts.

Credit insurance may be purchased on a single life or on a joint life basis. Credit insurance may be issued on an individual or group basis. Underwriting is generally limited in either event. The premiums usually are not age distinct. Joint life premiums are generally 50% higher than single life rates.

Credit reinsurance is generally administered by the ceding company, using bulk or simplified accounting procedures. Reinsurance may be ceded on either an excess or a quota share basis. The quota share method would be used to simplify administration or to relieve a surplus strain problem. It is not uncommon for the reinsurer to be owned by the distribution system.[1]

Credit reinsurance is almost always ceded on a coinsurance basis. The use of mod-co is fairly rare, but coinsurance using funds withheld by the ceding company or assets deposited in trust are common. This is largely the result of ceding to reinsurers that are licensed in only one state, usually not the ceding company's state of domicile.

Credit life insurance and credit disability insurance have differing degrees of complexity, reserving requirements, premium limitations, and profit levels and emergence patterns. Consequently, each is reinsured differently, as discussed below.

Credit Life

Of the two forms of credit insurance, credit life is the simplest and usually the more profitable form. Because the gross premium is usually in excess of the initial mortality reserves required on credit life, the surplus drain is much less than for credit disability insurance. In some cases, the commissions may be structured so that there is no surplus strain. Accordingly, reinsurers frequently insist on a share of the life insurance if they are requested to provide credit disability reinsurance.

---

[1] See Chapter 17, Captive Reinsurance.

Credit life insurance generally is purchased to cover the full amount of the loan. Such coverage is usually purchased on a single premium basis. If the insured pays the loan off early or decides to cancel the insurance, he is entitled to a refund of his unearned premium.

Critical period coverage has become more common recently as loan amounts have increased. This provides protection for a period of time less than the amortization period of the loan. This limitation is utilized to reduce costs to the consumer while providing protection during the period where the outstanding balance of the loan is at its highest. This coverage is more likely to be sold on a monthly premium basis.

Credit insurance is also solicited with most credit card or revolving credit accounts. The premiums for this coverage are added to the monthly billings of the creditor and vary with the loan balance. The benefit each month is the credit balance for that month.

In addition to mortality risk sharing, there are several reasons for a company to reinsure credit life insurance risks. These reasons include the need to offset the surplus strain resulting from morality reserves and acquisition expenses and the specific business purposes discussed in Chapter 17, Captive Reinsurance.

Credit Disability

Credit disability insurance is the more volatile of the two forms of credit insurance, and usually involves more surplus strain due to the unearned gross premium reserve requirements. Commissions on credit insurance are quite high, so the cash left to the insurer after paying commissions is inadequate to cover the unearned premium reserve.

Normal coinsurance of single premium credit insurance is considered to be ceded on a "written premium" basis, with premiums being paid to the reinsurer as they are written by the ceding company. If surplus strain is a problem for the reinsurer, as may be the case with a producer owned reinsurance company, credit disability reinsurance may be ceded on an "earned premium" basis. Under this method, the reinsurer receives premiums only as they are earned by the ceding company. The earned premium for each period is developed as the reinsurer's share of the corresponding reduction in the gross unearned premium reserve for the covered policies.

Under earned premium reinsurance, the reinsurer is relieved of the need to establish unearned premium reserves, as it has not received those unearned premiums. However, the reinsurer is responsible for claim reserves for claims which have been incurred.

Expense allowances are usually expressed as a percentage of the earned premiums. Each period, the ceding company remits to the reinsurer the earned premiums less earned expense allowances and less the reinsurer's share of paid claims. The ceding company also reports the information necessary for the reinsurer to establish the necessary claim reserves and liabilities so that it can report claims on an incurred basis.

If the sum of allowances and paid claims exceeds the earned premium for a given reporting period, the reinsurer must pay the deficit to the ceding company. In some instances, especially if the reinsurer is not accredited, the ceding company will hold all of the claim reserve and the reinsurer will pay any reserve increase to the ceding company. In essence, the claim reserve then is treated as a mod-co reserve.

Experience Rating

In the world of credit reinsurance, the term experience rating can refer to either of two calculations. In the first, the direct insurer may pay an experience based commission or profit sharing amount to the distribution source based on that account's experience. In the second, the reinsurer may pay an experience refund to the ceding company based on the experience of the reinsured block.

If the credit insurance program includes a provision for an experience commission or profit sharing to be paid to the agency or sponsoring company, the reinsurance agreement may include provision for the reinsurer to participate in the distribution. If not, the ceding company may find it has to share profits it does not have. Alternatively, the experience rating calculation may provide that reinsurance premiums and claims are netted out of the gross results in determining any refunds.

If the ceding company administers the business, it usually charges a fee to cover its administrative costs and to produce a profit. This fee is commonly known as the retention, not to be confused with the ceding company's retention of risk or retention limit. The retention charge normally is calculated as a percentage of premium, either written or earned, and treated as a deduction in the experience refund formula.

Credit reinsurance also can be subject to experience rating like any other reinsurance contract. However, in some credit reinsurance contracts, the experience rating provision can act in reverse of the normal procedure. If the experience on the reinsurance falls below an agreed upon level, the reinsurer can demand refund of part of the ceding commission. This provision is known as a contingent or sliding commission, or a claw-back.

For example, if the reinsurer grants a 60% allowance and the business develops losses of 38%, the reinsurer could recover enough allowance to cover its agreed upon retention, say 6%. There is usually a cap on the recoverable amount of the allowance, such as 15% of the original premium. Ceding companies usually do not reserve for this contingent cost; the cause of the payment is the same as that which would cause excess claim losses if the company had retained all the business. However, some state regulations may require reserving for this potential liability.

Special Considerations

Credit insurance normally involves small amounts of short-term coverage. If credit insurance is ceded on an excess basis, the volume of reinsurance ceded is normally quite low. The amount of underwriting information received is usually quite limited. Credit insurance is generally issued on a simplified underwriting basis using a two to four question application. Because of this, the mortality and morbidity experience will be significantly worse than individually underwritten life insurance.

Because competition in the credit insurance marketplace is at the distribution source level, rather than at the consumer level, a "reverse competition" situation exists. In short, the higher the premiums and commissions, the more likely that a company will sell through a given source. To provide some protection to the consumer, state regulators have placed limits on the premium and commission levels allowed. Credit insurance premiums may not exceed these maximum legislated premiums, called the *prima facie* rates, unless it can be demonstrated that a company's experience exceeds that level.

Some states employ mandated loss ratios, causing larger credit insurance groups to develop premium rates based on the experience of that group alone, even if that experience produces rates lower than the legislated maximum rates. The reinsurer should be aware of any maximum premium or commission rates or mandated loss ratios which apply to the risks that it will reinsure. The reinsurer should be aware of any changes in *prima facie* rates, mandated loss ratios, or commission rates and revise its allowances accordingly.

The reinsurance pricing actuary will use the same techniques as the ceding company actuary. While mortality, morbidity, and persistency experience may vary by the purpose of the loan, generalized assumptions are commonly used. Prior experience on the ceding company's credit business and on the specific block offered for reinsurance should be analyzed before establishing pricing assumptions.

Pricing techniques are usually fairly simple, often involving only the anticipated loss ratios and expenses. If the arrangement is to be conducted on an experience rated basis, a larger gross profit objective may be included in the assumptions. The credit reinsurance market is very competitive, and profit margins may be small.

Credit insurance is subject to an unusual risk in that it is not uncommon for a third party sponsor, such as a credit card issuer, to switch the insurance, both inforce and new issues, to a new carrier. Most coverage is group insurance and the group contract holder can move coverage at its will. The reinsurer must be aware of this possibility when setting its rates and allowance, especially if early losses are expected. It should examine the direct insurance contract and discuss the third party sponsor with the ceding company to determine its exposure to such switching.

GROUP LIFE AND AD&D INSURANCE

The demand for group life and accidental death and dismemberment (AD&D) reinsurance has grown as the demand for higher issue limits has grown. The demand for guaranteed issue or limited underwriting has also increased. Issue limits without evidence of $500,000, $1,000,000, or more are not uncommon. In order to provide such coverage, many companies have turned to reinsurers.

Group life and AD&D insurance can be reinsured on either an excess or a quota share basis. When using an excess basis, the ceding company reinsures amounts on lives in excess of the retention limit. Generally, the reinsurer will assume 100% of all risks in excess of the ceding company's group life retention limit. If that retention is small, the reinsurer may require the ceding company to retain a percentage of the excess in order to maintain an interest in properly insuring large risks without any underwriting evidence.

Excess reinsurance is sometimes further divided into excess risks and high limit or catastrophic risks. A working excess retention refers to a retention level set to produce a reasonable number of claims. A high limit, or catastrophic excess, refers to an excess situation where the retention limit is at a high level so that few reinsurance claims are anticipated. Pricing and the assessment of fluctuation should recognize the actual conditions of the situation.

Excess life reinsurance agreements are usually on a YRT basis, often with an experience refund provision. Typical requirements imposed by the reinsurer for a refunding arrangement include a minimum amount of premium, the use of a working excess type retention, and a cap on the maximum amount of insurance per life which may be included in the calculation of the refund. Amounts in excess of this limit are reinsured on a nonrefunding basis, usually with a different premium per unit.

The quota share method closely resembles the quota share method used for individual life reinsurance. The ceding company cedes a percentage of each risk. The reinsurer pays the ceding company an allowance to cover the ceding company's commissions and expenses. Under a quota share arrangement, the reinsurer may actually control the premium rates of the ceding company or at least participate in the rate setting process.

While quota share reinsurance of group life is usually on a coinsurance basis, YRT may also be used. Group AD&D is usually reinsured on a YRT basis and nearly always employs simplified administration.

Group insurance is usually term insurance, but group permanent insurance is also available. Reinsurance of group permanent is usually done on a YRT plan, based on the net amount at risk. Traditional coinsurance, applying allowances to the ceding company's premium rates, is feasible, but the volume may not justify the effort.

The term coinsurance as used in the group reinsurance field normally refers to a variation of quota share reinsurance. Under a coinsurance approach, the ceding company sets its own premium rates and the amount which the reinsurer pays to the ceding company is called the commission rather than a ceding allowance. Coinsurance arrangements are usually managed on a refunding basis.

Catastrophic reinsurance[2] refers to coverage of claims on the occurrence of a specified event. A cat cover usually requires a minimum number of deaths to occur in a single catastrophic event for a claim to be incurred and may provide for a deductible of three or more maximum retentions. The reinsurer then pays all or a percentage of excess claims, subject to a per event maximum.

Group life and AD&D retention limits are generally lower than individual life limits because of limited underwriting and lower total premiums in the group line.

Companies reinsure group life and AD&D coverages for largely the same reasons that they reinsure individual life. Examples of this include claim fluctuation protection, surplus relief, and service.[3] Other reasons for reinsuring group life and AD&D business include the need or desire to increase the limits for guaranteed or simplified underwriting issues, to minimize the negative effect of claims from a few large groups, and to minimize the fluctuations of a small line of business.

When pricing group life and AD&D reinsurance, the reinsurance actuary must consider underwriting guidelines, waiver of premium and other disability provisions, guaranteed issue limits, benefit structure, conversion rights, and optional amounts of insurance. The reinsurance actuary uses the same pricing techniques as the ceding company actuary. When pricing catastrophe coverage, the pricing actuary should consider the concentration of risks at any particular geographic location and any special hazards inherent to the group.

---

[2] See Chapter 15, Nonproportional Reinsurance.
[3] See Chapter 1, Introduction.

SELECT AND ULTIMATE TERM INSURANCE

Select and ultimate term and graded premium whole life (GPWL) products captured the lion's share of the term insurance market in the early 1980's. These products feature a premium scale which is dependent on the insured's original issue age and current duration. Select and ultimate products nearly always contain a re-entry provision allowing the insured to reenter, or receive rates similar to those for a new policy every few years. The premium rates of the reentered policy are based on the insured's current age and are normally substantially lower than the premiums based on the insured's original issue age and current duration.

For those who reenter, these products will result in substantial cost savings along with more commission income for the agent. The major problem with these products is that the group that does not qualify for re-entry will experience very substandard mortality. This poor mortality coupled with poor persistency inherent in the product's structure caused the experience to be much worse than originally anticipated. This, in turn, caused several reinsurers to cease reinsuring such products. Most of the reinsurers that remained in this market became much more cautious in their pricing.

Coinsurance has always been the favored method of reinsuring these term products. In many respects, developing coinsurance allowances is like developing a YRT rate scale for each product. Rules for medical and other underwriting evidence and overall underwriting practices vary significantly between the issuers of re-entry products. The major pricing consideration in reinsuring these products is for the reinsurance actuary to understand the rules for re-entry and the way in which the products are marketed. This knowledge will influence assumptions for both mortality and persistency. The treaty must be very clear on topics such as reentry underwriting and allowances. Policy continuation and change procedures are also very important.[4]

---

[4] See Chapter 22, Selected Additional Reinsurance Topics.

NONGUARANTEED ELEMENTS IN LIFE INSURANCE CONTRACTS

The introduction of universal life and excess interest whole life in the early 1980's changed the face of the life insurance market. The unique design of these products also changed reinsurance pricing and administration. These products featured somewhat modest interest rate guarantees and relatively high mortality charge guarantees with actual interest rates and mortality charges being redetermined periodically.

Setting credited interest rates is somewhat of an art. An insurer and its reinsurer can easily have different investment portfolios and reasons to credit different rates. The interest element in these products is very important from a marketing viewpoint. The ceding company has a direct relationship with the insured and needs to be able to set rates independently.

Reinsurance of non-guaranteed elements can be difficult because the interest credits to the policyholder and the mortality charges are not set in advance. The ceding company wants to be unrestricted by reinsurance considerations in setting the credited interest rate. While coinsurance is possible, it requires detailed cooperation and agreement between the ceding company and the reinsurer in establishing credited rates and investments. The considerations are essentially the same as those described for interest sensitive annuities in Chapter 20.

Mod-co allows the ceding company to retain control of the assets and, therefore, control over the credited interest rate. Even so, the reinsurer could still be vulnerable to aggressive, nonprofitable interest crediting strategies used by the direct insurer. Difficulties in developing mutually agreeable interest crediting strategies and profit objectives have inhibited the extensive use of mod-co for interest sensitive product reinsurance.

While coinsurance and modified coinsurance treaties involving interest sensitive products have been relatively infrequent, some do exist. When used, they have required careful discussion, negotiation, and documentation of mutually acceptable investment and interest crediting strategies.

Most reinsurance of interest sensitive products has involved YRT reinsurance or the "coinsurance" of the mortality element of the policy. The YRT scales used for reinsurance purposes on these products are generally made specifically for each product and are usually expressed in coinsurance terms, based on allowances applied to the cost of insurance rates used in the policy. In fact, because the mortality premiums in an interest sensitive product normally are expressed as ART premiums, there is no economic or cash flow difference between YRT and coinsurance of the cost of insurance rates. The difference lies largely in the choice of terminology; however, the use of coinsurance may result in Schedule S problems.

The three primary classes of life insurance products which feature non-guaranteed elements are interest sensitive whole life, universal life, and variable life. In addition, most term insurance plans and many ordinary life insurance plans feature indeterminate premiums, which are not guaranteed to remain at the initial level. These four general classes of products and some of the reinsurance considerations regarding them are discussed in this section.

Interest Sensitive Whole Life

Interest sensitive whole life is a fixed, level premium form of permanent life insurance. Like any level premium whole life product, it has guaranteed cash values to comply with the Standard Nonforfeiture Law. However, this product also has an accumulation element using insurer declared interest rates which are usually higher than the policy guaranteed rate. The actual cash surrender value is the greater of the accumulation fund and the guaranteed cash value. The products generally contains either front-end loads or surrender charges.

As with many interest sensitive life products, this level premium product generally is reinsured on a YRT basis. Most often, it is reinsured on a self-administered basis with the reinsurance premium calculation coinciding with the normal fund calculation, such as once a month. Because continued premium payment is required to keep the product from going on nonforfeiture status, the net amount at risk can be projected more accurately. Because of this, it is possible to use an individual cession approach or an annual premium approach.

Universal Life

Universal life products have flexible premiums which can be paid at any time and in any amount. Projections of future cash values are very difficult and largely futile, making normal individual cession accounting difficult. Accumulation amounts vary monthly and the projection of net amounts at risk is uncertain. Most universal life products are administered by the ceding company with monthly premiums based on the costs of insurance rates and individual notification of issues and terminations so the reinsurer can arrange for retrocession if needed.

The above discussion assumes that the ceding company wants to reinsure the exact amounts at risk. It is possible to use projected cash values and reinsure the resulting projected net amount at risk. Both reinsurance premiums and claims are then based on this predetermined net amount at risk. While not precisely matching the insurer's exposure, this method allows more simple and less costly administration.

Variable Life

Variable life insurance creates problems of administration and in projection of net amounts at risk similar to those of universal life. The solution is usually the same, utilizing self-administration and YRT premiums. Variable life has asset based fees for mortality, not cost of insurance rates, so regular YRT rates are used. Administration can be on an individual cession basis with approximate net amounts at risk or the ceding company may use exact calculations on a self administration basis.

As discussed earlier regarding variable annuities, reinsurance of separate accounts can be difficult. With variable life insurance, however, the rules specifically allow for mortality reinsurance using YRT. A current area of interest is an increasing demand for reinsurance of the minimum death benefit guarantees of a variable life contract.

Indeterminate Premium Policies

Many individual insurance products today do not guarantee gross premiums for future years, or may guarantee only that the future premium will not exceed a certain level. This level is usually at or above the statutory net valuation premium. This allows the insurer to avoid having to establish deficiency or additional reserves as it would have to do if it guaranteed rates at the initial level. The practice also provides the insurer some protection in that it can increase premiums if projected experience falls below that assumed in the initial pricing or the last repricing of the product. It may also reduce rates if experience and competition so indicate.

The use of indeterminate premiums provides some complications for the reinsurance agreement, however. Specifically, there are complications of establishing new allowances for coinsurance or modified coinsurance if the insurer changes rates, either up or down. If the reinsurer guarantees to always accept the same net cost, it could be held responsible for deficiency reserves the ceding company does not have to hold. If the reinsurer has an independent right to change premiums, then the ceding company could find itself in a position where its reinsurance premiums will exceed its gross premiums.

Some reinsurance agreements have addressed this concern by stating that the reinsurer will participate in the new rates with the original allowances. Other agreements give the reinsurer the right to change allowances in a manner that leaves the net amount of premium less allowance the same. In any event, it is advised that any reinsurance treaty covering indeterminate premium plans address this issue.

DEPOSIT TERM

Deposit term products present a unique reinsurance problem. These products feature an additional premium in the first year. This premium is several times larger than the basic term premium. The underlying term policy may be an ART, five year renewable term, or most common historically, a ten year renewable term product, followed by a whole life policy or a decreasing term policy to age 100. The excess of the initial premium over the basic first year term premium is referred to as the deposit.

In most products, the deposit normally grows at interest to two to three times its original size and is returned at the end of ten to twelve years. The deposit feature was created to improve persistency. In some cases, persistency did improve, but the profit improvement which would be expected was often negated by high first year commissions and agency financing costs.

The original deposit term policy did not develop cash values until near the end of the deposit period, but modifications in the Standard Nonforfeiture Law changed this situation and cash values are now required at early durations. Before the requirement of cash values, it was more profitable for the insurer if the insured lapsed before the end of the term period. Coinsurance was commonly used because the high commissions created considerable surplus strain. It was not unusual for the ceding company to request first year coinsurance allowances which exceeded the total first year premium including the deposit. In some instances, to avoid the risk of loss from lapse, the reinsurer would offer to coinsure the underlying term product and not participate in the deposit or investment element of the policy.

Reinsurance premiums may be paid either on the actual modal basis or annually, and may include or exclude the deposit. Allowances are usually annualized, at least in the first year. Frequently, allowances are calculated as a combination of percent of premium and an amount per policy issued or in force. When expressed as percentages of the basic first year premium, excluding the deposit, the allowance may be as much as 400% of the term premium. In this case, a chargeback is often required. The chargeback feature provides that if a policy terminates prior to a certain period or prior to the point where reinsurance premiums received exceed reinsurance allowances paid, the ceding company will return the excess of allowances paid over premiums collected.[5]

INCREASING BENEFITS

Products with increasing benefits can present special problems for the determination of reinsurance. One problem concerns policies which fall

---

[5] For further discussion of chargeback mechanics, see Chapter 9, Managing Assumed Reinsurance.

within the ceding companies retention limit at issue, but may in later years exceed the retention limit because of the increasing benefits. Since experience under benefit increases has demonstrated antiselection, reinsurers prefer to participate in a broad cross-section of business, not just in the increases. Unless special arrangements are made when the policy is issued, it is unlikely that a reinsurer would accept reinsurance arising from the increases.

The two principal types of increasing benefits are guaranteed insurability option (GIO) and cost of living adjustment (COLA), usually issued as riders. Both benefits allow the insured to increase the death benefit without any underwriting or evidence of insurability, regardless of any change in underwriting class, under specified conditions or at specific intervals.

A GIO rider provides the policyholder with options to purchase additional policies at certain specified intervals or at the occurrence of certain specified events, such as marriage or the birth of a child. The maximum amount of each benefit increase is defined in advance. The policyholder pays premiums for a standard issue at his then current age.

A COLA rider provides for death benefits on a policy to increase annually at the same rate as the change in a prescribed cost of living index, subject to some maximum limit. Normally, if the policyholder declines the increase in any year, he forfeits the right to exercise any future increases. Premiums on the policy are increased to reflect the new death benefits, usually treating these amounts as term insurance.

The simplest method for reinsuring increases is to employ YRT using point-in-scale rates. Coinsurance is also feasible, depending on policy design and rate structure. The presence of cash values may complicate administration.

The most important reinsurance consideration regarding such riders is that the agreement be clear as to the treatment of the future increases. At the outset of the treaty, it is necessary to determine how the increases will be apportioned between the ceding company and the reinsurer. Some reinsurers may be willing to absorb all the increases, but many prefer that the ceding company share the increases on a quota share basis.

The quota share method is used to ensure that the ceding company maintains an interest in the policy and has designed the benefits in a reasonable manner. For example, if the reinsurer has 35% of the initial risk, it will agree to assume 35% of all future increases in risk. It is common for a ceding company to reduce its initial retention to a point that its future share, if all options are exercised, will not exceed its maximum retention at issue of the policy. Others will assume their retention will increase in the future and keep a somewhat larger portion of the initial risk. The reinsurer may also place a cap on its participation.

On occasion, the reinsurer will agree to assume future increases with no participation in the initial risk. This procedure requires the ceding company to notify its reinsurer of any guaranteed insurability options issued. The reinsurer then indexes this information and treats its business as though it had a current risk, arranging retrocession for any other business it might receive on that life. Since the reinsurer guarantees future coverage, it charges a premium to the ceding company. This premium may be a single premium, an annual premium developed like that of a YRT scale, or coinsurance premiums based on the ceding company's premium for the option with coinsurance allowances.

ACCELERATED OR LIVING BENEFIT RIDERS

In the late 1980's, life insurance companies introduced a new group of benefits broadly classified as living benefits. The provisions allow the policyholder to collect some portion of the death benefit prior to death. There are several broad categories of benefits.

The premium paying, "dread disease" rider provides that a portion of the life policy, usually 25% or 50%, is payable if the insured develops a covered disease. Most commonly, the diseases include cancer, heart attack, coronary artery disease, stroke, and kidney failure. AIDS may be excluded because of anti-selection issues. The benefit is payable at the occurrence of the disease, not the severity.

The premium paying, Long Term Care (LTC) rider provides that a portion of the face amount, such as 2%, is paid monthly in the event the insured is required to be admitted to a nursing home.

A no-cost accelerated death benefit option pays the discounted face amount should the insured become terminally ill with a life expectancy of less than a specified period such as six months. Insurers and reinsurers usually require a statement from the insured's attending physician before it will make payments under this option.

Another no-cost accelerated benefit option provides benefits by means of a policy loan, with the balance of the loan being deducted from the proceeds at death.

For reinsurance purposes on premium paying accelerated death benefits, the treaty should state the portion of the benefit reinsured, the maximum benefit or maximum reinsurance benefit, the reinsurance premium, and the method for recapture after an increase in retention. If less than the full face amount is accelerated, the affect on continuing reinsurance should be described. If accelerated payments are made monthly, the treaty should indicate how reinsurance payments should be made, and how changes are made to the retention, the amount of reinsurance, and reinsurance premiums.

For no-cost benefits, the reinsurer may decline to participate in accelerated payments. If this occurs, and if 100% of the benefits are accelerated, then follow-up is necessary to get proof of death. If the reinsurer participates, the treaty should describe how it will share in the benefit, how the benefit will be calculated, and the maximum benefit or maximum reinsurance benefit.

The no-cost benefits may be made available to both new business and inforce policies. Agreement must be reached with all the reinsurers on administration and benefit payments.

If premium paying riders are made available to inforce policyholders, reinsurance becomes more complicated. Some reinsurers may choose not to participate. It is possible that the rider may be reinsured by one reinsurer with the base policy reinsured by another. Facultative risks, especially those where the ceding company held no retention, may require reinsurer approval at claim time.

JOINT LIFE

There are two types of joint life products, each with its own set of direct and reinsurance considerations. The traditional joint life plan insures two individuals, paying the stated benefit on the first death of the two. A more recently introduced product ensures two lives also, but pays the benefit only on the second death. In some instance, the first-to-die product may be, in effect, a small group plan with six or more insureds.

First-to-Die Policies

Most first-to-die policies have a Simultaneous Death Benefit Option which provides a benefit if the second death occurs within a specified time, such as 90 days, after the first death. Reinsurers will usually have a small charge for this benefit. If the policy provides a Survivors Benefit Option, allowing the survivor to purchase insurance after the first death without evidence of insurability, the reinsurer will typically have a special set of rates for the new policy. Agreements covering first-to-die policies with an Exchange or Split option will contain a set of rates for the individual policies.

Joint life policies may present problems in determining the retention limit if the company has several policies inforce on the lives. Alphabet splits may also present problems.

Second-to-Die Policies

Some second-to-die policies can be split into two single life policies on the occurrence of specific events. The reinsurer will provide special premium rates in this event. In second-to-die policies where the reserve does not increase on the first death, premiums are based on the joint equal age. If the reserve increases on the first death, the reinsurance on the survivors will be calculated on that individual's age. Problems may arise on last-to-die policies regarding notification of the first death. Notification is particularly important during the contestable period.

A similar situation may develop after the death of the primary insured. In this situation, the original policy is used as a single premium to purchase the new policy for a greatly increased amount. Point-in-scale rates are generally charged, although a single premium may be appropriate.

22 | Selected Additional Reinsurance Topics

The earlier chapters of this book have dealt with general issues regarding individual life, health, and annuity reinsurance. This chapter covers some special considerations which are unique to certain product features or to certain underwriting and issue programs. In addition, some of the special uses and concerns of reinsurance with affiliated companies are addressed.

DEFICIENCY RESERVES

Deficiency or additional reserves can be a major source of surplus strain. At times, the strain is so great that reinsurance is sought simply because of the need for surplus to cover the deficiency reserves.

In order to transfer deficiency reserves, coinsurance or modified coinsurance must be used. The use of YRT reinsurance will not transfer deficiency reserves. Mod-co can be used to fund the ceding company's deficiency reserve liability if the deficiency reserves are included in the mod-co reserves. Alternatively, a mod-co agreement can transfer deficiency reserves if the agreement specifies mod-co treatment of the basic plan reserves, but coinsurance for the deficiency reserves. In the latter case, the reinsurer must be admitted in the ceding company's state of domicile or some acceptable form of security must be employed. A basic tenet of reinsurance is that it is not possible to reinsure deficiency reserves alone, although it has been attempted.[1] This would be accounting entries only. The related policy benefits must also be reinsured. Otherwise, the ceding company would have no call on the funds represented by the deficiency reserves.

In the past, insurance products which had deficiency reserves sometimes were coinsured with companies located in jurisdictions, foreign or domestic, which had less stringent reserve requirements. In such transactions, the deficiency reserves sometimes vanished[2] as neither company held them.

If the reinsurer was an admitted reinsurer, the ceding company normally would take credit in its statement for all reserves, including deficiency reserves. However, some reinsurers would not hold the deficiency reserves if they were not required by their state of domicile. If the reinsurer was not admitted, it would purchase a letter of credit to cover the total reserves, including deficiency reserves, but only establish those reserves required by its domestic regulators. In either situation, the ceding company would take credit for reserves which the reinsurer did not hold.

Some regulators have expressed concern about these transactions and such treaties are subject to increased scrutiny. These regulators regard the regulatory reserve requirements as being designed to ensure that certain minimum reserves are established and that premiums are adequate to maintain reserves at that level. Vanishing reserves are believed to circumvent that system.

As a result of these concerns and some blatant exploitations of the system, regulators have pursued concepts such as mirror reserving[3] in an attempt to guarantee that total reserves of all insurers and reinsurers for a given policy are at least equal to the required minimum reserves.

---

[1] The Model Regulation on Credit for Life and Health Reinsurance prohibits taking credit or otherwise improving surplus due to a reinsurance agreement which covers only deficiency reserves. See Chapter 10, Reinsurance Regulation.

[2] See Chapter 10, Reinsurance Regulation.

[3] *Ibid.*

DIVIDEND OPTIONS

Insurers have developed many unique and creative dividend options. Many of these are used to purchase additional death benefits which may increase both gross death benefits and net amounts at risk. These increases in turn will affect the need for reinsurance. The considerations for reinsuring these benefits are similar to those for increasing benefits.[4]

Most frequently, reinsurance of these benefits is on a YRT basis. Participation by the reinsurer is proportionate to its participation in the base policy. Since most dividend options used to increase death benefits are applied as single premiums, coinsurance is a logical method for purchasing any needed reinsurance. However, applying YRT reinsurance to the net amount at risk is also simple and reasonable. The primary concern is to address the treatment of dividend purchases in the treaty so confusion or disagreement does not arise later.

CONVERSION, REISSUE, AND CHANGE

As noted in Chapter 6, the reinsurance treaty usually spells out specific rules concerning conversions, reissues, and other changes including reductions, terminations, and reinstatements.

A conversion is a contractual right of the insured to replace a term policy with a permanent plan without evidence of insurability. The new policy's premiums and values are based on the insured's attained age at the time of conversion. In essence, this is a new issue which has no evidence of insurability. Any reinsurance would continue with the original reinsurer using point-in-scale YRT rates.

Conversions may also be made based on the insured's original issue age and date. In this case, the policyholder will make up any deficiency in cash value or reserve between the old policy and the new one. The plan of reinsurance will depend on the original plan of reinsurance and the terms of the reinsurance treaty. Most commonly, reinsurance is on a YRT basis, with the net amount at risk based on the new reserve and point-in-scale rates.

---

[4] See Chapter 21, Reinsurance of Other Lines and Products.

Reissues usually involve treating the reinsurance in the same manner as would have applied to the new issue from inception. Both reissues and other policy changes usually involve adjusting both parties' shares of the risk proportionately.

REPLACEMENT PROGRAMS

Replacement programs, both internal and external, are sometimes major sources of business for insurers. Reinsurance for these programs can be complicated and should be clarified before the insurer initiates the programs. Otherwise, the insurer may find that its reinsurance on the policies involved is more costly than expected or even that it does not have reinsurance coverage. Reinsurance administration has also been complicated by replacement programs.

Internal Replacements

Some insurers have offered their policyholders the opportunity to exchange an existing policy for a new one based on a new policy form. Reasons insurance companies adopt such programs is to provide increased policyholder benefits and prevent replacement by other companies.

Typically, the insurer issues the new policy with a current issue date and issue age. Before initiating the internal replacement program, the insurer normally will analyze the net costs involved to determine the program's feasibility. This involves, among other things, repricing the replacement product to reflect its use in the replacement program instead of new issues. The mortality and persistency assumptions are different from those that entered into the original pricing of the replacement product since the insureds are not being reunderwritten.

The increased mortality costs are usually offset by the payment of lower commissions than were originally provided. The cost of reinsurance, if based on a point-in-scale approach, will be greater than originally assumed. Depending on the amount of the reinsurance involved, the program may prove to be economically infeasible using this reinsurance cost basis.

It is important that the insurer reach an agreement with the original reinsurer as to the basis for the reinsurance rates to be used for these programs before they are initiated. The reinsurer is likely to refuse to accept the replacement program issues, at least without modification in its rates, and the insurer could find itself with either expensive reinsurance or no reinsurance coverage at all.

External Replacements

External replacements may create even more problems for reinsurance. External replacement, in this discussion, refers to a company's program to replace the policy of another insurer with a new policy of its own without new underwriting. The ceding company's current automatic reinsurer is likely to deny coverage under its normal agreement because normal underwriting has not been followed. Unless the insurer negotiates reinsurance terms in advance, it likely will find that it has no reinsurance. The insurer may try to negotiate a special arrangement with the current reinsurer to cover the program and, if unsuccessful, may have to seek a new reinsurance carrier.

General Practices

Most reinsurers have evolved practices with respect to replacement programs which allow reinsurance coverage to be granted. While not firmly established, the following guidelines are contained in many reinsurance agreements:

(1) Internal replacements are treated as continuations or conversions, with reinsurance being continued with the original reinsurer at point-in-scale costs. Other terms may be negotiated between that reinsurer and the ceding company.
(2) Internal replacements may be reinsured with a new reinsurer if the original reinsurer gives its permission.
(3) External replacements can be reinsured with any reinsurer that will take the business. They are not covered by an agreement intended for new issues subject to normal underwriting unless the replacement program requires such underwriting or the reinsurer specifically agrees to terms and underwriting for the replacement program.

(4) Internal replacements involving full new business underwriting, full first year commissions, and new suicide and contestable periods can be viewed as new issues and reinsured with a new reinsurer.

REINSURANCE WITH AFFILIATES

Reinsurance between affiliated companies follows the same basic principles as reinsurance between unrelated parties. There are some special aspects to consider. This section addresses selected topics involving reinsurance from one affiliated insurance company to another. Neither party need be a professional reinsurer.

Uses

Reinsurance can provide strategic or tactical opportunities for company to better manage two or more life insurance subsidiaries. For example, reinsurance may provide an easy way to move capital from one insurance company to another using coinsurance with large initial allowances. No stock or debt instruments need to be involved, and movement of funds across state or national borders can be accomplished with relative ease. The capital and surplus repayment comes from statutory earnings, not dividends, and may receive more favorable tax treatment than would dividends.

Reinsurance can assist with capital needs in several ways. Allowances can be constructed so as to permit the financially stronger company to incur the acquisition expenses of the company in need of relief. Risks can also be transferred, reducing the need for surplus.

Reinsurance may be a tax preferred way to move surplus and risks, especially internationally. Capital contributions typically would be earned and taxed in one company, paid in dividends to another, taxed again, and contributed to the carrier needing surplus. On repayment, the whole process would be reversed.

On another level, reinsurance between affiliates can be used to maximize the retention of a commonly held group of companies, reducing the volume of reinsurance ceded outside the group. Presumably this will increase total profits by reducing the cost of reinsurance.

Other opportunities are available in which reinsurance may be creatively and legitimately used between affiliates. The key is to define the problem to be addressed and then apply the principles of unrelated party reinsurance to design an acceptable program.

Concerns

There are, naturally, some additional concerns to be addressed when dealing with reinsurance between affiliates. Many agreements between affiliates have developed serious problems because the treaties received inadequate attention at the time of drafting. It is advisable to devote at least the same time and attention to affiliated party reinsurance as to unrelated party agreements. Failure to do so may undermine tax strategies or corporate financial planning, especially with respect to statutory reporting.

One rule of thumb frequently used is whether or not the agreement meets the "arm's length" test. In other words, would each party enter into a similar agreement with an unrelated party with terms negotiated at arm's length. While it is not a guarantee, if the answer is affirmative, the agreement will likely meet most tests. If the answer is negative, the agreement may need to be reexamined to ensure that it meets all needs and will stand the test of time.

Another reason to devote as much time and effort to related party transactions as to others is that one or both companies may be sold and the parties might become unrelated. Several related party transactions have ended in arbitration or in court following the sale of one or both parties.

For the same reasons, administration of related party reinsurance should be just as fastidious and thorough as that for any other agreement. Lack of attention to items such as regulation, financial reporting, and taxation has caused some affiliated reinsurance agreements to fail to meet their objectives.

Regulation. Regulation of affiliated reinsurance is not very different than that of any other reinsurance. The terms should be those of an arm's length transaction. The reinsurance treaty provisions must be clear and the reinsurer must honor all commitments related to claims, benefits, and reserves.

The Model Holding Company Act developed by the NAIC contains provisions regarding reinsurance between affiliated companies. Most states have adopted modifications of this act or apply its guidelines in some manner. Companies considering an affiliated reinsurance transaction are advised to review this and other applicable laws before finalizing any agreement.

In particular, some states have adopted more stringent rules about accepting letters of credit for reserve credits if a related party is involved as either a reinsurer, a retrocessionaire, or the bank granting the letter of credit.

GAAP Reporting. GAAP accounting is usually on a consolidated basis for companies with common ownership. The effect of consolidated GAAP treatment of related party transactions should be that no net gain or loss from the transaction is reflected. If one company reports a GAAP gain, the other should show a corresponding GAAP loss. The earnings and balance sheet of the consolidated entity is not affected.

The GAAP provisions for taxes may not cancel out, however, since the ceding company and the reinsurer may be in different tax positions, taxed on different sources of profit, or taxed at different rates. Also, one party may be in an alternative minimum tax position and the other not, leading to tax results which may not offset each other.

Also, if ownership is not identical, say, for example, there is only partial overlap of ownership, then GAAP results may differ from those described.

Taxation. The IRS has tended to give careful scrutiny to related party reinsurance. Section 845(a) of the Internal Revenue Code specifically grants the IRS additional authority to reverse or reallocate the effects of reinsurance transactions when related parties are involved.[5] A arm's length argument may not be sufficient protection from IRS action.

The tax effects of consolidation must be considered when designing related party reinsurance. Expected benefits in one company could be more than offset by the tax effects on the other or in the consolidation. Internal allocations of taxes may be affected by reinsurance. The effects of the transaction on alternative minimum taxes should be anticipated.

---

[5] See Chapter 14, Tax Effects of Reinsurance.

REINSURANCE INTERMEDIARIES

In the property and casualty market, the majority of reinsurance is placed through reinsurance intermediaries, also referred to as brokers, because few property and casualty reinsurers employ a sales staff. In the traditional life reinsurance market, most professional reinsurers have sales personnel and the ceding companies' reinsurance needs are fairly straightforward, so intermediaries are infrequently encountered. However, reinsurance intermediaries are sometimes used for situations involving unusual or large transactions, such as financial reinsurance or stop loss, where special expertise or market access is needed. Brokerage involvement is common in the accident and health reinsurance marketplace.

In a typical transaction involving intermediaries, the intermediary works with the ceding company to put together a package to fill its reinsurance needs. The intermediary then approaches reinsurers with the package and negotiates terms and fees. The intermediary is generally paid on a continent fee basis. This fee is normally included in the cost of reinsurance and paid by the reinsurer. The ceding company is usually aware of the fee and, in some instances, may pay it directly to the intermediary.

In the life reinsurance market, any funds transferred for any reason generally flow directly between the reinsurer and the ceding company. However, for property and casualty reinsurance, funds typically pass through the intermediary. Because of this, the NAIC has recommended the Reinsurance Intermediary Model Act. This act provides for the licensing of reinsurance intermediaries and is designed to protect the ceding company against misappropriation of funds by the intermediary. The intermediary is required to have written authorization from the ceding company specifying the responsibilities of each party.

The act requires the intermediary to provide the ceding company with reports detailing all material transactions including commissions and fees. The act also requires the intermediary to keep a complete record of each transaction for at least ten years after the expiration of the contract. The records must include contract terms, reinsurance premium rates, commissions, records of financial transactions, names and addresses of all reinsurers, and proof of placement. The intermediary must also provide the ceding company with access to, and the right to copy and audit, all accounts and records. Conditions are also placed on the intermediary's handling of funds and bank accounts.

If the intermediary is allowed to settle claims on behalf of the reinsurer, the act provides that the intermediary must report all claims to the reinsurer on a timely basis and provide the reinsurer with a copy of the claim file in certain circumstances. These circumstances include, for example, claims that exceed the intermediary's settlement authority, involve coverage disputes, or have been open for more than six months.

Some intermediaries also serve as managers who have authority to perform underwriting services for the reinsurer and bind the reinsurer to risks. Depending upon their type of responsibilities and the independence of action, intermediaries may be required to have a bond and provide proof of errors and omissions insurance coverage.

At least two states, Texas and New York, place the risk of the intermediaries' insolvency or wrongful conduct on the reinsurer. These states require that payments made by the ceding company are deemed paid to the reinsurer when remitted to the intermediary, while payments made by the reinsurer are not deemed paid to the ceding company until received by the ceding company.

A | Sample Reinsurance Agreement[1]

YEARLY RENEWABLE TERM
REINSURANCE AGREEMENT
Effective as of January 1, 1995
between
ABC LIFE INSURANCE COMPANY
of
Cederville, USA,
referred to in this Agreement as "ABC Life" and
XYZ RE LIFE REINSURANCE COMPANY
of
Assumption GAAP, USA
referred to in this Agreement as "XYZ Re"

---

[1] This reinsurance treaty is provided to give an example of an indemnity agreement for YRT reinsurance coverage. It has been graciously provided by Lincoln National Life Insurance Company of Fort Wayne, Indiania.

This sample treaty is provided for reference purposes to enhance the reader's understanding. The authors do not endorse this particular treaty or any particular terms; each reinsurance treaty should be designed to reflect the agreement it covers and the requirements of the parties inovlved.

SECTION I. Reinsurance Coverage

A. ABC Life agrees to cede, and XYZ Re agrees to accept, reinsurance of the Policies specified in the Life Benefits Schedule. (The term "Policies" and certain other terms used in this Agreement are defined in the "Definitions" article.)
B. The death benefits provided by the Policies are reinsured. Supplemental benefits are reinsured if and as specified in applicable Addenda.
C. ABC Life agrees to either:
    (1) cede reinsurance of a Policy to XYZ Re as Automatic Reinsurance;
    (2) submit the Policy to XYZ Re for consideration as Facultative Reinsurance; or
    (3) cede insurance of a Policy as a Continuation.

SECTION II. Automatic Reinsurance

A. ABC Life agrees to cede the Reinsurance Amount of a Policy as Automatic Reinsurance if the following conditions are met:
    (1) it retains its Retention on the insured life when the Policy is issued;
    (2) it underwrites and issues the Policy in accordance with its underwriting rules and practices previously disclosed to XYZ Re;
    (3) the sum of (a) and (b) does not exceed the sum of its Retention and the Automatic Limit, where (a) equals the amount of individual life insurance issued by ABC Life then in force on the insured life, or in the case of individual life insurance with increasing death benefits, the Ultimate Amount of such policies, and (b) equals the amount of life insurance currently being applied for from ABC Life, or in the case of individual life insurance with increasing death benefits, the Ultimate Amount;
    (4) the sum of (a) and (b) does not exceed the Participation Limit, where (a) equals the amount of individual life insurance then in force on the insured life in all companies, or in the case of individual life insurance with increasing death benefits, the Ultimate Amount of such policies, and (b) equals the amount currently applied for on the insured life

from all companies, or in the case of individual life insurance with increasing death benefits, the Ultimate Amounts;
   (5) it has not submitted a facultative application to XYZ Re or any other insurance or reinsurance company for reinsurance of the current application; and
   (6) the Policy is not a Continuation.
B. A Policy shall not be ceded as Automatic Reinsurance if the Reinsurance Amount of the Policy is less than the minimum cession amount specified in the Administration Schedule.

SECTION III. Facultative Reinsurance

A. ABC Life agrees to submit Policies not satisfying the conditions for Automatic Reinsurance, and Policies which it does not wish to cede as Automatic Reinsurance, for consideration by XYZ Re as Facultative Reinsurance. ABC Life may also submit for consideration as Facultative Reinsurance any individual life insurance issued on a policy form that is not specified in the Life Benefits Schedule provided reinsurance terms and conditions are established and agreed upon by means of the Facultative Reinsurance application process.
B. An application for Facultative Reinsurance shall be made in the manner set forth in the Administration Schedule. Copies of all information which ABC Life has pertaining to the insurability of the proposed insured, including written summaries of any such information which cannot be copied, shall accompany the application.
C. Upon receipt of an application, XYZ Re agrees to promptly examine the underwriting information and communicate:
   (1) an offer to reinsure the Policy as applied for;
   (2) an offer to reinsure the Policy other than as applied for;
   (3) an offer to reinsure the Policy subject to the satisfaction of additional underwriting requirements;
   (4) a request for additional underwriting information; or
   (5) its unwillingness to make an offer to reinsure the Policy.
D. To accept an offer to reinsure made by XYZ Re, ABC Life agrees to (1) satisfy any conditions stated in the offer to reinsure and (2) follow the procedure for placing reinsurance into effect as specified in the Administration Schedule.

E. ABC Life agrees to inform XYZ Re immediately of any additional information pertaining to the insurability of a proposed insured which is brought to ABC Life's attention before the completion of the procedures for accepting XYZ Re's offer to reinsure. Upon its receipt of such information, XYZ Re may withdraw or modify its earlier offer to reinsure.
F. The terms of an offer to reinsure shall supercede the terms of this Agreement to the extent of any conflict between the parties. Otherwise, reinsurance of a Policy ceded as Facultative Reinsurance shall be in accordance with the terms of this Agreement.

SECTION IV. Continuations

A. If ABC Life issues a Continuation of a Policy within its normal continuation rules and practices, its agrees to reinsure the Continuation with XYZ Re. Reinsurance shall continue (1) under the reinsurance agreement between ABC Life and XYZ Re which provides reinsurance of the policy form of the Continuation or (2) under this Agreement if there is no such agreement.
B. A Policy which is a Continuation of a Policy that was not previously reinsured with XYZ Re may only be reinsured under this Agreement with the written consent of XYZ Re and the original reinsurer.
C. If the original Policy was ceded to XYZ Re as Facultative Reinsurance and ABC Life approves an increase in the face amount of the Continuation based upon receipt of any new information pertaining to the insurability of the proposed insured, ABC Life agrees to submit the Continuation to XYZ Re for consideration as Facultative Reinsurance. In such case, XYZ Re shall only be bound to reinsure the Continuation in accordance with its offer to reinsure the Continuation.
D. Reinsurance at issue of the Continuation shall not exceed the Reinsured Net Amount at Risk of the original Policy immediately prior to the issuance of the Continuation.
E. Premiums payable for reinsurance of a Continuation shall be calculated using the rate schedule applicable to the policy form of the Continuation as specified in the Reinsurance Premium Schedule. If there is no rate schedule applicable to the policy form of the Continuation, reinsurance premiums shall be payable using the rate schedule applicable to the original Policy.

F. If the Continuation results in a change in the life status of the insured risk from a single-insured plan to a joint- or multiple-insured plan, XYZ Re must consent to the Continuation.

SECTION V. Terms of Reinsurance

A. The plan of reinsurance shall be yearly renewable term reinsurance of the Reinsured Net Amount at Risk of a Policy.
B. Reinsurance of a Policy shall commence on the Policy date, except (1) in the case of Facultative Reinsurance, reinsurance shall commence on the Policy date only if XYZ Re's offer to reinsure is the best offer of reinsurance received by ABC Life as determined by ABC Life's published reinsurance placement rules in effect as of such date, and (2) if a premium receipt is issued by ABC Life in connection with an application for the Policy, reinsurance shall commence prior to the Policy date only if and as specified in a Premium Receipt Addendum.
C. ABC Life agrees not to use XYZ Re's name in connection with the sale of the Policies.
D. In no event shall reinsurance under this Agreement be in force with respect to a Policy unless the issuance and delivery of the Policy is in compliance with the laws of all applicable jurisdictions and ABC Life's corporate charter.
E. ABC Life agrees to maintain reinsurance of a Policy in force in accordance with the terms of this Agreement for as long as its Policy remains in force.

SECTION VI. Reinsurance Premiums

A. ABC Life agrees to pay XYZ Re premiums for reinsurance of a Policy equal to the appropriate rate specified in the Premium Schedule times the Reinsured Net Amount at Risk of the Policy.
B. The Premium Schedule specifies other monetary amounts which ABC Life agrees to take into account when calculating the amount due XYZ Re.
C. Reinsurance premiums shall be due and payable as specified in the Administration Schedule.
D. The payment of reinsurance premiums shall be a condition precedent to the liability of XYZ Re under this Agreement. If

reinsurance premiums are not paid when due, XYZ Re may give ABC Life thirty (30) days' written notice of its intent to terminate reinsurance because of ABC Life's failure to pay reinsurance premiums. Reinsurance of all Policies having reinsurance premiums in arrears shall terminate as of the date to which reinsurance premiums had previously been paid unless all premiums in arrears are paid before the end of the thirty (30) day notice period. If reinsurance on any Policy terminates because of ABC Life's failure to pay reinsurance premiums, reinsurance of Policies which premiums subsequently becoming due shall automatically terminate as of the date on which new reinsurance premiums become due.

E. So that XYZ Re need not maintain deficiency reserves in connection with reinsurance premiums payable pursuant to this Agreement, the premium rates specified in the Premium Schedule shall only be guaranteed for one Policy year. Nevertheless, XYZ Re shall anticipate continuing to accept reinsurance on the basis of such rates for all Policies originally ceded pursuant to such rates.

SECTION VII. Payment by XYZ Re

A. XYZ Re agrees to pay ABC Life the Reinsured Net Amount at Risk of any claim paid by ABC Life pursuant to a Policy in accordance with the "Settlement of Claims" article.

B. XYZ Re agrees to pay the Claims Ratio of any expenses incurred in connection with Policy claims except as set forth in the "Settlement of Claims" article.

C. The Premium Schedule specifies other monetary amounts that XYZ Re agrees to pay ABC Life pursuant to this Agreement.

SECTION VIII. Reinsurance Administration

The methods for placing reinsurance into effect, for paying reinsurance premiums, and for notifying XYZ Re of Policy lapses, reinstatements, reductions, continuations, increases in the Reinsured Net Amount at Risk, and other changes affecting reinsurance shall be specified in the Administration Schedule.

SECTION IX. Settlement of Claims

A. ABC Life agrees to give XYZ Re prompt written notice of its receipt of any claim on a Policy and to keep XYZ Re informed of any legal proceedings or settlement negotiations in connection with a claim. Copies of written materials relating to such claim, legal proceedings or negotiation shall be furnished to XYZ Re upon request.

B. ABC Life agrees to act in accord with its standard practices applicable to all claims in enforcing the terms and conditions of the Policies and with respect to the administration, negotiation, payment, denial, or settlement of any claim or legal proceeding.

C. XYZ Re agrees to accept the good faith decision of ABC Life in payment or settlement of any claim for which XYZ Re has received the required notice. XYZ Re agrees to pay ABC Life the Reinsured Net Amount at Risk on which reinsurance premiums have been computed upon receiving proper evidence that ABC Life has paid a Policy claim. Payment of the Reinsured Net Amount at Risk on account of death shall be made in one lump sum.

D. XYZ Re's liability shall include indemnification of the Claims Ratio of any expenses incurred by ABC Life in defending or investigating a Policy claim with the exception of:
   (1) salaries of employees or other internal expenses of ABC Life;
   (2) routine investigative or administrative expenses;
   (3) expenses incurred in connection with a dispute arising out of conflicting claims of entitlement to proceeds of a Policy that ABC Life admits are payable;
   (4) any gratuitous payments made by ABC Life; and
   (5) any punitive damages awarded against ABC Life, and expenses incurred in connection with such damages, that are based on the acts or omissions of ABC Life or its agents.

E. XYZ Re agrees to hold ABC Life harmless from certain expenses and liabilities that result from XYZ Re's own acts or omissions as provided in this section. For this purpose, XYZ Re agrees to indemnify ABC Life for XYZ Re's equitable share of those punitive and exemplary damages awarded against ABC Life, and expenses incurred in connection with a claim for such damages, if (1) XYZ Re actively participated in the acts or omissions, including the decision to deny a claim for Policy benefits, and (2) those acts or omissions serve as a material basis for the punitive or exemplary damages. XYZ Re's equitable share shall be determined by an assessment of XYZ Re's participation in the particular case.

F. If ABC Life should contest or compromise any claim and the amount of ABC Life's liability is thereby reduced, XYZ Re's liability shall be reduced by the Claims Ratio of the reduction.
G. If ABC Life should recover monies from any third party in connection with or arising out of any Policy, ABC Life agrees to pay XYZ Re the Claims Ratio of the recovery.
H. If the amount of insurance provided by a Policy is increased or reduced because of a misstatement of age or sex, XYZ Re's liability shall be increased or reduced by the Claims Ratio of the amount of the increase or reduction.
I. If ABC Life pays interest on a claim, XYZ Re agrees to pay the interest on the Reinsured Net Amount at Risk computed at the same rate and for the same period as that paid by ABC Life, but in no event later than the date the claim is finally adjudicated by ABC Life.
J. If ABC Life is required to pay penalties and interest imposed automatically by statute, XYZ Re shall indemnify ABC Life for the Claims Ratio of such penalties and interest.

SECTION X. Reinstatements

A. If ABC Life reinstates a lapsed Policy in accordance with the terms of the Policy and ABC Life's underwriting rules and practices, XYZ Re agrees to reinstate reinsurance of the Policy automatically unless XYZ Re's offer to reinsure the Policy specifies that reinsurance of the Policy may only be reinstated as Facultative Reinsurance.
B. If ABC Life collects premiums in arrears from the policyholder of a reinstated Policy, it agrees to pay XYZ Re all corresponding reinsurance premiums in arrears in connection with the reinstatement, plus XYZ Re's Proportionate Share of any interest received by ABC Life in connection with the reinstatement.

SECTION XI. Reductions in Insurance

If individual life insurance on a life reinsured under this Agreement terminates, the Reinsurance Amount shall be reduced as specified in the Administration Schedule.

SECTION XII. Increases in Policy Net Amount at Risk

A. If the Policy Net Amount at Risk on a Policy increases and the increase is subject to ABC Life's underwriting approval, the Reinsured Net Amount at Risk of the Policy shall only increase if the conditions of either the "Automatic Reinsurance" or "Facultative Reinsurance" articles are satisfied.
B. If the Policy Net Amount at Risk on a Policy increases causing the Reinsured Net Amount at Risk to exceed the Reinsurance Amount and the increase is not subject to ABC Life's underwriting approval, XYZ Re agrees to accept a portion of such increases only if and as specified in an Increasing Policy Addendum.

SECTION XIII. Changes in Retention

A. If ABC Life increases its Retention on new Policies, it agrees to notify XYZ Re in writing within (60) days of such increase. The notice shall specify the new Retention and the effective date thereof.
B. Whenever ABC Life increases its Retention on new Policies, it also agrees to indicate in its notice whether it wishes to (1) continue its previous retention on inforce Policies, or (2) increase its Retention on inforce Policies and recapture reinsurance. If ABC Life elects (2), ABC Life's new Retention on an in force Policy shall be calculated using the insured's age, mortality class, Policy form, and country of residence at issue of the Policy.
C. If ABC Life elects to increase its Retention on inforce Policies pursuant to Section B, its new Retention for such Policies shall become effective on the later of (1) the reinsurance renewal date of the Policy first following the effective date of its new Retention for new Policies, and (2) the policy anniversary date specified in the Administration Schedule. If ABC Life fails to initiate recapture of reinsurance within one hundred and eighty (180) days of when the first of its Policies becomes eligible for recapture, its election to recapture reinsurance shall be considered waived.
D. If an inforce Policy is subject to a waiver of premium claim on the date the Policy qualifies for a new Retention, the new Retention shall become effective on such date for purposes of life reinsurance only.
E. ABC Life may only elect to increase its Retention on inforce Policies if:

- (1) it maintained a Retention greater than $X at the time the Policy was issued and retained its Retention at such time;
- (2) its increases its Retention on all eligible inforce Policies; and
- (3) its retains the insurance recaptured from XYZ Re at its own risk without benefit of any proportional or nonproportional reinsurance other than catastrophe accident reinsurance.

F. Notwithstanding the preceding:
- (1) the recapture of the Reinsurance Amount shall be limited to XYZ Re's portion of all reinsurance on the life ceded by the ABC Life prior to the effective date of the recapture; and
- (2) if ABC Life gives notice of its intent to increase its Retention on inforce Policies within five (5) years following a merger with another insurance company or the date it accepts the Policies by means of an assignment, the new Retention applicable to such Policies shall be limited to 150% of the original reinsured's pre-merger or pre-assignment Retention.

G. For purposes of this article, Continuations shall be considered issued on the date of the original Policy.

SECTION XIV. Assignment of Reinsurance

If ABC Life sells, assumption reinsures or otherwise transfers the Policies to another insurer, it agrees to require that the other insurer assume all rights and obligations of ABC Life under this Agreement. XYZ Re may object to any such transfer that would result in a material adverse economic impact to XYZ Re. If XYZ Re so objects, ABC Life and XYZ Re agree to mutually calculate a termination charge which shall be paid by ABC Life to XYZ Re upon the transfer and this Agreement shall be terminated with respect to all Policies transferred by ABC Life.

SECTION XV. Material Changes

A. ABC Life agrees to notify XYZ Re in writing of any anticipated Material Change in any terms or conditions of the Policies, in ABC Life's underwriting rules and practices applicable to the Policies or in ABC Life's claims practices and procedures.

B. In the event of a Material Change to the Policies, to ABC Life's underwriting rules and practices or to its claims practices and procedures, XYZ Re may at its option:

(1) continue to reinsure the Policies under current terms;
(2) reinsure future Policies under modifies terms to reflect the Material Change; or
(3) consider future Policies as issued in a policy form that is not reinsured under this Agreement.

SECTION XVI. Errors

A. Any Error by either ABC Life or XYZ Re in the administration of reinsurance under this Agreement shall be corrected by restoring both ABC Life and XYZ Re to the positions they would have occupied had no Error occurred. Any monetary adjustments made between ABC Life and XYZ Re to correct an Error shall be without interest.
B. When a party claims that an Error should be corrected pursuant to Section A, that party agrees to investigate whether other instances of the Error have also occurred and agrees to report its findings to the other party.

SECTION XVII. Audits of Records and Procedures

A. XYZ Re or ABC Life may audit, at any reasonable time and at its own expense, all records and procedures relating to reinsurance under this Agreement. The party being audited agrees to cooperate in the audit, including providing any information requested by the other in advance of the audit.
B. Upon request, ABC Life agrees to furnish XYZ Re with copies of any underwriting information in ABC Life's files pertaining to a Policy.

SECTION XVIII. Arbitration

A. If ABC Life and XYZ Re cannot mutually resolve a dispute which arises out of or relates to this Agreement, the dispute shall be decided through arbitration as specified in the Arbitration Schedule. The arbitrators shall base their decision on the terms and conditions of this Agreement plus, as necessary, on the customs and practices of the insurance and reinsurance industry rather than solely on a strict interpretation of applicable law. There shall be no appeal from their decision, except that either party may petition a court having jurisdiction over the parties and the subject matter to reduce the arbitrators' decision to judgment.

B. The parties intend this article to be enforceable in accordance with the Federal Arbitration Act (9 U.S.C. §§1 *et seq.*), including any amendments to that Act which are subsequently adopted. If either party refuses to submit to arbitration as required by Section A, the other party may request a United States Federal District Court to compel arbitration in accordance with the Federal Arbitration Act. Both parties consent to the jurisdiction of such court to enforce this article and to confirm and enforce the performance of any award of the arbitrators.

SECTION XIX. Insolvency of ABC Life

A. In the event of the insolvency of ABC Life and the appointment of a conservator, liquidator or statutory successor of ABC Life, reinsurance shall be payable immediately upon demand to such conservator, liquidator or statutory successor, with reasonable provision for verification before payment, on the basis of claims allowed against ABC Life by any court of competent jurisdiction or by the conservator, liquidator or statutory successor of ABC Life without diminution because of the insolvency of ABC Life or because such conservator, liquidator or statutory successor has failed to pay all or a portion of any claims.

B. In the event of the insolvency of ABC Life, the liquidator, receiver, or other statutory successor of ABC Life agrees to give XYZ Re written notice of the pendency of a claim on a Policy within a reasonable time after such claim is filed in the insolvency proceeding. During the pendency of any such claim, XYZ Re may investigate the claim and interpose in the name of ABC Life (its conservator, liquidator, or statutory successor), but at its own expense, in the proceeding where such claim is to be adjudicated, any defense or defenses which XYZ Re may deem available to ABC Life or its conservator, liquidator, or statutory successor.

C. The Claims Ratio of the expense thus incurred by XYZ Re shall be charged, subject to court approval, against ABC Life as part of the expense of liquidation.

SECTION XX. Offset

Any debts or credits, matured or unmatured, liquidated or unliquidated, regardless of when they arose or were incurred, in favor of or against either ABC Life or XYZ Re with respect to this Agreement or any other reinsurance agreement between the parties, shall be offset and only the balance allowed or paid. If either ABC Life or XYZ Re is then under formal insolvency proceedings, this right of offset shall be subject to the laws of the state exercising primary jurisdiction over such proceedings.

SECTION XXI. Parties to the Agreement

This is an Agreement for indemnity reinsurance solely between ABC Life and XYZ Re. The acceptance of reinsurance under this Agreement shall not create any right or legal relation whatever between XYZ Re and an insured, policyholder, beneficiary, or any other party to or under any Policy.

SECTION XXII. Commencement and Termination

A. This Agreement shall be effective as of the date set forth on the cover page.
B. Either ABC Life or XYZ Re may terminate this Agreement for new reinsurance by giving ninety (90) days' written notice to the other party. In such case, ABC Life agrees to continue to cede, and XYZ Re agrees to continue to accept, reinsurance in accordance with this Agreement of Policies issued prior to the expiration of the ninety (90) day period. All reinsurance that has been placed in effect prior to such date shall remain in effect in accordance with terms of this Agreement, until the earlier of (1) the termination or expiration of the Policy and (2) the termination of this Agreement pursuant to Section C or D below.
C. Reinsurance of a Policy shall terminate as of the reinsurance premium renewal date on which the Reinsured Net Amount at Risk for such Policy is less than the automatic termination amount specified in the Administration Schedule, provided the reinsurance has been in force for the period specified in the Administration Schedule.

D. XYZ Re may terminate all reinsurance under this Agreement in accordance with Section D of the "Payments by ABC Life" article if ABC Life fails to pay reinsurance premiums when due.

SECTION XXIII. Entire Agreement

A. This Agreement represents the entire agreement between ABC Life and XYZ Re and supercedes any prior oral or written agreements between the parties regarding its subject matter.
B. No modification of this Agreement shall be effective unless set forth in a written amendment executed by both parties.
C. A waiver of a right created by this Agreement shall constitute a waiver only with respect to the particular circumstance for which it is given and not a waiver in any future circumstance.

SECTION XXIV
Deferred Acquisition Cost Tax Election

A. XYZ Re and ABC Life each acknowledge that it is subject to taxation under Subchapter "L" of the Internal Revenue Code of 1986 (the "Code").
B. With respect to this Agreement, XYZ Re and ABC Life agree to the following pursuant to Section 1.848-2(g)(8) of the Income Tax Regulations issued December 1992, whereby:
   (1) Each party agrees to attach a schedule to its federal income tax return which identifies this Agreement for which the joint election under the Regulation has been made;
   (2) The party with net positive consideration, as defined in the Regulation promulgated under Code Section 848, for this Agreement for each taxable year, agrees to capitalize specified policy acquisition expenses with respect to this Agreement without regard to the general deductions limitation of Section 848(c)(1);
   (3) Each party agrees to exchange information pertaining to the amount of net consideration under this Agreement each year to ensure consistency; and
   (4) This election shall be effective for the year that this Agreement was entered into and for all subsequent years that this Agreement remains in effect.

SECTION XXV. Definitions

A. **Automatic Limit** — the amount specified in the Life Benefits Schedule used to calculate the maximum Reinsurance Amount that may be ceded as Automatic Reinsurance.

B. **Automatic Reinsurance** — reinsurance satisfying certain conditions relating to the reinsurance as specified in the Agreement that is ceded to XYZ Re without obtaining a specific offer to reinsure from XYZ Re.

C. **Capacity Facultative Reinsurance** — Facultative Reinsurance for which ABC Life made facultative application to no reinsurer other than XYZ Re and on which ABC Life retained its full Retention on the Policy.

D. **Claims Ratio** — the Reinsured Net Amount at Risk on which reinsurance premiums have been computed divided by the Policy Net Amount at Risk calculated as of the date of the last premium payment.

E. **Continuation** — a new Policy replacing a Policy or a change in an existing Policy issued or made either (1) in compliance with the terms of the Policy, or (2) without (a) the same new underwriting information ABC Life would obtain in the absence of the Policy, (b) a suicide exclusion or contestable period as long as those contained in other new issues of Policies, or (c) the payment of the same commissions in the first year that ABC Life would have paid in the absence of the original Policy.

F. **Effective Date** — the date specified on the cover page on which this Agreement becomes binding on ABC Life and XYZ Re.

G. **Error** — any isolated deviation from the terms of this Agreement resulting from the act or omission of an employee of either ABC Life or XYZ Re whose principal function relates to the administration of reinsurance, whether such deviation results from inadvertence or a mistake in judgment. "Error" shall not include any failure to comply with the terms of an offer of Facultative Reinsurance or any negligent or deliberate deviation from the terms of this Agreement.

H. **Facultative Reinsurance** — reinsurance that is ceded to XYZ Re only after ABC Life has obtained and accepted a specific offer to reinsure made by XYZ Re. Such reinsurance may be ceded to XYZ Re only upon the terms specified by XYZ Re in its offer to reinsure and the terms of this Agreement that do not conflict with the specific offer to reinsure.

I. **XYZ Re's Proportionate Share** — the Reinsurance Amount divided by the death benefit of a Policy as of the date of issue or as of the date of a subsequent change to the Policy that affects the Reinsurance Amount.
J. **Material Change** — a change that a prudent insurance or reinsurance executive would consider as likely to impact upon a party's financial experience under this Agreement.
K. **Participation Limit** — the amount specified in the Life Benefits Schedule used as a condition for ceding Automatic Reinsurance.
L. **Policy** — an individual life insurance contract issued by ABC Life on any of the policy forms specified in the Life Benefits Schedule. A "Policy" shall include any attached riders and endorsements specified in the Life Benefits Schedule or any Addendum to this Agreement.
M. **Policy Net Amount at Risk** — on the reinsurance premium renewal date, the fact amount of a Policy less either the terminal reserve or, in the case of interest sensitive Policies, the accumulation account or cash value on the Policy, such difference taken to the nearest dollar. The terminal reserve or cash value shall be disregarded if a Policy is on either a level term plan of twenty years or less or on a decreasing term plan. The basis for determining the Policy Net Amount at Risk may be modified with the consent of both ABC Life and XYZ Re without the need for a formal amendment of this Agreement.
N. **Reinsurance Amount** — the Policy death benefit at issue less the Retention on the policy times the percentage of Automatic Reinsurance ceded to XYZ Re as specified in the Life Benefits Schedule. For Facultative Reinsurance, the "Reinsurance Amount" is that amount of the Policy death benefit at issue for which ABC Life accepts XYZ Re's offer to reinsure.
O. **Reinsured Net Amount at Risk** — the percentage of Automatic Reinsurance ceded to XYZ Re as specified in the Life Benefits Schedule or the percentage ceded as modified pursuant to the Facultative Reinsurance process times the remainder of (1) the Policy Net Amount at Risk less (2) the Retention on the Policy.
P. **Retention** — the amount specified in the Life Benefits Schedule that is held by ABC Life at its own risk on a life without the benefit of proportional reinsurance. In calculating the Retention, the sum retained by ABC Life on the life and in force as of the date of issue of the Policy shall be taken into account.

Q. **Ultimate Amount** — the projected maximum Policy Net Amount at Risk which a Policy could achieve based on reasonable assumptions made about the operation of certain characteristics of the policy form.

SECTION XXVI. Execution

ABC Life and XYZ Re, by their respective officers, executed this Agreement in duplicate on the dates shown below. As of the Effective Date, this Agreement consists of:

- this Yearly Renewable Term Reinsurance Agreement numbered 00;
- a Life Benefits Schedule;
- an Administration Schedule;
- a Premium Schedule;
- an Arbitration Schedule;
- a Waiver of Premium Addendum; and
- an Accidental Death Benefit Addendum.

FOR ABC LIFE   FOR XYZ RE

Signed at _____   Signed at _____

By   _____   By   _____
Title   _____   Title   _____
Date   _____   Date   _____

By   _____   By   _____
Title   _____   Title   _____
Date   _____   Date   _____

LIFE BENEFITS SCHEDULE
(Effective as of January 1, 1995)
to
Agreement Number 000 / 00

POLICIES REINSURED: ABC Life agrees to cede reinsurance in the listed percentages of Policies issued on the following Policy forms with issue dates from and until the dates listed below to insureds having surnames beginning with the letters of the alphabet shown. Any Addenda referred to in the last column shall also be applicable to reinsurance of the Policy.

Policy Form	Percent of Reinsurance Ceded to XYZ Re	Policy Issue Date From/Until	Alpha Split	Applicable Addenda

RETENTION: ABC Life agrees to hold the following face amounts, 100% of each Policy not to exceed the Retention limit below at its own risk on a life without the benefit of proportional reinsurance. In calculating its Retention, amounts retained by ABC Life on other individual life insurance Policies in force as of the issue date of the Policy shall be taken into account.

Ages	Standard-Table P

Sample Reinsurance Agreement

AUTOMATIC LIMITS: To bind Automatic Reinsurance, the maximum amount of life insurance inforce with ABC Life on a single life, or in the case of individual life insurance with increasing death benefits, the Ultimate Amounts, plus all amounts applied for from ABC Life on that life, or in the case of individual life insurance with increasing death benefits, the Ultimate Amounts, may not exceed the sum of the Retention on the life plus the following amounts.

<u>Ages</u>   <u>Standard-Table P</u>   <u>Over Table P</u>

PARTICIPATION LIMITS: To bind Automatic Reinsurance, the sum of (1) the maximum amount of individual life insurance in force on the insured in all companies or, in the case of individual life insurance with increasing death benefits, the Ultimate Amounts, as of the Policy Date of a Policy, and (2) the amount then being applied for by all companies, or in the case of individual life insurance with increasing death benefits, the Ultimate Amounts, on the insured, may not exceed the following amounts.

<u>Ages</u>   <u>Standard-Table P</u>   <u>Over Table P</u>

ADMINISTRATION SCHEDULE
(Effective as of January 1, 1995)
to
Agreement Number 000 / 00

TO PLACE REINSURANCE INTO EFFECT

(1) **For Automatic Reinsurance:** ABC Life agrees to cede Automatic Reinsurance of a Policy by including all required information about the Policy on the new business segment of the next self-administered statement submitted in accordance with the Reports section below following issuance of the Policy.

(2) **For Facultative Reinsurance:** ABC Life agrees to submit an application form for Facultative Reinsurance in substantial accord with the attached form. It agrees to allocate reinsurance in accordance with its published facultative placement rules among those reinsurers making facultative offers to reinsure a Policy. If according to such rules XYZ Re's offer is the one ABC Life intends to accept, ABC Life shall cede Facultative Reinsurance of the Policy by including all required information about the Policy on the new business segment of the next self-administered statement submitted in accordance with the **Reports** section below within one hundred twenty (120) days from the date of XYZ Re's facultative offer or the date specified in XYZ Re's approval of a written request from ABC Life to grant an extension to the facultative offer.

MINIMUM CESSION REQUIREMENT

ABC Life agrees not to cede any Policy as Automatic Reinsurance if the Reinsurance Amount of the Policy is less than $1,000.

REPORTS

Within thirty (30) days following the end of each month, ABC Life agrees to send XYZ Re the following three (3) reports:
(1) **A Billing Statement** containing Policy level detail in a form mutually acceptable to ABC Life and XYZ Re. At a minimum, it

shall contain the data elements specified in the attached Policy Detail Report. If the Policy contains supplemental benefits that are also reinsured, each segment of the Billing Statement shall include supplemental benefit detail.

The Billing Statement shall be segmented as follows:

- **New Issues** and first-year premiums due for new reinsurance.
- **Balance of first-year Policies** (Policies previously reported as new issues) and corresponding balance of first-year reinsurance premiums due for the reporting period.
- **Policies with anniversaries** during the reporting period and the corresponding renewal reinsurance premiums due.
- **Policies that have undergone a change** that affects reinsurance. Separate segments may be submitted for any change affecting reinsurance of a Policy, including:
    - reissues,
    - reinstatements,
    - terminations,
    - reductions,
    - changes in Retention,
    - changes in mortality ratings,
    - issuance of a Continuation, and
    - increases or decreases in the Net Amount at Risk

(2) **A Summary Accounting Report** that summarizes all financial transactions during the reporting period. The report shall separately total life and supplemental benefits for the first year reinsurance premiums are due, shall total life and supplemental benefits for renewal reinsurance premiums due, and shall identify all adjustments therefrom.

(3) **A Policy Exhibit Report** in substantial accord with the attached form that indicates inforce reinsurance as of the beginning of the reporting period, increases during the reporting period (new reinsurance, reinstatements, recoveries, or other increases) and all decreases during the reporting period (terminations, reductions, surrenders, death claims or other decreases); and the resulting inforce reinsurance as of the end of the reporting period.

ABC Life agrees to send XYZ Re within ten (10) working days following each quarter-end a **Reserve Report** in substantial accord with the attached form.

XYZ Re may request a change in the reporting requirements in order to obtain data it reasonably needs to properly administer this Agreement or to prepare its financial statements.

REINSURANCE PREMIUMS DUE

Reinsurance premiums are payable monthly in advance and are due with the reports submitted pursuant to the **Reports** section above.

INCREASE IN LIMIT OF RETENTION

If ABC Life elects to increase its Retention on inforce Policies, the increased Retention may not become effective for a Policy until the Policy's tenth anniversary date.

REDUCTIONS IN INSURANCE

(1) For purposes of this section only, the term "policy" shall refer to any life insurance issued by ABC Life on the insured person, whether or not reinsured with XYZ Re.

(2) If life insurance retained by ABC Life on an insured person reduces because a policy on that life lapses or reduces in accordance with the terms of a policy, the Reinsurance Amount shall be reduced as of the effective date of the termination or reduction in insurance to restore, as far as possible, the Retention of ABC Life on the life.

(3) Reinsurance shall first be reduced on the specific policy that was terminated or reduced. The balance, if any, of the reduction in the Reinsurance Amount shall be applied to reinsurance of other policies on the life beginning with the last policy issued.

(4) Notwithstanding the preceding, the reduction of the Reinsurance Amount shall not exceed to the amount of the reduction times XYZ Re's share of the total reinsurance on the life prior to the reduction and shall not include any policy ceded as Facultative Reinsurance on which, at the time of issue, ABC Life retained less than its Retention on the life.

AUTOMATIC TERMINATION

Reinsurance of a Policy shall terminate as of the beginning of the policy year during which the Reinsured Net Amount at Risk will be less than $10,000, provided reinsurance of the Policy has been in force for a period of a least 3 years.

CLAIMS ADMINISTRATION

Claims shall be individually reported as incurred using a form in substantial accord with the attached form. ABC Life may take credit for unearned reinsurance premiums from the date of death to the next Policy paid to date on its next billing statement.

PREMIUM TAX ADMINISTRATION

Payment to ABC Life from XYZ Re for any premium tax reimbursement shall be made annually following each year end.

Policy Detail Report
_____, 19 _____

For each policy show:

* Client Policy Number
* Effective Date of Tape or Statement
* Automatic/Facultative Indicator
* Name
  - Last Name
  - First Name
  - Middle Name
* Gender
* Date of Birth
* Smoker Indicator
* Original Plan Code
* Issue Age
* Table Rating
* Flat EXTRA1 Premium
* Length of Flat EXTRA1 (YR)
* Flat EXTRA2 Premium
* Length of Flat EXTRA2 (YR)
* Current Amount Reinsured
* Issue Monthly/Date/Century/Year
* Termination Date
* Reinstate Date
* Coverage Face
* Direct Face Issued
* Life Standard Premium
* Life Substandard Premium
* Gross Flat EXTRA1 Premium
* Gross Flat EXTRA2 Premium
* W.P. Premium
* ADB Premium
* Policy Fee
* Dividend
* Life Standard Allowance
* Life Substandard Allowance
* Gross Flat EXTRA1 Allowance
* Gross Flat EXTRA2 Allowance
* W.P. Allowance
* ADB Allowance

Additional Data Items (not required)

* Par/Nonpar Indicator
* State of Residency
* Type of Evidence
* Underwriting Indicator
* Social Security Number
* Coverage Sequence Number
* Account Number
* COX/MCX/RPR
* ER/NR
* Age Basis
* Gross Premium
* Allowance
* Tax Interest Rate
* Status Code
* Years From Issue to Conversion
* Reinsurance Premium Mode
* Retention Indicator
* Retention Amount
* Cash Value
* First Year/Renewal Indicator

Special Products (only required if applicable)

* Joint Insured Name
  - Joint Last Name
  - Joint First Name
  - Joint Middle Name
* Term Additions Indicator
* Accelerated Benefit Indicator
* Purchase Options

PREMIUM SCHEDULE
(Effective as of January 1, 1995)
to
Agreement Number 000 / 00

STANDARD REINSURANCE PREMIUMS

(1) <u>Basic Reinsurance Premium Rates</u>: The reinsurance premium rates for Automatic Reinsurance and Capacity Facultative Reinsurance ceded under this Agreement shall be the attached rates labeled "XXXX, NONSMOKER," "YYYY, SMOKER," "ZZZZ, AGGREGATE," and "Z1, SUBSTANDARD-EXTRA," nonrefunding and age nearest birthday."

(2) <u>For Reinsurance Amounts greater than $5,000,000</u>: Notwithstanding section (1) above, if the Reinsurance Amounts, or in the case of individual life insurance with increasing death benefits, Ultimate Amounts, on any one life ceded by ABC Life to XYZ Re under all reinsurance agreements exceeds $_____$, the reinsurance premium rate for the portion of such excess amount ceded under this Agreement (calculated by adding Reinsurance Amounts in effective date order) shall be the attached rates labeled "1XW3, NONSMOKER," "2XY3, SMOKER," and "3XX3, AGGREGATE," nonrefunding and age nearest birthday.

ADDITIONAL AMOUNTS PAID BY ABC LIFE:

(1) <u>Substandard Premiums</u>: For Policies written on substandard risks, the appropriate premium rate shall be adjusted by multiplying the rate by 25% for each table assessed the risk and adding such amount to the reinsurance premiums due.

(2) <u>Policy Fees</u>: ABC Life also agrees to pay XYZ Re any fees shown on the appropriate premium rates table.

(3) Temporary Flat Extra Premiums: ABC Life agrees to pay XYZ Re a temporary flat extra premium equal to the product of the flat extra premium assigned by ABC Life or XYZ Re on the Policy times the Reinsurance Amount minus an allowance of ten percent (10%) for all renewal years such premium is payable.

(4) Permanent Flat Extra Premiums: ABC Life agrees to pay XYZ Re's Proportionate Share of any permanent flat extra premium paid calculated on the Reinsurance Amount minus an allowance of seventy-five (75%) for the first year such premium is payable and ten percent (10%) for all renewal years such premium is payable.

(5) Continuations: Premiums payable for reinsurance of a Continuation shall be based on the age at issue and duration from issue of the original Policy. If the premium scale applicable to a Continuation contains a Policy fee, ABC Life agree to pay a first-year Policy fee on the Continuation if a Policy fee was not paid at issue of the original Policy.

ADDITIONAL AMOUNTS PAID BY XYZ RE:

(1) Premium Taxes: XYZ Re shall not reimburse ABC Life for state premium taxes.

(2) Experience Refunds: XYZ Re shall not pay an experience refund to ABC Life.

(3) Unearned Premiums: XYZ Re agrees to refund, without interest, any reinsurance premiums unearned as of the date of death of an insured person or as of the date of a reduction of reinsurance pursuant to the "Reductions" article.

ARBITRATION SCHEDULE
(Effective as of January 1, 1995)
to
Agreement Number 000 / 00

To initiate arbitration, either ABC Life or XYZ Re agrees to notify the other party in writing of its desire to arbitrate, stating the nature of its dispute and the remedy sought. The party to which the notice is sent agrees to respond in writing to the notification within ten (10) days of its receipt.

The arbitration hearing shall be held before a panel of three arbitrators, each of whom must be a present or former officer of a life insurance company. An arbitrator may not be a present or former officer, attorney, or consultant of ABC Life or XYZ Re, or either's affiliates.

ABC Life and XYZ Re agree to each name five (5) candidates to serve as an arbitrator. Each agree to choose one candidate from the other's list, and these two candidates shall serve as the first two arbitrators. If one or more candidates so chosen decline to serve as an arbitrator, the party that named the candidate shall add an additional candidate to its list, and the other party agrees to again choose one candidate from the list. This process shall continue until two arbitrators have been chosen and have accepted. ABC Life and XYZ Re agree to present their initial lists of five (5) candidates by written notification to the other party within twenty-five (25) days of the date of the mailing of the notification initiating the arbitration. Any subsequent additions to the list which are required shall be presented within ten (10) days of the date the naming party receives notice that a candidate who has been chosen declines to serve.

The two arbitrators shall select the third arbitrator from the eight (8) candidates remaining on the lists of ABC Life and XYZ Re within fourteen (14) days of the acceptance of their positions as arbitrators. If two arbitrators cannot agree on the choice of a third, then this choice shall be referred back to ABC Life and XYZ Re. ABC Life and XYZ Re agree to take turns striking the names of the remaining candidates from the initial eight (8) candidates until only one candidate remains. If the candidate so chosen shall decline to serve as the third arbitrator, this process shall continue until a candidate has been chosen and accepted.

This candidate shall serve as the third arbitrator. The first turn at striking the name of a candidate shall belong to the party that is responding to the other party's initiation of arbitration. Once chosen, the arbitrators are empowered to decide all substantive and procedural issues by a majority of votes.

It is agreed that each of the three arbitrators should be impartial regarding the dispute and should resolve the dispute on the basis described in the "Arbitration" article. At no time shall either ABC Life or XYZ Re contact or otherwise communicate with any person who is to be or has been designated as a candidate to serve as an arbitrators concerning the dispute, except upon the basis of jointly drafted communications provided by both ABC Life and XYZ Re to inform those candidates actually chosen as arbitrators of the nature and facts of the dispute. Likewise, any written or oral arguments provided to the arbitrators concerning the dispute shall be coordinated with the other party and shall be provided simultaneously to the other party or shall take place in the presence of the other party. Further, at no time shall any arbitrator be informed that he or she has been named or chosen by one party or the other.

The arbitration hearing shall be held on the date and in the location set by the arbitrators. In no event shall this date be later than six (6) months after the appointment of the third arbitrator. As soon as possible, the arbitrators shall establish prearbitration procedures as warranted by the facts and issues of the particular case. At least ten (10) days prior to the arbitration hearing, each party agrees to provide the other party and the arbitrators with a detailed statement of the facts and arguments it will present at the arbitration hearing. The arbitrators may consider any relevant evidence and agree to give the evidence such weight as they deem appropriate after consideration of any objections raised concerning it. The party initiating the arbitration shall have the burden of proving its case by a preponderance of the evidence. Each party may examine any witness who testifies at the arbitration hearing. Within twenty (20) days after the end of the arbitration hearing, the arbitrators shall issue a written decision that sets forth their findings and any award to be paid as a result of the arbitration, except that the arbitrators may not award punitive or exemplary damages. In their decision, the arbitrators shall apportion the costs of arbitration, which shall include, but not be limited to, their own fees and expenses.

WAIVER OF PREMIUM BENEFIT ADDENDUM
(Effective as of January 1, 1995)
to
Agreement Number 000 / 00

The provisions of the Agreement shall apply in all respects to reinsurance of the Waiver of Premium Benefit provided by the Policies except as otherwise set forth in this Addendum.

This Addendum is referred to as "WP" in the "Applicable Addendum" column of the **Policies Reinsured** section of the Life Benefits Schedule.

1. Definitions

1.1. XYZ Re's Proportionate Share — the face amount of the Waiver of Premium Benefit less ABC Life's Waiver of Premium retention divided by the face amount of the Waiver of Premium Benefit.

1.2. Policy Premiums — the insurance premiums, costs of insurance rates or other specified amounts due for the life insurance benefit of a Policy.

1.3. Waiver of Premium Benefit — a benefit provided pursuant to a Policy wherein ABC Life agrees to relinquish its right to Policy Premiums in the event of the policyowner's disability until such disability is ended.

2. Reinsurance Terms

2.1. ABC Life agrees to cede, and XYZ Re agrees to accept, XYZ Re's Proportionate Share of the Waiver of Premium Benefit if the following conditions are met:
    2.1.1. ABC Life retains the following amounts of Waiver of Premium Benefit on a life.

    an amount equal to its Retention of individual life insurance of the insured person.

2.1.2. the sum of Waiver Premium Benefit issued by ABC Life then in force on the insured life and the amount of Waiver of Premium Benefit then being applied for from the ABC Life does not exceed the sum of the ABC Life's Waiver of Premium retention and the following amounts:

<u>Ages</u>   <u>Standard-Table F</u>   <u>Over Table F</u>

2.1.3. the sum of the amount of Waiver of Premium Benefit then in force on the insured life in all companies and the amount of Waiver of Premium Benefit then being applied for on the insured life from all companies does not exceed the following amounts:

<u>Ages</u>   <u>Standard-Table F</u>

2.2. ABC Life agrees to place Waiver of Premium reinsurance into effect by following the procedures for placing life reinsurance into effect as set forth in the Administrative Schedule of the Agreement.

2.3. Waiver of Premium Benefits shall be coinsured with XYZ Re. Reinsurance shall follow the forms of ABC Life. ABC Life agree to pay XYZ Re reinsurance premiums for Waiver of Premium reinsurance equal to XYZ Re's Proportionate Share of the attached premium rates less an allowance of

75% of such premium in the first year and 10% in renewal years.

Waiver of Premium reinsurance premiums are payable with the same frequency as, and due with, the associated life reinsurance premium. Waiver of Premium reinsurance premiums shall not be due while a Waiver of Premium Benefit is being paid. However, while a Waiver of Premium is being paid, ABC Life agrees to continue to pay XYZ Re premiums for reinsurance of other benefits provided by the Policy in accordance with the Agreement or applicable addenda.

2.4. ABC Life agrees to give XYZ Re prompt notice of any Waiver of Premium claim, and upon request, agrees to provide proof of the insured person's continuing disability. XYZ Re's reinsurance liability for Waiver of Premium claims shall equal XYZ Re's Proportionate Share of Policy Premiums waived by ABC Life under the Policy. ABC Life agree to notify XYZ Re upon the termination of a Waiver of Premium claim and agrees to resume paying Waiver of Premium reinsurance premiums starting with the beginning of the first month following the date the person is no longer eligible for such Waiver of Premium Benefit.

2.5. ABC Life may elect to recapture reinsurance of in force Waiver of Premium reinsurance in accordance with the procedures set forth in the Agreement. If ABC Life elects to recapture such reinsurance but an insured person is subject to a Waiver of Premium claim when an increase of its Waiver of Premium retention would otherwise become effective, Waiver of Premium reinsurance shall remain at the current retention until the Policy returns to a premium-paying status. After such time, the intended recapture shall occur.

ACCIDENTAL DEATH BENEFIT ADDENDUM
(Effective as of January 1, 1995)
to
Agreement Number 000 / 00

The provisions of the Agreement shall apply in all respects to reinsurance of Accidental Death Benefits provided by the Policies except as otherwise set forth in this Addendum.

This Addendum is referred to as ADB in the "Applicable Addendum" column of the **Policies Reinsured** section of the Life Benefit Schedule.

1. Definitions

1.1   ADB — life insurance provided by the Policies which is payable in the event of the accidental death of the insured.

1.2. ADB Reinsurance Amount — the face amount of ADB provided by a Policy less the ABC Life's ADB retention.

2. Reinsurance Terms

2.1. The ABC Life agrees to cede, and XYZ Re agrees to accept, the ADB Reinsurance Amount as Automatic Reinsurance if

   2.1.1. the ABC Life retains the following amounts of ADB on a life:

   2.1.2. the sum of ADB issued by the ABC Life then in force on the insured life and the amount of ADB then being applied for from the ABC Life does not exceed the sum of the ABC Life's ADB retention and the following amounts:

   <u>Ages</u>   <u>Standard-Table F</u>

Sample Reinsurance Agreement

2.1.3. the sum of the amount of ADB then in force on the insured life in all companies and the amount of ADB then being applied for on the insured life from all companies does not exceed the following amounts:

Ages	Standard-Table F

2.2. Notwithstanding Section 2.1, ADB shall not be ceded if the ADB Reinsurance Amount at issue is less then $500.

2.3. The ABC Life agrees to place ADB reinsurance into effect by following the procedures for placing life reinsurance into effect as set forth in the Administrative Schedule of the Agreement.

2.4. Reinsurance of ADB shall be yearly renewal term reinsurance. ADB reinsurance premiums shall equal the ADB Reinsurance Amount times the appropriate rate shown below.

Based on the classification of the occupational manual of the ABC Life:

Classification	First Year	Renewal
Standard		
1 1/2 × Standard		
2 × Standard		
3 × Standard		
5 × Standard		

Reinsurance premiums are payable with the same frequency as, and due with, the associated life reinsurance premium. ADB reinsurance premiums shall be due even if a Policy is subject to a waiver of premium claim.

2.5. XYZ Re shall pay the ADB Reinsurance Amount of all ADB claims incurred during the term of this Addendum. Claims shall be reported and paid as incurred.

2.6. The ABC Life may elect to recapture reinsurance of in force ADB only if and when the associated life reinsurance benefit is recaptured in accordance with the terms of the Agreement and if it still has retention available on the life after first recapturing life reinsurance on the life.

2.7. Either the ABC Life or XYZ Re may terminate this Addendum for new ADB reinsurance by giving ninety (90) days' advance written notice to the other party.

B | Guidelines for the Reporting of Self-Administered Reinsurance[1]

INTRODUCTION

Reinsurance treaties are negotiated agreements. For many years the primary area of negotiation for most companies was price. Reinsurers traditionally performed the administrative functions associated with the business based on information transmitted on individual cession forms.

Times have changed. There has been a great development of self-administered reinsurance in recent years. These self-administered arrangements have generally resulted in lower costs for reinsurers, and consequently in lower reinsurance rates. For ceding companies, increased administrative costs have tended to offset the reinsurance rate decrease. Self-administering companies have gained a significant amount of control over reinsurance processing, but they have also assumed a greater responsibility for its accuracy and timeliness.

---

[1] The guidelines also include sample report forms, which have not been reproduced in this appendix.

With the advent of self-administered agreements, the range of negotiated items has expanded to include the question of what shall be reported to the reinsurer. The primary purpose of this document is to provide guidance to ceding companies and reinsurers alike on the information which should be reported through a self-administered arrangement.

Since there is a great deal of variation in the abilities of ceding companies, the needs of reinsurers, and the purposes for reinsurance, there is a correspondingly great variation in the terms of self-administered agreements. For example, there are certain arrangements which are reported on a "pure bulk" basis where only summary information is transferred. These arrangements frequently are used for financial planning reinsurance and are outside the scope of this document.

The agreements to which this document applies are those designed to replace individual cession reinsurer-administered agreements. These are frequently referred to as bordereau or listed-based reinsurance agreements. While the focus is on life insurance, the discussion can be generalized to other forms of insurance.

It is important to remember that self-administration is a two-way street. Ceding companies considering that option should weigh the savings generated by lower reinsurance rates and the additional control over handling against the higher self-administration costs and the added responsibility. For reinsurers, the reduced administration expenses must be weighed against the loss of direct control of the reinsurance processing and the reduced reinsurance rates.

The negotiated reporting requirements of an agreement can play a large role in its ultimate cost to both ceding companies and reinsurers.

CONSIDERING SELF-ADMINISTRATION: THOUGHTS ON SYSTEMS DEVELOPMENT

A ceding company which has never self-administered before or which is considering a revision of an existing self-administered agreement should consider many details in the course of developing the new self-administration system. Naturally, no single list of considerations can be completely comprehensive, particularly when products are evolving as rapidly as today, but the following list is presented to indicate the scope of matters that should be addressed before a ceding company decides to self-administer.

Responsibility

In cession basis reinsurance, the ceding company is responsible for the determination of facts regarding the reinsured policy (such as policy status and premium payments) and the transmission of these facts to the reinsurer. Self-administration requires the ceding company to assume some or all of the reinsurance support functions from the reinsurer (such as billing reports and annual statement information). The ceding company therefore becomes responsible for the timely and accurate reporting of the agreed items. Year-end timing can be especially critical.

EDP Resource Allocation

Developing and maintaining any reinsurance system will require a significant investment of EDP time and money. Many ceding companies find it difficult to assign a high priority to reinsurance systems work. If a company cannot devote sufficient EDP resources to the reinsurance system, it should not be self-administering. This source of expenses should be carefully examined by any ceding company which is considering self-administration. Some ceding companies reduce their EDP requirements by doing extensive systems work on local microcomputers instead of the company main frame. In this case, audit systems or procedures should be developed for the separate microcomputer systems to insure their accuracy.

Development Approach

A system might be more easily developed in piecemeal fashion than by attempting to handle the entire reinsurance process at once. Top priority would normally be given to major blocks of business currently being issued which require reinsurance. The piecemeal approach may be necessary if EDP resources are limited.

System Design

System design should be as flexible as possible in order to adapt to new situations without an inordinate amount of new programming. Adaptability could be required for new types of policies, new coinsurance allowances or YRT rates, and variations in the treatment of factors such as sex-distinct vs. unisex treatment, smoker/nonsmoker vs. composite rates or varying select periods.

Similarly, certain transactions may vary from agreement to agreement in the manner in which they are calculated. The optimal approach is to anticipate as much future variability as possible when building the system without encumbering it with overcomplexity.

Manual Processing

Most systems still require some degree of manual processing. It may not be realistic or cost effective to expect to program every-thing. Attempting to build too ambitious a system can result in delays and cost overruns.

External Constraints

Reinsurance is not governed solely by an agreement between ceding company and reinsurer. State regulations, tax rules and auditing requirements can all constrain a reinsurance arrangement.

Furthermore, such constraints are largely beyond the control of the ceding company and reinsurer and may change with little or no warning which may force changes in the self-administration system. A recent example is the development of the AICPA Statement of Position on Auditing Life Reinsurance.

Detail Reporting

In addition to the obvious reporting situations such as those described in later sections of this document, there are many ancillary issues which must be addressed. For example, how will the system handle the following:

Guidelines for the Reporting of Self-Administered Reinsurance

(1) Multiple inforce policies on the same life with different reinsurers.
(2) Multiple inforce policies on the same life with the same reinsurer.
(3) Multiple reinsurers on the same policy.
(4) Replacements and continuations (such as select term products).
(5) Automatic versus facultative treatment.
(6) The reinsurer's retrocession arrangements, particularly where additional information or different timing is a factor.
(7) Recapture and small amount cancellation rules.
(8) ADB retention (added to or included in basic life retention).
(9) Waiver of premium reinsurance which is frequently coinsured even though the other risks use a different form of reinsurance such as YRT.
(10) Coordination of ceded business with business being assumed from the same reinsurer.
(11) Changes in the retention level.

Errors and Omissions

The errors and omissions clause of a reinsurance contract is designed to address instances where a case has been processed incorrectly by accident. It is not intended to cover situations where a system is known to be deficient when it is put into production. A self-administration system should not be put into production until it is fully checked. The tendency of some ceding companies and reinsurers to negotiate an agreement first and worry about the self-administration later can put a great deal of pressure on the company to rush a system into production.

File Management

Some ceding companies have found that the best course is to build all necessary reinsurance information into a trailer on the policy master file. Others have preferred to set up a separate reinsurance master file which is coordinated with the policy master file. This decision is a fundamental one that should precede any systems work.

The advantage of using the policy master file itself is that handling problems caused by two separate systems can be eliminated. On the other hand, modifying the policy master file and its associated programs can be a more difficult and time-consuming task than creating an independent database. The advantage of setting up a separate reinsurance master is the complete control the reinsurance area has over its structure and operation. A disadvantage is the extra handling required to keep the reinsurance file in agreement with the policy master file.

There is another related consideration. User friendly languages and modern database management techniques may not be readily adaptable to the existing policy master file and programs. In order to take advantage of these advances, it may be necessary to build a separate reinsurance file.

Safeguards

Any production system should have documentation, backup files, hard copy records and security procedures to cope with accidental of intentional damage to the system.

Special Products

Products such as Universal and Variable Life can create different self-administration problems than traditional products. For example, how will the system handle the following:

(1) Varying risk amounts as they affect retention. Options include level retention, proportional retention or a combination of the two.
(2) Varying risk amounts as they affect the net amount at risk. Options include a fixed annual amount, monthly updating or exact adjustment. Reinsurance benefits can be paid for either the amount purchased or the actual amount of loss.
(3) Varying risk amounts that float above and below fixed retention limits.
(4) Varying risk amounts on other policies on the same life whether retained or reinsured.
(5) Varying risk amounts as they affect the establishment of future waiver of premium disability reserves.

(6) An alternate set of reinsurance premiums required for increasing benefit policies (*e.g.*, with a cost of living adjustment).

Report Formats

There are many options, once the above considerations are settled, as to how the information should be presented. The desired form of presentation may in some cases suggest or dictate other parts of the system.

Multiple benefits (*e.g.*, basic life, ADB, waiver of premium, other insured lives) can be reported together on one form or separately. Various transactions (*e.g.*, new issues, renewals, lapses, reduction, conversions) may require different information and different report formats.

Uniform Reporting

When a ceding company works with several reinsurers, it can be very helpful to have all of the reinsurers agree to a uniform reporting format. While this may take some initial work to negotiate, it will be very beneficial to the ceding company in the long run.

Management Reporting

Management reports can be produced relatively efficiently and inexpensively if they are designed as part of the overall self-administration system. They are likely to be neglected by the ceding company if they are not specified as part of the initial system. One useful report, particularly for YRT reinsurance arrangements, is a simple cash flow summary.

Summary

It is not possible to define one approach to the above considerations which is right for all companies. Nevertheless, in setting up a self-administration system, they must all be addressed to the satisfaction of both ceding company and reinsurer.

TRANSMISSION OF INFORMATION

When considering the transmission of information between ceding company and reinsurer, it is clear that a great many options are available to get the job done. This document does not recommend any particular approach. Each ceding company and reinsurer should consider its alternatives before negotiating the methods in which information will be transmitted. The areas which should be addressed include the following.

Mode of Transmission

Although historically information has been transferred almost exclusively by paper, in recent years ceding companies and reinsurers have been exploring other options such as the use of computer tapes, floppy disks and direct computer interfacing over telephone lines.

If one of the more sophisticated methods is contemplated, it must be carefully coordinated with the company which is to receive the data. Many ceding companies and reinsurers are not yet prepared to use or currently discourage the use of these methods.

Frequency and Timing

With the exception of some reporting such as Annual Statement work whose timing requirements are imposed by state regulators, there is room for ceding companies and reinsurers to negotiate whatever terms are appropriate. A typical provision might provide for the monthly or quarterly transfer of reports with a stated deadline (*e.g.*, 30 days after the end of the reporting period).

Format

No generally accepted standard format for reports currently exists, nor is one proposed. In many cases, the selection of the information to be transferred will have a lot to do with the report format. To the extent that electronic data transfer is contemplated, both parties must have a complete understanding of the format used in order for the transfer to be successful.

Summary vs. Detail

In self-administered reinsurance, much reporting is of summary information (*e.g.*, aggregate reserves, total premium due). One of the advantages of self-administration for the reinsurer is the greatly reduced amount of information that it is required to handle.

Under certain circumstances, however, significant amounts of detailed backup may be transferred between ceding company and reinsurer. New issues would normally be listed individually along with any information which the reinsurer needs to handle new issues according to the agreement.

A few general statements may provide some guidance to ceding companies and reinsurers in negotiating an agreement.

First, summary information such as statutory reserves that the ceding company has to calculate whether the business is reinsured or not should normally be reported to the reinsurer. Summary information that would not normally be calculated by the ceding company should be negotiated. An example of this might be a smaller company which does not have to calculate separate tax reserves while its reinsurer does. Obviously, if the ceding company must take on extra tasks, this tends to undermine the cost justification for self-administration.

Second, both detail and backup information should be provided to reinsurers when necessary for reinsurance support. Typical situations where detailed information might be required are new issue listings, premium reports (including new issues, renewals, adjustments and lapses) and audits. Such detailed information should be kept to a minimum and is generally required to support summary information.

Third, whether transmitted or not, the ceding company should maintain sufficiently detailed backup information in its office to provide documentation for claims and reinsurer audits.

Fourth, some reinsurers prefer to calculate certain summary items themselves. In particular, the reinsurer may need to value its statutory reserves on a different basis than the ceding company. In these cases, it is usually sufficient for the ceding company to provide the reinsurer with appropriate policy master file (or reinsurance file) information.

Summary

When developing a self-administration system, major decisions must be made in the transmission of information that are not as clearcut as in the past. The resolution of these questions can significantly affect the cost and ease of administration.

It is preferable to consider these questions openly between ceding company and reinsurer before entering into a self-administered agreement. Otherwise, there is the risk that the ceding company and reinsurer may have significantly different perceptions of how the information will be transferred.

PURPOSES OF SELF-ADMINISTERED REPORTS

Under the traditional individual reporting of cessions the reinsurer would maintain its own records as to policies in force, policy movements and reserves, would generate appropriate premium billings, and thus would usually be in a position to satisfy a wide range of reporting requirements including internal management reports as well as statutory and other external reports. Self-administered reports have to provide essentially the same information.

Statutory Reporting Requirements

Most life reinsurers doing business in the United States have to file an Annual Statement (Convention Blank) with one or more State Insurance Departments. As a minimum, they must have the information necessary to complete the following Annual Statement Schedules and Exhibits.

Exhibit 1 — Premiums and Annuity Considerations
Premiums and commissions, split by first year (other than single), single and renewal, must be reported.

Exhibit 8 — Aggregate Reserve for Life Policies and Contracts
Some reinsurers also are required to make quarterly reports of certain Annual Statement items such as reserves.

Exhibit 11 — Policy and Contract Claims
This is still reported on an individual claim basis by most ceding companies.

Exhibit of Life Insurance — Policy Exhibit
This summary includes the annual transactions on assumed reinsurance business.

Schedule S — Part 3C
This schedule gives data on reinsurance assumed as of December 31. For life reinsurance, amounts in force at end of year, reserves, premiums, and reinsurance payable on paid and unpaid losses must be shown.

Corresponding items will be used by the ceding company in its Annual Statement. These items may not be equal to the items in the reinsurer's statement if there are differences in timing, reserve basis, or valuation method.

Other Reporting Requirements

In addition to providing for statutory reporting requirements as set out above, many reinsurers find it necessary or desirable to obtain basic policy information for other purposes. The uses of such basic data include the following:

(1) Indexing (*e.g.*, alphabetic) policies to identity accumulations of coverage on a given life.
(2) Determining retrocession needs and producing retrocessions.
(3) Verifying the accuracy of self-administered reports (usually on a sampling basis), particularly with respect to premium calculations.
(4) Verifying that automatic binding requirements such as proper retention and treaty coverage are satisfied.
(5) Determining the disposition of facultative cases on file (*i.e.*, the reinsurer needs to close out pending case files).
(6) Verifying the inforce status and any preliminary claim amounts on death claim reimbursement requests from the ceding company.
(7) Developing statistics for internal management purposes such as projections of premiums, inforce, reserves, etc.

(8) Developing comparisons of actual versus expected mortality and persistency.
(9) Developing the reinsurer's GAAP reserves and tax reserves.

ADMINISTRATIVE REPORTING GUIDELINES

This section presents information that is transferred periodically (*e.g.*, monthly or quarterly) from ceding company to reinsurer in order to provide for the basic administration of the reinsurance. Uses of this information include those listed in the previous section under Other Reporting Requirements, items 1-6.

Although reinsurance agreements vary considerably in the specific information transferred, these guidelines list those items commonly reported. The details listed here are developed from list-based or bordereau reinsurance agreements. This is the most common form of self-administration in the amount of information provided.

Significant departures from this approach which transfer less information can be negotiated with reinsurers depending on factors such as the purpose of the agreement, the past experience of the ceding company with self-administration, and the ease of reinsurer audits.

Policy Details Generally Required

The following details are commonly required to be reported in self-administered reinsurance agreements. Where appropriate, items should be split by life, ADB, waiver of premium, and other ancillary benefits.

(1) Policy number of other cession identification. There is some interest in using social security numbers as identification.
(2) Name of insured (last name, first name and middle initial).
(3) Sex.
(4) Date of birth.
(5) Issue age.
(6) Attained age (or policy duration).
(7) Policy date.

Guidelines for the Reporting of Self-Administered Reinsurance 575

(8) The following transactions (with the appropriate details on the number of policies, amount and premium) plus a transaction code or other means to identify them:
   (a)   First year or renewal premiums.
   (b)   New business not previously reported (required when modal first year reinsurance premiums are used).
   (c)   Policies resulting from a continuation of coverage.
   (d)   Policy movements or changes such as
      (i)   Not taken
      (ii)   Surrender
      (iii) Lapse
      (iv) Reinstatement
      (v)   Conversion
      (vi) Increase in amount
      (vii) Decrease in amount
      (viii) Cancellation of reinsurance
      (ix) Recapture
      (x)   Death
      (xi) Expiry
      (xii) Other changes.

(9) Effective date of transaction.
(10) Table rating.
(11) Flat extra amount and term in years. If multiple flat extras are a possibility, the system should allow for it.
(12) Plan name or plan code.
(13) Underwriting or premium class (*e.g.*, smoker/nonsmoker/ preferred or special underwriting).
(14) Amount issued.
(15) Death benefit option (especially for Universal Life or similar plans).

(16) Reinsurance amount (separately for Life, ADB or WP if applicable). An alternative is to show the net amount at risk and the percent reinsured.
(17) Reinsurance premium due (separately for Life, ADB or WP).
(18) Reinsurance commission or allowance.
(19) Net amount due reinsurer or ceding company.
(20) Automatic or facultative indicator.

Additional Policy Details Not Always Required

Some ceding companies and reinsurers find it desirable to provide or obtain certain additional policy details not included in the above list.

(1) Retention indicator (*e.g.*, F=Full retention, P=Partial retention, N=Nothing retained). Provide either an indicator or actual amounts retained for both previous and new issues. This information is required both on a per cession and a per life basis.
(2) Large volume indicator (or a separate listing) where total reinsurance on an insured equals or exceeds a specified amount.
(3) Policy fee.
(4) Currency code.
(5) Amount reinsured at issue.
(6) Premium taxes to be reimbursed.
(7) Cash value to be reimbursed.
(8) Dividend to be reimbursed.
(9) Special risk class (*e.g.*, aviation, military, foreign).
(10) Joint life information.
(11) Policy duration and an indication of whether the duration is based on a previous policy.

One report that is not always required but which many reinsurers find useful is a list of pending facultative cessions.

Form of Administrative Reports

Some self-administered agreements specify separate listings for new issues, renewals, lapses and other adjustments. Others allow for the intermingling of various transactions on fewer listings.

From the reinsurer's point of view, it is usually more convenient to work with separate listings. For example, a new issue listing can be used to add policies to the reinsurer's database or to set up retrocessions. A separate lapse listing can be used to terminate retrocessions.

Another approach is to have only a couple of listings, but provide various subtotals. In general, a minimum of two listing is required:

(1) List of Risks Reinsured (including new issue and renewal information).
(2) List of Adjustments or Changes.

Each report should include appropriate subtotals and totals so that the reinsurer can readily record premiums and commissions in the proper categories (*e.g.*, First Year/Renewal/Single). In addition, subtotals split by new issue and renewal for each transaction type should be provided for policy movements (number of policies and amount).

In addition to the individual policy details set out above, a policy exhibit summary and a premium summary should be provided with each periodic listing. These summaries include totals of all transactions being reported with appropriate subtotals as required for the completing of Annual Statement Exhibit 1 and Exhibit of Life Insurance. Where applicable, corresponding totals for items such as expense allowances, dividends or cash values should be included.

Some method of transmitting information that does not affect premiums (*e.g.*, a name change) should also be included in the discussions between ceding company and reinsurer.

GUIDELINES FOR STATEMENT REPORTING

As was discussed earlier, one of the reinsurance support activities that is assumed to some degree by a self-administering ceding company is that of calculating statutory Annual Statement information for the reinsurer. In addition, there may be quarterly statements or GAAP statements prepared by the reinsurer for which it requires information.

In general, the ceding company has a clear responsibility to provide accurate and timely information for statutory statements. To the extent that reinsurers desire additional information for non-statutory purposes (*i.e.*, GAAP statements or internal management reports), these additional requests should be specifically discussed by the ceding company and reinsurer as a part of the negotiation process.

In some instances, reinsurers are willing to work from inforce files or other sources to generate some or all of the GAAP and statutory reports that are required.

A further question that should be agreed upon by the ceding company and reinsurer is how the various due and unpaid items listed below will be treated. In many cases, the emphasis is placed on "unusual" situations where the transactions are significantly past due. The more typical situations where there are simply timing differences between the ceding company and the reinsurer are not reported as due and unpaid.

Operating Statement Items

For the most part, the information necessary to complete Operating Statement items is available from the transactions made throughout the year. Exhibit 1 shows premiums, dividends, reinsurance expense allowances and reinsurance commissions. Exhibit 11 shows claims. Except where affected by due and unpaid items, this information is obtained directly from the paid entries to the reinsurer's accounting system. The ceding company normally does not do any special report of these items at year end.

Balance Sheet Items

These items represent the bulk of the extra statement reporting required. They can be grouped into two categories: the reinsurer's share of ceding company assets and liabilities, and due and unpaid adjustments to the reinsurer's paid accounts.

Reinsurer's Share of Assets and Liabilities

(1) *Reserves (Exhibit 8).* The reinsurer's share of any ceding company Exhibit 8 reserve is reported here. In addition to statutory reserves, some agreements may require the transfer of tax and/or GAAP reserves. It is also possible that some sort of detailed master file information is required in addition to, or in lieu of, summary information. This should all be negotiated between the ceding company and reinsurer.

(2) *Dividend Liability.* This is usually reported if the rein-surer participates in dividends.

(3) *Policy Loan Asset.* This is reported if the reinsurer participates in policy loans.
(4) *Deferred Premium Asset.* This is reported if the reinsurer participates in modal premiums.

Due and Unpaid Adjustments

(1) *Due and Unpaid Reinsurance Premiums.* As with the other due and unpaid items, the ceding company and reinsurer should agree on standards for declaring a premium payment due and unpaid.
(2) *Due and Unpaid Reinsurance Allowances or Commissions.*
(3) *Due and Unpaid Mean Reserve Transfer.* This is applicable to modified coinsurance reserve transfers.
(4) *Amounts Recoverable on Paid or Unpaid Losses.* This represents those claims that the ceding company has identified as payable by the reinsurer. The amount is split into claims paid by the ceding company and claims not yet paid (including claims in course of settlement).
(5) *Due and Unpaid Experience Refund.* Normally the reinsurer would perform this calculation and report the result to the ceding company.

Exhibit of Life Insurance (Policy Exhibit)

If this type of statement is prepared with every periodic statement as discussed previously, there will be little reporting required other than adding together the routine reports. If not, then some agreements provide for such an exhibit to be transferred at year end.

Some additional Policy Exhibit information may be requested by the reinsurer, specifically a split of Industrial and Ordinary insurance for dividend and other paid up additions, a split of term and whole life, a split of participating and non-participating insurance, and breakdowns of Credit and Group policies in several categories.

Statement of Ceding Company Actuarial Review

Any use of these statements should be discussed and agreed to by both the ceding company and the reinsurer. Their is no required use of this type of statement by any regulatory or professional body.

The Statement of Ceding Company Actuarial Review provides the reinsurer with a source of documentation to satisfy its auditors. Furthermore, it assures the reinsurer of appropriate ceding company review of the reported numbers.

From the ceding company point of view, completion of the Statement of Ceding Company Actuarial Review should not be a problem if the ceding company's numbers are reasonable. If not, the need to sign it might provide some incentive to the ceding company to improve its method of calculation.

The purpose of the Statement of Ceding Company Actuarial Review is not to cause second guessing and professional review of the actuaries completing the form. Actual professional standards on self-administered reinsurance have not been proposed, nor is there any expectation that they will be. Reinsurers simply want to rely on the normal professional competence and standards of an actuary who has reviewed the reported numbers.

GAAP Breakdowns of Inforce

Many reinsurers report on a GAAP as well as statutory basis. Those that do have developed a variety of approaches to obtaining inforce breakdowns for calculating deferred acquisition costs and related items. The three most common approaches are for the reinsurer to (a) calculate inforce breakdowns from the reinsurer's own inforce file, (b) ask the ceding company to calculate such a breakdown on the ceding company files, and (c) obtain an inforce file from the ceding company upon which the reinsurer can do its own breakdowns. The reinsurer might request additional information such as annual gross premium with the inforce breakdowns.

The three options result in varying degrees of timeliness, accuracy and control for the reinsurer as well as a varying amount of work for both parties. All three should be considered in entering a self-administration arrangement.

Auditing Requirements

Auditors are more concerned about reinsurance transactions today than has been the case in past years. A set of reporting and record-keeping requirements can be imposed on any reinsurance agreement by the auditing environment as it changes over time. The guidelines discussed in this document regarding all three types of reporting will be affected over time by changes in auditing standards.

A document that should be reviewed carefully by all ceding companies and reinsurers is the AICPA Statement of Position on Auditing Life Reinsurance which was published in November 1984.

GUIDELINES FOR STATISTICAL REPORTING

This section outlines the policy-level data needed by a reinsurer of self-administered life reinsurance business in other to conduct basic experience studies and analyses. This includes small scale studies of individual ceding companies by individual reinsurers and also large scale studies such as those sponsored by the Society of Actuaries. Topics often studied include lapse experience, mortality experience and overall financial results. Most of the data items needed for experience studies and statistical reporting are also needed for basic administrative and annual statement reporting. A few additional data items allow the reinsurer to perform additional analyses that have great potential value to both the reinsurer and the ceding company.

Although self-administered reinsurance business offers a number of advantages, one unfortunate disadvantage is that it has been difficult, if not impossible, to conduct experience studies on such business. This is because the reinsurer has not had sufficient data to perform such studies. Even in situations where the reinsurer has had sufficient data, often it has not been in a particularly usable form so that the studies would have had to be performed manually at a prohibitively high expense.

Ceding companies benefit in a number of ways if reinsurers are able to conduct experience studies. For example, some companies are unable to do their own experience studies. Analysis of their experience by a reinsurer, even if the analysis applies only to reinsured business, can provide helpful insights. In addition, industry risk classification practices seem to be under increasing scrutiny from regulators. Only reinsurers and very large direct writing companies have enough experience on various impaired lives to help support underwriting practices. But industry impairment mortality studies can be done on self-administered reinsurance business only if ceding companies are able to provide the necessary data.

Finally, and perhaps most important, experience studies enable reinsurers to establish more accurate pricing assumptions. In the long run, the use of more accurate pricing assumptions by reinsurers will mean lower reinsurance rates for ceding companies, since uncertainty in pricing assumptions requires larger contingency margins (or more conservative assumptions).

It is important to note that a reinsurer wishing to conduct experience studies on self-administered business faces two obstacles. First, the reinsurer must obtain the necessary data from the ceding company. Second, the reinsurer must obtain the data in a form compatible with its automated file maintenance and study systems. As mentioned earlier, the cost of conducting manual experience studies is probably prohibitive. The same is true of manually inputting all of the information from paper reports. All this points to the necessity of retransmitting administrative data in a different format suitable for studies.

A uniform format for reporting data on self-administered business would greatly facilitate the transmission process; however, no such format currently exists. The same considerations apply on an even larger scale when considering industry studies.

The types of data that are needed for statistical studies include the following:

(1) Identification information which allows for a clear description of the business being studied. This data is also useful in audit situations.
(2) Experience information (*e.g.*, deaths, lapses, amounts at risk) which is necessary for the study itself.
(3) Segmentation information (*e.g.*, impairment, line of business, smoker/nonsmoker) which allows the study results to be broken down by various factors.
(4) Special characteristics of the ceding company or the business which allow results to be specifically tailored to the business and which allow for the meaningful comparison and combination of results of various ceding companies and blocks of business.
(5) Policy change information which allows for the calculation of exposure data. Depending on the accuracy desired for the study, this type of information might be used very extensively or not at all.
(6) Expected results which enable actual vs. expected calculations to be made.

Guidelines for the Reporting of Self-Administered Reinsurance 583

Normally information which is being collected for studies is collected on a current year basis. For this reason, a reinsurer and ceding company might agree to regularly transfer only certain basic information for routine reinsurer studies. In special situations more substantial data might be transferred to do more extensive studies or to participate in a Society of Actuaries study.

The following data items are needed for statistical studies.

A. Summary Information
    (1) Client identification
    (2) Age basis
    (3) Type of reinsurance
    (4) Reinsurance agreement number

B. Information also Required for Administrative or Statement Reporting
    (1) Policy number
    (2) Primary insured's name
    (3) Primary insured's date of birth
    (4) Primary insured's sex
    (5) Primary insured's issue age
    (6) Issue date
    (7) Amount issued by ceding company
    (8) Amount reinsured*
    (9) Plan of insurance*
    (10) Death benefit option
    (11) Automatic or facultative indicator
    (12) Retention indicator (full, reduced, or none)
    (13) Risk classification (preferred, nonsmoker, smoker, standard, table rating, etc.)*
    (14) Flat extra per thousand,* and term in years
    (15) Policy status (premium paying, paid up, nonforfeiture option, terminated, etc.) and effective date
    (16) Termination type (cancellation, not taken, conversion, lapse, surrender, death, recapture, expiry, maturity) and effective date
    (17) Amount of accidental death benefit reinsured*
    (18) Amount of waiver of premium reinsured*

(19) Source (replacement, conversion, rollover, new business, etc.)
(20) Activity type (reinstatement, change in issued age, age, rating, plan, amount, or status) and effective date
(21) Currency code

C. Information Required only for Experience Analysis
   (1) Underwriting basis (guaranteed issue, simplified issue, nonmedical, paramedical, or medical)
   (2) Primary impairment code

*Include effective date if different from issue date (line 6)

A striking feature of the list of data items is that only two of them are needed strictly for experience studies. All other items are already needed for another reason. Thus supporting experience studies requires very little additional data from the ceding company.

Unfortunately, many ceding companies do not keep this information on any existing database. This should be considered as yet another matter for negotiation between ceding company and reinsurer when self-administration is being contemplated.

One point that cannot be overemphasized is that the reinsurer needs data in a form (disk or tape) compatible with its file maintenance and study systems. With the information in the proper form, the reinsurer is able to build automated records with historical information that can be used to analyze activity for a variety of time periods. Without the information, the industry, both ceding companies and reinsurers, risks running short of supporting data when it seems to be needed more than ever before.

With good planning and cooperation between ceding companies and reinsurers, it appears quite possible to improve the effectiveness of self-administered reinsurance without taking away the ability to perform valuable experience studies.

Guidelines for the Auditing of Administration and Reporting of Individual Life Reinsurance Assumed

INTRODUCTION

This paper is a sequel to the *Guidelines for the Reporting of Self-Administered Reinsurance* dated January 1, 1986, and includes guidelines which are intended to apply to the administration and reporting of individual life reinsurance which is covered by a treaty or other written agreement between the ceding company and reinsurer. In the absence of a written agreement setting out the terms and conditions of reinsurance, the rights and responsibilities of the parties to the reinsurance may be so unclear that an audit as considered in this paper might be inappropriate.

Prior to the 1980's it was very rare for reinsurers to perform on-site audits of the records of ceding companies. For a variety of reasons, it is becoming increasingly common for such audits to be performed.

This paper includes a brief review of some of the developments which led to the need to conduct on-site audits. In addition, some suggestions as to the scope of audit are included along with some ideas on how to make the process efficient for both the ceding company and audit team.

Reviews of surplus relief or other financial reinsurance arrangements are outside the scope of this paper. Likewise, audits of activities such as underwriting which require special expertise and techniques not applicable to audits of administration and reporting are not covered by this paper.

A properly conducted audit should be beneficial to both the ceding company and the reinsurer(s) conducting the audit. Through such a process, each of the parties should become more familiar with the needs of the other and the problems encountered in trying to meet those needs. One anticipated result is a strengthening of the once traditional "gentlemen's agreement" nature of the reinsured/reinsurer relationship.

TRADITIONAL METHOD OF ADMINISTRATION

Until recently, most ordinary life reinsurance in North America was administered under a traditional individual cession basis. The ceding company sent the reinsurer an individual "formal cession" or "application for reinsurance" documenting the details of each risk for which was sought. In turn, the reinsurer created a "reinsurance guarantee" or "reinsurance certificate" which was sent to the ceding company as written evidence of acceptance of the risk by the reinsurer.

The reinsurer maintained its own records as to risks reinsured based on the details contained in the formal cessions received from ceding companies. With this basis of administration, reinsurers rarely found it necessary to inspect the records of ceding companies for a variety of reasons including the following:

(1) The reinsurer sent monthly premium statements which were expected to be reviewed by the ceding company to identify any cases which had lapsed or been amended;

(2) Annual in force and reserve listings would typically be sent to each ceding company for comparison with its records to assure that the reinsurer was carrying appropriate cessions in force;

(3) Except for certain requirements, such as jumbo limits, formal cession details normally permitted the reinsurer to verify that treaty provisions were being met as to qualification for automatic cession, etc. (*e.g.*, letter of alphabet, amount retained, plan of insurance, mortality classification); and

(4) Facultative cessions were documented by a formal exchange of documents to support the reinsurer's acceptance of risk.

Reinsurer's concerns about ceding companies' internal controls over reinsurance ceded are minimal under the traditional individual cession basis of administration for reasons set out above. They are not, however, nonexistent.

It may well be that a ceding company whose reinsurance is administered solely on an individual cession basis will require an audit. The need for such an audit may become evident in a variety of ways (*e.g.*, from late-reported transactions or details of a claim). Specialized audits such as claims or underwriting audits which are not considered in this paper may be little affected by the basis of administration.

DEVELOPMENT OF THE NEED OF AUDITS

Self-Administration

Self-administration of reinsurance ceded has become very common in recent years. Several reinsurers have reported that over 50% of their business in force is self-administered by ceding companies, and the proportion seems to be increasing. Some of the factors influencing the shift to self-administration are as follows:

(1) The development of flexible-premium, variable-benefit products resulted in reinsurance administration by traditional methods becoming unwieldy;
(2) The development of interest-sensitive products led to more sophisticated data processing systems for policy administration, with increased capabilities to provide reinsurance reporting as a by-product of routine processing;
(3) Premium rate levels have continually declined in recent years, putting pressure on insurers and reinsurers to price for ever lower per-unit expenses; and
(4) Reinsurers sometimes provided more attractive allowances to ceding companies who agreed to self-administer their reinsured business. This is becoming less common, largely because both

ceding companies and reinsurers are finding that self-administration may not be as efficient and cost-effective as it was once thought to be.

The widespread shift to self-administration of reinsurance resulted in the transfer of considerable control over various reporting activities from reinsurers to ceding companies. The reinsurer may not maintain a database for individual risks reported on a self-administered basis. Ceding companies find that they are not always able to provide information on individual risks in a format consistent with the reinsurer's needs. The result is that reinsurers typically have somewhat limited access to the details of individual risks.

Another effect of the changes in administration is that reinsurers have lost some control over the timeliness of their own reporting because they may have to wait until reports are received from ceding companies before their own reports can be prepared.

Other Factors

Naturally, reinsurers have always been interested in the timeliness, completeness, and accuracy of the details of reinsurance assumed. Prudent business judgment dictates that a reinsurer take reasonable steps to assure that adequate information is received from ceding companies or other responsible parties such as brokers and intermediaries.

Besides the shift to self-administration, other factors have led reinsurers to expand their activities to assure that the internal controls of ceding companies (as they affect reinsurance ceded) are adequate. One of the main factors has been the increase in complexity of placing reinsurance; some of the reasons for this are as follows:

(1) Reinsurers may differ by plan and/or pricing classification;
(2) Reinsurers may change over time for a given plan as treaties are renegotiated;
(3) Exchange or replacement programs have led to confusion about how to reinsure replacement polices;
(4) Extreme price competition among reinsurers has led some companies to reduce their retention limits on selected (typically term) plans; and

(5) Rapid development of new products (*e.g.*, interest-sensitive plans, cost-of-living adjustments, flexible- or indeterminate-premium plans or variable life plans) has outstripped the ability of ceding companies to get administrative systems in place to support these products so that, in many cases, reinsurance administration has received little or no support.

Because of the complexity of placing reinsurance, the subject of controls over reinsurance ceded or assumed has attracted attention from auditors, regulators, and shareholders. This has resulted in actions by the following groups:

(1) The American Institute of Certified Public Accountants (AICPA) issued in November 1984, a *Statement of Position* (SOP) *on Auditing Life Reinsurance*;

(2) The National Association of Insurance Commissioner (NAIC) became increasingly interested in various aspects of reinsurance and established a Reinsurance and Antifraud Task Force which developed a Model Law on Credit for Reinsurance. In addition, the NAIC has developed a model regulation on surplus relief agreements and has formed a Study Group on Life Reinsurance that reports to the Accounting Practices and Procedures Task Force; and

(3) The foreign Corrupt Practices Act of 1977 amended the Securities Exchange Act of 1934 to require all publicly held companies to maintain accurate records and adequate systems of internal control. This places an added burden on the management of those publicly traded insurance companies who engage in significant reinsurance activities. Those insurers who assume business from a ceding company under self-administration arrangements appear to have an added obligation to ensure that the controls used by the cedent in preparation of the reports are adequate.

The AICPA's SOP on *Auditing Life Reinsurance*, in conjunction with the other factors discussed above, focuses considerable attention on reinsurance arrangements and seems to make it almost mandatory for a reinsurer to perform on-site audits of some ceding companies. For example, paragraph 22 of the SOP states that "The absence of adequate procedures by the assuming company to obtain assurance regarding the accuracy and reliability of data received from the ceding company, or the lack of reasonable assurance that such procedures are in use and operating as planned, may constitute a material weakness in the assuming company's system of internal accounting control."

Typically, a reinsurer's large accounts, especially those which are self-administering reinsurance ceded, will most likely be candidates for on-site audits based on SOP. Other reasons to audit may include recent adoption of self-administration by a particular company, prior audit experience, system changes, or changes in management or staff.

TERMINOLOGY: AUDIT OR REVIEW

The public accountant views the terms 'audit' and 'review' very specifically. An audit is an examination of financial statements in accordance with generally accepted auditing standards for the express purpose of giving an opinion of the fair and consistent presentation of those statements. A review has been defined by the Auditing Standards Division of the AICPA in their *Statement of Standards for Accounting and Review Services* issued in December 1978, and is significantly narrower in scope.

The procedures discussed in the writing of this paper are designed so that they may be performed by the staffs of the insurance companies involved and as such are not a true audit. Auditing techniques, however, are useful for helping to determine that all parties are properly complying with the terms of the reinsurance agreement.

A ceding company being audited should discuss any concerns it may have about terminology with the reinsurer conducting the audit. Naturally, the parties involved may agree upon whatever terminology convention they find most acceptable. Nevertheless, for convenience, the term "audit" is used in this paper to refer to the overall process of inspecting a company reinsurance procedures, controls, and records.

PURPOSE OF AUDIT

So far, we have described the general concerns which led to an increased interest in having reinsurers perform on-site audits of ceding companies. Each reinsurer wants to be sure that it is receiving all the reinsurance it is supposed to be getting, but *only* that which it should receive, that the reinsurance received is proper, that the correct premiums and allowances are paid, and that claims are paid only on valid, in force cases. Some specific goals for the audits are set out in this section.

(1) Ascertain that all transactions are accurately recorded, properly values, and reported in a timely manner;

(2) Verify that both the ceding company and the reinsurer have a mutual understanding of the terms and conditions of the applicable treaty covering the reinsured policy;

(3) Educate the reinsurer as to the day-to-day problems encountered by the ceding company in attempting to comply with treaty terms and conditions;

(4) Review the ceding company's internal controls to assure that treaty terms and conditions are being followed;

(5) Where confusion exists, clarify the ceding company's interpretation of treaty terms by reviewing the application to specific cases;

(6) Assist the ceding company by providing a relatively objective review of systems and procedures by an interested party;

(7) Establish a dialogue between ceding company and reinsurer to provide a framework for resolving misunderstandings which may arise from time to time;

(8) Satisfy the management needs of both the ceding company and reinsurer to gain reasonable assurance that appropriate systems, procedures, and controls governing reinsurance administration are in place; and

(9) Satisfy external auditors and regulators that the reinsurance relationship is functioning as intended, with appropriate controls to identify and correct administrative problems in a timely fashion. These controls should be of both a detective and a preventive nature.

Most reinsurer audits will pertain to reinsurance administration and will be general in nature. Occasionally, it may be necessary for the reinsurer to conduct a special purpose audit not covered by the guidelines in this paper. The scope of audit and audit procedures employed should be tailored to the particular purpose of such an audit.

SCOPE OF AUDIT

The reinsurer's audit is designed to permit a reasonable evaluation of a ceding company's internal controls over the receipt and initial setup of cases, including changes, and the related determination of the need for reinsurance. Although the audit will normally be restricted to an examination of ceding company records, systems and procedures which have a direct impact on the administration of reinsurance ceded, this may involve almost every aspect of the ceding company's policy issue and administration systems as well as claims administration. Where transactions affecting reinsurance involve processing with an EDP system, testing of input, processing, and output may be necessary.

Because of the potential exposure of the reinsurer due to actions or inactions of the ceding company's agency force, some reinsurers will want to review the ceding company's agency operations. The reinsurer will have an interest in the ceding company's attitude toward an agent that makes significant mistakes or intentionally takes positions adverse to the company and whether agents are required to maintain errors and omissions coverages.

It has to be appreciated that not all ceding companies and reinsurers will agree upon the interpretations to be given to specific treaty wordings. Similarly, there is not yet universal agreement in the life insurance/reinsurance industry as to how certain transactions are to be administered.

Because of the differing practices adopted by ceding companies and reinsurers, the scope of audit set out below may need to be modified in some respects to suit a particular situation. For example, the criteria for distinguishing new business from continuation policies may need to be worked out between the ceding company and reinsurer.

Most reinsurers do not want their audit teams to be put in the position of negotiating terms or conditions of reinsurance. Thus, the auditors typically are not authorized to make final decisions as to how particular transactions should be handled or how treaty terms are to be interpreted.

Accordingly, if a finding involves a financial adjustment or a significant question as to interpretation of treaty terms, the audit team will be expected to defer to its management to evaluate the situation and discuss the matter with the appropriate members of the management of the ceding company.

Specific items to be reviewed will typically include the following:

Reinsurance Agreements

(1) Provisions are maintained on a current basis
(2) Ceding company's and reinsurer's agreement files are consistent
(3) Essential details are disseminated fully and in a timely fashion to employees responsible for reinsurance administration

New Business Policies Requiring Reinsurance

(1) Issued only in accordance with written company guidelines
    (a) Issued per underwriting classification (including any required Aviation Exclusion or other endorsement)
    (b) Issued in accordance with the proposed insured's signed Application for Insurance
    (c) Initial premium received
    (d) Appropriate nonsmoker or other declarations signed by proposed insured
    (e) Conditional receipt rules begin followed
(2) Allocated appropriately to each reinsurer
    (a) Routed to appropriate person or department for processing
    (b) Identified whether or not overall retention is exceeded on the current policy
    (c) Confirmed that proper retention amount is kept (*e.g.*, for automatic reinsurance requirements)
    (d) Recorded properly in reinsurance inforce, premium billing, and valuation files

(e) Followed facultative submission requirements (and any additional requirements of the reinsurer)
(f) Followed automatic and jumbo limits
(g) Reported to correct reinsurer in a timely manner

Changes to Policies In Force

(1) Reinsurer notified in a timely manner
(2) Conversions, exchanges, reissues, rollovers, reinstatements, reentries, or other changes reported in accordance with the reinsurance treaty. Such changes are commonly categorized as either
   (a) *Continuation* to be reported to the original reinsurer even if that reinsurer is not a reinsurer for current new business; or
   (b) *New business* to be reported to the current reinsurer for the plan of insurance.
   Questions which may be involved in deciding whether a particular policy qualifies as new business for reinsurance purposes are as follows:
      (i) Was appropriate underwriting performed?
      (ii) Is the new policy unmodified as to suicide and incontestability?
      (iii) Was a full first year commission paid to the agent?
      (iv) Was any required nonsmoker declaration or other preferred risk documentation obtained?
(3) Appropriate reinsurer approvals obtained (*e.g.*, the reinsurer may need to underwrite reentries, reinstatements, or increases in amount)
(4) Appropriate endorsements included in continuation policies are
   (a) Suicide provision
   (c) Incontestability provision
   (d) Other (*e.g.*, Aviation Exclusion)
(5) Policy changes supported by appropriate forms signed by policy owner
(6) Termination documented
(7) Changes to Extended Term Insurance (ETI) or Reduced Paid UP (RPU) properly reported to the reinsurer, and consistent with policy form and any policy loans outstanding (the needs here will vary by type of treaty and whether or not the reinsurer participates in policy loans or surrender values)

(8) Contractual increases or decreases, such as COL adjustments, applied correctly
(9) Recaptures made according to the treaty

Claims (may be evaluated prior to audit)

(1) Prompt notification given to the reinsurer
(2) Appropriate details supplied to reinsurer
(3) Reinsurer's approval obtained (if required) before claim is settled

Valuation Reports

(1) All inforce reinsured cessions are included in the reserve listing
(2) Totals agree with reports to reinsurer
(3) Valuation factors and methods are appropriate (different factors of methods may apply to reinsurer)

Reinsurance Billings

(1) Proper calculation of premiums, allowances, etc.
(2) Proper payment of renewal premiums of allowances
(3) Timely payments to reinsurers
(4) Adequate controls on cash payments to assure that payments are consistent with amounts reported as due
(5) Adequate control of accounts receivable or payable items.

Although Financial or Management Control Reports may be outside the scope of an administrative audit, some reinsurers will find it convenient and appropriate to obtain and review such documents as part of the audit. The reports to be reviewed might include any or all of the following:

(1) Insurance Department Examination Report
(2) Independent Auditor's Report
(3) Internal Audit Reports
(4) Letter relating to the adequacy of internal accounting controls filed with regulatory authorities
(5) Annual Statement (Convention Blank)
(6) NAIC Early Warning Test
(7) GAAP Financial Statement

PREPARATION FOR AUDIT

Many steps can be taken by both the ceding company and reinsurer prior to the on-site audit to help minimize the amount of time spent in the offices of the ceding company. By performing as many of the required steps as possible in advance, the disruption of the ceding company's routine and staff can be kept to a minimum.

Setting the Audit Date

The date and duration of the audit should be set well in advance. For the convenience of both the ceding company and reinsurer, a lead time of as much as two or three months could be desirable.

It is important to time the audit so that appropriate ceding company personnel will be present. To the extent possible, the timing of the audit should be at the convenience of the ceding company. Factors for which allowances must be made include valuation periods, the extent of the audit, and vacations.

Reinsurers may find it desirable to establish an audit date by informal discussions between the reinsurer's marketing representative and appropriate personnel at the ceding company. Once the date has been set, reinsurer personnel involved in the audit may then take over and follow up with various details involved in conducting the audit.

Audit Preparations by the Ceding Company and the Reinsurer

The reinsurer's audit team will need to be selected. Some reinsurers have staff permanently assigned to do reinsurance audits as part of the internal audit function (typically including CPA's under the direction of the President, Treasurer, Controller, or possibly the Board of Directors). Such staff may need to be augmented by personnel drawn from other areas of the company.

For example, it is common to include individuals from the reinsurance Administration and Actuarial staff. Depending upon the nature of the audit and any special problems encountered or anticipated, it may be appropriate to include Claims or Underwriting staff on the audit team.

It is also important that the reinsurer send in writing to the ceding company the audit objectives as well as the items and procedures they will want to review. This type of communication should minimize the confusion and discomfort the ceding company may have about being audited.

The reinsurer may find it helpful to prepare a summary of the basic details of the treaties covering the business to be audited. It could be helpful to send a copy of such a summary to the ceding company for their review. Not only is this a possible helpful tool for the ceding company, it may facilitate early identification of any areas of misunderstanding of treaty terms.

The audit process can be further facilitated if the ceding company will send the audit team any written documentation setting out the general procedures, work flow land controls of the ceding company applicable to reinsurance administration. This will permit the team to focus more quickly on details and take up less of the coordinator's or other ceding company staff's time in becoming familiar with the administration system.

It is also helpful to have the ceding company send any necessary Financial and Management Control Reports to the audit team for its review prior to the on-site audit.

Some of the audit steps are best performed in the offices of the reinsurer prior to the on-site audit. For example, it may be possible for the reinsurer to verify most calculations of amounts at risk, premiums, allowances, bonuses, and chargebacks from the reports submitted by the ceding company.

Such a review should identify any systematic errors (EDP, or otherwise) that may be occurring. This early identification of calculation or other systematic problems will enable the audit team to quickly focus on problem areas during the on-site audit.

Another way to speed up the actual audit process is for the ceding company to give the audit team a set of sample forms identifying the fields which are relevant to reinsurance. The set could include, for example, various forms likely to be encountered in the policy files such as policy status sheets (showing status of policy according to the computer records) or underwriting worksheets showing the status of prior policies and the allocation of reinsurance on a current policy.

Depending on audit objectives, a sample of policy files to be reviewed should be made by the reinsurer prior to the audit. Such a sample would typically be drawn from self-administered reports submitted by the ceding company and might include the following information.

(1) A variety of plans of insurance
(2) Different years of issue
(3) Different transaction types such as
    (a) new business,
    (b) terminations,
    (c) reissues, reinstatements, exchanges, conversions, etc.,
    (d) increases and decreases in amount, and
    (e) claims (Life, WPD, ADB, etc.)

Most reinsurers make some effort to select the sample on a random basis. In addition, the sample size may be determined statistically based upon the amount of business covered by the treaty(ies) according to the ceding company reports. Naturally, if particular problems have been noted in the self-administered reports or on individual cessions, the sample selection may include more of the transactions in question than would arise from a purely random selection process.

Working exclusively from reports submitted by the ceding company may permit confirmation that reported cases are administered properly but cannot establish whether or not all cases are being properly reported. Accordingly, most audits will involve further samples selected on-site, possibly including a sample of cases drawn from the direct insurance master records of the ceding company.

If possible, the samples should be available in both alphabetical and numerical (by policy number) order. Some companies find it more convenient to access their files alphabetically while others prefer to utilize policy number.

The policy sample should be sent to the ceding company at least one or two weeks in advance of the audit. This gives the ceding company adequate time to pull the policy files requested (or any associated policy files which might affect the placement of reinsurance) without significantly disrupting normal operations.

Logistical Considerations

Audit Team. It is convenient for both the ceding company and reinsurer to know who will be involved in the audit. Where possible, the reinsurer should give the ceding company advance notice of who will be on the audit team and identify the team manager for purposes of coordination between the ceding company and the audit team.

Ceding Company Coordination. Similarly, the audit team needs to know with whom it will be working at the ceding company. It is expected that contacts with ceding company personnel will be coordinated through one individual assigned as coordinator and who would also provide access to policy registers (*e.g.*, new issues, terminations, changes, claims) or other records as needed.

The audit team should make it a point to know the name, location, and telephone number of the ceding company's coordinator and respect the wishes of the ceding company which may require that all staff contact be made through the coordinator. Ideally there should be a deputy coordinator to be contacted in case the principal coordinator is unavailable (*e.g.*, due to sickness or other business).

Access to Office. It will be necessary for the team members to know the usual office routine. For example, they will probably want to try to adhere to normal office hours. It may, however, be necessary for them to work before or after hours in order to get the job done. Accordingly, they need to know if work outside normal hours is acceptable to the ceding company and, if so, what special arrangements need to be made.

If there are special security procedures to be followed, the team will need to be informed. There may be a need for security passes or for the team to have someone accompany them while on the ceding company premises (either at all times or outside normal office hours).

Access to Records/Files. It is important for the audit team to know the forms in which the ceding company records are kept (*e.g.*, microfilm, microfiche, paper file, on-line computer record) land to have appropriate means of accessing those records (*e.g.*, microfilm reader, microfiche reader, video display terminal). If required access devices are not available, the audit team will have to provide its own.

The ceding company may wish to limit the degree to which the audit team has access to records. There may also be some concerns about the audit team making hard copies of ceding company records. These issues should be resolved early on, preferable long before the audit commences, so that there will be no misunderstanding about these important activities.

Other Items. Other minor points ideally should be addressed in advance of the audit. Most audit teams expect to provide their own usually portable) calculators; however, desk calculators are most convenient to use and some ceding companies choose to make them available to the audit team.

The audit team will have frequent need to contact the coordinator. For this reason it would be most convenient to have access to at least one telephone.

Naturally, the audit team will expect to make its own arrangements as to accommodations, meals, and travel. In special circumstances, the ceding company may find it desirable to advise the audit team.

PERFORMANCE OF THE AUDIT

Initial On-Site Meeting

It is important for the on-site audit process to begin with a meeting of the audit team with ceding company personnel who will be involved with the review process so they can get to know each other. In addition, a discussion about how the audit will proceed in line with the audit objectives sent earlier and the basic steps to be taken will help to alleviate any misgivings about the review process.

At this time, the logistical considerations can be reviewed and the team will be assigned to a work space. In order to acquaint the audit team with the environment in which they will be working, some ceding company coordinators may find it worthwhile to give the team a brief guided tour of their offices or other facilities.

This initial meeting is probably a good time to set up a closing conference to be held at the end of the on-site audit. Naturally, the duration of the audit may not be fixed, so the meeting time may have to be revised as circumstances warrant.

Interviews with Ceding Company Personnel

Interviews with ceding company reinsurance administrative personnel will help the audit team gain an understanding of the general nature of the reinsurance administration to help gain an understanding of the way the company administers its direct business and evaluates that business for reinsurance administration purposes. These interviews should be controlled by the company coordinator.

Overview of Administrative System

A good starting point for the audit itself is to trace the physical flow of paperwork associated with underwriting and issue of new business. This may be accomplished by reviewing the written work flow provided by the ceding company prior to the audit. Another possibility is to have a "walk-through" of the path followed by various transactions as they relate to ceded reinsurance.

This will usually give the team a good overall picture of how the administration system works in general, and will help them to know where to look for appropriate controls. Some audit teams find it helpful to create a simplified flowchart of the administrative system and have this reviewed by ceding company staff to assure that the audit team's understanding of the system flow is essentially correct. The extent to which such a flowchart is needed depends in part upon the documentation provided by the ceding company.

The basic steps involved in policy issue can be observed in brief. For example, the usage of an alpha index or similar controls for verifying previous in force will be seen in the walk-through should this take place.

Further Sample Selection

Depending upon audit objectives, audit teams may want to select additional samples on-site to supplement those previously selected from the reports submitted by the ceding company. This may include samples drawn from a recent verifiable in force or reserve listing, a new business register, a claims register, or a terminations changes register.

By making these sample selections early in the audit process, the ceding company staff can be assured of having adequate time to retrieve the appropriate policy files or other documentation.

Specific Review Assignments

In order to speed up the review process, audit team members may be assigned specific tasks to be undertaken concurrently. For example, one member may review treaty documentation while others are working on the system flowchart or selecting samples of new business or terminations/changes. The review of claims may also proceed separately from the review of individual policy files from the initial samples.

Peer Review

Insurance/reinsurance transactions have become very complicated in recent years. Some reinsurers have found it helpful to have audit members cross-check each other, at least on a number of cases, to make sure that they agree on their interpretation of the documentation and the application of treaty terms to specific cases and to assure that all recorded notes are both legible and intelligible.

Noting Discrepancies

It is recommended that detailed notes be made of any apparent discrepancies that are found. These will be helpful for further research or for discussion with the company coordinator.

The audit team should review and summarize the types of discrepancies found. This summary will be needed for discussion with the company coordinator, both in the course of the audit and in the closing conference to be held later.

It is desirable for the audit team to thoroughly review its findings in time to permit follow-up of any loose ends before the closing conference begins. It is helpful to have any audit findings summarized in approximately the same order as the scope of audit which itself may be taken as a rough guide for both the closing conference and the audit report.

Closing Conference

It is important to have a "wrap-up" or session of closing conference so that the audit team can discuss its findings with the ceding company. It is strongly recommended that the company coordinator arrange to have as many as possible of the people involved in the audit attend the conference which will help minimize the likelihood that the ceding company will be surprised by any of the findings reported in the audit report.

In addition, it may be that the audit team has misunderstood some documentation or procedure. By reporting and discussing what it perceived as "discrepancies," the audit team assures the ceding company staff of having an opportunity to correct any such misperceptions in a timely fashion.

The conference may also cover any plans the ceding company may have for correcting any discrepancies found or for strengthening internal controls where necessary.

If not already arranged it may, at this time, be decided to whom the audit report or summary letter will be submitted (original or copies). Normally, someone at the ceding company (typically the company coordinator) will want to review a draft audit report or summary letter before a final document is submitted to avoid unnecessary surprises. The final document is typically addressed to the ceding company management.

Other Audit Procedures

Other actions might be taken by some reinsurers. For example, it might be arranged for the reinsurer to obtain information from the ceding company's external auditor about steps taken by the auditor to confirm directly with policyholders information in the ceding company's in force policy files. This could save considerable duplication of work and effort. This information would be obtained through the company coordinator.

If suitable arrangements cannot be made to obtain assurances that the policy files have been adequately confirmed, some reinsurers may want to undertake an independent verification of policyholder information contained in the ceding company files and used as a basis for self-administered reinsurance. Such a measure would be somewhat unusual because the treaty is between the ceding company and the reinsurer who has no direct relationship with the policyholders, and could normally be undertaken only with appropriate ceding company permission and cooperation.

It may also be desirable for the reinsurer's audit team to meet with the ceding company's internal auditors to review the steps they have taken to confirm the adequacy of reinsurance systems and procedures and the reliability of information in the policy files.

AUDIT REPORT

The draft report should be prepared as quickly as possible after the audit. Invariably, some important points found or discussed will not have been reduced to writing; therefore, timely preparation of the audit report will maximize the likelihood that all important findings will be reflected in the report.

Some reinsurers prefer to address the audit report to their own management. They may send a copy of the formal report to the ceding company or, instead, they may send a letter summarizing the findings of audit.

The draft report or summary letter should be submitted to the coordinator of the ceding company for review and comments. There should be some agreement on the time frame for reviewing the draft report.

Once the comments of the ceding company have been reviewed and considered, the audit report can be put in final form. The report should then be submitted as agreed. The distribution of the report needs to be done with the approval of the ceding company.

As a rule, the audit report will stress the findings of the audit and should at least be copied to someone at a senior management level in the ceding company. In some cases, however, it may be appropriate to include reasons why certain things were done so as to avoid unnecessary questions and to put findings in the proper context.

The final audit report will probably contain a disclaimer to clarify that the audit may not necessarily disclose any or all material weaknesses in the ceding company's reinsurance administration systems and that the identification of, or failure to identify, specific problems or errors in any of the policies included in the review does not alter any of the terms or conditions of the governing reinsurance agreements.

FOLLOW-UP TO AUDIT

If the audit is to be of the greatest possible value to both the ceding company and reinsurer, there should be a definite plan for following up the findings and recommendations of the audit. This might involve having the reinsurer's marketing representative keep in touch on a regular basis with the ceding company to ascertain that appropriate steps are being taken to correct any deficiencies, strengthen internal controls, and so on.

Sometimes, audits lead to a need to revise treaty terms or conditions. For example, it may be found that it is not feasible for the ceding company to meet some treaty requirements. If that is the case, it may be possible to change the arrangement to put it on a more workable basis with requirements that the ceding company will be able to fulfill.

ALTERNATIVES TO ON-SITE AUDITS

Ceding companies frequently ask if there is anything they can do to eliminate or minimize the need for audits by reinsurers. For some companies, especially those which reinsure large volumes of reinsurance on a self-administered basis, there will be an ongoing need for reinsurer audits.

The frequency of such audits may, however, be reduced if current audits indicate that the ceding company has adequate procedures and controls to assure that policies requiring or involving reinsurance are properly identified and reported to the reinsurer in a complete, accurate, and timely manner. Obviously, if the company is seen to be doing a very responsible and thorough job in its reinsurance administration, the reinsurer will be inclined to spend its resources auditing other companies where the track record may not be as good. Such a demonstration might be made by sharing a copy of the audit report made by another reinsurer.

Audit Reports

Some reinsurers would be willing to have ceding companies conduct "self-audits" or quality control reviews and report the results to the reinsurer. Another method of supplying this information is through actuarial certification of reserves and in force. These reports would not replace reinsurer audits entirely, but could help reduce the frequency or extent of reinsurer audits by providing assurance that the ceding company has an ongoing program for reviewing its reinsurance administration.

A ceding company might find it helpful to obtain special letters of reports from its external auditors or state examiners covering the ceding company's reinsurance administration. If such letters or reports indicate that the ceding company has adequate internal controls over reinsurance ceded, the reinsurer may be able to defer or even forego an on-site audit.

Each of these sources must be reviewed in the light of the purpose served and the expertise with which each was executed. In any case these audits should not be relied upon solely.

Electronic Data Transfer

At least one reinsurer utilizes a procedure whereby the ceding company supplies the reinsurer with an abbreviated copy (*e.g.*, on magnetic tape) of their entire policy master file. The reinsurer then combines all policies on the same insured, based on name and birth date, and compares the total face amount to the retention of the ceding company as of each policy date.

If the sum of policy amounts is greater than the ceding company's retention and there is no reinsurance indicator, a listing of these policies is then printed out to be checked by the ceding company. If jumbo polices are involved they should be checked to make sure they were submitted facultatively.

If the sum of policy amounts is within the ceding company's retention but there is a reinsurance indicator, this information is also listed and reported to the ceding company. These cases should be checked to reconcile the apparent inconsistency.

If the ceding company denotes reinsurance by reinsurer, it is possible to compare all the policies that are reinsured against the reinsurer's records. The comparison is based on the ceding company's policy number. The reinsurer checks to make sure that each policy shown as reinsured with them is on its reinsurance master file, and any policy on its master file is also shown as an active policy on the ceding company's file. The reinsurer indicates discrepancies for the amount issued by the ceding company, birth date, policy date, and name of insured and reports this information to the ceding company for further investigation and appropriate corrective action.

JOINT-REINSURER OR SHARED AUDITS

There may be situations in which consideration should be given to the possibility of reinsurers sharing in an audit of a ceding company. The most common situation involves reinsurance pools. The audit can take the form of either two or more reinsurers providing personnel to make up a single audit team (joint-reinsurer audit), or one reinsurer undertaking the audit of a ceding company on behalf of all interested reinsurers and supplying the results directly to them (shared audit).

Some of the advantages of joint-reinsurer or shared audits include the following.

(1) Convenience to the ceding company (by reducing the number of on-site audits)
(2) Expense savings, primarily for the reinsurers but, to some extent, for the ceding company as well
(3) Increased likelihood that the several reinsurers will adopt consistent interpretations of treaty wordings which may not have originated with any one of them.

There can be distinct disadvantages to joint-reinsurer or shared audits; some of them are as follows.

(1) There may be issues regarding impermissible sharing of information between competitors (this is probably not significant if the only connections among the reinsurers and the ceding company relate to a common reinsurance pool)
(2) Some reinsurers may not wish to rely upon the standards and care used by another reinsurer conducting an audit

(3) If the lead (or other appointed) reinsurer performs an audit and reports to other reinsurers, there may be issues of (a) liability as to any problem not identified, and (b) disputes with the ceding company as to any negative comments communicated to third parties.

In many cases, the reinsurers may have agreements with the ceding company other than a pool agreement. If so, the reinsurers may have very different points of view about the significance of specific findings. For example, one reinsurer may have an ongoing relationship for reinsuring new business while other reinsurers may have only "runoff" agreements. In addition, some reinsurers may be reluctant to have the specific terms and correspondence, shared freely with other reinsurers.

Given the potentially serious concerns associated with joint-reinsurer or shared audits, such an undertaking should be approached very carefully. Good communication among all the parties involved in such an audit is a must.

The subject of joint-reinsurer or shared audits may, if sufficient interest is identified, be the subject of a separate paper.

Glossary[1]

Accredited Reinsurer

A *reinsurer* which is not licensed in a state may become accredited by showing that it meets the financial conditions of the state; it is licensed in at least one state; it submits to that state's jurisdiction and allows its books and records to be examined; and its directors and management personnel are of acceptable character and experience. A company ceding reinsurance to an accredited *reinsurer* will usually get full financial statement credit for reserves *ceded.*

Acquisition Costs

Expenses incurred by an insurer or *reinsurer* in the process of writing new or renewal business, including producer commissions.

---

[1] An important contribution to this glossary was made by Robert Kaufman, Ardian Gill, and Kirk Roeser, in the form of an earlier glossary of reinsurance terms which they prepared for Gill and Roeser, Inc., 535 Fifth Avenue, New York, NY 10017. We gratefully acknowledge their permission to incorporate that work into this glossary.

Admitted Assets
Cash and investments that meet criteria for liquidity and safety set by the National Association of Insurance Commissioners and by individual state commissioners. Only *admitted assets* are used in measuring the *capacity* and soundness of an insurer. *Non-admitted assets*, such as overdue receivables, are excluded from statutory assets and *surplus*.

Admitted Reinsurance
Reinsurance that is provided by a *reinsurer* licensed or authorized in the jurisdiction in question. *Ceding companies* may automatically take credit in that jurisdiction for *admitted reinsurance*. A *ceding company* may take credit for *non-admitted reinsurance* only if it is secured by a *letter of credit*, a *trust agreement* or *funds withheld* in a form acceptable to the regulators.

Aggregate Limit
The maximum sum of recoveries payable under those reinsurance agreements that provide an overall maximum loss limitation.

Aggregate Retention
An additional *retention* kept net by the *ceding company* of losses otherwise recoverable from the *reinsurer*. Only after the *aggregate retention* is exceeded can the *ceding company* recover from the *reinsurer*.

Alien Reinsurer
A non-U.S. domiciled *reinsurer* writing reinsurance in the U.S.

Alphabet Split
A method of allocating automatic reinsurance among several *reinsurers*. Using this method, each *reinsurer* is assigned a series of letters, and reinsurance is *ceded* based on the first letter of the insured's surname.

Arbitration Clause
A provision in reinsurance agreements that provides for non-judicial settlement of disputes between parties. Generally, each party chooses an arbiter, the arbiters agree on an umpire and these three agree on a resolution of the dispute. Under some clauses, an unsatisfied party may have the option to seek judicial relief following an arbitration finding.

Glossary

ASB
The Actuarial Standards Board is a body of actuaries charged with developing standards of actuarial standards of practice in the United States. ASB number 11 specifically addresses reinsurance transaction.

Assume
To accept or take over a risk, the converse of *cede*.

Assumption
A form of reinsurance under which policy administration and the contractual relationship with the insured, as well as all liabilities, pass to the *reinsurer*; the novation of liability is evidenced by an assumption certificate issued to the insured who, in some jurisdictions, has the right to refuse the change in insurers. See *Indemnity Reinsurance*.

Attachment Basis
A provision in many *stop loss* reinsurance agreements that determines whether, and in what manner, a reinsurance agreement covers a specific loss.

Authorized Reinsurer
A *reinsurer* which is licensed in the *ceding company's* state of domicile is said to be authorized. A company ceding reinsurance to an authorized reinsurer is usually allowed credit on its statutory financial statement for the reserves ceded.

Automatic Reinsurance
A reinsurance agreement under which the *reinsurer* is obligated to accept or *assume* risks which meet certain specific criteria based on the *ceding company's* underwriting.

Binding Limit
The amount of risk over the *ceding company's retention* which can be automatically *ceded* if all other conditions are met.

Bordereaux
A written schedule of insureds, premiums and losses submitted to *reinsurers* under certain types of reinsurance agreements. See *Self-Administration*.

Brokerage Market
Reinsurers who write business through reinsurance *intermediaries* or brokers. *Reinsurers* who do not generally accept such business are referred to as professional or direct *reinsurers*.

Calendar Year YRT
A *YRT* scale where the annual premium is due and payable on January 1 of each calendar year.

Capacity
The amount of *exposure* that a *reinsurer* is willing to accept on a risk, program, line of business or entire book of business.

Captive
An insurance or reinsurance subsidiary of an agent, group of agents, industrial company, trade association, or not-for-profit organization. *Captives* insure or reinsure parent-related business, non-parent business, or both. Though the number of domestic *captives* is increasing, most *captives* are still located in offshore domiciles such as Barbados, Bermuda or the U.K.'s Channel Islands.

Carryover Provisions
A multi-year rating device found in some reinsurance agreements which provides that a loss to *reinsurers* in a given time period may be applied to the results of a previous period (loss carryback) or may be applied to a future period (loss carryforward).

Catastrophe
A disaster involving multiple insureds and/or locations. Hurricanes, tornadoes, explosions and earthquakes are the most common *catastrophe* examples. *Catastrophe* is also sometimes used to designate a single large loss-generally $5,000,000 or more, or an event affecting a minimum number of lives, *e.g.*, three. *Catastrophe* reinsurance indemnifies the *ceding company* for such losses, subject to an agreed *retention, coinsurance,* and maximum limit.

Cede
To transfer an insurance risk from the company originally issuing the policy to another insurance company known as the *reinsurer*.

Glossary

Ceding Commission
The amount paid by the *reinsurer* to the *ceding company* to cover the *ceding company's acquisition costs* and overhead expenses, taxes, licenses and fees, and, perhaps, a share of expected profits, usually expressed as a percentage of the gross reinsurance premium.

Ceding Company
A ceding insurer or a ceding *reinsurer*. A ceding insurer is an insurer which underwrites and issues an original, primary policy to an insured and contractually transfers (cedes) a portion of the risk to a *reinsurer*. A *ceding reinsurer* is *reinsurer* which transfers (cedes) a portion of the underlying reinsurance to a *retrocessionnaire*.

Chargeback
A specified portion of the excess of reinsurance allowances paid over *ceded* premium which the *ceding* company returns to the *reinsurer* in the event of a lapse during a defined period. *Chargebacks* are used to protect the *reinsurer* in the event of early lapse.

Coinsurance
Indemnity life reinsurance under which the reserves as well as the risk are transferred to the *reinsurer*; the *ceding company* retains its liability to the contractual relationship with the insured. See *Modified Coinsurance* and *Assumption Reinsurance*.

Commutation
The *termination* of all obligations between the parties to a reinsurance agreement, normally accompanied by a final cash settlement. *Commutation* may be required by the reinsurance agreement or may be effected by mutual agreement.

Co Mod-co
See *Partially Modified Coinsurance*.

Conditional Automatic
A reinsurance arrangement where the reinsurer underwrites all cessions. Conditional *automatic reinsurance* is generally used only if the *ceding* company does not have underwriters or MIB facilities.

Conditional Receipt
A provision included in some life insurance policies providing coverage from the date of the application to the date at which the policy is either issued or declined.

Convention Blank
A summary of an insurance company's financial operations for a particular calendar year, supported by detailed exhibits and schedules, and filed with the state insurance department in each jurisdiction where the insurance company is licensed. It is also referred to as the annual statement. The *convention blank* is developed by the National Association of Insurance Commissioners (NAIC).

Cover Note
Confirmation by the *intermediary* to the *ceding company* of terms and conditions and percentage placed with each *reinsurer*.

Credibility
A statistical measure of the reliability of experience data, based on the size of the sample.

Cut Through Endorsement
An endorsement to a reinsurance agreement which requires that, in the event of the *ceding company's* insolvency, any loss covered under the reinsurance agreement be paid by the *reinsurer* directly to the insured (or a third party beneficiary). Also called assumption endorsement or assumption of liability endorsement (ALE).

Direct Premium Written
An insurer's premium income calculated before reflecting reinsurance inward or outward.

Errors and Omissions Clause
A provision in reinsurance agreements which is intended to neutralize any change in liability or benefits as a result of an inadvertent error by either party.

Escrow Account
An instrument used to segregate assets of one company for the benefit of another company.

Excess Reinsurance
A form of reinsurance under which recoveries are available when a given loss exceeds the *ceding company's retention* defined in the agreement. Also called excess of loss reinsurance.

Experience Rated
A reinsurance arrangement which allows the *ceding company* to share in a portion of any profits realized on the reinsurance.

Experience Refund
Under a reinsurance agreement, that part of the profits which is returned to the *ceding company* after recognition of contingency reserves, loss carryforward and loss carryback provisions. See *Carryover Provision*.

Experience Refund Reinsurance
A form of reinsurance, typically *yearly renewable term,* under which the premium *rates* are subject to an *experience refund* as opposed to being fixed (non-refund).

Exposure
Measure of vulnerability to loss, usually expressed in dollars or units.

Extended Wait
A retention method used in conjunction with long term disability and medical expense policies. Under this method, the *ceding company* is responsible for claims up to a certain predetermined limit. After the limit is reached, the *reinsurer* pays all or part of the claim.

Extra Contractual Obligations (ECO)
A generic term that, when used in reinsurance agreement, refers to damages awarded by a court against an insurer which are outside the provisions of the insurance policy, due to the insurer bad faith, fraud or gross negligence in the handling of a claim. Examples are *punitive damages* and *losses in excess of policy limits*.

Facultative
Reinsurance under which the *ceding company* has the option (faculty) of submitting and the *reinsurer* has the option of accepting or declining individual risks.

Facultative Obligatory
A form of life reinsurance which is a hybrid between *facultative* and *automatic*. A risk *ceded* is submitted to the *reinsurer* which has limited rights to decline individual risks.

FASB
The Financial Accounting Standards Board, better known as FASB, is a United States organization which makes pronouncements for the accounting profession regarding proper accounting procedures and guidelines. These standards are of importance to both *GAAP* and *statutory* accounting for life and health insurance and annuity providers in the United States.

FEGLI
A reinsurance *pool* established for the Federal Employees Group Life Insurance

Financial Reinsurance
A form of reinsurance which considers the time value of money and has loss containment provisions. Its primary objective is typically the enhancement of the *ceding company's* financial statements or operating ratios.

Flip-flop
A method of allocating *automatic reinsurance* among several *reinsurers* used in conjunction with *layering*. Under this method, each *reinsurer* is assigned a portion of the alphabet and receives the first *layer* of reinsurance on all insureds with surnames falling in its portion of the alphabet. It will receive the second *layer* of reinsurance on a different portion of the alphabet, and so on depending on the number of *layers*.

Follow the Fortunes
A provision in some reinsurance agreements, not always specifically identified as such, in which it is agreed that the *reinsurer* is bound to the same fate as the *ceding company* with respect to risks covered.

Foreign Reinsurer
A *reinsurer* chartered (domiciled) in one state writing business in another state is considered to be foreign in the non-domiciliary state. In its own state, the *reinsurer* is considered to be domestic.

Fronting
A situation where one insurance company issued policies to specified applicants and reinsures all or substantially all of the risks on the insurance to another insurance company for a fee or portion of the profits. *Fronting* typically is used in jurisdictions where the reinsuring company is not licensed to do business.

Funds Withheld
Assets that would normally be paid over to a *reinsurer* but are withheld by the *ceding company* to permit statutory credit for *non-admitted reinsurance*, to reduce a potential credit risk or to retain control over investments. Under certain conditions, the *reinsurer* may withhold funds from the *ceding company*.

Funds Withheld Mod-co
A form of modified *coinsurance* where the initial allowance which is normally paid to the *ceding company* is withheld by the *reinsurer* to lessen the *reinsurer's exposure* to risk.

Generally Accepted Accounting Principles (GAAP)
A method of reporting financial results in accordance with a going-concern basis.

Gentlemen's Agreement
A concept formerly applied to reinsurance agreements which emphasized the reliance upon the mutual integrity and good will of the parties to the agreement in order to solve disputes.

Guaranteed Cost Reinsurance
A form of reinsurance which has no adjustable or *experience refund* features. The final premium *rate* for the coverage is exactly as set forth *ab initio* in the contract.

Honorable Undertaking
A phrase in some older reinsurance agreements, usually in the following context: "This agreement is considered by the parties hereto as an *honorable undertaking*, the purpose of which is not to be defeated by a strict or narrow interpretation of the language thereof."

Incurred But Not Reported (IBNR)
The actuarial estimate or reserves required to pay *ultimate net losses* (UNL) after netting out existing reserves on reported but unpaid claims. This estimate includes an allowance for potential changes in such existing reserves as well as additional reserves for claims that have already occurred but are yet to be reported.

Indemnity Reinsurance
A form of reinsurance under which the risk but not the administration is passed to the *reinsurer* which indemnifies the *ceding company* for losses covered by the reinsurance agreement of *treaty*. The *ceding company* retains its liability to and its contractual relationship with the insured.

Indexing, Indexation
The adjustment of a *ceding company's retention* and the reinsurance limit by a measure of inflation such as the Consumer Price Index. Under *indexation*, the *ceding company's* original *retention* and the reinsurance limit are multiplied by the result of dividing the index on the settlement date by the index as of the effective date of the reinsurance agreement.

Individual Cession Administration
A reinsurance arrangement where the *reinsurer* sets up individual records for each cession and calculates the reinsurance premium, inforce, and reserve information for its financial reports.

Insolvency Clause
A provision in reinsurance agreements that provides for the continuance of payments of the obligations of the *reinsurer* as though no insolvency had occurred, with appropriate recognition of additional expenses of the *reinsurer* caused by the insolvency. Required in most states.

Intermediary
A third party in the design, negotiation and administration of a reinsurance agreement. Intermediaries recommend to *ceding companies* the type and amount of reinsurance to be purchased and negotiate the placement of coverage with *reinsurers*. Also called a broker. See *Brokerage Market*.

Intermediary Clause
A provision in reinsurance agreements which identifies the *intermediary* negotiating the agreement. Most *intermediary* clauses shift all credit risk to *reinsurers* by providing that (1) the *ceding company's* payments to the *intermediary* are deemed payments to the *reinsurer*, (2) the *reinsurer's* payments to the *intermediary* are not payments to the *ceding company* until actually received by the *ceding company*. This clause is mandatory in some states.

Jumbo Limit
A limit placed on the amount of coverage that may be inforce or applied for on an individual life for *automatic reinsurance* purposes. If such insurance exceeds the limit, the risk must be submitted for *facultative* review.

Layer
A horizontal segment of the liability insured, *e.g.*, the second $100,000 of a $500,000 liability is the first *layer* if the *ceding company* retains $100,000, but a higher *layer* if it retains a lesser amount. See *Pro Rata.*

Layering
A method of allocating *automatic reinsurance* among several *reinsurers.* Using this method, reinsurance is *ceded* in *layers.* The *layers* are defined in terms of amounts of insurance. One *reinsurer* will receive all reinsurance up to the limit of the first *layer.* A second *reinsurer* will receive all reinsurance in excess of the first *layer* up to the limit of the second *layer*, and so forth, depending on the number of *layers.*

Lead Reinsurer
The *reinsurer* who negotiates the terms, conditions and premium *rates* and first signs on to the *agreements; reinsurers* who subsequently accept those terms and conditions are considered following *reinsurers.* Uncommon in life reinsurance.

Letter of Credit
A financial guaranty issued by a bank that permits the party to which it is issued to draw funds from the bank in the event of a valid unpaid claim against the other party; in reinsurance, typically used to permit reserve credit to be taken with respect to non-*admitted reinsurance*; an

alternative to *funds withheld* and *modified coinsurance*. Also referred to as an LOC.

Lloyds
An insurance or reinsurance organization in which individuals or groups of individuals, called syndicates, rather than corporations, are at risk.

Loss Event
Any trigger for a recovery under an insurance of reinsurance agreement. Examples include *occurrence*, claims made, death or disability.

Losses in Excess of Policy Limits
A term that, when used in reinsurance agreements, refers to damages awarded by a court against an insurer in favor of the insured, due to the insurer's having failed to settle a third party claim against the insured within the policy limits by reason of bad faith, fraud or gross negligence. See *Extra Contractual Obligations* and *Punitive Damages*.

Losses Portfolio Transfer
A form of *financial reinsurance* for property and liability insurers involving the transfer of loss obligations already incurred which, when ultimately paid, will exceed the consideration paid to the *reinsurer* for undertaking such obligations. The amount by which the transferred obligations exceed the consideration paid is the resultant increase to the *ceding company's* statutory *surplus*.

Loss Ratio
Incurred losses (including applicable *IBNR*) dividend by *earned premium* for an accounting or *treaty* period. *Loss ratios* can be calculated on an accident year, calendar year, or underwriting year basis.

Loss Ratio Coverage
A form of *stop loss* reinsurance under which the *reinsurer* pays a portion of the claims represented by a *loss ratio* in excess of a specified *loss ratio*. For example, "20% on excess of 110%" will result in claims between 100% and 130% of premium being paid by the *reinsurer.*

Medical Information Bureau
A service bureau which compiles underwriting information. Member companies submit coded underwriting information on applicants to the MIB and receive coded information concerning impairments on new applicants from the bureau based on information compiled by other insurance company members. The company receiving information regarding an impairment must independently verify the information.

Minimum Cession
The smallest cession that a *reinsurer* will accept automatically. The minimum size is set to avoid the expenses associated with small cessions.

Mod-co Adjustment Interest Rate
In *modified coinsurance,* the interest rate used to calculate the amount payable by the *ceding company* in consideration of the reserves being transferred back by the *reinsurer*. See *Mod-co Reserve Adjustment.*

Mod-co Interest Rate
The interest rate used to determine the interest credited on the beginning reserves in a mod-co transaction.

Mod-co Reserve Adjustment
The net of two *modified coinsurance* items: the interest on reserves (payable by the *ceding company* to the *reinsurer*) and the increase in the reserve (payable by the *reinsurer* to the *ceding company*).

Modified Coinsurance
Indemnity life reinsurance that differs from *coinsurance* only in that the reserves are returned to the *ceding company* while the risk remains with the *reinsurer*; the *ceding company* is required to pay interest to replace that which would have been earned by the *reinsurer* if it had held the assets corresponding to the reserves in its own investment portfolio. Used to permit reserve credit to be taken with respect to a *non-admitted reinsurer*, to secure credit, and to retain control of investments. See *Funds Withheld Coinsurance* and *Assumption.*

Net Amount at Risk
The excess of the death benefit of a policy over the policy reserve.

Non-experience Rated
A reinsurance arrangement which does not allow the *ceding company* to share in any profits realized on the reinsurance. Premiums for *non-experience rated* reinsurance generally have smaller loads than premiums for *experience rated* reinsurance.

Nonproportional
A form of reinsurance where the *reinsurer*'s liability is not fixed in advance, but is dependent on the number or amount of claims incurred in a given period.

Normal Underwriting
One of the conditions for *automatic reinsurance*. The definition of what is normal for the plan is set at the inception of the agreement.

Occurrence
An adverse contingent accident or event neither expected nor intended from the point of view of the insured. With regard to limits on *occurrences*, catastrophe reinsurance agreements frequently define adverse events having a common cause and sometimes within a specified time frame, (for example, seventy-two hours) as being one *occurrence*. This definition prevents multiple *retentions* and reinsurance limits from being exposed in a single *catastrophe* loss.

Offset Clause
A provision in reinsurance agreements which permits each party to net amounts due against those payable before making payment; especially important in the event of insolvency of one party which ceases to remit amounts due to the other. This clause is often challenged by state insurance departments, creditors and others interested in maximizing the assets of the insolvent party. Also know as *set-off*.

Outstanding Surplus Account
A record kept by the reinsurer of the amount of *surplus* that it is carrying in a *financial reinsurance* arrangement.

Partially Modified Coinsurance (Part-co)
A combination of *coinsurance* and *modified coinsurance*. In most

situations a portion of the initial reserves equal to the initial allowance are held on a *coinsurance* basis, while the remaining reserves are held on a *mod-co* basis, eliminating any initial cash transfer. Also known as Co/Mod-co.

Participation Limit
A limit placed on the absolute amount of coverage that may be inforce or applied for on an individual life for reinsurance purposes. If the insurance exceeds the limit, the *reinsurer* will decline to *assume* any of the risk. This is most commonly applied to supplementary benefits such as accidental death coverage.

Persistency Bonus
An amount paid to the *ceding company* by the *reinsurer* if the reinsurance *ceded* in a given period meets certain persistency standards. *Persistency bonuses* are used to encourage the writing of persistent business.

Placement Ratio
The ratio of paid *facultative* cessions to number of *facultative* submissions. The *placement ratio* can be used to determine the effectiveness of the *reinsurer's facultative* underwriting and the cost per cession.

Point-in-Scale YRT
A term used in conjunction with a select and ultimate *YRT* scale. It refers to the premium rate appropriate for the insured's original issue age and duration.

Policy Expense Allowance
An amount payable to the *ceding company* by the *reinsurer* in lieu of actual commissions and expenses incurred by the *ceding company*.

Pool
A method of allocating reinsurance among several *reinsurers*. Using this method, each *reinsurer* receives a specified percentage of each risk *ceded* into the *pool*. Percentages may vary by *reinsurer*.

Premium (Written/Unearned/Earned)
Written premium is premium registered on the books of an insurer of *reinsurer* at the time a policy is issued and paid. Premium for a future *exposure* period is said to be *unearned premium*. For an individual policy, written premium minus *unearned premium* equals *earned premium*. *Earned premium* is income for the accounting period while *unearned premium* will be income in a future accounting period.

Production Bonus
An amount paid to the *ceding company* by the *reinsurer* if the amount of reinsurance *ceded* in a given period exceeds a specified amount. *Production bonuses* are used to encourage a *ceding company* to place reinsurance with a certain carrier.

Professional Reinsurers
Reinsurers that deal with the *ceding company* through their account executives, rather than through *intermediaries*. Also known as *direct reinsurers*. See *Brokerage Market*.

Profit Commission
A provision found in some reinsurance agreements which provides for profit sharing. Parties agree to a formula for calculating profit, an allowance for the *reinsurer's* expenses, and the *ceding company's* share of such profit after expenses. See *Adjustable Features, Risk Charge* and *Experience Refund*.

Proportional
A form of reinsurance where the amount *ceded* is defined at the time of cession, although the amount of the cession may vary with time by formula.

Pro Rata
See *Quota Share*.

Punitive Damages
A term that, when used in reinsurance agreements, refers to damages awarded by a court against an insured or against an insurer in addition

to compensatory damages. ***Punitive damages*** are intended to punish the insured or the insurer for willful and wanton misconduct and to serve as a deterrent. when the award is against an insurer, it is usually related to the conduct of the insurer in the handling of a claim, and can arise in both first party and third party coverage situations. See ***Extra Contractual Obligations*** and ***Losses in Excess of Policy Limits***.

Quota Share
A form of reinsurance in which premiums and losses are shared proportionately between ***ceding company*** and ***reinsurer***. One such reinsurance agreement is ***quota share***, in which the same percentage applies to all policies reinsured. Another is surplus share, in which the percentage may vary from policy to policy and usually increases as policy limits increase.

Rate
The premium ***rate*** is the amount of premium charged per ***exposure*** unit, *e.g.*, per $1,000.

Recapture
The process by which the ***ceding company*** recovers the liabilities transferred to a ***reinsurer***.

Reinsurance Pool
A ***multi-reinsurer*** agreement under which each ***reinsurer*** in the group or ***pool*** assumes a specified portion of each risk ***ceded*** to the ***pool***. Contrast with ***Reinsurance Wheel***.

Reinsurance Wheel
A procedure for retroceding individual life insurance risks in excess of a ***reinsurer's*** own ***retention*** to a group of ***retrocessionnaires*** (up to their subscribed limits) in rotation, the order being determined by their positions as spokes on an imaginary wheel. The spokes need not be of the same length, *i.e.*, limit, and a company may have more than one spoke. Contrast with ***Reinsurance Pool***.

Reinsurer
A ***reinsurer*** contractually accepts a portion of the ***ceding company's*** risk.

Retention
The dollar amount or percentage of each loss retained by the *ceding company* under a reinsurance agreement.

Retrocede
To transfer a reinsurance risk *assumed* by the *reinsurer* to another insurance company.

Retrocessionnaire
A *reinsurer* that contractually accepts from another *reinsurer* a portion of the *ceding company's* underlying reinsurance risk. The transfer is known as a retrocession.

Risk Charge
An amount identified in some reinsurance agreements as specifically to be retained by the *reinsurer* for assuming the risk under the policies reinsured; a share of the profits in excess of the *risk charge* is returned to the *ceding company* as an *experience refund.* Also known as profit and expense charge, risk and profit charge, or risk and expense charge.

Risk Premium Reinsurance (RPR)
Another name for *YRT* reinsurance.

Self-Administration
A reinsurance arrangement where the *ceding company* provides the *reinsurer* with periodic reports for reinsurance *ceded* giving premium, inforce, reserve, and any other information required by the *reinsurer* for its financial reports. Also known as *Bulk* or *Bordereaux.*

SGLI
A reinsurance *pool* established for the Servicemen's Group Life Insurance.

Sliding Scale Commission
A *ceding commission* which varies inversely with the *loss ratio* under the reinsurance agreement. The scales are not always one-to-one: for example, as the *loss ratio* decreases by 1%, the *ceding commission*

might increase only 1/2%. Sometimes used in reinsurance of credit insurance plans.

Spread Loss
A form of reinsurance under which premiums are paid during good years to build up a fund from which losses are recovered in bad years. This reinsurance has the effect of stabilizing a *ceding company's loss ratio* over an extended period of time.

Stop Loss
A form of reinsurance under which the *reinsurer* pays some of all of a *ceding company* aggregate retained losses in excess of a predetermined dollar amount or in excess of a percentage of premium. See *Loss Ratio Coverage.*

Surplus
The excess of assets over liabilities. Statutory *surplus* is an insurer's or *reinsurer's* capital as determined under statutory accounting rules. *Surplus* determines an insurer's or *reinsurer's capacity* to write business.

Surplus Relief
An increase in the *ceding company's surplus* through *financial reinsurance*. *Ceding companies* are able to use the increase in *surplus* to write more business while retaining reasonable operating ratios.

Termination
The formal ending of a reinsurance agreement by its natural expiry, cancellation or *commutation* by the parties. *Terminations* can be either on a cutoff or runoff basis. Undercutoff provisions, the parties' obligations are fixed as of the agreed cutoff date. Otherwise, obligations incurred while the agreement was in force are run off to their natural extinction.

Traditional Reinsurance Market
A reinsurance arrangement where risk sharing is the primary purpose.

Treaty

The legal contract defining the *reinsurance* agreement. A *treaty* contains common contract terms, such as a specific risk definition, data on limit and *retention,* and provisions for premium and duration, and is signed by representatives of both parties.

Trust Agreement

An agreement under which certain assets are deposited by one party (the grantor), for the sole benefit of another party (the beneficiary), into an account managed by a third party (the trustee). In reinsurance, such an agreement is most frequently used to permit a **ceding company** to take credit for *non-admitted reinsurance* up to the value of the assets in trust.

Unusual Expenses

In life reinsurance, non-routine expenses of the **ceding company** for claims investigation, legal defense or rescission actions. The *reinsurer* typically agrees to pay such expenses as distinct from *punitive,* exemplary or other noncontractual expenses which it does not agree to pay.

Yearly Renewable Term (YRT)

A form of life reinsurance under which the risks, but not the permanent plan reserves, are transferred to the *reinsurer* for a premium that varies each year with the amount at risk and the ages of the insureds.

Zero First Year YRT

A *YRT* scale with no premium in the first year.

Bibliography

1. Actuarial Standards Board, *Actuarial Standard of Practice No. 11, The Treatment of Reinsurance Transactions in Life and Health Insurance Company Financial Statements.* Chicago: Actuarial Standards Board, 1989.

2. Bowers, N. R., *et al.*, *Actuarial Mathematics.* Itasca: Society of Actuaries, 1984.

3. Bunner, Bruce, "Will Setoffs be Set Aside?" Best's Review, December 1989.

4. Coopers & Lybrand, *International Reinsurance Industry Guide.* London: Lloyds of London Press, Ltd., 1985.

5. Ernst & Ernst, *GAAP/Stock Life Insurance Companies.* Cleveland: Ernst & Ernst, 1974.

6. Grossman, Eli, *Life Reinsurance.* Atlanta: Life Office Management Association, 1981.

7. Financial Accounting Standards Board, *Statement of Financial Accounting Standards No. 60, Accounting Reporting for Insurance Enterprises*. Stamford: Financial Accounting Standards Board of the Financial Accounting Foundation, 1982.

8. _____, *Statement of Financial Accounting Standards No. 91, Accounting for Nonrefundable Fees and Costs Associated with Originating or Acquiring Loans and Initial Direct Costs of Leases*. Stamford: Financial Accounting Standards Board of the Financial Accounting Foundation, 1986.

9. _____, *Statement of Financial Accounting Standards No. 97, Accounting and Reporting by Insurance Enterprises for Certain Long-Duration Contacts and for Realized Gains and Losses from the Sale of Investments*. Stamford: Financial Accounting Standards Board of the Financial Accounting Foundation, 1987.

10. _____, *Statement of Financial Accounting Standards No. 109, Accounting for Income Taxes*. Norwalk: Financial Accounting Standards Board of the Financial Accounting Foundation, 1992.

11. _____, *Statement of Financial Accounting Standards No. 113, Accounting and Reporting for Reinsurance of Short-Duration and Long-Duration Contacts*. Norwalk: Financial Accounting Standards Board of the Financial Accounting Foundation, 1992.

12. _____, *Statement of Financial Accounting Standards No. 115, Accounting for Certain Investments in Debt and Equity Securities*. Norwalk: Financial Accounting Standards Board of the Financial Accounting Foundation, 1993.

13. _____, *Statement of Financial Accounting Standards No. 120, Accounting and Reporting by Mutual Life Insurance Enterprises and by Insurance Enterprises for Certain Long-Duration Contracts*. Norwalk: Financial Accounting Standards Board of the Financial Accounting Foundation, 1995.

14. Kempe, D. P., "Insolvency of Offshore Insurance Companies — Bermuda," Proceedings of ABA National Institute on Insurer Insolvency, June 7-8, 1986.

15. KPMG Peat Marwick, Llp., *Federal Taxation of Insurance Companies*. New York: Research Institute of America, 1994.

16. Patterson, W. S., "The New Life and Health Insurance Guaranty Association Model Act — Changes and Implications," Proceedings of ABA National Institute on Insurer Insolvency, June 7-8, 1986.

17. Peat, Marwick, Mitchell, *International Reinsurance*. New York: Peat, Marwick, Mitchell and Company, 1985.

18. Pentikäinen, T., "On the Net Retention and Solvency of Insurance Companies," Skand. Aktur. J., XXV (1952), 71.

19. Reinsurance Section Treaty Committee, *Discussion of Reinsurance Provisions in a Life Reinsurance Agreement*. Chicago: Society of Actuaries, 1984.

20. Robertson, R. S., "GAAP Accounting for Reinsurance Accepted" and "GAAP Accounting for Reinsurance Ceded," TSA XXVII (1975), 375.

21. Rosenthal, I., "Limits of Retention for Ordinary Life Insurance," RAIA, XXXVI (1947), 6.

22. Schibley, J. V., "A Sampler of Legal and Regulatory Issues Concerning Life Reinsurance," The Reinsurance Reporter (Lincoln National Life Insurance Company), First Quarter, 1990.

23. _____, "The Life Reinsurance Contract," unpublished presentation to the American Bar Association, August 10, 1987.

24. Semple, T. D. and R. M. Hall, "The Reinsurer's Liability," Proceedings of ABA National Institute on Insurer Insolvency, June 7-8, 1986.

25. Strain, R. W., *Reinsurance*. New York: College of Insurance, 1980.

26. Tiller, J. E., "Reinsurance — Current Financial Reporting Topics," RSA 11, No. 2 (1985), 1019.

27. Tract, H. M., "The Effect of the Insolvency of Reinsurer on Letters of Credit," Proceedings of ABA National Institute on Insurer Insolvency, June 7-8, 1986.

The reader is also referred to the proceedings and reports of various professional bodies, including the accounting, actuarial, and legal professions in Canada, the United Kingdom, and the United States. The various publications of the National Association of Insurance Commissioners is a major source of regulatory information in the United States. The Actuarial Standards of Practice published by the Actuarial Standards Board provide actuarial guidelines in the United States. For information regarding reinsurance in a specific country other than the United States, the reader is referred to the various professional, regulatory, and tax professionals in that country. The various study notes of the Society of Actuaries, both past and current, are sources of knowledge and additional detail.

Index

Accelerated benefit rider
  516-517
Accounting 22
  GAAP 355-382, 428
  Statutory 331-354, 428
  Tax 407-409
Accredited reinsurer 16-17
Actuarial opinion 23, 350
AD&D reinsurance 506-508
Administration 23, 183-194, 205-232, 500
Advantages
  Coinsurance financial 112
  Facultative reinsurance 50
  Funds withheld coinsurance 139-140
  Funds withhled mod-co 148
  Letters of credit 172
  Mod-co financial 130
  Part-co 156
  Trust (escrow) accounts 171
  YRT financial 119
Affiliate reinsurer 21, 524-526
Agent-owned reinsurance 21, 441-446
Alien reinsurers 312
Allowances 110, 182-183, 267
Alphabet split 38-39
Alternative minimum tax 403
American Arbitration Association 197
Analysis of increase in reserve 348
Ancillary benefits (see supplemental benefits)
Annuitization 499
Annuity reinsurance
  Considerations 495-500

Products 488-495
  Structure 500
Arbitration 197-198
Assignment 198
Asset control 495-496
Asset default 498
Assets 332-334
Assumed reinsurance 12, 257-281
Attracting producers 438
Assumed reinsurance 12, 257-281
Assumption 13, 308-311, 421-434
Auditing 229-231
Authorized reinsurer 16
Automatic reinsurance 14
  Amount of 36-38
  Considerations 42
  Multiple treaties 38-41
  Requirements for 26-36
  Treaty provisions 179-180
Australia 466

Bahamas 437, 469
Balance sheet 332-336
Barbados 437, 469
Benefit items 337-338
Bermuda 437, 469
Better experience 439
Binding limit 29-31
Bonuses 275
Buy back agreement 443

Canada 461-464
Capacity 252
Capital and surplus 338-339
Captive 20-21

Captive reinsurer 436-441
Cash flow 339-340
Cash values 260
Catastrophe reinsurance 10-11, 417
Cayman Islands 469
Ceded reinsurance 12, 233-256, 365-372
Ceding company
  Administration 208-218
  AORC considerations 444-446
  Assumption effects 427
  Credit captive considerations 448-449
  Facultative reinsurance considerations 49-52
  Increasing sales 8
  Insolvency 318, 323-324
  Motivation for captive reinsurance 438-439
  Nonproportional reserves 418-420
  Position under model act 318
  Stability 279-280
Certification of assumption 424
Changes 186-187, 521
Changing conditions 256
Chargebacks 275-278, 369-370, 375
Claims
  Administration 191-194
  Catastrophic 10-11
  Procedures (DI) 477
Coinsurance
  Advantages 121
  Cost evaluation 249
  Disadvantages 121-122

Experience refund 274
Financial reinsurance 120-129
Funds withheld 139-147
GAAP accounting 367-368, 373-374
Health reinsurance 475-476, 482
Illustrations 89-93, 122-129
Limit 183
Partly modified 156-167
Premiums and allowances 83-87
Traditional reinsurance 82-93
Uses 87
COLA 515
Commencement of liability
   Automatic 180
   Facultative 181
Commercial arbitration rules 197
Commissions 261-262
Compensatory damages 195
Compliance 22
Conditional automatic 57
Conditional receipt
   Automatic 180
   Facultative 181
Constant retention 70
Constant risk reinsured 70-71
Constructive receipt 444
Continental Europe 466-469
Continuations 34-35, 186-187
Conventional U.K. market 464-465
Conversion 188, 521
Corridors 243-244
Cost control 55

Cost evaluation 248-250, 254
Credit captive 20
Credit reinsurance 446-449, 501-506
Currency exchange risk 460
Cut-through clause 199, 319-320

Decreasing term 68
Deficiency reserves 519-120
DEFRA 391-392
Deposit term 513-514
Differences in reserves 298-299
Differences in taxation 454
Disability income reinsurance
   Plans 474-476
   Pricing 476-478
   Retention 472-474
Disadvantages
   Coinsurance financial 121-122
   Facultative reinsurance 50-52
   Funds withheld coinsurance 140
   Funds withheld mod-co 148
   Letters of credit 173
   Mod-co financial 131
   Part-co 157
   YRT financial 119-120
Distributions 268-269
Distribution systems 445
Divesting product line 7
Dividend options 521
Duration of agreement 201

Earnings 445
Economic factors 460-461
Effect of regulations 302-303
Electronic data imaging 49

Entire agreement 201
Errors (see oversights)
Escrow accounts
  (see trust accounts)
Evaluating costs 248
Excess capacity 45
Excess share 15, 36, 473
Excise tax 458-459
Exhibit of life insurance 349
Exhibits 340-344
Exemplary damages 195
Ex gratia payments 195
Expenses 191, 265-266, 337-338
Experience rating 15
Experience refund
  Assumed reinsurance
    271-275
  Credit reinsurance 504-505
  Financial reinsurance 111
  GAAP accounting 370-371,
    376-377
Experimental underwriting
  53-54
Extended deductible 481
Extended term 188
Extended wait 474
External changes 280
External replacements 523
Extra-contractual damages
  195-196

Facultative cessions 217, 372
Facultative exclusion 32-33
Facultative obligatory 57
Facultative pools 58
Facultative pricing 56
Facultative reinsurance 14-15,
  42-58, 278

Advantages of 50
Disadvantages of 50-52
Management of 253-254,
  267-268
Pricing for 56
Treaty provisions 180-181
FASB Statement 60 358-359
FASB Statement 91 361
FASB Statement 97 359-360
FASB Statement 109 361-362
FASB Statement 113 362
FASB Statement 115 364
FASB Statement 120 364-365
Federal income tax 267
FEGLI 17
Filing 203
Financial reinsurance 16,
  279-281
  Coinsurance 120-129
  Funds withheld coinsurance
    139-147
  Funds withheld mod-co
    148-156
  Management of 254-256
  Mod-co 129-138
  Part-co 156-167
  Regulation and taxation
    167-169
  Security considerations
    169-173
  Statutory accounting 350
  Terminology 110-112
  Uses of 107-109
  YRT 118-120
Financial reinsurer 18
First-to-die 518
Fixed share 473

Index

Flexible premium deferred annuity 489-490
Foreign tax planning 460
Foreign treaties 403-404
Form of reinsurance
   AORC's 442
   Credit captive 447-448
Formula retention 71
France 468
Frequency of review 243
Fronting 7, 232, 300
Full retention 27-29, 42
Functional responsibilities 209-212, 219-223, 231
Funds withheld coinsurance
   Advantages 139-140
   Disadvantages 140
   Illustrations 140-147
Funds withheld mod-co
   Advantages 148
   Disadvantages 148
   Illustrations 148-156

GAAP accounting 270, 355-365
   Assumed reinsurance 372-381
   Assumption 428
   Ceded reinsurance 365-372
   Financial reinsurance 381-382
   Reinsurance with affiliates 526
Gains and losses 393-394
Generalized experience refund formula 271-273
Germany 468-469
Group life insurance 506-508
Guaranteed benefit annuities 490-493

Guaranteed insurability option 515
Guaranteed investment contracts 492-493
Guaranty fund assessments 385-386

Health reinsurance
   Comprehensive 480-486
   Disability income 471-478
   Long-term care 478-480
   Major medical 480-486
   Other benefits 486
Holding company regulation 307-308

Illustrations
   Chargebacks 276-277
   Coinsurance 89-93, 122-129
   Funds withheld coinsurance 140-147
   Funds withheld mod-co 148-156
   Mod-co 100-106, 131-138
   Part-co 157-167
   Reinsurance treaty 529-562
   YRT 75-82
Improving operations 253
Income items 336-337
Income taxes 458
Increase in recapture 189
Increase in retention 189
Increased earnings 443
Increasing benefits 514-516
Indemnity 12, 218-231
Indeterminate premium policies 512-513
Individual cession 184, 185

Individual cession administration 223-225
Individual cession record 212-213
Industry practice 204
Inflation 460
Initial reinsurance premium 110
Insolvency
   Ceding company 318, 323-324
   Clause 318-323
   Management of 326-330
   Model act 316-318
   Policyholders rights 325
   Regulations 294
   Reinsurer 318, 324-325
   Treaty provisions 199-200
Inspection of records 196-197
Insurers Rehabilitation and Liquidation Model Act 199, 295-296
Intercompany reinsurance 307-308
Interest 267, 497
Interest sensitive products
   Annuities 488-490
   Whole life 511
Intermediaries 312, 527-528
Internal replacements 522-523
Internal Revenue Service 168
International reinsurance
   Business purposes 453
   Considerations of 454-461
   Motivations for 452-454
   Selected markets 461-470
Investment risk transfer 5
IRIS 313
Issue age 41

Japan 469
Joint life 517-518
Joint venture reinsurer 20
Jumbo limit 31

Key producers 438

Lapse risk transfer 4
Layering 40
Lead reinsurer 40
Legal authorization 35
Letters of credit 172-173, 201, 305-306
Level term policies 67-68
Level retention 70
Leverage 448
Liabilities 334-336
Life company status 397
Limited opinion 351
Limiting total claims 11
Living benefit riders 516-517
Lloyds of London 11, 465
Local taxes 386
Location of captive reinsurer 436-437
Long-term care 478-480
Loss carryovers 406
Loss recognition 380-381

Major medical 480-486
Managing insolvency 326-330
Managing reinsurance
   Assumed 257-281
   Ceded 233-256
Marketing 220-223, 279
Market value adjusted annuities 494-495
Minimum cession 29

Index 639

Mirror image reserves 297-299
Model insolvency act 316-318
Model Law on Credit for Reinsurance 287-290
Model Fronting Disclosure and Regulation Act 300-301
Model office projection 235-237
Modified coinsurance (mod-co)
    Advantages 130
    Cost evaluation 250
    Disability income 476
    Disadvantages 131
    Experience refund 274-275
    Financial reinsurance 129-138
    GAAP accounting 368-369, 374
    Illustrations 100-106, 131-138
    Premiums and allowances 96-97
    Reserve adjustment 97-99
    Traditional reinsurance 93-106
Monitoring results 255-256, 278
Morbidity risk transfer 4
Mortality 262-265, 498-499
Mortality risk transfer 4
Motivation for captive reinsurance 438-440
Motivation for international reinsurance 452-454
Multiple automatic treaties 38-41
Mutual company taxes 402

NAIC 173, 290
Net amount at risk 67-69, 260-261

Netherlands 467-468
New business 246-252
New business financing 5
Non-experience rated 15
Nonguaranteed elements 510-513
Nonproportional reinsurance 13-14
    Catastrophe 417
    Reserve considerations 418-420
    Spread loss 418
    Stop loss 414-416
Normal underwriting 33
Notification 183-184

OBRA 90 392-393
Occasional reinsurer 17
Offset 200, 296-297
Offshore sites 469-470
Offshore treaties 403-404
Omissions (see oversights)
Original insurer responsibilities 425-426
Original policy values 258
Outstanding surplus account 112, 125, 129, 138, 143, 147, 151, 155-156, 160
Oversights 194-195
Ownership of AORC's 442

Partially modified coinsurance (part-co)
    Advantages 156
    Disadvantages 157
    Illustrations 157-167
Participation in AORC's 442
Participation limit 31

Parties to the agreement 198-199
Pentikäinen's approach 240-242
Percentage ownership 444
Permanent policies 68-69
Persistency 264-265
Phase III 389-390, 398
Pitfalls in treaty preparation 204
Plan of insurance 35-36
Policy fees 260
Policy forms 182
Policy loans 333
Policyholder dividends 87-88, 189
Policyholder rights 325
Political factors 460-461
Political instability 461
Pooling 39-40
Pool participant 19
Practical considerations of retention limits 242-246
Pre-approval of treaty 203
Premiums 182-183, 258-260
   Accounting 184
   Coinsurance 83-87
   Initial reinsurance 110
   Mod-co 96-97
   YRT 71-74
Premium tax 266, 384-386
Previous submission 49
Pricing 23
   Assumptions 262-267
   Disability income 476-477
   Facultative considerations 267-268
   Long-term care 479
   Major medical 483-484
   Original policy values 258
   Techniques 268-270

Primary business source 52
Priority of distribution 317
Producer owned reinsurance 20
   AORC 441-446
   Captive 436-441
   Credit 446-449
   Special purpose 449-450
Product divesting 7
Product expertise 6, 251
Professional reinsurer 17
Profitability 23
   Ceding company 8
   Reinsurer 10
Profit objectives 269
Profit test years 269
Proportional reinsurance 13
Pro rata retention 69-70
Punitive damages 195
Purpose of captive reinsurer 436
Purpose of insolvency clause 319

Qualifications 179, 181
Qualified opinion 351
Quality control 52
Quota share 15
   Amount of automatic reinsurance 36-38
   Health insurance 473, 481

Ratio method 234-235
Recapture 189-190, 244-246, 253, 265, 370, 375-376, 477-478
Reciprocity 18
Reduced paid-up 188
Reductions 185-186
Re-entry 188
Refund (see experience refund)

Regulation
   Assumption 308-311
   Captive reinsurers 437-438
   Effect on operations 22
   Financial reinsurance 167-169
   Fronting 300
   International reinsurance 454-457
   Mirror image reserves 297-299
   Reinsurance with affiliates 525-526
   Reserve credit 286-297
   Unauthorized reinsurers 299-303
Reinstatement 190
Reinsurance report 125, 126, 138, 143, 144, 151, 155, 157, 164
Reinsurance treaty 177-204
Reinsurer
   Administration 218-232
   Captive 436-441
   Classification of 16-21
   Insolvency 318, 324-325
   Motivation for captive status 439-440
   Nonproportional reserves 420
   Position under model act 318
   Unauthorized 299-303
   Uses of facultative reinsurance 52-54
Reissue 521
Reliance 350-351
Replacements 34-35, 522-524
Reporting
   Ceding company administration 215-216

Reinsurer administration 227-229
Reserve credit 286-297
Reserves 260
   Annuities 495
   International reinsurance 455
   Nonproportional reinsurance 418-420
   Original policy values 258
Reserve adjustment (mod-co) 97-99, 135, 152, 160, 161
Residence 35
Retention
   Automatic reinsurance requirement 27-29
   Health reinsurance 472-474, 477, 481
   Increase in 189-190
   Management 270
   Methods 233-246
   Model office projection 235-237
   Pentikäinen's approach 240-242
   Practical consideration 242-246
   Ratio method 234-235
   Rosenthal's approximation 237-240
   Traditional reinsurance (YRT) 69-71
Retrocession 12, 224
   Agreements 270-271
   GAAP accounting 271
Retrocessionaire 19
Reviewing procedures 252
Risk charge 111
Risk participation 443-444
Risk premium reinsurance 62

Risk transfer 4-5, 290-294,
    362-363, 496-499
Robertson, R.S. 357
Rosenthal's approximation
    237-240

Schedule H 344
Schedule S 345-348
Schedule T 348
Second-to-die 518
SEC regulations 438
Section 818(c) 388-389
Section 820 388
Section 845 398-402
Section 848 392-393
Security considerations 169-173,
    303-306
Select and ultimate term insurance 509
Self-administration
    Ceding company 214-218
    GAAP accounting 371,
        377-380
    Managing inforce 278
    Reinsurer 225-229
    Statutory accounting 349-350
    Treaty provisions 184, 185
Sensitivity testing 269-270
Service 250-251, 254
Set-off 320-323
Sex 268-269
SGLI 17
Shopping 46-49
Side letters 203-204
Single premium deferred
    annuities 488-489
Small company status 398
Soliciting proposals 247-248
Solvency requirements 455-457

Special considerations
    Annuities 495-500
    Credit insurance 505-506
    Health reinsurance 485-486
Special provisions for GAAP
    369-371, 375-377
Special purpose reinsurer 18,
    449-450
Special treaty provisions
    194-202
Sponsor considerations 448-449
Spread loss 418
Stability 251, 279-280
Stamp duties 459
Standardization of provisions
    203
State taxes 304-386
Statutory accounting
    Assumption 428
    Balance sheet 332-336
    Capital and Surplus 338-339
    Exhibits 340-344
    Other items 348-349
    Schedules 344-348
    Summary of operations
        336-338
Stop loss 414-416, 482-483
Strategic business planning
    109, 429-434
Structured settlement annuities
    491-492
Summary of operations 336-338
Supplemental benefits 244
Surplus 336
    Account 338-339
    Management 8-9
    Planning 8-9
    Relief 108, 453-454
Surrender risk transfer 4-5

Index 643

Switzerland 468
Syndicates 11, 21
Systems design
   Ceding company 216-217
   Reinsurer 229
Tax
   Accounting 407-408
   Considerations for AORC's 443
   Considerations for captives 440-441
   Documentation 409
   Excise 458-459
   International reinsurance 454, 458-460
   Planning 9-10, 209, 404-406, 460
   Premium 266, 384-386
   Reinsurance with affiliates 526
   Reporting 428-429
   State 384-386
   U.S. federal income 386-404
   Withholding 459-460
Techniques of pricing 268-270
Terminations 185-186
Terminal funding annuities 493
Time lag 380
Traditional reinsurance 15
   Coinsurance 82-93
   Modified coinsurance 93-106
   YRT 62-82
Transfer 198
Treaty
   Administration 183-194
   Approval 307
   Definitions 179-181

Preparation 202-204
Special provisions 194-202
Terms and specifications 181-183
Trusts accounts 303-304
   Advantages 171
   Disadvantages 171-172

Unauthorized reinsurers 299-303
Underwriting
   Assistance through reinsurance 6
   Automatic reinsurance requirement 33
   Disability income 477
   Distributions for pricing 268-269
   Effect of reinsurance on 24
   Experimental programs 53-54
   Expertise 251
   Facultative reinsurance 42-58
   Insolvency 327-329
   Long-term care 479
Uniform Arbitration Act 197
United Kingdom 464-465
Universal life 69, 512
Uses of reinsurance 4-11

Valuation 478
Valuation actuary 23, 351-353
Vanishing reserves 299
Variable annuities 493-494
Variable life 512
Variations in retention limits 244
Virgin Islands 469
Voluntary terminations 498

Withholding tax 459-460

Yearly Renewable Term (YRT)
   Advantages 119
   Cost evaluation 248-249
   Disadvantages 119-120
   Disability income 474-475
   Financial reinsurance
     118-120

GAAP accounting 367, 372-373
Illustrations 75-82
Inforce management 274
Net amount at risk 67-69
New business management
   248-249
Premiums 71-74
Retention 69-71
Uses 74

About the Authors

DENISE FAGERBERG TILLER is a graduate of the University of Nebraska-Lincoln. She is a Fellow of the Society of Actuaries, a Member of the American Academy of Actuaries, and a Fellow of the Life Office Management Association.

Ms. Tiller began her actuarial career with CNA and worked at Maccabees Mutual Life Insurance Company prior to joining Transamerica Occidental Life Insurance Company as Manager of Reinsurance Pricing in 1980. She later moved to Tillinghast, a Towers Perrin company where she focused her consulting services on individual life insurance product development and reinsurance.

Ms. Tiller has served on the Section Council of the Reinsurance Section of the Society of Actuaries and chaired the Societies' Committee on Professional Development She was a faculty member for the 1988 Society of Actuaries Seminars on Financial Reinsurance, and has participated in a number of panels and workshops at Society meetings. Ms. Tiller also has served as president of the Los Angeles Actuarial Club.

Since 1983 she has been married to her coauthor. Other Tiller collaborations include daughters Elizabeth Elaine (1985), Victoria Jo (1990) and Alexandra Jean (1992). Since 1987 she has been employed as full-time chef, chauffeur, banker, social director, housekeeper, bookkeeper, zookeeper, wife, and mother of the Tiller family. In the midst of this disorder, she writes reinsurance books and outlines on demand. She currently is editing her first mystery, centered on a young, blond single actuary in Southern California, no doubt a desire to return to the "glory years" before kids. In her spare time, she runs to maintain her sanity — and to obtain some peace and quiet.

JOHN E. TILLER, JR. is a graduate of Harvey Mudd College in Claremont, California. He is a Fellow of the Society of Actuaries and a Member of the American Academy of Actuaries.

Mr. Tiller began his insurance career as a part-time insurance agent while in college. After pursuing an agency career for some fifteen months following college graduation, "he saw the light" and joined the actuarial student corp at Transamerica Occidental Life Insurance Company. Originally assigned the actuarial systems department, he escaped after three years to the reinsurance line of business where he became Vice-President and Actuary. During his reinsurance career at Transamerica, Mr. Tiller was responsible for product development and pricing, valuation and financial reporting, underwriting, contracts, sales and marketing, and strategic planning. He also was involved in corporate efforts regarding surplus allocation and management and tax planning.

Mr. Tiller then joined what is now Tillinghast, a Towers Perrin company, where he became a principle shareholder and unit manager for life insurance consulting in Irvine, California. His consulting activities involved a broad range of assignments, many of which were related to accepting or ceding indemnity reinsurance or assumption transactions.

Mr. Tiller subsequently became Executive Vice President and Chief Actuary for Resource Deployment, Inc., a subsidiary of what is now Travelers Insurance Group. In this role, Mr. Tiller oversaw the actuarial functions of over twenty insurance companies, including American Health and Life Insurance Company, Transport Life Insurance Company, Voyager Life Insurance, and Primerica Life Insurance Company.

In April 1993, Mr. Tiller became National Director of the Life Insurance Actuarial Consulting Practice of KPMG Peat Marwick LLP. While responsible for a wide range of actuarial and general consulting activities, he maintains his leadership role in reinsurance. He is frequently asked to review reinsurance activities on behalf of KPMG's clients and other.

Mr. Tiller was on the original Section Council of the Reinsurance Section of the Society of Actuaries. He has since been elected to another term on the council and has served as an officer during both terms on the Council. In between, he served on the Council of the Nontraditional Marketing Section Council, including terms as Vice-Chair and Chair. In the past, Mr. Tiller served as Chair of both the Program and Continuing Education Committees of the Society, as well as a member of many committees and task forces. Among these are the committees for Services to Members, Research Policy, and Professional Development and the first Task Force on AIDS. He chaired the ACLI's special task force on taxation of reinsurance transactions in the early 1980's and served on an Academy task force on risk classification.

Mr. Tiller is a frequent speaker or discussion leader at industry meetings, including both actuarial and non-actuarial groups. He was a faculty member for the Society's seminars on reinsurance in 1981 and 1988.

A native Texan, Mr. Tiller returned with his family to Texas in 1990 after almost twenty-five years in California. Surprisingly, cowboy boots still fit and the people are still friendly. Married to his coauthor since 1983, he spends his spare time trying to cope with an "actuarial housewife," five daughters (ranging in age from three to twenty at this writing), and a constantly changing assortment of dogs, cats, and occasional fish. A major ambition is to keep the poison ivy dormant long enough to use his much beloved but largely neglected sailboat.